投資助言業に係る規制

―ドイツ法との比較を中心として―

（令和３年３月16日開催）

報告者　神　作　裕　之
（東京大学大学院法学政治学研究科教授）

目　　次

金融商品取引法研究会出席者(令和3年3月16日)

報告者	神作裕之	東京大学大学院法学政治学研究科教授
会長代理	弥永真生	筑波大学ビジネスサイエンス系 ビジネス科学研究科教授
委員	飯田秀総	東京大学大学院法学政治学研究科准教授
〃	大崎貞和	野村総合研究所未来創発センターフェロー
〃	尾崎悠一	東京都立大学大学院法学政治学研究科教授
〃	加藤貴仁	東京大学大学院法学政治学研究科教授
〃	河村賢治	立教大学大学院法務研究科教授
〃	小出篤	学習院大学法学部教授
〃	後藤元	東京大学大学院法学政治学研究科教授
〃	武井一浩	西村あさひ法律事務所パートナー弁護士
〃	中東正文	名古屋大学大学院法学研究科教授
〃	藤田友敬	東京大学大学院法学政治学研究科教授
〃	松井智予	東京大学大学院法学政治学研究科教授
〃	松井秀征	立教大学法学部教授
〃	松尾健一	大阪大学大学院高等司法研究科教授
〃	松尾直彦	松尾国際法律事務所弁護士
〃	宮下央	ＴＭＩ総合法律事務所弁護士
オブザーバー	太田原和房	金融庁企画市場局市場課長
〃	岸田吉史	野村ホールディングス執行役員
〃	森忠之	大和証券グループ本社経営企画部担当部長兼法務課長
〃	森正孝	ＳＭＢＣ日興証券法務部長
〃	田中秀樹	みずほ証券法務部長
〃	窪久子	三菱ＵＦＪモルガン・スタンレー証券法務部長
〃	松本昌男	日本証券業協会自主規制本部長
〃	横田裕	日本証券業協会自主規制本部自主規制企画部長
〃	塚﨑由寛	日本取引所グループ総務部法務グループ課長
研究所	増井喜一郎	日本証券経済研究所理事長
〃	髙木隆	日本証券経済研究所常務理事
〃(幹事)	石川真衣	日本証券経済研究所研究員

(敬称略)

投資助言業に係る規制
—ドイツ法との比較を中心として—

神作会長　定刻になりましたので、ただいまから第15回金融商品取引法研究会を始めさせていただきます。

議事に入ります前に、本日は私からご報告をさせていただくことになっておりますので、議事の運営上、会長代理の弥永先生に司会を務めていただくことになりました。以下、弥永先生にお願いしたいと思います。どうかよろしくお願いいたします。

弥永会長代理　本日は、先ほど会長からもご挨拶がありましたように、神作裕之先生より「投資助言業に係る規制－ドイツ法との比較を中心として－」というテーマでご報告いただくことになっております。

それでは、神作先生、報告をよろしくお願いいたします。

［神作会長の報告］

神作会長　それでは、ご報告させていただきます。

私の本日のご報告のテーマは「投資助言業に係る規制－ドイツ法との比較を中心として－」です。

Ⅰ．はじめに

1．定義

はじめに、日本法における投資助言業の定義から申し上げます。投資助言業とは、「投資者の一方が相手方に対して、有価証券の価値等に関し、口頭、文書、その他の方法により助言を行うことを約し、相手方がそれに対し報酬を支払うことを約する投資顧問契約を締結し、当該契約に基づいて助言を行うことを業として行うこと（金商法28条3項1号・2条8項11号）」と定義されています。ポイントは、有価証券の価値等に関する助言を行うこと、及び報酬の支払いが要件となっている点です。

２．業法上の規制

我が国の投資助言業に対する規制の内容ですが、一般的な義務として、金商業者等に対して全般的に課されている誠実公正義務（金商法36条１項）があります。投資助言業者にはそれに加えて忠実義務及び善管注意義務が課されています。なお、私法上も投資顧問契約は準委任契約であって、民法の規定に基づき善管注意義務を負い、その中には忠実義務も含まれているというのが一般的な理解であると思われます。

次に行為規制ですが、投資助言業者には金融商品取引業者に一般的に課される行為規制が適用されるとともに、追加的に固有の行為規制が課されています。

まず､共通して適用される行為規制の中心は､業務管理体制の整備義務（金商法35条の３）や誠実公正義務（同法36条)、情報提供義務（同法37条の３等)、適合性の原則（同法41条１号）などです。

適合性原則は、本日の中心的なテーマとなりますが、例えば後ほどご紹介するドイツにおいては、投資助言業者には、一般の証券業者に加えてより高いレベルの説明義務とより高いレベルの適合性原則が課されています。日本の場合には、そのような考え方はとられておらず、投資助言業者であっても金融商品取引業に共通して適用される誠実公正義務や適合性原則のほか、忠実義務などの一般的義務が課されているにすぎません。このあたりは、後でまた詳しくお話をさせていただきます。

次に、投資助言に固有の行為として、例えば、投資顧問契約の締結や解約に関し、偽計・暴行・脅迫をする行為の禁止（金商法38条の２第１号）や顧客勧誘に際しての損失補填の約束の禁止（同条第２号)、他の顧客の利益を図るため特定の顧客の利益を害することとなる取引を行うことを内容とした助言の禁止や（金商法41条の２第１号)、顧客の取引に基づく価格等の変動を利用して、自己または第三者の利益を図る目的で正当な根拠を有しない助言を行うことが禁止されています（同条第２号）。

特に重要なのが、投資助言業務を行う金融商品取引業者に対しては、顧客を相手方として、または顧客のために有価証券の売買等を行うことが禁止されていることです（金商法41条の３）。ただし、この禁止には幾つかの例外があります。すなわち、第一種金融商品取引業や登録金融機関業務としてそのような取引を行う場合には、この禁止は適用されないこととなっています。また、顧客からの金銭・有価証券の預託の受け入れが禁止されています（金商法41条の４）。この禁止についても、金商法施行令で適用が除外される場合について幾つかの規定があります。

また、顧客に対する金銭・有価証券の貸付けも禁止されています（金商法41条の５）。

その他の規制として、投資助言業者には、営業保証金の供託義務があります。投資助言業者の規制を金融商品取引業者一般の規制と比較すると、例えば兼業規制、主要株主規制、自己資本比率規制、金融商品責任準備金制度の適用がないという点では、投資助言業に対する業規制は、緩和されています。すなわち、投資助言業者については、先ほど申しましたように忠実義務関係を中心に行為規制については強化されていますが、兼業規制とか開業規制についてはむしろ緩和されていると言えます。

３．手数料に関する最近の動向

証券会社や証券仲介業者の中に、従来型の個別の売買ごとに徴収する手数料にかえて、預かり資産の残高に応じてフィーを徴収する動きが生じています。後ほど、アメリカ法のところで申し上げますが、アメリカ法の理解では、一般的に、個々の取引ごとにコミッションを課す方式が通常の証券業務の提供に係る対価の徴収方法であるのに対して、資産残高に応じてフィーを徴収する方式は、投資顧問サービスもしくは投資助言サービスの対価の一般的な徴収方法であると言われています。

日本も、もし証券会社や証券仲介業者が、預かり資産の残高に応じてフィーを徴収する動きが定着してくると、有価証券の売買等に伴って助言ないし助言類似の行為がなされたときに、そのようなフィーが助言に対する報酬の支払であると認められて、投資助言業に当たることにならないのか、資産残高ベースでフィーを徴収する場合には、投資助言業への該当性の問題がより強く出てくるようにも思われます。

４．問題提起

投資助言業務と有価証券の売買･媒介等に係る金融商品取引業務の境界は、どのような基準に基づいて判断されるのでしょうか。また、投資助言業に係る業法上の規制には過不足がないのでしょうか。以上の２つの論点を中心に、投資助言業務と有価証券の売買・媒介等に係る金融商品取引業務を比較したいと思います。

なお、ソフトローのレベルでは、すなわち「顧客本位の業務運営の原則」を採用している金融事業者については、同原則の２で、「高度の専門性と職業倫理を保持し、顧客に対して誠実・公正に業務を行い、顧客の最善の利益を図るべきである」と定められています。このように、ソフトローのレベルでは、忠実義務を課されていない有価証券の売買・媒介等に係る金融商品取引業者についても、顧客の最善の利益を図るべき行為規範が、法的拘束力はないものの、課されています。

また、「顧客本位の業務運営の原則」６は、「金融事業者は、顧客の資産状況、取引経験、知識及び取引目的・ニーズを把握し、当該顧客にふさわしい金融商品･サービスの組成、販売･推奨等を行うべきである」と定めており、ここには「推奨」のみならず「販売」が含まれています。投資助言のみならず販売を行う際にも、当該顧客にふさわしい金融商品・サービスを販売すべきであることが、ソフトローのレベルにおいても定められています。

Ⅱ．米国法

1．投資助言業者の定義と適用除外

本日はドイツ法を中心にお話しいたしますが、日本法はどちらかというとドイツ法よりも米国法に近いので、まず米国法の状況を簡単に概観した後、ドイツ法を概観したいと思います。

米国における投資助言業の定義規定は、1940年の米国投資顧問業法202条（a）（11）です。資料1をご覧ください。投資助言業者とは、「報酬を得て、直接または出版物もしくは文書により、有価証券の価値、有価証券への投資、購入または販売の適切性に関して、他者に助言する業務に従事する者、並びに、報酬を得て、通常の業務の一環として、有価証券に関する分析もしくは報告を発行し、または公表する者」と定義されています。

この定義のポイントは2つです。第1は、有価証券に係る投資助言・推奨を行うことと、第2は上記サービスに対する報酬を受け取ることです。基本的に、先ほど述べた日本の投資助言業の定義と非常に近いと思われます。

ところが、米国では重要な適用除外があります。すなわち、ブローカー・ディーラー（証券会社）が投資助言を行う場合について、一定の場合には投資助言には当たらないとされています。そのための要件は、次の2つです。第1はブローカー・ディーラーが証券業務に付随して行う助言等が本業に「専ら付随して」なされることです。第2は、そのような本業に「専ら付随して」なされる助言等の行為について「特別の報酬」を受領していないことです。これら2つの要件を満たす場合には、投資助言業者には当たりません。

「専ら付随して」というのは英語ではsolely incidental、「特別の報酬」というのはspecial compensationと表記されています。このように、証券業者が証券の売買に関して助言を行う場合であっても、それが証券の売買やその媒介等という本業に専ら付随してなされ、かつそのための特別の報酬を得ていないときは、ブローカー・ディーラーは投資助言業者には当たらないという適用除外規定があります。条文では、1940年投資顧問業法202条（a）（11）

の後半部分です。資料1をご参照いただければと思います。

2．投資助言業者とブローカー・ディーラーの行為規制

米国では、投資助言業者とブローカー・ディーラーの法的地位がどのように違うと解されてきたかというと、投資助言業者はフィデューシャリー（fiduciary）であるのに対し、ブローカー・ディーラーは、フィデューシャリーではないというのが伝統的理解です。

米国においては、ブローカー・ディーラーと投資助言業者が個人顧客に対して助言を行うなど、実質的には同様のサービスを提供している場合があるにもかかわらず、両者の法的地位が異なるために、顧客が誤解や混乱に陥っていることが問題視されています。

ドッド＝フランク法は、SECにブローカー・ディーラーと投資助言業者の行為規制を制定する権限を付与するとともに、いずれの規範も、つまりブローカー・ディーラーの行為規範としても、投資助言業者の行為規範としても、「顧客の最善の利益」のために行為すべきものとする規制を制定しなければならないと定めました。さらに、先ほど定義規定をご紹介した投資顧問業法206条（1）及び（2）による基準、すなわち投資助言業者に課されている所定の基準よりも緩やかな基準を定めてはならないという制約を課しました。

ドッド＝フランク法に基づいて、2019年にレギュレーション・ベストインタレストが制定されました（SEC, 17 CFR Part 240, Release No. 34-86031; File No. S7-07-18, RIN 3235-AM35, Regulation Best Interest: The Broker-Dealer Standard of Conduct Regulation Best Interest）。ブローカー・ディーラーの行為規制として、次のような内容を定めています。なお、レギュレーション・ベストインタレストは、結局のところ、ブローカー・ディーラーと投資助言業者に共通の規範を提示しないで、ブローカー・ディーラーだけを対象にしています。したがって、ドッド＝フランク法が1つのあり方として描いていた投資助言業者とブローカー・ディーラーについて同一のルールは

実現しませんでした。ブローカー・ディーラーについてはベストインタレストということでレギュレーションの規律を適用する。投資助言業者についでは投資顧問業法を初めとする規制が適用されるという二本立ての規制が維持されています。

このように、ブローカー・ディーラーと投資助言会社の間には依然として法的差異が残ることになりました。しかし、規制の中身を見てみると、ブローカー・ディーラーの行為規制は、これはフィデューシャリーの定義にもよりますが、フィデューシャリーと言えなくもないというところがあります。ブローカー・ディーラーの行為規範として、個人顧客の最善の利益のために行為する義務が、ハードローとして課されることになったからです。

すなわち、ブローカー・ディーラーは、個人顧客に対して証券取引または証券を含む投資戦略を推奨するときは、推奨をしているブローカー・ディーラーやこれに関連する自然人の経済的またはその他の利益を個人顧客の利益に優先させることなく、推奨がなされる時点における個人顧客の最善の利益のために行動しなければなりません。このように、自分の利益や自分の関係者の利益を個人顧客の利益より優先してはなりません。そして、推奨がなされる時点における顧客のベストインタレストのために行動しなければならないという行為規範をハードローとして課しています。

その上で、これがベストインタレスト・レギュレーションの特徴的な規制手法だと思いますが、次の４つの義務を履行した場合には、ベストインタレストに従って行動したものとしています。

この４つは、次の通りです。

第１は、開示義務です。事前に、または推奨する時点で、個人顧客に対して書面をもって開示しなければならず、その内容は、重要な手数料およびコスト、提供される商品の範囲に重要な限定があるときには当該限定について開示しなければなりません。つまり、自分が取り扱う商品が限定されているときには、それを事前に示すことが要請されています。また、全ての利益相反に関する重要事項について開示すべきものとされています。さらに、開示すべきときは、「完全かつ公正な開示」を行うものとされています。

第2は、注意義務です。当該推奨に伴うリスク・利益・コストを理解した上で、それが個人顧客の少なくとも誰かの最善の利益にかなうと信じるに足る合理的な根拠があることが必要です。当該推奨が、特定の個人顧客の最善の利益にかない、かつ当該ブローカー・ディーラーの利益を当該顧客の利益に優先していないと信じるに足る合理的な根拠があることも求められています。個別の推奨のみならず、一連の推奨取引をあわせて見た場合に、当該個人顧客の投資プロファイルに照らして過大ではなく、当該個人顧客の最善の利益にかない、かつ当該ブローカー・ディーラーの利益を当該顧客の利益に優先していないと信じるに足る合理的な根拠があると言える程度の合理的な配慮、注意及び技能を用いた場合には、注意義務を尽くしたとされます。

第3は、利益相反に関する義務です。合理的に設計された利益相反についての方針・手続を策定し、実施し、エンフォースしなければなりません。当該推奨に係るあらゆる利益相反を特定し、開示するか、またはそれを排除することが求められます。この規制は、一般的なフィデューシャリーの規制よりも、むしろ厳しくなっていると言われています。と言いますのは、フィデューシャリー・デューティーの下では、従来は、利益相反関係について開示すれば足りると解されてきた面がありますが、開示するだけでは足りず、そのような利益相反関係を排除することが求められる場合が生じ得る点で、利益相反規制は厳格化されたと解されます。また、当該ブローカー・ディーラーと関係者の利益を個人顧客の利益よりも優先させる誘因になる全ての利益相反を特定し、これを緩和することが求められています。この点も、単に利益相反を特定するだけでなく、それに対して一定の緩和措置を講じることが必要になる点で厳格化しています。利益相反規制における開示の限界を意識し、開示を超えて、一定の利益相反を排除するとともに、顧客の最善の利益のために売買・媒介等をすることに対してバイアスを与え得る利益相反を特定した上で、緩和措置を講じるべきものとされています。恐らく実務に対して一番大きな影響が生じるのは、特定の期間内に特定の証券についてなされるあらゆる販売競争、販売ノルマ、ボーナス、現金以外の報酬を特定し、これを排除することです。販売競争やノルマは禁止されることになりました。

第４は、遵守義務です。上述した第１から第３までの義務、すなわち開示義務、注意義務、および、利益相反に関する義務を遵守するために合理的に設計された方針・手続を書面により策定し、それを実施しエンフォースする義務が課されています。第１から第３までの義務がきちんと遵守されているか、きちんと運用されているかを監視するコンプライアンス体制を構築して、それをきちんと運用し、エンフォースしなければなりません。

上述した、第１から第４の義務が履行されていれば、顧客のベストインタレストにかなう推奨をしたものとするという構造になっています。

先ほどドッド＝フランク法はブローカー・ディーラーと投資助言業者の行為規制をそろえるという選択肢を視野に入れていると申し上げましたけれども、結局差分は残っていると思われます。ただ、随分接近してきたとも言えます。接近したと評価できるのは、以下の点です。

まず、顧客のベストインタレストのために行動しなければならないという点は、両者に共通しており、ドッド＝フランク法の要請を満たしています。さらに、利益相反関係などに係る重要事項について、完全かつ公正な開示をしなければならないという点も共通しています。しかし、依然として両者の行為規制には差分が生じているように思われます。

第１は、規制のスタイルです。投資助言業者に課されるフィデューシャリー・デューティーは基本的にプリンシプル・ベースであるのに対して、ブローカー・ディーラーの顧客の最善の利益のために行動する義務は、具体的でルールベースの規範を含んでいる点です。これは恐らく、レギュレーション・ベストインタレストがFINRAのルールベースの自主規制を相当程度取り込んだということにもよると思われます。かなり具体的で詳細な規定が置かれています。これは、プリンシプル・ベースで規制をする投資顧問業法のスタイルとは大きく異なっています。

逆に、投資助言業者については、なぜルールベースで規制していないかというと、投資助言業者のビジネスモデルが非常に多様であるため、ルールベースで規制をすると過不足が生じるためであると推察されます。

第２に、投資助言業者は、完全かつ公正な開示と十分な情報に基づく同意によって利益相反に対処できるのに対して、ブローカー・ディーラーは、先ほど述べたように、一定の場合には開示だけでは足りずに、利益相反の緩和や排除が求められる点です。この点においては、むしろブローカー・ディーラーに対して、投資助言業者よりも厳格な規制が課されていると評価できる面もあると思われます。

第３に、投資助言業者の負うフィデューシャリー・デューティーは、顧客との関係全体について継続的に適用されます。これに対して、ブローカー・ディーラーのベストインタレストに係る義務は、顧客に対し助言・推奨を行う時点においてのみ適用されるにすぎません。このように、フィデューシャリーである投資助言業者は、顧客との間にフィデューシャリー関係がある間は、全面的かつ継続的にフィデューシャリー・デューティーを負うのに対して、ブローカー・ディーラーのベストインタレストに係る行為規範は、あくまでも顧客に対して推奨したり勧誘したりする局面だけに限られます。その結果、典型的には、投資助言業者は、顧客が口座を有している場合には、当該口座の監視義務があると言われていますが、ブローカー・ディーラーには顧客の証券口座について監視義務はないというのが米国の理解です。

３．投資助言業者のフィデューシャリー・デューティー

投資助言業者には、忠実義務が課されています。その内容は、どのようなものであるかというと、その内容は、次の３つです。

第１に、顧客の最善の利益に合致した助言を行わなければなりません。

第２に、取引の執行のために投資助言業者がブローカー・ディーラーを選択する責任がある場合には、最良執行を探らねばなりません。

第３に、顧客との関係が継続している限りにおいて、全期間を通して全面的に助言を行い、監視しなければなりません。

４．ブローカー・ディーラーの適用除外

ブローカー・ディーラーが投資助言を行っても、投資顧問業法の適用を除外される場合があることは前述しましたが、本日のご報告との関係ではこの点が大いに注目されます。

先ほど、ブローカー・ディーラーの助言行為が投資助言業に該当しないためには２つの要件があると申し上げました。「専ら（証券業務に）付随して」助言行為がなされることという要件と、それに対して「特別の報酬」を得ないことという要件の２つです。

SEC が「専ら（証券業務に）付随して」という要件についてどのように解釈しているかというと、提供されるサービスが口座について提供されるブローカレッジ・サービスに結びついたものであり、かつ合理的に関連しているものであれば「専ら付随して」に該当するというものです。顧客口座に対してブローカー・ディーラーが裁量権を行使する場合には、「専ら付随して」とは言えないのが原則です。ただし、投資裁量権がブローカー・ディーラーに認められている場合であっても、一定の限定、たとえば期間の限定ですとか対象の限定などがあったりすると、「専ら付随して」に該当する場合もあり得ます。

「専ら付随して」に該当するかどうかの判断にとって、SEC の解釈によれば、投資助言の重要性とか頻度は関係ありません。もっとも、この論点については、米国において争いがあります。一部の有力な説は、投資助言が「専ら付随して」に当たらないためには、時たま重要ではない助言行為を行うときだけに限ると解すべきであると解します。しかし、SEC はそのような見解にはくみせずに、投資助言が重要であっても、また、非常に頻繁に助言行為が行われる場合であっても、「専ら付随して」に当たることがあり得るという考え方に立っています。

助言が証券を販売するというブローカー・ディーラーの主要なビジネスに結びついているときにだけ「専ら付随して」に該当し、証券販売と結びついていなかったり、証券の販売が主要な業務ではなく助言が主要な業務であっ

たりする場合には、「専ら付随して」には該当しないことになります。しかし、ケース・バイ・ケースで判断されることになり、必ずしも基準が明確であるとはいえません。

スライドには具体例を幾つか挙げておりますが、時間の関係で省略します。

次に、「特別の報酬」です。ブローカレッジ・サービスを全面的に提供する場合と、ディスカウント・ブローカレッジ・サービスを提供する場合とで異なるレートを用いた手数料を収受しているということだけでは、「特別の報酬」を収受しているということにはならないと解されています。

なお、登録ブローカー・ディーラーは、投資顧問業法の適用を受けるサービスを提供し、かつ、報酬を収受している場合であっても、当該口座に関してのみ、投資助言業者になります。したがって、登録ブローカー・ディーラーが、投資助言業者になるかどうかは、あくまでも口座ごとに判断されることになります。

ここに、有名な、いわゆる「メリルリンチ・ルール」が登場してきます。SECは、ブローカー・ディーラーの適用除外規定に基づいて、証券会社が伝統的なコミッション・ベースの手数料ではなく、預かり資産残高に応じて手数料を徴収するフィー・ベースの手数料体系を採用するだけでは、投資顧問業法の適用を受ける投資助言業者になるわけではないという解釈通知を公表しました。これがメリルリンチ・ルールと呼ばれるものです。

メリルリンチがフィー・ベース、すなわち預かり資産残高に応じて手数料を徴収する場合であっても、一定の場合には投資顧問業法の適用を受けず、適用除外規定に当たり得るというのがSECの「メリルリンチ・ルール」と言われるものであったわけですが、このルールは判例によって否定されるに至っています。すなわち、2007年に有名な判例（Financial Planning Association v. SEC, 482 F.3d 481（D. C. Cir. 2007）が出されました。判旨は、「SECはブローカー・ディーラーが提供するフィー・ベースの手数料を収受する口座を投資顧問業法の適用から除外する権限はない」として、メリルリンチ・ルールを否定しました。

５．手数料・報酬の形態

口座の手数料・報酬の形態ですが、理念系としてはコミッション・ベースとフィー・ベースの２つがあります。コミッション・ベースの算定根拠は、個々の証券取引であり、取引に基づいて手数料を徴収することになります。これに対して、フィー・ベースの報酬体系の下では、口座の預かり資産残高に応じて手数料を徴収することになります。

利益相反については、コミッション・ベースの場合には過当な証券取引を誘導するおそれがある点に求められます。これに対して、フィー・ベースの場合にも利益相反のおそれがあると言われています。たしかに、コミッション・ベースに比べると利益相反のおそれは小さいと言われていますが、しかしフィー・ベースの場合には、むしろポートフォリオの見直し等に基づく必要な証券取引を抑制したり阻害したりするおそれがあると指摘されています。

業者のメリットとしては、コミッション・ベースの手数料体系は取引ごとに手数料を取りますので、必要なコストに応じて手数料を徴収することになります。これに対して、フィー・ベースの報酬体系は、証券取引の多寡に依存しない安定的な収益源を確保できるというメリットがあります。

業者のデメリットとしては、メリルリンチ・ルールが普及した大きな理由は、米国では、コミッション・ベースの手数料体系を採用していたのでは収益源が非常に不安定になるということが指摘されます。特にコミッション（手数料）の激しい引下げ競争があり、コミッション・ベースで競争に打ち勝つことはなかなか難しい。さらに、フィー・ベースに比べると規制コストが高くつくと言われています。特にコミッション・ベースの証券口座に対してはFINRAの自主規制において非常に細かなルールベースの規制がたくさんありますので、規制コストが高くつくと言われています。これに比べてフィー・ベースの報酬体系は、証券取引の多寡に依存しない安定的な収益源になるというメリットがある半面、証券取引が頻繁に行われると収益を圧迫する可能性が生じます。すなわち、証券取引に基づいては手数料を徴収できないというデメリットがあります。

コミッション・ベースとフィー・ベースの２つは理念系です。その中間に、いわばハイブリッドの報酬形態として、両者の良さをあわせ持つ報酬形態が多様に存在しています。

なお、スライドの表では、業者のメリット・デメリットについて記載しています。個人顧客のメリット・デメリットという形で記載していないのはどうしてかと申しますと、個人顧客にとっては証券取引の多寡や資産残高などに応じて、いずれの形態が有利になるかはケース・バイ・ケースで、一概にコミッション・ベースのほうが個人顧客に有利、フィー・ベースのほうが不利ということも言えないし、逆も言えないためです。

米国においてメリルリンチ・ルールが判例によって否定された後、基本的にどのような運用がなされているかというと、コミッション・ベースかフィー・ベースかを顧客が選択するというのが支配的な報酬体系になっているようです。すなわち、メリルリンチ・ルールが否定されて以降、証券口座はフィー・ベースとコミッション・ベースに分かれ、顧客によって選択がなされるというのが主流になっていると思われます。

レギュレーション・ベストインタレストのもとで、証券業者が開設する証券口座について、メリルリンチ・ルールを復活することが可能かという論点があります。レギュレーション・ベストインタレストを見ると、手数料について開示すべきことしか規定しておりません。したがって、手数料について公正かつ完全な開示をして、さらに、先ほど申し上げたブローカー・ディーラーの助言行為が「専ら（本業に）付随して」なされるものであって、かつ「特別の報酬」を受けていない場合には、証券業を営みながら助言行為を行なっても投資顧問行法の適用を受けないことも可能である、という結論になるのではないかと思いますが、この点については、ぜひ後ほどご議論いただければと思います。

６．実態

米国の実態です。

登録ブローカー・ディーラーの数、口座数、預かり資産の総額等をスライドに記載してあります。登録ブローカー・ディーラーのうち１割弱の363社は、同時に投資助言業者としても登録しています。口座全体の63％は、いわばデュアルレジスター、つまりブローカー・ディーラーの登録もしているし、投資助言業の登録もしています。このように証券業と投資助言業の双方の登録をしている業者によって開設されている口座数が、米国全体の口座数の６割に達しています。さらに、3764のブローカー・ディーラー業者のうち2098業者は、直接または間接に、投資助言業に従事する法人を支配し、またはそれによって支配され、または共通支配下にあるということです。半数以上の登録ブローカー・ディーラーは、何らかの形で投資助言業者と同一のグループに属しており､グループ全体として見てみるとブローカー･ディーラーと投資助言の両方を営んでいるケースがかなりあると言えます。

７．フォームCRS

注目すべきはフォームCRS（Client or Customer Relationship Summary）です。

フォームCRSは、1940年投資顧問業法に基づくフォームADVを改正するとともに､ブローカー･ディーラー向けに1934年証券取引所法を改正して､ブローカー・ディーラーについてはフォームCRSを追加するというものです。

フォームCRSのポイントは、投資助言業者及びブローカー・ディーラーが個人顧客と新たに関係をもとうとする場合には、みずからの法的地位について、顧客にその概要を説明するためのリレーションシップ・サマリーを交付しなければならないという点にあります。特に、ある業者が、証券業登録と投資顧問業登録をともにしている場合には、１枚のサマリーで説明するのが基本となります。別々のサマリーを作成して２枚のCRSをつくることが禁止されているわけではありませんが、そのような場合には、両方について均等に説明しなければならないとされています。

さらに、証券業登録か投資顧問業登録のいずれかしか登録していない場合であっても、関連会社が証券業または投資顧問業を営んでいる場合には、その旨を記載しなければなりません。そうすることで、グループレベルで、各会社が投資顧問と証券業のどちらを営んでいるのか、それぞれどのような関係にあるのかということについて開示されることになります。さらに、リレーションシップ・サマリーは、提供するサービス、手数料・コスト、利益相反、行為規範、会社及び登録証券外務員の懲戒歴などについても記載することとされています。

実務的には、フォーム CRS は、ドッド＝フランク法が対処しようとした課題に応えるために非常に有意義な入口規制になるように思われます。なお、利益相反については、レギュレーション・ベストインタレストでかなり詳細なルールベースの規制が行われていると申し上げましたが、そこで要求されている詳細な開示事項が、フォーム CRS の記載事項とされています。

Ⅲ．ドイツ法

1．投資助言の定義

次に、ドイツにおける投資助言業者の規制について概観します。

ドイツにおいて、投資助言は、「顧客またはその代理人に対する特定の金融商品に係る取引に関する、委任規則（EU）2017/565 第９条にいう個別の推奨であって、当該推奨が当該投資者個人に関する状況の検討に基づいてなされるものであるか、または、当該投資者に適合するものとして提示されるもの」と定義されています。

この定義の大きな特徴は、助言に対して報酬を受け取るかどうかは定義には全く入っていないという点です。さらに、これは米国でも日本でも、解釈上、確立していると思いますが、個別の推奨であって、当該投資者個人に関する状況の検討－これはノウユアカストマー・ルールを前提にしていますが

－を踏まえて顧客に対して推奨を行う、または当該投資者に適合するものとして提示することが明確に要件とされています。顧客のベストインタレストのために推奨を行うべきことが定義上明らかにされているのです。このような投資助言の定義はEU法を反映したものですが、非常に広範な定義規定となっています。

ただし、特定の金融商品に係る取引に関する推奨が、専ら情報伝達手段を通じてなされたり、公衆に向けて発せられたりする場合には、投資助言には該当しないものとされています。

ドイツにおいては、投資助言の特徴は、投資仲介や取次ぎなど、他の有価証券サービスとともになされることが通常であると認識されている点にあります。つまり、米国は、私の理解によれば、投資助言業と証券業をできるだけ明確に線引きしようとするという考え方に立っていると思いますが、ドイツでは発想がかなり違っており、そうではなく、むしろ証券業者というのは通常、投資助言業者でもあるという考え方に立っているものと思われます。それゆえ、個別の推奨に対して報酬を受領しているかどうかは、投資助言の定義にとって重要でないわけです。このような定義は、１つの魅力的な投資助言業の定義の仕方であると思います。

投資助言業に該当するかどうかの具体的な判断基準は、つぎの５つです。

第１に、単なる情報提供ではなく、推奨であること。推奨というのは、助言者の側の意見が含まれているということを意味します。もっとも、ここが難しいところだと思いますが、単なる情報の提供であっても、その情報提供を受ける側にとって、何らかの取捨選択、何らかの意思決定の助けのためになされる情報の提供であれば、推奨に該当することになるという点です。したがって、推奨と単なる情報提供の区別は非常に難しいということになります。しかしながら、基本的には推奨と情報提供の区別が第１の基準になります。

第２に、推奨が金融商品の取引に関するものであることです。特定の投資に関係しない助言は、一般的な助言であって、推奨とはなりません。

第3に、推奨が投資者にとって適合的なものとしてなされるか、または当該投資者の個別の状況に対する考慮に基づいてなされるものであることです。適合的なものとしてなされる推奨は、明示的でも黙示的でもよいと解されています。また、投資者の個別の状況に関する情報を利用しない推奨であっても、既に業者がそのような情報を収集しており、それを考慮して推奨がなされていると合理的に期待される場合には、投資者の個別の状況についての情報を利用しないで行った推奨であっても、それは個別の状況に対する考慮に基づいた推奨であるとみなされます。

第4に、推奨が配布・配信チャネルを通じて非排他的になされたものではなく、また、公衆に向けられたものでないということが要件になります。したがって、新聞、雑誌、インターネットのウェブページ、テレビ、ラジオなどを通じてなされる推奨は、投資助言には当たりません。ただし、電子メールなど、複数の者に向けられたメッセージの送付先が、投資勧誘のターゲットになっている場合や、メッセージの内容や用いられている言語など、個別の諸事情を考慮して、複数の者に電子メールを送信した場合であっても投資助言に当たるとされることがあり得ます。

第5に、推奨が、投資者またはその代理人を特定してなされたものであるか、見込み投資者またはその代理人を特定してなされるものであることです。逆に言うと、投資と無関係の者に対して推奨を行っても、それは投資助言とは言えません。もう一つが、コーポレート・ファイナンス上のアドバイスとの区別です。経済的なリターンやリスクヘッジのためではなく、産業上・戦略上・企業上の目的のためになされる助言はコーポレート・ファイナンスのための助言であって、投資助言ではないと解されています。

このように、EUやドイツでは、投資助言に当たるかどうかについて、その定義が非常に広いということもあって、かなり詳細な議論がなされています。この点については、資料7「Understanding the definition of advice under MiFID」をご参照いただければ幸いです。

投資助言業に該当する場合には、信用制度法によって適用が除外される場合があります。すなわち、一定の場合には、投資助言が有価証券サービス業者の定義から除外されています。投資助言の定義が広いために、EU およびドイツにおいては、充実した適用除外規定が置かれています。適用除外に当たらない場合には、投資助言は金融サービス業に当たります（信用制度法1条1ａ項)。それを他人のために営業として、または商人的な方法で営業することを必要とする規模で営む場合には、免許が必要です（信用制度法32条1項)。

条文については、お配りしている資料に抜き出してあります。資料6「参照条文」の中で言及する主要な法令を引用し、特にスライドに掲げてある条文は赤線を引いてありますので、ご参照いただければと思います。

それとともに、ドイツの大きな特徴は、信用制度法上、投資助言を行う業者を原則として金融サービス業者として規制するとともに、有価証券取引法上も規制している点です。有価証券取引法上も、投資助言業は有価証券サービス業に該当します。このように、投資助言業者に対しては、信用制度法上の規制と有価証券取引法上の規制が重畳的に適用されるのがドイツ法の特徴です。

ちなみに、投資助言は、旧法のもとでは有価証券サービス業ではなく、有価証券サービス付随業でした。新法のもとで、投資助言業は、付随業ではなく有価証券サービス業に格上げされたわけです。その理由は、投資助言が個人投資家にとってますます重要になってきており、個人投資家がますます個別の推奨に頼るようになってきているという事情があります。そのような実態を反映して、投資助言自体が有価証券サービスに該当するものとされ、より厳格な規制の対象になりました。

２．免許制

先ほど述べたように、ドイツ法の特徴は、投資助言業について、信用制度法と有価証券取引法による二重の規制体系をとっている点にあります。ただし、有価証券サービス業の範囲をできる限り信用制度法上の金融サービス業の範囲と一致させようとしています。この点も、工夫をしているところであると思います。ダブルで規制をかけますが、規制の対象は同一にして、規制をあまりに複雑にしないように留意しているのです。

なぜこのような二重の規制体系をとっているのかと言うと、有価証券取引法は資本市場法の観点から、それ以外の金融機関に比べて有価証券サービス業者に対して追加的な規制を課しており、したがって、投資助言業者の規制は加重されることになります。このように、規制を柔構造化して、一般的な銀行等の信用機関にプラスアルファの規制が、資本市場のプレーヤーである有価証券サービス業を営む業者に対して、マーケットの観点から課されているのです。なお、投資助言業者については、ほかの有価証券サービス業に比べると、投資仲介業者などとともに、参入要件はかなり緩やかなものとされています。

3. 投資助言業者の組織上の義務

始めに、投資助言業者の信用制度法上の地位について述べます。先ほど申しましたように、投資助言業者は信用制度法上の金融サービス提供機関になります。

金融サービス提供機関は、信用機関とともに金融機関と定義されています。そのため、投資助言業者には、金融機関にかかる一般的な義務が課されることになります。例えば、法令遵守態勢とかリスク管理態勢の整備義務です。

そして、有価証券サービス業務を提供する企業については特則があります。先ほど述べたように、柔構造化された規制体系が採用されており、有価証券取引法80条1項は、有価証券サービス業を提供する企業は、当該サービスを継続的かつ適正に行うことを確保するための態勢、及び利益相反管理態勢を整備しなければならないと規定しています。したがって、有価証券サービス業者の場合には、信用制度法上義務付けられている法令遵守態勢とリスク管理態勢に加えて、利益相反管理態勢の整備が必須とされています。

そのほか、例えば投資助言に従事する従業員は、十分な知識・能力を有することが求められています。すなわち、有価証券取引法87条1項は、投資助言に際しては、専門的知識を有し、かつ投資助言について信頼できると有価証券サービス業者が信じる従業員だけを使用することができると規定します。そして、当該従業員が投資助言をする前に、誰が投資助言をするのか等についてBaFinに届け出なければならないものとされています。このように、投資助言については上乗せ規制が課されています。

利益相反管理態勢整備義務は、時間の関係で省略しますが、投資助言業者が英米でいうフィデューシャリー・デューティー、ドイツ法の下では顧客の利益を擁護する義務を負うことから、利益相反について非常に厳格な組織上の義務を課されています。投資助言業者は、利益相反をきちんと検知して、それを回避し、コントロールするための態勢を整備すべきものとされています。

次に、ドイツにおける投資助言業者の行為規制を概観します。

まず柱になるのは、誠実・公正に、かつ専門家として顧客の最善の利益を擁護する義務です。このような一般的義務が課されるとともに、ノウユアカストマー・ルールを前提として「適合性の原則」に即して顧客に助言や推奨を行わなければなりません。以上が、投資助言業者の基本的な義務になります。

そして、有価証券の販売・媒介等の勧誘の過程で投資助言がなされる場合が多いという前提に立っているのがドイツの特徴で、私の理解では、ドイツの証券業者の多くは、投資助言も行うという前提で業務を行っています。例外的に、有価証券の販売・媒介等の勧誘の局面で投資助言が行われないのはどのような場合かというと、①エグゼキューションオンリーすなわち証券取引の執行だけを受託する場合と、②当該投資家に既に投資助言業者がついていて、当該投資助言者の指図に基づいて投資者が売買している場合です。このような場合には、投資助言業には当たらないとされますが、ドイツにおいては、投資助言に該当する場合が日本や米国に比較するとかなり広いと理解しています。ドイツは投資助言の範囲が非常に広くて、むしろ証券を売る場合には、投資助言がなされるのが通常であるという発想に立っているものと思われます。

4．投資助言業者の行為規制

投資助言業者の行為規制については、先に述べた組織上の義務に加えて、開示・情報提供義務が、一般の有価証券販売業者よりも加重されています。冒頭に述べたように、むしろ投資助言業者は、一般の証券会社よりも高いレベルの技能を要するという前提に立って、開示・情報提供義務が加重されていると考えられます。条文をご覧ください。まず、ドイツ有価証券取引法63条が、有価証券サービス業者の一般的な義務を定めています。資料６の11ページをご覧ください。63条の表題は、「一般的な行為規制：命令への授権（Allgemeine Verhaltensregeln; Verordnungsermächtigung）」です。この条文は、有価証券サービス業者の一般的な義務を定めており、説明義務とか適合性原則等について定めています。次に、資料６の16ページをご覧ください。ドイツ有価証券取引法64条は、「投資助言を行う際の特別の行為規制（Besondere Verhaltensregeln bei der Erbringung von Anlageberatung）」というタイトルです。有価証券サービス業者が投資助言をする場合の特別の行為規制として、一般の有価証券販売業者よりも重い義務が、有価証券取引法の64条に定められています。

例えばどのような点が加重されているかと言うと、投資分析が包括的・総合的に行われているのか、それとも、部分的に行われているのか、明らかにしなければならないものとされています。そのほか、有価証券取引の前に、基本情報書面が作成されない金融商品については、所定の情報を記載した情報提供書面を交付する義務を課しています。また、この後申し上げますが、投資助言業者は一般の証券業者よりも重い義務を課されますが、さらに投資助言業者を２つのカテゴリーに分けて、独立報酬投資助言業者というカテゴリーを設けています。独立報酬投資助言業者とは、顧客からだけ報酬を受け取る投資助言業者ですが、このような独立報酬投資助言業者については、通常の投資助言業者よりさらに上乗せされた規制が適用されます。３層構造の規制になっているのです。これもドイツ法の大きな特徴です。独立して顧客から報酬をいただいて投資助言を行う場合には、さらに追加的な情報提供義務などの規制が課されています。

まず、有価証券サービス業者の一般的な行為規制を定める有価証券取引法63条から見てまいります。第１項はベストインタレスト・ルールを定めています。すなわち、有価証券サービス業者は、誠実・公正に、かつ専門職業者として顧客の最善の利益を図り、証券業務とその付随業務を提供しなければならないと規定します。第２項は、利益相反管理態勢によっては、顧客の利益を侵害するリスクを回避できると評価し得ない場合には、顧客に対してリスクの範囲を明示する義務を課しています。すなわち、利益相反管理態勢に限界がある場合には、それをきちんと開示するという義務が一般的に課されています。

投資助言業者についての特則を定める有価証券取引法64条によると、それに加えて顧客に対してわかりやすい形で次の情報を提供するものとされています。すなわち、第１に、独立報酬投資助言者として助言を行うものか、それともコミッション・ベースで助言を行うものかの区別です。第２に、助言は包括的な分析に基づいて行われるものか、それとも限定された分析に基づいて行われるものかの区別です。第３に、投資助言が自己と密接な関係にある金融商品の提供者、またはその他の法的・経済的関係に密接な関係にあるため、投資助言の独立性を害し得る提供者または発行者の金融商品に限定して推奨を行うものかどうかの区別です。投資助言業者については、これらの事項に関する特別の開示義務が課されています。

第２の包括的・総合的な分析に基づく助言か、限定された分析に基づく助言かについては、単に包括的・総合的か、限定的かという文言を用いて説明するだけでは不十分であり、全ての種類の分析について、具体的な数を示しながら開示しなければならないものとされています。取り扱う金融商品の種類、発行者、リスク・コスト・複雑性など、どのような観点から推奨の対象に加えたのかということについても情報提供しなければなりません。投資助言業者の情報提供については、かなり厳しいルールが課されています。

次に、適合性の原則について述べます。学説も含めて非常に争われているのは、顧客に対して推奨した金融商品の適合性に係る判断について、定期的に判断を更新する義務があるかどうかがです。有価証券取引法64条1項3号によると、定期的に推奨した金融商品の適合性について審査を行うかどうかを投資者に知らせなければなりません。投資助言業者は、投資者に対して一回推奨したら、あとは放っておくのか、それともきちんと定期的に推奨判断を見直すのかについて事前に情報提供しなければなりません。

もっとも、一回推奨したらあとは放っておきますということが、先ほど述べた一般的な顧客に対する顧客の最善の利益の擁護義務に照らして許されるのかどうかが議論されています。定期的に適合性審査をレビューすることまでしなくても、一定の場合には見直さなければならないでしょうという議論がなされています。

ただし、定期的に推奨を見直すことについては、投資助言業者に対し、民事法上課されている説明義務の範囲を超えてしまっているという批判もあり、ドイツで活発に議論されている論点です。

有価証券サービス業者は、顧客に対して、当該顧客にとって適合的な金融商品または有価証券サービスを推奨しなければなりません。ロボアドバイザーなどを用いる場合でもルールは同じです。

推奨が適切かどうかの判断基準は次の３つです。第１は、推奨された金融商品が、顧客の投資目標とりわけ投資目的とリスク許容度にふさわしいものかどうかです。第２は、投資リスクが当該顧客にとって経済的に負担可能であるかどうかです。第３は、当該顧客は自己の知識と経験に照らして当該投資リスクを理解できるかどうかどうかです。これら３つの判断基準から、推奨が適合的なものかどうかが判断されることになります。

なお、プロ顧客については、基本的には十分な知識と経験があるということを前提に、情報収集の対象は、何のために投資するのかということと、当該投資者の財務状況に限定されると解されています。適格機関取引先には、そもそもノウユアカストマー・ルールは適用されませんから（有価証券取引法68条1項）、今までの議論は主としてリテール投資者に対する投資助言の話です。

適合性原則の前提は、ノウユアカストマー・ルールです。すなわち、適合性判断を適切に行うために必要な顧客の情報を、業者は収集しなければなりません。収集すべき顧客の関連情報は、①通常の収入の源とその額、②流動資産・投資商品・不動産を含む現在の資産価額、③通常の金融債務、④投資期間、負担するリスクに係る選好、リスクプロファイルおよび投資目的などの顧客の投資目標に関する情報です。有価証券サービス業者は、適切に適合性審査を行う前提として、これらの顧客情報を収集しなければならないとされています。

なお、学説でかなり争われている論点として、有価証券サービス業者は、上述した①から④までの事項について一般的な質問をすれば足りるのか、それとも具体的な知識と経験を問わなければならず、疑わしい場合には一般的な質問だけでは不十分であって、さらに踏み込んだ質問をしなければならないのかです。

次に、投資助言者に適用される適合性にのっとった助言義務に係る特則について申し上げます。

有価証券取引法64条は、投資助言業者などに課される行為規制の特則を定めます。投資助言業者は、収集した顧客情報に基づいて推奨を行うわけですが、その際、顧客を類型化して、一般顧客、プロ顧客、適格取引先のいずれかに分類する必要があります（同条3項）。必要な情報を収集できないときは、推奨を行ってはなりません。その場合には、顧客に対して助言できないことを明確に示すべきこととされています。顧客の側で誤った情報を提供し、かつ有価証券サービス業者がそのことを知らなかったか、もしくは誤っていることが明白でなかった場合には、助言を行うことができます。また、顧客が必要な情報を提供することを拒否した場合には、投資助言業者は推奨を行ってはならないとされています。

有価証券サービス業者は全ての情報を収集する必要はなく、具体的な助言に関して顧客を評価するために必要な情報だけを収集すれば足りる等々、ノウユアカストマーについては詳細な議論があります。時間の関係で、ここも省略いたします。

適合性については、ノウユアカストマー・ルールにのっとって情報を集めたら実際に適合性の有無について審査をしなければなりません。どのような観点から審査するかが問題になります。適合性審査においては、具体的な取引について、顧客の投資目標、投資リスク及び経済的に負担可能かどうかという観点から判断するほか、当該顧客がその者の知識をもって当該リスクを理解できるかどうかが審査の対象になります。

基本的に、ここで述べる適合性の審査の内容は、ドイツで判例上発展してきている、民事法上の適合性原則、ドイツにおいては「ふさわしい助言の原則」と言われますが、その内容とほぼ一致しています。

もっとも、先ほど少し述べましたように、民事法に係る判例法理とずれる可能性があるのは、一旦推奨した後に、その推奨を見直す義務が含まれるかどうかです。一般に、民事ルールではそこまでは認められないと解されており、もし金融監督法のほうでそれが認められるということになると、民事ルールと業者ルールが異なることになります。しかし、基本的には、ドイツの適合性の原則については、民事ルールと金融監督法上のルールが一致しています。

次に、これも大きな特徴ですが、ドイツには適合性報告という制度があります。投資助言業者は、契約を締結する前に適合性報告書を顧客に交付することが求められます（有価証券取引法64条4項）。従来は助言プロトコルという制度でした。助言プロトコルは、単に顧客と投資助言業者の会話のやりとりを記録するものでしたが、適合性報告にはかなり詳細な情報が記載されることになっています。すなわち、行った助言の概要と、行った推奨が、顧客の選好、投資目標及びその他の「顧客の属性」にどの程度適合するものであるかを具体的に記載しなければなりません。

この制度は、適合性報告によって、投資助言業者が行った推奨が本当に当該顧客にとって適合的なものであるかどうか、どの程度適合的なものであるかどうか、顧客に一瞥可能な形でわかりやすく伝え、顧客に再考の機会を与えることを目的とした制度であると解されています。適合性報告の内容、方式、様式は、規則において詳細に定められています。

適合性報告は何のために行われるかというと、先ほど申しましたように、顧客がもう一度、頭を冷やして考えるということのほかに、民事訴訟で用いることが想定されています。すなわち、適合性報告は、顧客が民事訴訟で争う場合の証明手段として役に立つことが期待されているわけです。もっとも、適合性報告制度は、決して証明責任を転換するものではありません。しかし、顧客を保護するために、金融監督法上、投資助言業者に義務付けられたものであって、訴訟において顧客の不利に援用することはできないと解されています。

次は、有価証券サービス業者の記録保存義務です（有価証券取引法83条1項）。顧客との電話や電子メールを保存しなければならない等の非常に細かなルールが定められています（同条3項）。これらの義務は、金融監督の実効性を確保するのみならず、顧客からの民事訴訟においても有用です。

5．独立報酬投資助言業者の特則

前述したように、ドイツには、独立報酬投資助言業者という制度があります。独立報酬投資助言業者とは、顧客だけから報酬を収受して助言をする業者です。この制度は2013年に導入されました。ドイツでは従来取引手数料（コミッション）に支えられて投資助言が行われてきましたけれども、手数料に支えられた投資助言とそれには支えられていない独立報酬投資助言とを顧客が意識的に選択できるように、誰が投資助言について報酬を支払っているかを明確にして投資助言を行うという制度です。

このような制度が2013年に導入されて、2018年に、内容的にはかなり共通しているのですが、独立報酬投資助言業者という制度に衣替えして、現行法に至っています。独立報酬投資助言者制度とは､従来のコミッション･ベースの報酬体系に基づく助言が、必ずしも投資者の最善の利益に合致してこなかったという問題意識から、顧客から報酬をきちんと得て、利益相反をきちんとコントロールした上で、しかも包括的な投資助言を行うことを目指したものです。

なお、3月13日現在、ドイツでは17社の独立報酬投資助言業者が存在しています。

独立報酬投資助言業者に対しては、さらに上乗せ規制が課されています。すなわち、独立報酬投資助言業者は、市場に提供されている十分に広範な金融商品の品ぞろえに配慮しなければなりません。金融商品全般に目配りをして投資助言を行うことを義務づけられているのです（有価証券取引法64条５項）。

自己の計算で顧客と取引することは原則禁止ですが、一定の例外があります（有価証券取引法64条６項）。

また、利害関係のある金融商品に係る取引を推奨する際に、利益相反関係について開示する義務が課されています。

顧客以外の者から報酬を受領することが禁じられています（有価証券取引法64条５項２号）。

さらに、リベートの供与についての開示義務があります（有価証券取引法70条１項１号）。リベートをもらわないと販売することのできない金融商品があり、そのような場合にはリベートを受け取ることはできるけれども、受領したリベートはできる限り速やかに顧客に全額返還しなければならないという相当に詳細かつ具体的な規定が置かれています。

Ⅳ．おわりに

以上、米国とドイツの投資助言業者の定義と法規制の概要について簡単に見てまいりました。日本法の投資助言業規制について参考になる論点として、第１に、投資助言の定義を見直す必要があるかどうかを挙げることができます。特に投資助言の対価として報酬を収受することの要否は、比較法的に大きく分かれていました。ドイツやＥＵ法のように報酬を収受することは、投資助言の要件から外した上で、顧客から報酬を得る場合には、上乗せ規制で対処するという規制も十分にあり得る手法であると思います。報酬を収受することを投資助言の要件とするかどうかは、大きな問題であると思います。

基本的に私の理解では、1940 年の米国の投資顧問業法で意識されたのは、証券会社が行っている助言的な行為と投資顧問をどのように区別するかでした。米国法は、報酬を受け取るかどうかで区別しました。つまり、当時の1940 年以前の米国の証券実務を前提にした米国に固有の定義が日本にそのまま移入されているように思います。これが合理的なのかどうか。米国においては、証券業という本業に付随してなされた助言であって、かつ、特別の報酬を受領しているかどうかという要件の双方を充足する場合には、投資助言業者の定義から除外することとし、それぞれの要件をめぐって非常に緻密な議論をして整理しています。そのような規制手法ももちろんあり得ると思いますけれども、証券会社および証券仲介業者の手数料ないし報酬の体系が預かり資産残高ベースのフィーに移行する傾向がある中で、米国の立法の沿革と証券実務を前提にした米国における投資助言の定義を維持するかどうかは、１つの問題であると思います。

次に、有価証券の売買等に伴う助言と、投資助言の場合とで、基本的に例えば適合性原則の内容とか情報提供は同一の規制で良いのかという問題があるかと思います。EU やドイツの考え方は、一般の証券業者ももちろんノウユアカストマーおよび適合性原則に服するわけですけれども、投資助言業者に対しては、先ほど述べたように、情報収集にしても、分析にしても、推奨にしても、より高いレベルの行為規範を課しています。米国でも日本でも、投資助言業者には一般的な忠実義務が課されてはいるのですが、ノウユアカストマー・ルールおよび適合性審査さらには適合性審査に係る報告などについてルール・ベースで定める必要はないのか、立法論として検討する必要があると思います。

特にノウユアカストマー・ルールが日本の金商法のもとで確立しているのかどうかは疑わしいと思っています。少なくとも投資助言業者については、ノウユアカストマー・ルールを、ハードローとしてきちんと定める必要があると思われます。また、顧客に対する情報提供、それから助言に実際に従事する者に対する規制が十分かどうか、これらの点についてＥＵ法やドイツ法には日本法にとって参考になる部分が少なくないと感じました。

具体的な提言には至っておらず、雑駁な報告になりましたけれども、私の報告は以上です。いろいろご教示をいただければと思います。

討　議

弥永会長代理　大変貴重なご報告をありがとうございました。

それでは、ただいまの神作先生のご報告に対しまして、どなたからでも結構でございますので、ご質問、ご意見をいただければと思います。

なお、恐縮ですが、ご発言される前にお名前を言っていただくようにお願いいたしたいと思います。

大崎委員　神作先生、非常に詳細なご報告、誠にありがとうございました。

１点感想的なことを申し上げて、もう一個は質問をしたいのです。

最後のところで先生も日本の制度への何らかの示唆はないかという問題提起をされていたと思いますので、そこに何か資するかもしれないという観点から申しますと、ドイツの制度としてご紹介いただいた投資助言業者の従業員に資格が求められるといいますか、一定の資質が求められる制度は、日本でもぜひ導入すべきではないかと思います。

ご承知のとおり、証券外務員登録制度というのがあるわけですが、日本の場合ですと、第一種金商業者等の役職員の登録が求められていて、歴史的に見れば、証券会社の店舗の外で活動する外務員を会社が常時コントロールできないという中で、一定の資格を要求したというようなこととか、アメリカの制度を受け入れたということがあったのだと思います。しかし、専門性の重要性という観点からは、投資助言を提供する人も、そういう専門性を備えていることを客観的に証明できるようにしておくことが重要ではないかと思います。

それから、ご質問したかったのは、フィー・ベースかコミッション・ベースかということで利益相反の問題が議論されてきたことは私も承知していますが、フィー・ベースでも利益相反があるという指摘をするときに、従来はフィーを徴収する割には取引をしない、つまり何もしないでお金を取っているということが批判されてきたかと思います。

そうした取引の回数、頻度という問題だけでなく、私が最近問題だと思っておりますのは、従来、投資助言や投資顧問という業務は、顧客資産の増大につながるよう努めていれば、基本的には顧客との利益相反はないという理解があったように思われることです。しかし、本当に人生に資するファイナンシャルプランニングということを考えれば、資産を取り崩して引き出していくというプロセスにおける適切なアドバイスというものも非常に重要だと思うのです。

ところが、資産を減らしていくことについてアドバイスをするということになると、投資助言業者からすると、顧客にとって良いアドバイスをすると、自分のフィー収入が、資産残高に応じたフィー・ベースの契約であっても減ることになるので、そこには根本的な利益相反があるのではないかと思います。最近アメリカのファイナンシャルプランナーの中にそういう問題提起する人がいたりするものですから、先生のご見解を伺いたいと思いました。

長くなりましてすみません。

神作会長　大崎先生、貴重なご指摘とご質問ありがとうございました。

フィー・ベースの場合に、利益相反が生じ得る事項として、本来必要な有価証券の売買を行うことに対するディスインセンティブが生じるほか、むしろ資産が減少していく側面でも顧客にとって貴重なアドバイスというのがあるのに、きちんと助言がなされて資産が取り崩される場合には、資産残高が減少するため、フィー・ベースの報酬体系ではうまくいかないのではないかというご質問をいただきました。これはご指摘のとおりだと思います。

特に高齢化が進んでいくなどして、むしろ資産を取り崩して、それをどうやって生活費等に充てていくかという状況の下では、例えば有価証券を売却するときに一体どの銘柄から売却していくのかについて適切な助言をすることも、大変重要な任務であると思います。したがって、特に日本の場合には、少子高齢化の進展に照らして、むしろ資産を取り崩していくという局面において、適切な助言を投資助言業者が行うためのインセンティブを付与する報酬体系は、確かに大崎先生が指摘されたように、資産をふやしていくという方向で考えてきたフィー・ベースの報酬体系とはかなり異なる発想に基づく報酬体系が必要になるであろうと思います。非常に重要なご指摘をいただいたと思います。

基本的には、実務において、恐らくいろいろな工夫がなされていくことになると思います。フィー・ベースとコミッション・ベースというのはあくまでも２つの理念型にすぎませんので、この２つの間にさまざまな報酬体系があり得ます。さらに、個別の証券取引や預かり資産残高以外の要素を盛り込んだ報酬体系ももちろん考えられるでしょうし、基本的には業者がそれぞれ工夫して開発した報酬体系を、どのような設計思想に基づいて、誰がどのくらい負担しているのかということをきちんと開示して、顧客がその中から選択していくという方向に向かっていくのではないかと推測しています。大崎先生の言われるように、資産を取り崩していく局面における投資助言のあり方というのは、これまで日本ではあまり議論されてこなかった問題ではないかと思いますが、大変に重要な論点だと思います。

大崎先生から、何かご知見がありましたら、ぜひご教示いただければありがたいと思います。

大崎委員　アメリカのファイナンシャルプランナーでそういう問題意識を持っている人と議論したときは、それが本当に適切かというのはちょっと疑問もあるのですが、例えば顧客の所得水準に連動するようなフィーを考えるとか、そのようないろいろな試行錯誤をしているという話は聞きました。単純な資産残高連動だと、完全な利益相反になるのだということを強調しておりました。

小出委員　ご報告、大変勉強になりました。ありがとうございます。私も神作先生にご指導いただいて､別の研究会でアメリカのブローカー･ディーラーに関するレギュレーション・ベストインタレストについては勉強したこともあるのですけれども、ドイツに関しては全く勉強しておりませんで、非常におもしろく伺いました。

やや漠然としたコメントというか質問で大変申しわけないのですけれども、今日せっかくドイツの話とアメリカの話と日本の話のいずれもお聞きしましたので、３つの国それぞれの方向性について教えていただきたいと思うのです。

まず初めに、先生のご報告に基づくドイツ法に対する理解の確認です。ドイツ法については基本的に規制の対象も広いし、見ていると、かなり手取り足取りというか、ルールベースで相当細かく投資助言業に対する規制がかかるようになっているという理解ですけれども、この理解が正しいのかということがまず１つです。

仮にこの理解が正しいとしますと、他方でアメリカについての私の理解を申し上げると、アメリカでレギュレーション・ベストインタレストができた背景にあるのがドッド＝フランク法にであったというのは、私は非常に重要な意味があったと思っています。すなわち、もともとアメリカというところは、リテールによる投資が大変盛んであった。それがあまりにも過熱した部分があったことが､金融危機の一因であった。それに対する反省に基づいて、リテールの証券業者の投資助言業務に対しても規制強化を図るべきこととされ、そこで、ドッド＝フランク法の中で、レギュレーション・ベストインタレストにつながるようなブローカー・ディーラーに対する規制強化が織り込まれた、私はそういう理解をしております。

業者に対する規制を強化して、一般投資家を保護していかなければいけないという考え方自体に対してはいろいろな評価がありうるとは思うのですけれども、レギュレーション・ベストインタレストというのは、そうした考え方に基づいて、それまでのアメリカのフィデューシャリー・デューティーというプリンシプル・ベースのものに比べると、ルールベースの規制を取り入れて、ドイツほどではないにせよ、細かい規制を入れていったというふうに理解をしています。

一方、日本でも、先生ご紹介のとおり、顧客本位の業務運営ということが言われるようになりましたけれども、それが、アメリカのこういったレギュレーション・ベストインタレストと同じような時期であったというのはたまたまであって、日本における立法事実というか、あれは「立法」ではありませんけれども、日本においてああいうような考え方が提唱されるようになったというのは、日本では逆にリテール投資家があまり証券市場に投資をしてくれないということが前提にあって、そうした証券市場をうまくリテール投資家、家計資産につなげていくために、投資家保護を強化して、それで安心して投資できるようにしていこうという目的で、ああいった考え方が導入されたのだというふうに私は理解しています。

日本とアメリカというのは、もちろんもともと金商法上の規制と証券法上の規制とは非常に類似している中で、最近も同じ方向を向いているように見えるのだけれども、その背景にある実態は違っているように思うのです。そう考えたとき、ドイツにこのように非常に詳細な規制が入った背景は何であったのかというのが、非常に興味があるところです。

私はドイツの状況をよく知らないのですけれども、ドイツは比較的最近リテール投資が伸びているという状況があるという話も伺っています。そういったリテール投資が伸びている状況があるから、アメリカみたいにそれに伴って生じてきた弊害を除去する目的でこういう厳しい規制が入ってきたのか。それとも、むしろ逆に、こういう厳しい規制が入ったからこそ、ドイツは非常にリテール投資が伸びたと言えるのか。

これは日本にとっても非常に参考になると思っておりまして、仮にドイツがこういう厳しい規制が入っているから、リテール投資家が安心して投資できるようになったと考えるのであれば、日本もこれを見習って、顧客本位の業務運営のようなプリンシプル・ベースの規制よりも、もう少し厳しいルールベースの規制を入れていくことによって、よりリテール投資家の心理を安心させるということも考えられるように思います。

そうではなくて、ドイツは元々リテールによる投資が盛んであったという状況があったのであれば、まだ日本でここまで厳しい規制を入れる必要はなくて、むしろ日本ではプリンシプル・ベースのような形で緩やかに規制して、証券業者がより熱心に投資助言や勧誘できるようにした上で、弊害が生じたら、こういった規制を入れていくという方向性もあり得るのかなと思っております。そこで、ドイツにこういった規制が入った背景というか、立法事実というものを教えていただければと思います。

長くなってしまって申しわけありません。

神作会長　小出先生、非常に貴重なコメントとご質問をありがとうございます。

いただいたご質問に直接答えることにはならないとも思うのですが、私が注目しているのは、ドイツにおいて、投資助言業者に対して非常に詳細なルールベースの適合性原則ですとか、情報提供義務が規定された背景には、むしろ私法、すなわち民事法上、既に判例法理によって、投資助言業者や証券業者等に対して相当厳しい情報提供義務や適合性原則が課されていたことがあると思います。この点が、日本との大きな違いであるという感想を持っています。

そして、ドイツにおいては、むしろ業者ルールは、民事ルールとしてかなり定着していたルールを業法のレベルでも確立するとともに、先ほど申しましたような金融監督法においては適合性報告書のような民事訴訟を支える機能を営む制度を創設し、民事法によるエンフォースメントを補助しています。このように、民事法的なエンフォースメントというのがまずベースにあって、それを基礎として、かなり具体的かつ詳細なルールベースの行為規制が導入されているものと理解しています。日本では、情報提供義務や適合性原則は、むしろ、業法上の行為規制が先行し、民事ルールは、業者ルールを追随する形で発展してきたと理解していますが、この点が日本とドイツではかなり状況が異なると思います。

ＥＵ加盟国の中でもさまざまだとは思いますけれども、ドイツについては、ＥＵ法の定める業者ルールとしての詳細な情報提供義務や適合性原則ルールを導入することについて、抵抗があまりなかったと思います。情報提供義務や適合性原則については、ほとんど民事ルールと同じルールが業法上も導入されたというのが一般的な理解だったと思います。

このように、民事法上もかなり認められていた証券業者や投資助言業者の情報提供義務や適合性原則が、EU 指令の国内法化や EU 規則を通じて業者ルールになり、ドイツの有価証券サービス業者は、BaFin の監督等に服するとともに、先ほど申しましたように、適合性報告書制度や記録保存義務などの業者ルールによって、監督の実効性を確保するとともに、民事ルールに基づいて顧客が業者と争うときの武器が、リテール投資家に与えられたという側面があると思います。私の印象ですと、適合性原則ですとか情報提供義務というのは、監督機関とか、自主規制団体だけで十分なエンフォースメントができるかというと、限界が大きく、結局、個々の投資家が行動を起こすことによって、エンフォースしていくというのが、実効性確保の中心になるという考え方がドイツでは強いと理解しています。

そのような理解からすると、ご報告で述べたルールベースのさまざまな規制が、業法としていきなり入ったのではなくて、あくまでも民事ルールとして既にかなり具体的に確立していた規範を業者ルールとして取り込むとともに、それを整備して、場合によってはプラスアルファしたと理解できると思います。

では、業法上の行為規制としても導入されたことによって、ドイツの資本市場がどのようになったのかということは、私はきちんと研究してないのですけれども、ドイツでも昔から富裕層はかなり存在し、富裕層は証券投資を活発に行ってきたと思います。ただ、投資家の裾野がなかなか広がらないというのがドイツの資本市場の大きな問題点でした。ドイツでも、日本と同様、直接金融市場が間接金融市場に比べて脆弱であり、資本市場を強化する必要があるとしてそのような政策が採られてきました。したがって、小出先生ご指摘のとおり、政策的に投資家保護を図りつつ、業者規制を充実させるという面があったことも確かだと思われます。少なくとも、資本市場振興政策が導入されて以降、ドイツ証券取引所の株価は相当上昇しており、株価という面からは一定の成果があったとも考えられますが、それが法改正によるものであると申し上げるだけの知見がありません。

なお、ドイツでは、「灰色の市場」と呼ばれてきた、きちんと法規制されていない市場にどちらかというと洗練されていない個人投資家が勧誘されて、情報開示が不十分で不透明な中で、リスクがきわめて高く、詐欺的な投資をさせられるという問題が深刻でした。「灰色の市場」とは、資本市場法の適用を受けない民法上の組合や人的会社に対する持分、有限会社の社員たる地位、匿名組員としての参加や信託受益権などが販売されて、投資者詐欺事件などが頻発しました。ドイツでは「灰色の市場」に対しては取引所法や目論見書法の規制が適用されず長い間立法措置も講じられなかったため、裁判所が事後的に民事法に基づいて投資者を保護してきました。すなわち、「灰色の市場」に関して判例は、目論見書責任や説明義務に基づく損害賠償責任など民事上の規律によって投資者保護を図ってきました。2004 年の投資者保護改善法による改正販売目論見書法によって、ドイツにおいて「灰色の市場」で流通している金融商品についてもようやく公法上の目論見書義務と民事法上の目論見書責任の特則が適用されることになり、一般投資家の信頼もかなり高まった面があると思います。一般に、資本市場の規律づけは、民事法上の規律と監督法上の規制があいまって、投資者保護および資本市場の機能向上という目的をよりよく実現できるのだと思います。

なお、相当に詳細なルールベースの業者ルール、特に利益相反規制は、業者のためでもあると言われています。すなわち、民事訴訟が頻発するドイツにおいて、業者の側では、業者規制はきちんと遵守していることを主張して、民事訴訟においてむしろ業者をディフェンドする意味もあると言われています。この点も、日本とは随分状況が違うと思います。

すなわち、ドイツでは、厳格な民事ルールや民事紛争が生じやすいことを背景に、むしろ業者の側もこういった業者ルールを求めるという面があるようです。基本的には、情報提供義務や適合性原則は、民事ルールとして課されているわけですので、むしろ業者ルールとしてもきちんとやることはやっていますよと業者の側は反論するわけです。もっとも、ここでは民事法と業法の関係という論点が生じますから、業者ルールを守っていれば、民事責任を負わないかというと、単純にはそのようなことは申せません。しかし、例えば先ほどの法令遵守体制とか利益相反管理体制等をしっかりつくって、監督に服しながら法令を遵守して業務を行っていますということは、民事訴訟において、業者にとってプラスになる面もあるということが指摘されています。

小出委員　今伺っていて、日本も、もともと民事法、私法のほうは大陸法であるドイツ法と親和的な部分が多いと思いますので、その意味では、ドイツが民事法をベースに規制を発展させてきた経験というのは非常に参考になるし、今後日本でも検討していく価値が十分あるという感想を持ちました。

松井（智）委員　大変詳細なご報告をありがとうございました。

私も別の研究会でこの問題について少し別の観点で調べたことがありました。説明義務をこのように投資助言業のほうに近づけていったときには、レギュレーションコストの顧客への転嫁が進む結果、それに耐えられない零細規模の投資家が市場から排除されて、逆に投資における格差が進むのではないかという問題があるのではないかというようなことが、そのときの研究会でいろいろと指摘があったかと記憶しています。

その観点で、例えばアメリカなどではロボアドバイザーのような機械的な推奨をどういうふうに扱うかとか、いろいろな議論があったかと思うのです。したがって、ドイツでは例えばフィー・ベースのほうが望ましいといったような実務慣行があるのかどうかとか、ロボアドバイザーのようなものをレギュレーション上どうやって扱うのかといったようなことについて伺えればと思います。

神作会長　ご質問どうもありがとうございました。

松井先生ご指摘のとおり、特に米国の議論においては、ブローカー・ディーラーの説明義務や適合性原則と、投資助言業者の義務とを完全に一致させることに対する最も強い反対の論拠は、松井先生がご指摘された点であったと理解しています。そして、米国では、結局、そのような意見が多数を占め、2019年にSECが制定したレギュレーション・ベストインタレストは、ブローカー・ディーラーだけを規制対象とし、両者の行為規範を完全に一致させることを断念しました。したがって、松井先生のご指摘は、大変に重要だと思います。すなわち、ブローカー・ディーラーに対して極めて厳格な、いわばsole interest ruleに基づく行為規範をルール化してしまうと、ブローカー・ディーラーがコストとリターンへの考慮などから、相手にしない一般投資家がかなり出てきてしまって、その人たちは結局のところ、証券市場すなわち資本市場にアクセスする道を遮断されてしまうのではないかという観点は、確かに大変重要であると思います。

しかし、ドイツではあまりそのような議論はなされておりません。おそらく民事ルールが基本にあるからではないかと推測しますけれども、不適切もしくは不適合な金融商品を販売してはらならいというルールが民事法上確立していて、逆に言うと、資本市場の観点あるいは証券投資の促進という観点から、業者規制が形づくられるというよりも、むしろ民事ルールをベースに監督規制を形づくっている。これがドイツやＥＵの大きな特徴であると思います。情報提供や適合性原則については、業者ルールが民事ルールをベースにしているという点で、業者ルールをかなりの自由度をもって政策的に設計できる国とは事情がかなり異なると考えます。

そこのところが、米国などの議論と違うところがあるのかもしれませんが、ご指摘いただいた点は本当におっしゃるとおりです。米国において一般投資家、特に零細な投資家が証券投資にアクセスし、多様な商品を購入できる。

そのようなチャンスを与えることが非常に重要であるという発想が、とくに米国では強いと思います。業者規制が不適切に厳し過ぎたりすると、むしろ業者がそのようなビジネスから撤退してしまう。それはよくないという発想があるのはご指摘のとおりと思います。

次に、松井先生がご指摘されたロボアドバイザーに対する規制のあり方です。ドイツでも、ロボアドバイザーはかなり発展しており広く利用されています。もっとも、ドイツ法およびEU法においては、ロボアドバイザーも基本的には人間が投資助言をする場合とまったく同一のルールに服するということが確立しています。したがって、基本的には、ロボアドバイザーによって投資者に推奨されている商品というのは、現状では非常に安全性が高くて、現段階では、大半の投資者にとって適合的なものが多いと言われています。

しかし、この後、ロボアドバイザーがどのような金融商品を扱い、どのように展開していくかは、簡単には予測できず、いろいろな可能性があると思います。したがって、将来的には大きな問題が生じるかもしれませんけれども、現状ではあまり問題が生じてないというか、問題が生じないような運用や利用がなされている段階であると認識しています。

最後に、報酬体系については、ドイツにおいても、フィー・ベースの方が望ましいという議論が有力であるというわけでは必ずしもなく、報酬体系や報酬の額について開示をし、投資者がその中から選択するという方向が志向されていると理解しています。

十分なお答えになっておりませんけれども、松井先生から、さらにコメントとかご意見がありましたら、ぜひご指摘、ご教示いただければと思います。

松井（智）委員　私にも特に良いアイデアはないのですが、ただ、そのような規制が入ったことによって、全体としての投資額がどういう影響を受けたのかとか、どういう報酬体系で業務を遂行する人たちが増えたのかとか、そういったことがわかると、影響としてわかりやすいのかなと感じました。

神作会長　報酬の実態については、米国のものは、ある程度統計を見つけることができたのですけれども、ドイツについては、少し探してみたのですが、ご紹介できるような統計を見つけることができませんでした。もしわかりましたら、補充させていただきたいと思います。

松尾（直）委員　神作先生、非常に詳細なご説明をいただきましてありがとうございます。

私からご質問させていただきたいのは、ご承知のとおり、もともとアメリカでは、1934年証券取引所法と1940年投資顧問業法があって、異なる根拠法となっています。ブローカー・ディーラーのいわゆる投資助言業務については、間にある中間的なもので、その扱いをどうするかということが議論になったのだと思います。

日本はご承知のとおり、法律は別建てだったのですけれども、金商法に金融商品取引業ということで、投資助言業務も証券取引法時代の証券業も統合された。ただ、過去の別法体系をベースに、金融商品取引業を類型化して、規制内容が多少とも異なるところがあります。

ドイツの場合は、ドイツ法を存じ上げませんけれども、もともとＥＵのMiFIDがあって、投資サービス業という概念において幅広い業務が入っているわけです。

今回ご報告をお伺いして思ったのは、投資助言業務について厳しいことです。日本は、相対的に投資顧問業については、投資一任業務は別として、純粋な助言業務については、結局、投資家からすると、投資判断は自分が行って、取引発注も自分で行って、助言を受けるだけなのです。ですから、相対的に軽い規制になっているという考えだろうと思われるのですけれども、ドイツは、投資サービス業の中で、投資助言業について、投資家は助言を受けるだけなのに、なぜこれほど重い規制をかけられているのか。英米法的なフィデューシャリーだけでは多分説明し切れないと思うのですけれども、その辺、先生に教えていただければと思います。

神作会長　松尾先生、ご質問どうもありがとうございます。

基本的にはドイツにおいて投資助言者に対して重い義務が課されているのは、何度も繰り返しで恐縮ですけれども、既に民事法上そのような義務が課されていまして、民事法上は、投資助言契約は準委任契約であると解されています。準委任であるため、受任者である投資助言業者は、委任者である顧客に対して、利益相反規制を含む善管注意義務や誠実義務を負っていると解されています。これは英米におけるフィデューシャリー・デューティーの議論とも共通する点だと思いますけれども、助言を行うというのは基本的には専門家すなわち顧客よりも専門性のある人がより専門性の少ない人に対して一定のアドバイスを行うということなので、依存関係が生じるのが通常であろうと解されているものと思われます。

確かに松尾先生がおっしゃったように、助言を受けても、最終的に投資判断をするのは投資者本人ではないかというのはご指摘のとおりと思います。けれども、英米においては、専門家等のフィデューシャリー･デューティー、ドイツにおいては、(準)委任関係に基づく誠実義務(Treuepflicht)、あるいは委託者の利益を擁護する義務が課され、一定の事項について推奨したり助言を与えたりするものについては、投資助言に限らず、一般的にかなり厳しい義務が民事法上課されていると理解しています。

少し脱線するかもしれませんけれども、日本でなかなか専門家が育たない一つの理由は、専門家に係る法的ルールが、表現の仕方は適切でないかもしれませんが、日本法の場合にはやや甘いところがあるのではないかと思います。むしろ、英米やＥＵのように、専門家は、きちんと職業専門人として公正かつ誠実に、顧客の方を向いて仕事をしていくという法規範を確立する必要があると思います。さらに、特に本日のテーマで問題になっているのは、マーケットに係る投資助言ですので､マーケットに係る投資助言については、マーケットを向いて仕事をするのだということに留意すべきだと思います。ドイツでは、民事法上も、また業法上も、先ほど述べたようにかなり厳格かつ詳細な助言業者の義務が課されていることに加えて、マーケットの観点から、有価証券取引法は、さらにそれに追加して規制を上乗せしているという構造になっています。

専門家に対して、どのような法的ルールを課すかという、投資助言の領域だけの問題ではなくて、日本法全体にかかわる問題であると思いますけれども、日本では専門家責任というのがなかなか発展しないということの裏腹の問題だと思います。私は、少なくともマーケットを背景とした金融商品に係る投資助言については、少なくとも欧米並みのルールを導入するのが適切ではないかと考えています。

松尾（直）委員　少し追加ですが、投資助言はちょっと軽いと申しましたけれども、善管注意義務と忠実義務が入っていまして、旧証券業には入れてないです。ですから、投資助言業のほうが重くなっている面もあります。

あと、やや脱線するかもしれませんが、先生がおっしゃった専門家という点ですけれども、私も専門家なのです。ただ、提供しているサービスの内容が違うということと、金融の専門家の最大の難しさは、自己の専門的知見だけでは必ずしも顧客の満足度を高められないことだと思います。医師でも、弁護士でも、結果を保証することはできないのですけれども、金融商品取引業では、結果を保証できないというか、損失補填の規制があるから、むしろ結果を保証してはいけないことになっています。顧客は収益を上げたい、あるいは損失を回避したい。でも、それはマーケットによって左右されるわけです。私は自分で異なる分野の専門家をやっていて、金融の専門家というのは難しいだろうなと常に思っているのです。

そういう議論はドイツにはないのですか。要は、マーケットによって顧客の目的である収益性、損失回避が左右されてしまって、専門家もコントロールできないのです。これは医師や弁護士以上にコントロールできないと思います。そういう特殊な専門家である金融の専門家について、何かそういう議論はないのでしょうか。一般論過ぎて申しわけないのですが、あるいは先生のお考えみたいなものはないでしょうか。

神作会長　まさにおっしゃるとおりで、結果がどうなるかは本当に誰にもわかりません。ただし、専門家であろうとも、結果責任を負うものではないということは確かだと思います。専門家責任は結果責任を負わせるものではありません。しかし、顧客との関係で、たとえ損失が出ても、あるいは期待したような利益が出なくても、法的請求はできないということを正当化するためには、情報提供ですとか適合性の原則ですとか、特に利益相反規制ですとか、そのような投資助言業者が遵守すべきルールをきちっと守ってやっていれば、結果がどうであれ、責任を問われることはないという考え方に立つことになります。むしろ結果責任を問われないためにも、態勢整備義務などの組織上の義務を含む、金融監督法上のさまざまなルールが置かれている面があると思います。

さらに投資助言の場合の大きな特徴は、マーケットを常に意識していて、特に顧客だけから報酬を受け取る独立報酬助言業者というのは、ドイツにおいては、原則として、マーケットに流通している金融商品全般に目配りをして投資助言をしなければならないこととされています。顧客だけではなくて、マーケットも意識して、注意義務を資本市場の機能発揮に資するようにアレンジしている面があると思います。そういう意味では、まさに松尾先生ご指摘のとおり、市場はどうなるかわからないという特徴をドイツはむしろ非常に強く意識して、こういった法体系を構築していると理解しています。

松尾（直）委員　もう一点、セルサイドのいわゆるアナリスト、証券会社に所属するアナリストのアナリストレポートは、投資助言との関係では、ドイツではどのように位置づけられているのでしょうか。

神作会長　ご報告の中でも申し上げました５つの基準、単なる情報提供か推奨か、また、金融商品の取引に関するものか、などスライドの 25 ～ 26 ページの①から⑤の基準を適用して判断することになります。

アナリストレポートについてもっとも問題になるのは、④の要件、すなわち、「推奨が配布・配信チャネルを通じて排他性を否定する態様でなされたものではなく、また、公衆に向けられたものでないこと」の要件です。そして、投資リサーチの配信については、この要件を満たさないものとされています。解釈上、明確化が図られており、「投資リサーチの配信は、投資助言に当たらない」ものとされています。もっとも、典型的な投資リサーチの範囲を超えたタイプの配信がされたようなとき、例えば特定のグループに対してだけ、そのグループのメンバーだけをターゲットにして勧誘的な要素が含まれる配信がなされる場合には、④の要件を充足する場合があり得、先ほどの①から⑤までの基準を満たせば、推奨に当たるとされます。

なお、上述した５つの基準は、そもそもドイツの基準というわけではなく、ＥＵレベルの基準ですけれども、日本法にとってもかなり参考になる基準であると感じています。

河村委員　ご報告、大変勉強になりました。どうもありがとうございました。

今の助言に関する規制が厳しいという点にも関係するのですけれども、ドイツの実態として、証券会社が投資助言をして、その助言の結果としての発注を自社につなげていく。こういうことがあったのではないのかなということを勝手に推測したのですけれども、もしそういうことがあったとすると、それが原因で助言のところの規制が厳しくなり、また投資助言の定義についても、必ずしも報酬を要件としないということにつながっていったのではないかと思ったのですが、そのあたりの実態について改めて教えていただければと思います。もしかすると、既にお話しいただいているかもしれませんけれども、お願いします。

それからもう一点ですが、先ほどもともと民事責任、民事の部分が発展していたというお話があったと思うのですけれども、違う点として、情報提供義務のところでしょうか、一旦推奨した後も継続的に見直していかなくてはいけないというところで、その議論が出てきた背景に何があったのでしょうか。例えば高齢者との関連の話とか、そのあたりの議論があったのかというところも教えていただければ幸いです。

神作会長　河村先生、２つのご質問どうもありがとうございました。

まず前者のご質問です。もう少しきちんと調べたり、インタビューしたりしなければならないのですが、本日は調査が間に合っておりません。したがって推測に止まりますが、ドイツでは、投資助言の範囲が広いことと相まって、ドイツの証券会社は、証券業、すなわち証券の売買やその媒介等についての免許と、投資助言についての免許の両方を持っている場合が多いと推測しています。米国でも、ブローカー・ディーラーの登録と投資顧問の登録の両方をする業者が一定程度存在することを申し上げましたけれども、むしろドイツは、そのようなビジネスモデルが主流であると予想しています。

そうしますと、河村先生のおっしゃるとおり、利益相反の危険性が相当に大きくなるわけですけれども、基本的に米国と同様に、ドイツやＥＵにおいても、投資助言業者に対しては、自己が当該顧客の取引の当事者になってはならないとされます。このルールは、投資助言業者の行為規範として、日米独に共通と理解しています。投資助言業者は、投資助言に係る取引について自ら本人となって取引をしてはならないというルールが課されますが、ドイツの場合には、実は例外が結構広く認められています。すなわち、事前に顧客から書面による同意を得て、かつ、一定の条件のもとであれば行うことができるとされています。実は、証券業務との兼営から生じる利益相反については、かなり規制が甘いといえると思います。

そのような行為から顧客を保護するために期待されているのが、証券業者に課される最良執行義務であると理解しています。すなわち、投資者にとっては最良執行がなされれば、不利益はないであろうという割り切りをしているとも考えられます。

また、ご報告でも申し上げたとおり、ドイツでは、投資助言業者に対しては、有価証券サービス業者として、有価証券取引法において、一般的な利益相反管理態勢整備義務が導入されており、組織上の義務を課すことによって利益相反の問題に組織的に対処しようとしています。

なお、ドイツの有価証券取引法は、有価証券サービス業者に対して一般的に利益相反管理態勢整備義務を課すとともに、どうしてもそれによってもクリアできない利益相反については、投資者に対してきちんと開示しなければならないと規定します。このように、業法および金融監督法上の規制によって、一定の対応をしようとしています。さらに、最良執行義務についても同様で、業者ルールによって利益相反によって生じ得る不利益を実質的に排除するための措置が講じられています。しかし、それで十分かと言われると、これらの規制の実効性が必ずしも高いわけではないこともあり、河村先生ご指摘のとおり、業法上厳格な規制を導入するという方向に進んだと考えられるように思います。

確かにご指摘いただいた利益相反の問題は、ドイツにおいても非常に深刻な問題で、監督法上の規制が入れられたことによって、実態としてどれだけ実質的な利益相反の問題が解消しているのかについては、まだまだ調べなければいならないところが多く、不十分なお答えに止めざるを得ません。

２つ目のご質問について申し上げます。適合性判断について継続的な見直しを要するかどうか、論点になっている背景についてのご質問をいただきました。高齢者というのも一要素だと思いますけれども、典型的なケースというのは、投資者の財政状態や経済状態が大きく変わってしまったようなケースです。例えば投資者が行っていたビジネスが破綻したり、仕事を失って失業してしまったりといったケースです。何らかの事情によって経常的な収入が得られなくなったというのが、典型的なケースです。そのほか、例えば人生において大きな出来事、たとえば事故に遭ったり、病気になったり、離婚したり、そういったさまざまな財政状態とか社会経済生活上の環境が刻々と変化していくわけで、高齢化もその一例ですが、それだけに限らず、そういったさまざまな状況や環境の変化について、投資助言業者は特に重要な事項については情報を収集し直して、推奨判断を変えていく必要があるかどうかが議論されています。このような定期的な適合性審査が顧客の利益擁護義務から導かれるとして、一部の研究者は民事ルールとしても認めるべきであると主張していますが、民事ルールとしてはそこまでは認められないとする見解が多いようです。

業者ルールとしては、先ほど申し上げたように、有価証券取引法において、適合性審査について定期的にレビューする義務があるとまでは規定してないのですけれども、定期的な見直しをするかしないかということを顧客に対してきちんと開示しなければならないというルールになっています。

松井（秀）委員　非常に詳細なご報告をありがとうございました。アメリカ、ドイツ、日本も含めて比較をしていただきまして、それぞれの制度が相対化され、私自身、投資助言業についてあまり詳しくないのですけれども、理解が深まりました。

１点、実は先ほどの河村先生のご質問とほぼ重なってしまうので、もうお答えいただいたようなものですけれども、先生のご報告の24ページの「投資助言業の定義」に関するドイツの部分で、一番下に「ドイツにおいては、投資助言の特徴は、投資仲介や取次ぎなどの他の有価証券サービスとともになされることが通常である」というご指摘をくださっております。この点が実はドイツの制度に影響を与えているのではないか、というのが気になったところです。

先ほど河村先生からもありましたが、投資助言に報酬という概念が含まれない。これはヨーロッパの影響もあるのかもしれませんけれども、報酬概念を含めてしまうと、ある種の規制すべき対象が漏れ落ちてしまう。あるいはドイツのさまざまな事情があるかとも思いますけれども、他のサービスを兼ねているがゆえに、投資助言だけを切り離してクリアに規制をすることができない。上乗せ規制になるというのはまさにそういうことだろうと思うのです。そのようなドイツの固有の事情は、規制のあり方に反映しているのではないか。また、そのように理解することによって、アメリカや日本の制度を今後考えるときに、ドイツとどのような事情が同じで、何が違っているかを見ていくことができるのではないかと思った次第であります。

以上の次第で、ドイツの投資助言の実態と、先生がご紹介くださったドイツの制度のある種の規制の重さや広さというところとが結びついているのではないか。このあたりの認識について、以上の理解でよいかどうかをお伺いできればと思っておりました。ただ、先ほど河村先生とのやりとりでかなり答えていただいたようにも思いますので、もし既にお答えいただいているということであれば十分でございます。どうぞよろしくお願いいたします。

神作会長　松井先生、ご質問どうもありがとうございました。

私の認識が間違っているかもしれないのですが、証券会社が行っていること自体は、日本も米国もドイツもあまり違わないのではないかという気がしています。

すなわち、証券の売買やその媒介等を行う際に、証券会社やその従業員等が助言的な行為を行うというのは、どこの国でも一定程度行っているものと推測します。

米国の場合には、証券業規制が先に存在しており、それに加えて新たに投資顧問業法を制定するというときに、松尾先生からご指摘いただいたように、両者を別の法律で規制することにして、両者の適用範囲をどのように線引きするかが非常に大きな問題になりました。その結果、報酬の収受をようけんとする投資助言の定義とブローカー・ディーラーの適用除外という、米国に独特な規制体系が形成されました。

これに対してドイツにおいては、有価証券サービスという包括的な概念の下に、有価証券の売買、その媒介等などとともに投資助言も含められ、同一の法律によって規制されています。かつては、投資助言自体が有価証券サービス付随業務であったことに象徴されるように、ドイツにおいては、投資助言について独立して当該サービスの対価として報酬を収受しているかどうかは直接的には問題にしません。業者がビジネスとして行っているわけですから、どこかでコストは回収していると思われるわけですけれども、報酬の収受を投資助言の要件とはせず、したがって投資助言の範囲は日米に比較するとかなり広範になります。米国のような一種のフィクションというか、特別な報酬でなければ、そして証券業に専ら付随してなされる分には、ブローカー・ディーラーは助言的な行為を行っても、投資助言業には該当しないという整理をしたわけですけれども、ドイツ法は、そのような整理をせずに、機能的に投資助言をとらえて規制していると思います。

私から見ると、むしろ米国の規制のほうがやや特殊と申しますか、先ほど申しましたように、規制の沿革ですとか、当時、証券会社が行っていた実務を背景に、投資顧問業法の規制が証券会社に適用されてしまうと、米国の場合には、本人として取引することが原則としてできなくなるので、ブローカー・ディーラーにとっては、投資顧問業者とされるとビジネスモデルに大きな影響が生じることになるのだと思います。まさにそのことは、労働省がフィデューシャリー・ルールに関する規則案を公表したときに、業界が大変な騒ぎになった原因であると思います。もっとも、投資助言業者になると原則として本人として顧客と取引できないというルール自体は、ドイツ法にも存在し、ドイツはそちらについて適用除外規定によって調整しているわけですので、どこで調整をするかという問題にすぎないのかもしれません。ドイツでは、有価証券サービス業者が、他の多くのサービスを兼ねているがゆえに、その中で投資助言だけを切り離してクリアに規制をすることができず、上乗せ規制にならざるを得ないという松井先生のご指摘は、なるほどと思うとともに、投資助言業を証券業から切り離して規制する米国法の規制、が経路依存によってやや特殊な道を進んでいるような印象を受けます。日本法は、平成18年証取法改正によって、投資助言業務を金融商品取引業に取り込んだわけですから、ドイツ法のように投資助言業を定義し、規制することも、一考に値すると思いますが、民事ルールや最良執行義務などの業者規制全体を見通しながら、議論を進める必要があると思います。

松井（秀）委員　私自身もあまり詳しく研究したことがないものですから、むしろなるほどと思いながら、本日、お伺いをいたしました。

法律の制度としてのたてつけ、できた順序、あるいはアメリカの場合に関しては、先生がおっしゃったように規制の中身ゆえに、業者のインセンティブが変わって、動きが変わっているということがわかりました。いずれにしても、各国の制度のありようや、業者の成り立ちが影響しているということは、非常に抽象度の高いレベルですけれども、理解をいたしました。どうもありがとうございました。また考えさせていただけばと存じます。

弥永会長代理　それでは、まだご議論もあろうかとは思いますけれども、時間も参りましたので、本日の研究会の質疑を終了させていただきたいと思います。神作先生、どうもありがとうございました。

次回の研究会は、お手元の議事次第にございますように、5月27日の午後１時から、宮下央先生よりご報告いただく予定でございます。

なお、会場は、本日と同じくこの証券団体会議室となりますが、新型コロナウイルスの感染状況等に大きな変化が見られない場合には、今回同様、リアルとオンライン併用のハイブリッドでの開催を想定しております。

それでは、本日の研究会はこれで閉会させていただきたいと思います。

報告者レジュメ

金融商品取引法研究会

投資助言業に係る規制 ―ドイツ法との比較を中心として―

2021年3月16日

東京大学　神作裕之

目次

I. はじめに
II. 米国法
III. ドイツ法
IV. おわりに

2

Ⅰ　はじめに

1. 定義
2. 業法上の規制
3. 手数料に関する最近の動向
4. 問題提起

3

Ⅰ　はじめに

1.　定義

投資助言業＝投資者の一方が相手方に対して、有価証券の価値等に関し、口頭、文書その他の方法により助言を行うことを約し、相手方がそれに対し報酬を支払うことを約する投資顧問契約を締結し、当該契約に基づいて助言を行うことを業として行うこと（金商法28条3項1号・2条8項11号）

- 有価証券の価値等に関する助言
- 報酬の支払

2.　業法上の規制

①　一般的義務

- 誠実公正義務（金商法36条1項）
- 忠実義務および善管注意義務（金商法41条1項・2項）

なお、投資助言業者は、私法上も、準委任契約である投資顧問契約に基づき、善管注意義務（民法644条）を負い、それには忠実義務が含まれると解される

4

Ⅰ　はじめに

②行為規制

- 金融商品取引業に共通して適用される行為規制の適用を受ける

金商法上の情報提供義務および適合性原則等（金商法37条の3・38条9号・金商業府令117条1項1号・40条1号）

- 投資助言に固有の禁止行為（金商法41条の2、金商業府令126条）

✓顧客の取引に基づく価格等の変動を利用して自己または第三者の利益を図る目的で、正当な根拠を有しない助言を行うことの禁止など（同法41条の2第2号）

✓投資助言業務を行う金融商品取引業者は、顧客を相手方として、または顧客のために有価証券の売買等を行うことの禁止（金商法41条の3）

ただし、第一種金融商品取引業や登録金融機関業務として行う場合等には、適用されない（金商法施行令16条の8）

✓顧客からの金銭・有価証券の預託の受入れの禁止（金商法41条の4）

ただし、登録金融機関が信託業務として行う場合や内閣府令で定める場合には、適用されない（金商法施行令16条の9）

5

Ⅰ　はじめに

②行為規制

- 金銭・有価証券の貸付けの禁止（金商法41条の5）

ただし、政令で定める場合には、適用が除外される（金商法施行令16条の11）

③その他の規制

- 営業保証金の供託義務

➡兼業規制、主要株主規制、自己資本比率規制、金融商品責任準備金制度の適用はない

6

Ⅰ　はじめに

3.　手数料に関する近時の動向

証券会社や証券仲介業者の中に、従来型の個別の売買毎の手数料に変えて、預かり資産の残高に応じてフィーを徴収する動き

【例】

- A証券株式会社

個人顧客の預かり資産残高に応じて一定の報酬を受け取る仕組み（レベルフィー）を2年以内に全支店で展開することを目指す

- B証券株式会社

2022年にも、株式や債券など預かり資産の残高に応じた手数料体系を本格的に導入

なお、投資信託の販売手数料については、購入時に支払うか、運用残高に応じて支払うか、顧客側が選べるサービスをすでに開始

7

Ⅰ　はじめに

4　問題提起

- 投資助言業務と有価証券の売買・媒介等に係る金融商品取引業務の境界？
- 投資助言業に係る業法上の規制は過不足がないか？

有価証券の売買・媒介等に係る金融商品取引業者も、説明義務および適合性原則に服する

さらに、ソフトローのレベルでは、顧客本位の業務運営の原則が適用される場合がある

高度の専門性と職業倫理を保持し、顧客に対して誠実・公正に業務を行い、顧客の最善の利益を図るべきである（原則2）

金融事業者は、顧客の資産状況、取引経験、知識及び取引目的・ニーズを把握し、当該顧客にふさわしい金融商品・サービスの組成、販売・推奨等を行うべきである（原則6）

8

Ⅱ　米国法

1. 投資助言業者の定義と適用除外
2. 投資助言業者とブローカー・ディーラーの行為規制
3. 投資助言業者のフィデューシャリー・デューティー
4. ブローカー・ディーラーの適用除外
5. 手数料・報酬の形態
6. 実態
7. フォームCRS

9

1　投資助言業者の定義と適用除外

➢定義

1940年米国投資顧問業法202条(a)(11)

投資助言業者＝「報酬を得て、直接または出版物もしくは文書により、有価証券の価値、有価証券への投資、購入または販売の適切性に関して、他者に助言する業務に従事する者、並びに、報酬を得て、通常の業務の一環として、有価証券に関する分析もしくは報告を発行し、または公表する者」

- 有価証券に係る投資助言・推奨を行うこと
- 上記のサービスに対する報酬を受け取ること

➢ブローカー・ディーラーに関する適用除外

ブローカー・ディーラーの助言などの行為が、本業に「専ら付随して(solely incidental)」なされるにすぎず、かつ、その行為について「特別の報酬(special compensation)」を受領していなければ、投資助言業者には当たらない

10

2　投資助言業者とブローカー・ディーラーの行為規制

➢受認者（フィデューシャリー）かどうか？

投資助言業者は、フィデューシャリーであるのに対し、ブローカー・ディーラーは、フィデューシャリーではないというのが伝統的理解

➢米国における問題意識

ブローカー・ディーラーと投資助言業者が、個人顧客に対し助言を行うなど実質的に類似・同種のサービスを提供している場合があるにもかかわらず、両者の法的地位が異なり、顧客が誤解または混乱に陥っていることを問題視

➢ドッド＝フランク法

SECにブローカー・ディーラーと投資助言業者の行為規制を制定する権限を付与するとともに、いずれの規範も「顧客の最善の利益（best interest of the customer）」のために行為することを要求するものでなければならず、投資顧問業法206条（1）および（2）の定める基準より緩和されたものであってはならない（ドッド＝フランク法913条（g））

11

2　投資助言業者とブローカー・ディーラーの行為規制

➢レギュレーション・ベストインタレスト（SEC, 17 CFR Part 240, Release No. 34-86031; File No. S7-07-18, RIN 3235-AM35, Regulation Best Interest: The Broker-Dealer Standard of Conduct Regulation Best Interest)

ブローカー・ディーラーの行為規制

個人顧客の最善の利益ために行為する義務

(1)　個人顧客に対して証券取引または証券を含む投資戦略を推奨するときは、推奨をしているブローカー＝ディーラーやこれに関連する自然人の経済的またはその他の利益を個人顧客の利益に優先させることなく、推奨する時点において、個人顧客の最善の利益のために行動しなければならない

(2)　(1)の義務は、次の場合には履行されたものとする

① 開示義務

- 事前に、または推奨する時点で、個人顧客に対し、書面をもって行う
- 重要な手数料やコスト、提供される商品の範囲に重要な限定があることなどについて開示する
- すべての利益相反に関する重要事項について開示する
- 「完全かつ公正な開示」を行う

12

2　投資助言業者とブローカー・ディーラーの行為規制

➢ レギュレーション・ベストインタレスト

②注意義務

つぎの根拠を充たす程度の合理的な配慮、注意および技能を用いたこと

- 当該推奨に伴うリスク・利益・コストを理解した上で、それが個人顧客の少なくともだれかの最善の利益に適うと信じるに足る合理的な根拠があること
- 当該推奨が、特定の個人顧客の最善の利益に適い、かつ、当該ブローカー・ディーラーの利益を当該顧客の利益に優先していないと信じるに足る合理的な根拠があること
- 個別の推奨のみならず、一連の推奨取引をあわせて見た場合にも、当該個人顧客の投資プロファイルに照らして、過大ではなく、当該個人顧客の最善の利益に適い、かつ、当該ブローカー・ディーラーの利益を当該顧客の利益に優先していないと信じるに足る合理的な根拠があること

③利益相反に関する義務

- 合理的に設計された書面による方針・手続を策定・実施・エンフォースする義務
- 当該推奨に係るあらゆる利益相反を特定し、開示するか、またはそれを排除すること
- 当該ブローカー・ディーラーと関係者の利益を個人顧客の利益よりも優先させる誘因になるすべての利益相反を特定し、緩和すること
- 特定の期間内に特定の証券についてなされるあらゆる販売競争、販売ノルマ、ボーナス、現金以外の報酬を特定し、排除すること

④遵守義務

上記①～③の義務を遵守するために合理的に設計された書面による方針・手続の策定・実施・エンフォースする義務

13

2　投資助言業者とブローカー・ディーラーの行為規制

➢ レギュレーション・ベストインタレストに基づくブローカー・ディーラーの義務と投資助言業者の義務の異同

✓ 両者の義務は、次の点で接近したと評価できる

- 顧客の最善の利益のために行動すべきこと
- 利益相反関係などに係る重要事項について完全かつ公正な開示をすべきこと

✓ しかし、依然として、両者の行為義務には差分が生じている

- 投資助言業者に課されるフィデューシャリー・デューティーはプリンシプル・ベースであるのに対して、ブローカー・ディーラーの顧客の最善の利益のために行動する義務は、より具体的かつルールベースであること

⇐FINRAのルールベースの自主規制を一部取り込んでいるためと考えられる

⇐投資助言業者のビジネスモデルが非常に多様であるためと考えられる

- 投資助言業者は、完全かつ公正な開示と、十分な情報に基づく同意によって利益相反に対処できるのに対し、ブローカー・ディーラーは、一定の場合には開示だけでは足りず、利益相反の緩和や排除が求められる
- 投資助言業者の負うフィデューシャリー・デューティーは、顧客との間の関係全体におよび継続的に適用されるのに対し、ブローカー・ディーラーの義務は、顧客に対する推奨の時点においてのみ適用されるにすぎない

➡投資助言業者に認められる口座等の監視義務は、ブローカー・ディーラーには認められない

14

3　投資助言業者のフィデューシャリー・デューティー

投資助言業者の忠実義務の具体的内容

①顧客の最善の利益に合致した助言を行わねばならない

②顧客の取引を執行するために投資助言業者がブローカー・ディーラーを選択する責任がある場合には、最良執行を探らねばならない

③顧客との関係が継続している期間を通して全面的に助言を行い、監視しなければならない

15

4　ブローカー・ディーラーの適用除外

➢ブローカー・ディーラーの助言行為が投資助言業者に該当しないための要件

①本業に「専ら付随して（solely incidental）」なされること

②当該行為について「特別の報酬（special compensation）」を受領していないこと

SECの解釈

①「専ら（証券業務に）付随して」

- 提供されるサービスが口座について提供されるブローカレッジ・サービスに結び付いたものであり、かつ、合理的に関連しているものであれば、「専ら付随して」に該当する
- 顧客口座に対してブローカー・ディーラーが裁量権を行使する場合には、「専ら付随して」とはいえないのが原則
- 投資裁量がブローカー・ディーラーに認められている場合であっても、例外的に、期間および対象が限定されており、かつ、包括的で継続的な投資裁量の性質を欠いているものであれば、「専ら付随して」に該当し得る
- 「専ら付随して」に該当するかどうかの判断にとって、投資助言の重要性や頻度は関係ない
- 助言が証券を販売するという主要なビジネスに結びついているときにだけ「専ら付随して」に該当し、証券販売と結び付いていなかったり、証券の販売が主要な業務ではなく助言が主要な業務であったりする場合には、「専ら付随して」には該当しない
- 具体的には、ブローカー・ディーラーの事業をめぐる事実関係と状況、提供されている特別のサービス、ブローカー・ディーラーと顧客との関係等に基づいて個別に判断される

16

4　ブローカー・ディーラーの適用除外

➢ブローカー・ディーラーの助言行為が投資助言業者に該当しないための要件

①「専ら付随して」

【具体例】

- 顧客が一定期間、口座を利用できないときは、ブローカー・ディーラーが証券を購入または売却できる旨を「数か月」にわたって授権する場合には、「専ら付随して」に該当しない
- マージン要件を満たしたり、顧客がとくに定めた顧客の義務を履行したりするために証券の売買をすることは、「専ら付随して」に該当する
- 顧客のポジションに税制上の損失を実現させるために、特定の債券や証券を売却することは、「専ら付随して」に該当する

②「特別の報酬」

- ブロカレッジ・サービスを全面的に提供する場合とディスカウント・ブローカレッジ・サービスとで異なるレートを用いた手数料を収受しているということだけで、「特別の報酬」を収受していることにはならない
- 登録ブローカー・ディーラーは、投資顧問業法の適用を受けるサービスを提供し、または報酬を収受している口座に関してのみ、投資助言業者となる

17

4　ブローカー・ディーラーの適用除外

➢いわゆる「メリルリンチ・ルール」

SEC,　Certain Broker-Dealers Deemed Not to be Investment Advisers, Investment Advisers　Act Release No. 2376 (Apr. 12, 2005) [70 FR 20424 (Apr. 19, 2005)]

SECは、ブローカー・ディーラーの適用除外規定に基づいて、証券会社が伝統的なコミッション・ベースの手数料（取引ごとに課される手数料）ではなく、フィー・ベースの手数料（預かり資産の残高に応じて課される手数料）を収受するだけで、投資顧問業法の適用を受ける投資助言業者になるわけではないとの解釈通知を公表

➢判例により「メリルリンチ・ルール」が無効になる

Financial Planning Association v. SEC, 482 F.3d 481 (D.C. Cir. 2007)

【判旨】 SECは、ブローカー・ディーラーが提供するフィー・ベースの手数料を収受する口座を投資顧問業法の適用から除外する権限を有しない

18

5　手数料・報酬の形態

手数料・報酬の形態	算定根拠	利益相反のおそれ	業者のメリット	業者のデメリット
コミッション・ベース	個々の証券取引に基づいて手数料を徴収	過当な証券取引を誘導するおそれ	必要なコストに応じた手数料を徴収	・不安定な収益源 ・激しい競争 ・規制コストがフィー・ベースに比べると高いとされる
フィー・ベース	口座の預かり資産残高に応じて手数料を徴収	ポートフォリオの見直し等に基づく必要な証券取引を抑制・阻害するおそれ	証券取引の多寡に依存しない安定的な収益源	・証券取引が頻繁に行われる場合には、収益を圧迫 ・証券取引に基づく手数料を徴収できない

＊コミッション・ベースとフィー・ベースのハイブリッド形態として、両者の要素を併せ持つ報酬形態が多様に存在する

＊個人顧客にとっては、証券取引の多寡や資産残高などに応じて、いずれの形態が有利かはケースバイケース

19

5　手数料・報酬の形態

メリルリンチ・ルールが否定されて以降、証券口座は、取引手数料を徴取するタイプと預かり資産の残高に応じてフィーを支払うタイプのものに分かれ、顧客によって選択されることが主流になったとされる

【論点】

レギュレーション・ベストインタレストの下で、証券業者が開設する証券口座について、預かり資産の残高に応じてフィー・ベースの手数料を徴収することは可能か？

レギュレーション・ベストインタレストの下では、手数料・コストについて、フィー・ベースであることを開示し、かつ、ブローカー・ディーラーの助言などの行為が本業に「専ら付随して(solely incidental)」なされるにすぎず、かつ、その行為について「特別の報酬(special compensation)」を受領していなければ、可能であるようにも思われる

20

6　実態

＊2018年12月時点

登録ブローカー・ディーラー　3，764業者

顧客口座数　1．4億口座

預かり総資産4.3兆ドル

3，764業者のうち、1割弱の363業者は、同時に、投資助言業者としても登録

顧客口座数　9千万口座（証券口座全体の約63%）

3，764業者のうち、2098業者は、直接または間接に、投資助言業に従事する法人を支配し、それに支配され、または共通支配下にある

登録投資助言業者の19．57%に当たる2，691業者は、ブローカー・ディーラーである関連会社をもっており、投資助言業者が管理する総資産の約74%がこれら2，691の登録投資助言業者によって運用・運用指図されている

21

7　フォームCRS

フォームCRS（Client or Customer Relationship Summary）

- 法的位置づけ

1940年投資顧問法に基づくフォームADVの改正

同時に、1934年証券取引所法の下に新たにフォームCRSを追加

- 投資助言業者およびブローカー・ディーラーが個人顧客との関係を新たに開始する際に、自己の法的地位について顧客にその概要を説明するためのリレーションシップ・サマリーの交付を義務付け

とくに、証券業登録と投資顧問業登録をしている場合には、1枚のサマリーで説明するか、別々のサマリーを作成するにしても均等に説明しなければならない

さらに、証券業登録か投資顧問業登録のいずれかしか登録していない場合であっても、関連会社が証券業または投資顧問業を営んでいる場合には、その旨を記載しなければならない

- リレーションシップ・サマリーのその他の記載事項

提供するサービス、手数料・コスト、利益相反、行為規範、会社および登録証券外務員の懲戒歴など

なお、利益相反については、レギュレーション・ベストインタレストの利益相反に係る規制において開示が求められている事項も記載事項とされる

22

Ⅲ　ドイツ法

1. 投資助言の定義
2. 免許制
3. 投資助言業者の組織上の義務
4. 投資助言業者の行為規制
5. 独立報酬投資助言業者の特則

23

1　投資助言業の定義

投資助言＝「顧客またはその代理人に対する特定の金融商品に係る取引に関する、委任規則(EU)2017/565第9条にいう個別の推奨であって、当該推奨が当該投資者個人に関する状況の検討に基づいてなされるものであるか、または、当該投資者に適合するものとして提示されるもの」(有価証券取引法2条8項10号)

ただし、専ら情報伝達手段を通じてなされたり、公衆に向けて発せられたりするものは、除外される(有価証券取引法2条8項10号)

日本の金融商品取引法や米国の投資顧問業法における投資助言の定義と異なり、報酬を支払うことを約し、または報酬を得て個別の推奨を行うことが要件とされていない

投資助言の概念は、日米に比較してかなり広い

➡ドイツにおいては、投資助言は、投資仲介や取次ぎなどの他の有価証券サービスとともになされることが通常であると認識されている

24

1　投資助言業の定義

➢ 投資助言の該当するかどうかの判断基準（Question & Answers, Understanding the definition of advice under MiFID）

①　単なる情報提供ではなく、推奨であること

- 推奨は、単なる事実や数字の表明ではなく、助言者の側の意見が含まれる
- 情報の取捨選択を助けるためになされる情報の提供は、推奨に該当することがある

②　推奨が金融商品の取引に関するものであること

- 特定の投資に関係しない助言は、一般的な助言にすぎず推奨ではない
- 特定の顧客の個別の状況の評価に基づかない投資に関する推奨は、一般的推奨であって、投資助言ではない

③　推奨が適合的なものとしてなされるか、または、当該投資者の個別の状況に対する考慮に基づいてなされるものであること

- 適合的なものとしてなされる推奨は、明示的でも黙示的でもよい
- 投資者の個別の状況についての情報を利用しないことによっても、そのような情報を収集しており、それを考慮することが合理的に見て期待される場合には、個別の状況に対する考慮に基づくものとされる

25

1　投資助言業の定義

➢ 投資助言の該当するかどうかの判断基準（Question & Answers, Understanding the definition of advice under MiFID）

④　推奨が配布・配信チャネルを通じて排他性を否定する態様でなされたものではなく、また、公衆に向けられたものでないこと

- 新聞、雑誌、インターネットのウェブページ、テレビ、ラジオなどを通じて公衆に向けてなされる推奨は、投資助言には当たらない
- インターネットを用いる場合には、公衆一般に向けられた場合には投資助言の要件を満たさないが、特定の投資者や特定の状況にある者にとっては適合的であるものとして提示された場合には、投資助言に当たり得る
- 電子メールなど複数の者に向けられたメッセージは、メッセージを送られた者がターゲットであること、メッセージの内容、用いられた言語など個別の事情を考慮して、投資助言に当たる場合があり得る
- 投資リサーチの配信は、投資助言に当たらない

⑤　推奨が投資者またはその代理人を特定してなされたものであるか、見込み投資者またはその代理人を特定してなされるものであること

- 投資者ないし見込み投資者としての立場にない者に対する推奨は、投資助言に当たらない
- 経済的なリターンやリスクヘッジのためでなく、産業上・戦略上・企業上の目的のために助言を求める場合には、企業財務のための助言であって、投資助言には当たらない

26

1　投資助言業の定義

➢信用制度法による適用除外

① 国内の「機関」や資本管理会社等と顧客の間で、専ら投資管理会社など所定の会社が発行する国内投資財産（ヘッジファンドは除く。）に対する持分または株式に関する投資助言と投資仲介のみを金融サービスとして提供している場合であって、かつ、これらの金融サービスを提供するに際し、申出を行うそのための許可を得た場合を除き、顧客の金銭または持分に対し所有または占有を取得する権限を付与されていない企業（同法2条6項8号）

② 専ら他の職業上の活動の範囲内で、当該投資助言に対して特別の報酬を受けることなく、同法1条1a項第1文にいう金融サービス（投資助言が含まれる。）を提供する企業（同法2条6項15号）

このことに対応して、有価証券取引法において、これら2つの企業は、有価証券サービス業者の定義から除外されている（有価証券取引法3条1項7号・12号）

27

2　免許制

➢信用制度法上の金融サービス業に該当

投資助言は、金融商品の売買（取次ぎや媒介を含む）等とともに金融サービス業である（信用制度法1条1a項）

他人のために営業として、または商人的な方法で営業することを必要とする規模で金融サービス業を営むためには、免許を必要とする（信用制度法32条1項）

➢有価証券取引法上の有価証券サービス業に該当

他方、金融商品の売買等と投資助言は、有価証券取引法により、有価証券サービス業に該当する（有価証券取引法1条8項）

なお、投資助言は、旧法の下では有価証券サービス付随業務であった（有価証券取引法改正前2条3a項3号）

しかし、現行法の下では、有価証券サービスとされた上で、前述したように詳細に定義されている（有価証券取引法2条8項10号）

【立法趣旨】投資助言が有価証券サービス業に格上げされたのは、個人投資家はますます個別の推奨に頼るようになってきているという実態を反映したもの

28

2　免許制

➢ドイツ法の特徴

信用制度法と有価証券取引法による二重の監督法上の規制体系

ただし、有価証券サービス業の範囲をできる限り信用制度法上の金融サービス業の範囲と一致させている

有価証券サービス業者は、有価証券サービス業者として有価証券取引法の監督に服するとともに、信用制度法上も金融サービス提供機関として、同法に基づく監督にも服する

資本市場法の観点から、有価証券取引法において追加的な規制が有価証券サービス業者に課されている

もっとも、投資助言業者は、投資仲介業者、締結媒介業者、投資運用業者、金融ポートフォリオ運用業者などとともに、その金融サービス業務を遂行するに際し、顧客の金銭・有価証券を所有または占有する権限を有さず、かつ、自己の計算で金融商品を取引する権限を有しないときは、最低5万ユーロの当初資本金を有すれば足りる(信用制度法33条1項1号a)

投資助言業への参入要件は、かなり緩やか

29

3　投資助言業者の組織上の義務

➢金融サービス業者の信用制度法上の地位

金融サービス提供機関(信用制度法1条1a項1a号)

金融サービス提供機関は、信用機関とともに金融機関とされる(信用制度法1条1b項)

➢金融機関の組織上の義務

金融機関は、法令遵守のための態勢整備と適切かつ有効なリスク管理態勢を整備し運用する義務を負う(信用制度法25a条1項)

➢有価証券サービス業務を提供する企業の組織上の義務の特則

それに加え、有価証券サービス業およびその付随業務を提供する企業は、当該サービスを継続的かつ適正に行うことを確保するための態勢、および、利益相反管理態勢を整備しなければならない(有価証券取引法80条1項1号・2号)

30

3　投資助言業者の組織上の義務

➢有価証券サービス業務を提供する企業の組織上の義務の特則

有価証券サービス業およびその付随業務を提供する企業は、当該サービスを継続的かつ適正に行うことを確保するための態勢、および、利益相反管理態勢を整備しなければならない（有価証券取引法80条1項1号・2号）

MiFID25条1項では投資助言、金融商品についての情報提供、投資サービス等を提供する個人の知識・能力の確保を有価証券サービス業者に求める

ESMA「知識・能力の評価に関するガイダンス」

＜https://www.esma.europa.eu/document/guidelines-assessment-knowledge-and-competence＞

31

3　投資助言業者の組織上の義務

➢専門的知識があり信頼できる従業員の使用

- 投資助言に際しては、専門的知識があり、かつ投資助言について信頼できると有価証券サービス業者が信じる従業員だけを使用することができる（有価証券取引法87条1項）
- 有価証券サービス業者は、当該従業員が投資助言をする前に、BaFinに、次の事項を届け出なければならない

①当該従業員

②当該有価証券サービス業者が、その組織上の理由により当該従業員に直接流通を受託する権限を付与するときは、その旨

■ESMA, Guidelines for the assessment of knowledge and competence, 3 January 2017/ ESMA71-1154262120-153

32

3　投資助言業者の組織上の義務

➢利益相反管理態勢整備義務（有価証券取引法80条1項1号・2号）

- 利益相反は、証券業者・そのグループ企業およびその経営者・従業員と顧客、ならびにそれらの顧客相互間の利益衝突に及ぶ
- また、第三者からの特別利益や報酬プランによって惹起される利益相反にも及ぶ
- これらの利益相反を検知し、回避し、コントロールするための態勢を整備しなければならない
- なお、情報を移転する場合には、情報の偽造や外部からの攻撃のリスクを最小限にし、情報の正確性・安全性を維持するための態勢を整備しなければならない

33

3　投資助言業者の組織上の義務

➢利益相反管理態勢整備義務（有価証券取引法80条1項1号・2号）

- 利益相反管理態勢の中心は、情報隔壁
- 情報障壁の内容と運用は、米国のそれと類似している
- 利益相反が生じ得る部門間の物理的な遮断
- 情報へのアクセスに対する制限とその例外
- 情報障壁を超えて伝達される情報とそのための要件については、need to knowの原則に基づきルール化
- 上記ルールに従って取引や業務が行われているかどうかを独立したコンプライアンス部門が監視・統制（コンプライアンス責任者が設置される）
- 情報隔壁を超えて管理すべき情報が伝達され利用されるのは、任務の遂行のために当該情報へのアクセス・利用が必要であり、かつ、それによって機密性を害しない場合に限られる

➡利益相反管理体制の一環として設置される情報隔壁の運用に際し、所定の機密情報がウォールを超えて移転・利用される場合には、コンプライアンス部門のチェックを受けることが必要

- 上記の情報隔壁の仕組み自体に対する監視・監督
- 顧客の苦情処理手続との連動によるコントロールも重要

34

4　投資助言業者の行為規制

➢概観

有価証券サービス業者は、行為規制に服し、誠実・公正に、かつ、専門家として顧客の最善の利益を擁護する一般的義務や、利益相反に関する具体的な行為規制に服する

ノウユアカストマー・ルールを前提に、適合性原則に即して顧客に情報を提供する義務がもっとも中心的な義務（有価証券取引法64条3項）

ドイツでは、基本的に、販売業者に対しても、これらの監督法上の義務が課されているほか、民事法上も、販売等の場合であっても、適合性すなわち顧客の人的特性に着目した説明義務が課される

それゆえ、有価証券の勧誘の過程では、投資助言がなされる場合が多いと解されている

実務もそのことを前提に動いている模様

【例外的に、投資助言業に該当しない場合】

①執行だけを依頼する場合

②他に、投資助言業者が存在しその者の助言に基づいて発注している場合

35

4　投資助言業者の行為規制

➢概観

一般の有価証券販売業者より加重された開示・情報提供義務

投資助言が独立した立場でなされているかどうか、投資分析が包括的・総合的に行われているか、それとも部分的に行われているか等についての開示義務（有価証券取引法64条1項）

有価証券取引の前に、基本情報書面が作成されない金融商品について所定の情報を記載した情報提供書面の交付義務（有価証券取引法64条2項）

✓独立して投資助言を行う業者の追加的な開示・情報提供義務

独立して投資助言を行う業者は、分散投資に留意すべきことや、投資助言に基づく顧客から報酬を受領できるとともに報酬についての監督法上の規制に服する（有価証券取引法64条4項）

独立して投資助言を行う業者は、自己または密接関係者が発行者である有価証券を推奨する際には、それに先立ち当該事実その他の所定の情報を開示しなければならない（有価証券取引法64条5項）

➡投資助言業者は、販売業者より加重された行為規制に服し、独立報酬投資助言業者はさらに加重された義務を負う

36

4　投資助言業者の行為規制

➢概観

✓証券業者に対する一般的な行為規制（有価証券取引法63条）

- 誠実、公正に、かつ専門職業者として、顧客の最善の利益を図り、証券業務とその付随業務を提供しなければならない（同条1項）
- 利益相反管理態勢によっては、合理的に見て顧客の利益を侵害するリスクが回避されるとは評価し得ない場合には、有価証券サービス業者は、取引を行う前に、利益相反の一般的な種類とそれが生じつつあること、顧客の利益が害されるおそれのあるリスクの範囲について明示的に表示しなければならない（同条2項）

37

4　投資助言業者の行為規制

➢情報提供義務

（1）助言をする前に、次の事項について、顧客に分かりやすい形式で情報提供しなければならない

- 有価証券サービス業者は、独立報酬投資助言者として助言を行うものか、それともコミッション・ベースで助言を行うものかについて、情報提供をしなければならない（有価証券取引法64条1項1号）
- 助言が包括的な分析に基づき行われるものか、それとも、限定された分析に基づいて行われるものか、および、自己の投資助言が自己と密接な関係にある提供者またはその他の法的・経済的関係に密接な関係にあるため、投資助言の独立性を害し得る提供者または発行者の金融商品に限定されているかどうか（有価証券取引法64条1項2号）➡スライド39ページ参照
- 当該業者が顧客に定期的に推奨する金融商品の適合性についての判断を提供するかどうか（有価証券取引法64条1項3号）➡スライド40・44ページ
- これらの情報は、定型的な形式で提供することができる（同法63条7項を準用する64条1項）

38

4　投資助言業者の行為規制

➢情報提供義務

（2）包括的・総合的な分析に基づく助言か、限定された分析に基づく助言かについての説明義務

- 有価証券サービス業者は、自らの投資助言が金融商品の包括的・総合的な分析に基づくものか、限定された分析に基づくものかを顧客に詳細に説明しなければならない（有価証券取引法64条1項2号）
- 分析が包括的・総合的か、限定的かという文言を用いる説明では不十分であり、すべての種類の分析の具体的な数を示さなければならない
- さらに、取り扱う金融商品の種類、発行者、リスク・コスト・複雑性などどのような観点から推奨の対象に加えたか等についても情報提供しなければならない（規則52条3項）

39

4　投資助言業者の行為義務

➢情報提供義務

（3）顧客に対し推奨した金融商品について適合性の判断について定期的に知らせるかどうかについて情報提供する義務

投資助言業者は、定期的に推奨した金融商品の適合性について審査を行うかどうかを知らせなければならない（有価証券取引法64条1項3号）

審査を行うとした場合には、その頻度、どの程度の審査を行い、かつて収集した情報をどの程度再評価の対象にするか、実際に新たな推奨をするにあたりどのようにそれを顧客に伝えるかを知らせなければならない（規則52条5項）

もっとも、この情報提供義務は、民事法上の契約締結後の説明義務の範囲を超えたものであるという批判がある

他方、継続的な危険が生じている場合には民事法上もそのような義務が認められるとの反論もある

（4）プロ顧客に対して有価証券サービスを提供する場合には、要保護性が低いことから情報提供義務は限定される

40

4　投資助言業者の行為義務

➢ 適合性（Geeignetheit）の審査

（1）ノウユアカストマー・ルール

- 有価証券サービス業者は、顧客に対し、当該顧客にとって適合的な金融商品または有価証券サービスを推奨しなければならない
- 全面的にあるいは部分的に自動化されたロボアドバイザーなどのシステムを用いる投資助言についても、当該サービスを提供する際の適合性の審査に係る義務と責任は、原則どおり（規則54条1項）
- 推奨が適切かどうかの判断基準（規則54条2項）

① 推奨された金融商品は、顧客の投資目標とりわけ投資目的とリスク許容度に対応したものかどうか

② 投資リスクが当該顧客にとって経済的に負担可能であるかどうか

③ 当該顧客は、自己の知識と経験に照らして当該投資リスクを理解できるかどうか

- プロ顧客については、ある取引のリスクを理解するために必要な知識と経験を有していることを前提にすることができるため、情報収集の対象は、投資目標と財務状況に限定される
- さらに、適格機関取引先には、そもそもノウユアカストマー・ルールは適用されない（有価証券取引法68条1項）

41

4　投資助言業者の行為義務

➢適合性（Geeignetheit）の審査

（1）ノウユアカストマー・ルール

- 収集すべき顧客の関連情報

① 通常の収入の源とその額

② 流動資産・投資商品・不動産を含む現在の資産価額

③ 通常の金融債務

④ 顧客の投資目標に関する情報として、投資期間、負担するリスクに係る選好、リスクプロファイルおよび投資の目的

なお、有価証券サービス業者は、一般的な質問をもって足りるのか、それとも、具体的な知識と経験を問わなければならず、疑わしい場合には一般的な質問だけでは不十分であるとする見解とに分かれる

42

4 投資助言業者の行為義務

➢適合性（Geeignetheit）に則った助言義務

- 有価証券サービス業者は、収集した顧客情報に基づいて適切な金融商品および有価証券サービスだけを推奨しなければならない（有価証券取引法64条3項2文）
- 有価証券サービス業者は、まず有価証券取引法が予定している顧客の類型すなわち一般顧客、プロ顧客および適格取引先のいずれかに分類しなければならない（有価証券取引法64条3項）
- 必要な情報を収集しないときは、推奨を行ってはならず、その場合には、顧客に対して助言をすることができない旨を明確に示さなければならない
- 顧客が不適切な情報を提供し、かつ有価証券サービス業者がそのことを知らなかったかもしくは誤っていることが明白でなかった場合には、助言を行うことに支障はない（有価証券取引法65条2項、規則55条3項）
- 必要な情報を提供することを顧客が明確に拒否した場合には、推奨を行うことは許されない（規則54条8項）

43

4 投資助言業者の行為義務

➢ 適合性（Geeignetheit）に則った助言義務

- 有価証券サービス業者は、すべての情報を収集する必要はなく、具体的な助言に関して顧客を評価するために必要な情報だけを収集すれば足りる
- その際、有価証券サービス業者は、状況が変わったという根拠がない限り、これまでの助言に係る会話に頼ることができ、顧客の過去の投資行動を考慮することもできる
- 起こり得る変化を考慮するために、取引関係が長い場合には、重要な要素については定期的に更新されなければならない
- しかしながら、従来の投資や預金の構成から当該投資者の知識、経験、投資目標およびリスクに対する考え方を推論し、投資推奨の基礎として利用することは認められる
- 反対に、顧客の職業から金融商品のリスク許容性に関する一般的な知識を推し量ることはできず、具体的な経験に焦点を当てる必要がある
- 有価証券サービス業者は、顧客の情報が正確かつ完全であると信頼することができ、形式的に不正確であることが自明である場合を除き、顧客から取得した情報を検証したり審査したりする義務を負わない
- ドイツでも議論が収束していないのは、有価証券サービス業者は、定期的に顧客の情報を更新する義務があるかどうか

投資助言をする際には顧客の財政状況や投資目標を考慮しなければならない有価証券サービス業者の義務と、時間の経過によりこれらは変化し得ることに鑑み、検証したり更新したり義務があるとする説が有力であるが、そのような説も変化の徴表があった場合に限ると解している

44

4　投資助言業者の行為義務

➢ 適合性（Geeignetheit）審査義務

- 有価証券サービス業者は、顧客の類型ごとの分類と顧客情報に基づいて、適合性審査を行わなければならない（有価証券取引法64条3項）
- 適合性審査においては、具体的な取引について、顧客の投資目標、顧客の投資リスクおよび経済的に負担可能かどうかという観点から判断がなされるほか、当該顧客がその者の知識をもってして当該リスクを理解できるかどうかが審査の対象になる
- 顧客の個別の状況と金融商品の双方を考慮した推奨がなされなければならず、監督法上の適合性審査義務は民事法における判例法理として発展してきた投資家にふさわしい助言の原則と対応しているとされる
- さらに、MiFIDⅡに対応して、適合性審査において、損失負担能力とリスク許容性についても審査すべきことが明文化された（有価証券取引法64条3項2号）
- 具体的にどのような情報に基づいてこれらについて判断するか明確でないが、財政状況、家族関係、年齢、職業の状況および流動性資産に対する必要性などが考慮すべき要素とされている
- 債務については取得すべき情報には挙げられておらず、上記情報だけで判断すれば足りるのか不明であるが、学説においては、リスク負担能力について追加の情報を得て判断するとともに、投資目標について情報を得る際にリスク許容度についても質問をした上で顧客と議論すべきであるとする説がある

45

4　投資助言業者の行為義務

➢ 適合性報告

- 投資助言業者は、従来の助言プロトコルに替えて、適合性報告を契約を締結する前に交付しなければならない（有価証券取引法64条4項）
- ただし、遠隔通信手段による金融商品の売買のため、事前に適合性報告を交付できないときは、例外的に、契約締結後遅滞なく交付することについて顧客の同意があり、かつ、顧客が適合性報告を受領した後に取引を実行する機会を顧客が提供している場合には、契約締結後に交付することができる（有価証券取引法64条4項）
- 助言プロトコルは会話のやり取りを記録するものであったが、適合性報告には、行った助言の概要と行った推奨が顧客の選好、投資目標およびその他の「顧客の属性」にどの程度適合するものであるかが記載される
- 適合性報告によって、行った推奨が本当に適合的なものであるかどうか、どの程度適合的であるかどうかを顧客に一瞥させ再考の機会を与えることになる
- 適合性報告の内容、方式および様式は、規則で詳細に定められている（規則54条12項）
- 適合性報告は、顧客が民事訴訟で争う場合に証明手段として役に立つことが期待されている
- 適合性報告制度は、顧客に有利に証明責任を転換するものではないけれども、顧客を保護するために監督法上、投資助言業者に義務付けられたものであって、訴訟において顧客の不利に利用することはできない

46

4　投資助言業者の行為義務

➢記録保存義務

●記録および顧客との電話・電子メールの保存の義務付け

有価証券サービス業者は、提供する有価証券サービス業務および有価証券サービス付随業務ならびに従事した取引について、規則の定める義務に業者が従っているかどうかをBaFinが検査または監査することができるように、記録を保存しなければならない（有価証券取引法83条1項）

有価証券サービス業者は、顧客の委託の引受け・媒介・実行に関し有価証券サービスを提供するに当たり、証拠保全のために電話や電子通信手段の通話や通信を保存しなければならない（有価証券取引法83条3項）

有価証券サービス業者は、顧客に対し、電話や電子的通信手段の通話や通信を保存することを顧客に知らせなければならない（有価証券取引法83条5項）

顧客に事前に知らせなかった場合または顧客が保存に異議を述べた場合には、当該顧客の委託に係る有価証券サービスを提供してはならない（有価証券取引法83条5項）

詳細については、規則76条参照

47

5　独立報酬投資助言業者の特則

➢独立報酬投資助言業者制度の沿革

2013年報酬投資助言業者法により、報酬投資助言者制度を導入

【立法趣旨】

投資助言業者がどのようにして報酬を得ているかについての透明性を向上させる目的

➡コミッションに支えらえた投資助言と、手数料に支えられていない報酬投資助言とを顧客が意識的に選択できるように、だれが投資助言について支払いをしているかを明確にする

立法当時、ドイツでは、コミッションに支えられた投資助言が主流であり、金融商品の提供者または発行者から投資助言業者はコミッションを受領していた

しかも、多くの顧客は、そのような事実を、リベートの開示に係る法律上の義務が課されているのにもかかわらず、知らされることがなかった

報酬投資助言業者に対する行為規制により、報酬投資助言業者は、市場に目を向けて顧客の利益のために、顧客からのみ報酬を受領して、投資助言を行うことが期待されている

48

5　独立報酬投資助言業者の特則

➢独立報酬投資助言業者制度の沿革

✓手数料に基づく従来の投資助言の報酬体系の問題点

投資助言業者にとって高額な手数料を得ることのできる取引が必ずしも投資者の最善の利益に合致しない場合であっても、そのような取引を投資者に推奨する危険

しかも、従来型のビジネスモデルによる投資助言を受けてきた顧客は、投資助言業者がそもそも手数料収入を得ていたり、金融商品の販売によりその組成者や提供者からリベートを受領していたりすることすら知らず、あるいはほとんど知らない場合が多かったとされる

➡手数料に基づく投資助言により生じる利益相反を回避するための選択肢として、独立報酬投資助言業者が競争上次第にその地歩を固めてきた

➡そのような実務の流れを受け、2018年1月施行の改正有価証券取引法により、ドイツは独立報酬投資助言業者という制度に衣替えし、独立報酬投資助言業者はBaFinに登録するものとするとともに、その商号に対し一定の法的保護を与えることにした

49

5　独立報酬投資助言業者の特則

➢独立報酬投資助言業者の実態

2021年3月13日現在、ドイツでは、17社の独立報酬投資助言業者が登録されている

BaFin, Register unabhängiger Honorar-Anlageberater

< https://portal.mvp.bafin.de/database/HABInfo/>

50

5　独立報酬投資助言業者の特則

➢独立報酬投資助言業者の行為規制

独立報酬投資助言者は、投資助言者と同様の一般的な行為規制に服するほか（有価証券取引法63条・64条）、次の特別の行為規制を課される

【趣旨】

従来型のビジネスモデルである手数料収入に依存しない独立報酬投資助言者という制度があることを明示的に意識した上で、顧客が選択を行うことが期待されている

（1）市場に提供されている十分に広範な金融商品の品揃えに配慮すべき義務（有価証券取引法64条5項）

独立報酬投資助言者の取扱う金融商品は、その種類と発行者について十分に分散されていることを要し（有価証券取引法64条5項1号）、自らまたは自らと密接な関係にある者が発行したり提供したりする金融商品に限定してはならない（同条同項2号）

もし、独立報酬投資助言者自身またはその密接関係者が発行しまたは提供する金融商品に係る契約締結を推奨するときは、顧客に対してその旨を明示しなければならない（有価証券取引法64条6項、有価証券サービス業者の行為規制及び組織化要件に関する規則3条（WpDVerOV））

51

5　独立報酬投資助言業者の特則

➢独立報酬投資助言業者の行為規制

（2）自己の計算で顧客と取引することの禁止

- 有価証券サービス業者は、自己が行った独立報酬投資助言に基づいて当該顧客と取引を行う場合には、自己の計算で固定価格または特定し得る価格（固定価格取引：Festpreisgeschäfte）で当該取引を実行してはならない（有価証券取引法64条6項）
- ただし、固定価格取引が、当該有価証券サービス業者自身が提供者であるか発行者である金融商品に係る取引である場合は、この限りではない（有価証券取引法64条6項）

（3）利害関係のある金融商品に係る取引を推奨する際の、自らの収益に関する利益の所在について表示する義務

- 自己が当該金融商品の提供者もしくは発行者である場合、または当該金融商品の提供者もしくは発行者と密接な関係その他の経済的利害関係を有する場合
- 上記の事実のほか、自己の収益に関する利益、または自己の利害関係者の利益等について、開示しなければならない
- もっとも、その額については開示する必要はない

52

5 独立報酬投資助言業者の特則

➢独立報酬投資助言業者の行為規制

（4）顧客以外の者から報酬を受領することの禁止

- 独立報酬投資助言業者は、顧客からのみ報酬を受領することができる（有価証券取引法64条5項2号）
- 第三者からリベートまたは非金銭的なリベート（たとえばインセンティブのための海外旅行など）を収受することも原則として禁止される（同法同項同号）
- 例外が認められるのは、金融商品または同様の性質をもつ金融商品をリベートの受領なしには入手することができず、かつ、当該リベートをできる限り速やかに全額顧客に返却する場合に限る（同法同条同項）
- 非金銭的なリベートは、顧客に返還できないため、禁止される

（5）リベートの供与に係る開示義務

- 独立報酬投資助言者としてではなく第三者に対してリベートを供与する場合には、リベートを供与しているかどうか、供与している場合にはその額はいくらかについて、顧客に誤解のないように情報提供しなければならない（有価証券取引法70条1項1号）

53

Ⅳ おわりに

➢ドイツ法からの示唆

- 投資助言業の定義

報酬を収受することを要件にするかどうか

〔参考〕

米国法：報酬の収受を要件とした上で、ブローカー・ディーラーが助言行為を行う場合には、証券業に「専ら付随して」なされ、かつ「特別の報酬」を受領していない場合には、投資顧問業法の適用を除外

報酬体系のあり方に対して一定のバイアスを与える結果になっていないか？

- 投資助言業に対する行為規制は十分か？

忠実義務は課されているものの、情報提供義務や適合性原則は、金融商品取引業者一般に課されているものと同様の内容

法的にフィデューシャリーであることから、ドイツ法のように上乗せ規制が検討されるべき

とくにノウユアカストマー・ルールについては、法的根拠が薄弱

54

資　料

【配布資料】

資料1　INVESTMENT ADVISERS ACT OF 1940

資料2　SECURITIES AND EXCHANGE COMMISSION　17 CFR Part 276
[Release No. IA-5249]　Commission Interpretation Regarding the Solely Incidental Prong of the Broker-Dealer Exclusion from the Definition of Investment Adviser

資料3　SECURITIES AND EXCHANGE COMMISSION　17 CFR Part 276
[Release No. IA-5248; File No. S7-07-18]　RIN: 3235-AM36
Commission Interpretation Regarding Standard of Conduct for Investment Advisers

資料4　SECURITIES AND EXCHANGE COMMISSION　17 CFR Part 275
[Release No. IA-2653; File No. S7-23-07]　RIN 3235-AJ96
Temporary Rule Regarding Principal Trades with Certain Advisory Clients

資料5　DIRECTIVE 2014/65/EU OF THE EUROPEAN PARLIAMENT AND OF COUNCIL of 15 May 2014

資料6　参照条文（ドイツ法関係）

資料7　Understanding the definition of advice under MiFID

資料8　esma Guidelines for the assessment of knowledge and competence

資料9　REGULATIONS COMMISSION DELEGATED REGULATION (EU) 2017/565 of 25 April 2016

資料 1

INVESTMENT ADVISERS ACT OF 1940

[References in brackets [ ] are to title 15, United States Code]

[Title II of Chapter 686 of the 76th Congress]

[As Amended Through P.L. 115–417, Enacted January 03, 2019]

[Currency: This publication is a compilation of the text of title II of chapter 686 of the 76th Congress. It was last amended by the public law listed in the As Amended Through note above and below at the bottom of each page of the pdf version and reflects current law through the date of the enactment of the public law listed at https://www.govinfo.gov/app/collection/comps/]

[Note: While this publication does not represent an official version of any Federal statute, substantial efforts have been made to ensure the accuracy of its contents. The official version of Federal law is found in the United States Statutes at Large and in the United States Code. The legal effect to be given to the Statutes at Large and the United States Code is established by statute (1 U.S.C. 112, 204).]

TITLE II—INVESTMENT ADVISERS

FINDINGS

SEC. 201. [80b–1] Upon the basis of facts disclosed by the record and report of the Securities and Exchange Commission made pursuant to section 30 of the Public Utility Holding Company Act of 1935, and facts otherwise disclosed and ascertained, it is hereby found that investment advisers are of national concern, in that, among other things—

(1) their advice, counsel, publications, writings, analyses, and reports are furnished and distributed, and their contracts, subscription agreements, and other arrangements with clients are negotiated and performed, by the use of the mails and means and instrumentalities of interstate commerce;

(2) their advice, counsel, publications, writings, analyses, and reports customarily relate to the purchase and sale of securities traded on national securities exchanges and in interstate over-the-counter markets, securities issued by companies engaged in business in interstate commerce, and securities issued by national banks and member banks of the Federal Reserve System; and

(3) the foregoing transactions occur in such volume as substantially to affect interstate commerce, national securities exchanges, and other securities markets, the national banking system and the national economy.

DEFINITIONS

SEC. 202. [80b–2] (a) When used in this title, unless the context otherwise requires, the following definitions shall apply:

G:\COMP\SEC\INVESTMENT ADVISERS ACT OF 1940.XML

(1) "Assignment" includes any direct or indirect transfer or hypothecation of an investment advisory contract by the assignor or of a controlling block of the assignor's outstanding voting securities by a security holder of the assignor; but if the investment adviser is a partnership, no assignment of an investment advisory contract shall be deemed to result from the death or withdrawal of a minority of the members of the investment adviser having only a minority interest in the business of the investment adviser, or from the admission to the investment adviser of one or more members who, after such admission, shall be only a minority of the members and shall have only a minority interest in the business.

(2) "Bank" means (A) a banking institution organized under the laws of the United States or a Federal savings association, as defined in section 2(5) of the Home Owners' Loan Act, (B) a member bank of the Federal Reserve System, (C) any other banking institution, savings association, as defined in section 2(4) of the Home Owners' Loan Act, or trust company, whether incorporated or not, doing business under the laws of any State or of the United States, a substantial portion of the business of which consists of receiving deposits or exercising fiduciary powers similar to those permitted to national banks under the authority of the Comptroller of the Currency, and which is supervised and examined by State or Federal authority having supervision over banks or savings associations, and which is not operated for the purpose of evading the provisions of this title, and (D) a receiver, conservator, or other liquidating agent of any institution or firm included in clauses (A), (B), or (C) of this paragraph.

(3) The term "broker" has the same meaning as given in section 3 of the Securities Exchange Act of 1934.

(4) "Commission" means the Securities and Exchange Commission.

(5) "Company" means a corporation, a partnership, an association, a joint-stock company, a trust, or any organized group of persons, whether incorporated or not; or any receiver, trustee in a case under title 11 of the United States Code, or similar official, or any liquidating agent for any of the foregoing, in his capacity as such.

(6) "Convicted" includes a verdict, judgment, or plea of guilty, or a finding of guilt on a plea of nolo contendere, if such verdict, judgment, plea, or finding has not been reversed, set aside, or withdrawn, whether or not sentence has been imposed.

(7) The term "dealer" has the same meaning as given in section 3 of the Securities Exchange Act of 1934, but does not include an insurance company or investment company.

(8) "Director" means any director of a corporation or any person performing similar functions, with respect to any organization, whether incorporated or unincorporated.

(9) "Exchange" means any organization, association, or group of persons, whether incorporated or unincorporated, which constitutes, maintains, or provides a market place or facilities for bringing together purchasers and sellers of securi-

ties or for otherwise performing with respect to securities the functions commonly performed by a stock exchange as that term is generally understood, and includes the market place and the market facilities maintained by such exchange.

(10) "Interstate commerce" means trade, commerce, transportation, or communication among the several States, or between any foreign country and any State, or between any State and any place or ship outside thereof.

(11) "Investment adviser" means any person who, for compensation, engages in the business of advising others, either directly or through publications or writings, as to the value of securities or as to the advisability of investing in, purchasing, or selling securities, or who, for compensation and as part of a regular business, issues or promulgates analyses or reports concerning securities; but does not include (A) a bank, or any bank holding company as defined in the Bank Holding Company Act of 1956, which is not an investment company, except that the term "investment adviser" includes any bank or bank holding company to the extent that such bank or bank holding company serves or acts as an investment adviser to a registered investment company, but if, in the case of a bank, such services or actions are performed through a separately identifiable department or division, the department or division, and not the bank itself, shall be deemed to be the investment adviser; (B) any lawyer, accountant, engineer, or teacher whose performance of such services is solely incidental to the practice of his profession; (C) any broker or dealer whose performance of such services is solely incidental to the conduct of his business as a broker or dealer and who receives no special compensation therefor; (D) the publisher of any bona fide newspaper, news magazine or business or financial publication of general and regular circulation; (E) any person whose advice, analyses, or reports relate to no securities other than securities which are direct obligations of or obligations guaranteed as to principal or interest by the United States, or securities issued or guaranteed by corporations in which the United States has a direct or indirect interest which shall have been designated by the Secretary of the Treasury, pursuant to section 3(a)(12) of the Securities Exchange Act of 1934, as exempted securities for the purposes of that Act; (F) any nationally recognized statistical rating organization, as that term is defined in section 3(a)(62) of the Securities Exchange Act of 1934, unless such organization engages in issuing recommendations as to purchasing, selling, or holding securities or in managing assets, consisting in whole or in part of securities, on behalf of others;;[1] (G) any family office, as defined by rule, regulation, or order of the Commission, in accordance with the purposes of this title; or (H) such other persons not within the intent of

[1] Effective on July 21, 2011, section 409(a) of Public Law 111–203 amends section 202(a)(11) by striking "or (G)" and inserting the following: "; (G) any family office, as defined by rule, regulation, or order of the Commission, in accordance with the purposes of this title; or (H)" (shown above). Such amendment probably should not have included a semicolon at the beginning of the inserted language.

this paragraph, as the Commission may designate by rules and regulations or order.

(12) "Investment company", affiliated person, and "insurance company" have the same meanings as in the Investment Company Act of 1940. "Control" means the power to exercise a controlling influence over the management or policies of a company, unless such power is solely the result of an official position with such company.

(13) "Investment supervisory services" means the giving of continuous advice as to the investment of funds on the basis of the individual needs of each client.

(14) "Means or instrumentality of interstate commerce" includes any facility of a national securities exchange.

(15) "National securities exchange" means an exchange registered under section 6 of the Securities Exchange Act of 1934.

(16) "Person" means a natural person or a company.

(17) The term "person associated with an investment adviser" means any partner, officer, or director of such investment adviser (or any person performing similar functions), or any person directly or indirectly controlling or controlled by such investment adviser, including any employee of such investment adviser, except that for the purposes of section 203 of this title (other than subsection (f) thereof), persons associated with an investment adviser whose functions are clerical or ministerial shall not be included in the meaning of such term. The Commission may by rules and regulations classify, for the purposes of any portion or portions of this title, persons, including employees controlled by an investment adviser.

(18) "Security" means any note, stock, treasury stock, security future, bond, debenture, evidence of indebtedness, certificate of interest or participation in any profit-sharing agreement, collateral-trust certificate, preorganization certificate or subscription, transferable share, investment contract, voting-trust certificate, certificate of deposit for a security, fractional undivided interest in oil, gas, or other mineral rights, any put, call, straddle, option, or privilege on any security (including a certificate of deposit) or on any group or index of securities (including any interest therein or based on the value thereof), or any put, call, straddle, option, or privilege entered into on a national securities exchange relating to foreign currency, or, in general, any interest or instrument commonly known as a "security", or any certificate of interest or participation in, temporary or interim certificate for, receipt for, guaranty of, or warrant or right to subscribe to or purchase any of the foregoing.

(19) "State" means any State of the United States, the District of Columbia, Puerto Rico, the Virgin Islands, or any other possession of the United States.

(20) "Underwriter" means any person who has purchased from an issuer with a view to, or sells for an issuer in connection with, the distribution of any security, or participates or has a direct or indirect participation in any such undertaking, or participates or has a participation in the direct or indirect

underwriting of any such undertaking; but such term shall not include a person whose interest is limited to a commission from an underwriter or dealer not in excess of the usual and customary distributor's or seller's commission. As used in this paragraph the term "issuer" shall include in addition to an issuer, any person directly or indirectly controlling or controlled by the issuer, or any person under direct or indirect common control with the issuer.

(21) "Securities Act of 1933", "Securities Exchange Act of 1934", and "Trust Indenture Act of 1939", mean those Acts, respectively, as heretofore or hereafter amended.

(22) "Business development company" means any company which is a business development company as defined in section 2(a)(48) of title I of this Act and which complies with section 55 of title I of this Act, except that—

(A) the 70 per centum of the value of the total assets condition referred to in sections 2(a)(48) and 55 of title I of this Act shall be 60 per centum for purposes of determining compliance therewith;

(B) such company need not be a closed-end company and need not elect to be subject to the provisions of sections 55 through 65 of title I of this Act; and

(C) the securities which may be purchased pursuant to section 55(a) of title I of this Act may be purchased from any person.

For purposes of this paragraph, all terms in sections 2(a)(48) and 55 of title I of this Act shall have the same meaning set forth in such title as if such company were a registered closed-end investment company, except that the value of the assets of a business development company which is not subject to the provisions of sections 55 through 65 of title I of this Act shall be determined as of the date of the most recent financial statements which it furnished to all holders of its securities, and shall be determined no less frequently than annually.

(23) "Foreign securities authority" means any foreign government, or any governmental body or regulatory organization empowered by a foreign government to administer or enforce its laws as they relate to securities matters.

(24) "Foreign financial regulatory authority" means any (A) foreign securities authority, (B) other governmental body or foreign equivalent of a self-regulatory organization empowered by a foreign government to administer or enforce its laws relating to the regulation of fiduciaries, trusts, commercial lending, insurance, trading in contracts of sale of a commodity for future delivery, or other instruments traded on or subject to the rules of a contract market, board of trade or foreign equivalent, or other financial activities, or (C) membership organization a function of which is to regulate the participation of its members in activities listed above.

(25) "Supervised person" means any partner, officer, director (or other person occupying a similar status or performing similar functions), or employee of an investment adviser, or other person who provides investment advice on behalf of the

investment adviser and is subject to the supervision and control of the investment adviser.

(26) The term "separately identifiable department or division" of a bank means a unit—

(A) that is under the direct supervision of an officer or officers designated by the board of directors of the bank as responsible for the day-to-day conduct of the bank's investment adviser activities for one or more investment companies, including the supervision of all bank employees engaged in the performance of such activities; and

(B) for which all of the records relating to its investment adviser activities are separately maintained in or extractable from such unit's own facilities or the facilities of the bank, and such records are so maintained or otherwise accessible as to permit independent examination and enforcement by the Commission of this Act or the Investment Company Act of 1940 and rules and regulations promulgated under this Act or the Investment Company Act of 1940.

(27) The terms "security future" and "narrow-based security index" have the same meanings as provided in section 3(a)(55) of the Securities Exchange Act of 1934.

(28) The term "credit rating agency" has the same meaning as in section 3 of the Securities Exchange Act of 1934.

(29) The term "private fund" means an issuer that would be an investment company, as defined in section 3 of the Investment Company Act of 1940 (15 U.S.C. 80a–3), but for section 3(c)(1) or 3(c)(7) of that Act.

(30) The term "foreign private adviser" means any investment adviser who—

(A) has no place of business in the United States;

(B) has, in total, fewer than 15 clients and investors in the United States in private funds advised by the investment adviser;

(C) has aggregate assets under management attributable to clients in the United States and investors in the United States in private funds advised by the investment adviser of less than $25,000,000, or such higher amount as the Commission may, by rule, deem appropriate in accordance with the purposes of this title; and

(D) neither—

(i) holds itself out generally to the public in the United States as an investment adviser; nor

(ii) acts as—

(I) an investment adviser to any investment company registered under the Investment Company Act of 1940; or

(II) a company that has elected to be a business development company pursuant to section 54 of the Investment Company Act of 1940 (15 U.S.C. 80a–53), and has not withdrawn its election.

(29)[2] The terms "commodity pool", "commodity pool operator", "commodity trading advisor", "major swap participant", "swap", "swap dealer", and "swap execution facility" have the same meanings as in section 1a of the Commodity Exchange Act (7 U.S.C. 1a).

(b) No provision in this title shall apply to, or be deemed to include, the United States, a State, or any political subdivision of a State, or any agency, authority, or instrumentality of any one or more of the foregoing, or any corporation which is wholly owned directly or indirectly by any one or more of the foregoing, or any officer, agent, or employee of any of the foregoing acting as such in the course of his official duty, unless such provision makes specific reference thereto.

(c) CONSIDERATION OF PROMOTION OF EFFICIENCY, COMPETITION, AND CAPITAL FORMATION.—Whenever pursuant to this title the Commission is engaged in rulemaking and is required to consider or determine whether an action is necessary or appropriate in the public interest, the Commission shall also consider, in addition to the protection of investors, whether the action will promote efficiency, competition, and capital formation.

REGISTRATION OF INVESTMENT ADVISERS

SEC. 203. [80b–3] (a) Except as provided in subsection (b) and section 203A[3], it shall be unlawful for any investment adviser, unless registered under this section, to make use of the mails or any means or instrumentality of interstate commerce in connection with his or its business as an investment adviser.[4]

(b) The provisions of subsection (a) shall not apply to—

(1) any investment adviser, other than an investment adviser who acts as an investment adviser to any private fund, all of whose clients are residents of the State within which such investment adviser maintains his or its principal office and place of business, and who does not furnish advice or issue analyses or reports with respect to securities listed or admitted to unlisted trading privileges on any national securities exchange;

(2) any investment adviser whose only clients are insurance companies;

(3) any investment adviser that is a foreign private adviser;

(4) any investment adviser that is a charitable organization, as defined in section 3(c)(10)(D) of the Investment Company Act of 1940, or is a trustee, director, officer, employee, or volunteer of such a charitable organization acting within the scope of such person's employment or duties with such organization, whose advice, analyses, or reports are provided only to one or more of the following:

(A) any such charitable organization;

(B) a fund that is excluded from the definition of an investment company under section 3(c)(10)(B) of the Investment Company Act of 1940; or

(C) a trust or other donative instrument described in section 3(c)(10)(B) of the Investment Company Act of 1940, or the trustees, administrators, settlors (or potential settlors), or beneficiaries of any such trust or other instrument;

(5) any plan described in section 414(e) of the Internal Revenue Code of 1986, any person or entity eligible to establish and maintain such a plan under the Internal Revenue Code of 1986, or any trustee, director, officer, or employee of or volunteer for any such plan or person, if such person or entity, acting in such capacity, provides investment advice exclusively to, or with respect to, any plan, person, or entity or any company, account, or fund that is excluded from the definition of an investment company under section 3(c)(14) of the Investment Company Act of 1940;

(6)(A) any investment adviser that is registered with the Commodity Futures Trading Commission as a commodity trading advisor whose business does not consist primarily of acting as an investment adviser, as defined in section 202(a)(11) of this title, and that does not act as an investment adviser to—

(i) an investment company registered under title I of this Act; or

(ii) a company which has elected to be a business development company pursuant to section 54 of title I of this Act and has not withdrawn its election; or

(B) any investment adviser that is registered with the Commodity Futures Trading Commission as a commodity trading advisor and advises a private fund, provided that, if after the date of enactment of the Private Fund Investment Advisers Registration Act of 2010, the business of the advisor should become predominately the provision of securities-related advice, then such adviser shall register with the Commission;

(7) any investment adviser, other than any entity that has elected to be regulated or is regulated as a business development company pursuant to section 54 of the Investment Company Act of 1940 (15 U.S.C. 80a–54), who solely advises—

(A) small business investment companies that are licensees under the Small Business Investment Act of 1958;

(B) entities that have received from the Small Business Administration notice to proceed to qualify for a license as a small business investment company under the Small Business Investment Act of 1958, which notice or license has not been revoked; or

(C) applicants that are affiliated with 1 or more licensed small business investment companies described in subparagraph (A) and that have applied for another license under the Small Business Investment Act of 1958, which application remains pending; or

[2] Effective July 21, 2011, sections 402(a) and 770 of Public Law 111–203 provides for amendments to insert new paragraphs (29)–(30) and a second paragraph (29), respectively (shown above). The second paragraph (29) that precedes subsection (b) probably should be redesignated as paragraph (31).

[3] Section 303(d) of the National Securities Markets Improvment Act of 1996 (P.L. 104–290; 110 Stat. 3438) amended section 203 of the Investment Advisers Act of 1940 by striking "subsection (b) *of this section*" and inserting "subsection (b) and section 203A". This compilation reflects this amendment even though the italicized words were not in the underlying law at the time of the amendment.

[4] See also 7 U.S.C. 2, 2a, 6m. [Printed in appendix to this volume.]

(8) any investment adviser, other than an entity that has elected to be regulated or is regulated as a business development company pursuant to section 54 of the Investment Company Act of 1940 (15 U.S.C. 80a–53), who solely advises—

(A) rural business investment companies (as defined in section 384A of the Consolidated Farm and Rural Development Act (7 U.S.C. 2009cc)); or

(B) companies that have submitted to the Secretary of Agriculture an application in accordance with section 384D(b) of the Consolidated Farm and Rural Development Act (7 U.S.C. 2009cc–3(b)) that—

(i) have received from the Secretary of Agriculture a letter of conditions, which has not been revoked; or

(ii) are affiliated with 1 or more rural business investment companies described in subparagraph (A).

(c)(1) An investment adviser, or any person who presently contemplates becoming an investment adviser, may be registered by filing with the Commission an application for registration in such form and containing such of the following information and documents as the Commission, by rule, may prescribe as necessary or appropriate in the public interest or for the protection of investors:

(A) the name and form of organization under which the investment adviser engages or intends to engage in business; the name of the State or other sovereign power under which such investment adviser is organized; the location of his or its principal office, principal place of business, and branch offices, if any; the names and addresses of his or its partners, officers, directors, and persons performing similar functions or, if such an investment adviser be an individual, of such individual; and the number of his or its employees;

(B) the education, the business affiliations for the past ten years, and the present business affiliations of such investment adviser and of his or its partners, officers, directors, and persons performing similar functions and of any controlling person thereof;

(C) the nature of the business of such investment adviser, including the manner of giving advice and rendering analyses or reports;

(D) a balance sheet certified by an independent public accountant and other financial statements (which shall, as the Commission specifies, be certified);

(E) the nature and scope of the authority of such investment adviser with respect to clients' funds and accounts;

(F) the basis or bases upon which such investment adviser is compensated;

(G) whether such investment adviser, or any person associated with such investment adviser, is subject to any disqualification which would be a basis for denial, suspension, or revocation of registration of such investment adviser under the provisions of subsection (e) of this section; and

(H) a statement as to whether the principal business of such investment adviser consists or is to consist of acting as investment adviser and a statement as to whether a substan-

tial part of the business of such investment adviser, consists or is to consist of rendering investment supervisory services.

(2) Within forty-five days of the date of the filing of such application (or within such longer period as to which the applicant consents) the Commission shall—

(A) by order grant such registration; or

(B) institute proceedings to determine whether registration should be denied. Such proceedings shall include notice of the grounds for denial under consideration and opportunity for hearing and shall be concluded within one hundred twenty days of the date of the filing of the application for registration. At the conclusion of such proceedings the Commission, by order, shall grant or deny such registration. The Commission may extend the time for conclusion of such proceedings for up to ninety days if it finds good cause for such extension and publishes its reasons for so finding or for such longer period as to which the applicant consents.

The Commission shall grant such registration if the Commission finds that the requirements of this section are satisfied and that the applicant is not prohibited from registering as an investment adviser under section 203A. The Commission shall deny such registration if it does not make such a finding or if it finds that if the applicant were so registered, its registration would be subject to suspension or revocation under subsection (e) of this section.

(d) Any provision of this title (other than subsection (a) of this section) which prohibits any act, practice, or course of business if the mails or any means or instrumentality of interstate commerce are used in connection therewith shall also prohibit any such act, practice, or course of business by any investment adviser registered pursuant to this section or any person acting on behalf of such an investment adviser, irrespective of any use of the mails or any means or instrumentality of interstate commerce in connection therewith.

(e) The Commission, by order, shall censure, place limitations on the activities, functions, or operations of, suspend for a period not exceeding twelve months, or revoke the registration of any investment adviser if it finds, on the record after notice and opportunity for hearing, that such censure, placing of limitations, suspension, or revocation is in the public interest and that such investment adviser, or any person associated with such investment adviser, whether prior to or subsequent to becoming so associated—

(1) has willfully made or caused to be made in any application for registration or report required to be filed with the Commission under this title, or in any proceeding before the Commission with respect to registration, any statement which was at the time and in the light of the circumstances under which it was made false or misleading with respect to any material fact, or has omitted to state in any such application or report any material fact which is required to be stated therein.

(2) has been convicted within ten years preceding the filing of any application for registration or at any time thereafter of any felony or misdemeanor or of a substantially equivalent crime by a foreign court of competent jurisdiction which the Commission finds—

(A) involves the purchase or sale of any security, the taking of a false oath, the making of a false report, bribery, perjury, burglary, any substantially equivalent activity however denominated by the laws of the relevant foreign government, or conspiracy to commit any such offense;

(B) arises out of the conduct of the business of a broker, dealer, municipal securities dealer, investment adviser, bank, insurance company, government securities broker, government securities dealer, fiduciary, transfer agent, credit rating agency, foreign person performing a function substantially equivalent to any of the above, or entity or person required to be registered under the Commodity Exchange Act or any substantially equivalent statute or regulation;

(C) involves the larceny, theft, robbery, extortion, forgery, counterfeiting, fraudulent concealment, embezzlement, fraudulent conversion, or misappropriation of funds or securities or substantially equivalent activity however denominated by the laws of the relevant foreign government; or

(D) involves the violation of section 152, 1341, 1342, or 1343 or chapter 25 or 47 of title 18, United States Code, or a violation of substantially equivalent foreign statute.

(3) has been convicted during the 10-year period preceding the date of filing of any application for registration, or at any time thereafter, of—

(A) any crime that is punishable by imprisonment for 1 or more years, and that is not described in paragraph (2); or

(B) a substantially equivalent crime by a foreign court of competent jurisdiction.

(4) is permanently or temporarily enjoined by order, judgment, or decree of any court of competent jurisdiction, including any foreign court of competent jurisdiction, from acting as an investment adviser, underwriter, broker, dealer, municipal securities dealer, government securities broker, government securities dealer, transfer agent, credit rating agency, foreign person performing a function substantially equivalent to any of the above, or entity or person required to be registered under the Commodity Exchange Act or any substantially equivalent statute or regulation, or as an affiliated person or employee of any investment company, bank, insurance company, foreign entity substantially equivalent to any of the above, or entity or person required to be registered under the Commodity Exchange Act or any substantially equivalent statute or regulation, or from engaging in or continuing any conduct or practice in connection with any such activity, or in connection with the purchase or sale of any security.

(5) has willfully violated any provision of the Securities Act of 1933, the Securities Exchange Act of 1934, the Investment Company Act of 1940, this title, the Commodity Exchange Act, or the rules or regulations under any such statutes or any rule

of the Municipal Securities Rulemaking Board, or is unable to comply with any such provision.

(6) has willfully aided, abetted, counseled, commanded, induced, or procured the violation by any other person of any provision of the Securities Act of 1933, the Securities Exchange Act of 1934, the Investment Company Act of 1940, this title, the Commodity Exchange Act, the rules or regulations under any of such statutes, or the rules of the Municipal Securities Rulemaking Board, or has failed reasonably to supervise, with a view to preventing violations of the provisions of such statutes, rules, and regulations, another person who commits such a violation, if such other person is subject to his supervision. For the purposes of this paragraph no person shall be deemed to have failed reasonably to supervise any person, if—

(A) there have been established procedures, and a system for applying such procedures, which would reasonably be expected to prevent and detect, insofar as practicable, any such violation by such other person, and

(B) such person has reasonably discharged the duties and obligations incumbent upon him by reason of such procedures and system without reasonable cause to believe that such procedures and system were not being complied with.

(7) is subject to any order of the Commission barring or suspending the right of the person to be associated with an investment adviser;

(8) has been found by a foreign financial regulatory authority to have—

(A) made or caused to be made in any application for registration or report required to be filed with a foreign securities authority, or in any proceeding before a foreign securities authority with respect to registration, any statement that was at the time and in light of the circumstances under which it was made false or misleading with respect to any material fact, or has omitted to state in any application or report to a foreign securities authority any material fact that is required to be stated therein;

(B) violated any foreign statute or regulation regarding transactions in securities or contracts of sale of a commodity for future delivery traded on or subject to the rules of a contract market or any board of trade; or

(C) aided, abetted, counseled, commanded, induced, or procured the violation by any other person of any foreign statute or regulation regarding transactions in securities or contracts of sale of a commodity for future delivery traded on or subject to the rules of a contract market or any board of trade, or has been found, by the foreign finanical regulatory authority, to have failed reasonably to supervise, with a view to preventing violations of statutory provisions, and rules and regulations promulgated thereunder, another person who commits such a violation, if such other person is subject to his supervision; or

(9) is subject to any final order of a State securities commission (or any agency or officer performing like functions),

State authority that supervises or examines banks, savings associations, or credit unions, State insurance commission (or any agency or office performing like functions), an appropriate Federal banking agency (as defined in section 3 of the Federal Deposit Insurance Act (12 U.S.C. 1813(q))), or the National Credit Union Administration, that—

(A) bars such person from association with an entity regulated by such commission, authority, agency, or officer, or from engaging in the business of securities, insurance, banking, savings association activities, or credit union activities; or

(B) constitutes a final order based on violations of any laws or regulations that prohibit fraudulent, manipulative, or deceptive conduct.

(f) The Commission, by order, shall censure or place limitations on the activities of any person associated, seeking to become associated, or, at the time of the alleged misconduct, associated or seeking to become associated with an investment adviser, or suspend for a period not exceeding 12 months or bar any such person from being associated with an investment adviser, broker, dealer, municipal securities dealer, municipal advisor, transfer agent, or nationally recognized statistical rating organization, if the Commission finds, on the record after notice and opportunity for hearing, that such censure, placing of limitations, suspension, or bar is in the public interest and that such person has committed or omitted any act or omission enumerated in paragraph (1), (5), (6), (8), or (9) of subsection (e) or has been convicted of any offense specified in paragraph (2) or (3) of subsection (e) within ten years of the commencement of the proceedings under this subsection, or is enjoined from any action, conduct, or practice specified in paragraph (4) of subsection (e). It shall be unlawful for any person as to whom such an order suspending or barring him from being associated with an investment adviser is in effect willfully to become, or to be, associated with an investment adviser without the consent of the Commission, and it shall be unlawful for any investment adviser to permit such a person to become, or remain, a person associated with him without the consent of the Commission, if such investment adviser knew, or in the exercise of reasonable care, should have known, of such order.

(g) Any successor to the business of an investment adviser registered under this section shall be deemed likewise registered hereunder, if within thirty days from its succession to such business it shall file an application for registration under this section, unless and until the Commission, pursuant to subsection (c) or subsection (e) of this section, shall deny registration to or revoke or suspend the registration of such successor.

(h) Any person registered under this section may, upon such terms and conditions as the Commission finds necessary in the public interest or for the protection of investors, withdraw from registration by filing a written notice of withdrawal with the Commission. If the Commission finds that any person registered under this section, or who has pending an application for registration filed under this section, is no longer in existence, is not engaged in business as an investment adviser, or is prohibited from reg-

istering as an investment adviser under section 203A, the Commission shall by order cancel the registration of such person.

(i) MONEY PENALTIES IN ADMINISTRATIVE PROCEEDINGS.—

(1) AUTHORITY OF COMMISSION.—

(A) IN GENERAL.—In any proceeding instituted pursuant to subsection (e) or (f) against any person, the Commission may impose a civil penalty if it finds, on the record after notice and opportunity for hearing, that such penalty is in the public interest and that such person—

(i) has willfully violated any provision of the Securities Act of 1933, the Securities Exchange Act of 1934, the Investment Company Act of 1940, or this title, or the rules or regulations thereunder;

(ii) has willfully aided, abetted, counseled, commanded, induced, or procured such a violation by any other person;

(iii) has willfully made or caused to be made in any application for registration or report required to be filed with the Commission under this title, or in any proceeding before the Commission with respect to registration, any statement which was, at the time and in the light of the circumstances under which it was made, false or misleading with respect to any material fact, or has omitted to state in any such application or report any material fact which was required to be stated therein; or

(iv) has failed reasonably to supervise, within the meaning of subsection (e)(6), with a view to preventing violations of the provisions of this title and the rules and regulations thereunder, another person who commits such a violation, if such other person is subject to his supervision;[5]

(B) CEASE-AND-DESIST PROCEEDINGS.—In any proceeding instituted pursuant to subsection (k) against any person, the Commission may impose a civil penalty if the Commission finds, on the record, after notice and opportunity for hearing, that such person—

(i) is violating or has violated any provision of this title, or any rule or regulation issued under this title; or

(ii) is or was a cause of the violation of any provision of this title, or any rule or regulation issued under this title.

(2) MAXIMUM AMOUNT OF PENALTY.—

(A) FIRST TIER.—The maximum amount of penalty for each act or omission described in paragraph (1) shall be $5,000 for a natural person or $50,000 for any other person.

(B) SECOND TIER.—Notwithstanding subparagraph (A), the maximum amount of penalty for each such act or omission shall be $50,000 for a natural person or $250,000 for any other person if the act or omission described in para-

[5] So in law. The semicolon at the end of subparagraph (A)(iv) probably should be a period.

graph (1) involved fraud, deceit, manipulation, or deliberate or reckless disregard of a regulatory requirement.

(C) THIRD TIER.—Notwithstanding subparagraphs (A) and (B), the maximum amount of penalty for each such act or omission shall be $100,000 for a natural person or $500,000 for any other person if—

(i) the act or omission described in paragraph (1) involved fraud, deceit, manipulation, or deliberate or reckless disregard of a regulatory requirement; and

(ii) such act or omission directly or indirectly resulted in substantial losses or created a significant risk of substantial losses to other persons or resulted in substantial pecuniary gain to the person who committed the act or omission.

(3) DETERMINATION OF PUBLIC INTEREST.—In considering under this section whether a penalty is in the public interest, the Commission may consider—

(A) whether the act or omission for which such penalty is assessed involved fraud, deceit, manipulation, or deliberate or reckless disregard of a regulatory requirement;

(B) the harm to other persons resulting either directly or indirectly from such act or omission;

(C) the extent to which any person was unjustly enriched, taking into account any restitution made to persons injured by such behavior;

(D) whether such person previously has been found by the Commission, another appropriate regulatory agency, or a self-regulatory organization to have violated the Federal securities laws, State securities laws, or the rules of a self-regulatory organization, has been enjoined by a court of competent jurisdiction from violations of such laws or rules, or has been convicted by a court of competent jurisdiction of violations of such laws or of any felony or misdemeanor described in section 203(e)(2) of this title;

(E) the need to deter such person and other persons from committing such acts or omissions; and

(F) such other matters as justice may require.

(4) EVIDENCE CONCERNING ABILITY TO PAY.—In any proceeding in which the Commission may impose a penalty under this section, a respondent may present evidence of the respondent's ability to pay such penalty. The Commission may, in its discretion, consider such evidence in determining whether such penalty is in the public interest. Such evidence may relate to the extent of such person's ability to continue in business and the collectability of a penalty, taking into account any other claims of the United States or third parties upon such person's assets and the amount of such person's assets.

(j) AUTHORITY TO ENTER AN ORDER REQUIRING AN ACCOUNTING AND DISGORGEMENT.—In any proceeding in which the Commission may impose a penalty under this section, the Commission may enter an order requiring accounting and disgorgement, including reasonable interest. The Commission is authorized to adopt rules, regulations, and orders concerning payments to investors, rates of

interest, periods of accrual, and such other matters as it deems appropriate to implement this subsection.

(k) CEASE-AND-DESIST PROCEEDINGS.—

(1) AUTHORITY OF THE COMMISSION.—If the Commission finds, after notice and opportunity for hearing, that any person is violating, has violated, or is about to violate any provision of this title, or any rule or regulation thereunder, the Commission may publish its findings and enter an order requiring such person, and any other person that is, was, or would be a cause of the violation, due to an act or omission the person knew or should have known would contribute to such violation, to cease and desist from committing or causing such violation and any future violation of the same provision, rule, or regulation. Such order may, in addition to requiring a person to cease and desist from committing or causing a violation, require such person to comply, or to take steps to effect compliance, with such provision, rule, or regulation, upon such terms and conditions and within such time as the Commission may specify in such order. Any such order may, as the Commission deems appropriate, require future compliance or steps to effect future compliance, either permanently or for such period of time as the Commission may specify, with such provision, rule, or regulation with respect to any security, any issuer, or any other person.

(2) HEARING.—The notice instituting proceedings pursuant to paragraph (1) shall fix a hearing date not earlier than 30 days nor later than 60 days after service of the notice unless an earlier or a later date is set by the Commission with the consent of any respondent so served.

(3) TEMPORARY ORDER.—

(A) IN GENERAL.—Whenever the Commission determines that the alleged violation or threatened violation specified in the notice instituting proceedings pursuant to paragraph (1), or the continuation thereof, is likely to result in significant dissipation or conversion of assets, significant harm to investors, or substantial harm to the public interest, including, but not limited to, losses to the Securities Investor Protection Corporation, prior to the completion of the proceedings, the Commission may enter a temporary order requiring the respondent to cease and desist from the violation or threatened violation and to take such action to prevent the violation or threatened violation and to prevent dissipation or conversion of assets, significant harm to investors, or substantial harm to the public interest as the Commission deems appropriate pending completion of such proceedings. Such an order shall be entered only after notice and opportunity for a hearing, unless the Commission, notwithstanding section 211(c) of this title, determines that notice and hearing prior to entry would be impracticable or contrary to the public interest. A temporary order shall become effective upon service upon the respondent and, unless set aside, limited, or suspended by the Commission or a court of competent jurisdiction, shall remain effective and enforceable pending the completion of the proceedings.

(B) APPLICABILITY.—This paragraph shall apply only to a respondent that acts, or, at the time of the alleged misconduct acted, as a broker, dealer, investment adviser, investment company, municipal securities dealer, government securities broker, government securities dealer, or transfer agent, or is, or was at the time of the alleged misconduct, an associated person of, or a person seeking to become associated with, any of the foregoing.

(4) REVIEW OF TEMPORARY ORDERS.—

(A) COMMISSION REVIEW.—At any time after the respondent has been served with a temporary cease-and-desist order pursuant to paragraph (3), the respondent may apply to the Commission to have the order set aside, limited, or suspended. If the respondent has been served with a temporary cease-and-desist order entered without a prior Commission hearing, the respondent may, within 10 days after the date on which the order was served, request a hearing on such application and the Commission shall hold a hearing and render a decision on such application at the earliest possible time.

(B) JUDICIAL REVIEW.—Within—

(i) 10 days after the date the respondent was served with a temporary cease-and-desist order entered with a prior Commission hearing, or

(ii) 10 days after the Commission renders a decision on an application and hearing under subparagraph (A), with respect to any temporary cease-and-desist order entered without a prior Commission hearing,

the respondent may apply to the United States district court for the district in which the respondent resides or has its principal office or place of business, or for the District of Columbia, for an order setting aside, limiting, or suspending the effectiveness or enforcement of the order, and the court shall have jurisdiction to enter such an order. A respondent served with a temporary cease-and-desist order entered without a prior Commission hearing may not apply to the court except after hearing and decision by the Commission on the respondent's application under subparagraph (A) of this paragraph.

(C) NO AUTOMATIC STAY OF TEMPORARY ORDER.—The commencement of proceedings under subparagraph (B) of this paragraph shall not, unless specifically ordered by the court, operate as a stay of the Commission's order.

(D) EXCLUSIVE REVIEW.—Section 213 of this title shall not apply to a temporary order entered pursuant to this section.

(5) AUTHORITY TO ENTER AN ORDER REQUIRING AN ACCOUNTING AND DISGORGEMENT.—In any cease-and-desist proceeding under paragraph (1), the Commission may enter an order requiring accounting and disgorgement, including reasonable interest. The Commission is authorized to adopt rules,

regulations, and orders concerning payments to investors, rates of interest, periods of accrual, and such other matters as it deems appropriate to implement this subsection.

(l) EXEMPTION OF VENTURE CAPITAL FUND ADVISERS.—

(1) IN GENERAL.—No investment adviser that acts as an investment adviser solely to 1 or more venture capital funds shall be subject to the registration requirements of this title with respect to the provision of investment advice relating to a venture capital fund. Not later than 1 year after the date of enactment of this subsection, the Commission shall issue final rules to define the term "venture capital fund" for purposes of this subsection. The Commission shall require such advisers to maintain such records and provide to the Commission such annual or other reports as the Commission determines necessary or appropriate in the public interest or for the protection of investors.

(2) ADVISERS OF SBICS.—For purposes of this subsection, a venture capital fund includes an entity described in subparagraph (A), (B), or (C) of subsection (b)(7) (other than an entity that has elected to be regulated or is regulated as a business development company pursuant to section 54 of the Investment Company Act of 1940).

(3) ADVISERS OF RBICS.—For purposes of this subsection, a venture capital fund includes an entity described in subparagraph (A) or (B) of subsection (b)(8) (other than an entity that has elected to be regulated as a business development company pursuant to section 54 of the Investment Company Act of 1940 (15 U.S.C. 80a–53)).

(m) EXEMPTION OF AND REPORTING BY CERTAIN PRIVATE FUND ADVISERS.—

(1) IN GENERAL.—The Commission shall provide an exemption from the registration requirements under this section to any investment adviser of private funds, if each of such investment adviser acts solely as an adviser to private funds and has assets under management in the United States of less than $150,000,000.

(2) REPORTING.—The Commission shall require investment advisers exempted by reason of this subsection to maintain such records and provide to the Commission such annual or other reports as the Commission determines necessary or appropriate in the public interest or for the protection of investors.

(3) ADVISERS OF SBICS.—For purposes of this subsection, the assets under management of a private fund that is an entity described in subparagraph (A), (B), or (C) of subsection (b)(7) (other than an entity that has elected to be regulated or is regulated as a business development company pursuant to section 54 of the Investment Company Act of 1940) shall be excluded from the limit set forth in paragraph (1).

(4) ADVISERS OF RBICS.—For purposes of this subsection, the assets under management of a private fund that is an entity described in subparagraph (A) or (B) of subsection (b)(8) (other than an entity that has elected to be regulated or is regulated as a business development company pursuant to section

54 of the Investment Company Act of 1940 (15 U.S.C. 80a–53)) shall be excluded from the limit set forth in paragraph (1).

(n) REGISTRATION AND EXAMINATION OF MID-SIZED PRIVATE FUND ADVISERS.—In prescribing regulations to carry out the requirements of this section with respect to investment advisers acting as investment advisers to mid-sized private funds, the Commission shall take into account the size, governance, and investment strategy of such funds to determine whether they pose systemic risk, and shall provide for registration and examination procedures with respect to the investment advisers of such funds which reflect the level of systemic risk posed by such funds.

SEC. 203A. [80b–3a] STATE AND FEDERAL RESPONSIBILITIES.

(a) ADVISERS SUBJECT TO STATE AUTHORITIES.—

(1) IN GENERAL.—No investment adviser that is regulated or required to be regulated as an investment adviser in the State in which it maintains its principal office and place of business shall register under section 203, unless the investment adviser—

(A) has assets under management of not less than $25,000,000, or such higher amount as the Commission may, by rule, deem appropriate in accordance with the purposes of this title; or

(B) is an adviser to an investment company registered under title I of this Act.

(2) TREATMENT OF MID-SIZED INVESTMENT ADVISERS.—

(A) IN GENERAL.—No investment adviser described in subparagraph (B) shall register under section 203, unless the investment adviser is an adviser to an investment company registered under the Investment Company Act of 1940, or a company which has elected to be a business development company pursuant to section 54 of the Investment Company Act of 1940, and has not withdrawn the election, except that, if by effect of this paragraph an investment adviser would be required to register with 15 or more States, then the adviser may register under section 203.

(B) COVERED PERSONS.—An investment adviser described in this subparagraph is an investment adviser that—

(i) is required to be registered as an investment adviser with the securities commissioner (or any agency or office performing like functions) of the State in which it maintains its principal office and place of business and, if registered, would be subject to examination as an investment adviser by any such commissioner, agency, or office; and

(ii) has assets under management between—

(I) the amount specified under subparagraph (A) of paragraph (1), as such amount may have been adjusted by the Commission pursuant to that subparagraph; and

(II) $100,000,000, or such higher amount as the Commission may, by rule, deem appropriate in accordance with the purposes of this title.

(3) DEFINITION.—For purposes of this subsection, the term "assets under management" means the securities portfolios with respect to which an investment adviser provides continuous and regular supervisory or management services.

(b) ADVISERS SUBJECT TO COMMISSION AUTHORITY.—

(1) IN GENERAL.—No law of any State or political subdivision thereof requiring the registration, licensing, or qualification as an investment adviser or supervised person of an investment adviser shall apply to any person—

(A) that is registered under section 203 as an investment adviser, or that is a supervised person of such person, except that a State may license, register, or otherwise qualify any investment adviser representative who has a place of business located within that State;

(B) that is not registered under section 203 because that person is excepted from the definition of an investment adviser under section 202(a)(11); or[6]

(C) that is not registered under section 203 because that person is exempt from registration as provided in subsection (b)(7) of such section, or is a supervised person of such person; or

(D) that is not registered under section 203 because that person is exempt from registration as provided in subsection (b)(8) of such section, or is a supervised person of such person.

(2) LIMITATION.—Nothing in this subsection shall prohibit the securities commission (or any agency or office performing like functions) of any State from investigating and bringing enforcement actions with respect to fraud or deceit against an investment adviser or person associated with an investment adviser.

(c) EXEMPTIONS.—Notwithstanding subsection (a), the Commission, by rule or regulation upon its own motion, or by order upon application, may permit the registration with the Commission of any person or class of persons to which the application of subsection (a) would be unfair, a burden on interstate commerce, or otherwise inconsistent with the purposes of this section.

(d) STATE ASSISTANCE.—Upon request of the securities commissioner (or any agency or officer performing like functions) of any State, the Commission may provide such training, technical assistance, or other reasonable assistance in connection with the regulation of investment advisers by the State.[7]

[6] The word "or" after the semicolon in paragraph (1)(B) probably should not appear.

[7] Section 307 of the National Securities Markets Improvement Act of 1996 (P.L. 104–290; 110 Stat. 3438) provides as follows:

SEC. 307. [15 U.S.C. 80b–3a note] CONTINUED STATE AUTHORITY.

(a) PRESERVATION OF FILING REQUIREMENTS.—Nothing in this title or any amendment made by this title prohibits the securities commission (or any agency or office performing like functions) of any State from requiring the filing of any documents filed with the Commission pursuant to the securities laws solely for notice purposes, together with a consent to service of process and any required fee.

ANNUAL AND OTHER REPORTS

SEC. 204. [80b–4] (a) IN GENERAL.—Every investment adviser who makes use of the mails or of any means or instrumentality of interstate commerce in connection with his or its business as an investment adviser (other than one specifically exempted from registration pursuant to section 203(b) of this title), shall make and keep for prescribed periods such records (as defined in section 3(a)(37) of the Securities Exchange Act of 1934), furnish such copies thereof, and make and disseminate such reports as the Commission, by rule, may prescribe as necessary or appropriate in the public interest or for the protection of investors. All records (as so defined) of such investment advisers are subject at any time, or from time to time, to such reasonable periodic, special, or other examinations by representatives of the Commission as the Commission deems necessary or appropriate in the public interest or for the protection of investors.

(b) RECORDS AND REPORTS OF PRIVATE FUNDS.—

(1) IN GENERAL.—The Commission may require any investment adviser registered under this title—

(A) to maintain such records of, and file with the Commission such reports regarding, private funds advised by the investment adviser, as necessary and appropriate in the public interest and for the protection of investors, or for the assessment of systemic risk by the Financial Stability Oversight Council (in this subsection referred to as the "Council"); and

(B) to provide or make available to the Council those reports or records or the information contained therein.

(2) TREATMENT OF RECORDS.—The records and reports of any private fund to which an investment adviser registered under this title provides investment advice shall be deemed to be the records and reports of the investment adviser.

(3) REQUIRED INFORMATION.—The records and reports required to be maintained by an investment adviser and subject to inspection by the Commission under this subsection shall include, for each private fund advised by the investment adviser, a description of—

(A) the amount of assets under management and use of leverage, including off-balance-sheet leverage;

(b) PRESERVATION OF FEES.—Until otherwise provided by law, rule, regulation, or order, or other administrative action of any State, or any political subdivision thereof, adopted after the date of enactment of this Act, filing, registration, or licensing fees shall, notwithstanding the amendments made by this title, continue to be paid in amounts determined pursuant to the law, rule, regulation, or order, or other administrative action as in effect on the day before such date of enactment.

(c) AVAILABILITY OF PREEMPTION CONTINGENT ON PAYMENT OF FEES.—

(1) IN GENERAL.—During the period beginning on the date of enactment of this Act and ending 3 years after that date of enactment, the securities commission (or any agency or office performing like functions) of any State may require registration of any investment adviser that fails or refuses to pay the fees required by subsection (b) in or to such State, notwithstanding the limitations on the laws, rules, regulations, or orders, or other administrative actions of any State, or any political subdivision thereof, contained in subsection (a), if the laws of such State require registration of investment advisers.

(2) DELAYS.—For purposes of this subsection, delays in payment of fees or underpayments of fees that are promptly remedied in accordance with the applicable laws, rules, regulations, or orders, or other administrative actions of the relevant State shall not constitute a failure or refusal to pay fees.

(B) counterparty credit risk exposure;

(C) trading and investment positions;

(D) valuation policies and practices of the fund;

(E) types of assets held;

(F) side arrangements or side letters, whereby certain investors in a fund obtain more favorable rights or entitlements than other investors;

(G) trading practices; and

(H) such other information as the Commission, in consultation with the Council, determines is necessary and appropriate in the public interest and for the protection of investors or for the assessment of systemic risk, which may include the establishment of different reporting requirements for different classes of fund advisers, based on the type or size of private fund being advised.

(4) MAINTENANCE OF RECORDS.—An investment adviser registered under this title shall maintain such records of private funds advised by the investment adviser for such period or periods as the Commission, by rule, may prescribe as necessary and appropriate in the public interest and for the protection of investors, or for the assessment of systemic risk.

(5) FILING OF RECORDS.—The Commission shall issue rules requiring each investment adviser to a private fund to file reports containing such information as the Commission deems necessary and appropriate in the public interest and for the protection of investors or for the assessment of systemic risk.

(6) EXAMINATION OF RECORDS.—

(A) PERIODIC AND SPECIAL EXAMINATIONS.—The Commission—

(i) shall conduct periodic inspections of the records of private funds maintained by an investment adviser registered under this title in accordance with a schedule established by the Commission; and

(ii) may conduct at any time and from time to time such additional, special, and other examinations as the Commission may prescribe as necessary and appropriate in the public interest and for the protection of investors, or for the assessment of systemic risk.

(B) AVAILABILITY OF RECORDS.—An investment adviser registered under this title shall make available to the Commission any copies or extracts from such records as may be prepared without undue effort, expense, or delay, as the Commission or its representatives may reasonably request.

(7) INFORMATION SHARING.—

(A) IN GENERAL.—The Commission shall make available to the Council copies of all reports, documents, records, and information filed with or provided to the Commission by an investment adviser under this subsection as the Council may consider necessary for the purpose of assessing the systemic risk posed by a private fund.

(B) CONFIDENTIALITY.—The Council shall maintain the confidentiality of information received under this paragraph in all such reports, documents, records, and information, in a manner consistent with the level of confidentiality established for the Commission pursuant to paragraph (8). The Council shall be exempt from section 552 of title 5, United States Code, with respect to any information in any report, document, record, or information made available, to the Council under this subsection.

(8) COMMISSION CONFIDENTIALITY OF REPORTS.—Notwithstanding any other provision of law, the Commission may not be compelled to disclose any report or information contained therein required to be filed with the Commission under this subsection, except that nothing in this subsection authorizes the Commission—

(A) to withhold information from Congress, upon an agreement of confidentiality; or

(B) prevent the Commission from complying with—

(i) a request for information from any other Federal department or agency or any self-regulatory organization requesting the report or information for purposes within the scope of its jurisdiction; or

(ii) an order of a court of the United States in an action brought by the United States or the Commission.

(9) OTHER RECIPIENTS CONFIDENTIALITY.—Any department, agency, or self-regulatory organization that receives reports or information from the Commission under this subsection shall maintain the confidentiality of such reports, documents, records, and information in a manner consistent with the level of confidentiality established for the Commission under paragraph (8).

(10) PUBLIC INFORMATION EXCEPTION.—

(A) IN GENERAL.—The Commission, the Council, and any other department, agency, or self-regulatory organization that receives information, reports, documents, records, or information from the Commission under this subsection, shall be exempt from the provisions of section 552 of title 5, United States Code, with respect to any such report, document, record, or information. Any proprietary information of an investment adviser ascertained by the Commission from any report required to be filed with the Commission pursuant to this subsection shall be subject to the same limitations on public disclosure as any facts ascertained during an examination, as provided by section 210(b) of this title.

(B) PROPRIETARY INFORMATION.—For purposes of this paragraph, proprietary information includes sensitive, nonpublic information regarding—

(i) the investment or trading strategies of the investment adviser;

(ii) analytical or research methodologies;

(iii) trading data;

(iv) computer hardware or software containing intellectual property; and

(v) any additional information that the Commission determines to be proprietary.

(11) ANNUAL REPORT TO CONGRESS.—The Commission shall report annually to Congress on how the Commission has used the data collected pursuant to this subsection to monitor the markets for the protection of investors and the integrity of the markets.

(c) FILING DEPOSITORIES.—The Commission may, by rule, require an investment adviser—

(1) to file with the Commission any fee, application, report, or notice required to be filed by this title or the rules issued under this title through any entity designated by the Commission for that purpose; and

(2) to pay the reasonable costs associated with such filing and the establishment and maintenance of the systems required by subsection (c).

(d) ACCESS TO DISCIPLINARY AND OTHER INFORMATION.—

(1) MAINTENANCE OF SYSTEM TO RESPOND TO INQUIRIES.—

(A) IN GENERAL.—The Commission shall require the entity designated by the Commission under subsection (b)(1) to establish and maintain a toll-free telephone listing, or a readily accessible electronic or other process, to receive and promptly respond to inquiries regarding registration information (including disciplinary actions, regulatory, judicial, and arbitration proceedings, and other information required by law or rule to be reported) involving investment advisers and persons associated with investment advisers.

(B) APPLICABILITY.—This subsection shall apply to any investment adviser (and the persons associated with that adviser), whether the investment adviser is registered with the Commission under section 203 or regulated solely by a State, as described in section 203A.

(2) RECOVERY OF COSTS.—An entity designated by the Commission under subsection (b)(1) may charge persons making inquiries, other than individual investors, reasonable fees for responses to inquiries described in paragraph (1).

(3) LIMITATION ON LIABILITY.—An entity designated by the Commission under subsection (b)(1) shall not have any liability to any person for any actions taken or omitted in good faith under this subsection.

(d)[8] RECORDS OF PERSONS WITH CUSTODY OR USE.—

(1) IN GENERAL.—Records of persons having custody or use of the securities, deposits, or credits of a client, that relate to such custody or use, are subject at any time, or from time to time, to such reasonable periodic, special, or other examinations and other information and document requests by representatives of the Commission, as the Commission deems necessary or appropriate in the public interest or for the protection of investors.

(2) CERTAIN PERSONS SUBJECT TO OTHER REGULATION.—Any person that is subject to regulation and examination by a Federal financial institution regulatory agency (as such term is

[8] So in law. There are two subsection (d)'s. See amendments made by sections 404(1) and 929Q(b) of Public Law 111–203 (124 Stat. 1571, 1866).

defined under section 212(c)(2) of title 18, United States Code) may satisfy any examination request, information request, or document request described under paragraph (1), by providing the Commission with a detailed listing, in writing, of the securities, deposits, or credits of the client within the custody or use of such person.

PREVENTION OF MISUSE OF NONPUBLIC INFORMATION

SEC. 204A. [80b–4a] Every investment adviser subject to section 204 of this title shall establish, maintain, and enforce written policies and procedures reasonably designed, taking into consideration the nature of such investment adviser's business, to prevent the misuse in violation of this Act or the Securities Exchange Act of 1934, or the rules or regulations thereunder, of material, nonpublic information by such investment adviser or any person associated with such investment adviser. The Commission, as it deems necessary or appropriate in the public interest or for the protection of investors, shall adopt rules or regulations to require specific policies or procedures reasonably designed to prevent misuse in violation of this Act or the Securities Exchange Act of 1934 (or the rules or regulations thereunder) of material, nonpublic information.

INVESTMENT ADVISORY CONTRACTS

SEC. 205. [80b–5] (a) No investment adviser registered or required to be registered with the Commission shall enter into, extend, or renew any investment advisory contract, or in any way perform any investment advisory contract entered into, extended, or renewed on or after the effective date of this title, if such contract—

(1) provides for compensation to the investment adviser on the basis of a share of capital gains upon or capital appreciation of the funds or any portion of the funds of the client;

(2) fails to provide, in substance, that no assignment of such contract shall be made by the investment adviser without the consent of the other party by the contract; or

(3) fails to provide, in substance, that the investment adviser, if a partnership, will notify the other party to the contract of any change in the membership of such partnership within a reasonable time after such change.

(b) Paragraph (1) of subsection (a) shall not—

(1) be construed to prohibit an investment advisory contract which provides for compensation based upon the total value of a fund averaged over a definite period, or as of definite dates, or taken as of a definite date;

(2) apply to an investment advisory contract with—

(A) an investment company registered under title I of this Act, or

(B) any other person (except a trust, governmental plan, collective trust fund, or separate account referred to in section 3(c)(11) of title I of this Act), provided that the contract relates to the investment of assets in excess of $1 million,

if the contract provides for compensation based on the asset value of the company or fund under management averaged over a specified period and increasing and decreasing proportionately with the investment performance of the company or fund over a specified period in relation to the investment record of an appropriate index of securities prices or such other measure of investment performance as the Commission by rule, regulation, or order may specify;

(3) apply with respect to any investment advisory contract between an investment adviser and a business development company, as defined in this title, if (A) the compensation provided for in such contract does not exceed 20 per centum of the realized capital gains upon the funds of the business development company over a specified period or as of definite dates, computed net of all realized capital losses and unrealized capital depreciation, and the condition of section 61(a)(4)(B)(iii) of title I of this Act is satisfied, and (B) the business development company does not have outstanding any option, warrant, or right issued pursuant to section 61(a)(4)(B) of title I of this Act and does not have a profit-sharing plan described in section 57(n) of title I of this Act;

(4) apply to an investment advisory contract with a company excepted from the definition of an investment company under section 3(c)(7) of title I of this Act; or

(5) apply to an investment advisory contract with a person who is not a resident of the United States.

(c) For purposes of paragraph (2) of subsection (b), the point from which increases and decreases in compensation are measured shall be the fee which is paid or earned when the investment performance of such company or fund is equivalent to that of the index or other measure of performance, and an index of securities prices shall be deemed appropriate unless the Commission by order shall determine otherwise.

(d) As used in paragraphs (2) and (3) of subsection (a), "investment advisory contract" means any contract or agreement whereby a person agrees to act as investment adviser to or to manage any investment or trading account of another person other than an investment company registered under title I of this Act.

(e) The Commission, by rule or regulation, upon its own motion, or by order upon application, may conditionally or unconditionally exempt any person or transaction, or any class or classes of persons or transactions, from subsection (a)(1), if and to the extent that the exemption relates to an investment advisory contract with any person that the Commission determines does not need the protections of subsection (a)(1), on the basis of such factors as financial sophistication, net worth, knowledge of and experience in financial matters, amount of assets under management, relationship with a registered investment adviser, and such other factors as the Commission determines are consistent with this section. With respect to any factor used in any rule or regulation by the Commission in making a determination under this subsection, if the Commission uses a dollar amount test in connection with such factor, such as a net asset threshold, the Commission shall, by order, not later than 1 year after the date of enactment of the Private Fund Investment Advisers Registration Act of 2010, and every 5 years thereafter, adjust for the effects of inflation on such test. Any such adjustment that is not a multiple of $100,000 shall be rounded to the nearest multiple of $100,000.

(f) AUTHORITY TO RESTRICT MANDATORY PRE-DISPUTE ARBITRATION.—The Commission, by rule, may prohibit, or impose conditions or limitations on the use of, agreements that require customers or clients of any investment adviser to arbitrate any future dispute between them arising under the Federal securities laws, the rules and regulations thereunder, or the rules of a self-regulatory organization if it finds that such prohibition, imposition of conditions, or limitations are in the public interest and for the protection of investors.

PROHIBITED TRANSACTIONS BY REGISTERED INVESTMENT ADVISERS

SEC. 206. [80b–6] It shall be unlawful for any investment adviser, by use of the mails or any means or instrumentality of interstate commerce, directly or indirectly—

(1) to employ any device, scheme, or artifice to defraud any client or prospective client;

(2) to engage in any transaction, practice, or course of business which operates as a fraud or deceit upon any client or prospective client;

(3) acting as principal for his own account, knowingly to sell any security to or purchase any security from a client, or acting as broker for a person other than such client, knowingly to effect any sale or purchase of any security for the account of such client, without disclosing to such client in writing before the completion of such transaction the capacity in which he is acting and obtaining the consent of the client to such transaction. The prohibitions of this paragraph (3) shall not apply to any transaction with a customer of a broker or dealer if such broker or dealer is not acting as an investment adviser in relation to such transaction; or

(4) to engage in any act, practice, or course of business which is fraudulent, deceptive, or manipulative. The Commission shall, for the purposes of this paragraph (4) by rules and regulations define, and prescribe means reasonably designed to prevent, such acts, practices, and courses of business as are fraudulent, deceptive, or manipulative.

EXEMPTIONS

SEC. 206A. [80b–6a] The Commission, by rules and regulations, upon its own motion, or by order upon application, may conditionally or unconditionally exempt any person or transaction, or any class or classes of persons, or transactions, from any provision or provisions of this title or of any rule or regulation thereunder, if and to the extent that such exemption is necessary or appropriate in the public interest and consistent with the protection of investors and the purposes fairly intended by the policy and provisions of this title.

MATERIAL MISSTATEMENTS

SEC. 207. [80b–7] It shall be unlawful for any person willfully to make any untrue statement of a material fact in any registration application or report filed with the Commission under section 203 or 204, or willfully to omit to state in any such application or report any material fact which is required to be stated therein.

GENERAL PROHIBITIONS

SEC. 208. [80b–8] (a) It shall be unlawful for any person registered under section 203 of this title to represent or imply in any manner whatsoever that such person has been sponsored, recommended, or approved, or that his abilities or qualifications have in any respect been passed upon by the United States or any agency or any officer thereof.

(b) No provision of subsection (a) shall be construed to prohibit a statement that a person is registered under this title or under the Securities Exchange Act of 1934, if such statement is true in fact and if the effect of such registration is not misrepresented.

(c) It shall be unlawful for any person registered under section 203 of this title to represent that he is an investment counsel or to use the name "investment counsel" as descriptive of his business unless (1) his or its principal business consists of acting as investment adviser, and (2) a substantial part of his or its business consists of rendering investment supervisory services.

(d) It shall be unlawful for any person indirectly, or through or by any other person, to do any act or thing which it would be unlawful for such person to do directly under the provisions of this title or any rule or regulation thereunder.

ENFORCEMENT OF TITLE

SEC. 209. [80b–9] (a) Whenever it shall appear to the Commission, either upon complaint or otherwise, that the provisions of this title or of any rule or regulation prescribed under the authority thereof, have been or are about to be violated by any person, it may in its discretion require, and in any event shall permit, such person to file with it a statement in writing, under oath or otherwise, as to all the facts and circumstances relevant to such violation, and may otherwise investigate all such facts and circumstances.

(b) For the purposes of any investigation or any proceeding under this title, any member of the Commission or any officer thereof designated by it is empowered to administer oaths and affirmations, subpena witnesses, compel their attendance, take evidence, and require the production of any books, papers, correspondence, memoranda, contracts, agreements, or other records which are relevant or material to the inquiry. Such attendance of witnesses and the production of any such records may be required from any place in any State or in any Territory or other place subject to the jurisdiction of the United States at any designated place of hearing.

(c) In case of contumacy by, or refusal to obey a subpena issued to, any person, the Commission may invoke the aid of any court of the United States within the jurisdiction of which such investigation or proceeding is carried on, or where such person resides or carries on business, in requiring the attendance and testimony of witnesses and the production of books, papers, correspondence, memoranda, contracts, agreements, and other records. And such court may issue an order requiring such person to appear before the Commission or member or officer designated by the Commission, there to produce records, if so ordered or to give testimony touching the matter under investigation or in question; and any failure to obey such order of the court may be punished by such court as a contempt thereof. All process in any such case may be served in the judicial district whereof such person is an inhabitant or wherever he may be found. Any person who without just cause shall fail or refuse to attend and testify or to answer any lawful inquiry or to produce books, papers, correspondence, memoranda, contracts, agreements, or other records, if in his or its power so to do, in obedience to the subpena of the Commission, shall be guilty of a misdemeanor, and upon conviction shall be subject to a fine of not more than $1,000 or to imprisonment for a term of not more than one year, or both.

(d) Whenever it shall appear to the Commission that any person has engaged, is engaged, or is about to engage in any act or practice constituting a violation of any provision of this title, or of any rule, regulation, or order hereunder, or that any person has aided, abetted, counseled, commanded, induced, or procured, is aiding, abetting, counseling, commanding, inducing, or procuring, or is about to aid, abet, counsel, command, induce, or procure such a violation, it may in its discretion bring an action in the proper district court of the United States, or the proper United States court of any Territory or other place subject to the jurisdiction of the United States, to enjoin such acts or practices and to enforce compliance with this title or any rule, regulation, or order hereunder. Upon a showing that such person has engaged, is engaged, or is about to engage in any such act or practice, or in aiding, abetting, counseling, commanding, inducing, or procuring any such act or practice, a permanent or temporary injunction or decree or restraining order shall be granted without bond. The Commission may transmit such evidence as may be available concerning any violation of the provisions of this title, or of any rule, regulation, or order thereunder, to the Attorney General, who, in his discretion, may institute the appropriate criminal proceedings under this title.

(e) MONEY PENALTIES IN CIVIL ACTIONS.—

(1) AUTHORITY OF COMMISSION.—Whenever it shall appear to the Commission that any person has violated any provision of this title, the rules or regulations thereunder, or a cease-and-desist order entered by the Commission pursuant to section 203(k) of this title, the Commission may bring an action in a United States district court to seek, and the court shall have jurisdiction to impose, upon a proper showing, a civil penalty to be paid by the person who committed such violation.

(2) AMOUNT OF PENALTY.—

(A) FIRST TIER.—The amount of the penalty shall be determined by the court in light of the facts and circumstances. For each violation, the amount of the penalty shall not exceed the greater of (i) $5,000 for a natural per-

son or $50,000 for any other person, or (ii) the gross amount of pecuniary gain to such defendant as a result of the violation.

(B) SECOND TIER.—Notwithstanding subparagraph (A), the amount of penalty for each such violation shall not exceed the greater of (i) $50,000 for a natural person or $250,000 for any other person, or (ii) the gross amount of pecuniary gain to such defendant as a result of the violation, if the violation described in paragraph (1) involved fraud, deceit, manipulation, or deliberate or reckless disregard of a regulatory requirement.

(C) THIRD TIER.—Notwithstanding subparagraphs (A) and (B), the amount of penalty for each such violation shall not exceed the greater of (i) $100,000 for a natural person or $500,000 for any other person, or (ii) the gross amount of pecuniary gain to such defendant as a result of the violation, if—

(I) the violation described in paragraph (1) involved fraud, deceit, manipulation, or deliberate or reckless disregard of a regulatory requirement; and

(II) such violation directly or indirectly resulted in substantial losses or created a significant risk of substantial losses to other persons.

(3) PROCEDURES FOR COLLECTION.—

(A) PAYMENT OF PENALTY TO TREASURY.—A penalty imposed under this section shall be payable into the Treasury of the United States, except as otherwise provided in section 308 of the Sarbanes-Oxley Act of 2002 and section 21F of the Securities Exchange Act of 1934.

(B) COLLECTION OF PENALTIES.—If a person upon whom such a penalty is imposed shall fail to pay such penalty within the time prescribed in the court's order, the Commission may refer the matter to the Attorney General who shall recover such penalty by action in the appropriate United States district court.

(C) REMEDY NOT EXCLUSIVE.—The actions authorized by this subsection may be brought in addition to any other action that the Commission or the Attorney General is entitled to bring.

(D) JURISDICTION AND VENUE.—For purposes of section 214 of this title, actions under this paragraph shall be actions to enforce a liability or a duty created by this title.

(4) SPECIAL PROVISIONS RELATING TO A VIOLATION OF A CEASE-AND-DESIST ORDER.—In an action to enforce a cease-and-desist order entered by the Commission pursuant to section 203(k), each separate violation of such order shall be a separate offense, except that in the case of a violation through a continuing failure to comply with the order, each day of the failure to comply shall be deemed a separate offense.

(f) AIDING AND ABETTING.—For purposes of any action brought by the Commission under subsection (e), any person that knowingly or recklessly has aided, abetted, counseled, commanded, induced, or procured a violation of any provision of this Act, or of any rule, regulation, or order hereunder, shall be deemed to be in violation of such provision, rule, regulation, or order to the same extent as the person that committed such violation.

PUBLICITY

SEC. 210. [80b–10] (a) The information contained in any registration application or report or amendment thereto filed with the Commission pursuant to any provision of this title shall be made available to the public, unless and except insofar as the Commission, by rules and regulations upon its own motion, or by order upon application, finds that public disclosure is neither necessary nor appropriate in the public interest or for the protection of investors. Photostatic or other copies of information contained in documents filed with the Commission under this title and made available to the public shall be furnished to any person at such reasonable charge and under such reasonable limitations as the Commission shall prescribe.

(b) Subject to the provisions of subsections (c) and (d) of section 209 of this title and section 24(c) of the Securities Exchange Act of 1934, the Commission, or any member, officer, or employee thereof, shall not make public the fact that any examination or investigation under this title is being conducted, or the results of or any facts ascertained during any such examination or investigation; and no member, officer, or employee of the Commission shall disclose to any person other than a member, officer, or employee of the Commission any information obtained as a result of any such examination or investigation except with the approval of the Commission. The provisions of this subsection shall not apply—

(1) in the case of any hearing which is public under the provisions of section 212; or

(2) in the case of a resolution or request from either House of Congress.

(c) No provision of this title shall be construed to require, or to authorize the Commission to require any investment adviser engaged in rendering investment supervisory services to disclose the identity, investments, or affairs of any client of such investment adviser, except insofar as such disclosure may be necessary or appropriate in a particular proceeding or investigation having as its object the enforcement of a provision or provisions of this title or for purposes of assessment of potential systemic risk.

SEC. 210A. [80b–10a] CONSULTATION.

(a) EXAMINATION RESULTS AND OTHER INFORMATION.—

(1) The appropriate Federal banking agency shall provide the Commission upon request the results of any examination, reports, records, or other information to which such agency may have access—

(A) with respect to the investment advisory activities of any—

(i) bank holding company or savings and loan holding company;

(ii) bank; or

(iii) separately identifiable department or division of a bank,

that is registered under section 203 of this title; and

(B) in the case of a bank holding company or savings and loan holding company or bank that has a subsidiary or a separately identifiable department or division registered under that section, with respect to the investment advisory activities of such bank or bank holding company or savings and loan holding company.

(2) The Commission shall provide to the appropriate Federal banking agency upon request the results of any examination, reports, records, or other information with respect to the investment advisory activities of any bank holding company or savings and loan holding company, bank, or separately identifiable department or division of a bank, which is registered under section 203 of this title.

(3) Notwithstanding any other provision of law, the Commission and the appropriate Federal banking agencies shall not be compelled to disclose any information provided under paragraph (1) or (2). Nothing in this paragraph shall authorize the Commission or such agencies to withhold information from Congress, or prevent the Commission or such agencies from complying with a request for information from any other Federal department or agency or any self-regulatory organization requesting the information for purposes within the scope of its jurisdiction, or complying with an order of a court of the United States in an action brought by the United States, the Commission, or such agencies. For purposes of section 552 of title 5, United States Code, this paragraph shall be considered a statute described in subsection (b)(3)(B) of such section 552.

(b) EFFECT ON OTHER AUTHORITY.—Nothing in this section shall limit in any respect the authority of the appropriate Federal banking agency with respect to such bank holding company or savings and loan holding company (or affiliates or subsidiaries thereof), bank, or subsidiary, department, or division or a bank under any other provision of law.

(c) DEFINITION.—For purposes of this section, the term "appropriate Federal banking agency" shall have the same meaning as given in section 3 of the Federal Deposit Insurance Act.

RULES, REGULATIONS, AND ORDERS

SEC. 211. [80b–11] (a) The Commission shall have authority from time to time to make, issue, amend, and rescind such rules and regulations and such orders as are necessary or appropriate to the exercise of the functions and powers conferred upon the Commission elsewhere in this title, including rules and regulations defining technical, trade, and other terms used in this title, except that the Commission may not define the term "client" for purposes of paragraphs (1) and (2) of section 206 to include an investor in a private fund managed by an investment adviser, if such private fund has entered into an advisory contract with such adviser. For the purposes of its rules or regulations the Commission may classify persons and matters within its jurisdiction and prescribe different requirements for different classes of persons or matters.

(b) Subject to the provisions of chapter 15 of title 44, United States Code, and regulations prescribed under the authority thereof, the rules and regulations of the Commission under this title, and amendments thereof, shall be effective upon publication in the manner which the Commission shall prescribe, or upon such later date as may be provided in such rules and regulations.

(c) Orders of the Commission under this title shall be issued only after appropriate notice and opportunity for hearing. Notice to the parties to a proceeding before the Commission shall be given by personal service upon each party or by registered mail or certified mail or confirmed telegraphic notice to the party's last known business address. Notice to interested persons, if any, other than parties may be given in the same manner or by publication in the Federal Register.

(d) No provision of this title imposing any liability shall apply to any act done or omitted in good faith in conformity with any rule, regulation, or order of the Commission, notwithstanding that such rule, regulation, or order may, after such act or omission, be amended or rescinded or be determined by judicial or other authority to be invalid for any reason.

(e) DISCLOSURE RULES ON PRIVATE FUNDS.—The Commission and the Commodity Futures Trading Commission shall, after consultation with the Council but not later than 12 months after the date of enactment of the Private Fund Investment Advisers Registration Act of 2010, jointly promulgate rules to establish the form and content of the reports required to be filed with the Commission under subsection 204(b) and with the Commodity Futures Trading Commission by investment advisers that are registered both under this title and the Commodity Exchange Act (7 U.S.C. 1a et seq.).

(g)[9] STANDARD OF CONDUCT.—

(1) IN GENERAL.—The Commission may promulgate rules to provide that the standard of conduct for all brokers, dealers, and investment advisers, when providing personalized investment advice about securities to retail customers (and such other customers as the Commission may by rule provide), shall be to act in the best interest of the customer without regard to the financial or other interest of the broker, dealer, or investment adviser providing the advice. In accordance with such rules, any material conflicts of interest shall be disclosed and may be consented to by the customer. Such rules shall provide that such standard of conduct shall be no less stringent than the standard applicable to investment advisers under section 206(1) and (2) of this Act when providing personalized investment advice about securities, except the Commission shall not ascribe a meaning to the term "customer" that would include an investor in a private fund managed by an investment adviser, where such private fund has entered into an advisory contract with such adviser. The receipt of compensation based on commission or fees shall not, in and of itself, be considered a violation of such standard applied to a broker, dealer, or investment adviser.

[9] So in law. There is no subsection (f).

(2) RETAIL CUSTOMER DEFINED.—For purposes of this subsection, the term "retail customer" means a natural person, or the legal representative of such natural person, who—

(A) receives personalized investment advice about securities from a broker, dealer, or investment adviser; and

(B) uses such advice primarily for personal, family, or household purposes.

(h) OTHER MATTERS.—The Commission shall—

(1) facilitate the provision of simple and clear disclosures to investors regarding the terms of their relationships with brokers, dealers, and investment advisers, including any material conflicts of interest; and

(2) examine and, where appropriate, promulgate rules prohibiting or restricting certain sales practices, conflicts of interest, and compensation schemes for brokers, dealers, and investment advisers that the Commission deems contrary to the public interest and the protection of investors.

(i) HARMONIZATION OF ENFORCEMENT.—The enforcement authority of the Commission with respect to violations of the standard of conduct applicable to an investment adviser shall include—

(1) the enforcement authority of the Commission with respect to such violations provided under this Act; and

(2) the enforcement authority of the Commission with respect to violations of the standard of conduct applicable to a broker or dealer providing personalized investment advice about securities to a retail customer under the Securities Exchange Act of 1934, including the authority to impose sanctions for such violations, and

the Commission shall seek to prosecute and sanction violators of the standard of conduct applicable to an investment adviser under this Act to same extent as the Commission prosecutes and sanctions violators of the standard of conduct applicable to a broker or dealer providing personalized investment advice about securities to a retail customer under the Securities Exchange Act of 1934.

HEARINGS

SEC. 212. [80b–12] Hearings may be public and may be held before the Commission, any member or members thereof, or any officer or officers of the Commission designated by it, and appropriate records thereof shall be kept.

COURT REVIEW OF ORDERS

SEC. 213. [80b–13] (a) Any person or party aggrieved by an order issued by the Commission under this title may obtain a review of such order in the court of appeals of the United States within any circuit wherein such person resides or has his principal office or place of business, or in the United States Court of Appeals for the District of Columbia, by filing in such court, within sixty days after the entry of such order, a written petition praying that the order of the Commission be modified or set aside in whole or in part. A copy of such petition shall be forthwith transmitted by the clerk of the court to any member of the Commission, or any officer thereof designated by the Commission for that purpose, and thereupon the Commission shall file in the court the record upon which the order complained of was entered, as provided in section 2112 of title 28, United States Code. Upon the filing of such petition such court shall have jurisdiction, which upon the filing of the record shall be exclusive, to affirm, modify, or set aside such order, in whole or in part. No objection to the order of the Commission shall be considered by the court unless such objection shall have been urged before the Commission or unless there were reasonable grounds for failure so to do. The findings of the Commission as to the facts, if supported by substantial evidence, shall be conclusive. If application is made to the court for leave to adduce additional evidence, and it is shown to the satisfaction of the court that such additional evidence is material and that there were reasonable grounds for failure to adduce such evidence in the proceeding before the Commission, the court may order such additional evidence to be taken before the Commission and to be adduced upon the hearing in such manner and upon such terms and conditions as to the court may seem proper. The Commission may modify its findings as to the facts by reason of the additional evidence so taken, and it shall file with the court such modified or new findings, which, if supported by substantial evidence, shall be conclusive, and its recommendation, if any, for the modification or setting aside of the original order. The judgment and decree of the court affirming, modifying, or setting aside, in whole or in part, any such order of the Commission shall be final, subject to review by the Supreme Court of the United States upon certiorari or certification as provided in section 1254 of title 28, United States Code.

(b) The commencement of proceedings under subsection (a) shall not, unless specifically ordered by the court, operate as a stay of the Commission's order.

JURISDICTION OF OFFENSES AND SUITS

SEC. 214. [80b–14] (a) IN GENERAL.—The district courts of the United States and the United States courts of any Territory or other place subject to the jurisdiction of the United States shall have jurisdiction of violations of this title or the rules, regulations, or orders thereunder, and, concurrently with State and Territorial courts, of all suits in equity and actions at law brought to enforce any liability or duty created by, or to enjoin any violation of this title or the rules, regulations, or orders thereunder. Any criminal proceeding may be brought in the district wherein any act or transaction constituting the violation occurred. Any suit or action to enforce any liability or duty created by, or to enjoin any violation of this title or rules, regulations, or orders thereunder, may be brought in any such district or in the district wherein the defendant is an inhabitant or transacts business, and process in such cases may be served in any district of which the defendant is an inhabitant or transacts business or wherever the defendant may be found. In any action or proceeding instituted by the Commission under this title in a United States district court for any judicial district, a subpoena issued to compel the attendance of a witness or the production of documents or tangible things (or both) at a hearing or trial may be served at any place within the United

States. Rule 45(c)(3)(A)(ii) of the Federal Rules of Civil Procedure shall not apply to a subpoena issued under the preceding sentence. Judgments and decrees so rendered shall be subject to review as provided in sections 1254, 1291, 1292, and 1294 of title 28, United States Code. No costs shall be assessed for or against the Commission in any proceeding under this title brought by or against the Commission in any court.

(b) EXTRATERRITORIAL JURISDICTION.—The district courts of the United States and the United States courts of any Territory shall have jurisdiction of an action or proceeding brought or instituted by the Commission or the United States alleging a violation of section 206 involving—

(1) conduct within the United States that constitutes significant steps in furtherance of the violation, even if the violation is committed by a foreign adviser and involves only foreign investors; or

(2) conduct occurring outside the United States that has a foreseeable substantial effect within the United States.

VALIDITY OF CONTRACTS

SEC. 215. [80b–15] (a) Any condition, stipulation, or provision binding any person to waive compliance with any provision of this title or with any rule, regulation, or order thereunder shall be void.

(b) Every contract made in violation of any provision of this title and every contract heretofore or hereafter made, the performance of which involves the violation of, or the continuance of any relationship or practice in violation of any provision of this title, or any rule, regulation, or order thereunder, shall be void (1) as regards the rights of any person who, in violation of any such provision, rule, regulation, or order, shall have made or engaged in the performance of any such contract, and (2) as regards the rights of any person who, not being a party to such contract, shall have acquired any right thereunder with actual knowledge of the facts by reason of which the making or performance of such contract was in violation of any such provision.

ANNUAL REPORTS OF COMMISSION

SEC. 216. [80b–16] The Commission shall submit annually a report to the Congress covering the work of the Commission for the preceding year and including such information, data, and recommendations for further legislation in connection with the matters covered by this title as it may find advisable.

PENALTIES [10]

SEC. 217. [80b–17] Any person who willfully violates any provision of this title, or any rule, regulation, or order promulgated by the Commission under authority thereof, shall, upon conviction, be fined not more than $10,000, imprisoned for not more than five years, or both.

[10] See also 18 U.S.C. 3571. [Printed in appendix to this volume.]

HIRING AND LEASING AUTHORITY OF THE COMMISSION

SEC. 218. [80b–18] The provisions of section 4(b) of the Securities Exchange Act of 1934 shall be applicable with respect to the power of the Commission—

(1) to appoint and fix the compensation of such other employees as may be necessary for carrying out its functions under this title, and

(2) to lease and allocate such real property as may be necessary for carrying out its functions under this title.

SEPARABILITY OF PROVISIONS

SEC. 219. [80b–19] If any provision of this title or the application of such provision to any person or circumstances shall be held invalid, the remainder of the title and the application of such provision to persons or circumstances other than those as to which it is held invalid shall not be affected thereby.

SHORT TITLE

SEC. 220. [80b–20] This title may be cited as the "Investment Advisers Act of 1940".

EFFECTIVE DATE

SEC. 221. [80b–21] This title shall become effective on November 1, 1940.

SEC. 222. [80b–18a] STATE REGULATION OF INVESTMENT ADVISERS.

(a) JURISDICTION OF STATE REGULATORS.—Nothing in this title shall affect the jurisdiction of the securities commissioner (or any agency or officer performing like functions) of any State over any security or any person insofar as it does not conflict with the provisions of this title or the rules and regulations thereunder.

(b) DUAL COMPLIANCE PURPOSES.—No State may enforce any law or regulation that would require an investment adviser to maintain any books or records in addition to those required under the laws of the State in which it maintains its principal office and place of business, if the investment adviser—

(1) is registered or licensed as such in the State in which it maintains its principal office and place of business; and

(2) is in compliance with the applicable books and records requirements of the State in which it maintains its principal office and place of business.

(c) LIMITATION ON CAPITAL AND BOND REQUIREMENTS.—No State may enforce any law or regulation that would require an investment adviser to maintain a higher minimum net capital or to post any bond in addition to any that is required under the laws of the State in which it maintains its principal office and place of business, if the investment adviser—

(1) is registered or licensed as such in the State in which it maintains its principal office and place of business; and

(2) is in compliance with the applicable net capital or bonding requirements of the State in which it maintains its principal office and place of business.

(d) NATIONAL DE MINIMIS STANDARD.—No law of any State or political subdivision thereof requiring the registration, licensing, or qualification as an investment adviser shall require an investment adviser to register with the securities commissioner of the State (or any agency or officer performing like functions) or to comply with such law (other than any provision thereof prohibiting fraudulent conduct) if the investment adviser—

(1) does not have a place of business located within the State; and

(2) during the preceding 12-month period, has had fewer than 6 clients who are residents of that State.

SEC. 223. [15 U.S.C. 80b–18b] CUSTODY OF CLIENT ACCOUNTS.

An investment adviser registered under this title shall take such steps to safeguard client assets over which such adviser has custody, including, without limitation, verification of such assets by an independent public accountant, as the Commission may, by rule, prescribe.

SEC. 224. [15 U.S.C. 80b–18c] RULE OF CONSTRUCTION RELATING TO THE COMMODITIES EXCHANGE ACT.

Nothing in this title shall relieve any person of any obligation or duty, or affect the availability of any right or remedy available to the Commodity Futures Trading Commission or any private party, arising under the Commodity Exchange Act (7 U.S.C. 1 et seq.) governing commodity pools, commodity pool operators, or commodity trading advisors.

SECURITIES AND EXCHANGE COMMISSION

17 CFR Part 276

[Release No. IA-5249]

Commission Interpretation Regarding the Solely Incidental Prong of the Broker-Dealer Exclusion from the Definition of Investment Adviser

AGENCY: Securities and Exchange Commission.

ACTION: Interpretation.

SUMMARY: The Securities and Exchange Commission (the "SEC" or the "Commission") is publishing an interpretation of a section of the Investment Advisers Act of 1940 (the "Advisers Act" or the "Act"), which excludes from the definition of "investment adviser" any broker or dealer that provides advisory services when such services are "solely incidental" to the conduct of the broker or dealer's business and when such incidental advisory services are provided for no special compensation.

DATES: Effective July 12, 2019.

FOR FURTHER INFORMATION CONTACT: James McGinnis, Senior Counsel, Investment Adviser Regulation Office, at (202) 551-6787 or IArules@sec.gov; and Benjamin Kalish, Attorney-Advisor, or Parisa Haghshenas, Branch Chief, Chief Counsel's Office at (202) 551-6825 or IMOCC@sec.gov, Division of Investment Management, Securities and Exchange Commission, 100 F Street NE, Washington, DC 20549-8549.

SUPPLEMENTARY INFORMATION: The Commission is publishing an interpretation of the solely incidental prong of the broker-dealer exclusion in section 202(a)(11)(C) of the Advisers Act [15 U.S.C. 80b].[1]

TABLE OF CONTENTS

I. INTRODUCTION

The Advisers Act regulates the activities of certain "investment advisers," who are defined in section 202(a)(11) of the Advisers Act in part as persons who, for compensation, engage in the business of advising others about securities. Section 202(a)(11)(C) excludes from the definition of investment adviser—and thus from the application of the Advisers Act—a broker or dealer "whose performance of such advisory services is solely incidental to the conduct of his business as a broker or dealer and who receives no special compensation" for those services (the "broker-dealer exclusion"). The broker-dealer exclusion shows, on the one hand, that at the time the Advisers Act was enacted Congress recognized broker-dealers commonly provided some investment advice to their customers in the course of their business as broker-dealers and that it would be inappropriate to bring broker-dealers within the scope of the

[1] 15 U.S.C. 80b. Unless otherwise noted, when we refer to the Advisers Act, or any paragraph of the Advisers Act, we are referring to 15 U.S.C. 80b of the United States Code, at which the Advisers Act is codified.

Advisers Act because of this aspect of their business.[2] On the other hand, the limitations of the exclusion show that Congress excluded broker-dealer advisory services from the scope of the Advisers Act only under certain circumstances—namely, when those services are solely incidental to the broker-dealer's regular business as a broker-dealer (the "solely incidental prong") and when the broker-dealer receives no special compensation (the "special compensation prong").[3]

On April 18, 2018, the Commission proposed a rulemaking intended to enhance the standard of conduct for broker-dealers when providing recommendations.[4] The Commission also proposed an interpretation intended to reaffirm and in some cases clarify the standard of conduct for investment advisers,[5] as well as a rulemaking intended to provide retail investors with clear and succinct information regarding key aspects of their brokerage and advisory relationships.[6] The Reg. BI Proposal discussed the broker-dealer exclusion and requested

2 *Opinion of General Counsel Relating to Section 202(a)(11)(C) of the Investment Advisers Act of 1940*, Investment Advisers Act Release No. 2 (Oct. 28, 1940) ("Advisers Act Release No. 2").

3 *See Regulation Best Interest*, Securities Exchange Act Release No. 83062 (April 18, 2018) [83 FR 21574 (May 9, 2018)] ("Reg. BI Proposal"), at n.343. The broker-dealer exclusion is conjunctive—that is, the broker-dealer must both provide investment advice that is solely incidental to the conduct of his business as a broker-dealer *and* the broker-dealer must receive no special compensation. In the event that a broker-dealer's investment advice fits within the guidance of this Release with respect to the solely incidental prong, that broker-dealer must also receive no special compensation for the advisory service to be consistent with the broker-dealer exclusion.

4 *See id.*

5 *Proposed Commission Interpretation Regarding Standard of Conduct for Investment Advisers; Request for Comment on Enhancing Investment Adviser Regulation*, Investment Advisers Act Release No. 4889 (April 18, 2018) [83 FR 21203 (May 9, 2018)] (the "Proposed Fiduciary Interpretation").

6 *See Form CRS Relationship Summary; Amendments to Form ADV; Required Disclosures in Retail Communications and Restrictions on the Use of Certain Names or Titles*, Investment Advisers Act Release No. 4888 (April 18, 2018) [83 FR 21416 (May 9, 2018)] ("Relationship Summary Proposal"). Concurrently with this interpretation, we also are adopting the final versions of the rules and interpretations proposed in the Relationship Summary Proposal, the Reg. BI Proposal, and the Proposed Fiduciary Interpretation. *See Form CRS Relationship Summary; Amendments to Form ADV*, Investment Advisers Act Release No. 5247 (June 5, 2019) (the "Relationship Summary Adoption"); *Regulation Best Interest: The Broker-Dealer Standard of Conduct*, Exchange Act Release No. 86031 (June 5, 2019) ("Reg. BI

comment on the scope of the exclusion as applied to a broker-dealer's exercise of investment discretion.[7] While some commenters addressed when a broker-dealer's advisory services are "solely incidental to the conduct of his business as a broker or dealer" in the context of the exercise of investment discretion, more commenters addressed this prong more generally.[8] For example, many commenters requested general guidance on or expressed views about the meaning of the solely incidental prong[9] and the permissibility under this prong of various broker-dealer activities that relate to the investment advice they provide in light of the Reg. BI Proposal and the Relationship Summary Proposal.[10] Other commenters suggested that our approach to the Reg. BI Proposal was inconsistent with the solely incidental prong of the broker-dealer exclusion. One commenter suggested that the Reg. BI Proposal, if adopted, would allow broker-dealers to provide investment advice beyond what the solely incidental prong should "reasonably be interpreted to permit," arguing that to qualify for exclusion from regulation under

Adoption"); and *Commission Interpretation Regarding Standard of Conduct for Investment Advisers*, Investment Advisers Act Release No. 5248 (June 5, 2019) ("Final Fiduciary Interpretation").

7 *See* Reg. BI Proposal, *supra* footnote 3, at nn.342–67 and accompanying text.

8 We considered comments submitted in File No. S7-07-18 (Reg. BI Proposal, *supra* footnote 3); File No. S7-08-18 (Relationship Summary Proposal, *supra* footnote 6); and File No. S7-09-18 (Proposed Fiduciary Interpretation, *supra* footnote 5). Those comments are available on the Commission's website at https://www.sec.gov/comments/s7-07-18/s70718.htm, https://www.sec.gov/comments/s7-08-18/s70818.htm, and https://www.sec.gov/comments/s7-09-18/s70918.htm, respectively.

9 *See, e.g.*, Comment Letter of North American Securities Administrators Association, Inc. (Aug. 23, 2018) ("NASAA Letter"); Comment Letter of CFA Institute (Aug. 7, 2018) ("CFA Institute Letter") (noting the "need to give guidance" on the broker-dealer exclusion and noting that the Commission has legal authority to provide needed clarification); Comment Letter of the Institute for the Fiduciary Standard (Aug. 6, 2018) ("IFS Letter") (arguing that when a broker's investment advice is solely incidental to its business is one of a number of "questions the SEC should address"); Comment Letter of the Consumer Federation of America (Aug. 7, 2018) ("CFA Letter") (arguing that the Commission failed to "engage" on "just how far the 'solely incidental' exclusion stretches"); Comment Letter of the Investment Adviser Association (Aug. 6, 2018) ("IAA Letter") ("[T]he Commission should reconsider when broker-dealers should be able to rely on the Solely Incidental [prong]."); Comment Letter of Michael Kitces (Aug. 2, 2018) ("Kitces Letter") (arguing that the Commission's prior interpretations of the solely incidental prong are inconsistent with the plain meaning and legislative history of the term).

10 *See, e.g.*, CFA Letter; Kitces Letter.

the Advisers Act, broker-dealers should only "be able to provide very limited advice…."[11] Two commenters thought that the Commission's expressed support for maintaining the "broker-dealer model as an option for retail customers seeking investment advice"[12] was inconsistent with the solely incidental prong.[13] Another commenter called the Commission's previously articulated interpretation of the solely incidental prong "vague."[14] The comments we received demonstrate that there is disagreement about when the provision of broker-dealer investment advice is consistent with the solely incidental prong.[15] In light of these comments, we are adopting this interpretation to confirm and clarify the Commission's position with respect to the solely incidental prong. To illustrate how the interpretation functions, we discuss its application to two advisory services that a broker or dealer may provide, namely: (i) exercising investment discretion over customer accounts and (ii) account monitoring.[16] Our interpretation complements each of the rules and forms we are adopting, which, among other things, are

[11] *See* NASAA Letter.

[12] *See* Reg. BI Proposal, *supra* footnote 3, at text accompanying n.31.

[13] *See* CFA Letter (stating that certain aspects of the Relationship Summary Proposal and the Reg. BI Proposal indicated that broker-dealers were in an "advice relationship" in a manner that does not "remotely sound like advice that is 'solely incidental to' the conduct of their business as a broker or dealer"); Kitces Letter (arguing that referring to the broker-dealer model as a "model for advice" is in contravention of the broker-dealer exclusion because "advice can only be incidental if it occurs by chance, as a *consequence* of a product sale, or *without* intent to give advice").

[14] *See* Comment Letter of Securities Arbitration Clinic, St. Vincent DePaul Legal Program, Inc., St. John's University School of Law (Aug. 7, 2018) ("St. John's Clinic Letter").

[15] Furthermore, interested parties have for years expressed their views to the Commission on what they believe the broker-dealer exclusion requires, including disagreements with the Commission's interpretation of the exclusion. *See, e.g.*, Comment Letter of Consumer Federation of America (Sept. 20, 2004) (arguing that the Commission should "define 'solely incidental' in a way that hews closely to what commenters described as Congress's clear intent to provide only a very narrow exclusion"), *available at* https://www.sec.gov/rules/proposed/s72599/s72599-1101.pdf.

[16] We received comments requesting guidance with respect to the solely incidental prong on both activities. *See infra* section II.C.

intended individually and collectively to enhance investor understanding of the relationships and services offered by investment advisers and broker-dealers.[17]

II. Interpretation and Application

A. Historical Context and Legislative History

When the Advisers Act was enacted in 1940, broker-dealers regularly provided investment advice.[18] They did so in two distinct ways: as an auxiliary part of traditional brokerage services for which their brokerage customers paid fixed commissions and, alternatively, as a distinct advisory service for which their advisory clients separately contracted and paid a fee.[19] The advice that broker-dealers provided as an auxiliary component of traditional brokerage services was referred to as "brokerage house advice" in a leading study of

[17] *See* Reg. BI Adoption; Relationship Summary Adoption; Final Fiduciary Interpretation, *supra* footnote 6. We also received a few comments in response to the Reg. BI Proposal and the Relationship Summary Proposal requesting that the Commission provide guidance on the special compensation prong. *See, e.g.*, CFA Letter (arguing, among other points, that special compensation would constitute any compensation other than commissions for trade execution); Comment Letter of Coalition of Mutual Fund Investors (Aug. 8, 2018) ("Mutual Fund Investors Letter") (arguing that special compensation should include all asset-based compensation and third-party fees from mutual funds and their advisers). We are not providing guidance on the special compensation prong in this Release as we do not believe our views on this prong require additional clarification. The Commission has considered the meaning of the special compensation prong on previous occasions. *See, e.g.*, *Interpretive Rule Under the Advisers Act Affecting Broker-Dealers*, Investment Advisers Act Release No. 2652 (Sept. 24, 2007) ("2007 Proposing Release"); *Certain Broker-Dealers Deemed Not to Be Investment Advisers*, Investment Advisers Act Release No. 2376 (Apr. 12, 2005) ("2005 Adopting Release," in which, as discussed *infra* at footnote 38 and accompanying text, the Commission adopted a rule that a court vacated on grounds that did not address our interpretive positions relating to the solely incidental prong). The comments we received in response to requests for comment to the Reg. BI Proposal and the Relationship Summary Proposal did not demonstrate that there is significant disagreement with our interpretation of that prong.

[18] For an extensive discussion of broker-dealer practice in the years leading up to enactment of the Advisers Act, from which this summary is drawn, *see* 2005 Adopting Release, *supra* footnote 17; *Certain Broker-Dealers Deemed Not to Be Investment Advisers*, Investment Advisers Act Release No. 2340 (Jan. 6, 2005) ("2005 Proposing Release").

[19] *See, e.g.*, *Investment Trusts and Investment Companies: Hearings on S. 3580 Before a Subcomm. of the Senate Committee on Banking and Currency*, 76th Cong., 3d Sess. 736 (1940) ("Hearings on S. 3580") (testimony of Dwight C. Rose, president of the Investment Counsel Association of America) ("Most . . . investment dealers . . . and brokers advise on investment problems, either as an auxiliary service without charge, or for specific charges allocated to this specific function.").

the time.[20] "Brokerage house advice" was extensive and varied,[21] and included information about various corporations, municipalities, and governments;[22] broad analyses of general business and financial conditions;[23] market letters and special analyses of companies' situations;[24] information about income tax schedules and tax consequences;[25] and "chart reading."[26] The second way in which broker-dealers dispensed advice was to charge a distinct fee for advisory services, which typically were provided through special "investment advisory departments" within broker-dealer firms that advised customers for a fee in the same manner as firms whose sole business was providing "investment counsel" services.[27]

20 *See* Twentieth Century Fund, THE SECURITY MARKETS (1935) ("SECURITY MARKETS") at 633–46 (discussing "brokerage house advice"); *see also* Charles F. Hodges, WALL STREET (1930) ("WALL STREET") at 253–85; SEC, REPORT ON INVESTMENT COUNSEL, INVESTMENT MANAGEMENT, INVESTMENT SUPERVISORY, AND INVESTMENT ADVISORY SERVICES (1939) (H.R. Doc. No. 477) ("INVESTMENT COUNSEL REPORT") at n.1.

21 *See, e.g.*, REPORT OF PUBLIC EXAMINING BD. ON CUSTOMER PROTECTION TO N.Y. STOCK EXCHANGE (Aug. 31, 1939), at 3:

> The customer entrusts the broker with information regarding his financial affairs and dealings which he expects to be kept in strict confidence. Frequently he looks to the broker to perform a whole series of functions relating to the investment of his funds and the care of his securities. Although he could secure similar services at his bank, he asks his broker, as a matter of choice and convenience, to hold credit balances of cash pending instructions; to retain securities in safekeeping and to collect dividends and interest; to advise him respecting investments; and to lend him money on suitable collateral.

22 SECURITY MARKETS, *supra* footnote 20, at 633; WALL STREET, *supra* footnote 20, at 254 ("This information includes current and comparative data for a number of years on earning and earnings records, capitalization, financial position, dividend record, comparative balance sheets and income statements . . . production and operating statistics, territory and markets served, officers and directors of the company and much other information of value to the investor in appraising the value of a security.").

23 SECURITY MARKETS, *supra* footnote 20, at 634; WALL STREET, *supra* footnote 20, at 254.

24 SECURITY MARKETS, *supra* footnote 20, at 640–43; WALL STREET, *supra* footnote 20, at 277–85.

25 SECURITY MARKETS, *supra* footnote 20, at 641.

26 *Id.* at 643 (defining "chart reading" as "the study of the charted course of prices and volume of trading over a long period of time in order to discover typical conformations recurring in the past with sufficient frequency to be utilized in the present as a basis of judgment as to impending price changes").

27 *See* Advisers Act Release No. 2, *supra* footnote 2; *see also* SECURITY MARKETS, *supra* footnote 20, at 646, 653 (referring to "investment supervisory departments" and "special investment management departments" of broker-dealers). In general, contemporaneous literature used the term "investment counsel" or "investment counselor" to refer to those who provided investment advice for a fee and whose advisory

Between 1935 and 1939, the Commission conducted a congressionally mandated study of investment trusts and investment companies and in connection with this study surveyed investment advisers, including broker-dealers with investment advisory departments.[28] In a report to Congress (the "Investment Counsel Report"), the Commission informed Congress that the Commission's study had identified two broad classes of problems relating to investment advisers that warranted legislation: "(a) the problem of distinguishing between bona fide investment counselors and 'tipster' organizations; and (b) those problems involving the organization and operation of investment counsel institutions."[29] Based on the findings of the Investment Counsel Report, representatives of the Commission testified at the congressional hearings on what ultimately became the Advisers Act in favor of regulating the persons engaged in the business of providing investment advice for compensation.

Congress responded by passing the Advisers Act. Section 202(a)(11) of the Act defined "investment adviser"—those subject to the requirements of the Act—broadly to include "any person who, for compensation, engages in the business of advising others, either directly or through publications or writings, as to the value of securities or as to the advisability of investing in, purchasing, or selling securities, or who, for compensation and as part of a regular business, issues or promulgates analyses or reports concerning securities...." In adopting this broad definition, Congress necessarily rejected arguments presented during its hearings that legitimate

relationship with clients had a supervisory or managerial character. *See id.* at 646 (defining "investment counselor" as "an individual, institution, organization, or department of an institution or organization which undertakes for a fee to advise or to supervise the investment of funds by, and on occasion to manage the investment accounts of, clients"). Under the Advisers Act, "investment counsel" is a defined subset of the "investment advisers" to whom the Act applies. *See* section 208(c) of the Act.

28 INVESTMENT COUNSEL REPORT, *supra* footnote 20, at 1. The study was conducted pursuant to section 30 of the Public Utility Holding Company Act of 1935 [15 U.S.C. 79z-4]; *see* Hearings on S. 3580, *supra* footnote 19, at 995–96.

29 INVESTMENT COUNSEL REPORT, *supra* footnote 20, at 27.

investment counselors[30] should be free from any oversight except, perhaps, by the few states that had passed laws regulating investment counselors and by private organizations, such as the Investment Counsel Association of America.[31] Instead, in responding to such views, congressional committee members repeatedly observed that those whose business was limited to providing investment advice for compensation were subject to little if any regulatory oversight, and questioned why they should not be subject to regulation even though other professionals were.[32]

Conversely, the Advisers Act specifically excluded persons, among others, from the broad definition of "investment adviser" to the extent that such persons rendered investment advice incidental to their primary business.[33] Broker-dealers were among these excluded

30 Hearings on S. 3580, *supra* footnote 19, at 745–48; *see also* 2005 Adopting Release, *supra* footnote 17, at n.62.

31 Hearings on S. 3580, *supra* footnote 19, at 716–18, 736–38, 740-41, 744–45, 760, 763.

32 *Id.* at 738–39, 745–49, 751–53 (Senators Wagner and Hughes). David Schenker, chief counsel for the Commission's study, offered the following observations in response to investment counselors' arguments against the registration and regulation required by the Act:

> Then there is another curious thing, Senator, that those people who are subject to supervision by some authoritative body of some kind, such as securities dealers or investment bankers have to register with us as brokers and dealers. People, who are brokers and members of stock exchanges and are supervised by the stock exchanges. Curiously enough, the people in the investment-counsel business who are supervised are not eligible for membership in the investment counsel association; because the association says that if you are in the brokerage or banking business you cannot be a member of the association.
>
> So the situation is that if you take their analysis, the only ones who would not be subject to regulation by the S.E.C. would be the people who are not subject to regulation by anybody at all. These investment counselors who appeared here are no different from the over-the-counter brokers and dealers or the members of the New York Stock Exchange.

Id. at 995–96. Eventually, members of the investment counsel industry agreed with the proposed legislation. *See id.* at 1124; *Investment Trusts and Investment Companies: Hearings on H.R. 10065 Before a Subcomm. of the House Committee on Interstate and Foreign Commerce*, 76th Cong., 3d Sess. (1940) ("Hearings on H.R. 10065"); *see also* S. REP. NO. 76-1775, 76th Cong., 3d Sess. 21 (1940); H.R. REP. NO. 76-2639, 76th Cong., 3d Sess. 27 (1940).

33 The exclusion for certain professionals in Advisers Act section 202(a)(11) is very similar to certain state-law provisions governing investment counselors at the time, which excepted "brokers, attorneys, banks, savings and loan associations, trust companies, and certified public accountants." *See* STATUTORY REGULATION OF INVESTMENT ADVISERS (prepared by the Research Department of the Illinois Legislative

persons, as section 202(a)(11)(C) of the Act excludes from the definition of "investment adviser" a broker-dealer who provides investment advice that is "solely incidental to the conduct of his business as a broker or dealer and who receives no special compensation therefor"—*i.e.*, the broker-dealer exclusion.

B. Scope of the Solely Incidental Prong of the Broker-Dealer Exclusion

The Commission and its staff have on several occasions discussed the scope of the broker-dealer exclusion.[34] In adopting a rule regarding fee-based brokerage accounts in 2005, for example, the Commission stated that investment advisory services are "solely incidental to" the conduct of a broker-dealer's business when the services are offered in connection with and are reasonably related to the brokerage services provided to an account.[35] The interpretation was consistent with the Commission's contemporaneous construction of the Advisers Act as excluding broker-dealers whose investment advice is given "solely as an incident of their regular business."[36] The 2005 interpretation stated that the importance or frequency of the investment advice was not a determinant of whether the solely incidental prong was satisfied; the Commission rejected the view that only minor, insignificant, or infrequent advice qualifies for

Council) reprinted in Hearings on S. 3580, *supra* footnote 19, at 1007. That report stated that "the investment advice furnished by these excepted groups would seem to be merely incidental to some other function being performed by them." *Id.*

34 *See, e.g.*, Advisers Act Release No. 2, *supra* footnote 2; *Applicability of the Investment Advisers Act to Certain Brokers and Dealers; Interpretation of the Term 'Special Compensation'*, Investment Advisers Act Release No. 640 (Oct. 5, 1978); *Applicability of the Investment Advisers Act to Financial Planners, Pension Consultants, and Other Persons Who Provide Investment Advisory Services as a Component of Other Financial Services*, Investment Advisers Act Release No. 1092 (Oct. 8, 1987).

35 2005 Adopting Release, *supra* footnote 17; 2005 Proposing Release, *supra* footnote 18.

36 *See* Advisers Act Release No. 2, *supra* footnote 2; *see also* 2005 Adopting Release, *supra* footnote 17.

the broker-dealer exclusion, noting that the advice broker-dealers gave as part of their brokerage services in 1940 was often substantial and important to customers.[37]

On March 30, 2007, the Court of Appeals for the District of Columbia Circuit in *Financial Planning Association v. SEC* vacated the rule regarding fee-based brokerage accounts, but not on grounds that addressed our interpretive positions relating to the solely incidental prong.[38] In September 2007, we proposed to reinstate these interpretive positions.[39]

Since that time, a federal appellate court has addressed the solely incidental prong. In 2011, in *Thomas v. Metropolitan Life Insurance Company*, the Court of Appeals for the Tenth Circuit addressed the scope of the broker-dealer exclusion in the context of a private suit alleging that a broker had violated the Advisers Act by failing to disclose incentives to sell proprietary products.[40] As part of its analysis of the exclusion, the court looked to the interpretation of the solely incidental prong that we advanced in 2005 and 2007. The court found these interpretations to be "persuasive" in light of its own analysis of the text of the solely incidental prong of the broker-dealer exclusion as well as the legislative history and historical background of the Advisers Act.[41] The court concluded that a broker-dealer's investment advice is solely incidental to its conduct as a broker-dealer if the advice is given "only in connection with the primary business of selling securities."[42] Thus, the court explained, "broker-dealers who give advice that is not connected to the sale of securities—or whose primary business consists of

37 *See* 2005 Adopting Release, *supra* footnote 17, at nn.139–42 and accompanying text.

38 *See* 482 F.3d 481 (D.C. Cir. 2007).

39 2007 Proposing Release, *supra* footnote 17.

40 631 F.3d 1153 (10th Cir. 2011).

41 *Id.* at 1163–64.

42 *Id.* at 1164.

giving advice—do not meet the [solely incidental] prong" of the broker-dealer exclusion.[43] The court also agreed with the Commission's interpretations that the solely incidental prong does not hinge upon "the quantum or importance" of a broker-dealer's advice but on its relationship to the broker-dealer's primary business.[44] In the court's view, "[t]he quantum or importance of the broker-dealer's advice is relevant only insofar as the advice cannot supersede the sale of the product as the 'primary' goal of the transaction or the 'primary' business of the broker-dealer."[45]

Based on the text and history of the solely incidental prong, our previous interpretations of the prong, the *Thomas* decision, and the comments we have received, we are providing the following interpretation.[46] We interpret the statutory language to mean that a broker-dealer's provision of advice as to the value and characteristics of securities or as to the advisability of transacting in securities[47] is consistent with the solely incidental prong if the advice is provided in connection with and is reasonably related to the broker-dealer's primary business of effecting securities transactions.[48] If a broker-dealer's primary business is giving advice as to the value

43 *Id.*

44 *Id.* at 1163.

45 *Id.* at 1166. In *Thomas*, the brokerage firm's representative had conducted an analysis of the plaintiffs' financial situation and advised them to purchase a particular financial product based in part on that analysis. The plaintiffs alleged that the firm's policy "required [representatives] to provide investment advice to potential customers as a means to sell more proprietary products" and that this policy was "so pervasive that [representatives] allegedly gave financial advice to every customer to whom they sold a product." *Id.* at 1157. The Court rejected the plaintiffs' contention that these facts rendered the advice so central to the transaction that it could not be considered "solely incidental" to it. Because the representative's advice "was closely related to the sale of the [product] and selling the [product] was the primary object of the transaction," the Court concluded, the advice was "solely incidental" to the representative's conduct as a broker. *Id.* at 1167.

46 To the extent that this interpretation is inconsistent with the Commission's prior interpretations with respect to the solely incidental prong, this interpretation supersedes those interpretations.

47 *See* Advisers Act section 202(a)(11) (definition of "investment adviser").

48 *Cf.* 2005 Adopting Release, *supra* footnote 17 ("In general, investment advice is 'solely incidental to' the conduct of a broker-dealer's business within the meaning of section 202(a)(11)(C) and to 'brokerage services' provided to accounts… when the advisory services rendered are in connection with and reasonably related to the brokerage services provided."). We have modified the wording of our

and characteristics of securities or the advisability of transacting in securities, or if the advisory services are not offered in connection with or are not reasonably related to the broker-dealer's business of effecting securities transactions, the broker-dealer's advisory services are not solely incidental to its business as a broker-dealer.[49] Whether advisory services provided by a broker-dealer satisfy the solely incidental prong is assessed based on the facts and circumstances surrounding the broker-dealer's business, the specific services offered, and the relationship between the broker-dealer and the customer.

The quantum or importance of investment advice that a broker-dealer provides to a client is not determinative as to whether or not the provision of advice is consistent with the solely incidental prong. Advice need not be trivial, inconsequential, or infrequent to be consistent with the solely incidental prong. Indeed, our simultaneous adoption of (i) Regulation Best Interest, which raises the standard of conduct that applies to broker-dealer recommendations, and (ii) the relationship summary, which provides information about broker-dealer recommendation services to customers, underscores that broker-dealer investment advice can be consequential even when it is offered in connection with and reasonably related to the primary business of effecting securities transactions.

interpretation to make clear that the broker-dealer's primary business must also be effecting securities transactions.

49 Nothing in this interpretation alters the Commission's 2006 interpretation of section 28(e) of the Exchange Act, which, in the context of a client commission arrangement that otherwise satisfies section 28(e), permits a broker-dealer to be paid out of a pool of commissions for its research even if that broker-dealer did not effect a securities transaction. *See* Commission Guidance Regarding Client Commission Practices Under Section 28(e) of the Securities Exchange Act of 1934, Securities Exchange Act Release No. 54165 (July 18, 2006), 71 FR 41978 (July 24, 2006).

To illustrate the application of this interpretation in practice, we provide the following guidance on the application of the interpretation to (i) exercising investment discretion over customer accounts and (ii) account monitoring.

C. Guidance on Applying the Interpretation of the Solely Incidental Prong

1. Investment Discretion

The Commission has for many years considered issues related to a broker-dealer's exercise of investment discretion over customer accounts and the extent to which such practices could be considered solely incidental to the business of a broker-dealer.[50] The Commission has stated that discretionary brokerage relationships "have many of the characteristics of the relationships to which the protections of the Advisers Act are important."[51] In particular, the Commission has explained that when a broker-dealer exercises investment discretion, it is not providing *advice* to customers that is in connection with and reasonably related to effecting securities transactions; rather, the broker-dealer is making investment *decisions* relating to the purchase or sale of securities on behalf of customers on an ongoing basis.[52] At the same time, the Commission has taken the position that some limited exercise of discretionary authority by broker-dealers could be considered solely incidental to their business.[53]

We requested comment in the Reg. BI Proposal on a broker-dealer's exercise of investment discretion over customer accounts and the extent to which the exercise of investment

50 *See* Reg. BI Proposal, *supra* footnote 3, at nn.343–62 and accompanying text.

51 *Final Extension of Temporary Exemption from the Investment Advisers Act for Certain Brokers and Dealers*, Investment Advisers Act Release No. 626 (Apr. 27, 1978) ("Advisers Act Release No. 626").

52 *See* 2005 Proposing Release, *supra* footnote 18.

53 *See* Reg. BI Proposal, *supra* footnote 3, at nn.355–62 and accompanying text. *Cf.* NASD rule 2510 (allowing discretion only if a customer "has given prior written authorization to a stated individual or individuals… in accordance with [FINRA] rule 3010").

discretion should be considered solely incidental to the business of a broker-dealer.[54] Commenters agreed that the exercise of unlimited discretion should not be considered "solely incidental" investment advice.[55] Commenters expressed varying views, however, on the extent to which the exercise of temporary or limited discretion could be considered solely incidental to the business of a broker-dealer. Several commenters suggested that the exercise of any investment discretion should be governed by the Advisers Act.[56] One commenter suggested that the Commission should interpret the solely incidental prong through the lens of the definition of "investment discretion" in section 3(a)(35) of the Securities Exchange Act of 1934 (the "Exchange Act"),[57] noting that section 3(a)(35) focuses on "the level of authority, decision-making ability, influence – and ultimately, control – an intermediary has over another's money" and arguing that those with section 3(a)(35) investment discretion have a heightened likelihood of mismanagement and abuse of another's money.[58] Another commenter suggested that, while

54 *See* Relationship Summary Proposal, *supra* footnote 6, at nn.363–67 and accompanying text; *see also id.* at nn.343–62 and accompanying text for a description of the Commission's historical approaches.

55 *See, e.g.*, Comment Letter of Financial Planning Coalition (Aug. 7, 2018) ("FPC Letter") ("[A] broker-dealer's provision of unfettered discretionary investment advice should never be considered 'solely incidental' to its business as a broker-dealer." (emphasis removed)); CFA Letter; IFS Letter.

56 *See, e.g.*, Comment Letter of Invesco Advisers, Inc. (Aug. 7, 2018) ("Discretionary management over an account, whether or not temporary, is not within the scope of the 'solely incidental' exclusion."); IAA Letter; CFA Institute Letter.

57 Under Exchange Act section 3(a)(35), a person exercises "investment discretion" with respect to an account if, directly or indirectly, such person (A) is authorized to determine what securities or other property shall be purchased or sold by or for the account, (B) makes decisions as to what securities or other property shall be purchased or sold by or for the account even though some other person may have responsibility for such investment decisions, or (C) otherwise exercises such influence with respect to the purchase and sale of securities or other property by or for the account as the Commission, by rule, determines, in the public interest or for the protection of investors, should be subject to the operation of the provisions of this title and the rules and regulations thereunder. 15 U.S.C. 78c(a)(35).

58 *See* FPC Letter (noting also that several federal and state courts have used factors similar to those in section 3(a)(35) to impose a fiduciary standard). Another commenter also suggested using Exchange Act section 3(a)(35) "investment discretion" as a basis for establishing whether discretion is not solely incidental for purposes of the broker-dealer exclusion, with an exception for investment discretion "that a customer grants on a temporary or limited basis." *See* Comment Letter of Pickard Djinis and Pisarri (Aug. 14, 2018) ("Pickard Letter").

discretion generally should subject a broker-dealer to the Advisers Act, there are certain cases where temporary or limited discretion does not have the supervisory or managerial character of the investment discretion warranting the protections of the Advisers Act.[59]

Applying our interpretation of the solely incidental prong, a broker-dealer's exercise of unlimited discretion[60] would not be solely incidental to the business of a broker-dealer consistent with the meaning of section 202(a)(11)(C).[61] It would be inconsistent with the solely incidental prong for broker-dealers to exercise "investment discretion" as that term is defined in section 3(a)(35) of the Exchange Act with respect to any of its accounts, except for certain instances of investment discretion granted by a customer on a temporary or limited basis, as discussed below. A broker-dealer with unlimited discretion to effect securities transactions possesses ongoing authority over the customer's account indicating a relationship that is primarily advisory in nature; such a level of discretion by a broker-dealer is so comprehensive and continuous that the provision of advice in such context is not incidental to effecting securities transactions.

We recognize, however, that there are situations where a broker-dealer may exercise temporary or limited discretion in a way that is not indicative of a relationship that is primarily advisory in nature. Generally, these are situations where the discretion is limited in time, scope, or other manner and lacks the comprehensive and continuous character of investment discretion

59 *See* Comment Letter of the Securities Industry and Financial Markets Association (Aug. 7, 2018) ("SIFMA Letter").

60 We view unlimited investment discretion as a person having the ability or authority to buy and sell securities on behalf of a customer without consulting the customer—*i.e.*, having responsibility for a customer's trading decisions.

61 The Commission has in the past stated that the quintessentially supervisory or managerial character of investment discretion warrants the protection of the Advisers Act. *See Amendment and Extension of Temporary Exemption from the Investment Advisers Act for Certain Brokers and Dealers*, Investment Advisers Act Release No. 471 (Aug. 20, 1975); *see also* 2005 Proposing Release, *supra* footnote 18; 2005 Adopting Release, *supra* footnote 17.

that would suggest that the relationship is primarily advisory. The totality of the facts and circumstances would be relevant to determining whether temporary or limited discretion is consistent with the solely incidental prong. Taking into consideration specific examples that commenters have suggested in the past, instances of temporary or limited investment discretion that, standing alone, would not support the conclusion that a relationship is primarily advisory—and therefore outside the scope of the solely incidental prong—include discretion: (i) as to the price at which or the time to execute an order given by a customer for the purchase or sale of a definite amount or quantity of a specified security; (ii) on an isolated or infrequent basis, to purchase or sell a security or type of security when a customer is unavailable for a limited period of time; (iii) as to cash management, such as to exchange a position in a money market fund for another money market fund or cash equivalent;[62] (iv) to purchase or sell securities to satisfy margin requirements, or other customer obligations that the customer has specified; (v) to sell specific bonds or other securities and purchase similar bonds or other securities in order to permit a customer to realize a tax loss on the original position; (vi) to purchase a bond with a specified credit rating and maturity; and (vii) to purchase or sell a security or type of security limited by specific parameters established by the customer. We view these examples of temporary or limited discretion as typically consistent with the broker-dealer exclusion because

[62] Certain changes to money market fund regulation and operations have been implemented since our prior interpretations. *See Money Market Fund Reform; Amendments to Form PF*, Investment Company Act Release No. 31166 (Jul. 23, 2014) (removing an exemption that permitted institutional non-government money market funds to maintain a stable net asset value, while maintaining such exemption for certain other money market funds, and applying certain fees and gates reforms to institutional non-government money market funds and retail money market funds but not to government money market funds, among other changes). In light of these changes, differently categorized money market funds may have different investment characteristics. Accordingly, we anticipate that FINRA will be reviewing the application of the rules that apply to the exercise of broker-dealer discretion in this context. The Commission staff also will evaluate broker-dealer exercise of discretionary cash management to consider whether additional measures may be necessary.

they are in connection with and reasonably related to a broker-dealer's business of effecting securities transactions and do not suggest that the broker-dealer's primary business is providing investment advice.

We have previously described a similar list of situations that we would consider temporary or limited discretion that may be consistent with the solely incidental prong.[63] We make three refinements.

First, we are not including authority for a period "not to exceed a few months" relating to the time a broker-dealer may purchase or sell a security or type of security when a customer is unavailable for a limited period of time. Depending on the facts and circumstances, a period of discretion lasting a few months may be indicative of a business or customer relationship that is primarily advisory in nature.

Second, we would view it as consistent with our interpretation of the solely incidental prong for broker-dealers to purchase or sell securities to satisfy margin requirements, *or other customer obligations that the customer has specified* (new wording italicized). In our view, there may be similar obligations to a broker-dealer or a third party whereby a broker-dealer may be authorized to make a purchase or sale, such as a sale to satisfy a collateral call.

Third, we would view it as consistent with our interpretation of the solely incidental prong for broker-dealers to sell specific bonds *or other securities* in order to permit a customer to realize a tax loss on the original position (new wording italicized). We see no distinction between bonds or other securities in this particular context.

2. Account Monitoring

[63] *See* 2005 Adopting Release, *supra* footnote 17, at nn.178–81 and accompanying text; 2007 Proposing Release, *supra* footnote 17, at n.13 and accompanying text.

We received several comments regarding the extent to which a broker-dealer may monitor the status and performance of a customer's account while relying on the broker-dealer exclusion. Some commenters suggested that a broker-dealer's agreement to provide ongoing monitoring for the purpose of recommending changes to a customer's investments is not an advisory service that is solely incidental to the primary securities transaction business of a broker-dealer and thus the broker-dealer exclusion should not be available to broker-dealers who provide such services.[64] Another commenter suggested that broker-dealers providing personalized investment advice about securities on an ongoing basis should not be able to rely on the broker-dealer exclusion.[65] Commenters also suggested that providing services that cause overseen assets to meet the definition of "regulatory assets under management" under Form ADV (*i.e.*, securities portfolios for which the broker-dealer provides "continuous and regular supervisory or management services") should subject a broker-dealer to the Advisers Act.[66]

We disagree with commenters who suggested that *any* monitoring of customer accounts would not be consistent with the solely incidental prong. A broker-dealer that agrees to

64 *See* FPC Letter ("[B]roker-dealers that enter into agreements with retail customers to provide ongoing monitoring for purposes of recommending changes in investments should be considered investment advisers and subject to fiduciary obligations under the Advisers Act. Entering into an agreement to provide ongoing monitoring… goes beyond advice that is solely incidental to the conduct of business as a broker-dealer…."); IAA Letter (same quotation as the FPC Letter); IAA Letter ("[A] broker-dealer that agrees to provide a retail customer ongoing monitoring for purposes of recommending changes in investments would not be providing services that are solely incidental to its business as a broker-dealer under the 2007 interpretation."); Fisher Letter ("Brokers can give ongoing investment advice… yet still not be required to register as an investment adviser…. [T]he boundaries [between brokers and investment advisers] have practically been erased.").

65 *See* Mutual Fund Investors Letter ("[The SEC] should… subject broker-dealers to the Advisers Act when they are providing personalized investment advice about securities on an ongoing basis… The term 'solely incidental' should be interpreted narrowly and only include personalized investment advice that is one-time, temporary, or limited in scope.").

66 *See* IAA Letter; Pickard Letter.

monitor[67] a retail customer's account on a periodic basis for purposes of providing buy, sell, or hold recommendations may still be considered to provide advice in connection with and reasonably related to effecting securities transactions.[68] In contrast, when a broker-dealer, voluntarily and without any agreement with the customer, reviews the holdings in a retail customer's account for the purposes of determining whether to provide a recommendation to the customer—and, if applicable, contacts that customer to provide a recommendation based on that voluntary review—the broker-dealer's actions are in connection with and reasonably related to the broker-dealer's primary business of effecting securities transactions. Absent an agreement with the customer (which would be required to be disclosed pursuant to Regulation Best Interest), we do not consider this voluntary review to be "account monitoring."[69]

We decline to delineate every circumstance where agreed-upon monitoring is and is not solely incidental to a broker-dealer's brokerage business. Broker-dealers may consider adopting policies and procedures that, if followed, would help demonstrate that any agreed-upon monitoring is in connection with and reasonably related to the broker-dealer's primary business

67 The guidance in this section applies when a broker-dealer agrees to monitor a customer's account. *See* Reg. BI Adoption, *supra* footnote 6, at section II.B.2 for a discussion of what constitutes such an agreement.

68 *See id.* Monitoring agreed to by the broker-dealer would result in a recommendation to purchase, sell, or hold a security each time the agreed-to monitoring occurs and would be covered by Regulation Best Interest. *See id.* ("For example, if a broker-dealer agrees to monitor the retail customer's account on a quarterly basis, the quarterly review and each resulting recommendation to purchase, sell, or hold, will be a recommendation subject to Regulation Best Interest.").

In agreeing to provide any monitoring services, broker-dealers should also consider that a broker-dealer that separately contracts or charges a separate fee for advisory services is providing investment advice that is inconsistent with the broker-dealer exclusion. *See, e.g.*, 2005 Adopting Release, *supra* footnote 17. Broker-dealers should also consider that, even where such monitoring is consistent with the solely incidental prong, the broker-dealer must also receive no special compensation for the activity to be eligible for the broker-dealer exclusion. Broker-dealers receive special compensation where there is a clearly definable charge for investment advice. *See* Advisers Act Release No. 626, *supra* footnote 51; *see also* Advisers Act Release No. 2, *supra* footnote 2; 2007 Proposing Release, *supra* footnote 17 (describing this interpretation as the Commission's "longstanding view").

69 *See* Reg. BI Adoption, *supra* footnote 6, at section II.B.2.b. Any recommendation made to the retail customer as a result of such voluntary review would be subject to Regulation Best Interest. *See id.*

of effecting securities transactions. For example, broker-dealers may include in their policies and procedures that a registered representative may agree to monitor a customer's account at specific time frames (*e.g.*, quarterly) for the purpose of determining whether to provide a buy, sell, or hold recommendation to the customer.[70] However, such policies and procedures should not permit a broker-dealer to agree to monitor a customer account in a manner that in effect results in the provision of advisory services that are not in connection with or reasonably related to the broker-dealer's primary business of effecting securities transactions, such as providing continuous monitoring.[71] Additionally, dually registered firms may similarly consider adopting policies and procedures that distinguish the level and type of monitoring in advisory and brokerage accounts.[72]

The Commission will consider further comment on its interpretation of the solely incidental prong of the broker-dealer exclusion and its application to certain brokerage activities

70 As noted in the Reg. BI Adoption, and consistent with the relationship summary adopted in the Relationship Summary Adoption, the scope and frequency of a broker-dealer's monitoring is a material fact relating to the type and scope of services provided to a retail customer and thus is required to be disclosed under Regulation Best Interest. *See id.* at section II.B.2; *cf.* Relationship Summary Adoption, *supra* footnote 6. A broker-dealer disclosing to a customer that the broker-dealer will provide monitoring constitutes an agreement to monitor. *See supra* footnote 67.

71 The two examples of advisory services we discuss in this Release—investment discretion and monitoring—cannot be viewed and interpreted in isolation. For example, it would not be consistent with the solely incidental prong for a broker-dealer to exercise unlimited investment discretion over a customer account even if its monitoring activities do comport with the solely incidental prong. Thus, any policies and procedures that a broker-dealer adopts to ensure that the broker-dealer's activities are in connection with and reasonably related to the broker-dealer's primary business of effecting securities transactions similarly should not grant the broker-dealer the ability or authority to buy and sell securities on behalf of a customer as part of periodic account monitoring, except in circumstances of temporary or limited discretion that would be consistent with the solely incidental prong, as discussed above.

72 In the Final Fiduciary Interpretation, we note that investment advisers may consider whether written policies and procedures relating to monitoring would be appropriate under Advisers Act rule 206(4)-7. *See* Final Fiduciary Interpretation, *supra* footnote 6, at section II.B.3.

Additionally, the Reg. BI Adoption confirms that a dual registrant is an investment adviser solely with respect to those accounts for which a dual registrant provides investment advice or receives compensation that subjects it to the Advisers Act. *See* Reg. BI Adoption, *supra* footnote 6, at section II.B.3.d. Determining the capacity in which a dual registrant is making a recommendation is a facts and circumstances test. *See id.*

to evaluate whether additional guidance might be appropriate in the future. Based on any comments received, the Commission may, but need not, supplement this interpretation.

III. Economic Considerations

The Commission's interpretation above is intended to advise the public of its understanding of the solely incidental prong of the broker-dealer exclusion. The interpretation does not itself create any new legal obligations for broker-dealers. Nonetheless, the Commission recognizes that to the extent a broker-dealer's practices are not consistent with this interpretation of the solely incidental prong, the interpretation could have potential economic effects. We discuss these effects below.

A. Background

The Commission's interpretation regarding the solely incidental prong of the broker-dealer exclusion would affect broker-dealers and their associated persons as well as the customers of those broker-dealers, and the market for financial advice more broadly.[73] As of December 2018, there were approximately 3,764 registered broker-dealers with over 140 million customer accounts. In total, these broker-dealers have over $4.3 trillion in total assets, which are total broker-dealer assets as reported on Form X-17a-5.[74] Of the broker-dealers registered with the Commission as of December 2018, 363 broker-dealers were dually registered with the Commission as investment advisers.[75] Dual registrant firms hold over 90 million (63%) of the

73 *See* Relationship Summary Adoption, *supra* footnote 6, at section IV.B (discussing the market for financial advice generally).

74 Assets are estimated by Total Assets (allowable and non-allowable) from Part II of the FOCUS filings (Form X-17A-5 Part II, *available at* https://www.sec.gov/files/formx-17a-5_2.pdf) and correspond to balance sheet total assets for the broker-dealer. The Commission does not have an estimate of the total amount of customer assets for broker-dealers. We estimate broker-dealer size from the total balance sheet assets as described above.

75 For purposes of this analysis, a dual registrant is any firm that is dually registered with the Commission as an investment adviser and a broker-dealer. Because this number does not include the number of broker-

overall 140 million customer accounts held by broker dealers.[76] As part of the Reg. BI Proposal, we requested data and other information related to the nature and magnitude of discretionary services offered by broker-dealers,[77] but did not receive any data or information to inform our analysis of potential economic effects stemming from this interpretation.

B. Potential Economic Effects

Broker-dealers currently incur ongoing costs related to compliance with their legal and regulatory obligations, including costs related to understanding their practices and structuring their practices to be consistent with the solely incidental prong of the broker-dealer exclusion. This interpretation generally confirms the scope of the solely incidental prong of the broker-dealer exclusion.

Generally, we believe that few, if any, broker-dealers take the view that they act consistently with the solely incidental prong with respect to any accounts over which the broker-dealer exercises more than temporary or limited investment discretion.[78] As with other circumstances in which the Commission speaks to the legal obligations of regulated entities, we

dealers who are also registered as state investment advisers, the number undercounts the full number of broker-dealers that operate in both capacities.

76 Some broker-dealers may be affiliated with investment advisers without being dually registered. From Question 10 on Form BD, 2,098 broker-dealers report that directly or indirectly, they either control, are controlled by, or under common control with an entity that is engaged in the securities or investment advisory business. Comparatively, 2,691 (19.57%) SEC-registered investment advisers report an affiliate that is a broker-dealer in Section 7A of Schedule D of Form ADV, including 1,916 SEC-registered investment advisers that report an affiliate that is a registered broker-dealer. Approximately 74% of total assets under management of investment advisers are managed by these 2,691 investment advisers.

77 *See* Reg. BI Proposal, *supra* footnote 3.

78 *See* Comment Letter of UBS (noting that broker-dealers have existing arrangements where they exercise temporary or limited discretion, such as discretion as to time and price, and that those types of discretion "do not present the sort of risks about which the SEC is concerned with respect to the exercise of *unfettered discretion*") (emphasis added); SIFMA Letter (noting that there are instances in which temporary or limited discretion, such as discretion as to prices at which securities can be purchased, does not have the supervisory or managerial character of the investment discretion warranting the protections of the Advisers Act).

acknowledge that affected firms, including those whose practices are consistent with the Commission's interpretation, incur costs to evaluate the Commission's interpretation and assess its applicability to them. Further, to the extent certain broker-dealers currently understand the scope of permissible monitoring or other permissible advisory activities under the solely incidental prong to be different from what is set forth in this interpretation, there could be some economic effects.[79]

This interpretation may produce economic effects to the extent that it causes any broker-dealers to recognize that their practices are inconsistent with the solely incidental prong and to adjust their practices to make them consistent. In particular, broker-dealers that have interpreted the solely incidental prong to conduct more advisory activities than this interpretation permits may choose to no longer provide such services to customers. This could result in a loss of certain customers, a reduction in certain business activities, and could preclude those broker-dealers from further developing certain services for their customers, except to the extent those broker-dealers are dually registered firms and their customers are also advisory clients. This may, in turn, result in decreased competition in the market for certain services, increased fees for those services, or a diminished number of broker-dealers offering commission-based services to investors.[80]

79 The above application of our interpretation of the solely incidental prong to the exercise of investment discretion is generally consistent with the position taken in the 2005 Adopting Release and preliminarily taken in the 2007 Proposing Release. We believe that many broker-dealers changed their practices with respect to investment discretion in light of those releases, and thus those practices likely are consistent with our interpretation of the solely incidental prong.

80 For example, to the extent that broker-dealers respond to the interpretation by limiting the levels of discretion that they provide for their customers, execution quality (including the execution price) may be affected due to the delays encountered when the broker-dealer must contact a customer to proceed with a transaction.

To the extent any broker-dealers have been providing advisory services beyond the scope of this interpretation, their customers may receive fewer advisory services if these broker-dealers choose not to register as investment advisers and adjust their business practices in light of this interpretation. To the extent that this interpretation would lead to a decline in the supply of certain services offered by broker-dealers (or a decline in broker-dealers offering services to particular customers), it could reduce the efficiency of portfolio construction for those investors who might otherwise benefit from broker-dealers providing investment advice with respect to their account and would find similar advice from investment advisers to be too costly or unattainable (*e.g.*, due to account minimum requirements). For example, certain broker-dealers may incur costs to adopt or revise policies and procedures to ensure that the account monitoring that they may agree to provide their customers is consistent with this interpretation and may choose instead to stop offering such monitoring services. Further, to the extent that any broker-dealers determine that their services are not consistent with this interpretation, they may choose to register as investment advisers with the Commission, or one or more states, as applicable. Such broker-dealers would bear costs in choosing to register as investment advisers to continue providing those services, and their clients may face higher fees as a result. Alternatively, broker-dealers that have investment adviser affiliates may seek to place existing customers in advisory accounts instead of brokerage accounts.

Broker-dealers that determine they must change business practices as a result of this interpretation will choose their responses based on their circumstances. For example, if broker-dealers with affiliated advisers are able to utilize their existing regulatory infrastructure and compliance policies and procedures to account for activities that are inconsistent with the solely incidental exclusion they may face lower costs associated with migration of brokerage accounts

and activities to investment advisory accounts. By contrast, we expect the costs of regulatory registration and compliance to be greater for any standalone broker-dealers that choose to become registered investment advisers, as they are more likely to need to undertake new systems, procedures, and policies.

To the extent that broker-dealers choose to discontinue providing certain services, register as investment advisers, or encourage migration of customer's brokerage accounts to advisory accounts of affiliates, this interpretation could result in a shift in the demand for the services of different types of financial service providers, decreasing the demand for services of broker-dealers and increasing the demand for the services of investment advisers.[81]

This interpretation may also produce some overall economic effects to the extent that it causes any broker-dealers that to date have avoided performing limited discretion and other activities to recognize that they may perform such activities consistent with the solely incidental prong of the broker-dealer exclusion. Such broker-dealers may respond to this interpretation by increasing the amount of limited discretionary services or monitoring services that they agree to provide to their customers. Investors that have established relationships with such broker-dealers may benefit from more efficient access to these services and may demand these services from broker-dealers rather than becoming clients of investment advisers. While additional provision of these services by broker-dealers also raises the risk of regulatory arbitrage because similar activities would be regulated under different regimes, we believe this risk will be mitigated by

81 To the extent this interpretation results in altered compliance costs for standalone broker-dealers, non-affected standalone broker-dealers (*i.e.*, those standalone broker-dealers that already are in compliance with the solely incidental prong as we have interpreted it), dual registrants, investment advisers, and other financial intermediaries that are not required to register as investment advisers (such as banks, trust companies, insurance companies, commodity trading advisers, and municipal advisors) may to a varying degree gain business at these affected broker-dealers' expense.

the adoption of rules that enhance the standard of conduct that applies to broker-dealer recommendations.

List of Subjects in 17 CFR Part 276

Securities.

Amendments to the Code of Federal Regulations

For the reasons set out above, the Commission is amending title 17, chapter II of the Code of Federal Regulations as set forth below:

PART 276–INTERPRETATIVE RELEASES RELATING TO THE INVESTMENT ADVISERS ACT OF 1940 AND GENERAL RULES AND REGULATIONS THEREUNDER

1. Part 276 is amended by adding Release No. IA–5249 and the release date of June 5, 2019, to the end of the list of interpretive releases to read as follows:

Subject	Release No.	Date	Fed. Reg. Vol. and Page
* *	*	* *	* *
Commission Interpretation Regarding the Solely Incidental Prong of the Broker-Dealer Exclusion from the Definition of Investment Adviser	IA-5249	June 5, 2019	[Insert FR Volume Number] FR [Insert FR Page Number]

By the Commission.

Dated: June 5, 2019

Vanessa A. Countryman,

Acting Secretary.

資料3

Conformed to Federal Register version

SECURITIES AND EXCHANGE COMMISSION

17 CFR Part 276

[Release No. IA-5248; File No. S7-07-18]

RIN: 3235-AM36

Commission Interpretation Regarding Standard of Conduct for Investment Advisers

AGENCY: Securities and Exchange Commission.

ACTION: Interpretation.

SUMMARY: The Securities and Exchange Commission (the "SEC" or the "Commission") is publishing an interpretation of the standard of conduct for investment advisers under the Investment Advisers Act of 1940 (the "Advisers Act" or the "Act").

DATES: Effective July 12, 2019.

FOR FURTHER INFORMATION CONTACT: Olawalé Oriola, Senior Counsel; Matthew Cook, Senior Counsel; or Jennifer Songer, Branch Chief, at (202) 551-6787 or *IArules@sec.gov*, Investment Adviser Regulation Office, Division of Investment Management, Securities and Exchange Commission, 100 F Street NE, Washington, DC 20549-8549.

SUPPLEMENTARY INFORMATION: The Commission is publishing an interpretation of the standard of conduct for investment advisers under the Advisers Act [15 U.S.C. 80b].[1]

[1] 15 U.S.C. 80b. Unless otherwise noted, when we refer to the Advisers Act, or any paragraph of the Advisers Act, we are referring to 15 U.S.C. 80b of the United States Code, at which the Advisers Act is codified, and when we refer to rules under the Advisers Act, or any paragraph of these rules, we are referring to title 17, part 275 of the Code of Federal Regulations [17 CFR 275], in which these rules are published.

TABLE OF CONTENTS

I. INTRODUCTION

Under federal law, an investment adviser is a fiduciary.[2] The fiduciary duty an investment adviser owes to its client under the Advisers Act, which comprises a duty of care and a duty of loyalty, is important to the Commission's investor protection efforts. Also important to the Commission's investor protection efforts is the standard of conduct that a broker-dealer owes to a retail customer when it makes a recommendation of any securities transaction or investment strategy involving securities.[3] Both investment advisers and broker-dealers play an important

[2] *SEC v. Capital Gains Research Bureau, Inc.*, 375 U.S. 180, 194 (1963) ("SEC v. Capital Gains"); *see also infra* footnotes 34–44 and accompanying text; Investment Adviser Codes of Ethics, Investment Advisers Act Release No. 2256 (July 2, 2004); Compliance Programs of Investment Companies and Investment Advisers, Investment Advisers Act Release No. 2204 (Dec. 17, 2003); Electronic Filing by Investment Advisers; Proposed Amendments to Form ADV, Investment Advisers Act Release No. 1862 (Apr. 5, 2000). Investment advisers also have antifraud liability with respect to prospective clients under section 206 of the Advisers Act.

[3] *See* Regulation Best Interest, Exchange Act Release No. 34-86031 (June 5, 2019) ("Reg. BI Adoption"). This final interpretation regarding the standard of conduct for investment advisers under the Advisers Act ("Final Interpretation") interprets section 206 of the Advisers Act, which is applicable to both SEC- and

role in our capital markets and our economy more broadly. Investment advisers and broker-dealers have different types of relationships with investors, offer different services, and have different compensation models. This variety is important because it presents investors with choices regarding the types of relationships they can have, the services they can receive, and how they can pay for those services.

On April 18, 2018, the Commission proposed rules and forms intended to enhance the required standard of conduct for broker-dealers[4] and provide retail investors with clear and succinct information regarding the key aspects of their brokerage and advisory relationships.[5] In connection with the publication of these proposals, the Commission published for comment a separate proposed interpretation regarding the standard of conduct for investment advisers under the Advisers Act ("Proposed Interpretation").[6] We stated in the Proposed Interpretation, and we continue to believe, that it is appropriate and beneficial to address in one release and reaffirm—and in some cases clarify—certain aspects of the fiduciary duty that an investment adviser owes

state-registered investment advisers, as well as other investment advisers that are exempt from registration or subject to a prohibition on registration under the Advisers Act. This Final Interpretation is intended to highlight the principles relevant to an adviser's fiduciary duty. It is not, however, intended to be the exclusive resource for understanding these principles. Separately, in various circumstances, case law, statutes (such as the Employee Retirement Income Security Act of 1974 ("ERISA")), and state law impose obligations on investment advisers. In some cases, these standards may differ from the standard enforced by the Commission.

4 Regulation Best Interest, Exchange Act Release No. 83062 (Apr. 18, 2018) ("Reg. BI Proposal").

5 Form CRS Relationship Summary; Amendments to Form ADV; Required Disclosures in Retail Communications and Restrictions on the use of Certain Names or Titles, Investment Advisers Act Release No. 4888 (Apr. 18, 2018) ("Relationship Summary Proposal").

6 Proposed Commission Interpretation Regarding Standard of Conduct for Investment Advisers; Request for Comment on Enhancing Investment Adviser Regulation, Investment Advisers Act Release No. 4889 (Apr. 18, 2018).

to its clients under section 206 of the Advisers Act.[7] After considering the comments received, we are publishing this Final Interpretation with some clarifications to address comments.[8]

A. Overview of Comments

We received over 150 comment letters on our Proposed Interpretation from individuals, investment advisers, trade or professional organizations, law firms, consumer advocacy groups, and bar associations.[9] Although many commenters generally agreed that the Proposed Interpretation was useful,[10] some noted the challenges inherent in a Commission interpretation covering the broad scope of the fiduciary duty that an investment adviser owes to its clients under the Advisers Act.[11] Some of these commenters suggested modifications to or withdrawal

7 Further, the Commission recognizes that many advisers provide impersonal investment advice. *See, e.g.*, Advisers Act rule 203A-3 (defining "impersonal investment advice" in the context of defining "investment adviser representative" as "investment advisory services provided by means of written material or oral statements that do not purport to meet the objectives or needs of specific individuals or accounts"). This Final Interpretation does not address the extent to which the Advisers Act applies to different types of impersonal investment advice.

8 In the Proposed Interpretation, the Commission also requested comment on: licensing and continuing education requirements for personnel of SEC-registered investment advisers; delivery of account statements to clients with investment advisory accounts; and financial responsibility requirements for SEC-registered investment advisers, including fidelity bonds. We are continuing to evaluate the comments received in response.

9 Comment letters submitted in File No. S7-09-18 are available on the Commission's website at https://www.sec.gov/comments/s7-09-18/s70918.htm. We also considered those comments submitted in File No. S7-08-18 (Comments on Relationship Summary Proposal) and File No. S7-07-18 (Comments on Reg. BI Proposal). Those comments are available on the Commission's website at https://www.sec.gov/comments/s7-08-18/s70818.htm and https://www.sec.gov/comments/s7-07-18/s70718.htm.

10 *See, e.g.*, Comment Letter of North American Securities Administrators Association (Aug. 23, 2018) ("NASAA Letter") (stating that the Proposed Interpretation is a "useful resource"); Comment Letter of Invesco (Aug. 7, 2018) ("Invesco Letter") (agreeing that "there are benefits to having a clear statement regarding the fiduciary duty that applies to an investment adviser").

11 *See, e.g.*, Comment Letter of Pickard Djinis and Pisarri LLP (Aug. 7, 2018) ("Pickard Letter") (noting the Commission's "efforts to synthesize case law, legislative history, academic literature, prior Commission releases and other sources to produce a comprehensive explanation of the fiduciary standard of conduct"); Comment Letter of Dechert LLP (Aug. 7, 2018) ("Dechert Letter") ("It is crucial that any universal interpretation of an adviser's fiduciary duty be based on sound and time-tested principles. Given the difficulty of defining and encompassing all of an adviser's responsibilities to its clients, while also accommodating the diversity of advisory arrangements, interpretive issues will arise in the future."); Comment Letter of the Hedge Funds Subcommittee of the Federal Regulation of Securities Committee of the Business Law Section of the American Bar Association (Aug. 24, 2018) ("ABA Letter") ("We note at

of the Proposed Interpretation.[12] Although most commenters agreed that an investment adviser's fiduciary duty comprises a duty of care and a duty of loyalty, as described in the Proposed Interpretation, they had differing views on aspects of the fiduciary duty and in some cases sought clarification on its application.[13]

Some commenters requested that we adopt rule text instead.[14] The relationship between an investment adviser and its client has long been based on fiduciary principles not generally set forth in specific statute or rule text. We believe that this principles-based approach should continue as it expresses broadly the standard to which investment advisers are held while allowing them flexibility to meet that standard in the context of their specific services. In our view, adopting rule text is not necessary to achieve our goal in this Final Interpretation of reaffirming and in some cases clarifying certain aspects of the fiduciary duty.

the outset that it is difficult to capture the nature of an investment adviser's fiduciary duty in a broad statement that has universal applicability.").

12 *See, e.g.*, Comment Letter of L.A. Schnase (Jul. 30, 2018) (urging the Commission not to issue the Proposed Interpretation in final form, or at least not without substantial rewriting or reshaping); Comment Letter of Money Management Institute (Aug. 7, 2018) ("MMI Letter") (urging the Commission to "revise the interpretation so that it reflects the common law principles in which an investment adviser's fiduciary duty is grounded"); Dechert Letter (recommending that we withdraw the Proposed Interpretation and instead rely on existing authority and sources of law, as well as existing Commission practices for providing interpretive guidance, in order to define the source and scope of an investment adviser's fiduciary duty).

13 *See, e.g.*, Comment Letter of Cambridge Investment Research Inc. (Aug. 7, 2018) ("Cambridge Letter") (stating that "greater clarity on all aspects of an investment adviser's fiduciary duty will improve the ability to craft such policies and procedures, as well as support the elimination of confusion for retail clients and investment professionals"); Comment Letter of Institutional Limited Partners Association (Aug. 6, 2018) ("ILPA Letter 1") ("Interpretation will provide more certainty regarding the fiduciary duties owed by private fund advisers to their clients."); Comment Letter of New York City Bar Association (Jun. 26, 2018) ("NY City Bar Letter") (stating that the uniform interpretation of an investment adviser's fiduciary duty is necessary).

14 Some commenters suggested that we codify the Proposed Interpretation. *See, e.g.*, Comment Letter of Roy Tanga (Apr. 25, 2018); Comment Letter of Financial Engines (Aug. 6, 2018) ("Financial Engines Letter"); ILPA Letter 1; Comment Letter of AARP (Aug. 7, 2018) ("AARP Letter"); Comment Letter of Gordon Donohue (Aug. 6, 2018); Comment Letter of Financial Planning Coalition (Aug. 7, 2018) ("FPC Letter").

II. Investment Advisers' Fiduciary Duty

The Advisers Act establishes a federal fiduciary duty for investment advisers.[15] This fiduciary duty is based on equitable common law principles and is fundamental to advisers' relationships with their clients under the Advisers Act.[16] The investment adviser's fiduciary duty is broad and applies to the entire adviser-client relationship.[17] The fiduciary duty to which advisers are subject is not specifically defined in the Advisers Act or in Commission rules, but reflects a Congressional recognition "of the delicate fiduciary nature of an investment advisory relationship" as well as a Congressional intent to "eliminate, or at least to expose, all conflicts of interest which might incline an investment adviser—consciously or unconsciously—to render advice which was not disinterested."[18] An adviser's fiduciary duty is imposed under the

15 *Transamerica Mortgage Advisors, Inc. v. Lewis*, 444 U.S. 11, 17 (1979) ("Transamerica Mortgage v. Lewis") ("§ 206 establishes federal fiduciary standards to govern the conduct of investment advisers.") (quotation marks omitted); *Santa Fe Industries, Inc. v. Green*, 430 U.S. 462, 471, n.11 (1977) (in discussing SEC v. Capital Gains, stating that the Supreme Court's reference to fraud in the "equitable" sense of the term was "premised on its recognition that Congress intended the Investment Advisers Act to establish federal fiduciary standards for investment advisers"); SEC v. Capital Gains, *supra* footnote 2; Amendments to Form ADV, Investment Advisers Act Release No. 3060 (July 28, 2010) ("Investment Advisers Act Release 3060") ("Under the Advisers Act, an adviser is a fiduciary whose duty is to serve the best interests of its clients, which includes an obligation not to subrogate clients' interests to its own," citing Proxy Voting by Investment Advisers, Investment Advisers Act Release No. 2106 (Jan. 31, 2003) ("Investment Advisers Act Release 2106")).

16 *See* SEC v. Capital Gains, *supra* footnote 2 (discussing the history of the Advisers Act, and how equitable principles influenced the common law of fraud and changed the suits brought against a fiduciary, "which Congress recognized the investment adviser to be").

17 The Commission has previously recognized the broad scope of section 206 of the Advisers Act in a variety of contexts. *See, e.g.*, Investment Advisers Act Release 2106, *supra* footnote 15; Timbervest, LLC, et al., Advisers Act Release No. 4197 (Sept. 17, 2015) (Commission Opinion) (" [O]nce an investment advisory relationship is formed, the Advisers Act does not permit an adviser to exploit that fiduciary relationship by defrauding his client in any investment transaction connected to the advisory relationship."); *see also SEC v. Lauer*, 2008 WL 4372896, at 24 (S.D. Fla. Sept. 24, 2008) ("Unlike the antifraud provisions of the Securities Act and the Exchange Act, Section 206 of the Advisers Act does not require that the activity be 'in the offer or sale of any' security or 'in connection with the purchase or sale of any security.'"); Thomas P. Lemke & Gerald T. Lins, Regulation of Investment Advisers (2013 ed.), at § 2:30 ("[T]he SEC has … applied [sections 206(1) and 206(2)] where fraud arose from an investment advisory relationship, even though the wrongdoing did not specifically involve securities.").

18 *See* SEC v. Capital Gains, *supra* footnote 2; *see also* In the Matter of Arleen W. Hughes, Exchange Act Release No. 4048 (Feb. 18, 1948) ("Arleen Hughes") (Commission Opinion) (discussing the relationship of

Advisers Act in recognition of the nature of the relationship between an investment adviser and a client and the desire "so far as is presently practicable to eliminate the abuses" that led to the enactment of the Advisers Act.[19] It is made enforceable by the antifraud provisions of the Advisers Act.[20]

An investment adviser's fiduciary duty under the Advisers Act comprises a duty of care and a duty of loyalty.[21] This fiduciary duty requires an adviser "to adopt the principal's goals,

trust and confidence between the client and a dual registrant and stating that the registrant was a fiduciary and subject to liability under the antifraud provisions of the Securities Act of 1933 and the Securities Exchange Act of 1934).

19 *See* SEC v. Capital Gains, *supra* footnote 2 (noting that the "declaration of policy" in the original bill, which became the Advisers Act, declared that "the national public interest and the interest of investors are adversely affected … when the business of investment advisers is so conducted as to defraud or mislead investors, or to enable such advisers to relieve themselves of their fiduciary obligations to their clients. It is hereby declared that the policy and purposes of this title, in accordance with which the provisions of this title shall be interpreted, *are to mitigate and, so far as is presently practicable to eliminate* the abuses enumerated in this section") (citing S. 3580, 76th Cong., 3d Sess., § 202 and Investment Trusts and Investment Companies, Report of the Securities and Exchange Commission, Pursuant to Section 30 of the Public Utility Holding Company Act of 1935, on Investment Counsel, Investment Management, Investment Supervisory, and Investment Advisory Services, H.R. Doc. No. 477, 76th Cong. 2d Sess., 1, at 28) (emphasis added).

20 *Id.*; Transamerica Mortgage v. Lewis, *supra* footnote 15 ("[T]he Act's legislative history leaves no doubt that Congress intended to impose enforceable fiduciary obligations."). Some commenters questioned the standard to which the Advisers Act holds investment advisers *See, e.g.,* Comment Letter of Stark & Stark, PC (undated) ("The duty of care at common law and under the Advisers Act only requires that advisers not be negligent in performing their duties.") (internal citation omitted); Comment Letter of Institutional Limited Partners Association (Nov. 21, 2018) ("ILPA Letter 2") ("The Advisers Act standard is a lower simple 'negligence' standard."). Claims arising under Advisers Act section 206(2) are not scienter-based and can be adequately pled with only a showing of negligence. *Robare Group, Ltd., et al. v. SEC*, 922 F.3d 468, 472(D.C. Cir. 2019) ("Robare v. SEC"); *SEC v. Steadman*, 967 F.2d 636, 643, n.5 (D.C. Cir. 1992) (citing SEC v. Capital Gains, *supra* footnote 2) ("[A] violation of § 206(2) of the Investment Advisers Act may rest on a finding of simple negligence."); *SEC v. DiBella*, 587 F.3d 553, 567 (2d Cir. 2009) ("the government need not show intent to make out a section 206(2) violation"); *SEC v. Gruss*, 859 F. Supp. 2d 653, 669 (S.D.N.Y. 2012) ("Claims arising under Section 206(2) are not scienter-based and can be adequately pled with only a showing of negligence."). However, claims arising under Advisers Act section 206(1) require scienter. *See, e.g.*, Robare v. SEC; *SEC v. Moran*, 922 F. Supp. 867, 896 (S.D.N.Y. 1996); *Carroll v. Bear, Stearns & Co.*, 416 F. Supp. 998, 1001 (S.D.N.Y. 1976).

21 *See, e.g.*, Investment Advisers Act Release 2106, *supra* footnote 15. These duties were generally recognized by commenters. *See, e.g.*, Comment Letter of Consumer Federation of America (Aug. 7, 2018) ("CFA Letter"); Comment Letter of the Investment Adviser Association (Aug. 6, 2018) ("IAA Letter"); Comment Letter of Investments & Wealth Institute (Aug. 6, 2018); Comment Letter of Raymond James (Aug. 7, 2018); FPC Comment Letter. *But see* Dechert Letter (questioning the sufficiency of support for a duty of care).

objectives, or ends."[22] This means the adviser must, at all times, serve the best interest of its client and not subordinate its client's interest to its own. In other words, the investment adviser cannot place its own interests ahead of the interests of its client. This combination of care and loyalty obligations has been characterized as requiring the investment adviser to act in the "best interest" of its client at all times.[23] In our view, an investment adviser's obligation to act in the best interest of its client is an overarching principle that encompasses both the duty of care and the duty of loyalty. As discussed in more detail below, in our view, the duty of care requires an investment adviser to provide investment advice in the best interest of its client, based on the client's objectives. Under its duty of loyalty, an investment adviser must eliminate or make full and fair disclosure of all conflicts of interest which might incline an investment adviser—consciously or unconsciously—to render advice which is not disinterested such that a client can provide informed consent to the conflict.[24] We believe this is another part of an investment adviser's obligation to act in the best interest of its client.

A. Application of Duty Determined by Scope of Relationship

An adviser's fiduciary duty is imposed under the Advisers Act in recognition of the

22 Arthur B. Laby, *The Fiduciary Obligations as the Adoption of Ends*, 56 Buffalo Law Review 99 (2008); *see also* Restatement (Third) of Agency, §2.02 Scope of Actual Authority (2006) (describing a fiduciary's authority in terms of the fiduciary's reasonable understanding of the principal's manifestations and objectives).

23 Investment Advisers Act Release 3060, *supra* footnote 15 (adopting amendments to Form ADV and stating that "under the Advisers Act, an adviser is a fiduciary whose duty is to serve the best interests of its clients, which includes an obligation not to subrogate clients' interests to its own," citing Investment Advisers Act Release 2106, *supra* footnote 15). *See SEC v. Tambone*, 550 F.3d 106, 146 (1st Cir. 2008) ("SEC v. Tambone") ("Section 206 imposes a fiduciary duty on investment advisers to act at all times in the best interest of the fund…"); *SEC v. Moran*, 944 F. Supp. 286, 297 (S.D.N.Y 1996) ("SEC v. Moran") ("Investment advisers are entrusted with the responsibility and duty to act in the best interest of their clients."). Although most commenters agreed that an adviser has an obligation to act in its client's best interest, some questioned whether the Proposed Interpretation appropriately considered the best interest obligation as part of the duty of care, or whether it instead should be considered part of the duty of loyalty. *See, e.g.*, MMI Letter; Comment Letter of Investment Company Institute (Aug. 7, 2018) ("ICI Letter").

24 *See infra* footnotes 67-70 and accompanying text for a more detailed discussion of informed consent and how it is generally considered on an objective basis and may be inferred.

nature of the relationship between an adviser and its client—a relationship of trust and confidence.[25] The adviser's fiduciary duty is principles-based and applies to the entire relationship between the adviser and its client. The fiduciary duty follows the contours of the relationship between the adviser and its client, and the adviser and its client may shape that relationship by agreement, provided that there is full and fair disclosure and informed consent.[26] With regard to the scope of the adviser-client relationship, we recognize that investment advisers provide a wide range of services, from a single financial plan for which a client may pay a one-time fee, to ongoing portfolio management for which a client may pay a periodic fee based on the value of assets in the portfolio. Investment advisers also serve a large variety of clients, from retail clients with limited assets and investment knowledge and experience to institutional clients with very large portfolios and substantial knowledge, experience, and analytical resources.[27] In our experience, the principles-based fiduciary duty imposed by the Advisers Act has provided sufficient flexibility to serve as an effective standard of conduct for investment advisers, regardless of the services they provide or the types of clients they serve.

Although all investment advisers owe each of their clients a fiduciary duty under the Advisers Act, that fiduciary duty must be viewed in the context of the agreed-upon scope of the

[25] *See, e.g.*, Hearings on S. 3580 before Subcommittee of the Senate Committee on Banking and Currency, 76th Cong., 3d Sess. (leading investment advisers emphasized their relationship of "trust and confidence" with their clients); SEC v. Capital Gains, *supra* footnote 2 (citing same).

[26] Several commenters asked that we clarify that an adviser and its client can tailor the scope of the relationship to which the fiduciary duty applies through contract. *See, e.g.*, MMI Letter; Financial Engines Letter; ABA Letter.

[27] This Final Interpretation also applies to automated advisers, which are often colloquially referred to as "robo-advisers." Automated advisers, like all SEC-registered investment advisers, are subject to all of the requirements of the Advisers Act, including the requirement that they provide advice consistent with the fiduciary duty they owe to their clients. *See* Division of Investment Management, Robo Advisers, IM Guidance Update No. 2017-02 (Feb. 2017), *available at* https://www.sec.gov/investment/im-guidance-2017-02.pdf (describing Commission staff's guidance as to three distinct areas under the Advisers Act that automated advisers should consider, due to the nature of their business model, in seeking to comply with their obligations under the Advisers Act).

relationship between the adviser and the client. In particular, the specific obligations that flow from the adviser's fiduciary duty depend upon what functions the adviser, as agent, has agreed to assume for the client, its principal. For example, the obligations of an adviser providing comprehensive, discretionary advice in an ongoing relationship with a retail client (*e.g.*, monitoring and periodically adjusting a portfolio of equity and fixed income investments with limited restrictions on allocation) will be significantly different from the obligations of an adviser to a registered investment company or private fund where the contract defines the scope of the adviser's services and limitations on its authority with substantial specificity (*e.g.*, a mandate to manage a fixed income portfolio subject to specified parameters, including concentration limits and credit quality and maturity ranges).[28]

While the application of the investment adviser's fiduciary duty will vary with the scope of the relationship, the relationship in all cases remains that of a fiduciary to the client. In other words, an adviser's federal fiduciary duty may not be waived, though it will apply in a manner that reflects the agreed-upon scope of the relationship.[29] A contract provision purporting to waive the adviser's federal fiduciary duty generally, such as (i) a statement that the adviser will not act as a fiduciary, (ii) a blanket waiver of all conflicts of interest, or (iii) a waiver of any

[28] *See, e.g., infra* text following footnote 35.

[29] Because an adviser's federal fiduciary obligations are enforceable through section 206 of the Advisers Act, we would view a waiver of enforcement of section 206 as implicating section 215(a) of the Advisers Act, which provides that "any condition, stipulation or provision binding any person to waive compliance with any provision of this title. . . shall be void." *See also* Restatement (Third) of Agency, § 8.06 Principal's Consent (2006) ("[T]he law applicable to relationships of agency as defined in § 1.01 imposes mandatory limits on the circumstances under which an agent may be empowered to take disloyal action. These limits serve protective and cautionary purposes. Thus, an agreement that contains general or broad language purporting to release an agent in advance from the agent's general fiduciary obligation to the principal is not likely to be enforceable. This is because a broadly sweeping release of an agent's fiduciary duty may not reflect an adequately informed judgment on the part of the principal; if effective, the release would expose the principal to the risk that the agent will exploit the agent's position in ways not foreseeable by the principal at the time the principal agreed to the release. In contrast, when a principal consents to specific transactions or to specified types of conduct by the agent, the principal has a focused opportunity to assess risks that are more readily identifiable.").

specific obligation under the Advisers Act, would be inconsistent with the Advisers Act,[30] regardless of the sophistication of the client.[31]

30 *See* sections 206 and 215(a). Commenters generally agreed that a client cannot waive an investment adviser's fiduciary duty through agreement. *See* Dechert Letter; Comment Letter of Ropes & Gray LLP (Aug. 7, 2018) ("Ropes & Gray Letter"), at n.20; *see also supra* footnote 29. In the Proposed Interpretation, we stated that "the investment adviser cannot disclose or negotiate away, and the investor cannot waive, the federal fiduciary duty." One commenter disputed this broad statement, believing that it called into question "the ability of an investment adviser and client to define the scope of the adviser's services and duties." ABA Letter; *see also* Financial Engines Letter. We have modified this statement to clarify that a general waiver of the fiduciary duty would violate that duty and to provide examples of such a general waiver.

31 Some commenters mentioned a 2007 No-Action Letter in which staff indicated that whether a clause in an advisory agreement that purports to limit an adviser's liability under that agreement (a so-called "hedge clause") would violate sections 206(1) and 206(2) of the Advisers Act depends on all of the surrounding facts and circumstances. Heitman Capital Management, LLC, SEC Staff No-Action Letter (Feb. 12, 2007) ("Heitman Letter"). A few commenters indicated that the Heitman Letter expanded the ability of investment advisers to private funds, and potentially other sophisticated clients, to disclaim their fiduciary duties under state law in an advisory agreement. *See, e.g.*, ILPA Letter 1; ILPA Letter 2. The commenters' descriptions of the Heitman Letter suggest that it may have been applied incorrectly. The Heitman Letter does not address the scope or substance of an adviser's federal fiduciary duty; rather, it addresses the extent to which hedge clauses may be misleading in violation of the Advisers Act's antifraud provisions. Another commenter agreed with this reading of the Heitman Letter. *See* Comment Letter of American Investment Council (Feb. 25, 2019). In response to these comments, we express below the Commission's views about an adviser's obligations under sections 206(1) and 206(2) of the Advisers Act with respect to the use of hedge clauses. Accordingly, because we are expressing our views in this Final Interpretation, the Heitman Letter is withdrawn.

This Final Interpretation makes clear that an adviser's federal fiduciary duty may not be waived, though its application may be shaped by agreement. This Final Interpretation does not take a position on the scope or substance of any fiduciary duty that applies to an adviser under applicable state law. *See supra* footnote 3. The question of whether a hedge clause violates the Advisers Act's antifraud provisions depends on all of the surrounding facts and circumstances, including the particular circumstances of the client (*e.g.*, sophistication). In our view, however, there are few (if any) circumstances in which a hedge clause in an agreement with a retail client would be consistent with those antifraud provisions, where the hedge clause purports to relieve the adviser from liability for conduct as to which the client has a non-waivable cause of action against the adviser provided by state or federal law. Such a hedge clause generally is likely to mislead those retail clients into not exercising their legal rights, in violation of the antifraud provisions, even where the agreement otherwise specifies that the client may continue to retain its non-waivable rights. Whether a hedge clause in an agreement with an institutional client would violate the Advisers Act's antifraud provisions will be determined based on the particular facts and circumstances. To the extent that a hedge clause creates a conflict of interest between an adviser and its client, the adviser must address the conflict as required by its duty of loyalty.

B. Duty of Care

As fiduciaries, investment advisers owe their clients a duty of care.[32] The Commission has discussed the duty of care and its components in a number of contexts.[33] The duty of care includes, among other things: (i) the duty to provide advice that is in the best interest of the client, (ii) the duty to seek best execution of a client's transactions where the adviser has the responsibility to select broker-dealers to execute client trades, and (iii) the duty to provide advice and monitoring over the course of the relationship.

1. Duty to Provide Advice that is in the Best Interest of the Client

The duty of care includes a duty to provide investment advice that is in the best interest of the client, including a duty to provide advice that is suitable for the client.[34] In order to

32 *See* Investment Advisers Act Release 2106, *supra* footnote 15 (stating that under the Advisers Act, "an adviser is a fiduciary that owes each of its clients duties of care and loyalty with respect to all services undertaken on the client's behalf, including proxy voting," which is the subject of the release, and citing SEC v. Capital Gains *supra* footnote 2, to support this point). This Final Interpretation does not address the specifics of how an investment adviser might satisfy its fiduciary duty when voting proxies. *See also* Restatement (Third) of Agency, § 8.08 (discussing the duty of care that an agent owes its principal as a matter of common law); Tamar Frankel & Arthur B. Laby, The Regulation of Money Managers (updated 2017) ("Advice can be divided into three stages. The first determines the needs of the particular client. The second determines the portfolio strategy that would lead to meeting the client's needs. The third relates to the choice of securities that the portfolio would contain. The duty of care relates to each of the stages and depends on the depth or extent of the advisers' obligation towards their clients.").

33 *See, e.g.*, Suitability of Investment Advice Provided by Investment Advisers; Custodial Account Statements for Certain Advisory Clients, Investment Advisers Act Release No. 1406 (Mar. 16, 1994) ("Investment Advisers Act Release 1406") (stating that advisers have a duty of care and discussing advisers' suitability obligations); Interpretive Release Concerning the Scope of Section 28(e) of the Securities Exchange Act of 1934 and Related Matters, Exchange Act Release No. 23170 (Apr. 28, 1986) ("Exchange Act Release 23170") ("an adviser, as a fiduciary, owes its clients a duty of obtaining the best execution on securities transactions"). We highlight certain contexts, but not all, in which the Commission has addressed the duty of care. *See, e.g.*, Investment Advisers Act Release 2106, *supra* footnote 15.

34 In 1994, the Commission proposed a rule that would have made express the fiduciary obligation of investment advisers to make only suitable recommendations to a client. Investment Advisers Act Release 1406, *supra* footnote 33. Although never adopted, the rule was designed, among other things, to reflect the Commission's interpretation of an adviser's *existing* suitability obligation under the Advisers Act. In addition, we do not cite Investment Advisers Act Release 1406 as the source of authority for the view we express here, which at least one comment letter suggested, but cite it merely to show that the Commission has long held this view. *See* Comment Letter of the Managed Funds Association and the Alternative Investment Management Association (Aug. 7, 2018) (indicating that the Commission's failure to adopt the proposed suitability rule means "investment advisers are not subject to an express 'suitability' standard

provide such advice, an adviser must have a reasonable understanding of the client's objectives. The basis for such a reasonable understanding generally would include, for retail clients, an understanding of the investment profile, or for institutional clients, an understanding of the investment mandate.[35] The duty to provide advice that is in the best interest of the client based on a reasonable understanding of the client's objectives is a critical component of the duty of care.

Reasonable Inquiry into Client's Objectives

How an adviser develops a reasonable understanding will vary based on the specific facts and circumstances, including the nature of the client, the scope of the adviser-client relationship, and the nature and complexity of the anticipated investment advice.

In order to develop a reasonable understanding of a retail client's objectives, an adviser should, at a minimum, make a reasonable inquiry into the client's financial situation, level of financial sophistication, investment experience, and financial goals (which we refer to collectively as the retail client's "investment profile"). For example, an adviser undertaking to formulate a comprehensive financial plan for a retail client would generally need to obtain a

under existing regulation"). We believe that this obligation to make only suitable recommendations to a client is part of an adviser's fiduciary duty to act in the best interest of its client. Accordingly, an adviser must provide investment advice that is suitable for its client in providing advice that is in the best interest of its client. *See* SEC v. Tambone, *supra* footnote 23 ("Section 206 imposes a fiduciary duty on investment advisers to act at all times in the best interest of the fund…."); SEC v. Moran, *supra* footnote 23 ("Investment advisers are entrusted with the responsibility and duty to act in the best interest of their clients.").

35 Several commenters stated that the duty to make a reasonable inquiry into a client's investment profile may not apply in the institutional client context. *See, e.g.*, Comment Letter of BlackRock, Inc. (Aug. 7, 2018); Comment Letter of Teachers Insurance and Annuity Association of America (Aug. 7, 2018); Comment Letter of Allianz Global Investors U.S. LLC (Aug. 7, 2018) ("Allianz Letter"); Comment Letter of John Hancock Life Insurance Company (U.S.A.) (Aug. 3, 2018). Accordingly, we are describing the duty as a duty to have a reasonable understanding of the client's objectives. While not every client will have an investment profile, every client will have objectives. For example, an institutional client's objectives may be ascertained through its investment mandate.

range of personal and financial information about the client such as current income, investments, assets and debts, marital status, tax status, insurance policies, and financial goals.[36]

In addition, it will generally be necessary for an adviser to a retail client to update the client's investment profile in order to maintain a reasonable understanding of the client's objectives and adjust the advice to reflect any changed circumstances.[37] The frequency with which the adviser must update the client's investment profile in order to consider changes to any advice the adviser provides would itself turn on the facts and circumstances, including whether the adviser is aware of events that have occurred that could render inaccurate or incomplete the investment profile on which the adviser currently bases its advice. For instance, in the case of a financial plan where the investment adviser also provides advice on an ongoing basis, a change in the relevant tax law or knowledge that the client has retired or experienced a change in marital status could trigger an obligation to make a new inquiry.

By contrast, in providing investment advice to institutional clients, the nature and extent of the reasonable inquiry into the client's objectives generally is shaped by the specific investment mandates from those clients. For example, an investment adviser engaged to advise on an institutional client's investment grade bond portfolio would need to gain a reasonable understanding of the client's objectives within that bond portfolio, but not the client's objectives

36 Investment Advisers Act Release 1406, *supra* footnote 33. After making a reasonable inquiry into the client's investment profile, it generally would be reasonable for an adviser to rely on information provided by the client (or the client's agent) regarding the client's financial circumstances, and an adviser should not be held to have given advice not in its client's best interest if it is later shown that the client had misled the adviser concerning the information on which the advice was based.

37 Such updating would not be needed with one-time investment advice. In the Proposed Interpretation, we stated that an adviser "must" update a client's investment profile in order to adjust the advice to reflect any changed circumstances. We believe that any obligation to update a client's investment profile, like the nature and extent of the reasonable inquiry into a retail client's objectives, turns on what is reasonable under the circumstances. Accordingly, we have revised the wording of this statement in this Final Interpretation.

within its entire investment portfolio. Similarly, an investment adviser whose client is a registered investment company or a private fund would need to have a reasonable understanding of the fund's investment guidelines and objectives. For advisers acting on specific investment mandates for institutional clients, particularly funds, we believe that the obligation to update the client's objectives would not be applicable except as may be set forth in the advisory agreement.

Reasonable belief that advice is in the best interest of the client

An investment adviser must have a reasonable belief that the advice it provides is in the best interest of the client based on the client's objectives. The formation of a reasonable belief would involve considering, for example, whether investments are recommended only to those clients who can and are willing to tolerate the risks of those investments and for whom the potential benefits may justify the risks.[38] Whether the advice is in a client's best interest must be evaluated in the context of the portfolio that the adviser manages for the client and the client's objectives.

For example, when an adviser is advising a retail client with a conservative investment objective, investing in certain derivatives may be in the client's best interest when they are used to hedge interest rate risk or other risks in the client's portfolio, whereas investing in certain directionally speculative derivatives on their own may not. For that same client, investing in a particular security on margin may not be in the client's best interest, even if investing in that same security without the use of margin may be in the client's best interest. However, for

[38] Item 8 of Part 2A of Form ADV requires an investment adviser to describe its methods of analysis and investment strategies and disclose that investing in securities involves risk of loss which clients should be prepared to bear. This item also requires that an adviser explain the material risks involved for each significant investment strategy or method of analysis it uses and particular type of security it recommends, with more detail if those risks are significant or unusual. Accordingly, investment advisers are required to identify and explain certain risks involved in their investment strategies and the types of securities they recommend. An investment adviser needs to consider those same risks in determining the clients to which the adviser recommends those investments.

example, when advising a financially sophisticated client, such as a fund or other sophisticated client that has an appropriate risk tolerance, it may be in the best interest of the client to invest in such derivatives or in securities on margin, or to invest in other complex instruments or other products that may have limited liquidity.

Similarly, when an adviser is assessing whether high risk products—such as penny stocks or other thinly-traded securities—are in a retail client's best interest, the adviser should generally apply heightened scrutiny to whether such investments fall within the retail client's risk tolerance and objectives. As another example, complex products such as inverse or leveraged exchange-traded products that are designed primarily as short-term trading tools for sophisticated investors may not be in the best interest of a retail client absent an identified, short-term, client-specific trading objective and, to the extent that such products are in the best interest of a retail client initially, they would require daily monitoring by the adviser.[39]

A reasonable belief that investment advice is in the best interest of a client also requires that an adviser conduct a reasonable investigation into the investment sufficient not to base its advice on materially inaccurate or incomplete information.[40] We have taken enforcement action where an investment adviser did not independently or reasonably investigate securities before recommending them to clients.[41]

[39] *See* Exchange-Traded Funds, Securities Act Release No. 10515 (June 28, 2018); SEC staff and FINRA, Investor Alert, Leveraged and Inverse ETFs: Specialized Products with Extra Risks for Buy-and-Hold Investors (Aug. 1, 2009); SEC Office of Investor Education and Advocacy, Investor Bulletin: Exchange-Traded Funds (ETFs) (Aug. 2012); *see also* FINRA Regulatory Notice 09-31, Non-Traditional ETFs – FINRA Reminds Firms of Sales Practice Obligations Relating to Leveraged and Inverse Exchange-Traded Funds (June 2009).

[40] *See, e.g.*, Concept Release on the U.S. Proxy System, Investment Advisers Act Release No. 3052 (July 14, 2010) (indicating that a fiduciary "has a duty of care requiring it to make a reasonable investigation to determine that it is not basing its recommendations on materially inaccurate or incomplete information").

[41] *See, e.g.*, In the Matter of Larry C. Grossman, Investment Advisers Act Release No. 4543 (Sept. 30, 2016) (Commission Opinion) ("*In re* Grossman") (in connection with imposing liability on a principal of a

The cost (including fees and compensation) associated with investment advice would generally be one of many important factors—such as an investment product's or strategy's investment objectives, characteristics (including any special or unusual features), liquidity, risks and potential benefits, volatility, likely performance in a variety of market and economic conditions, time horizon, and cost of exit—to consider when determining whether a security or investment strategy involving a security or securities is in the best interest of the client. When considering similar investment products or strategies, the fiduciary duty does not necessarily require an adviser to recommend the lowest cost investment product or strategy.

Moreover, an adviser would not satisfy its fiduciary duty to provide advice that is in the client's best interest by simply advising its client to invest in the lowest cost (to the client) or least remunerative (to the investment adviser) investment product or strategy without any further analysis of other factors in the context of the portfolio that the adviser manages for the client and the client's objective. Rather, the adviser could recommend a higher-cost investment or strategy if the adviser reasonably concludes that there are other factors about the investment or strategy that outweigh cost and make the investment or strategy in the best interest of the client, in light of that client's objectives. For example, it might be consistent with an adviser's fiduciary duty to advise a client with a high risk tolerance and significant investment experience to invest in a private equity fund with relatively higher fees and significantly less liquidity as compared with a fund that invests in publicly-traded companies if the private equity fund was in the client's best

registered investment adviser for recommending offshore private investment funds to clients), *stayed in part,* Investment Advisers Act No. 4563 (Nov. 1, 2016), *response to remand*, Investment Advisers Act Release No. 4871 (Mar. 29, 2018) (reinstating the Sept. 30, 2016 opinion and order, except with respect to the disgorgement and prejudgment interest in light of the Supreme Court's decision in *Kokesh v. SEC*, 137 S. Ct. 1635 (2017)).

interest because it provided exposure to an asset class that was appropriate in the context of the client's overall portfolio.

An adviser's fiduciary duty applies to all investment advice the investment adviser provides to clients, including advice about investment strategy, engaging a sub-adviser, and account type.[42] Advice about account type includes advice about whether to open or invest through a certain type of account (*e.g.*, a commission-based brokerage account or a fee-based advisory account) and advice about whether to roll over assets from one account (*e.g.*, a retirement account) into a new or existing account that the adviser or an affiliate of the adviser manages.[43] In providing advice about account type, an adviser should consider all types of accounts offered by the adviser and acknowledge to a client when the account types the adviser offers are not in the client's best interest.[44]

42 In addition, with respect to prospective clients, investment advisers have antifraud liability under section 206 of the Advisers Act, which, among other things, applies to transactions, practices, or courses of business which operate as a fraud or deceit upon prospective clients, including those regarding investment strategy, engaging a sub-adviser, and account type. We believe that, in order to avoid liability under this antifraud provision, an investment adviser should have sufficient information about the prospective client and its objectives to form a reasonable basis for advice before providing any advice about these matters. At the point in time at which the prospective client becomes a client of the investment adviser (*e.g.*, at account opening), the fiduciary duty applies. Accordingly, while advice to prospective clients about these matters must comply with the antifraud provisions under section 206 of the Advisers Act, the adviser must also satisfy its fiduciary duty with respect to any such advice (*e.g.*, regarding account type) when a prospective client becomes a client.

43 We consider advice about "rollovers" to include advice about account type, in addition to any advice regarding the investments or investment strategy with respect to the assets to be rolled over, as the advice necessarily includes the advice about the account type into which assets are to be rolled over. As noted below, as a general matter, an adviser's duty to monitor extends to all personalized advice it provides to the client, including, for example, in an ongoing relationship, an evaluation of whether a client's account or program type (for example, a wrap account) continues to be in the client's best interest. *See infra* text accompanying footnote 52.

44 Accordingly, in providing advice to a client or customer about account type, a financial professional who is dually licensed (*i.e.*, an associated person of a broker-dealer and a supervised person of an investment adviser (regardless of whether the professional works for a dual registrant, affiliated firms, or unaffiliated firms)) should consider all types of accounts offered (*i.e.*, both brokerage accounts and advisory accounts) when determining whether the advice is in the client's best interest. A financial professional who is only a supervised person of an investment adviser (regardless of whether that advisory firm is a dual registrant or affiliated with a broker-dealer) may only recommend an advisory account the adviser offers when the account is in the client's best interest. If a financial professional who is only a supervised person of an

2. Duty to Seek Best Execution

An investment adviser's duty of care includes a duty to seek best execution of a client's transactions where the adviser has the responsibility to select broker-dealers to execute client trades (typically in the case of discretionary accounts).[45] In meeting this obligation, an adviser must seek to obtain the execution of transactions for each of its clients such that the client's total cost or proceeds in each transaction are the most favorable under the circumstances. An adviser fulfills this duty by seeking to obtain the execution of securities transactions on behalf of a client with the goal of maximizing value for the client under the particular circumstances occurring at the time of the transaction. Maximizing value encompasses more than just minimizing cost. When seeking best execution, an adviser should consider "the full range and quality of a broker's services in placing brokerage including, among other things, the value of research provided as well as execution capability, commission rate, financial responsibility, and responsiveness" to the adviser.[46] In other words, the "determinative factor" is not the lowest possible commission cost, "but whether the transaction represents the best qualitative execution."[47] Further, an

investment adviser chooses to advise a client to consider a non-advisory account (or to speak with other personnel at a dual registrant or affiliate about a non-advisory account), that advice should be in the best interest of the client. This same framework applies in the case of a prospective client, but any advice or recommendation given to a prospective client would be subject to the antifraud provisions of the federal securities laws. *See supra* footnote 42 and Reg. BI Adoption, *supra* footnote 3.

45 *See* Commission Guidance Regarding Client Commission Practices Under Section 28(e) of the Securities Exchange Act of 1934, Exchange Act Release No. 54165 (July 18, 2006) (stating that investment advisers have "best execution obligations"); Investment Advisers Act Release 3060, *supra* footnote 15 (discussing an adviser's best execution obligations in the context of directed brokerage arrangements and disclosure of soft dollar practices); *see also* Advisers Act rule 206(3)-2(c) (referring to adviser's duty of best execution of client transactions).

46 Exchange Act Release 23170, *supra* footnote 33.

47 *Id.*

investment adviser should "periodically and systematically" evaluate the execution it is receiving for clients.[48]

3. Duty to Provide Advice and Monitoring over the Course of the Relationship

An investment adviser's duty of care also encompasses the duty to provide advice and monitoring at a frequency that is in the best interest of the client, taking into account the scope of the agreed relationship.[49] For example, when the adviser has an ongoing relationship with a client and is compensated with a periodic asset-based fee, the adviser's duty to provide advice and monitoring will be relatively extensive as is consistent with the nature of the relationship.[50] Conversely, absent an express agreement regarding the adviser's monitoring obligation, when the adviser and the client have a relationship of limited duration, such as for the provision of a

48 *Id.* The Advisers Act does not prohibit advisers from using an affiliated broker to execute client trades. However, the adviser's use of such an affiliate involves a conflict of interest that must be fully and fairly disclosed and the client must provide informed consent to the conflict. *See also* Interpretation of Section 206(3) of the Investment Advisers Act of 1940, Investment Advisers Act Release No. 1732 (Jul. 17, 1998) (discussing application of section 206(3) of the Advisers Act to certain principal and agency transactions). Two commenters requested that we prescribe specific obligations related to best execution. Comment Letter of the Healthy Markets Association (Aug. 7, 2018); Comment Letter of ICE Data Services (Aug. 7, 2018). However, prescribing specific requirements of how an adviser might satisfy its best execution obligations is outside of the scope of this Final Interpretation.

49 *Cf.* SEC v. Capital Gains, *supra* footnote 2 (describing advisers' "basic function" as "furnishing to clients on a personal basis competent, unbiased, and continuous advice regarding the sound management of their investments" (quoting Investment Trusts and Investment Companies, Report of the Securities and Exchange Commission, Pursuant to Section 30 of the Public Utility Holding Company Act of 1935, on Investment Counsel, Investment Management, Investment Supervisory, and Investment Advisory Services, H.R. Doc. No. 477, 76th Cong. 2d Sess., 1, at 28)). *Cf.* Barbara Black, *Brokers and Advisers-What's in a Name?*, 32 Fordham Journal of Corporate and Financial Law XI (2005) ("[W]here the investment adviser's duties include management of the account, [the adviser] is under an obligation to monitor the performance of the account and to make appropriate changes in the portfolio."); Arthur B. Laby, *Fiduciary Obligations of Broker-Dealers and Investment Advisers*, 55 Villanova Law Review 701 (2010) ("Laby Villanova Article") (stating that the scope of an adviser's activity can be altered by contract and that an adviser's fiduciary duty would be commensurate with the scope of the relationship) (internal citations omitted).

50 However, an adviser and client may scope the frequency of the adviser's monitoring (*e.g.*, agreement to monitor quarterly or monthly and as appropriate in between based on market events), provided that there is full and fair disclosure and informed consent. We consider the frequency of monitoring, as well as any other material facts relating to the agreed frequency, such as whether there will also be interim monitoring when there are market events relevant to the client's portfolio, to be a material fact relating to the advisory relationship about which an adviser must make full and fair disclosure and obtain informed consent as required by its fiduciary duty.

one-time financial plan for a one-time fee, the adviser is unlikely to have a duty to monitor. In other words, in the absence of any agreed limitation or expansion, the scope of the duty to monitor will be indicated by the duration and nature of the agreed advisory arrangement.[51] As a general matter, an adviser's duty to monitor extends to all personalized advice it provides to the client, including, for example, in an ongoing relationship, an evaluation of whether a client's account or program type (for example, a wrap account) continues to be in the client's best interest.[52]

C. Duty of Loyalty

The duty of loyalty requires that an adviser not subordinate its clients' interests to its own.[53] In other words, an investment adviser must not place its own interest ahead of its client's interests.[54] To meet its duty of loyalty, an adviser must make full and fair disclosure to its clients

51 *See also* Laby Villanova Article, *supra* footnote 49, at 728 (2010) ("If an adviser has agreed to provide continuous supervisory services, the scope of the adviser's fiduciary duty entails a continuous, ongoing duty to supervise the client's account, regardless of whether any trading occurs. This feature of the adviser's duty, even in a non-discretionary account, contrasts sharply with the duty of a broker administering a non-discretionary account, where no duty to monitor is required.") (internal citations omitted).

52 Investment advisers also may consider whether written policies and procedures relating to monitoring would be appropriate under Advisers Act rule 206(4)-7, which requires any investment adviser registered or required to be registered under the Advisers Act to adopt and implement written policies and procedures reasonably designed to prevent violation of the Advisers Act and the rules thereunder by the adviser and its supervised persons.

53 Investment Advisers Act Release 3060, *supra* footnote 15 (adopting amendments to Form ADV and stating that "[u]nder the Advisers Act, an adviser is a fiduciary whose duty is to serve the best interests of its clients, which includes an obligation not to subrogate clients' interests to its own," citing Investment Advisers Act Release 2106, *supra* footnote 15). The duty of loyalty applies not just to advice regarding potential investments, but to all advice the investment adviser provides to an existing client, including advice about investment strategy, engaging a sub-adviser, and account type. *See supra* text accompanying footnotes 42-43.

54 For example, an adviser cannot favor its own interests over those of a client, whether by favoring its own accounts or by favoring certain client accounts that pay higher fee rates to the adviser over other client accounts. The Commission has brought numerous enforcement actions against advisers that allocated trades to their own accounts and allocated less favorable or unprofitable trades to their clients' accounts. *See, e.g.*, *SEC v. Strategic Capital Management, LLC and Michael J. Breton*, Litigation Release No. 23867 (June 23, 2017) (partial settlement) (adviser placed trades through a master brokerage account and then allocated profitable trades to adviser's account while placing unprofitable trades into the client accounts in

of all material facts relating to the advisory relationship.[55] Material facts relating to the advisory relationship include the capacity in which the firm is acting with respect to the advice provided. This will be particularly relevant for firms or individuals that are dually registered as broker-dealers and investment advisers and who serve the same client in both an advisory and a brokerage capacity. Thus, such firms and individuals generally should provide full and fair disclosure about the circumstances in which they intend to act in their brokerage capacity and the circumstances in which they intend to act in their advisory capacity. This disclosure may be accomplished through a variety of means, including, among others, written disclosure at the beginning of a relationship that clearly sets forth when the dual registrant would act in an advisory capacity and how it would provide notification of any changes in capacity.[56] Similarly, a dual registrant acting in its advisory capacity should disclose any circumstances under which its advice will be limited to a menu of certain products offered through its affiliated broker-dealer or affiliated investment adviser.

violation of fiduciary duty and contrary to disclosures). In the Proposed Interpretation, we stated that the duty of loyalty requires an adviser to "put its client's interest first." One commenter suggested that the requirement of an adviser to put its client's interest "first" is very different from a requirement not to "subordinate" or "subrogate" clients' interests, and is inconsistent with how the duty of loyalty had been applied in the past. *See* Comment Letter of the Asset Management Group of the Securities Industry and Financial Markets Association (Aug. 7, 2018) ("SIFMA AMG Letter"). Accordingly, we have revised the description of the duty of loyalty in this Final Interpretation to be more consistent with how we have previously described the duty. *See* Investment Advisers Act Release 3060, *supra* footnote 15 ("Under the Advisers Act, an adviser is a fiduciary whose duty is to serve the best interests of its clients, which includes an obligation not to subrogate clients' interests to its own.") (citing Investment Advisers Act Release 2106, *supra* footnote 15). In practice, referring to putting a client's interest first is a plain English formulation commonly used by investment advisers to explain their duty of loyalty in a way that may be more understandable to retail clients.

55 *See* SEC v. Capital Gains, *supra* footnote 2 ("Failure to disclose material facts must be deemed fraud or deceit within its intended meaning."); Investment Advisers Act Release 3060, *supra* footnote 15 ("as a fiduciary, an adviser has an ongoing obligation to inform its clients of any material information that could affect the advisory relationship"); *see also* General Instruction 3 to Part 2 of Form ADV ("Under federal and state law, you are a fiduciary and must make full disclosure to your clients of all material facts relating to the advisory relationship.").

56 *See also* Reg. BI Adoption, *supra* footnote 3, at 99.

In addition, an adviser must eliminate or at least expose through full and fair disclosure all conflicts of interest which might incline an investment adviser—consciously or unconsciously—to render advice which was not disinterested.[57] We believe that while full and fair disclosure of all material facts relating to the advisory relationship or of conflicts of interest and a client's informed consent prevent the presence of those material facts or conflicts themselves from violating the adviser's fiduciary duty, such disclosure and consent do not themselves satisfy the adviser's duty to act in the client's best interest.[58] To illustrate what

57 In the Proposed Interpretation, we stated that an adviser must seek to avoid conflicts of interest with its clients. Proposed Interpretation, *supra* footnote 6. Some commenters requested clarity on what it means to "seek to avoid" conflicts of interest. *See, e.g.*, Comment Letter of Schulte Roth & Zabel LLP (Aug. 8, 2018); ABA Letter (stating that this wording could be read to require an adviser to first seek to avoid a conflict, before addressing a conflict through disclosure, rather than being able to provide full and fair disclosure of a conflict, and only seek avoidance if the conflict cannot be addressed through disclosure). The Commission first used this phrasing when adopting amendments to the Form ADV Part 2 instructions. *See* Investment Advisers Act Release 3060, *supra* footnote 15 and General Instruction 3 to Part 2 of Form ADV ("As a fiduciary, you also must seek to avoid conflicts of interest with your clients, and, at a minimum, make full disclosure of all material conflicts of interest between you and your clients that could affect the advisory relationship."). The release adopting this instruction clarifies the Commission's intent that it capture the fiduciary duty described in SEC v. Capital Gains and Arleen Hughes. *See* Investment Advisers Act Release 3060, *supra* footnote 15, at n.4 and accompanying text (citing SEC v. Capital Gains, *supra* footnote 2, and Arleen Hughes, *supra* footnote 18, as the basis of this language). Both of these cases emphasized that the adviser, as a fiduciary, should seek to avoid conflicts, but at a minimum must make full and fair disclosure of the conflict and obtain the client's informed consent. *See* SEC v. Capital Gains, *supra* footnote 2 ("The Advisers Act thus reflects . . . a congressional intent to eliminate, or at least to expose, all conflicts of interest which might incline an investment adviser—consciously or unconsciously—to render advice which was not disinterested."); Arleen Hughes, *supra* footnote 18 ("Since loyalty to his trust is the first duty which a fiduciary owes to his principal, it is the general rule that a fiduciary must not put himself into a position where his own interests may come in conflict with those of his principal" but if a fiduciary "chooses to assume a role in which she is motivated by conflicting interests, . . . she may do so if, but only if, she obtains her client's consent after disclosure . . ."). We believe the Commission's reference to "seek to avoid" conflicts in the Form ADV Part 2 instructions is consistent with the Final Interpretation's statement that an adviser "must eliminate or at least expose all conflicts of interest which might incline an investment adviser—consciously or unconsciously—to render advice which was not disinterested" as well as the substantively identical statements in SEC v. Capital Gains, *supra* footnote 2, and Arleen Hughes, *supra* footnote 18. While an adviser may satisfy its duty of loyalty by making full and fair disclosure of conflicts of interest and obtaining the client's informed consent, an adviser is prohibited from overreaching or taking unfair advantage of a client's trust.

58 As noted above, an investment adviser's obligation to act in the best interest of its client is an overarching principle that encompasses both the duty of care and the duty of loyalty. *See* SEC v. Tambone, *supra* footnote 23 (stating that Advisers Act section 206 "imposes a fiduciary duty on investment advisers to act at all times in the best interest of the fund . . . and *includes* an obligation to provide 'full and fair disclosure of all material facts'") (emphasis added) (citing SEC v. Capital Gains, *supra* footnote 2). We describe

constitutes full and fair disclosure, we are providing the following guidance on (i) the appropriate level of specificity, including the appropriateness of stating that an adviser "may" have a conflict, and (ii) considerations for disclosure regarding conflicts related to the allocation of investment opportunities among eligible clients.

In order for disclosure to be full and fair, it should be sufficiently specific so that a client is able to understand the material fact or conflict of interest and make an informed decision whether to provide consent.[59] For example, it would be inadequate to disclose that the adviser has "other clients" without describing how the adviser will manage conflicts between clients if and when they arise, or to disclose that the adviser has "conflicts" without further description.

above in this Final Interpretation how the application of an investment adviser's fiduciary duty to its client will vary with the scope of the advisory relationship. *See supra* section II.A.

59 Arleen Hughes, *supra* footnote 18, at 4 and 8 (stating, "[s]ince loyalty to his trust is the first duty which a fiduciary owes to his principal, it is the general rule that a fiduciary must not put himself into a position where his own interests may come in conflict with those of his principal. To prevent any conflict and the possible subordination of this duty to act solely for the benefit of his principal, a fiduciary at common law is forbidden to deal as an adverse party with his principal. An exception is made, however, where the principal gives his informed consent to such dealings," and adding that, "[r]egistrant has an affirmative obligation to disclose all material facts to her clients in a manner which is clear enough so that a client is fully apprised of the facts and is in a position to give his informed consent."); *see also Hughes v. Securities and Exchange Commission*, 174 F.2d 969 (1949) (affirming the SEC decision in Arleen Hughes); General Instruction 3 to Part 2 of Form ADV (stating that an adviser's disclosure obligation "requires that [the adviser] provide the client with sufficiently specific facts so that the client is able to understand the conflicts of interest [the adviser has] and the business practices in which [the adviser] engage[s], and can give informed consent to such conflicts or practices or reject them"); Investment Advisers Act Release 3060, *supra* footnote 15; Restatement (Third) of Agency §8.06 ("Conduct by an agent that would otherwise constitute a breach of duty as stated in §§ 8.01, 8.02, 8.03, 8.04, and 8.05 [referencing the fiduciary duty] does not constitute a breach of duty if the principal consents to the conduct, provided that (a) in obtaining the principal's consent, the agent (i) acts in good faith, (ii) discloses all material facts that the agent knows, has reason to know, or should know would reasonably affect the principal's judgment unless the principal has manifested that such facts are already known by the principal or that the principal does not wish to know them, and (iii) otherwise deals fairly with the principal; and (b) the principal's consent concerns either a specific act or transaction, or acts or transactions of a specified type that could reasonably be expected to occur in the ordinary course of the agency relationship."). *See infra* footnotes 67-70 and accompanying text for a more detailed discussion of informed consent and how it is generally considered on an objective basis and may be inferred.

Similarly, disclosure that an adviser "may" have a particular conflict, without more, is not adequate when the conflict actually exists.[60] For example, we would consider the use of "may" inappropriate when the conflict exists with respect to some (but not all) types or classes of clients, advice, or transactions without additional disclosure specifying the types or classes of clients, advice, or transactions with respect to which the conflict exists. In addition, the use of "may" would be inappropriate if it simply precedes a list of all possible or potential conflicts regardless of likelihood and obfuscates actual conflicts to the point that a client cannot provide informed consent. On the other hand, the word "may" could be appropriately used to disclose to a client a potential conflict that does not currently exist but might reasonably present itself in the future.[61]

Whether the disclosure is full and fair will depend upon, among other things, the nature of the client, the scope of the services, and the material fact or conflict. Full and fair disclosure for an institutional client (including the specificity, level of detail, and explanation of terminology) can differ, in some cases significantly, from full and fair disclosure for a retail client because institutional clients generally have a greater capacity and more resources than

60 We have brought enforcement actions in such cases. *See, e.g.,* In the Matter of The Robare Group, Ltd., et al., Investment Advisers Act Release No. 4566 (Nov. 7, 2016) (Commission Opinion) (finding, among other things, that adviser's disclosure that it *may* receive a certain type of compensation was inadequate because it did not reveal that the adviser actually had an arrangement pursuant to which it received fees that presented a potential conflict of interest); *aff'd in part and rev'd in part on other grounds Robare* v. SEC, *supra* footnote 20; *In re Grossman, supra* footnote 41 (indicating that "the use of the prospective 'may' in [the relevant Form ADV disclosures] is misleading because it suggested the mere possibility that [the broker] would make a referral and/or be paid 'referral fees' at a later point, when in fact a commission-sharing arrangement was already in place and generating income"). *Cf. Dolphin & Bradbury, Inc. v. SEC,* 512 F.3d 634, 640 (D.C. Cir. 2008) ("The Commission noted the critical distinction between disclosing the risk that a future event *might* occur and disclosing actual knowledge the event *will* occur.") (emphasis in original). For Form ADV Part 2 purposes, advisers are instructed that when they have a conflict or engage in a practice with respect to some (but not all) types or classes of clients, advice, or transactions, to indicate as such rather than disclosing that they "may" have the conflict or engage in the practice. General Instruction 2 to Part 2 of Form ADV.

61 We have added this example of a circumstance where "may" could be appropriately used in response to the request of some commenters. *See, e.g.,* Pickard Letter; ICI Letter; Ropes & Gray Letter; IAA Letter.

retail clients to analyze and understand complex conflicts and their ramifications.[62] Nevertheless, regardless of the nature of the client, the disclosure must be clear and detailed enough for the client to make an informed decision to consent to the conflict of interest or reject it.

When allocating investment opportunities among eligible clients, an adviser may face conflicts of interest either between its own interests and those of a client or among different clients.[63] If so, the adviser must eliminate or at least expose through full and fair disclosure the conflicts associated with its allocation policies, including how the adviser will allocate investment opportunities, such that a client can provide informed consent.[64] When allocating investment opportunities, an adviser is permitted to consider the nature and objectives of the client and the scope of the relationship.[65] An adviser need not have *pro rata* allocation policies, or any particular method of allocation, but, as with other conflicts and material facts, the

62 *Arleen Hughes, supra* footnote 18 (the "method and extent of disclosure depends upon the particular client involved," and an unsophisticated client may require "a more extensive explanation than the informed investor").

63 *See* Restatement (Third) of Agency, § 8.01 General Fiduciary Principle (2006) ("Unless the principal consents, the general fiduciary principle, as elaborated by the more specific duties of loyalty stated in §§ 8.02 to 8.05, also requires that an agent refrain from using the agent's position or the principal's property to benefit the agent or a third party.").

64 The Commission has brought numerous enforcement actions alleging that advisers unfairly allocated client trades to preferred clients without making full and fair disclosure. *See* Staff of the U.S. Securities and Exchange Commission, *Study on Investment Advisers and Broker-Dealers As Required by Section 913 of the Dodd-Frank Wall Street Reform and Consumer Protection Act* (Jan. 2011), *available at* https://www.sec.gov/news/studies/2011/913studyfinal.pdf, at 23–24 (citing enforcement actions). This Final Interpretation sets forth the Commission's views regarding what constitutes full and fair disclosure. *See, e.g., supra* text accompanying footnote 59; *see also* Barry Barbash and Jai Massari, *The Investment Advisers Act of 1940; Regulation by Accretion*, 39 Rutgers Law Journal 627 (2008) (stating that under section 206 of the Advisers Act and traditional notions of fiduciary and agency law, an adviser must not give preferential treatment to some clients or systematically exclude eligible clients from participating in specific opportunities without providing the clients with appropriate disclosure regarding the treatment).

65 An adviser and a client may even agree that certain investment opportunities or categories of investment opportunities will not be allocated or offered to a client.

adviser's allocation practices must not prevent it from providing advice that is in the best interest of its clients.[66]

While most commenters agreed that informed consent is a component of the fiduciary duty, a few commenters objected to what they saw as subjectivity in the use of the term "informed" to describe a client's consent to a disclosed conflict.[67] The fact that disclosure must be full and fair such that a client can provide informed consent does not require advisers to make an affirmative determination that a particular client understood the disclosure and that the client's consent to the conflict of interest was informed. Rather, disclosure should be designed to put a client in a position to be able to understand and provide informed consent to the conflict of interest. A client's informed consent can be either explicit or, depending on the facts and circumstances, implicit.[68] We believe, however, that it would not be consistent with an adviser's fiduciary duty to infer or accept client consent where the adviser was aware, or reasonably should have been aware, that the client did not understand the nature and import of the conflict.[69]

66 In the Proposed Interpretation, we stated that "in allocating investment opportunities among eligible clients, an adviser must treat all clients fairly." Some commenters interpreted this statement to mean that it would be impermissible for an adviser to allocate a particular investment to one eligible client instead of a second eligible client, even when the second client had received full and fair disclosure and provided informed consent to such an investment being allocated to the first client. *See, e.g.*, Ropes & Gray Letter; SIFMA AMG Letter. We have removed that sentence from this Final Interpretation and replaced it with this discussion that clarifies our views regarding allocation of investment opportunities.

67 *See, e.g.*, Comment Letter of LPL Financial LLC (Aug. 7, 2018); Ropes & Gray Letter.

68 We do not interpret an adviser's fiduciary duty to require that full and fair disclosure or informed consent be achieved in a written advisory contract or otherwise in writing. For example, an adviser could provide a client full and fair disclosure of all material facts relating to the advisory relationship as well as full and fair disclosure of all conflicts of interest which might incline the adviser, consciously or unconsciously, to render advice that was not disinterested, through a combination of Form ADV and other disclosure and the client could implicitly consent by entering into or continuing the investment advisory relationship with the adviser.

69 *See* Arleen Hughes, *supra* footnote 18 ("Registrant cannot satisfy this duty by executing an agreement with her clients which the record shows some clients do not understand and which, in any event, does not contain the essential facts which she must communicate."). In the Proposed Interpretation, we stated that inferring or accepting client consent to a conflict would not be consistent with the fiduciary duty where "the material facts concerning the conflict could not be fully and fairly disclosed." Some commenters expressed

In some cases, conflicts may be of a nature and extent that it would be difficult to provide disclosure to clients that adequately conveys the material facts or the nature, magnitude, and potential effect of the conflict sufficient for a client to consent to or reject it.[70] In other cases, disclosure may not be specific enough for a client to understand whether and how the conflict could affect the advice it receives. For retail clients in particular, it may be difficult to provide disclosure regarding complex or extensive conflicts that is sufficiently specific, but also understandable. In all of these cases where an investment adviser cannot fully and fairly disclose a conflict of interest to a client such that the client can provide informed consent, the adviser should either *eliminate* the conflict or adequately *mitigate* (*i.e.*, modify practices to reduce) the conflict such that full and fair disclosure and informed consent are possible.

Full and fair disclosure of all material facts relating to the advisory relationship, and all conflicts of interest which might incline an investment adviser—consciously or unconsciously—to render advice which was not disinterested, can help clients and prospective clients in evaluating and selecting investment advisers. Accordingly, we require advisers to deliver to their clients a "brochure," under Part 2A of Form ADV, which sets out minimum disclosure requirements, including disclosure of certain conflicts.[71] Investment advisers are required to

agreement with this statement. *See, e.g.*, CFA Letter (agreeing that "advisers should be precluded from inferring or accepting client consent to a conflict" where the material facts concerning the conflict could not be fully and fairly disclosed). Other commenters expressed doubt that such disclosure could be impossible. *See, e.g.*, Allianz Letter ("[W]e have not encountered a situation in which we could not fully and fairly disclose the material facts, including the nature, extent, magnitude and potential effects of the conflict."). In response to commenters, we have replaced the general statement about an inability to fully and fairly disclose material facts about the conflict with more specific examples of how advisers can make such full and fair disclosure. *See supra* text accompanying footnotes 59-66.

70 As discussed above, institutional clients generally have a greater capacity and more resources than retail clients to analyze and understand complex conflicts and their ramifications. *See supra* text accompanying footnote 62.

71 Investment Advisers Act Release 3060, *supra* footnote 15; General Instruction 3 to Part 2 of Form ADV ("Under federal and state law, you are a fiduciary and must make full disclosure to your clients of all material facts relating to the advisory relationship. As a fiduciary, you also must seek to avoid conflicts of

deliver the brochure to a prospective client at or before entering into a contract so that the prospective client can use the information contained in the brochure to decide whether or not to enter into the advisory relationship.[72] In a concurrent release, we are requiring all investment advisers to deliver to retail investors, at or before the time the adviser enters into an investment advisory agreement, a relationship summary, which would include, among other things, a plain English summary of certain of the firm's conflicts of interest, and would encourage retail investors to inquire about those conflicts.[73]

III. Economic Considerations

As noted above, this Final Interpretation is intended to reaffirm, and in some cases clarify, certain aspects of an investment adviser's fiduciary duty under the Advisers Act. The Final Interpretation does not itself create any new legal obligations for advisers. Nonetheless, the Commission recognizes that to the extent an adviser's practices are not consistent with the Final Interpretation provided above, the Final Interpretation could have potential economic effects. We discuss these potential effects below.

interest with your clients, and, at a minimum, make full disclosure of all material conflicts of interest between you and your clients that could affect the advisory relationship. This obligation requires that you provide the client with sufficiently specific facts so that the client is able to understand the conflicts of interest you have and the business practices in which you engage, and can give informed consent to such conflicts or practices or reject them."). *See also* Robare v. SEC, *supra* footnote 20 ("[R]egardless of what Form ADV requires, [investment advisers have] a fiduciary duty to fully and fairly reveal conflicts of interest to their clients.").

72 Investment Advisers Act rule 204-3. *See* Investment Advisers Act Release 3060, *supra* footnote 15 (adopting amendments to Form ADV and stating that, "A client may use this disclosure to select his or her own adviser and evaluate the adviser's business practices and conflicts on an ongoing basis. As a result, the disclosure clients and prospective clients receive is critical to their ability to make an informed decision about whether to engage an adviser and, having engaged the adviser, to manage that relationship."). To the extent that the information required for inclusion in the brochure does not satisfy an adviser's disclosure obligation, the adviser "may have to disclose to clients information not specifically required by Part 2 of Form ADV or in more detail than the brochure items might otherwise require" and this disclosure may be made "in [the] brochure or by some other means." General Instruction 3 to Part 2 of Form ADV.

73 Form CRS Relationship Summary; Amendments to Form ADV; Required Disclosures in Retail Communications and Restrictions on the use of Certain Names or Titles, Investment Advisers Act Release No. 5247 (June 5, 2019) ("Relationship Summary Adoption").

A. Background

The Commission's interpretation of the standard of conduct for investment advisers under the Advisers Act set forth in this Final Interpretation would affect investment advisers and their associated persons as well as the clients of those investment advisers, and the market for financial advice more broadly.[74] As of December 31, 2018, there were 13,299 investment advisers registered with the Commission with over $84 trillion in assets under management as well as 17,268 investment advisers registered with states with approximately $334 billion in assets under management and 3,911 investment advisers who submit Form ADV as exempt reporting advisers.[75] As of December 31, 2018, there are approximately 41 million client accounts advised by SEC-registered investment advisers.[76]

These investment advisers currently incur ongoing costs related to their compliance with their legal and regulatory obligations, including costs related to understanding the standard of conduct. We believe, based on the Commission's experience, that the interpretations set forth in this Final Interpretation are generally consistent with investment advisers' current understanding of their fiduciary duty under the Advisers Act.[77] However, we recognize that as the scope of the

74 *See* Relationship Summary Proposal, *supra* footnote 5, at section IV.A (discussing the market for financial advice generally).

75 Data on investment advisers is based on staff analysis of Form ADV, particularly Item 5.F.(2)(c) of Part 1A for Regulatory Assets under Management. Because this Final Interpretation interprets an adviser's fiduciary duty under section 206 of the Advisers Act, this interpretation would be applicable to both SEC- and state-registered investment advisers, as well as other investment advisers that are exempt from registration or subject to a prohibition on registration under the Advisers Act.

76 Item 5.F.(2)(f) of Part 1A of Form ADV.

77 *See supra* section II.B.i. For example, some commenters asked that we clarify from the Proposed Interpretation that an adviser and its client can tailor the scope of the relationship to which the fiduciary duty applies, through contract. *See, e.g.*, MMI Letter; Financial Engines Letter; ABA Letter. *See supra* footnotes 67–69 and accompanying text, including clarifications addressing these commenters' concerns. More generally, some commenters requested clarifications from the Proposed Interpretation, and we are issuing this Final Interpretation to address those issues raised by commenters, as discussed in more detail above.

adviser-client relationship varies and in many cases can be broad, there may be certain current circumstances where investment advisers interpret their fiduciary duty to require something less, and other current circumstances where they interpret their fiduciary duty to require something more, than this Final Interpretation. We lack data to identify which investment advisers currently understand their fiduciary duty to require something different from the standard of conduct articulated in this Final Interpretation. Based on our experience over decades of interacting with the investment management industry as its primary regulator, however, we generally believe that it is not a significant portion of the market.

One commenter suggested that the Proposed Interpretation's discussion of how an adviser fulfills its fiduciary duty appeared to be based in the context of having as a client an individual investor, and not a fund.[78] This commenter indicated its concerns about the ability of a fund manager to infer consent from a client that is a fund, and that issues regarding inferring consent from funds could significantly increase compliance costs for venture capital funds.[79] Our discussion above in this Final Interpretation includes clarifications to address comments, and expressly acknowledges that while all investment advisers owe each of their clients a fiduciary duty, the specific application of the investment adviser's fiduciary duty must be viewed in the context of the agreed-upon scope of the adviser-client relationship.[80] This Final Interpretation, as compared to the Proposed Interpretation, includes significantly more examples of the application of the fiduciary duty to institutional clients, and clarifies the Commission's interpretation of what constitutes full and fair disclosure and informed consent, acknowledging a number of comments

[78] *See* Comment Letter of National Venture Capital Association (Aug. 7, 2018) ("NVCA Letter").

[79] *Id.*

[80] *See supra* section II.A.

on this topic.[81] We believe that these clarifications will help address some of this commenter's concerns with respect to increased compliance costs for venture capital funds, in part by clarifying how the fiduciary duty can apply to institutional clients. We continue to believe, based on our experience with investment advisers to different types of clients, that advisers understand their fiduciary duty to be generally consistent with the standards of this Final Interpretation.

B. Potential Economic Effects

Based on our experience as the long-standing regulator of the investment adviser industry, the Commission's interpretation of the fiduciary duty under section 206 of the Advisers Act described in this Final Interpretation generally reaffirms the current practices of investment advisers. Therefore, we expect there to be no significant economic effects from this Final Interpretation. However, as with other circumstances in which the Commission speaks to the legal obligations of regulated entities, we acknowledge that affected firms, including those whose practices are consistent with the Commission's interpretation, incur costs to evaluate the Commission's interpretation and assess its applicability to them. Further, to the extent certain investment advisers currently understand the practices necessary to comply with their fiduciary duty to be different from those discussed in this Final Interpretation, there could be some economic effects, which we discuss below.

Clients of investment advisers

The typical relationship between an investment adviser and a client is a principal-agent relationship, where the principal (the client) hires an agent (the investment adviser) to perform

[81] In particular, this Final Interpretation expressly notes our belief that a client generally may provide its informed consent implicitly "by entering into or continuing the investment advisory relationship with the adviser" after disclosure of a conflict of interest. *See supra* footnote 68.

some service (investment advisory services) on the principal's behalf.[82] Because investors and investment advisers are likely to have different preferences and goals, the investment adviser relationship is subject to agency problems, including those resulting from conflicts: that is, investment advisers may take actions that increase their well-being at the expense of investors, thereby imposing agency costs on investors.[83] A fiduciary duty, such as the duty investment advisers owe their clients, can mitigate these agency problems and reduce agency costs by deterring investment advisers from taking actions that expose them to legal liability.[84]

To the extent this Final Interpretation causes a change in behavior of those investment advisers, if any, who currently interpret their fiduciary duty to require something different from this Final Interpretation, we expect a potential reduction in agency problems and, consequently, a reduction of agency costs to the client.[85] For example, an adviser that, as part of its duty of loyalty, fully and fairly discloses[86] a conflict of interest and receives informed consent from its client with respect to the conflict may reduce agency costs by increasing the client's awareness of the conflict and improving the client's ability to monitor the adviser with respect to this conflict. Alternatively, the client may choose to not consent given the information the adviser

82 *See, e.g.*, James A. Brickley, Clifford W. Smith, Jr. & Jerold L. Zimmerman, *Managerial Economics and Organizational Architecture* (2004), at 265 ("An agency relationship consists of an agreement under which one party, the principal, engages another party, the agent, to perform some service on the principal's behalf."); *see also* Michael C. Jensen & William H. Meckling, *Theory of the Firm: Managerial Behavior, Agency Costs and Ownership Structure*, 3 Journal of Financial Economics 305-360 (1976) ("Jensen and Meckling").

83 *See, e.g.*, Jensen and Meckling, *supra* footnote 82.

84 *See, e.g.*, Frank H. Easterbrook & Daniel R. Fischel, *Contract and Fiduciary Duty*, 36 Journal of Law & Economics 425-46 (1993).

85 To the extent that this Final Interpretation clarifies the fiduciary duty for investment advisers, one commenter suggested it may then clarify what clients expect of their investment advisers. *See* Cambridge Letter (stating that "greater clarity on all aspects of an investment adviser's fiduciary duty will improve the ability to craft such policies and procedures, as well as support the elimination of confusion for retail clients and investment professionals").

86 As discussed above, whether such a disclosure is full and fair will depend upon, among other things, the nature of the client, the scope of the services, and the conflict. *See supra* section II.C.

discloses about a conflict of interest if the perceived risk associated with the conflict is too significant, and instead try to renegotiate the contract with the adviser or look for an alternative adviser or other financial professional. In addition, the obligation to fully and fairly disclose a current conflict may cause the adviser to take other actions, for example eliminating or adequately mitigating (*i.e.*, modifying practices to reduce) that conflict rather than taking the risk that the client will not provide informed consent or will look for an alternative adviser or other financial professional. The extent to which agency costs would be reduced by such a disclosure is difficult to assess given that we are unable to ascertain the total number of investment advisers that currently interpret their fiduciary duty to require something different from the Commission's interpretation,[87] and consequently we are not able to estimate the agency costs such advisers currently impose on investors. In addition, we believe that there may be potential benefits for clients of those investment advisers, if any, to the extent this Final Interpretation is effective at strengthening investment advisers' understanding of their obligations to their clients. Further, to the extent that this Final Interpretation enhances the understanding of any investment advisers of their duty of care, it may potentially raise the quality of investment advice and also lead to increased compliance with the duty to monitor, for example whether advice about an account or program type remains in the client's best interest, thereby increasing the likelihood that the advice fits with a client's objectives.

In addition, to the extent that this Final Interpretation causes some investment advisers to properly identify circumstances in which conflicts may be of a nature and extent that it would be

87 One commenter did not agree that the discussion of fiduciary obligations in the Proposed Interpretation applied to advisers to funds as well as advisers to retail investors. *See* NVCA Letter. As discussed above, this Final Interpretation has clarified the discussion to address this commenter's concerns and acknowledges that the application of the fiduciary duty of an adviser to a retail client would be different from the specific application of the fiduciary duty of an adviser to a registered investment company or private fund.

difficult to provide disclosure to clients that adequately conveys the material facts or nature, magnitude, and potential effect of the conflict sufficient for clients to consent to it or reject it, or in which the disclosure may not be specific enough for clients to understand whether and how the conflict could affect the advice they receive, this Final Interpretation may lead those investment advisers to take additional steps to improve their disclosures or to determine whether adequately mitigating (*i.e.,* modifying practices to reduce) the conflict may be appropriate such that full and fair disclosure and informed consent are possible. This Final Interpretation may also cause some investment advisers to conclude in some circumstances that they cannot fully and fairly disclose a conflict of interest to a client such that the client can provide informed consent. We would expect that these advisers would either eliminate the conflict or adequately mitigate (*i.e.,* modify practices to reduce) the conflict such that full and fair disclosure and informed consent would be possible. Thus, to the extent this Final Interpretation would cause investment advisers to better understand their obligations and therefore to modify their business practices in ways that (i) reduce the likelihood that conflicts and other agency costs will cause an adviser to place its interests ahead of the interests of the client or (ii) help those advisers to provide full and fair disclosure, it would be expected to ameliorate the agency conflict between investment advisers and their clients. In turn, this may improve the quality of advice that the clients receive and therefore produce higher overall returns for clients and increase the efficiency of portfolio allocation. However, as discussed above, we would generally expect these effects to be minimal because we believe that the interpretations we are setting forth in this Final Interpretation are generally consistent with investment advisers' current understanding of their fiduciary duty under the Advisers Act. Finally, this Final Interpretation would also benefit

clients of investment advisers to the extent it assists the Commission in its oversight of investment advisers' compliance with their regulatory obligations.

Investment advisers and the market for investment advice

In general, we expect this Final Interpretation to affirm investment advisers' understanding of the fiduciary duty they owe their clients under the Advisers Act, reduce uncertainty for advisers, and facilitate their compliance. Further, by addressing in one release certain aspects of the fiduciary duty that an investment adviser owes to its clients under the Advisers Act, this Final Interpretation could reduce investment advisers' costs associated with comprehensively assessing their compliance obligations. We acknowledge that, as with other circumstances in which the Commission speaks to the legal obligations of regulated entities, affected firms, including those whose practices are consistent with the Commission's interpretation, incur costs to evaluate the Commission's interpretation and assess its applicability to them. Moreover, as discussed above, there may be certain investment advisers who currently understand their fiduciary duty to require something different from the fiduciary duty described in this Final Interpretation. Those investment advisers would experience an increase in their compliance costs as they change their systems, processes, disclosures, and behavior, and train their supervised persons, to align with this Final Interpretation. However, this increase in costs would be mitigated by potential benefits in efficiency for investment advisers that are able to understand aspects of their fiduciary duty by reference to a single Commission release that reaffirms—and in some cases clarifies—certain aspects of the fiduciary duty.[88] In addition, and as discussed above, in the case of an investment adviser that believed it owed its clients a lower

[88] As noted above, *supra* footnote 3, this Final Interpretation is intended to highlight the principles relevant to an adviser's fiduciary duty. It is not, however, intended to be the exclusive resource for understanding these principles.

standard of conduct, there will be client benefits from the ensuing adaptation of a higher standard of conduct and related change in policies and procedures.

Moreover, to the extent any investment advisers that understood their fiduciary duty to require something different from the fiduciary duty described in this Final Interpretation change their behavior to align with this Final Interpretation, there could also be some economic effects on the market for investment advice. For example, any improved compliance may not only reduce agency costs in current investment advisory relationships and increase the value of those relationships to current clients, it may also increase trust in the market for investment advice among all investors, which may result in more investors seeking advice from investment advisers. This may, in turn, benefit investors by improving the efficiency of their portfolio allocation. To the extent it is costly or difficult, at least in the short term, to expand the supply of investment advisory services to meet an increase in demand, any such new demand for investment advisory services could put some upward price pressure on fees. At the same time, however, if any such new demand increases the overall profitability of investment advisory services, then we expect it would encourage entry by new investment advisers—or hiring of new representatives by current investment advisers—such that competition would increase over time. Indeed, the recent growth in the investment adviser segment of the market, both in terms of number of firms and number of representatives,[89] may suggest that the costs of expanding the supply of investment advisory services are currently relatively low.

Additionally, we acknowledge that to the extent certain investment advisers recognize, as a result of this Final Interpretation, that their fiduciary duty is stricter than the fiduciary duty as they currently interpret it, it could potentially affect competition. Specifically, this Final

[89] *See* Relationship Summary Proposal, *supra* footnote 5, at section IV.A.1.d.

Interpretation of certain aspects of the standard of conduct for investment advisers may result in additional compliance costs for investment advisers seeking to meet their fiduciary duty. This increase in compliance costs, in turn, may discourage competition for client segments that generate lower revenues, such as clients with relatively low levels of financial assets, which could reduce the supply of investment advisory services and raise fees for these client segments. However, the investment advisers who already are complying with the understanding of their fiduciary duty reflected in this Final Interpretation, and who may therefore currently have a comparative cost disadvantage, could find it more profitable to compete for the clients of those investment advisers who would face higher compliance costs as a result of this Final Interpretation, which would mitigate negative effects on the supply of investment advisory services. Further, as noted above, there has been a recent growth trend in the supply of investment advisory services, which is likely to mitigate any potential negative supply effects from this Final Interpretation.[90]

One commenter discussed that, in its view, any statement in the Proposed Interpretation that certain circumstances may require the elimination of material conflicts, rather than full and fair disclosure or the mitigation of such conflicts, could lead to an effect on the market and costs to advisers, if such a requirement would cause advisers who had not shared that interpretation to change their business models or product offerings or the ways in which they interact with

[90] Beyond having an effect on competition in the market for investment adviser services, it is possible that this Final Interpretation could affect competition between investment advisers and other providers of financial advice, such as broker-dealers, banks, and insurance companies. This may be the case if certain investors base their choice between an investment adviser and another provider of financial advice, at least in part, on their perception of the standards of conduct each owes to their customers. To the extent that this Final Interpretation increases investors' trust in investment advisers' overall compliance with their standard of conduct, certain of these investors may become more willing to hire an investment adviser rather than one of their non-investment adviser competitors. As a result, investment advisers as a group may become more competitive compared to that of other types of providers of financial advice. On the other hand, if this Final Interpretation raises costs for investment advisers, they could become less competitive with other financial advice providers.

clients.[91] We disagree that this Final Interpretation includes a requirement to eliminate conflicts of interest. As discussed in more detail above, elimination of a conflict is one method of addressing that conflict; when appropriate advisers may also address the conflict by providing full and fair disclosure such that a client can provide informed consent to the conflict.[92] Further, we believe that any potential costs or market effects resulting from investment advisers addressing conflicts of interest may be decreased by the flexibility advisers have to meet their federal fiduciary duty in the context of the specific scope of services that they provide to their clients, as discussed in this Final Interpretation.

The commenter also drew particular attention to the question of whether the Commission's discussion of the fiduciary duty in the Proposed Interpretation applied to advisers to institutional clients as well as those to retail clients. The same commenter indicated that failing to accommodate the application of the concepts in the Proposed Interpretation to sophisticated clients could risk changing the marketplace or limiting investment opportunities for sophisticated clients, increasing compliance burdens for advisers to sophisticated clients, or chilling innovation. As explained above, this Final Interpretation, as compared to the Proposed Interpretation, discusses in more detail the ability of investment advisers and different types of clients to shape the scope of the relationship to which the fiduciary duty applies.[93] In particular, this Final Interpretation acknowledges that while advisers owe each of their clients a fiduciary duty, the specific obligations of, for example, an adviser providing comprehensive, discretionary advice in an ongoing relationship with a retail client will be significantly different from the

91 *See* Dechert Letter.

92 *See supra* section II.C.

93 *See supra* footnotes 78-81 and accompanying text.

obligations of an adviser to an institutional client, such as a registered investment company or private fund, where the contract defines the scope of the adviser's services and limitations on its authority with substantial specificity.[94]

Finally, to the extent this Final Interpretation causes some investment advisers to reassess their compliance with their duty of loyalty, it could lead to a reduction in the expected profitability of advice relating to particular investments for which compliance costs would increase following the reassessment.[95] As a result, the number of investment advisers willing to advise a client to make these investments may be reduced. A decline in the supply of investment adviser advice regarding these types of investments could affect efficiency for investors; it could reduce the efficiency of portfolio allocation for those investors who might otherwise benefit from investment adviser advice regarding these types of investments and are no longer able to receive such advice. At the same time, if providing full and fair disclosure and appropriate monitoring for highly complex products (*e.g.*, those with a complex payout structure, such as those that include variable or contingent payments or payments to multiple parties) results in these products becoming less profitable for investment advisers, investment advisers may be discouraged from supplying advice regarding such products. However, investors may benefit from (1) no longer receiving inadequate disclosure or monitoring for such products, (2) potentially receiving advice regarding other, less complex or expensive products that may be more efficient for the investor, and (3) only receiving recommendations for highly complex or high cost products for which an

94 *See supra* section II.A.

95 For example, such products could include highly complex, high cost products with risk and return characteristics that are hard for retail investors to fully understand, or where the investment adviser and its representatives receive complicated payments from affiliates that create conflicts of interest that are difficult for retail investors to fully understand.

investment adviser can provide full and fair disclosure regarding its conflicts and appropriate monitoring.

List of Subjects in 17 CFR Part 276

Securities.

Amendments to the Code of Federal Regulations

For the reasons set out above, the Commission is amending Title 17, chapter II of the Code of Federal Regulations as set forth below:

PART 276–INTERPRETATIVE RELEASES RELATING TO THE INVESTMENT ADVISERS ACT OF 1940 AND GENERAL RULES AND REGULATIONS THEREUNDER

1. Part 276 is amended by adding Release No. IA–5428 and the release date of June 5, 2019, to the end of the list of interpretive releases to read as follows"

Subject	Release No.	Date	Fed. Reg. Vol. and Page
* * * * * * *			
Commission Interpretation Regarding Standard of Conduct for Investment Advisers	IA-5248	June 5, 2019	[Insert FR Volume Number] FR [Insert FR Page Number]

By the Commission.

Dated: June 5, 2019.

Vanessa A. Countryman,

Acting Secretary.

SECURITIES AND EXCHANGE COMMISSION

17 CFR Part 275

[Release No. IA-2653; File No. S7-23-07]

RIN 3235-AJ96

Temporary Rule Regarding Principal Trades with Certain Advisory Clients

AGENCY: Securities and Exchange Commission.

ACTION: Interim final temporary rule; Request for comments.

SUMMARY: The Commission is adopting a temporary rule under the Investment Advisers Act of 1940 that establishes an alternative means for investment advisers who are registered with the Commission as broker-dealers to meet the requirements of section 206(3) of the Advisers Act when they act in a principal capacity in transactions with certain of their advisory clients. The Commission is adopting the temporary rule on an interim final basis as part of its response to a recent court decision invalidating a rule under the Advisers Act, which provided that fee-based brokerage accounts were not advisory accounts and were thus not subject to the Advisers Act. As a result of the Court's decision, which takes effect on October 1, fee-based brokerage customers must decide whether they will convert their accounts to fee-based accounts that are subject to the Advisers Act or to commission-based brokerage accounts. We are adopting the temporary rule to enable investors to make an informed choice between those accounts and to continue to have access to certain securities held in the principal accounts of certain advisory firms while remaining protected from certain conflicts of interest. The temporary rule will expire and no longer be effective on December 31, 2009.

DATES: *Effective Date*: September 30, 2007, except for 17 CFR 275.206(3)-3T will be effective from September 30, 2007 until December 31, 2009.

Comment Date: Comments on the interim final rule should be received on or before November 30, 2007.

ADDRESSES: Comments may be submitted by any of the following methods:

Electronic comments:

- Use the Commission's Internet comment form (http://www.sec.gov/rules/final.shtml); or
- Send an e-mail to *rule-comments@sec.gov*. Please include File Number S7-23-07 on the subject line; or
- Use the Federal eRulemaking Portal (http://www.regulations.gov). Follow the instructions for submitting comments.

Paper comments:

- Send paper comments in triplicate to Nancy M. Morris, Secretary, Securities and Exchange Commission, 100 F Street, NE, Washington, DC 20549-1090.

All submissions should refer to File Number S7-23-07. This file number should be included on the subject line if e-mail is used. To help us process and review your comments more efficiently, please use only one method. The Commission will post all comments on the Commission's Internet Web site (http://www.sec.gov/rules/final.shtml). Comments are also available for public inspection and copying in the Commission's Public Reference Room, 100 F Street, NE, Washington, DC 20549, on official business days between the hours of 10:00 am and 3:00 pm. All comments received will be posted without change; we do not edit personal identifying information from submissions. You should submit only information that you wish to make available publicly.

FOR FURTHER INFORMATION CONTACT: David W. Blass, Assistant Director, Daniel S. Kahl, Branch Chief, or Matthew N. Goldin, Attorney-Adviser, at (202) 551-6787 or *IArules@sec.gov*, Office of Investment Adviser Regulation, Division of Investment Management, U.S. Securities and Exchange Commission, 100 F Street, NE, Washington, DC 20549-5041.

SUPPLEMENTARY INFORMATION: The Securities and Exchange Commission ("Commission") is adopting temporary rule 206(3)-3T [17 CFR 275.206(3)-3T] under the Investment Advisers Act of 1940 [15 U.S.C. 80b] as an interim final rule.

We are soliciting comments on all aspects of the rule. We will carefully consider the comments that we receive and respond to them in a subsequent release.

I. BACKGROUND

A. The *FPA* Decision

On March 30, 2007, the Court of Appeals for the District of Columbia Circuit (the "Court"), in *Financial Planning Association v. SEC* ("*FPA* decision"), vacated rule 202(a)(11)-1 under the Investment Advisers Act of 1940 ("Advisers Act" or "Act").[1] Rule 202(a)(11)-1 provided, among other things, that fee-based brokerage accounts were not advisory accounts and were thus not subject to the Advisers Act.[2] As a consequence

[1] 482 F.3d 481 (D.C. Cir. 2007).

[2] Fee-based brokerage accounts are similar to traditional full-service brokerage accounts, which provide a package of services, including execution, incidental investment advice, and custody. The primary difference between the two types of accounts is that a customer in a fee-based brokerage account pays a fee based upon the amount of assets on account (an asset-based fee) and a customer in a traditional full-service brokerage account pays a commission (or a mark-up or mark-down) for each transaction.

of the *FPA* decision, broker-dealers offering fee-based brokerage accounts became subject to the Advisers Act with respect to those accounts, and the client relationship became fully subject to the Advisers Act. Broker-dealers would need to register as investment advisers, if they had not done so already, act as fiduciaries with respect to those clients, disclose all potential material conflicts of interest, and otherwise fully comply with the Advisers Act, including the Act's restrictions on principal trading.

We filed a motion with the Court on May 17, 2007 requesting that the Court temporarily withhold the issuance of its mandate and thereby stay the effectiveness of the *FPA* decision.[3] We estimated at the time that customers of broker-dealers held $300 billion in one million fee-based brokerage accounts.[4] We sought the stay to protect the interests of those customers and to provide sufficient time for them and their brokers to discuss, make, and implement informed decisions about the assets in the affected accounts. We also informed the Court that we would use the period of the stay to consider whether further rulemaking or interpretations were necessary regarding the application of the Act to fee-based brokerage accounts and other issues arising from the Court's decision. On June 27, 2007, the Court granted our motion and stayed the issuance of its mandate until October 1, 2007.[5]

[3] May 17, 2007, Motion for the Stay of Mandate, in *FPA v. SEC*.

[4] *Id.*

[5] *See* June 27, 2007, Order of the U.S. Court of Appeals for the District of Columbia Circuit, in *FPA v. SEC*.

B. Section 206(3) of the Advisers Act and the Issue of Principal Trading

We and our staff received several letters regarding the *FPA* decision and about particular consequences to customers who hold fee-based brokerage accounts.[6] Our staff followed up with, and has been engaged in an ongoing dialogue with, representatives of investors, financial planners, and broker-dealers regarding the implications of the *FPA* decision. During that process, firms that offered fee-based brokerage accounts informed us that, unless the Commission acts before October 1, 2007, one group of fee-based

[6] *See, e.g.*, Letter from Barbara Roper, Director of Investor Protection, Consumer Federation of America, et al., to Christopher Cox, Chairman, U.S. Securities and Exchange Commission, dated April 24, 2007; E-mail from Timothy J. Sagehorn, Senior Vice President – Investments, UBS Financial Services Inc., to Christopher Cox, Chairman, U.S. Securities and Exchange Commission, dated May 15, 2007; Letter from Kurt Schacht, Managing Director, CFA Institute Centre for Financial Market Integrity, to Christopher Cox, Chairman, U.S. Securities and Exchange Commission, dated May 23, 2007; Letter from Joseph P. Borg, President, North American Securities Administrators Association, Inc., to Christopher Cox, Chairman, U.S. Securities and Exchange Commission, dated June 18, 2007; Letter from Daniel P. Tully, Chairman Emeritus, Merrill Lynch & Co., Inc., to Christopher Cox, Chairman, U.S. Securities and Exchange Commission, dated June 21, 2007; Letter, with Exhibit, from Ira D. Hammerman, Senior Managing Director and General Counsel, Securities Industry and Financial Markets Association, to Robert E. Plaze, Associate Director, Division of Investment Management, U.S. Securities and Exchange Commission, and Catherine McGuire, Chief Counsel, Division of Market Regulation, U.S. Securities and Exchange Commission, dated June 27, 2007 ("SIFMA Letter"); Letter from Raymond A. "Chip" Mason, Chairman and CEO, Legg Mason, Inc., to Christopher Cox, Chairman, U.S. Securities and Exchange Commission, dated July 10, 2007; Letter from Robert J. McCann, Vice Chairman and President – Global Private Client, Merrill Lynch, to Christopher Cox, Chairman, U.S. Securities and Exchange Commission, dated July 11, 2007; Letter from Samuel L. Hayes, III, Jacob Schiff Professor of Investment Banking Emeritus, Harvard Business School, to Christopher Cox, Chairman, U.S. Securities and Exchange Commission, dated July 12, 2007; Letter from Duane Thompson, Managing Director, Washington Office, Financial Planning Association, to Robert E. Plaze, Associate Director, Division of Investment Management, U.S. Securities and Exchange Commission, dated July 27, 2007 ("FPA Letter"); Letter from Richard Bellmer, Chair, and Ellen Turf, CEO, National Association of Personal Financial Advisors, to Robert E. Plaze, Associate Director, Division of Investment Management, U.S. Securities and Exchange Commission, dated August 14, 2007 ("NAPFA Letter"); Letter from Congressman Dennis Moore, et al., to Christopher Cox, Chairman, U.S. Securities and Exchange Commission, dated July 13, 2007; and Letter from Congressman Spencer Bachus, Ranking Member, Committee on Financial Services, to Christopher Cox, Chairman, U.S. Securities and Exchange Commission,

brokerage customers is particularly likely to be harmed by the consequences of the *FPA* decision: customers who depend both on access to principal transactions with their brokerage firms and on the protections associated with a fee-based (rather than transaction-based) compensation structure. Firms explained that section 206(3) of the Advisers Act, the principal trading provision, poses a significant practical impediment to continuing to meet the needs of those customers.

Section 206(3) of the Advisers Act makes it unlawful for any investment adviser, directly or indirectly "acting as principal for his own account, knowingly to sell any security to or purchase any security from a client …, without disclosing to such client in writing before the completion of such transaction the capacity in which he is acting and obtaining the consent of the client to such transaction."[7] Section 206(3) requires an adviser entering into a principal transaction with a client to satisfy these disclosure and consent requirements on a transaction-by-transaction basis.[8] An adviser may provide the

dated July 10, 2007. Each of these letters is available at: www.sec.gov/comments/s7-23-07.

[7] 15 U.S.C. 80b-6(3). Section 206(3) also addresses "agency cross transactions," imposing the same procedural requirements regarding prior disclosure and consent on those transactions as it imposes on principal transactions. Agency cross transactions are transactions for which an investment adviser provides advice and the adviser, or a person controlling, controlled by, or under common control with the adviser, acts as a broker for that advisory client and for the person on the other side of the transaction. *See Method for Compliance with Section 206(3) of the Investment Advisers Act of 1940 with Respect to Certain Transactions*, Investment Advisers Act Release No. 557 (Dec. 2, 1976) [41 FR 53808] ("Rule 206(3)-2 Proposing Release").

[8] *See Commission Interpretation of Section 206(3) of the Investment Advisers Act of 1940*, Investment Advisers Act Release No. 1732 (July 17, 1998) [63 FR 39505 (July 23, 1998)] ("Section 206(3) Release") ("[A]n adviser may comply with Section 206(3) either by obtaining client consent prior to execution of a principal or agency transaction, or after execution but prior to settlement of the transaction."). *See also* Investment Advisers Act Release No. 40 (Jan. 5, 1945) [11 FR 10997] ("[T]he requirements of written disclosure and of consent contained in this clause must be satisfied before the completion of each separate transaction. A blanket disclosure and consent in a general agreement between investment adviser and client would not suffice.").

written disclosure to a client and obtain the client's consent at or prior to the completion of the transaction.[9]

During our discussions, firms informed our staff that the written disclosure and the client consent requirements of section 206(3) act as an operational barrier to their ability to engage in principal trades with their clients. Firms that are registered both as broker-dealers and investment advisers generally do not offer principal trading to current advisory clients (or do so on a very limited basis), and the rule vacated in the *FPA* decision had allowed broker-dealers to offer fee-based accounts without complying with the Advisers Act, including the requirements of section 206(3). Most informed us that they plan to discontinue fee-based brokerage accounts as a result of the *FPA* decision because of the application of the Advisers Act. They also informed us of their view that, unless they are provided an exemption from, or an alternative means of complying with, section 206(3) of the Advisers Act, they would be unable to provide the same range of services to those fee-based brokerage customers who elect to become advisory clients and would expect few to elect to do so.[10]

9 Section 206(3) Release ("Implicit in the phrase 'before the completion of such transaction' is the recognition that a securities transaction involves various stages before it is 'complete.' The phrase 'completion of such transaction' on its face would appear to be the point at which all aspects of a securities transaction have come to an end. That ending point of a transaction is when the actual exchange of securities and payment occurs, which is known as 'settlement.'").

10 The firms explained that they plan to consult with their customers and obtain customers' consent to convert the fee-based accounts to one or more other types of accounts already operating on pre-existing business platforms. We understand that in most cases customers will be able to choose among different types of brokerage accounts, paying commissions for securities, and advisory accounts, paying asset-based fees. Firms indicated to us that, if we provide an alternative means of complying with section 206(3), they believe a significant number of their fee-based brokerage customers will elect to convert their accounts to non-discretionary advisory accounts. Those accounts operate in many respects like fee-based brokerage accounts, but fiduciary duties apply to the adviser, and the other obligations of the Advisers Act also apply. Firms offering these

Several broker-dealers and the Securities Industry and Financial Markets Association ("SIFMA") contended that providing written disclosure before completion of each securities transaction, as required by section 206(3) of the Advisers Act, makes it not feasible for an adviser to offer customers principal transactions for several reasons. Firms explained that there are timing and mechanical impediments to complying with section 206(3)'s written disclosure requirement. SIFMA explained that, for example, the combination of rapid electronic trading systems and the limited availability of many of the securities traded in principal markets means that an adviser may be unable to provide written disclosure and obtain consent in sufficient time to obtain such securities at the best price or, in some cases, at all.[11] Similarly, SIFMA contended that trade-by-trade written disclosure prior to execution is not practicable because "discussions between investment advisers and non-discretionary clients about a trade or strategy may occur before a particular transaction is effected, but at the time that discussion occurs the representative may not know whether the transaction will be effected on an agency or a principal basis."[12]

Firms also explained that they engage in thousands – in many cases, tens of thousands – of principal trades a day and that, due to the sheer volume of transactions, providing a written notice to all the clients with whom they conduct trades in a principal

accounts provide investment advice, but clients retain decision making authority over their investment selections.

11 SIFMA Letter, at 21 ("Many fixed income securities, including municipal securities, that have limited availability are quoted, purchased and sold quickly through electronic communications networks utilized by bond dealers. . . . In today's principal markets, investment advisers do not necessarily have 'sufficient opportunity to secure the client's specific prior consent' and provide trade-by-trade disclosure, and opportunities to achieve best execution may be lost if the adviser does not act immediately on current market prices.") (quoting Rule 206(3)-2 Proposing Release).

capacity may only be done using automated systems.[13] One such automated system is the system broker-dealers use to provide customers with transaction-specific written notifications, or trade confirmations, that include the information required by rule 10b-10 under the Exchange Act.[14] Under rule 10b-10, a broker-dealer must disclose on its confirmation if it acts as principal for its own account with respect to a transaction.[15] However, confirmations are provided to customers too late to satisfy the requirements of section 206(3). This is because trade confirmations are *sent*, rather than *delivered*, at completion of a transaction and much of the information required to be disclosed by rule 10b-10 may only be available at completion of a transaction, not before. Thus, even if firms were to rely on the Commission's 1998 interpretation of section 206(3), under which disclosure and consent may be obtained after execution but before settlement of a transaction,[16] no automated system currently exists that could ensure compliance.[17]

---

12 *Id.*

13 Firms asserted that, while possible, providing written notifications by fax or email prior to a transaction is impractical. Clients may not have ready access to either at the time they wish to conduct a trade and delaying the trade in order to provide the written notification likely would not be in the client's best interest, in particular as market prices may change rapidly.

14 17 CFR 240.10b-10. Rule 10b-10 under the Exchange Act requires a broker-dealer, at or before completion of a transaction, to give or send to its customer a written confirmation containing specified information about the transaction.

15 Rule 10b-10(a)(2) under the Exchange Act [17 CFR 240.10b-10(a)(2)].

16 *See* Section 206(3) Release.

17 It may be possible for firms to upgrade their confirmation delivery systems to provide an additional written disclosure that satisfies the content and chronological requirements of section 206(3) of the Act. Based on our experience with changes to confirmation delivery systems (largely in response to our changes to Exchange Act rule 10b-10), any such upgrade could take years to accomplish and would not be available by October 1, 2007, the date the *FPA* decision becomes effective. Furthermore, even if an automated system were developed to provide those written disclosures at or before completion of the transaction, no such automated system exists to obtain the required consent from advisory clients. We also are mindful of the burdens associated with such a system change. SIFMA has submitted to us that "[t]rade confirmation production systems are among the

Additionally, even if an automated system existed to enable the disclosure and consent after execution of a trade but before its completion in satisfaction of section 206(3), firms indicated that they would be unlikely to trade on such a basis. The firms explained that they do not seek post-execution consent because allowing a client until settlement to consent to a trade that has already been executed creates too great a risk that intervening market changes or other factors could lead a client to withhold consent to the disadvantage of the firm.

Access to securities held in a firm's principal accounts is important to many investors. We believe, based on our discussions with industry representatives and others throughout the transition process, that many customers may wish to access the securities inventory of a diversified broker-dealer through their non-discretionary advisory accounts.[18] For example, the Financial Planning Association ("FPA") noted that principal trades in a fiduciary relationship could be beneficial to investors, stating:

> Depending on the circumstances, clients may benefit from principal trades, but only in the context of a fiduciary relationship with the best interests of the client being paramount. In favorable circumstances, advisers may obtain access to a broader range of investment opportunities, better trade execution, and more

---

most expensive and most difficult to alter anywhere in the brokerage industry, because of the mass nature of confirmations, the sensitive and private nature of the information, and the extremely short deadlines for their production and mailing." Letter from Ira D. Hammerman, Senior Vice President and General Counsel, Securities Industry and Financial Markets Association, to Jonathan G. Katz, Secretary, U.S. Securities and Exchange Commission, U.S. Securities and Exchange Commission, dated April 4, 2005, available at: www.sec.gov/rules/proposed/s70604/ihammerman040405.pdf.

18 We have previously expressed our view that some principal trades may serve clients' best interests. *See* Section 206(3) Release.

favorable transaction prices for the securities being bought or sold than would otherwise be available.[19]

As a result of the *FPA* decision, customers must elect on or before October 1, 2007, to convert their fee-based brokerage accounts to advisory accounts or to traditional commission-based brokerage accounts. Several firms emphasized to our staff that the inability of a client to access certain securities held in the firm's principal accounts – particularly municipal securities and other fixed income securities that they contend have limited availability and are dealt through a firm's account using electronic communications networks – may be a determinative factor in whether the client selects (or the firm makes available) a non-discretionary advisory account to replace the client's fee-based brokerage account. As discussed in this Release, many firms informed us that, because of the practical difficulties with complying with the trade-by-trade written disclosure requirements of section 206(3) discussed above, they simply refrain from engaging in principal trading with their advisory clients. Accordingly, customers who wish to access firms' principal inventories may, as a practical matter, have no choice but to open a traditional brokerage account in which they will pay transaction-based compensation, rather than convert their fee-based brokerage account to an advisory account.

While we do not agree with SIFMA that an exemption from section 206(3) of the Act in its entirety is appropriate, we do believe that there may be substantial benefits to many of the investors holding an estimated $300 billion in approximately one million fee-based brokerage accounts if their accounts are converted to advisory accounts instead

19 FPA Letter, at 3.

of traditional brokerage accounts.[20] Those investors will continue to be able to avoid transaction-based compensation and the incentives such a compensation arrangement creates for a broker-dealer, a reason they may have initially opened fee-based brokerage accounts.[21] They also will enjoy, as the Court pointed out in the *FPA* decision, the protections of the "federal fiduciary standard [that] govern[s] the conduct of investment advisers."[22]

To address the concerns described above and to protect the interests of customers who previously held fee-based brokerage accounts, we are adopting a temporary rule, on an interim final basis, that provides an alternative method for advisers who also are registered as broker-dealers to comply with section 206(3) of the Act. We believe this rule both protects investors' choice – fee-based brokerage customers would be able to choose an account that offers a similar set of services (including access to the same securities) that were available to them in fee-based brokerage accounts – and avoids

20 SIFMA asserted that firms should be exempt entirely from section 206(3) of the Act in order to "preserve the [fee-based brokerage] client's ability to access certain securities that are best – or only – available through trades with the adviser or an affiliate of the adviser." SIFMA Letter, at 3. SIFMA further requested that we provide broker-dealers an exemption from all of the provisions of the Advisers Act with respect to their fee-based brokerage accounts. We are not adopting such a broad exemption.

21 A brokerage industry committee formed in 1994 at the suggestion of then-Commission Chairman Arthur Levitt concluded that fee-based compensation would better align the interests of broker-dealers and their customers and allow registered representatives to focus on what the committee described as their most important role – providing investment advice to individual customers, not generating transaction revenues. *See Report of the Committee on Compensation Practices* (Tully Report) (Apr. 10, 1995). We already have sought and received public comment on the potential benefits to investors of fee-based accounts, *see Certain Broker-Dealers Deemed Not to be Investment Advisers*, Investment Advisers Act Release No. 2376 (Apr. 12, 2005) [70 FR 20424 (Apr. 19, 2005]; *Certain Broker-Dealers Deemed Not to be Investment Advisers*, Investment Advisers Act Release No. 2340 (Jan. 6, 2005) [70 FR 2716 (Jan. 14, 2005)]; and *Certain Broker-Dealers Deemed Not to be Investment Advisers*, Investment Advisers Act Release No. 1845 (Nov. 4, 1999) [64 FR 61226 (Nov. 10, 1999)].

disruption to, and confusion among, investors who may wish to access and sell securities only available through a firm acting in a principal capacity and who, as a result, may no longer be offered any fee-based account. We believe the temporary rule will allow fee-based brokerage customers to maintain their existing relationships with, and receive roughly the same services from, their broker-dealers. We believe further that making the rule temporary allows us an opportunity to observe how those firms use the alternative means of compliance provided by the rule, and whether those firms serve their clients' best interests.

II. DISCUSSION

A. Overview of Temporary Rule 206(3)-3T

Congress intended section 206(3) of the Advisers Act to address concerns that an adviser might engage in principal transactions to benefit itself or its affiliates, rather than the client.[23] In particular, Congress appears to have been concerned that advisers might use advisory accounts to "dump" unmarketable securities or those the advisers fear may decline in value.[24] Congress chose not to prohibit advisers from engaging in principal and agency transactions, but rather to prescribe a means by which an adviser must disclose and obtain the consent of its client to the conflicts of interest involved.

22 *FPA* decision, at 16, *citing Transamerica Mortgage Advisors Inc. v. Lewis*, 444 U.S. 11, 17 (1979).

23 *See* Investment Trusts and Investment Companies: Hearings on S. 3580 Before the Subcomm. of the Comm. on Banking and Currency, 76th Cong., 3d Sess. 320 (1940) (statement of David Schenker, Chief Counsel, Securities and Exchange Commission Investment Trust Study) ("Senate Hearings"). As noted above, section 206(3) also addresses agency cross transactions, which raise similar concerns regarding an adviser engaging in transactions to benefit itself or its affiliates, as well as the concern that an adviser may be subject to divided loyalties.

24 *See* Senate Hearings at 322 ("[i]f a fellow feels he has a sour issue and finds a client to whom he can sell it, then that is not right. . . .") (statement of David Schenker, Chief Counsel, Securities and Exchange Commission Investment Trust Study).

Congress's concerns were and continue to be significant. Self-dealing by investment advisers involves serious conflicts of interest and a substantial risk that the proprietary interests of the adviser will prevail over those of its clients.[25]

In light of these concerns and the important protections provided by section 206(3) of the Advisers Act, rule 206(3)-3T provides advisers an alternative means to comply with the requirements of that section that is consistent with the purposes, and our prior interpretations, of the section. The temporary rule continues to provide the protection of transaction-by-transaction disclosure and consent, subject to several conditions.[26] Specifically, temporary rule 206(3)-3T permits an adviser, with respect to a non-discretionary advisory account, to comply with section 206(3) of the Advisers Act by, among other things: (i) providing written prospective disclosure regarding the conflicts arising from principal trades; (ii) obtaining written, revocable consent from the client prospectively authorizing the adviser to enter into principal transactions; (iii) making certain disclosures, either orally or in writing, and obtaining the client's consent before each principal transaction; (iv) sending to the client confirmation statements disclosing the capacity in which the adviser has acted and disclosing that the adviser informed the client that it may act in a principal capacity and that the client authorized the transaction; and (v) delivering to the client an annual report itemizing the principal

25 As we have stated before "where an investment adviser effects a transaction as principal with his advisory account client, the terms of the transaction are necessarily not established by arm's-length negotiation. Instead, the investment adviser is in a position to set, or to exert influence potentially affecting, the terms by which he participates in such trade. The pressures of self-interest which may be present in such principal transactions may require the prophylaxis of the disclosures [required by section 206(3).]" Rule 206(3)-2 Proposing Release.

26 We similarly provided, in a rule of analogous scope and structure to rule 206(3)-3T, an alternative means of compliance with the disclosure and consent requirements of section 206(3) relating to "agency cross transactions." *See* rule 206(3)-2 under the Advisers Act.

transactions. The rule also requires that the investment adviser be registered as a broker-dealer under section 15 of the Exchange Act and that each account for which the adviser relies on this rule be a brokerage account subject to the Exchange Act, and the rules thereunder, and the rules of the self-regulatory organization(s) of which it is a member.[27]

These conditions, discussed below, are designed to prevent overreaching by advisers by requiring an adviser to disclose to the client the conflicts of interest involved in these transactions, inform the client of the circumstances in which the adviser may effect a trade on a principal basis, and provide the client with meaningful opportunities to refuse to consent to a particular transaction or revoke the prospective general consent to these transactions. We note that we have previously stated that "Section 206(3) should be read together with Sections 206(1) and (2) to require the adviser to disclose facts necessary to alert the client to the adviser's potential conflicts of interest in a principal or agency transaction."[28] We request comment generally on the need for the rule and its potential impact on clients of the advisers. Will the advantages described above that we believe accompany rule 206(3)-3T be beneficial to investors? Have we struck an appropriate balance between investor choice and investor protection? Does the alternative means of compliance contained in rule 206(3)-3T provide all the necessary investor protections?[29]

---

27 *See* Section II.B.7 of this Release.

28 Section 206(3) Release. For a further discussion, see Section II.B.8 of this Release.

29 In this regard, see NAPFA Letter ("express[ing] its strong reservations regarding the possible grant of principal trading relief").

B. Section-by-Section Description of Rule 206(3)-3T

Rule 206(3)-3T deems an investment adviser to be in compliance with the provisions of section 206(3) of the Advisers Act when the adviser, or a person controlling, controlled by, or under common control with the investment adviser, acting as principal for its own account, sells to or purchases from an advisory client any security, provided that certain conditions discussed below are met. The scope and structure of the rule are similar to our rule 206(3)-2 under the Advisers Act, which, as noted above, provides an alternative means of complying with the limitations on "agency cross transactions," also contained in section 206(3).

We have applied section 206(3) not only to principal transactions engaged in or effected by an adviser, but also to certain situations in which an adviser causes a client to enter into a principal transaction that is effected by a broker-dealer that controls, is controlled by, or is under common control with the adviser.[30] Accordingly, rule 206(3)-3T would be available if the adviser acts as principal by causing the client to engage in a transaction with a broker-dealer that is an affiliate of the adviser – that is, a broker-dealer that controls, is controlled by, or is under common control with the investment adviser.

1. Non-Discretionary Accounts

Rule 206(3)-3T applies to principal trades with respect to accounts over which the client has not granted "investment discretion, except investment discretion granted by the advisory client on a temporary or limited basis."[31] Availability of the rule to

---

30 *See* Section 206(3) Release at n. 3.

31 Rule 206(3)-3T(a)(1). For purposes of the rule, the term "investment discretion" has the same meaning as in section 3(a)(35) of the Exchange Act [15 U.S.C. 78c(a)(35)], except that it excludes investment discretion granted by a customer on a temporary or limited basis. Section 3(a)(35) of the Exchange Act provides that a person exercises "investment discretion" with respect to an account if, directly or indirectly, such person: (A) is

discretionary accounts would be inconsistent with the requirement of the rule, discussed below, that the adviser obtains consent (which may be oral consent) from the client for each principal transaction.[32] In addition, we are of the view that the risk of relaxing the procedural requirements of section 206(3) of the Advisers Act when a client has ceded substantial, if not complete, control over the account raises significant risks that the client will not be, or is not in a position to be, sufficiently involved in the management of the account to protect himself or herself from overreaching by the adviser.

The rule would apply to all non-discretionary advisory accounts, not only those that were originally established as fee-based brokerage accounts.[33] As noted above, some portion of the customers converting fee-based brokerage accounts into advisory accounts will be converting those accounts into non-discretionary accounts offered by the

authorized to determine what securities or other property shall be purchased or sold by or for the account; (B) makes decisions as to what securities or other property shall be purchased or sold by or for the account even though some other person may have responsibility for such investment decisions; or (C) otherwise exercises such influence with respect to the purchase and sale of securities or other property by or for the account as the Commission, by rule, determines, in the public interest or for the protection of investors, should be subject to the operation of the provisions of this title and rules and regulations thereunder.

We would view a broker-dealer's discretion to be temporary or limited within the meaning of rule 206(3)-3T(a)(1) when the broker-dealer is given discretion: (i) as to the price at which or the time to execute an order given by a customer for the purchase or sale of a definite amount or quantity of a specified security; (ii) on an isolated or infrequent basis, to purchase or sell a security or type of security when a customer is unavailable for a limited period of time not to exceed a few months; (iii) as to cash management, such as to exchange a position in a money market fund for another money market fund or cash equivalent; (iv) to purchase or sell securities to satisfy margin requirements; (v) to sell specific bonds and purchase similar bonds in order to permit a customer to take a tax loss on the original position; (vi) to purchase a bond with a specified credit rating and maturity; and (vii) to purchase or sell a security or type of security limited by specific parameters established by the customer.

32 Rule 206(3)-3T(a)(4). *See* Section II.B.4 of this Release.

33 We have not extended the rule to advisory accounts that are held only at investment advisers, as opposed to firms that are both investment advisers and registered broker-dealers. *See* Section II.B.7 of this Release.

same firm. We understand from our discussions with broker-dealers that maintaining principal trading distinctions between advisory accounts that were once fee-based brokerage accounts and those that were not would be very difficult. Trade execution routing for investment advisory programs often is derived through unified programs or electronic codes allowing or prohibiting certain kinds of trades uniformly for all accounts that are of the same type. As such, limiting relief to accounts that were formerly in fee-based brokerage programs would make the requested relief impractical for firms and would neither serve the best interests of clients (because the effect would be to limit their ability to continue to access the inventory of securities held by their brokerage firm) nor be administratively feasible to firms affected by the Court's ruling with respect to the transition and ongoing servicing of these and other accounts subject to the Advisers Act. We accordingly determined not to limit the availability of the temporary rule only to those non-discretionary advisory accounts that were fee-based brokerage accounts.

We welcome comment on this aspect of our interim final rule. Are we correct that the potential for abuse through self-dealing is less in non-discretionary accounts, where clients may be better able to protect themselves and monitor trading activity, than in accounts where clients have granted discretion and may not be in a position to protect themselves sufficiently? Should we further limit the availability of the rule so that it is only available for transactions with wealthy or sophisticated clients who, for other purposes under the Act, we have presumed are capable of protecting themselves? For example, should it apply only with respect to transactions with a "qualified client" as defined in Advisers Act rule 205-3?

Should we limit the relief provided by the rule to accounts that originally were fee-based brokerage accounts? Do the operational burdens and complexities identified by the broker-dealers support application of the rule to all non-discretionary advisory accounts?

2. Issuer and Underwriter Limitations

Rule 206(3)-3T is not available for principal trades of securities if the investment adviser or a person who controls, is controlled by, or is under common control with the adviser ("control person") is the issuer or is an underwriter of the security.[34] The rule includes one exception – an adviser may rely on the rule for trades in which the adviser or a control person is an underwriter of non-convertible investment-grade debt securities.

One benefit an investor may gain by establishing a brokerage account with a large broker-dealer is the ability to obtain access to potentially profitable public offerings of securities. These securities are typically purchased by the broker-dealer participating in the underwriting as part of its allotment of the offering and then sold to customers in principal transactions. As noted above, many broker-dealers have not made such offerings available to advisory clients because of the requirements of section 206(3).

A broker-dealer participating in an underwriting typically has a substantial economic interest in the success of the underwriting, which might be different from the interests of investors. When a broker-dealer acts as an underwriter with respect to a

[34] Rule 206(3)-3T(a)(2). The term "underwriter" is defined in section 202(a)(20) of the Advisers Act to mean "any person who has purchased from an issuer with a view to, or sells for an issuer in connection with, the distribution of any security, or participates or has a direct or indirect participation in any such undertaking, or participates or has a participation in the direct or indirect underwriting of any such undertaking; but such term shall not include a person whose interest is limited to a commission from an underwriter or dealer not in excess of the usual and customary distributor's or seller's commission."

security, it is compensated precisely for the service of distributing that security.[35] A successful distribution not only offers the possibility of a concession on the securities (the spread between the underwriter's purchase price from the issuer and the public offering price), but also often an over-allotment option, and potentially future business (whether as an underwriter, lender, adviser or otherwise) with the issuer. The incentives may bias the advice being provided or lead the adviser to exert undue influence on its client's decision to invest in the offering or the terms of that investment. As such, the broker-dealer's incentives to "dump" securities it is underwriting are greater for sales by a broker-dealer acting as an underwriter than for sales by a broker-dealer not acting as an underwriter of other securities from its inventory.

A broker-dealer acting as an issuer has similar, if not greater, proprietary interests that are likely to adversely affect the objectivity of its advice. We therefore are of the view that an investment adviser who (or whose affiliate) is the issuer or underwriter of a security has such a significant conflict of interest as to make such a transaction, with one exception, an inappropriate subject of the relief we are providing today.

We have, however, provided an exception for principal transactions in non-convertible investment grade debt securities underwritten by the adviser or a person who controls, is controlled by, or is under common control with the adviser.[36] Non-convertible investment grade debt securities may be less risky and therefore less likely to be "dumped" on clients. Also, it may be easier for clients to identify whether the price

[35] The act of underwriting is purchasing "with a view to . . . the distribution of any security." Section 202(a)(20) of the Advisers Act [17 CFR 275.202(a)(20)].

[36] "Investment grade debt securities" are defined in the rule to mean any non-convertible debt security that is rated in one of the four highest rating categories of at least two nationally recognized statistical rating organizations (as defined in section 3(a)(62) of the Exchange Act [15 U.S.C. 78c(a)(62)]). Rule 206(3)-3T(c).

they are being quoted for a non-convertible investment grade debt security is fair given the relative comparability, and the significant size, of the non-convertible investment grade debt markets.

Moreover, as the staff has discussed the effects of the *FPA* decision with broker-dealers, those broker-dealers have asserted that it is in the interest of investors to permit them to conduct principal trades with their advisory clients involving these securities, even where they or their affiliates are underwriters. Those firms argue that clients may face difficulties and higher costs in obtaining these debt instruments, particularly municipal bonds, through an advisory account if the adviser is not permitted to rely on the interim final rule's alternative means of complying with section 206(3).

The limitation on issuer transactions makes the rule unavailable for principal transactions in traditional equity or debt offerings of the investment adviser or a control person of the adviser. It also makes the rule unavailable in connection with – and thus requires compliance with section 206(3)'s trade-by-trade written disclosure requirements before – non-discretionary placement by an adviser of a proprietary structured product, such as a structured note, with an advisory client.[37] We request comment on whether we

[37] There is no uniform definition of what constitutes a structured product and the term is not defined in the temporary rule. Structured products include, among other things, securitizations of pools of assets, such as asset-backed securities which are supported by a discrete pool of financial assets (*e.g.*, mortgages or other receivables). *See generally* Securities Act Release No. 8518 (Dec. 22, 2004) [70 FR 1506 (Jan. 7, 2005)]. The Financial Industry Regulatory Authority, Inc. ("FINRA"), the self-regulatory organization that oversees broker-dealers, defines structured products as "securities derived from or based on a single security, a basket of securities, an index, a commodity, a debt issuance and/or a foreign currency." FINRA Notice to Members 05-59 (Sept. 2005). FINRA has notified its members that they should consider only recommending structured products to customers who have been approved for options trading. *Id.* at 4. *See also* FINRA Notice to Members 03-71 (Nov. 2003) (expressing concern that investors, particularly retail investors, may not fully understand the risks associated with non-conventional investments – such as structured securities – and cautioning members

should consider expanding the availability of the rule to apply to structured products, and if so, on what terms.

We also request comment on our exclusion for securities issued or underwritten by the adviser or its control persons. Do commenters agree with our assessment of the risks to clients and our interpretation of the purposes of section 206(3)? Should we consider making the rule available for principal transactions in all securities (including those issued or subject to an underwriting by the adviser or a control person) in light of the clients' interest in obtaining access to public offerings? Alternatively, is there an approach we might take that could distinguish types of underwriting arrangements that do not present unacceptable risks of conflicts for the adviser? In this regard, we request comment on the one exception we have provided for non-convertible investment grade debt securities. Is the exception appropriate under the circumstances? Are there other circumstances in which an adviser should be able to rely on the rule when it (or a control person) is an issuer or underwriter of securities in certain circumstances?

3. Written Prospective Consent Following Written Disclosure

An adviser may rely on rule 206(3)-3T only after having secured its client's written, revocable consent prospectively authorizing the adviser directly or indirectly acting as principal for its own account, to sell any security to or purchase any security from such client.[38] The consent must be obtained only after the adviser provides the client with written disclosure about: (i) the circumstances under which the investment adviser may engage in principal transactions with the client; (ii) the nature and

to ensure that their sales conduct procedures fully and accurately address any of the special circumstances presented by the sale of these products).

[38] Rule 206(3)-3T(a)(3).

significance of the conflicts the investment adviser has with its clients' interests as a result of those transactions; and (iii) how the investment adviser addresses those conflicts.[39] We anticipate that this consent normally would be obtained by the adviser when the client establishes the advisory account.[40]

Rule 206(3)-3T is not exclusive. An adviser would still be able to effect principal trades with a client who either never grants the prospective consent required under paragraph (a)(3) of the rule 206(3)-3T, or subsequently revokes that consent after having granted it, so long as the adviser complies with the terms of section 206(3) of the Act.

Will the disclosure required by paragraph (a)(3) be meaningful for clients in understanding the conflicts and risks inherent in principal trading by a fiduciary counterparty? Are there alternative approaches that we could adopt to make the prospective disclosures more meaningful to clients? Should we require disclosure to be prominent or, alternatively, require disclosure in a separately executed document to assure that the client has separately given attention to the request for consent?

With each written disclosure, confirmation, and request for written prospective consent, the investment adviser must include a conspicuous, plain English statement clarifying that the prospective general consent may be revoked at any time.[41] Thus, the client must be able to revoke his or her prospective consent at any time, thereby preventing an adviser from relying on rule 206(3)-3T with respect to that account going

[39] The FPA recommended a similar condition. *See* FPA Letter, at 3.

[40] No additional disclosure regarding the principal capacity in which the adviser may be acting need be made pursuant to rule 206(3)-3T(a)(3) at the time of the transaction, provided the disclosure required by paragraph (a)(3) of the rule has been made and is correct in all material respects.

[41] Rule 206(3)-3T(a)(8). The FPA recommended a similar condition. *See* FPA Letter, at 4.

forward.[42] Do these provisions adequately ensure that client consent is voluntary? Will advisers make a client's consent a condition to participation in non-discretionary advisory accounts they offer? If so, should we add a provision to the rule to address this issue, such as prohibiting advisers from doing so?

The written prospective consent need only be executed once. Should we require that the client's consent be renewed periodically? What benefit would be gained by such a provision in light of the client's right to revoke his or her consent at any time?

4. Trade-by-Trade Consent Following Disclosure

The temporary rule requires an investment adviser, before the execution of *each* principal transaction, to: (i) inform the client of the capacity in which the adviser may act with respect to the transaction; and (ii) obtain consent from the client for the investment adviser to act as principal for its own account with respect to each such transaction.[43] The trade-by-trade disclosure and consent may be written or oral. Although representatives of the brokerage industry have requested that we eliminate the requirement for transaction-by-transaction disclosure and consent,[44] we have determined that such disclosure and consent continues to be important to alert clients to the potential for conflicted advice they may be receiving on individual transactions. In light of the conflicts inherent in these transactions, generally notifying the client that a transaction may be effected on a principal basis close in time to the carrying out of such a trade is appropriate.

[42] The right to revoke prospective consent is not intended to allow a client to rescind, after execution but prior to settlement, a particular trade to which the client provided specific consent prior to execution.

[43] Rule 206(3)-3T(a)(4).

[44] SIFMA Letter, at 3.

Given the frequency and speed of trading in some advisory accounts as well as the increasing complexity of securities products available in the marketplace, trade-by-trade disclosure and consent, even if oral, might be a more effective protection against misunderstanding by advisory clients of the nature of a transaction and the conflicts inherent in it as well as a meaningful safeguard for investment advisers seeking to comply with their fiduciary obligations. We understand, however, that in many instances the adviser may not know whether a particular transaction will be effected on a principal basis. Accordingly, the rule permits advisers to disclose to clients that they "may" act in a principal capacity with respect to the transaction.

We do not believe the obligation to make oral disclosure will impose a significant burden on investment advisers of non-discretionary accounts who must, in most cases, obtain consent for each transaction regardless of whether the transaction will be done on a principal basis.[45] We are interested in learning from investors whether this consent requirement is informative and helpful. We also are interested in learning from advisers whether they intend to document receipt of the oral consent and, if so, whether they will be able to do so efficiently.

We request comment regarding whether investment advisers find useful the flexibility to provide oral instead of written disclosure on a trade-by-trade basis. Or, will advisers instead view the relief as unworkable?

5. Written Confirmation

The investment adviser must send to each client with which it effects a principal trade pursuant to rule 206(3)-3T a written confirmation, at or before the completion of the

[45] *See* rule 206(3)-3T(a)(1) (limiting the availability of the rule to accounts over which the adviser does not exercise discretionary authority).

transaction.[46] In addition to the other information required to be in a confirmation by Exchange Act rule 10b-10,[47] the confirmation must include a conspicuous, plain English statement informing the advisory client that the adviser disclosed to the client prior to the execution of the transaction that the adviser may act in a principal capacity in connection with the transaction, that the client authorized the transaction, and that the adviser sold the security to or bought the security from the client for its own account.[48] An investment adviser need not send a duplicate confirmation. An adviser may satisfy its obligations under paragraph (a)(5) by including, or causing an affiliated broker-dealer to include, the additional required disclosure on a confirmation otherwise sent to the client with respect to a particular principal transaction.

The requirement to provide a trade-by-trade confirmation is designed to ensure that clients are given a written notice and reminder of each transaction that the investment adviser effects on a principal basis and that conflicts of interest are inherent in such transactions.[49] We request comment on our written confirmation condition. Is there additional information that should be included in the confirmation? Are there circumstances in which commenters believe it is appropriate for us to permit investment advisers to rely on rule 206(3)-3T and also deliver confirmations to clients pursuant to the alternative periodic reporting provisions of rule 10b-10(b)?

[46] For a discussion of the meaning of "completion" of the transaction, see Section 206(3) Release. The temporary rule does not permit advisers to deliver confirmations using the alternative periodic reporting provisions of rule 10b-10(b) under the Exchange Act.

[47] 17 CFR 240.10b-10.

[48] Rule 206(3)-3T(a)(5).

[49] Rule 206(3)-2 under the Advisers Act, our agency cross transaction rule, requires similar confirmation disclosure.

6. Annual Summary Statement

The investment adviser must deliver to each client, no less frequently than once a year, written disclosure containing a list of all transactions that were executed in the account in reliance on rule 206(3)-3T, including the date and price of such transactions.[50] The annual summary statement is designed to ensure that clients receive a periodic record of the principal trading activity in their accounts and are afforded an opportunity to assess the frequency with which their adviser engages in such trades. As with each other disclosure required pursuant to rule 206(3)-3T, to be able to rely on the rule the investment adviser must include a conspicuous, plain English statement that its client's written prospective consent may be revoked at any time.[51]

We request comment generally on this aspect of the interim final rule. Should a summary statement be provided more or less frequently than annually? Is there additional information that we should require to be included in each summary statement? For example, we are not requiring advisers to disclose in an annual statement the total amount of all commissions or other remuneration they receive in connection with transactions with respect to which they are relying on this rule. Although that disclosure is required with respect to agency cross transactions pursuant to rule 206(3)-2(a)(3), we are concerned that disclosure of such amounts for principal trades may not accurately reflect the actual economic benefit to the adviser with respect to those trades or the consequence to the client for consenting to those trades. Are our concerns justified? Commenters are invited to submit suggestions for possible enhancements to the

[50] Rule 206(3)-3T(a)(6). Rule 206(3)-2(a)(3) contains a similar annual report requirement with respect to agency cross transactions. In addition, the FPA recommended a similar condition. *See* FPA Letter, at 4.

disclosures in annual statements that could enhance the disclosure to clients of the significance of their consenting to principal trades.

7. Advisory Account Must be a Brokerage Account

Rule 206(3)-3T is only available to an investment adviser that also is registered with us as a broker-dealer. Each account for which the investment adviser relies on this section must be a brokerage account subject to the Exchange Act, the rules thereunder, and the rules of applicable self-regulatory organizations (*e.g.*, FINRA).[52] The rule therefore requires that the protections of both the Advisers Act and the Exchange Act apply when advisers enter into principal transactions with clients in reliance on the rule.

The temporary rule permits, subject to compliance with the rule's conditions, an adviser that also is registered as a broker-dealer to execute a principal trade directly (out of its own account) or indirectly (out of an account of another person who is a control person of the adviser). Because we have decided to apply the rule only to advisers who also are registered as broker-dealers, an adviser who is not also a registered broker-dealer would be unable to rely on rule 206(3)-3T if it causes a client to enter into a principal trade with a control person, even if that control person is a registered broker-dealer.

Our decision not to extend the rule to advisory accounts that are held only at investment advisers, as opposed to entities that are both investment advisers and broker dealers, is based on several considerations. First, firms that are both broker-dealers and investment advisers and their employees must comply with the comprehensive set of Commission and self-regulatory organization sales practice and best execution rules that apply to the relationship between a broker-dealer and its customer in addition to the

[51] Rule 206(3)-3T(a)(8).

fiduciary duties an adviser owes a client. We believe that it is important to maintain the application of the laws and rules regarding broker-dealers to these accounts.[53] Second, as a practical matter, advisory clients most frequently need and desire principal trading services from firms that are dually registered as an adviser and a broker-dealer because they generally carry large inventories of securities. Providing a variation in the method of complying with section 206(3) of the Advisers Act for advisers that also are registered as broker-dealers thus addresses a large category of the situations in which clients are likely to benefit from access to the inventory of the adviser/broker-dealer without sacrificing pricing or other sales practice protections.

We request comment on this aspect of the interim final rule. What will be the benefit to customers of maintaining the sales practice rules of self-regulatory organizations? What will be the impact of the rule on advisers that are not themselves registered as broker-dealers? Would they choose to register as a broker-dealer in order to take advantage of the new rule? Are there particular requirements of broker-dealer regulation that are clearly duplicative or clearly inapplicable to the regulation of investment advisers and so are unnecessary in this context?

8. Other Obligations Unaffected

Rule 206(3)-3T(b) clarifies that the temporary rule does not relieve in any way an investment adviser from its obligation to act in the best interests of each of its advisory clients, including fulfilling the duty with respect to the best price and execution for a

52 Rule 206(3)-3T(a)(7).

53 We note that fee-based brokerage accounts have been subject to Commission and self-regulatory organization sales practice and best execution rules since their inception.

particular transaction.[54] Compliance with rule 206(3)-3T also does not relieve an investment adviser from its fiduciary obligation imposed by sections 206(1) or (2) of the Advisers Act or by other applicable provisions of federal law.[55]

We note specifically that an adviser engaging in principal transactions is subject to rule 206(4)-7, which, among other things, requires an investment adviser registered with us to adopt and implement written policies and procedures reasonably designed to prevent violations of the Advisers Act (and the rules thereunder) by the adviser or any of its supervised persons.[56] Thus, an adviser relying on rule 206(3)-3T as an alternative means of complying with section 206(3) must have adopted and implemented written policies and procedures reasonably designed to comply with the requirements of the rule. In addition, rule 204-2,[57] as well as Exchange Act rules 17a-3[58] and 17a-4,[59] requires the adviser to make, keep, and retain records relating to the principal trades the adviser effects.

54 Rule 206(3)-2(e) contains a similar provision.

55 Section 206(3) Release. *See also* SIFMA Memo at Exhibit page 23 (noting that, in connection with any relief provided under section 206(3), "[t]he adviser will continue to act in the best interests of the client, including a duty to provide best execution, and will be required to meet all disclosure obligations imposed by Sections 206(1) and (2) of the Advisers Act and by other applicable provisions of the federal securities laws and rules of SROs"); section 406 of the Employee Retirement Income Security Act of 1974 ("ERISA") (describing "prohibited transactions" of fiduciaries subject to ERISA); section 4975(c)(1) of the Internal Revenue Code (the "Code") (describing "prohibited transactions" of fiduciaries governed by the Code).

56 Rule 206(4)-7(a) [17 CFR 275.206(4)-7(a)].

57 17 CFR 275.204-2.

58 17 CFR 240.17a-3.

59 17 CFR 240.17a-4.

9. Limited Duration of Relief

Rule 206(3)-3T(d) contains a sunset provision. Absent further action by the Commission, the temporary rule will expire on December 31, 2009, which is about 27 months from its effective date.[60] Setting a termination date for the rule will necessitate further Commission action no later than the end of that period if the Commission intends to continue the same or similar relief.

We believe limiting the duration of the rule will give us an opportunity to observe how firms comply with their disclosure obligations under the rule, and whether, when they conduct principal trades with their clients, they put their clients' interests first. A significantly shorter period than the one we have established, however, may have disadvantaged former fee-based brokerage customers because of the uncertainty about the continuation of access through their advisory accounts to the securities in the inventory of their brokerage firm. Those customers also could have faced renewed disruption and confusion if the rule on principal trades were abolished or substantially modified in the short term. Similarly, broker-dealers would have faced the same uncertainty about the continuation of the rule, which could have caused some broker-dealers to decide not to make the necessary expenditures and investments to offer advisory accounts with access to principal trades.

We request comment on whether the 27-month time frame is appropriate. We also welcome comment on any other aspects of the rule that commenters believe should be modified.

[60] The FPA recommended a similar condition. *See* FPA Letter, at 2.

10. Other Matters

This rulemaking action must be: (i) necessary or appropriate in the public interest; (ii) consistent with the protection of investors; and (iii) consistent with the purposes fairly intended by the policy and provisions of the Advisers Act.[61] We also need to consider the effect of the rule on competition, efficiency, and capital formation, which we address below in Section VII of this Release. For the reasons described in this Release, we believe that the rule is necessary or appropriate in the public interest and consistent with the protection of investors. We also believe that the temporary rule is consistent with the purposes fairly intended by the policy and provisions of the Advisers Act.

In the *FPA* decision, the Court described the purposes of the Act, emphasizing that the "overall statutory scheme of the [Advisers Act] addresses the problems identified to Congress in two principal ways: First, by establishing a federal fiduciary standard to govern the conduct of investment advisers, broadly defined, . . . and second, by requiring full disclosure of all conflicts of interest."[62] The Congressional intent was to eliminate or expose all conflicts of interest that might incline an investment adviser, consciously or unconsciously, to render advice that was not disinterested.[63] The Court further noted that Congress's purpose in enacting the Advisers Act was to establish fiduciary standards and require full disclosure of all conflicts of interests of investment advisers.[64]

The temporary rule adopted today meets those purposes and adheres closely to the text of section 206(3), which reflects the basic conflict disclosure purposes of the Act.

[61] *See* 15 U.S.C. 80b-6a.

[62] *FPA* decision, at 490.

[63] *Id.*

[64] *Id.*

That section provides that an adviser, before engaging in a principal trade with an advisory client, must disclose to the client in writing before completion of the transaction the capacity in which the adviser is acting and must obtain the consent of the client to the transaction. As we have stated before, "[i]n adopting Section 206(3), Congress recognized the potential for [abuses such as price manipulation or the placing of unwanted securities into client accounts], but did not prohibit advisers entirely from engaging in all principal and agency transactions with clients. Rather, Congress chose to address these particular conflicts of interest by imposing a disclosure and client consent requirement in Section 206(3) of the Advisers Act."[65]

The temporary rule complies with Congressional intent. It provides an alternative procedural means of complying with section 206(3) that retains transaction-by-transaction disclosure and consent (as required by section 206(3) of the Act), but adds additional investor protections measures by requiring an adviser:

- at the outset of the relationship with the client, to disclose in writing the circumstances under which the investment adviser directly or indirectly may engage in principal transactions, the nature and significance of conflicts with its client's interests as a result of the transactions, and how the investment adviser addresses those conflicts;
- to obtain prospective written consent of the client in response to that initial disclosure;
- before each transaction, to inform the advisory client, orally or in writing, that the adviser may act in a principal capacity with respect to the transaction and

[65] Section 206(3) Release at text accompanying note 5.

to obtain the consent from the advisory client, orally or in writing, for the transaction;

- to send to the client, at or before completion of the transaction, a written trade confirmation that, in addition to the information required by rule 10b-10 under the Exchange Act, discloses that the adviser informed the client prior to the execution of the transaction that the adviser may be acting in a principal capacity in connection with the transaction, that the client authorized the transaction, and that the adviser sold the security to, or bought the security from, the client for its own account;
- to send to the advisory client an annual statement listing each principal transaction during the preceding year and the date and price of each such transaction; and
- to acknowledge explicitly in each required disclosure the right of the client to revoke his or her prospective consent at any time.

We believe that these transaction-specific steps, taken together, fulfill the Congressional purpose behind section 206(3) of the Act.

Another significant protection is that, as we discuss in Section II.B.7 above, to benefit from the rule, the investment adviser must also be a broker-dealer registered with us. Therefore, the firm must comply with the comprehensive set of Commission and self-regulatory organization sales practice and best execution rules that apply to the relationship between a broker-dealer and customer in addition to the fiduciary duties an adviser owes a client.

We further believe that the temporary nature of the rule will give us an opportunity to observe how firms comply with their obligations, and whether, when they conduct principal trades with their clients, they put their clients' interests first. The rule therefore employs a range of features to achieve the transaction-by-transaction conflict disclosure and consent purposes and policies of the Advisers Act. The rule additionally enables the adviser to discharge its fiduciary duties by bolstering them with broker-dealer responsibilities.

11. Effective Date

This temporary rule takes effect on September 30, 2007. For several reasons, including those discussed above, we have acted on an interim final basis.

In the time since the *FPA* decision, the Commission staff has had numerous communications with affected customers, broker-dealers, and investment advisers about areas in which Commission action or relief might be required to protect the interests of investors as a result of the Court's decision. One area of significance identified as our deliberative process continued was the area of principal trades. Under the rule vacated in the *FPA* decision, principal trades in fee-based brokerage accounts were not subject to section 206(3) of the Act. Through the process of discussions with interested parties, it was brought to our attention that a large number of fee-based brokerage customers favor having the choice of advisory accounts with access to the inventory of a diversified broker-dealer and that for certain customers the access to such securities – many of which would otherwise be unavailable – was a critical component of their investment strategy. We also learned that, as discussed above, the traditional method for complying with the principal trading restrictions on an adviser in section 206(3) – written disclosure and

consent before completion of each securities transaction – made it not feasible for an adviser to engage in principal trading with its clients. The Commission received requests for principal trading relief from firms and the staff engaged in discussions with representatives of investors, financial planners, and broker-dealers about the terms of relief, considered their specific comments, and took those comments into account in developing the temporary rule we are adopting today.

Because of the *FPA* decision and the October 1, 2007 expiration of the stay of the issuance of the Court's mandate to vacate the former rule, investors with fee-based brokerage accounts must now consider whether they should convert their accounts to advisory accounts or to traditional commission-based brokerage accounts. It is not possible for those customers to make a meaningful, well-informed decision if they do not know what services will be offered in advisory accounts. For example, it would be critical to a customer who invests primarily in fixed income securities (which generally are traded by firms on a principal basis) to know whether he or she could continue to access a firm's inventory of those securities (or sell those securities to the firm) in an advisory account. But firms informed us that they would not permit that kind of trading without a rule that is effective and that provides an alternative means of complying with section 206(3) of the Act. Until we could publish a rule for comment, receive and analyze those comments, and adopt a final rule, that customer would be left with the choice between a traditional brokerage account without the ability to pay a fee based on assets – presumably the customer's preferred manner of payment – or a fee-based advisory account without the ability to invest in fixed income products.

Changing accounts and methods of payments can be highly disruptive and confusing to many investors, requiring a series of communications between the investor and one or more firms about the options available to give the investor the information he or she needs to make informed decisions about the services available in each type of account. We believe that it serves such investors' interests best to adopt the rule on an interim final basis, which permits them to continue the same kind of account, with similar services, that they had when they were fee-based brokerage customers.

We are aware that, as a result of the *FPA* decision, the process for converting as many as one million fee-based brokerage accounts to non-discretionary advisory or other accounts requires a great deal of time and imposes significant conversion costs on firms. For example, in order to comply with the October 1 deadline, those firms needed to draft or revise agreements, policies, and other documents, hire and train employees, and make changes to data and record keeping, order entry, billing, and other systems. The firms offering fee-based brokerage accounts urged us to reduce the burdens that apply to them by adopting a rule that is effective on or before October 1 and that permits an alternative method of complying with section 206(3) of the Act (or, alternatively, to exempt them from section 206(3) altogether). They informed us that this would simplify the process of communicating with their customers and reduce investor confusion. This is mostly because the services and manner of payments would be substantially similar in non-discretionary advisory accounts as they were in fee-based brokerage accounts – the firms would not have to explain why the services a customer has become accustomed to are changing, or why the manner of payment is changing.

The firms also were concerned that, without a rule that is effective by the date the *FPA* decision takes effect, fee-based brokerage customers may elect (or the firm may recommend) a commission-based brokerage account in order to have access to their firm's inventory of securities, then elect an advisory account only after a rule subject to notice and comment is finalized. This type of serial account change is costly to firms for the same reasons it is costly for them to convert accounts pursuant to the *FPA* decision. Moreover, such switching of account types can be confusing to customers if it is the firm that is recommending the changes.

Those factors led to this rule and similarly explain why the rule needs to be available at the same time the broker-dealers complete the transition from fee-based brokerage to advisory or other accounts. Otherwise, the risk of disrupting services to the investors, depriving them of the choice of an advisory account with a broker-dealer, and confusing them with a series of changes to the services available to them would have been substantial. Obtaining a further postponement of the stay of the mandate to allow advance notice and comment rulemaking did not appear feasible. For these reasons, issuance of an immediately effective rule is necessary to ameliorate the likely harm to investors.

Furthermore, we emphasize that we are requesting comments on the rule and will carefully consider and respond to them in a subsequent release. Moreover, this is a temporary rule. Setting a 27-month termination date for the rule will necessitate further Commission action no later than the end of that period if the Commission intends to continue the same or similar relief. The sunset provision will result in the Commission assessing the operation of the rule and intervening developments, as well public comment letters, and considering whether to continue the rule with or without modification or not at all.

A significantly shorter period than the 27-month period we have established could have disadvantaged investors. They would have faced uncertainty about the continuation of having access through their advisory accounts to the securities in the inventory of their brokerage firm and could have faced renewed disruption and confusion if the rule on principal trades were abolished or substantially modified in the short term. Similarly, broker-dealers would have faced the same uncertainty about the continuation of the rule, which could have caused some broker-dealers to decide not to make the necessary expenditures and investments to offer advisory accounts with access to principal trades.

As a result, the Commission finds that it has good cause to have the rule take effect on September 30, 2007, and that notice and public procedure in advance of the effectiveness of the rule are impracticable, unnecessary, and contrary to the public interest. In addition, the rule in part has interpretive aspects and is a rule that recognizes an exemption and relieves a restriction.

III. REQUEST FOR COMMENTS

The Commission is requesting comments from all members of the public during the next 60 days. We will carefully consider the comments that we receive and respond to them in a subsequent release.

In addition, we are awaiting a report being prepared by RAND Corporation comparing how the different regulatory systems that apply to broker-dealers and advisers affect investors (the "RAND Study"). As we have previously announced, the Commission commissioned a study comparing the levels of protection afforded

customers of broker-dealers and investment advisers under the federal securities laws.[66] The Commission will have another opportunity to assess the operation and terms of the rule when it receives the results of the RAND Study comparing how the different regulatory systems that apply to broker-dealers and advisers affect investors. The RAND Study is expected to be delivered to the Commission no later than December 2007, several months ahead of schedule. The results of the RAND Study are expected to provide an important empirical foundation for the Commission to consider what action to take to improve the way investment advisers and broker-dealers provide financial services to customers. One option then available to the Commission will be making the RAND Study results available to the public and seeking comments on them and their bearing on the terms of this rule.

IV. TRANSITION GUIDANCE

We are today providing guidance to assist broker-dealers who have offered fee-based brokerage accounts and are seeking the consent of their clients to convert those accounts to advisory accounts and meet the requirements of this rule by October 1, 2007.

A. Client Consent

Broker-dealers have asked whether they must, before October 1, 2007, obtain written consent from each of their fee-based brokerage customers to enter into an advisory agreement that meets the requirements of the Advisers Act, in particular section 205 of the Act. Broker-dealers have informed us that, as a practical matter, it is not feasible for them to do so and, if written consent is required, many fee-based brokerage

[66] *Commission Seeks Time for Investors and Brokers to Respond to Court Decision on Fee-Based Accounts*, SEC Press Release No. 2007-95 (May 14, 2007).

customers will experience interrupted service or will be placed in traditional commission-based brokerage accounts, which may not be best for them.

Interim final rule 206(3)-3T(a)(3) requires an adviser wishing to rely on the rule's alternative means for complying with section 206(3) of the Act to obtain a written prospective consent from each client authorizing the investment adviser to engage in principal transactions with the client. We understand that it likely will be impossible for advisers to obtain these written consents from fee-based brokerage customers who convert their accounts to non-discretionary advisory accounts prior to October 1, 2007. To make the alternative means provided in the interim final rule useful immediately upon its effective date to those customers, we will not object if an adviser obtains the required written consent no later than January 1, 2008 from each fee-based customer who converts his or her account to a non-discretionary advisory account. During this transitional period, investment advisers must comply with the other conditions of rule 206(3)-3T, including the condition in paragraph (a)(4) of the rule, which requires that the adviser make certain disclosures and obtain client consent before effecting a principal trade with the client. They also must provide a client with the written disclosure required by paragraph (a)(3) of the temporary rule prior to effecting the first trade with that client in reliance on this rule.

B. Client Brochures

Advisers Act rule 204-3 requires an investment adviser to furnish its advisory clients with a disclosure statement, or brochure, containing at least the information required to be in Part II of Form ADV at the time of, or prior to, entering into an advisory

contract.[67] In light of the time constraints firms face in complying with the October 1st deadline, we will not object if, with respect to the fee-based brokerage customers that convert to non-discretionary advisory accounts, advisers deliver this statement no later than January 1, 2008.

V. PAPERWORK REDUCTION ACT

A. Background

Rule 206(3)-3T contains "collection of information" requirements within the meaning of the Paperwork Reduction Act of 1995.[68] The collection of information is new. We submitted these requirements to the Office of Management and Budget ("OMB") for review in accordance with 44 U.S.C. 3507(j) and 5 CFR 1320.13. Separately, we have submitted the collection of information to OMB for review and approval in accordance with 44 U.S.C. 3507(d) and 5 CFR 1320.11. The OMB has approved the collection of information on an emergency basis with an expiration date of March 31 , 2008. An agency may not conduct or sponsor, and a person is not required to respond to, a collection of information unless it displays a currently valid OMB control number. The title for the collection of information is: "Temporary rule for principal trades with certain advisory clients, rule 206(3)-3T" and the OMB control number for the collection of information is 3235-0630.

---

[67] The Advisers Act does not specify any means by which a client must execute a new advisory contract or agree to changes in an existing one. For purposes of transitioning clients from fee-based brokerage accounts, advisers presumably must look to the terms of the contracts they have in place, as well as applicable contract law, to determine the manner in which they need to enter into new contract or amend existing contracts in order to come into compliance with the Act.

[68] 44 U.S.C. 3501 *et seq.*

Rule 206(3)-3T provides an alternative method for investment advisers that are registered with us as broker-dealers to meet the requirements of section 206(3) when they act in a principal capacity with respect to transactions with certain of their advisory clients. In the absence of this rule, an adviser must provide a written disclosure and obtain consent for each transaction in which the adviser acts in a principal capacity. Rule 206(3)-3T permits an adviser, with respect to a non-discretionary advisory account, to comply with section 206(3) by: (i) making certain written disclosures; (ii) obtaining written, revocable consent from the client prospectively authorizing the adviser to enter into principal trades; (iii) making oral or written disclosure that the adviser may act in a principal capacity and obtaining the client's consent orally or in writing prior to the execution of each principal transaction; (iv) sending to the client confirmation statements disclosing the capacity in which the adviser has acted and indicating that the adviser disclosed to the client that it may act in a principal capacity and that the client authorized the transaction; and (v) delivering to the client an annual report itemizing the principal transactions.

B. Collections of Information and Associated Burdens

Under rule 206(3)-3T, there are four distinct collection burdens. Our estimate of the burden of each of the collections reflects the fact that the alternative means of compliance provided by the rule is substantially similar to the approach advisers currently employ to comply with the disclosure and consent obligations of section 206(3) of the Advisers Act and the approach that broker-dealers employ to comply with the confirmation requirements of rule 10b-10 under the Exchange Act. Thus, as discussed below, we estimate that rule 206(3)-3T will impose only small additional burdens.

Providing the information required by rule 206(3)-3T is necessary to obtain the benefit of the alternative means of complying with section 206(3) of the Advisers Act. The rule contains two types of collections of information: information provided by an adviser to its advisory clients and information collected from advisory clients by an adviser. With respect to each type of collection, the information would be maintained by the adviser. Under Advisers Act rule 204-2(e), an adviser must preserve for five years the records required by the collection of information pursuant to rule 206(3)-3T. Although the rule does not call for any of the information collected to be provided to us, to the extent advisers include any of the information required by the rule in a filing, such as Form ADV, the information will not be kept confidential. The collection of information delivered by investment advisers pursuant to rule 206(3)-3T would be provided to clients and also would be maintained by investment advisers. The collection of information delivered by clients to advisers would be subject to the confidentiality strictures that govern those relationships, and we would expect them to be confidential communications.

Collections of Information

Prospective Disclosure and Consent: Pursuant to paragraph (a)(3) of the rule, an investment adviser must provide written, prospective disclosure to the client explaining: (i) the circumstances under which the investment adviser directly or indirectly may engage in principal transactions; (ii) the nature and significance of conflicts with its client's interests as a result of the transactions; and (iii) how the investment adviser addresses those conflicts. Pursuant to paragraph (a)(8) of the rule, the written, prospective disclosure must include a conspicuous, plain English statement that a client's written, prospective consent may be revoked without penalty at any time by written notice to the investment adviser from the client. And, for the adviser to be able to rely on rule 206(3)-3T with respect to an account, the client must have executed a written, revocable consent after receiving such written, prospective disclosure.

The first part of this collection of information involves the preparation and distribution of a written disclosure statement, which we anticipate will be largely uniform for clients in non-discretionary advisory accounts with a particular firm. This collection of information is necessary to explain to investors how their interests might be different from the interests of their investment adviser when the adviser engages in principal trades with them. It is designed to provide investors with sufficient information to be able to decide whether to consent to such trades.

We anticipate that the cost of this collection will mostly be borne upfront as advisers develop and deliver the required disclosure. This will require drafting and distributing the required disclosure to clients with respect to the accounts for which the investment adviser seeks to rely on the rule.[69] Once the disclosure has been developed and is integrated into materials provided upon opening a non-discretionary advisory account, the ongoing burden will be minimal.

We estimate that the average burden for drafting the required prospective disclosure for each eligible adviser, taking into account both those advisers that previously engaged in principal trades with their non-discretionary advisory clients, will be approximately 5 hours on average. We expect that some advisers, particularly the

[69] We note that disclosure about the conflicts of interest for an adviser that engages in principal trades already is required to be disclosed by investment advisers in Form ADV. *See* Item 8 of Part 1A of Form ADV; Item 9 of Part II of Form ADV; Item 7(l) of Schedule H to Part II of Form ADV.

large financial services firms, may take significantly longer to draft the required disclosure because they may have more principal trading practices, and potentially more conflicts, to describe.[70] Other advisers may take significantly less time and some eligible advisers may choose not to rely on rule 206(3)-3T. Further, we expect the drafting burden will be uniform with respect to each eligible adviser regardless of how many individual non-discretionary advisory accounts that adviser administers or seeks to engage with in principal trading. As of August 1, 2007, there were 634 advisers that were eligible to rely on the temporary rule (*i.e.*, also registered as broker-dealers), 395 of which indicate that they have non-discretionary advisory accounts.[71] We estimate that 90 percent of those 395 advisers, or a total of 356 of those advisers, will rely on this rule.[72] Of the 239 eligible advisers that do not currently provide non-discretionary advisory services, we estimate that 10 percent of these advisers, or 24 advisers, will create non-discretionary advisory programs and rely on the alternative means of compliance provided by this rule.[73] Thus, the total number of advisers we anticipate will rely on the

[70] The opportunities to engage in principal trades with advisory clients will vary greatly among eligible investment advisers. We believe many of these advisers are registered as broker-dealers for limited purposes and do not engage in market-making activities or otherwise carry extensive inventories of securities. These firms likely would limit their principal trading operations significantly. For example, they may choose to engage only in riskless principal trades, which may pose limited conflicts of interest resulting in brief disclosures. Investment advisers with large inventories of securities and multi-faceted operations, however, likely will have much more extensive disclosure.

[71] IARD data as of August 1, 2007, for Items 6.A(1) and 5.F(2)(e) of Part 1A of Form ADV.

[72] We anticipate that most dually-registered advisers will make use of the rule to engage in, at a minimum, riskless principal transactions to limit the need for these advisers to process trades for their advisory clients with other broker-dealers. We estimate that 10% of these firms will determine that the costs involved to comply with the rule are too significant in relation to the benefits that the adviser, and their clients, will enjoy.

[73] We estimate that 10% of the dually-registered advisers that do not currently have non-discretionary advisory programs will create them due to a combination of market forces

rule is 380.[74] Accordingly, we estimate that the total drafting burden for the prospective disclosure statement for the estimated 380 advisers that will rely on the rule will be 1,900 hours.[75]

The prospective disclosure will need to be distributed to all clients who have non-discretionary advisory accounts for which an adviser seeks to rely on rule 206(3)-3T. Registration data indicates that there are approximately 3,270,000 existing non-discretionary advisory accounts held with eligible advisers.[76] Discussions with eligible advisers indicate that approximately: (i) 90 percent of these non-discretionary advisory accounts administered by them, or 2,943,000 accounts, are in programs to which the rule will not apply, such as mutual fund asset allocation programs; and (ii) 40 percent of the remaining 327,000 non-discretionary advisory accounts administered by them, or 130,800 accounts, are retirement accounts, and thus unlikely to participate in principal trading,[77] leaving 196,200 existing non-retirement non-discretionary advisory accounts administered by eligible advisers.[78]

---

and the ability to enter into principal trades more efficiently as a result of the rule. We base this estimate on discussions with industry representatives.

74 356 dually-registered advisers that currently have non-discretionary advisory account programs + 24 dually-registered advisers that do not currently have non-discretionary advisory programs, but we expect will initiate them = 380 eligible advisers that will have non-discretionary advisory programs.

75 5 hours per adviser x 380 eligible advisers that will rely on the rule = 1,900 total hours.

76 IARD data as of August 1, 2007, for Item 5.F(2)(e) of Part 1A of Form ADV.

77 We have based this estimate on discussions with industry representatives. The Code and ERISA impose restrictions on certain types of transactions involving certain retirement accounts. We do not take a position on whether the Code or ERISA limits the availability of rule 206(3)-3T.

78 3,270,000 existing non-discretionary advisory accounts among eligible advisers – 2,943,000 accounts in wrap fee and other programs to which the rule will not apply – 130,800 retirement accounts = 196,200 non-retirement, non-discretionary advisory accounts among eligible advisers.

As noted in Section I.B of this Release and confirmed by discussions with several firms, we anticipate that most fee-based brokerage accounts will be converted to non-discretionary advisory accounts. For purposes of our analysis, we have assumed that all of the estimated 1 million fee-based brokerage accounts will be converted to non-discretionary advisory accounts.[79] Of those accounts, we estimate that substantially all of them are held at investment advisers that also are registered as broker-dealers.[80] Discussion with broker-dealers that have fee-based brokerage programs have informed us that approximately 40 percent of the existing fee-based brokerage accounts are retirement accounts, and are unlikely to engage in principal trading. We anticipate that all eligible advisers that are converting fee-based brokerage accounts to non-discretionary advisory accounts will conduct principal trading in reliance on the rule. Thus, we estimate that eligible investment advisers will distribute the prospective disclosure to approximately 600,000 former fee-based brokerage customers. When aggregated with the 196,200 existing non-retirement, non-discretionary advisory accounts we believe likely will receive the prospective disclosure, we estimate the total number of accounts for which clients will receive prospective disclosure to be 796,200.[81]

We estimate that the burden for administering the distribution of the prospective disclosure will be approximately 0.1 hours (six minutes) for every account. Based on the

---

79 This assumption may result in the estimated paperwork burdens and costs of proposed rule 206(3)-3T being overstated.

80 Industry representatives have informed us that substantially all fee-based brokerage accounts are held with twelve broker-dealers, all of which also are registered as investment advisers according to IARD data as of August 1, 2007.

81 196,200 existing non-retirement, non-discretionary advisory accounts we estimate are likely to receive prospective disclosures + 600,000 fee-based brokerage accounts we estimate will be converted to non-discretionary advisory accounts = 796,200 total

discussion above, we estimate that the prospective disclosure will be distributed to a total of approximately 796,200 eligible existing non-discretionary advisory accounts and eligible former fee-based brokerage accounts. We estimate the total hour burden under paragraph (a)(3) of rule 206(3)-3T for distribution of the prospective written disclosure to be 79,620 hours.[82]

We estimate an average one-time cost of preparation of the prospective disclosure to include outside legal fees for approximately three hours of review to total $1,200 per eligible adviser on average,[83] for a total of $456,000.[84] As we discuss above, advisers that rely on the rule will face widely varying numbers and severity of conflicts of interest with their clients. We believe that those advisers that engage in riskless principal trading, are unlikely to seek outside legal services in drafting the prospective disclosure. On the other hand, advisers with more significant conflicts are likely to engage outside legal services to assist in preparation of the prospective written disclosure. We also estimate a one-time average cost for printing and physical distribution of the various disclosure documents, including a disclosure and consent form and, if necessary, a revised account agreement, to be approximately $1.50 per account,[85] for a total of $1,194,300.[86]

accounts we expect to receive the prospective disclosure addressed in paragraph (a)(3) of rule 206(3)-3T.

82 0.1 hours (six minutes) per account x 796,200 accounts = 79,620 hours.

83 Outside legal fees are in addition to the projected 5 hour per adviser burden discussed in note 75 and accompanying text.

84 $400 per hour for legal services x 3 hours per adviser x 380 eligible advisers that we expect to rely on the rule = $456,000. The hourly cost estimate is based on our consultation with advisers and law firms who regularly assist them in compliance matters.

85 This estimate is based on discussions with firms. It represents our estimate of the average cost for printing and distribution, which we expect will include distribution of hard copies for approximately 85% of accounts and distribution of electronic copies for approximately 15% of accounts.

The second part of this burden is that the adviser must receive from each client an executed written, revocable consent prospectively authorizing the investment adviser, or a broker-dealer affiliate of the adviser, to act as principal for its own account, to sell any security to or purchase any security from the advisory client. This collection of information is necessary to verify that a client has provided the required prospective consent. It is designed to ensure that advisers that wish to engage in principal trades with their clients in reliance on the rule inform their clients that they have a right not to consent to such transactions.

Compliance with this part of the temporary rule will require advisers to collect executed written, prospective consent from advisory clients. We anticipate that the bulk of the burden of this collection will be borne upfront. We expect that the consent solicitation for existing non-discretionary advisory accounts and fee-based brokerage accounts being converted to non-discretionary advisory accounts will be integrated into the prospective written disclosure. For new clients, we anticipate that the consent solicitation provision will be included in the account agreement signed by a client upon opening a non-discretionary advisory account. Once the consent solicitation has been integrated into the account-opening paperwork, the ongoing burden will be minimal.

We believe that the burden and costs to advisers of soliciting consent is included in the burdens and costs of drafting and distributing the notices described above. This is because we expect the consent solicitation to be integrated into the firm's prospective written disclosure. We estimate an average burden per accountholder of 0.05 hours (three minutes) in connection with reviewing the consent solicitation, asking questions,

86 $1.50 per account x 796,200 accounts = $1,194,300.

providing consent, and, for those that so wish, revoking that consent at a later date. Assuming that there are 796,200 accountholders who receive prospective disclosure and a prospective consent solicitation we estimate a total burden of 39,810 hours on accountholders for reviewing and/or returning consents.[87] We further estimate that 90 percent of these accountholders, or 716,580 accountholders, will execute and return the consent.[88]

Finally, we estimate that the burden of updating the disclosure, maintaining records on prospective consents provided, and processing consent revocations and prospective consents granted subsequent to the initial solicitation will be approximately 100 hours per eligible adviser per year. We estimate that the total burden for all advisers to keep prospective consent information up to date will be 38,000 hours.[89]

Trade-By-Trade Disclosure and Consent: Pursuant to paragraph (a)(4) of the rule, an investment adviser, prior to the execution of each principal transaction, must inform the advisory client, orally or in writing, of the capacity in which it may act with respect to such transaction. Also pursuant to paragraph (a)(4) of the rule, an investment adviser, prior to the execution of each principal transaction, must obtain oral or written consent from the advisory client to act as principal for its own account with respect to such transaction. This collection of information is necessary to alert an advisory client that a

87 0.05 hours (three minutes) per accountholder x 796,200 accountholders executing and returning the consent = 39,810 total burden hours on accountholders with respect to returning consents.

88 796,200 eligible accountholders x 90 percent = 716,580 accountholders who will return their prospective consents. We refer herein to these 716,580 accountholders who return their consents, and whose advisers are therefore eligible to rely on the rule with respect to them, as "eligible accountholders."

specific trade may be executed as principal and provide the client with the opportunity to withhold its authorization for the trade to be executed on a principal basis.

We note that section 206(3) of the Advisers Act requires written trade-by-trade disclosure in connection with principal trades. We believe that complying with this part of rule 206(3)-3T provides an alternative method of compliance that is likely to be less costly than compliance with section 206(3) in many situations. However, to the extent that advisers are not currently engaging in principal trades with non-discretionary advisory accountholders (and thus are not preparing and providing written disclosure regarding conflicts of interest associated with principal trading in particular securities), advisers electing to rely on the rule will need to begin to prepare such disclosure and communicate it to clients. Based on discussions with industry and their experience with fee-based brokerage accounts and existing non-discretionary advisory programs, we estimate conservatively that non-discretionary advisory accountholders at eligible advisers engage in an average of approximately 50 trades per year and that, for purposes of this analysis, all those trades are principal trades for which the investment adviser seeks to rely on rule 206(3)-3T.[90] We estimate, based on our discussions with broker-dealers, a burden of 0.0083 hours (approximately 30 seconds) per trade on average for preparation and communication of the requisite disclosure to a client, and for the client to consent, for an estimated total burden of approximately 297,381 hours per year.[91]

89 100 hours per eligible adviser x 380 eligible advisers that will rely on the rule = a total burden of 38,000 hours for updating disclosure, maintaining records, and processing new consents and revocations.

90 These assumptions may result in the estimated paperwork burdens and costs of proposed rule 206(3)-3T being overstated.

91 50 trades per account per year x 716,580 accountholders that will provide prospective consent and therefore enable their advisers to rely on the rule with respect to them x

Trade-By-Trade Confirmations: Pursuant to paragraph (a)(5) of the rule, an investment adviser must deliver to its client a written confirmation at or before completion of each principal transaction that includes, in addition to the information required by rule 10b-10 under the Exchange Act [17 CFR 240.10b-10], a conspicuous, plain English statement that the investment adviser: (i) informed the advisory client that it may be acting in a principal capacity in connection with the transaction and the client authorized the transaction; and (ii) owned the security sold to the advisory client (or bought the security from the client for its own account). Pursuant to paragraph (a)(8) of the rule, each confirmation must include a conspicuous, plain English statement that the written, prospective consent described above may be revoked without penalty at any time by written notice to the investment adviser from the client. This collection of information is necessary to ensure that an advisory client is reminded that a particular trade was made on a principal basis and is given the opportunity to revoke prospective consent to such trades.

The majority of the information required in this collection of information is already required to be assembled and communicated to clients pursuant to requirements under the Exchange Act. As such, we do not believe that there will be an ongoing hour burden associated with this requirement. We estimate a one-time cost burden for reprogramming computer systems that generate confirmations to ensure that all the

0.0083 hours (approximately 30 seconds) per trade for disclosure = a burden of 297,381 hours per year.

information required for purposes of paragraphs (a)(5) and (a)(8) of rule 206(3)-3T is included in such confirmations of $20,000 per eligible adviser for a total of $7,600,000.[92]

Principal Transactions Report: Pursuant to paragraph (a)(6) of the rule, the investment adviser must deliver to each client, no less frequently than annually, written disclosure containing a list of all transactions that were executed in the account in reliance upon the rule, and the date and price of such transactions. This report will require a collection of information that should already be available to the adviser or its broker-dealer affiliate executing the client's transactions. Pursuant to paragraph (a)(8) of the rule, each principal transactions report must include a conspicuous, plain English statement that the written, prospective consent described above may be revoked without penalty at any time by written notice to the investment adviser from the client. This collection of information is necessary to ensure that clients receive a periodic record of the principal trading activity in their accounts and are afforded an opportunity to assess the frequency with which their adviser engages in such trades.

We estimate that other than the actual aggregation and delivery of this statement, the burden of this collection will not be substantial because the information required to be contained in the statement is already maintained by investment advisers and/or broker-dealers executing trades for their clients. Advisers and broker-dealers already send periodic or annual statements to clients.[93] Thus, to comply, advisers will need to add

[92] $20,000 to program system generating confirmations per adviser x 380 eligible advisers that will rely on the rule = $7,600,000 total programming costs for confirmations. Our estimate for the cost to program the confirmation system was derived from discussions with broker-dealers.

[93] For example, investment advisers that are qualified custodians for purposes of rule 206(4)-2 under the Advisers Act and that maintain custody of their advisory clients' assets must, at a minimum, send quarterly account statements to their clients pursuant to rule 206(4)-2(a)(3).

information they already maintain to documents they already prepare and send. We expect that there will be a one-time burden associated with this requirement relating to programming computer systems to generate the report, aggregating information that is already available and maintained by advisers or their broker-dealer affiliates. We estimate this burden to be on average approximately 5 hours per eligible firm for a total of 1,900 hours.[94] We also estimate that in addition to the hour burden, firms may have costs associated with retaining outside professionals to assist in programming. We estimate these costs to average $10,000 per adviser for a total upfront cost of $3,800,000.[95] Once computer systems enable these reports to be generated electronically, we estimate that the average ongoing burden of generating the reports and delivering them to clients will be 0.05 hours (three minutes) per eligible non-discretionary advisory account, or a total of 35,829 hours per year.[96]

94 5 hours per eligible adviser for programming relating to the principal trade report x 380 advisers = a total programming burden relating to the principal trade report of 1,900 hours. Advisers that use proprietary systems will likely devote considerably more time to programming reports. However, these advisers are also likely to have already programmed systems to meet the requirements of rule 206(3)-2(a)(3), which contains a similar annual report requirement with respect to agency cross transactions. Other advisers may be using commercial software to track and report trades in accounts. These software packages should take little time for an adviser to implement, and consequently should impose significantly less than a 5 hour burden.

95 $10,000 for retaining outside professionals to assist in programming in connection with the principal transactions report per adviser x 380 advisers = $3,800,000 in outside programming costs in connection with the principal transactions report. We based our outside programming cost estimate on a rate of $250 per hour for 40 hours of programming consultant time. We anticipate that the advisers that rely on commercial software solutions, many of which will be components to trading software they already have acquired, will not have to retain outside programming consultants.

96 0.05 hours (three minutes) per eligible accountholder to generate and deliver reports x 716,580 eligible accountholder = 35,829 hours total burden for generating and delivering reports to accountholders. Because, as we note above, the information required by the rule will be added to documents advisers already send to clients, we estimate that there is no added cost associated with delivering the reports to clients (*e.g.*, postage costs).

C. Summary of Estimated Paperwork Burden

For purposes of the Paperwork Reduction Act, we estimate an annual incremental increase in the burden for investment advisers and their affiliated broker-dealers to comply with the alternative means for compliance with section 206(3) of the Advisers Act contained in rule 206(3)-3T. As discussed above, our estimates reflect the fact that the alternative means of compliance is similar to the approach advisers currently employ to comply with the disclosure and consent obligations of section 206(3) of the Advisers Act and also is similar to the approach broker-dealers employ to comply with certain of the requirements of rule 10b-10 under the Exchange Act.

Some amount of training of personnel on compliance with the rule and developing, acquiring, installing, and using technology and systems for the purpose of collecting, validating and verifying information may be necessary. In addition, as discussed above, some amount of time, effort and expense may be required in connection with processing and maintaining information. We estimate that the total amount of costs, including capital and start-up costs, for compliance with the rule is approximately $13,050,300.[97] We estimate that the hour burden will be 494,440 hours.[98]

97 $456,000 for outside professional fees associated with preparation of the prospective disclosure + $1,194,300 for printing and physical distribution costs associated with the prospective disclosure + $7,600,000 for programming costs for outside professionals for rendering trade confirmations compliant with the rule + $3,800,000 for programming costs for outside professionals to create principal trading reports = a total of $13,050,300.

98 1,900 hours for drafting prospective disclosure + 79,620 hours for administering distribution of prospective disclosure to accountholders + 39,810 hours for review by accountholders of the consent solicitation and returning consents + 38,000 hours for advisers maintaining and updating consent information + 297,381 hours for preparation and communication of trade-by-trade disclosure and consent + 1,900 hours for programming to create principal trading reports + 35,829 hours for ongoing generation of principal trading reports = a total of 494,440 hours.

D. Request for Comment

We invite comment on each of these estimates and the underlying assumptions. Pursuant to 44 U.S.C. 3506(c)(2)(B), we request comment with respect to the collections described in this section of this Release in order to: (i) evaluate whether the collections of information are necessary for the proper performance of our functions, including whether the information will have practical utility; (ii) evaluate the accuracy of our estimate of the burden of the collections of information; (iii) determine whether there are ways to enhance the quality, utility, and clarity of the information to be collected; and (iv) evaluate whether there are ways to minimize the burden of the collections of information on those who respond, including through the use of automated collection techniques or other forms of information technology.[99]

Persons submitting comments on the collection of information requirements should direct the comments to the Office of Management and Budget, Attention: Desk Officer for the Securities and Exchange Commission, Office of Information and Regulatory Affairs, Washington, DC 20503, and should send a copy to Nancy M. Morris, Secretary, Securities and Exchange Commission, 100 F Street, NE, Washington, DC 20549-1090, with reference to File No. S7-23-07. Requests for materials submitted to OMB by the Commission with regard to these collections of information should be in writing, refer to File No. S7-23-07, and be submitted to the Securities and Exchange Commission, Records Management, Office of Filings and Information Services, Washington, DC 20549. The OMB is required to make a decision concerning the collection of information between 30 and 60 days after publication of this release.

99 Comments are requested pursuant to 44 U.S.C. 3506(c)(2)(B).

Consequently, a comment to OMB is assured of having its full effect if OMB receives it within 30 days of publication.

VI. COST-BENEFIT ANALYSIS

A. Background

We are adopting, as an interim final temporary rule, rule 206(3)-3T under the Advisers Act, which provides an alternative means for investment advisers that are registered with us as broker-dealers to meet the requirements of section 206(3) when they act in a principal capacity with respect to transactions with certain of their advisory clients. We are adopting this rule as part of our response to a recent court decision invalidating rule 202(a)(11)-1, which provided that fee-based brokerage accounts were not advisory accounts and were thus not subject to the Advisers Act. As a result of the court's decision, these fee-based accounts are advisory accounts subject to the fiduciary duty and other requirements of the Advisers Act, unless converted to commission-based brokerage accounts. To maintain investor choice and protect the interests of investors holding an estimated $300 billion in approximately one million fee-based brokerage accounts, we are adopting rule 206(3)-3T.

B. Summary of Temporary Rule

Rule 206(3)-3T permits an adviser, with respect to a non-discretionary advisory account, to comply with section 206(3) by: (i) making certain written disclosures; (ii) obtaining written, revocable consent from the client prospectively authorizing the adviser to enter into principal trades; (iii) making oral or written disclosure of the capacity in which the adviser may act and obtaining the client's consent orally or in writing prior to the execution of each principal transaction; (iv) sending to the client confirmation statements disclosing the capacity in which the adviser has acted and indicating that the adviser disclosed to the client that it may act in a principal capacity and that the client authorized the transaction; and (v) delivering to the client an annual report itemizing the principal transactions. These conditions are designed to require an adviser to fully apprise the client of the conflicts of interest involved in these transactions, inform the client of the circumstances in which the adviser may effect a trade on a principal basis, and provide the client with meaningful opportunities to revoke prospective consent or refuse to authorize a particular transaction.

To avoid disruption that would otherwise occur to customers who currently hold fee-based brokerage accounts, we are adopting rule 206(3)-3T on an interim final basis so that it will be available when the Court's decision takes effect on October 1, 2007.[100] For reasons explained below, we are adopting the rule on a temporary basis so that it will expire on December 31, 2009.

C. Benefits

As discussed above, the principal benefit of rule 206(3)-3T is that it maintains investor choice and protects the interests of investors holding an estimated $300 billion in one million fee-based brokerage accounts. It is our understanding that investors favor having the choice of advisory accounts with access to the inventory of a diversified broker-dealer but that meeting the requirements set out in section 206(3) is not feasible for advisers affiliated with broker-dealers or advisers that also are registered as broker-dealers. By complying with what we believe to be relatively straightforward procedural requirements, investment advisers can avoid what they have indicated to us is a critical impediment to their providing access to certain securities which they hold in their own

[100] *See supra* note 5 and accompanying text.

accounts—namely, written trade-by-trade disclosure. These advisers have communicated to us that the trade-by-trade written disclosure requirement is so impracticable in today's markets that it effectively stands in the way of their being able to give clients access to certain securities that might most cheaply or quickly be traded with a client on a principal basis. In fact, with respect to some securities, for which the risks might be relatively low (such as investment-grade debt securities), absent principal trading, clients may not have access to them at all. For other securities, execution may be improved where the adviser or affiliated broker-dealer can provide the best execution of the transaction.

A resulting second benefit of the rule is that non-discretionary advisory clients of dually registered firms will have easier access to a wider range of securities. This in turn will likely increase liquidity in the markets for these securities and promote capital formation in these areas.

A third benefit of the rule is that it provides the protections of the sales practice rules of the Exchange Act and the relevant self-regulatory organizations because an adviser relying on the rule must also be a registered broker-dealer. As a result, clients will have the benefit of the fiduciary duties imposed on the investment adviser by the Advisers Act and of the Commission's rules and regulations under the Exchange Act as well as those of the SROs.

Another benefit of Rule 206(3)-3T is that it provides a lower cost alternative for an adviser to engage in principal transactions. As discussed above, in the absence of this rule our view has been that an adviser must provide written disclosure and obtain consent for each specific principal transaction. Rule 206(3)-3T permits an adviser to comply with section 206(3) by, among other things, providing oral disclosure prior to the execution of each principal transaction. As discussed above, we understand traditional compliance is difficult and costly. This alternative means of compliance should be, consistent with the protection of investors, less costly and less burdensome.

D. Costs

Prospective Disclosure and Consent: Pursuant to paragraph (a)(3) of the rule, an investment adviser must provide written, prospective disclosure to the client explaining: (i) the circumstances under which the investment adviser directly or indirectly may engage in principal transactions; (ii) the nature and significance of conflicts with its client's interests as a result of the transactions; and (iii) how the investment adviser addresses those conflicts. Pursuant to paragraph (a)(8) of the rule, the written, prospective disclosure must include a conspicuous, plain English statement that a client's written, prospective consent may be revoked without penalty at any time by written notice to the investment adviser from the client. And, for the adviser to be able to rely on rule 206(3)-3T with respect to an account, the client must have executed a written, revocable consent after receiving such written, prospective disclosure. The principal costs associated with this requirement include: (i) preparation of the prospective disclosure and consent solicitation; (ii) distribution of the disclosure and consent solicitation to clients; and (iii) ongoing management of information, including revocations of consent and grants of consent that occur subsequent to the account opening process.

We estimate that the costs of preparing the prospective disclosure and consent solicitation will be borne upfront. Once these items have been generated by eligible advisers, such advisers will be able to include them in other materials already required to be delivered to clients. For purposes of the Paperwork Reduction Act, we have estimated

the number of hours and costs the average adviser would spend in the initial preparation of their prospective disclosure and consent solicitation.[101] Based on those estimates, we estimate that advisers would incur costs of approximately $1,480 on average per adviser, including a conflicts review process, drafting efforts and consultation with clients, and legal consultation.[102] Assuming there are 380 eligible advisers (*i.e.*, advisers that also are registered broker-dealers) that will prepare the prospective disclosure and consent solicitation, we estimate that the total costs will be $562,400.[103]

For purposes of the Paperwork Reduction Act, we have estimated the number of hours and costs the average adviser would spend on the distribution of their prospective disclosure and consent solicitation as 210 hours and $3,143.[104] We expect that the costs of distribution of the prospective disclosure and solicitation consent to existing non-

---

101 *See* section V.B of this Release. We estimate the following burdens and/or costs: (i) for drafting the required prospective disclosure, approximately 5 hours on average per eligible adviser, of which we estimate there are 380, for a total of 1,900 hours; and (ii) for utilizing outside legal professionals in the preparation of the prospective disclosure, approximately $1,200 on average per eligible adviser, for a total of $456,000.

102 We expect that the internal preparation function will most likely be performed by compliance professionals. Data from the SIFMA's *Report on Office Salaries in the Securities Industry 2006* ("Industry's Salary Report"), modified to account for an 1,800-hour work-year and multiplied by 2.93 to account for bonuses, firm size, employee benefits and overhead, suggest that the cost for a Compliance Clerk is approximately $56 per hour. $56 per hour x 5 hours on average per adviser = $280 on average per adviser of internal costs for preparation of the prospective disclosure. $280 on average per adviser of internal costs + $1,200 on average per adviser of costs for external consultants = $1,480 on average per adviser.

103 $1,480 on average per adviser in costs for preparation of the prospective disclosure x 380 advisers = $562,400 in total costs for preparation of the prospective disclosure.

104 *See* section V.B of this Release. We estimate the following burdens and/or costs: (i) for printing the prospective disclosure (including a disclosure and consent form and, if necessary, a revised Form ADV brochure and account agreement), approximately $1.50 on average per eligible account, of which we estimate there are approximately 796,200, for a total of $1,194,300 (which, if divided by the estimated 380 eligible advisers, equals a total cost for printing of approximately $3,143 on average per adviser); (ii) for distributing the prospective disclosure, approximately 0.1 hours on average per eligible

discretionary advisory clients and fee-based brokerage accountholders converting their accounts to non-discretionary advisory accounts will include duplication charges, postage and other mailing related expenses. We estimate that these costs will be approximately $5.60 on average per client, for a total of $4,458,720.[105]

For purposes of the Paperwork Reduction Act, we have estimated the number of hours the average accountholder would spend on reviewing the written disclosure document and, if it wishes, returning an executed consent.[106] We estimate that the costs corresponding to this hour burden will be approximately $0.50 on average per eligible accountholder. Assuming that there are 796,200 eligible accountholders who will receive the written disclosure document and 716,580 that will provide consent during the transitional solicitation, we estimate that the total cost to clients will be $398,100.[107]

account, for a total of 79,620 hours (which, if divided by the estimated 380 eligible advisers, equals a total burden of 210 hours on average per adviser).

105 We expect that the distribution function for the prospective written disclosure and consent solicitation will most likely be performed by a general clerk. Data from the Industry's Salary Report, modified to account for an 1,800-hour work-year and multiplied by 2.93 to account for bonuses, firm size, employee benefits and overhead, suggest that cost for a General Clerk is approximately $41 per hour. $41 per hour x 0.1 hours on average for distribution per account = approximately $4.10 on average per account for distribution. $1.50 on average printing cost per account + $4.10 on average distribution cost per account = $5.60 on average per account. $5.60 on average per account x 796,200 accounts to which we expect the disclosure to be distributed = a total printing and distribution cost for the prospective disclosure and consent solicitation of $4,458,720 (which, if divided by the estimated 380 eligible advisers, equals a total cost for distribution of approximately $11,733 on average per eligible adviser).

106 *See* section V.B of this Release. We estimate that the burden per client account that will return an executed consent (eligible accountholder), of which we estimate that there will be approximately 716,580, will be 0.05 hours (3 minutes) on average, for a total burden of 35,829 hours. We do not believe there will be a significant difference in burden between those clients that consent and those that do not.

107 $0.50 on average for each accountholder who receives a written prospective disclosure document x 796,200 eligible accountholders = $398,100. We do not believe there will be a significant difference in burden between those accountholders that consent and those that do not.

For purposes of the Paperwork Reduction Act, we have estimated the number of hours the average adviser would spend in ongoing maintenance of prospective disclosure and consent solicitation efforts.[108] Based on those estimates, we estimate that the average cost of updating the written prospective disclosure, maintaining records on prospective consents provided, and processing consent revocations and consents granted subsequent to the initial solicitation will be approximately $5,600 on average per eligible adviser per year.[109] We estimate that the annual cost for all eligible advisers to keep consent information up to date will be $2,128,000.[110]

Based on the discussion above, we estimate the costs relating to paragraph (a)(3) of rule 206(3)-3T to be on average approximately: (i) $13,213 per adviser in one-time costs;[111] (ii) $5,600 per adviser in ongoing costs; and (iii) $0.50 per client account in costs. As such, we estimate the total costs associated with the prospective written disclosure and consent requirement of the rule to be $7,547,040.[112]

108 *See* section V.B of this Release. We estimate that the burden per eligible adviser of ongoing maintenance of the prospective disclosure and consent solicitation efforts will be approximately 100 hours on average per year, for a total of 38,000 hours.

109 We expect that this function will most likely be performed by compliance professionals at $56 per hour. *See* Industry's Salary Report. 100 hours on average per adviser per year x $56 per hour = $5,600 on average per adviser per year.

110 $5,600 on average per adviser per year x 380 eligible advisers = $2,128,000.

111 $1,480 on average per adviser in costs for preparation of the prospective disclosure and consent solicitation + $11,733 on average per adviser in costs for printing and distributing the prospective disclosure and consent solicitation = total one-time costs for preparation, printing and distribution of the prospective disclosure and consent solicitation of $13,213 on average per adviser.

112 ($13,213 average one time cost per adviser x 380 eligible advisers) + ($5,600 average ongoing costs per adviser x 380 eligible advisers) + ($0.50 average costs per accountholder x 796,200 accountholders who will review the written disclosure) = $5,020,940 + $2,128,000 + $398,100 = $7,547,040 total cost of compliance with paragraph (a)(3) of rule 206(3)-3T.

Trade-by-Trade Disclosure and Consent: Pursuant to paragraph (a)(4) of the rule, an investment adviser, prior to the execution of each principal transaction, must inform the advisory client, orally or in writing, of the capacity in which it may act with respect to such transaction. Also pursuant to paragraph (a)(4) of the rule, an investment adviser, prior to the execution of each principal transaction, must obtain oral or written consent from the advisory client to act as principal for its own account with respect to such transaction. Further, investment advisers likely will want to document for their own evidentiary purposes the receipt of trade-by-trade consent by their representatives.

As noted in our Paperwork Reduction Act analysis, section 206(3) of the Advisers Act already requires written trade-by-trade disclosure in connection with principal trades. We believe that complying with this requirement of rule 206(3)-3T provides an alternative method of compliance that is likely to be less costly than compliance with section 206(3). To the extent that advisers are not currently engaging in principal trades with non-discretionary advisory accountholders (and thus are not preparing and providing written disclosure regarding conflicts of interest associated with principal trading in particular securities), advisers electing to rely on the rule will need to begin to prepare such tailored disclosure and communicate it to clients.

We estimate that the costs of preparing and communicating trade-by-trade disclosures to clients and obtaining their consents could include: (i) preparing disclosure relating to the conflicts associated with executing that transaction on a principal basis; and (ii) communicating that disclosure to clients. For purposes of the Paperwork Reduction Act, we have estimated the number of hours advisers would spend on

providing trade-by-trade disclosure and consent solicitation.[113] Based on those estimates, we estimate that the cost of preparing each trade-by-trade disclosure will be approximately $0.47 on average.[114] For purposes of the Paperwork Reduction Act analysis, we have estimated that eligible clients engage in an average of approximately 50 trades per year, all of which we have conservatively assumed are principal trades. We further estimate that communicating the disclosure to clients orally will be at most a minimal cost (note that system programming costs are discussed separately under the subsection entitled "Related Costs" below). As such, we estimate the total annual cost for compliance with paragraph (a)(4) of rule 206(3)-3T to be approximately $16,662,240.[115]

Trade-by-Trade Confirmations: Pursuant to paragraph (a)(5) of the rule, an investment adviser must deliver to its client a written confirmation at or before completion of each principal transaction that includes, in addition to the information required by rule 10b-10 under the Exchange Act [17 CFR 240.10b-10], a conspicuous, plain English statement that the investment adviser: (i) informed the advisory client that it may be acting in a principal capacity in connection with the transaction and the client

---

113 *See* section V.B of this Release. We estimate that based on discussions with industry representatives that there will be approximately 50 trades (which we conservatively assume will be principal trades) on average made per year per eligible account. We estimate a burden of 0.0083 hours (30 seconds) on average per trade for communication of the requisite disclosure to an eligible accountholder, of which we estimate there will be 716,580, for an estimated total burden of approximately 297,381 hours per year. The burden for the average adviser would thus be 297,381 total hours per year ÷ 380 eligible advisers = approximately 783 hours on average per adviser per year.

114 We expect that this function will most likely be performed by compliance professionals at $56 per hour (*see* Industry's Salary Report) and that the preparation and communication of trade-by-trade disclosure will comprise an average burden of approximately 0.0083 hours (30 seconds) per trade. 0.0083 hours on average per trade x $56 per hour = approximately $0.47 on average per trade.

115 783 hours on average per adviser per year x $56 per hour = $43,848 on average per adviser per year. $43,848 on average per eligible adviser per year x 380 eligible advisers = $16,662,240 total costs per year.

authorized the transaction; and (ii) owned the security sold to the advisory client (or bought the security from the client for its own account). As noted above in the Paperwork Reduction Act section of this Release, the majority of the information that this provision requires to be delivered to clients is already required to be assembled and communicated to clients pursuant to requirements under the Exchange Act. We expect that the costs associated with conforming trade confirmations to the requirements of paragraph (a)(5) of rule 206(3)-3T will stem principally from programming computer systems that generate confirmations to ensure that all the required information is contained in the confirmations. Costs associated with programming are described under the subsection entitled "Related Costs" below.

Principal Transactions Report: Pursuant to paragraph (a)(6) of the rule, the investment adviser must deliver to each client, no less frequently than annually, written disclosure containing a list of all transactions that were executed in the account in reliance upon the rule, and the date and price of such transactions. This report will require advisers to aggregate and distribute information that should already be available to the adviser or its broker-dealer affiliate executing the client's transactions.

As noted in the Paperwork Reduction Act section of this Release, we estimate that other than the actual aggregation and delivery of this statement, the burden of this collection will not be substantial because the information required to be contained in the statement is already collected and maintained by investment advisers and/or broker-dealers executing trades for their clients. Advisers and broker-dealers already send periodic or annual statements to clients. Thus, to comply, advisers will need to add information they already maintain to documents they already prepare and send. We

expect that there will be a one-time cost associated with this requirement relating to programming computer systems to generate the report, aggregating information that is already available and maintained by advisers or their broker-dealer affiliates. Costs associated with programming are described under the subsection entitled "Related Costs" below.

Related Costs: We expect that the bulk of the costs of compliance with rule 206(3)-3T relate to: (i) the initial distribution of prospective disclosure and collection of consents (described above); (ii) systems programming costs to ensure that trade confirmations contain all of the information required by paragraph (a)(4) of the rule; and (iii) systems programming costs to aggregate already-collected information to generate compliant principal transactions reports. For purposes of the Paperwork Reduction Act, we have estimated the cost an average adviser would incur on programming their computer systems, regardless of the size of their non-discretionary advisory account programs, to prepare compliant confirmations and principal transaction reports and to be able to track both prospective and trade-by-trade consents. For purposes of the Paperwork Reduction Act analysis, we have estimated the number of hours the average adviser would spend on programming computer systems to facilitate compliance with the rule.[116] Based on those estimates, we estimate the costs of programming, generating and

---

116 *See* section V.B of this Release. We estimate the following burdens and costs: (i) for programming computer systems to generate trade confirmations compliant with rule 206(3)-3T, approximately $20,000 on average per eligible adviser, of which we estimate there are approximately 380, for a total of $7,600,000; (ii) for the internal burden associated with programming computer systems relating to principal trade reports compliant with rule 206(3)-3T, approximately five hours on average per eligible adviser, for a total of 1,900 hours; (iii) for assistance of outside professionals to assist in programming computer systems to generate principal trade reports, approximately $10,000 on average per eligible adviser, for a total of $3,800,000; and (iv) for generation and delivery of annual principal trade reports each year, approximately 0.05 hours (three

delivering compliant confirmations and principal trade reports to be approximately $34,201 on average per eligible adviser,[117] for a total of $12,996,289.[118]

For those advisers that are converting fee-based brokerage accounts to non-discretionary advisory accounts, we are providing transition relief, described in section IV of this Release, that is designed, among other things, to avoid disruptions to clients and minimize costs to advisers.

Total Costs: The total overall costs, including estimated costs for all eligible advisers and eligible accounts, relating to compliance with rule 206(3)-3T are $37,205,569.[119]

minutes) on average per eligible account, of which we estimate there are approximately 716,580, for a total of 35,829 hours total per year.

117 We expect that the internal programming function most likely will be performed by computer programmers. Data from the Industry's Salary Report, modified to account for an 1,800-hour work-year and multiplied by 2.93 to account for bonuses, firm size, employee benefits and overhead, suggest that cost for a Sr. Computer Operator is approximately $67 per hour. Five hours on average per adviser x $67 per hour = $335 on average per adviser (or, across all 380 eligible advisers, $127,300). We expect that the generation and delivery of annual principal trade reports will most likely be performed by general clerks at $41 per hour. $41 per hour x 35,829 total hours per year = $1,468,989 (or, if divided among all 380 eligible advisers, approximately $3,866 on average per adviser per year). $20,000 on average per adviser for programming to generate compliant trade confirmations + $335 on average per adviser for internal programming costs in connection with developing an annual principal trades report + $10,000 on average per adviser for outside computing assistance in developing the annual principal trade report + $3,866 on average per adviser for generation and delivery of annual principal trade reports per year = approximately $34,201 on average per adviser in connection with compliance with the confirmation and principal trade report requirements.

118 $7,600,000 for programming to generate compliant trade confirmations + $127,300 for internal programming costs in connection with developing an annual principal trades report + $3,800,000 for outside computing assistance in developing the annual principal trade report + $1,468,989 for generation and delivery of annual principal trade reports per year = $12,996,289 total costs in connection with compliance with the confirmation and principal trade report requirements.

119 $7,547,040 total costs in connection with compliance with the prospective disclosure and consent requirements of the rule + $16,662,240 total costs in connection with compliance with the trade-by-trade disclosure and consent requirements of the rule + $12,996,289 total costs in connection with compliance with the confirmation and principal trade report

E. Request for Comment

- We solicit quantitative data to assist with our assessment of the benefits and costs of rule 206(3)-3T.
- What, if any, additional costs are involved in complying with the rule? What are the types of costs, and what are the amounts? Should the rule be modified in any way to mitigate costs? If so, how?
- Does the rule's requirement that a report be provided to each client, at least annually, of the transactions undertaken with the client in reliance on the rule result in a meaningful identification of an adviser's trading patterns with its clients that will enable the client to evaluate more effectively than it would simply with prospective disclosure and trade-by-trade disclosure prior to the execution of a principal transaction whether it should continue to consent, or revoke its consent, to principal trading in reliance on the rule?
- What will the effect of the rule be on the availability of account services and securities to clients who do not consent to principal transactions?
- Have we accurately estimated the costs of compliance with the rule?
- We assumed that firms already collect much of the information that the rule would require for the principal trading reports. Are we correct? We solicit comments on the extent to which firms already aggregate the information that the rule will require to be disclosed in the principal trading reports?

requirements of the rule = $37,205,569 total costs in connection with compliance with the rule.

VII. PROMOTION OF EFFICIENCY, COMPETITION AND CAPITAL FORMATION

Section 202(c) of the Advisers Act mandates that the Commission, when engaging in rulemaking that requires it to consider or determine whether an action is necessary or appropriate in the public interest, consider, in addition to the protection of investors, whether the action will promote efficiency, competition, and capital formation.[120]

Rule 206(3)-3T permits an investment adviser, with respect to a non-discretionary advisory account, to comply with section 206(3) by: (i) making certain written disclosures; (ii) obtaining written, revocable consent from the client prospectively authorizing the adviser to enter into principal trades; (iii) making oral or written disclosure and obtaining the client's consent orally or in writing prior to the execution of each principal transaction; (iv) sending to the client confirmation statements for each principal trade that disclose the capacity in which the adviser has acted and indicating that the client consented to the transaction; and (v) delivering to the client an annual report itemizing the principal transactions.

Rule 206(3)-3T may increase efficiency by providing an alternative means of compliance with section 206(3) of the Advisers Act that we believe will be less costly and less burdensome. As discussed above, by permitting oral trade-by-trade disclosure, advisers may be more willing to engage in principal trades with advisory clients. As a result, advisers may provide access to certain securities the adviser or its affiliate has in inventory. Clients might want access to securities an adviser, or an affiliated broker-dealer, has in inventory, despite the conflicts inherent in principal trading, if those

120 15 U.S.C. 80b-2(c).

securities are scarce or hard to acquire. Firms have argued that purchasing such securities from, or selling them to, an adviser could lead to faster or less expensive execution, advantages a client may deem to outweigh the risks presented by principal trading with an adviser.[121]

We expect that rule 206(3)-3T will promote competition because it preserves investor choice for different types of advisory accounts. As a practical matter, advisers did not frequently engage in principal trades. By relying on the rule, advisers that are also are registered broker-dealers will be able to offer advisory clients access to their (and their affiliates') inventory. Advisers that are not also registered as broker-dealers may seek to market their services without principal trades and their associated costs and benefits. We are not able to predict with certainty the effect of the rule on them, but it is possible that some advisers may elect to register as broker-dealers in order to rely on rule 206(3)-3T.

We believe that if rule 206(3)-3T has any effect on capital formation it is likely to be positive, although indirect. We understand that most investment advisers will not trade with non-discretionary advisory client accounts on a principal basis so long as they must provide trade-by-trade written disclosure. Providing an alternative to the traditional requirements of trade-by-trade written disclosure might serve to broaden the potential universe of purchasers of securities, in particular investment grade debt securities for the reasons described above, opening the door to greater investor participation in the securities markets with a potential positive effect on capital formation.

121 *See, e.g.*, SIFMA Letter.

The Commission requests comment on whether the proposed amendments are likely to promote efficiency, competition, and capital formation.

VIII. FINAL REGULATORY FLEXIBILITY ANALYSIS

This Final Regulatory Flexibility Analysis ("FRFA") has been prepared in accordance with 5 U.S.C. 604. It relates to rule 206(3)-3T, which we are adopting in this Release.[122]

A. Need for and Objectives of the Rule

Sections I and II of this Release describe the reasons for and objectives of rule 206(3)-3T. As we discuss in detail above, our reasons include the need to facilitate the transition of customers in fee-based brokerage accounts in the wake of the *FPA* decision and to address the stated inability of the sponsors of those accounts to offer clients some of the services the clients desire in the non-discretionary advisory accounts to which they will be transitioned.

B. Small Entities Affected by the Rule

Rule 206(3)-3T is an alternative method of complying with Advisers Act section 206(3) and is available to all investment advisers that: (i) are registered as broker-dealers under the Exchange Act; and (ii) effect trades with clients directly or indirectly through a broker-dealer controlling, controlled by or under common control with the investment adviser, including small entities. Under Advisers Act rule 0-7, for purposes of the Regulatory Flexibility Act an investment adviser generally is a small entity if it: (i) has assets under management having a total value of less than $25 million; (ii) did not have

[122] Although the requirements of the Regulatory Flexibility Act are not applicable to rules adopted under the Administrative Procedure Act's "good cause" exception, *see* 5 U.S.C. 601(2) (defining "rule" and notice requirements under the Administrative Procedures Act), we nevertheless prepared a FRFA.

total assets of $5 million or more on the last day of its most recent fiscal year; and (iii) does not control, is not controlled by, and is not under common control with another investment adviser that has assets under management of $25 million or more, or any person (other than a natural person) that had $5 million or more on the last day of its most recent fiscal year.[123]

We have opted not to make the relief available to all investment advisers, but have instead restricted it to investment advisers that are dually registered as broker-dealers under the Exchange Act. We have taken this approach because, as more fully discussed above, in the context of principal trades which implicate potentially significant conflicts of interest, and which are executed through broker-dealers, we believe it is important that the protections of both the Advisers Act and the Exchange Act, which includes well developed sales practice rules, apply to advisers entering into principal transactions with clients.

The Commission estimates that as of August 1, 2007, 597 investment advisers were small entities.[124] The Commission assumes for purposes of this FRFA that 29 of these small entities (those that are both as investment advisers and broker-dealers) could rely on rule 206(3)-3T, and that all of these small entities would rely on the new rule.[125] We welcome comment on the availability of the rule to small entities. Do small investment advisers believe an alternative means of compliance with section 206(3) of the Advisers Act should be available to more of them? Do they believe that the dual registration requirement of the rule is too onerous for small advisers despite the

[123] *See* 17 CFR 275.0-7.

[124] IARD Data as of August 1, 2007.

[125] *Id.*

discussion in subsection F below? If so, how do they propose replicating the additional protections afforded to clients by the broker-dealer regulations?

C. Projected Reporting, Recordkeeping, and Other Compliance Requirements

The provisions of rule 206(3)-3T would impose certain new reporting or recordkeeping requirements, but are not expected to materially alter the time required for investment advisers that also are registered as broker-dealers to engage in transactions with their clients on a principal basis. Rule 206(3)-3T is designed to provide an alternative means of compliance with the requirements of section 206(3) of the Advisers Act. Investment advisers taking advantage of the rule with respect to non-discretionary advisory accounts would be required to make certain disclosures to clients on a prospective, trade-by-trade and annual basis. Specifically, rule 206(3)-3T permits an adviser, with respect to a non-discretionary advisory account, to comply with section 206(3) of the Advisers Act by, among other things: (i) making certain written disclosures; (ii) obtaining written, revocable consent from the client prospectively authorizing the adviser to enter into principal trades; (iii) making oral or written disclosure and obtaining the client's consent orally or in writing prior to the execution of each principal transaction; (iv) sending to the client confirmation statements for each principal trade that disclose the capacity in which the adviser has acted and indicating that the client consented to the transaction; and (v) delivering to the client an annual report itemizing the principal transactions. Advisers are already required to communicate the content of many of the disclosures pursuant to their fiduciary obligations to clients. Other disclosures are already required by rules applicable to broker-dealers.

D. Agency Action to Minimize Effect on Small Entities

Small entities registered with the Commission as investment advisers seeking to rely on the rule would be subject to the same disclosure requirements as larger entities. In each case, however, an investment adviser, whether large or small, would only be able to rely on the rule if it also is registered with us as a broker-dealer. As noted above, we estimate that 25 small entities are registered as both advisers and broker-dealers and therefore those small entities are eligible to rely on the rule. In developing the requirements of the rule, we considered the extent to which they would have a significant impact on a substantial number of small entities, and included flexibility where possible, calling for disclosures that are already generated by the relevant firms in one form or another wherever possible in light of the objectives of the rule, to reduce the corresponding burdens imposed.

E. Duplicative, Overlapping, or Conflicting Federal Rules

The Commission believes that there are no rules that duplicate or conflict with rule 206(3)-3T, which presents an alternative means of compliance with the procedural requirements of section 206(3) of the Advisers Act that relate to principal transactions.

The Commission notes, however, that rule 10b-10 under the Exchange Act is a separate confirmation rule that requires broker-dealers to provide certain information to their customers regarding the transactions they effect. Furthermore, FINRA Rule 2230 requires broker-dealers that are members of FINRA to deliver a written notification containing certain information, including whether the member is acting as a broker for the customer or is working as a dealer for its own account. Brokers and dealers typically deliver this information in confirmations that fulfill the requirements of rule 10b-10 under the Exchange Act. Rule G-15 of the Municipal Securities Rulemaking Board also contains a separate confirmation rule that governs member transactions in municipal securities, including municipal fund securities. In addition, investment advisers that are qualified custodians for purposes of rule 206(4)-2 under the Advisers Act and that maintain custody of their advisory clients' assets must send quarterly account statements to their clients pursuant to rule 206(4)-2(a)(3) under the Advisers Act.

These rules overlap with certain elements of rule 206(3)-3T, but the Commission has designed the temporary rule to work efficiently together with existing rules by permitting firms to incorporate the required disclosure into one confirmation statement.

F. Significant Alternatives

The Regulatory Flexibility Act directs us to consider significant alternatives that would accomplish our stated objective, while minimizing any significant adverse impact on small entities.[126] Alternatives in this category would include: (i) establishing different compliance or reporting standards or timetables that take into account the resources available to small entities; (ii) clarifying, consolidating, or simplifying compliance requirements under the rule for small entities; (iii) using performance rather than design standards; and (iv) exempting small entities from coverage of the rule, or any part of the rule.

The Commission believes that special compliance or reporting requirements or timetables for small entities, or an exemption from coverage for small entities, may create the risk that the investors who are advised by and effect securities transactions through such small entities would not receive adequate disclosure. Moreover, different disclosure

[126] *See* 5 U.S.C. 603(c).

requirements could create investor confusion if it creates the impression that small investment advisers have different conflicts of interest with their advisory clients in connection with principal trading than larger investment advisers. We believe, therefore, that it is important for the disclosure protections required by the rule to be provided to advisory clients by all advisers, not just those that are not considered small entities. Further consolidation or simplification of the proposals for investment advisers that are small entities would be inconsistent with the Commission's goals of fostering investor protection.

We have endeavored through rule 206(3)-3T to minimize the regulatory burden on all investment advisers eligible to rely on the rule, including small entities, while meeting our regulatory objectives. It was our goal to ensure that eligible small entities may benefit from the Commission's approach to the new rule to the same degree as other eligible advisers. The condition that advisers seeking to rely on the rule must also be registered as broker-dealers and that each account with respect to which a dually-registered adviser seeks to rely on the rule must be a brokerage account subject to the Exchange Act, and the rules thereunder, and the rules of the self-regulatory organization(s) of which it is a member, reflect what we believe is an important element of our balancing between easing regulatory burdens (by affording advisers an alternative means of compliance with section 206(3) of the Act) and meeting our investor protection objectives.[127] Finally, we do not consider using performance rather than design standards to be consistent with our statutory mandate of investor protection in the present context.

[127] *See* Section II.B.7 of this Release.

G. General Request for Comments

We solicit written comments regarding our analysis. We request comment on whether the rule will have any effects that we have not discussed. We request that commenters describe the nature of any impact on small entities and provide empirical data to support the extent of the impact.

IX. STATUTORY AUTHORITY

The Commission is adopting Rule 206(3)-3T pursuant to sections 206A and 211(a) of the Advisers Act.

TEXT OF RULE

List of Subjects in 17 CFR Part 275

Investment advisers, Reporting and recordkeeping requirements.

For the reasons set out in the preamble, Title 17, Chapter II of the Code of Federal Regulations is amended as follows:

PART 275 -- RULES AND REGULATIONS, INVESTMENT ADVISERS ACT OF 1940

1. The general authority citation for Part 275 is revised to read as follows:

Authority: 15 U.S.C. 80b-2(a)(11)(G), 80b-2(a)(17), 80b-3, 80b-4, 80b-4a, 80b-6(4), 80b-6a, and 80b-11, unless otherwise noted.

* * * * *

2. Section 275.206(3)-3T is added to read as follows:

§ 275.206(3)-3T Temporary rule for principal trades with certain advisory clients.

(a) An investment adviser shall be deemed in compliance with the provisions of section 206(3) of the Advisers Act (15 U.S.C. 80b-6(3)) when the adviser directly or indirectly, acting as principal for its own account, sells to or purchases from an advisory

client any security if:

(1) The investment adviser exercises no "investment discretion" (as such term is defined in section 3(a)(35) of the Securities Exchange Act of 1934 ("Exchange Act") (15 U.S.C. 78c(a)(35))), except investment discretion granted by the advisory client on a temporary or limited basis, with respect to the client's account;

(2) Neither the investment adviser nor any person controlling, controlled by, or under common control with the investment adviser is the issuer of, or, at the time of the sale, an underwriter (as defined in section 202(a)(20) of the Advisers Act (15 U.S.C. 80b-2(a)(20))) of, the security; *except that* the investment adviser or a person controlling, controlled by, or under common control with the investment adviser may be an underwriter of an investment grade debt security (as defined in paragraph (c) of this section);

(3) The advisory client has executed a written, revocable consent prospectively authorizing the investment adviser directly or indirectly to act as principal for its own account in selling any security to or purchasing any security from the advisory client, so long as such written consent is obtained after written disclosure to the advisory client explaining:

(i) The circumstances under which the investment adviser directly or indirectly may engage in principal transactions;

(ii) The nature and significance of conflicts with its client's interests as a result of the transactions; and

(iii) How the investment adviser addresses those conflicts;

(4) The investment adviser, prior to the execution of each principal transaction:

(i) Informs the advisory client, orally or in writing, of the capacity in which it may act with respect to such transaction; and

(ii) Obtains consent from the advisory client, orally or in writing, to act as principal for its own account with respect to such transaction;

(5) The investment adviser sends a written confirmation at or before completion of each such transaction that includes, in addition to the information required by 17 CFR 240.10b-10, a conspicuous, plain English statement informing the advisory client that the investment adviser:

(i) Disclosed to the client prior to the execution of the transaction that the adviser may be acting in a principal capacity in connection with the transaction and the client authorized the transaction; and

(ii) Sold the security to, or bought the security from, the client for its own account;

(6) The investment adviser sends to the client, no less frequently than annually, written disclosure containing a list of all transactions that were executed in the client's account in reliance upon this section, and the date and price of such transactions;

(7) The investment adviser is a broker-dealer registered under section 15 of the Exchange Act (15 U.S.C. 78o) and each account for which the investment adviser relies on this section is a brokerage account subject to the Exchange Act, and the rules thereunder, and the rules of the self-regulatory organization(s) of which it is a member; and

(8) Each written disclosure required by this section includes a conspicuous, plain English statement that the client may revoke the written consent referred to in paragraph (a)(3) of this section without penalty at any time by written notice to the investment adviser.

(b) This section shall not be construed as relieving in any way an investment adviser from acting in the best interests of an advisory client, including fulfilling the duty with respect to the best price and execution for the particular transaction for the advisory client; nor shall it relieve such person or persons from any obligation that may be imposed by sections 206(1) or (2) of the Advisers Act or by other applicable provisions of the federal securities laws.

(c) For purposes of paragraph (a)(2) of this section, an *investment grade debt security* means a non-convertible debt security that, at the time of sale, is rated in one of the four highest rating categories of at least two nationally recognized statistical rating organizations (as defined in section 3(a)(62) of the Exchange Act (15 U.S.C. 78c(a)(62))).

(d) This section will expire and no longer be effective on December 31, 2009.

By the Commission.

Nancy M. Morris
Secretary

September 24, 2007

資料5

MiFID II（抜粋）

DIRECTIVE 2014/65/EU OF THE EUROPEAN PARLIAMENT AND OF THE COUNCIL

of 15 May 2014

on markets in financial instruments and amending Directive 2002/92/EC and Directive 2011/61/EU

(recast)

(Text with EEA relevance)

THE EUROPEAN PARLIAMENT AND THE COUNCIL OF THE EUROPEAN UNION,

Having regard to the Treaty on the Functioning of the European Union, and in particular Article 53(1) thereof,

Having regard to the proposal from the European Commission,

After transmission of the draft legislative act to the national parliaments,

Having regard to the opinion of the European Central Bank [1],

Having regard to the opinion of the European Economic and Social Committee [2],

Acting in accordance with the ordinary legislative procedure [3],

Whereas:

(1) Directive 2004/39/EC of the European Parliament and of the Council [4] has been substantially amended several times [5]. Since further amendments are to be made, it should be recast in the interests of clarity.

(2) Council Directive 93/22/EEC [6] sought to establish the conditions under which authorised investment firms and banks could provide specified services or establish branches in other Member States on the basis of home country authorisation and supervision. To that end, that Directive aimed to harmonise the initial authorisation and operating requirements for investment firms including conduct of business rules. It also provided for the harmonisation of some conditions governing the operation of regulated markets.

(3) In recent years more investors have become active in the financial markets and are offered an even more complex wide-ranging set of services and instruments. In view of those developments the legal framework of the Union should encompass the full range of investor-oriented activities. To that end, it is necessary to provide for the degree of harmonisation needed to offer investors a high level of protection and to allow investment firms to provide services throughout the Union, being an internal market, on the basis of home country supervision. Directive 93/22/EEC was therefore replaced by Directive 2004/39/EC.

(4) The financial crisis has exposed weaknesses in the functioning and in the transparency of financial markets. The evolution of financial markets has exposed the need to strengthen the framework for the regulation of markets in financial instruments, including where trading in such markets takes place over-the-counter (OTC), in order to increase transparency, better protect investors, reinforce confidence, address unregulated areas, and ensure that supervisors are granted adequate powers to fulfil their tasks.

[1] OJ C 161, 7.6.2012, p. 3.
[2] OJ C 191, 29.6.2012, p. 80.
[3] Position of the European Parliament of 15 April 2014 (not yet published in the Official Journal) and decision of the Council of 13 May 2014.
[4] Directive 2004/39/EC of the European Parliament and of the Council of 21 April 2004 on markets in financial instruments amending Council Directives 85/611/EEC and 93/6/EEC and Directive 2000/12/EC of the European Parliament and of the Council and repealing Council Directive 93/22/EEC (OJ L 145, 30.4.2004, p. 1).
[5] See Annex III, Part A.
[6] Council Directive 93/22/EEC of 10 May 1993 on investment services in the securities field (OJ L 141, 11.6.1993, p. 27).

(b) a natural or legal person not subject to supervision under this Directive or Directives 2009/65/EC, 2009/138/EC or 2013/36/EU.

4. If the competent authorities, upon completion of the assessment, decide to oppose the proposed acquisition, they shall, within two working days, and not exceeding the assessment period, inform the proposed acquirer in writing and provide the reasons for that decision. Subject to national law, an appropriate statement of the reasons for the decision may be made accessible to the public at the request of the proposed acquirer. This shall not prevent a Member State from allowing the competent authority to make such disclosure in the absence of a request by the proposed acquirer.

5. If the competent authorities do not oppose the proposed acquisition within the assessment period in writing, it shall be deemed to be approved.

6. The competent authorities may fix a maximum period for concluding the proposed acquisition and extend it where appropriate.

7. Member States may not impose requirements for the notification to and approval by the competent authorities of direct or indirect acquisitions of voting rights or capital that are more stringent than those set out in this Directive.

8. ESMA shall develop draft regulatory technical standards to establish an exhaustive list of information, referred to in Article 13(4) to be included by proposed acquirers in their notification, without prejudice to paragraph 2 of this Article.

ESMA shall submit those draft regulatory technical standards to the Commission by 1 January 2014.

Power is delegated to the Commission to adopt the regulatory technical standards referred to in the first subparagraph in accordance with Articles 10 to 14 of Regulation (EU) No 1095/2010.

9. ESMA shall develop draft implementing technical standards to determine standard forms, templates and procedures for the modalities of the consultation process between the relevant competent authorities as referred to in Article 11(2).

ESMA shall submit those draft implementing technical standards to the Commission by 1 January 2014.

Power is conferred on the Commission to adopt the implementing technical standards referred to in the first subparagraph in accordance with Article 15 of Regulation (EU) No 1095/2010.

Article 13

Assessment

1. In assessing the notification provided for in Article 11(1) and the information referred to in Article 12(2), the competent authorities shall, in order to ensure the sound and prudent management of the investment firm in which an acquisition is proposed, and having regard to the likely influence of the proposed acquirer on the investment firm, appraise the suitability of the proposed acquirer and the financial soundness of the proposed acquisition against all of the following criteria:

(a) the reputation of the proposed acquirer;

(b) the reputation and experience of any person who will direct the business of the investment firm as a result of the proposed acquisition;

(c) the financial soundness of the proposed acquirer, in particular in relation to the type of business pursued and envisaged in the investment firm in which the acquisition is proposed;

(d) whether the investment firm will be able to comply and continue to comply with the prudential requirements based on this Directive and, where applicable, other Directives, in particular Directives 2002/87/EC and 2013/36/EU, in particular, whether the group of which it will become a part has a structure that makes it possible to exercise effective supervision, effectively exchange information among the competent authorities and determine the allocation of responsibilities among the competent authorities;

(e) whether there are reasonable grounds to suspect that, in connection with the proposed acquisition, money laundering or terrorist financing within the meaning of Article 1 of Directive 2005/60/EC is being or has been committed or attempted, or that the proposed acquisition could increase the risk thereof.

The Commission shall be empowered to adopt delegated acts in accordance with Article 89 which adjust the criteria set out in the first subparagraph of this paragraph.

2. The competent authorities may oppose the proposed acquisition only if there are reasonable grounds for doing so on the basis of the criteria set out in paragraph 1 or if the information provided by the proposed acquirer is incomplete.

3. Member States shall neither impose any prior conditions in respect of the level of holding that must be acquired nor allow their competent authorities to examine the proposed acquisition in terms of the economic needs of the market.

4. Member States shall make publicly available a list specifying the information that is necessary to carry out the assessment and that must be provided to the competent authorities at the time of notification referred to in Article 11(1). The information required shall be proportionate and adapted to the nature of the proposed acquirer and the proposed acquisition. Member States shall not require information that is not relevant for a prudential assessment.

5. Notwithstanding Article 12(1), (2) and (3), where two or more proposals to acquire or increase qualifying holdings in the same investment firm have been notified to the competent authority, the latter shall treat the proposed acquirers in a non-discriminatory manner.

Article 14

Membership of an authorised investor compensation scheme

The competent authority shall verify that any entity seeking authorisation as an investment firm meets its obligations under Directive 97/9/EC at the time of authorisation.

The obligation laid down in the first paragraph shall be met in relation to structured deposits where the structured deposit is issued by a credit institution which is a member of a deposit guarantee scheme recognised under Directive 2014/49/EU.

Article 15

Initial capital endowment

Member States shall ensure that the competent authorities do not grant authorisation unless the investment firm has sufficient initial capital in accordance with the requirements of Regulation (EU) No 575/2013 having regard to the nature of the investment service or activity in question.

Article 16

Organisational requirements

1. The home Member State shall require that investment firms comply with the organisational requirements laid down in paragraphs 2 to 10 of this Article and in Article 17.

2. An investment firm shall establish adequate policies and procedures sufficient to ensure compliance of the firm including its managers, employees and tied agents with its obligations under this Directive as well as appropriate rules governing personal transactions by such persons.

3. An investment firm shall maintain and operate effective organisational and administrative arrangements with a view to taking all reasonable steps designed to prevent conflicts of interest as defined in Article 23 from adversely affecting the interests of its clients.

An investment firm which manufactures financial instruments for sale to clients shall maintain, operate and review a process for the approval of each financial instrument and significant adaptations of existing financial instruments before it is marketed or distributed to clients.

The product approval process shall specify an identified target market of end clients within the relevant category of clients for each financial instrument and shall ensure that all relevant risks to such identified target market are assessed and that the intended distribution strategy is consistent with the identified target market.

An investment firm shall also regularly review financial instruments it offers or markets, taking into account any event that could materially affect the potential risk to the identified target market, to assess at least whether the financial instrument remains consistent with the needs of the identified target market and whether the intended distribution strategy remains appropriate.

An investment firm which manufactures financial instruments shall make available to any distributor all appropriate information on the financial instrument and the product approval process, including the identified target market of the financial instrument.

Where an investment firm offers or recommends financial instruments which it does not manufacture, it shall have in place adequate arrangements to obtain the information referred to in the fifth subparagraph and to understand the characteristics and identified target market of each financial instrument.

The policies, processes and arrangements referred to in this paragraph shall be without prejudice to all other requirements under this Directive and Regulation (EU) No 600/2014, including those relating to disclosure, suitability or appropriateness, identification and management of conflicts of interests, and inducements.

4. An investment firm shall take reasonable steps to ensure continuity and regularity in the performance of investment services and activities. To that end the investment firm shall employ appropriate and proportionate systems, resources and procedures.

5. An investment firm shall ensure, when relying on a third party for the performance of operational functions which are critical for the provision of continuous and satisfactory service to clients and the performance of investment activities on a continuous and satisfactory basis, that it takes reasonable steps to avoid undue additional operational risk. Outsourcing of important operational functions may not be undertaken in such a way as to impair materially the quality of its internal control and the ability of the supervisor to monitor the firm's compliance with all obligations.

An investment firm shall have sound administrative and accounting procedures, internal control mechanisms, effective procedures for risk assessment, and effective control and safeguard arrangements for information processing systems.

Without prejudice to the ability of competent authorities to require access to communications in accordance with this Directive and Regulation (EU) No 600/2014, an investment firm shall have sound security mechanisms in place to guarantee the security and authentication of the means of transfer of information, minimise the risk of data corruption and unauthorised access and to prevent information leakage maintaining the confidentiality of the data at all times.

6. An investment firm shall arrange for records to be kept of all services, activities and transactions undertaken by it which shall be sufficient to enable the competent authority to fulfil its supervisory tasks and to perform the enforcement actions under this Directive, Regulation (EU) No 600/2014, Directive 2014/57/EU and Regulation (EU) No 596/2014, and in particular to ascertain that the investment firm has complied with all obligations including those with respect to clients or potential clients and to the integrity of the market.

7. Records shall include the recording of telephone conversations or electronic communications relating to, at least, transactions concluded when dealing on own account and the provision of client order services that relate to the reception, transmission and execution of client orders.

Such telephone conversations and electronic communications shall also include those that are intended to result in transactions concluded when dealing on own account or in the provision of client order services that relate to the reception, transmission and execution of client orders, even if those conversations or communications do not result in the conclusion of such transactions or in the provision of client order services.

For those purposes, an investment firm shall take all reasonable steps to record relevant telephone conversations and electronic communications, made with, sent from or received by equipment provided by the investment firm to an employee or contractor or the use of which by an employee or contractor has been accepted or permitted by the investment firm.

An investment firm shall notify new and existing clients that telephone communications or conversations between the investment firm and its clients that result or may result in transactions will be recorded.

Such a notification may be made once, before the provision of investment services to new and existing clients.

An investment firm shall not provide, by telephone, investment services and activities to clients who have not been notified in advance about the recording of their telephone communications or conversations, where such investment services and activities relate to the reception, transmission and execution of client orders.

Orders may be placed by clients through other channels, however such communications must be made in a durable medium such as mails, faxes, emails or documentation of client orders made at meetings. In particular, the content of relevant face-to-face conversations with a client may be recorded by using written minutes or notes. Such orders shall be considered equivalent to orders received by telephone.

An investment firm shall take all reasonable steps to prevent an employee or contractor from making, sending or receiving relevant telephone conversations and electronic communications on privately-owned equipment which the investment firm is unable to record or copy.

The records kept in accordance with this paragraph shall be provided to the client involved upon request and shall be kept for a period of five years and, where requested by the competent authority, for a period of up to seven years.

8. An investment firm shall, when holding financial instruments belonging to clients, make adequate arrangements so as to safeguard the ownership rights of clients, especially in the event of the investment firm's insolvency, and to prevent the use of a client's financial instruments on own account except with the client's express consent.

9. An investment firm shall, when holding funds belonging to clients, make adequate arrangements to safeguard the rights of clients and, except in the case of credit institutions, prevent the use of client funds for its own account.

10. An investment firm shall not conclude title transfer financial collateral arrangements with retail clients for the purpose of securing or covering present or future, actual or contingent or prospective obligations of clients.

11. In the case of branches of investment firms, the competent authority of the Member State in which the branch is located shall, without prejudice to the possibility of the competent authority of the home Member State of the investment firm to have direct access to those records, enforce the obligation laid down in paragraphs 6 and 7 with regard to transactions undertaken by the branch.

Member States may, in exceptional circumstances, impose requirements on investment firms concerning the safeguarding of client assets additional to the provisions set out in paragraphs 8, 9 and 10 and the respective delegated acts as referred to in paragraph 12. Such requirements must be objectively justified and proportionate so as to address, where investment firms safeguard client assets and client funds, specific risks to investor protection or to market integrity which are of particular importance in the circumstances of the market structure of that Member State.

Member States shall notify, without undue delay, the Commission of any requirement which they intend to impose in accordance with this paragraph and at least two months before the date appointed for that requirement to come into force. The notification shall include a justification for that requirement. Any such additional requirements shall not restrict or otherwise affect the rights of investment firms under Articles 34 and 35.

The Commission shall within two months of the notification referred to in the third subparagraph provide its opinion on the proportionality of and justification for the additional requirements.

Member States may retain additional requirements provided that they were notified to the Commission in accordance with Article 4 of Directive 2006/73/EC before 2 July 2014 and that the conditions laid down in that Article are met.

The Commission shall communicate to Member States and make public on its website the additional requirements imposed in accordance with this paragraph.

12. The Commission shall be empowered to adopt delegated acts in accordance with Article 89 to specify the concrete organisational requirements laid down in paragraphs 2 to 10 of this Article to be imposed on investment firms and on branches of third-country firms authorised in accordance with Article 41 performing different investment services and/or activities and ancillary services or combinations thereof.

Article 17

Algorithmic trading

1. An investment firm that engages in algorithmic trading shall have in place effective systems and risk controls suitable to the business it operates to ensure that its trading systems are resilient and have sufficient capacity, are subject to appropriate trading thresholds and limits and prevent the sending of erroneous orders or the systems otherwise functioning in a way that may create or contribute to a disorderly market. Such a firm shall also have in place effective systems and risk controls to ensure the trading systems cannot be used for any purpose that is contrary to Regulation (EU) No 596/2014 or to the rules of a trading venue to which it is connected. The investment firm shall have in place effective business continuity arrangements to deal with any failure of its trading systems and shall ensure its systems are fully tested and properly monitored to ensure that they meet the requirements laid down in this paragraph.

2. An investment firm that engages in algorithmic trading in a Member State shall notify this to the competent authorities of its home Member State and of the trading venue at which the investment firm engages in algorithmic trading as a member or participant of the trading venue.

4. The Commission shall be empowered to adopt delegated acts in accordance with Article 89 to:

(a) define the steps that investment firms might reasonably be expected to take to identify, prevent, manage and disclose conflicts of interest when providing various investment and ancillary services and combinations thereof;

(b) establish appropriate criteria for determining the types of conflict of interest whose existence may damage the interests of the clients or potential clients of the investment firm.

Section 2

Provisions to ensure investor protection

Article 24

General principles and information to clients

1. Member States shall require that, when providing investment services or, where appropriate, ancillary services to clients, an investment firm act honestly, fairly and professionally in accordance with the best interests of its clients and comply, in particular, with the principles set out in this Article and in Article 25.

2. Investment firms which manufacture financial instruments for sale to clients shall ensure that those financial instruments are designed to meet the needs of an identified target market of end clients within the relevant category of clients, the strategy for distribution of the financial instruments is compatible with the identified target market, and the investment firm takes reasonable steps to ensure that the financial instrument is distributed to the identified target market.

An investment firm shall understand the financial instruments they offer or recommend, assess the compatibility of the financial instruments with the needs of the clients to whom it provides investment services, also taking account of the identified target market of end clients as referred to in Article 16(3), and ensure that financial instruments are offered or recommended only when this is in the interest of the client.

3. All information, including marketing communications, addressed by the investment firm to clients or potential clients shall be fair, clear and not misleading. Marketing communications shall be clearly identifiable as such.

4. Appropriate information shall be provided in good time to clients or potential clients with regard to the investment firm and its services, the financial instruments and proposed investment strategies, execution venues and all costs and related charges. That information shall include the following:

(a) when investment advice is provided, the investment firm must, in good time before it provides investment advice, inform the client:

(i) whether or not the advice is provided on an independent basis;

(ii) whether the advice is based on a broad or on a more restricted analysis of different types of financial instruments and, in particular, whether the range is limited to financial instruments issued or provided by entities having close links with the investment firm or any other legal or economic relationships, such as contractual relationships, so close as to pose a risk of impairing the independent basis of the advice provided;

(iii) whether the investment firm will provide the client with a periodic assessment of the suitability of the financial instruments recommended to that client;

(b) the information on financial instruments and proposed investment strategies must include appropriate guidance on and warnings of the risks associated with investments in those instruments or in respect of particular investment strategies and whether the financial instrument is intended for retail or professional clients, taking account of the identified target market in accordance with paragraph 2;

(c) the information on all costs and associated charges must include information relating to both investment and ancillary services, including the cost of advice, where relevant, the cost of the financial instrument recommended or marketed to the client and how the client may pay for it, also encompassing any third-party payments.

The information about all costs and charges, including costs and charges in connection with the investment service and the financial instrument, which are not caused by the occurrence of underlying market risk, shall be aggregated to allow the client to understand the overall cost as well as the cumulative effect on return of the investment, and where the client so requests, an itemised breakdown shall be provided. Where applicable, such information shall be provided to the client on a regular basis, at least annually, during the life of the investment.

5. The information referred to in paragraphs 4 and 9 shall be provided in a comprehensible form in such a manner that clients or potential clients are reasonably able to understand the nature and risks of the investment service and of the specific type of financial instrument that is being offered and, consequently, to take investment decisions on an informed basis. Member States may allow that information to be provided in a standardised format.

6. Where an investment service is offered as part of a financial product which is already subject to other provisions of Union law relating to credit institutions and consumer credits with respect to information requirements, that service shall not be additionally subject to the obligations set out in paragraphs 3, 4 and 5.

7. Where an investment firm informs the client that investment advice is provided on an independent basis, that investment firm shall:

(a) assess a sufficient range of financial instruments available on the market which must be sufficiently diverse with regard to their type and issuers or product providers to ensure that the client's investment objectives can be suitably met and must not be limited to financial instruments issued or provided by:

(i) the investment firm itself or by entities having close links with the investment firm; or

(ii) other entities with which the investment firm has such close legal or economic relationships, such as contractual relationships, as to pose a risk of impairing the independent basis of the advice provided;

(b) not accept and retain fees, commissions or any monetary or non-monetary benefits paid or provided by any third party or a person acting on behalf of a third party in relation to the provision of the service to clients. Minor non-monetary benefits that are capable of enhancing the quality of service provided to a client and are of a scale and nature such that they could not be judged to impair compliance with the investment firm's duty to act in the best interest of the client must be clearly disclosed and are excluded from this point.

8. When providing portfolio management the investment firm shall not accept and retain fees, commissions or any monetary or non-monetary benefits paid or provided by any third party or a person acting on behalf of a third party in relation to the provision of the service to clients. Minor non-monetary benefits that are capable of enhancing the quality of service provided to a client and are of a scale and nature such that they could not be judged to impair compliance with the investment firm's duty to act in the best interest of the client shall be clearly disclosed and are excluded from this paragraph.

9. Member States shall ensure that investment firms are regarded as not fulfilling their obligations under Article 23 or under paragraph 1 of this Article where they pay or are paid any fee or commission, or provide or are provided with any non-monetary benefit in connection with the provision of an investment service or an ancillary service, to or by any party except the client or a person on behalf of the client, other than where the payment or benefit:

(a) is designed to enhance the quality of the relevant service to the client; and

(b) does not impair compliance with the investment firm's duty to act honestly, fairly and professionally in accordance with the best interest of its clients.

The existence, nature and amount of the payment or benefit referred to in the first subparagraph, or, where the amount cannot be ascertained, the method of calculating that amount, must be clearly disclosed to the client, in a manner that is comprehensive, accurate and understandable, prior to the provision of the relevant investment or ancillary service. Where applicable, the investment firm shall also inform the client on mechanisms for transferring to the client the fee, commission, monetary or non-monetary benefit received in relation to the provision of the investment or ancillary service.

The payment or benefit which enables or is necessary for the provision of investment services, such as custody costs, settlement and exchange fees, regulatory levies or legal fees, and which by its nature cannot give rise to conflicts with the investment firm's duties to act honestly, fairly and professionally in accordance with the best interests of its clients, is not subject to the requirements set out in the first subparagraph.

10. An investment firm which provides investment services to clients shall ensure that it does not remunerate or assess the performance of its staff in a way that conflicts with its duty to act in the best interests of its clients. In particular, it shall not make any arrangement by way of remuneration, sales targets or otherwise that could provide an incentive to its staff to recommend a particular financial instrument to a retail client when the investment firm could offer a different financial instrument which would better meet that client's needs.

11. When an investment service is offered together with another service or product as part of a package or as a condition for the same agreement or package, the investment firm shall inform the client whether it is possible to buy the different components separately and shall provide for a separate evidence of the costs and charges of each component.

Where the risks resulting from such an agreement or package offered to a retail client are likely to be different from the risks associated with the components taken separately, the investment firm shall provide an adequate description of the different components of the agreement or package and the way in which its interaction modifies the risks.

ESMA, in cooperation with EBA and EIOPA, shall develop by 3 January 2016, and update periodically, guidelines for the assessment and the supervision of cross-selling practices indicating, in particular, situations in which cross-selling practices are not compliant with obligations laid down in paragraph 1.

12. Member States may, in exceptional cases, impose additional requirements on investment firms in respect of the matters covered by this Article. Such requirements must be objectively justified and proportionate so as to address specific risks to investor protection or to market integrity which are of particular importance in the circumstances of the market structure of that Member State.

Member States shall notify the Commission of any requirement which they intend to impose in accordance with this paragraph without undue delay and at least two months before the date appointed for that requirement to come into force. The notification shall include a justification for that requirement. Any such additional requirements shall not restrict or otherwise affect the rights of investment firms under Articles 34 and 35 of this Directive.

The Commission shall within two months from the notification referred to in the second subparagraph provide its opinion on the proportionality of and justification for the additional requirements.

The Commission shall communicate to Member States and make public on its website the additional requirements imposed in accordance with this paragraph.

Member States may retain additional requirements that were notified to the Commission in accordance with Article 4 of Directive 2006/73/EC before 2 July 2014 provided that the conditions laid down in that Article are met.

13. The Commission shall be empowered to adopt delegated acts in accordance with Article 89 to ensure that investment firms comply with the principles set out in this Article when providing investment or ancillary services to their clients, including:

(a) the conditions with which the information must comply in order to be fair, clear and not misleading;

(b) the details about content and format of information to clients in relation to client categorisation, investment firms and their services, financial instruments, costs and charges;

(c) the criteria for the assessment of a range of financial instruments available on the market;

(d) the criteria to assess compliance of firms receiving inducements with the obligation to act honestly, fairly and professionally in accordance with the best interest of the client.

In formulating the requirements for information on financial instruments in relation to point b of paragraph 4 information on the structure of the product shall be included, where applicable, taking into account any relevant standardized information required under Union law.

14. The delegated acts referred to in paragraph 13 shall take into account:

(a) the nature of the service(s) offered or provided to the client or potential client, taking into account the type, object, size and frequency of the transactions;

(b) the nature and range of products being offered or considered including different types of financial instruments;

(c) the retail or professional nature of the client or potential clients or, in the case of paragraphs 4 and 5, their classification as eligible counterparties.

Article 25

Assessment of suitability and appropriateness and reporting to clients

1. Member States shall require investment firms to ensure and demonstrate to competent authorities on request that natural persons giving investment advice or information about financial instruments, investment services or ancillary services to clients on behalf of the investment firm possess the necessary knowledge and competence to fulfil their obligations under Article 24 and this Article. Member States shall publish the criteria to be used for assessing such knowledge and competence.

2. When providing investment advice or portfolio management the investment firm shall obtain the necessary information regarding the client's or potential client's knowledge and experience in the investment field relevant to the specific type of product or service, that person's financial situation including his ability to bear losses, and his investment objectives including his risk tolerance so as to enable the investment firm to recommend to the client or potential client the investment services and financial instruments that are suitable for him and, in particular, are in accordance with his risk tolerance and ability to bear losses.

Member States shall ensure that where an investment firm provides investment advice recommending a package of services or products bundled pursuant to Article 24(11), the overall bundled package is suitable.

3. Member States shall ensure that investment firms, when providing investment services other than those referred to in paragraph 2, ask the client or potential client to provide information regarding that person's knowledge and experience in the investment field relevant to the specific type of product or service offered or demanded so as to enable the investment firm to assess whether the investment service or product envisaged is appropriate for the client. Where a bundle of services or products is envisaged pursuant to Article 24(11), the assessment shall consider whether the overall bundled package is appropriate.

Where the investment firm considers, on the basis of the information received under the first subparagraph, that the product or service is not appropriate to the client or potential client, the investment firm shall warn the client or potential client. That warning may be provided in a standardised format.

Where clients or potential clients do not provide the information referred to under the first subparagraph, or where they provide insufficient information regarding their knowledge and experience, the investment firm shall warn them that the investment firm is not in a position to determine whether the service or product envisaged is appropriate for them. That warning may be provided in a standardised format.

4. Member States shall allow investment firms when providing investment services that only consist of execution or reception and transmission of client orders with or without ancillary services, excluding the granting of credits or loans as specified in Section B.1 of Annex I that do not comprise of existing credit limits of loans, current accounts and overdraft facilities of clients, to provide those investment services to their clients without the need to obtain the information or make the determination provided for in paragraph 3 where all the following conditions are met:

(a) the services relate to any of the following financial instruments:

(i) shares admitted to trading on a regulated market or on an equivalent third-country market or on a MTF, where those are shares in companies, and excluding shares in non-UCITS collective investment undertakings and shares that embed a derivative;

(ii) bonds or other forms of securitised debt admitted to trading on a regulated market or on an equivalent third country market or on a MTF, excluding those that embed a derivative or incorporate a structure which makes it difficult for the client to understand the risk involved;

(iii) money-market instruments, excluding those that embed a derivative or incorporate a structure which makes it difficult for the client to understand the risk involved;

(iv) shares or units in UCITS, excluding structured UCITS as referred to in the second subparagraph of Article 36(1) of Regulation (EU) No 583/2010;

(v) structured deposits, excluding those that incorporate a structure which makes it difficult for the client to understand the risk of return or the cost of exiting the product before term;

(vi) other non-complex financial instruments for the purpose of this paragraph.

For the purpose of this point, if the requirements and the procedure laid down under the third and the fourth subparagraphs of Article 4(1) of Directive 2003/71/EC are fulfilled, a third-country market shall be considered to be equivalent to a regulated market.

(b) the service is provided at the initiative of the client or potential client;

(c) the client or potential client has been clearly informed that in the provision of that service the investment firm is not required to assess the appropriateness of the financial instrument or service provided or offered and that therefore he does not benefit from the corresponding protection of the relevant conduct of business rules. Such a warning may be provided in a standardised format;

(d) the investment firm complies with its obligations under Article 23.

5. The investment firm shall establish a record that includes the document or documents agreed between the investment firm and the client that set out the rights and obligations of the parties, and the other terms on which the investment firm will provide services to the client. The rights and duties of the parties to the contract may be incorporated by reference to other documents or legal texts.

6. The investment firm shall provide the client with adequate reports on the service provided in a durable medium. Those reports shall include periodic communications to clients, taking into account the type and the complexity of financial instruments involved and the nature of the service provided to the client and shall include, where applicable, the costs associated with the transactions and services undertaken on behalf of the client.

When providing investment advice, the investment firm shall, before the transaction is made, provide the client with a statement on suitability in a durable medium specifying the advice given and how that advice meets the preferences, objectives and other characteristics of the retail client.

Where the agreement to buy or sell a financial instrument is concluded using a means of distance communication which prevents the prior delivery of the suitability statement, the investment firm may provide the written statement on suitability in a durable medium immediately after the client is bound by any agreement, provided both the following conditions are met:

(a) the client has consented to receiving the suitability statement without undue delay after the conclusion of the transaction; and

(b) the investment firm has given the client the option of delaying the transaction in order to receive the statement on suitability in advance.

Where an investment firm provides portfolio management or has informed the client that it will carry out a periodic assessment of suitability, the periodic report shall contain an updated statement of how the investment meets the client's preferences, objectives and other characteristics of the retail client.

7. If a credit agreement relating to residential immovable property, which is subject to the provisions concerning creditworthiness assessment of consumers laid down in Directive 2014/17/EU of the European Parliament and the Council ([1]), has as a prerequisite the provision to that same consumer of an investment service in relation to mortgage bonds specifically issued to secure the financing of and having identical terms as the credit agreement relating to residential immovable property, in order for the loan to be payable, refinanced or redeemed, that service shall not be subject to the obligations set out in this Article.

8. The Commission shall be empowered to adopt delegated acts in accordance with Article 89 to ensure that investment firms comply with the principles set out in paragraphs 2 to 6 of this Article when providing investment or ancillary services to their clients, including information to obtain when assessing the suitability or appropriateness of the services and financial instruments for their clients, criteria to assess non-complex financial instruments for the purposes of point (a)(vi) of paragraph 4 of this Article, the content and the format of records and agreements for the provision of services to clients and of periodic reports to clients on the services provided. Those delegated acts shall take into account:

(a) the nature of the service(s) offered or provided to the client or potential client, having regard to the type, object, size and frequency of the transactions;

(b) the nature of the products being offered or considered, including different types of financial instruments;

(c) the retail or professional nature of the client or potential clients or, in the case of paragraph 6, their classification as eligible counterparties.

9. ESMA shall adopt by 3 January 2016 guidelines specifying criteria for the assessment of knowledge and competence required under paragraph 1.

10. ESMA shall develop by 3 January 2016, and update periodically, guidelines for the assessment of:

(a) financial instruments incorporating a structure which makes it difficult for the client to understand the risk involved in accordance with points (a)(ii) and (a)(iii) of paragraph 4;

(b) structured deposits incorporating a structure which makes it difficult for the client to understand the risk of return or the cost of exiting the product before term, in accordance with point (a)(v) of paragraph 4.

11. ESMA may develop guidelines, and update them periodically, for the assessment of financial instruments being classified as non-complex for the purpose of point (a)(vi) of paragraph 4, taking into account the delegated acts adopted under paragraph 8.

Article 26

Provision of services through the medium of another investment firm

Member States shall allow an investment firm receiving an instruction to provide investment or ancillary services on behalf of a client through the medium of another investment firm to rely on client information transmitted by the latter investment firm. The investment firm which mediates the instructions will remain responsible for the completeness and accuracy of the information transmitted.

([1]) Directive 2014/17/EU of the European Parliament and of the Council of 4 February 2014 on credit agreements for consumers relating to residential immovable property and amending Directives 2008/48/EC and 2013/36/EU and Regulation (EU) No 1093/2010 (OJ L 60, 28.2.2014, p. 34).

ANNEX I

LISTS OF SERVICES AND ACTIVITIES AND FINANCIAL INSTRUMENTS

SECTION A

Investment services and activities

(1) Reception and transmission of orders in relation to one or more financial instruments;

(2) Execution of orders on behalf of clients;

(3) Dealing on own account;

(4) Portfolio management;

(5) Investment advice;

(6) Underwriting of financial instruments and/or placing of financial instruments on a firm commitment basis;

(7) Placing of financial instruments without a firm commitment basis;

(8) Operation of an MTF;

(9) Operation of an OTF.

SECTION B

Ancillary services

(1) Safekeeping and administration of financial instruments for the account of clients, including custodianship and related services such as cash/collateral management and excluding maintaining securities accounts at the top tier level;

(2) Granting credits or loans to an investor to allow him to carry out a transaction in one or more financial instruments, where the firm granting the credit or loan is involved in the transaction;

(3) Advice to undertakings on capital structure, industrial strategy and related matters and advice and services relating to mergers and the purchase of undertakings;

(4) Foreign exchange services where these are connected to the provision of investment services;

(5) Investment research and financial analysis or other forms of general recommendation relating to transactions in financial instruments;

(6) Services related to underwriting.

(7) Investment services and activities as well as ancillary services of the type included under Section A or B of Annex 1 related to the underlying of the derivatives included under points (5), (6), (7) and (10) of Section C where these are connected to the provision of investment or ancillary services.

SECTION C

Financial instruments

(1) Transferable securities;

(2) Money-market instruments;

(3) Units in collective investment undertakings;

(4) Options, futures, swaps, forward rate agreements and any other derivative contracts relating to securities, currencies, interest rates or yields, emission allowances or other derivatives instruments, financial indices or financial measures which may be settled physically or in cash;

(5) Options, futures, swaps, forwards and any other derivative contracts relating to commodities that must be settled in cash or may be settled in cash at the option of one of the parties other than by reason of default or other termination event;

(6) Options, futures, swaps, and any other derivative contract relating to commodities that can be physically settled provided that they are traded on a regulated market, a MTF, or an OTF, except for wholesale energy products traded on an OTF that must be physically settled;

(7) Options, futures, swaps, forwards and any other derivative contracts relating to commodities, that can be physically settled not otherwise mentioned in point 6 of this Section and not being for commercial purposes, which have the characteristics of other derivative financial instruments;

(8) Derivative instruments for the transfer of credit risk;

(9) Financial contracts for differences;

(10) Options, futures, swaps, forward rate agreements and any other derivative contracts relating to climatic variables, freight rates or inflation rates or other official economic statistics that must be settled in cash or may be settled in cash at the option of one of the parties other than by reason of default or other termination event, as well as any other derivative contracts relating to assets, rights, obligations, indices and measures not otherwise mentioned in this Section, which have the characteristics of other derivative financial instruments, having regard to whether, inter alia, they are traded on a regulated market, OTF, or an MTF;

(11) Emission allowances consisting of any units recognised for compliance with the requirements of Directive 2003/87/EC (Emissions Trading Scheme).

SECTION D

Data reporting services

(1) Operating an APA;

(2) Operating a CTP;

(3) Operating an ARM.

ANNEX II

PROFESSIONAL CLIENTS FOR THE PURPOSE OF THIS DIRECTIVE

Professional client is a client who possesses the experience, knowledge and expertise to make its own investment decisions and properly assess the risks that it incurs. In order to be considered to be professional client, the client must comply with the following criteria:

I. CATEGORIES OF CLIENT WHO ARE CONSIDERED TO BE PROFESSIONALS

The following shall all be regarded as professionals in all investment services and activities and financial instruments for the purposes of the Directive.

(1) Entities which are required to be authorised or regulated to operate in the financial markets. The list below shall be understood as including all authorised entities carrying out the characteristic activities of the entities mentioned: entities authorised by a Member State under a Directive, entities authorised or regulated by a Member State without reference to a Directive, and entities authorised or regulated by a third country:

(a) Credit institutions;

(b) Investment firms;

(c) Other authorised or regulated financial institutions;

(d) Insurance companies;

(e) Collective investment schemes and management companies of such schemes;

(f) Pension funds and management companies of such funds;

(g) Commodity and commodity derivatives dealers;

(h) Locals;

(i) Other institutional investors;

(2) Large undertakings meeting two of the following size requirements on a company basis:

— balance sheet total: EUR 20 000 000

— net turnover: EUR 40 000 000

— own funds: EUR 2 000 000

(3) National and regional governments, including public bodies that manage public debt at national or regional level, Central Banks, international and supranational institutions such as the World Bank, the IMF, the ECB, the EIB and other similar international organisations.

(4) Other institutional investors whose main activity is to invest in financial instruments, including entities dedicated to the securitisation of assets or other financing transactions.

The entities referred to above are considered to be professionals. They must however be allowed to request non-professional treatment and investment firms may agree to provide a higher level of protection. Where the client of an investment firm is an undertaking referred to above, the investment firm must inform it prior to any provision of services that, on the basis of the information available to the investment firm, the client is deemed to be a professional client, and will be treated as such unless the investment firm and the client agree otherwise. The investment firm must also inform the customer that he can request a variation of the terms of the agreement in order to secure a higher degree of protection.

It is the responsibility of the client, considered to be a professional client, to ask for a higher level of protection when it deems it is unable to properly assess or manage the risks involved.

This higher level of protection will be provided when a client who is considered to be a professional enters into a written agreement with the investment firm to the effect that it shall not be treated as a professional for the purposes of the applicable conduct of business regime. Such agreement shall specify whether this applies to one or more particular services or transactions, or to one or more types of product or transaction.

II. CLIENTS WHO MAY BE TREATED AS PROFESSIONALS ON REQUEST

II.1. Identification criteria

Clients other than those mentioned in section I, including public sector bodies, local public authorities, municipalities and private individual investors, may also be allowed to waive some of the protections afforded by the conduct of business rules.

Investment firms shall therefore be allowed to treat any of those clients as professionals provided the relevant criteria and procedure mentioned below are fulfilled. Those clients shall not, however, be presumed to possess market knowledge and experience comparable to that of the categories listed in Section I.

Any such waiver of the protection afforded by the standard conduct of business regime shall be considered to be valid only if an adequate assessment of the expertise, experience and knowledge of the client, undertaken by the investment firm, gives reasonable assurance, in light of the nature of the transactions or services envisaged, that the client is capable of making investment decisions and understanding the risks involved.

The fitness test applied to managers and directors of entities licensed under Directives in the financial field could be regarded as an example of the assessment of expertise and knowledge. In the case of small entities, the person subject to that assessment shall be the person authorised to carry out transactions on behalf of the entity.

In the course of that assessment, as a minimum, two of the following criteria shall be satisfied:

— the client has carried out transactions, in significant size, on the relevant market at an average frequency of 10 per quarter over the previous four quarters,

— the size of the client's financial instrument portfolio, defined as including cash deposits and financial instruments exceeds EUR 500 000,

— the client works or has worked in the financial sector for at least one year in a professional position, which requires knowledge of the transactions or services envisaged.

Member States may adopt specific criteria for the assessment of the expertise and knowledge of municipalities and local public authorities requesting to be treated as professional clients. Those criteria can be alternative or additional to those listed in the fifth paragraph.

II.2. Procedure

Those clients may waive the benefit of the detailed rules of conduct only where the following procedure is followed:

— they must state in writing to the investment firm that they wish to be treated as a professional client, either generally or in respect of a particular investment service or transaction, or type of transaction or product,

— the investment firm must give them a clear written warning of the protections and investor compensation rights they may lose,

— they must state in writing, in a separate document from the contract, that they are aware of the consequences of losing such protections.

Before deciding to accept any request for waiver, investment firms must be required to take all reasonable steps to ensure that the client requesting to be treated as a professional client meets the relevant requirements stated in Section II.1.

However, if clients have already been categorised as professionals under parameters and procedures similar to those referred to above, it is not intended that their relationships with investment firms shall be affected by any new rules adopted pursuant to this Annex.

Firms must implement appropriate written internal policies and procedures to categorise clients. Professional clients are responsible for keeping the investment firm informed about any change, which could affect their current categorisation. Should the investment firm become aware however that the client no longer fulfils the initial conditions, which made him eligible for a professional treatment, the investment firm shall take appropriate action.

【参照条文】

●KWG（抜粋）

§ 1 Begriffsbestimmungen

(1) 1Kreditinstitute sind Unternehmen, die Bankgeschäfte gewerbsmäßig oder in einem Umfang betreiben, der einen in kaufmännischer Weise eingerichteten Geschäftsbetrieb erfordert. 2Bankgeschäfte sind

1.die Annahme fremder Gelder als Einlagen oder anderer unbedingt rückzahlbarer Gelder des Publikums, sofern der Rückzahlungsanspruch nicht in Inhaber- oder Orderschuldverschreibungen verbrieft wird, ohne Rücksicht darauf, ob Zinsen vergütet werden (Einlagengeschäft),

1a.die in § 1 Abs. 1 Satz 2 des Pfandbriefgesetzes bezeichneten Geschäfte (Pfandbriefgeschäft),

2.die Gewährung von Gelddarlehen und Akzeptkrediten (Kreditgeschäft),

3.der Ankauf von Wechseln und Schecks (Diskontgeschäft),

4.die Anschaffung und die Veräußerung von Finanzinstrumenten im eigenen Namen für fremde Rechnung (Finanzkommissionsgeschäft),

5.die Verwahrung und die Verwaltung von Wertpapieren für andere (Depotgeschäft),

6.die Tätigkeit als Zentralverwahrer im Sinne des Absatzes 6,

7.die Eingehung der Verpflichtung, zuvor veräußerte Darlehensforderungen vor Fälligkeit zurückzuerwerben,

8.die Übernahme von Bürgschaften, Garantien und sonstigen Gewährleistungen für andere (Garantiegeschäft),

9.die Durchführung des bargeldlosen Scheckeinzugs (Scheckeinzugsgeschäft), des Wechseleinzugs (Wechseleinzugsgeschäft) und die Ausgabe von Reiseschecks (Reisescheckgeschäft),

10.die Übernahme von Finanzinstrumenten für eigenes Risiko zur Plazierung oder die Übernahme gleichwertiger Garantien (Emissionsgeschäft),

11. [aufgehoben]

12.die Tätigkeit als zentrale Gegenpartei im Sinne von Absatz 31.

(1a) 1Finanzdienstleistungsinstitute sind Unternehmen, die Finanzdienstleistungen für andere gewerbsmäßig oder in einem Umfang erbringen, der einen in kaufmännischer Weise eingerichteten Geschäftsbetrieb erfordert, und die keine Kreditinstitute sind. 2Finanzdienstleistungen sind

1.die Vermittlung von Geschäften über die Anschaffung und die Veräußerung von Finanzinstrumenten (Anlagevermittlung),

1a.die Abgabe von persönlichen Empfehlungen an Kunden oder deren Vertreter, die sich auf Geschäfte mit bestimmten Finanzinstrumenten beziehen, sofern die Empfehlung auf eine Prüfung der persönlichen Umstände des Anlegers gestützt oder als für ihn geeignet dargestellt wird und nicht ausschließlich über Informationsverbreitungskanäle oder für die Öffentlichkeit bekannt gegeben wird (Anlageberatung),

1b.der Betrieb eines multilateralen Systems, das die Interessen einer Vielzahl von Personen am Kauf und Verkauf von Finanzinstrumenten innerhalb des Systems und nach festgelegten Bestimmungen in einer Weise zusammenbringt, die zu einem Vertrag über den Kauf dieser Finanzinstrumente führt (Betrieb eines

multilateralen Handelssystems),

1c.das Platzieren von Finanzinstrumenten ohne feste Übernahmeverpflichtung (Platzierungsgeschäft),

1d.der Betrieb eines multilateralen Systems, bei dem es sich nicht um einen organisierten Markt oder ein multilaterales Handelssystem handelt und das die Interessen einer Vielzahl Dritter am Kauf und Verkauf von Schuldverschreibungen, strukturierten Finanzprodukten, Emissionszertifikaten oder Derivaten innerhalb des Systems auf eine Weise zusammenführt, die zu einem Vertrag über den Kauf dieser Finanzinstrumente führt (Betrieb eines organisierten Handelssystems),

2.die Anschaffung und Veräußerung von Finanzinstrumenten im fremden Namen für fremde Rechnung (Abschlußvermittlung),

3.die Verwaltung einzelner in Finanzinstrumenten angelegter Vermögen für andere mit Entscheidungsspielraum (Finanzportfolioverwaltung),

4.der Eigenhandel durch das

a)kontinuierliche Anbieten des An- und Verkaufs von Finanzinstrumenten zu selbst gestellten Preisen für eigene Rechnung unter Einsatz des eigenen Kapitals,

b)häufige organisierte und systematische Betreiben von Handel für eigene Rechnung in erheblichem Umfang außerhalb eines organisierten Marktes oder eines multilateralen oder organisierten Handelssystems, wenn Kundenaufträge außerhalb eines geregelten Marktes oder eines multilateralen oder organisierten Handelssystems ausgeführt werden, ohne dass ein multilaterales Handelssystem betrieben wird (systematische Internalisierung),

c)Anschaffen oder Veräußern von Finanzinstrumenten für eigene Rechnung als Dienstleistung für andere oder

d)Kaufen oder Verkaufen von Finanzinstrumenten für eigene Rechnung als unmittelbarer oder mittelbarer Teilnehmer eines inländischen organisierten Marktes oder eines multilateralen oder organisierten Handelssystems mittels einer hochfrequenten algorithmischen Handelstechnik, die gekennzeichnet ist durch

aa)eine Infrastruktur zur Minimierung von Netzwerklatenzen und anderen Verzögerungen bei der Orderübertragung (Latenzen), die mindestens eine der folgenden Vorrichtungen für die Eingabe algorithmischer Aufträge aufweist: Kollokation, Proximity Hosting oder direkter elektronischer Hochgeschwindigkeitszugang,

bb)die Fähigkeit des Systems, einen Auftrag ohne menschliche Intervention im Sinne des Artikels 18 der Delegierten Verordnung (EU) 2017/565 der Kommission vom 25. April 2016 zur Ergänzung der Richtlinie 2014/65/EU des Europäischen Parlaments und des Rates in Bezug auf die organisatorischen Anforderungen an Wertpapierfirmen und die Bedingungen für die Ausübung ihrer Tätigkeit sowie in Bezug auf die Definition bestimmter Begriffe für die Zwecke der genannten Richtlinie (ABl. L 87 vom 31.3.2017, S. 1) in der jeweils geltenden Fassung, einzuleiten, zu erzeugen, weiterzuleiten oder auszuführen und

cc)ein hohes untertägiges Mitteilungsaufkommen im Sinne des Artikels 19 der Delegierten Verordnung (EU) 2017/565 in Form von Aufträgen, Kursangaben oder Stornierungen

auch ohne dass eine Dienstleistung für andere vorliegt (Hochfrequenzhandel),

5.die Vermittlung von Einlagengeschäften mit Unternehmen mit Sitz außerhalb des Europäischen Wirtschaftsraums (Drittstaateneinlagenvermittlung),

6.die Verwahrung, die Verwaltung und die Sicherung von Kryptowerten oder privaten kryptografischen Schlüsseln, die dazu dienen, Kryptowerte zu halten, zu speichern oder zu übertragen, für andere (Kryptoverwahrgeschäft),

7.der Handel mit Sorten (Sortengeschäft),

8. [aufgehoben]

9.der laufende Ankauf von Forderungen auf der Grundlage von Rahmenverträgen mit oder ohne Rückgriff (Factoring),

10.der Abschluss von Finanzierungsleasingverträgen als Leasinggeber und die Verwaltung von Objektgesellschaften im Sinne des § 2 Absatz 6 Satz 1 Nummer 17 außerhalb der Verwaltung eines Investmentvermögens im Sinne des § 1 Absatz 1 des Kapitalanlagegesetzbuchs (Finanzierungsleasing),

11.die Anschaffung und die Veräußerung von Finanzinstrumenten außerhalb der Verwaltung eines Investmentvermögens im Sinne des § 1 Absatz 1 des Kapitalanlagegesetzbuchs für eine Gemeinschaft von Anlegern, die natürliche Personen sind, mit Entscheidungsspielraum bei der Auswahl der Finanzinstrumente, sofern dies ein Schwerpunkt des angebotenen Produktes ist und zu dem Zweck erfolgt, dass diese Anleger an der Wertentwicklung der erworbenen Finanzinstrumente teilnehmen (Anlageverwaltung),

12.die Verwahrung und die Verwaltung von Wertpapieren ausschließlich für alternative Investmentfonds (AIF) im Sinne des § 1 Absatz 3 des Kapitalanlagegesetzbuchs (eingeschränktes Verwahrgeschäft).

3Die Anschaffung und die Veräußerung von Finanzinstrumenten für eigene Rechnung, die nicht Eigenhandel im Sinne des § 1 Absatz 1a Satz 2 Nummer 4 ist (Eigengeschäft), gilt als Finanzdienstleistung, wenn das Eigengeschäft von einem Unternehmen betrieben wird, das

1.dieses Geschäft, ohne bereits aus anderem Grunde Institut zu sein, gewerbsmäßig oder in einem Umfang betreibt, der einen in kaufmännischer Weise eingerichteten Geschäftsbetrieb erfordert, und

2.einer Instituts-, einer Finanzholding- oder gemischten Finanzholding-Gruppe oder einem Finanzkonglomerat angehört, der oder dem ein CRR-Kreditinstitut angehört.

4Ein Unternehmen, das als Finanzdienstleistung geltendes Eigengeschäft nach Satz 3 betreibt, gilt als Finanzdienstleistungsinstitut. 5Die Sätze 3 und 4 gelten nicht für Abwicklungsanstalten nach § 8a Absatz 1 Satz 1 des Stabilisierungsfondsgesetzes. 6Ob ein häufiger systematischer Handel im Sinne des Satzes 2 Nummer 4 Buchstabe b vorliegt, bemisst sich nach der Zahl der Geschäfte außerhalb eines Handelsplatzes im Sinne des § 2 Absatz 22 des Wertpapierhandelsgesetzes (OTC-Handel) mit einem Finanzinstrument zur Ausführung von Kundenaufträgen, die für eigene Rechnung durchgeführt werden. 7Ob ein Handel in erheblichem Umfang im Sinne des Satzes 2 Nummer 4 Buchstabe b vorliegt, bemisst sich entweder nach dem Anteil des OTC-Handels an dem Gesamthandelsvolumen des Unternehmens in einem bestimmten Finanzinstrument oder nach dem Verhältnis des OTC-Handels des Unternehmens zum Gesamthandelsvolumen in einem bestimmten Finanzinstrument in der Europäischen Union. 8Die

Voraussetzungen der systematischen Internalisierung sind erst dann erfüllt, wenn sowohl die in den Artikeln 12 bis 17 der Delegierten Verordnung (EU) 2017/565 bestimmte Obergrenze für häufigen systematischen Handel als auch die in der vorgenannten Delegierten Verordnung bestimmte einschlägige Obergrenze für den Handel in erheblichem Umfang überschritten werden oder wenn ein Unternehmen sich freiwillig den für die systematische Internalisierung geltenden Regelungen unterworfen und einen entsprechenden Erlaubnisantrag bei der Bundesanstalt gestellt hat.

(1b) Institute im Sinne dieses Gesetzes sind Kreditinstitute und Finanzdienstleistungsinstitute.

(2) (以下、略)

§ 2 Ausnahmen

(6) 1Als Finanzdienstleistungsinstitute gelten nicht

1.die Deutsche Bundesbank und vergleichbare Institutionen in den anderen Staaten der Europäischen Union, die Mitglieder des Europäischen Systems der Zentralbanken sind;

1a.von zwei oder mehr Mitgliedstaaten der Europäischen Union gegründete internationale Finanzinstitute, die dem Zweck dienen, Finanzmittel zu mobilisieren und seinen Mitgliedern Finanzhilfen zu gewähren, sofern diese von schwerwiegenden Finanzierungsproblemen betroffen oder bedroht sind;

2.die Kreditanstalt für Wiederaufbau;

3.die öffentliche Schuldenverwaltung des Bundes oder eines Landes, eines ihrer Sondervermögen oder eines anderen Staates des Europäischen Wirtschaftsraums und deren Zentralbanken;

4.private und öffentlich-rechtliche Versicherungsunternehmen;

5.Unternehmen, die Finanzdienstleistungen im Sinne des § 1 Absatz 1a Satz 2 ausschließlich für ihre Mutterunternehmen oder ihre Tochter- oder Schwesterunternehmen erbringen;

5a.Kapitalverwaltungsgesellschaften und extern verwaltete Investmentgesellschaften, sofern sie nur die kollektive Vermögensverwaltung erbringen oder neben der kollektiven Vermögensverwaltung ausschließlich die in § 20 Absatz 2 und 3 des Kapitalanlagegesetzbuchs aufgeführten Dienstleistungen oder Nebendienstleistungen als Finanzdienstleistungen erbringen;

5b.EU-Verwaltungsgesellschaften und ausländische AIF-Verwaltungsgesellschaften, sofern sie nur die kollektive Vermögensverwaltung erbringen oder neben der kollektiven Vermögensverwaltung ausschließlich die in Artikel 6 Absatz 3 der Richtlinie 2009/65/EG oder die in Artikel 6 Absatz 4 der Richtlinie 2011/61/EU aufgeführten Dienstleistungen oder Nebendienstleistungen als Finanzdienstleistungen erbringen;

6.Unternehmen, deren Finanzdienstleistung für andere ausschließlich in der Verwaltung eines Systems von Arbeitnehmerbeteiligungen an den eigenen oder an mit ihnen verbundenen Unternehmen besteht;

7.Unternehmen, die ausschließlich Finanzdienstleistungen im Sinne sowohl der Nummer 5 als auch der Nummer 6 erbringen;

8.Unternehmen, die als Finanzdienstleistungen für andere ausschließlich die Anlageberatung und die Anlagevermittlung zwischen Kunden und

a)inländischen Instituten,
b)Instituten oder Finanzunternehmen mit Sitz in einem anderen Staat des Europäischen Wirtschaftsraums, die die Voraussetzungen nach § 53b Abs. 1 Satz 1 oder Abs. 7 erfüllen,
c)Unternehmen, die auf Grund einer Rechtsverordnung nach § 53c gleichgestellt oder freigestellt sind,
d)Kapitalverwaltungsgesellschaften, extern verwalteten Investmentgesellschaften, EU-Verwaltungsgesellschaften oder ausländischen AIF-Verwaltungsgesellschaften oder
e)Anbietern oder Emittenten von Vermögensanlagen im Sinne des § 1 Absatz 2 des Vermögensanlagengesetzes
betreiben, sofern sich diese Finanzdienstleistungen auf Anteile oder Aktien an inländischen Investmentvermögen, die von einer Kapitalverwaltungsgesellschaft ausgegeben werden, die eine Erlaubnis nach § 7 oder § 97 Absatz 1 des Investmentgesetzes in der bis zum 21. Juli 2013 geltenden Fassung erhalten hat, die für den in § 345 Absatz 2 Satz 1, Absatz 3 Satz 2, in Verbindung mit Absatz 2 Satz 1, oder Absatz 4 Satz 1 des Kapitalanlagegesetzbuchs vorgesehenen Zeitraum noch fortbesteht, oder eine Erlaubnis nach den §§ 20, 21 oder §§ 20, 22 des Kapitalanlagegesetzbuchs erhalten hat oder die von einer EU-Verwaltungsgesellschaft ausgegeben werden, die eine Erlaubnis nach Artikel 6 der Richtlinie 2009/65/EG oder der Richtlinie 2011/61/EU erhalten hat, oder auf Anteile oder Aktien an EU-Investmentvermögen oder ausländischen AIF, die nach dem Kapitalanlagegesetzbuch vertrieben werden dürfen, mit Ausnahme solcher AIF, die nach § 330a des Kapitalanlagegesetzbuchs vertrieben werden dürfen, oder auf Vermögensanlagen im Sinne des § 1 Absatz 2 des Vermögensanlagengesetzes, die erstmals öffentlich angeboten werden, beschränken und die Unternehmen nicht befugt sind, sich bei der Erbringung dieser Finanzdienstleistungen Eigentum oder Besitz an Geldern oder Anteilen von Kunden zu verschaffen, es sei denn, das Unternehmen beantragt und erhält eine entsprechende Erlaubnis nach § 32 Abs. 1; Anteile oder Aktien an Hedgefonds im Sinne von § 283 des Kapitalanlagegesetzbuchs gelten nicht als Anteile an Investmentvermögen im Sinne dieser Vorschrift;
（・・・・略）
15.Unternehmen, die als Finanzdienstleistung im Sinne des § 1 Abs. 1a Satz 2 ausschließlich die Anlageberatung im Rahmen einer anderen beruflichen Tätigkeit erbringen, ohne sich die Anlageberatung besonders vergüten zu lassen;
（以下、略）

●WpHG（抜粋）

§ 2 Begriffsbestimmungen
(1) Wertpapiere im Sinne dieses Gesetzes sind, auch wenn keine Urkunden über sie ausgestellt sind, alle Gattungen von übertragbaren Wertpapieren mit Ausnahme von Zahlungsinstrumenten, die ihrer Art nach auf den Finanzmärkten handelbar sind, insbesondere
1.Aktien,

2.andere Anteile an in- oder ausländischen juristischen Personen, Personengesellschaften und sonstigen Unternehmen, soweit sie Aktien vergleichbar sind, sowie Hinterlegungsscheine, die Aktien vertreten,
3.Schuldtitel,
a)insbesondere Genussscheine und Inhaberschuldverschreibungen und Orderschuldverschreibungen sowie Hinterlegungsscheine, die Schuldtitel vertreten,
b)sonstige Wertpapiere, die zum Erwerb oder zur Veräußerung von Wertpapieren nach den Nummern 1 und 2 berechtigen oder zu einer Barzahlung führen, die in Abhängigkeit von Wertpapieren, von Währungen, Zinssätzen oder anderen Erträgen, von Waren, Indices oder Messgrößen bestimmt wird; nähere Bestimmungen enthält die Delegierte Verordnung (EU) 2017/565 der Kommission vom 25. April 2016 zur Ergänzung der Richtlinie 2014/65/EU des Europäischen Parlaments und des Rates in Bezug auf die organisatorischen Anforderungen an Wertpapierfirmen und die Bedingungen für die Ausübung ihrer Tätigkeit sowie in Bezug auf die Definition bestimmter Begriffe für die Zwecke der genannten Richtlinie (ABl. L 87 vom 31.3.2017, S. 1), in der jeweils geltenden Fassung.
(2) Geldmarktinstrumente im Sinne dieses Gesetzes sind Instrumente, die üblicherweise auf dem Geldmarkt gehandelt werden, insbesondere Schatzanweisungen, Einlagenzertifikate, Commercial Papers und sonstige vergleichbare Instrumente, sofern im Einklang mit Artikel 11 der Delegierten Verordnung (EU) 2017/565
1.ihr Wert jederzeit bestimmt werden kann,
2.es sich nicht um Derivate handelt und
3.ihre Fälligkeit bei Emission höchstens 397 Tage beträgt,
es sei denn, es handelt sich um Zahlungsinstrumente.
(3) Derivative Geschäfte im Sinne dieses Gesetzes sind
1.als Kauf, Tausch oder anderweitig ausgestaltete Festgeschäfte oder Optionsgeschäfte, die zeitlich verzögert zu erfüllen sind und deren Wert sich unmittelbar oder mittelbar vom Preis oder Maß eines Basiswertes ableitet (Termingeschäfte) mit Bezug auf die folgenden Basiswerte:
a)Wertpapiere oder Geldmarktinstrumente,
b)Devisen, soweit das Geschäft nicht die in Artikel 10 der Delegierten Verordnung (EU) 2017/565 genannten Voraussetzungen erfüllt, oder Rechnungseinheiten,
c)Zinssätze oder andere Erträge,
d)Indices der Basiswerte der Buchstaben a, b, c oder f, andere Finanzindizes oder Finanzmessgrößen,
e)derivative Geschäfte oder
f)Berechtigungen nach § 3 Nummer 3 des Treibhausgas-Emissionshandelsgesetzes, Emissionsreduktionseinheiten nach § 2 Nummer 20 des Projekt-Mechanismen-Gesetzes und zertifizierte Emissionsreduktionen nach § 2 Nummer 21 des Projekt-Mechanismen-Gesetzes, soweit diese jeweils im Emissionshandelsregister gehalten werden dürfen (Emissionszertifikate);
2.Termingeschäfte mit Bezug auf Waren, Frachtsätze, Klima- oder andere physikalische Variablen, Inflationsraten oder andere volkswirtschaftliche Variablen oder sonstige Vermögenswerte, Indices oder

Messwerte als Basiswerte, sofern sie

a)durch Barausgleich zu erfüllen sind oder einer Vertragspartei das Recht geben, einen Barausgleich zu verlangen, ohne dass dieses Recht durch Ausfall oder ein anderes Beendigungsereignis begründet ist,

b)auf einem organisierten Markt oder in einem multilateralen oder organisierten Handelssystem geschlossen werden und nicht über ein organisiertes Handelssystem gehandelte Energiegroßhandelsprodukte im Sinne von Absatz 20 sind, die effektiv geliefert werden müssen, oder

c)die Merkmale anderer Derivatekontrakte im Sinne des Artikels 7 der Delegierten Verordnung (EU) 2017/565 aufweisen und nichtkommerziellen Zwecken dienen,

und sofern sie keine Kassageschäfte im Sinne des Artikels 7 der Delegierten Verordnung (EU) 2017/565 sind;

3.finanzielle Differenzgeschäfte;

4.als Kauf, Tausch oder anderweitig ausgestaltete Festgeschäfte oder Optionsgeschäfte, die zeitlich verzögert zu erfüllen sind und dem Transfer von Kreditrisiken dienen (Kreditderivate);

5.Termingeschäfte mit Bezug auf die in Artikel 8 der Delegierten Verordnung (EU) 2017/565 genannten Basiswerte, sofern sie die Bedingungen der Nummer 2 erfüllen.

(4) Finanzinstrumente im Sinne dieses Gesetzes sind

1.Wertpapiere im Sinne des Absatzes 1,

2.Anteile an Investmentvermögen im Sinne des § 1 Absatz 1 des Kapitalanlagegesetzbuchs,

3.Geldmarktinstrumente im Sinne des Absatzes 2,

4.derivative Geschäfte im Sinne des Absatzes 3,

5.Emissionszertifikate,

6.Rechte auf Zeichnung von Wertpapieren und

7.Vermögensanlagen im Sinne des § 1 Absatz 2 des Vermögensanlagengesetzes mit Ausnahme von Anteilen an einer Genossenschaft im Sinne des § 1 des Genossenschaftsgesetzes sowie Namensschuldverschreibungen, die mit einer vereinbarten festen Laufzeit, einem unveränderlich vereinbarten festen positiven Zinssatz ausgestattet sind, bei denen das investierte Kapital ohne Anrechnung von Zinsen ungemindert zum Zeitpunkt der Fälligkeit zum vollen Nennwert zurückgezahlt wird, und die von einem CRR-Kreditinstitut im Sinne des § 1 Absatz 3d Satz 1 des Kreditwesengesetzes, dem eine Erlaubnis nach § 32 Absatz 1 des Kreditwesengesetzes erteilt worden ist, oder von einem in Artikel 2 Absatz 5 Nummer 5 der Richtlinie 2013/36/EU namentlich genannten Kreditinstitut, das über eine Erlaubnis verfügt, Bankgeschäfte im Sinne von § 1 Absatz 1 Satz 2 Nummer 1 und 2 des Kreditwesengesetzes zu betreiben, ausgegeben werden, wenn das darauf eingezahlte Kapital im Falle des Insolvenzverfahrens über das Vermögen des Instituts oder der Liquidation des Instituts nicht erst nach Befriedigung aller nicht nachrangigen Gläubiger zurückgezahlt wird.

(5) Waren im Sinne dieses Gesetzes sind fungible Wirtschaftsgüter, die geliefert werden können; dazu zählen auch Metalle, Erze und Legierungen, landwirtschaftliche Produkte und Energien wie Strom.

(6) Waren-Spot-Kontrakt im Sinne dieses Gesetzes ist ein Vertrag im Sinne des Artikels 3 Absatz 1 Nummer 15 der Verordnung (EU) Nr. 596/2014.

(7) Referenzwert im Sinne dieses Gesetzes ist ein Kurs, Index oder Wert im Sinne des Artikels 3 Absatz 1 Nummer 29 der Verordnung (EU) Nr. 596/2014.

(8) 1Wertpapierdienstleistungen im Sinne dieses Gesetzes sind

1.die Anschaffung oder Veräußerung von Finanzinstrumenten im eigenen Namen für fremde Rechnung (Finanzkommissionsgeschäft),

2.das

a)kontinuierliche Anbieten des An- und Verkaufs von Finanzinstrumenten an den Finanzmärkten zu selbst gestellten Preisen für eigene Rechnung unter Einsatz des eigenen Kapitals (Market-Making),

b)häufige organisierte und systematische Betreiben von Handel für eigene Rechnung in erheblichem Umfang außerhalb eines organisierten Marktes oder eines multilateralen oder organisierten Handelssystems, wenn Kundenaufträge außerhalb eines geregelten Marktes oder eines multilateralen oder organisierten Handelssystems ausgeführt werden, ohne dass ein multilaterales Handelssystem betrieben wird (systematische Internalisierung),

c)Anschaffen oder Veräußern von Finanzinstrumenten für eigene Rechnung als Dienstleistung für andere (Eigenhandel) oder

d)Kaufen oder Verkaufen von Finanzinstrumenten für eigene Rechnung als unmittelbarer oder mittelbarer Teilnehmer eines inländischen organisierten Marktes oder eines multilateralen oder organisierten Handelssystems mittels einer hochfrequenten algorithmischen Handelstechnik im Sinne von Absatz 44, auch ohne Dienstleistung für andere (Hochfrequenzhandel),

3.die Anschaffung oder Veräußerung von Finanzinstrumenten in fremdem Namen für fremde Rechnung (Abschlussvermittlung),

4.die Vermittlung von Geschäften über die Anschaffung und die Veräußerung von Finanzinstrumenten (Anlagevermittlung),

5.die Übernahme von Finanzinstrumenten für eigenes Risiko zur Platzierung oder die Übernahme gleichwertiger Garantien (Emissionsgeschäft),

6.die Platzierung von Finanzinstrumenten ohne feste Übernahmeverpflichtung (Platzierungsgeschäft),

7.die Verwaltung einzelner oder mehrerer in Finanzinstrumenten angelegter Vermögen für andere mit Entscheidungsspielraum (Finanzportfolioverwaltung),

8.der Betrieb eines multilateralen Systems, das die Interessen einer Vielzahl von Personen am Kauf und Verkauf von Finanzinstrumenten innerhalb des Systems und nach nichtdiskretionären Bestimmungen in einer Weise zusammenbringt, die zu einem Vertrag über den Kauf dieser Finanzinstrumente führt (Betrieb eines multilateralen Handelssystems),

9.der Betrieb eines multilateralen Systems, bei dem es sich nicht um einen organisierten Markt oder ein multilaterales Handelssystem handelt und das die Interessen einer Vielzahl Dritter am Kauf und Verkauf von Schuldverschreibungen, strukturierten Finanzprodukten, Emissionszertifikaten oder Derivaten innerhalb des Systems auf eine Weise zusammenführt, die zu einem Vertrag über den Kauf dieser Finanzinstrumente führt

(Betrieb eines organisierten Handelssystems),

10.die Abgabe von persönlichen Empfehlungen im Sinne des Artikels 9 der Delegierten Verordnung (EU) 2017/565 an Kunden oder deren Vertreter, die sich auf Geschäfte mit bestimmten Finanzinstrumenten beziehen, sofern die Empfehlung auf eine Prüfung der persönlichen Umstände des Anlegers gestützt oder als für ihn geeignet dargestellt wird und nicht ausschließlich über Informationsverbreitungskanäle oder für die Öffentlichkeit bekannt gegeben wird (Anlageberatung).

2Das Finanzkommissionsgeschäft, der Eigenhandel und die Abschlussvermittlung umfassen den Abschluss von Vereinbarungen über den Verkauf von Finanzinstrumenten, die von einem Wertpapierdienstleistungsunternehmen oder einem Kreditinstitut ausgegeben werden, im Zeitpunkt ihrer Emission. 3Ob ein häufiger systematischer Handel vorliegt, bemisst sich nach der Zahl der Geschäfte außerhalb eines Handelsplatzes (OTC-Handel) mit einem Finanzinstrument zur Ausführung von Kundenaufträgen, die von dem Wertpapierdienstleistungsunternehmen für eigene Rechnung durchgeführt werden. 4Ob ein Handel in erheblichem Umfang vorliegt, bemisst sich entweder nach dem Anteil des OTC-Handels an dem Gesamthandelsvolumen des Wertpapierdienstleistungsunternehmens in einem bestimmten Finanzinstrument oder nach dem Verhältnis des OTC-Handels des Wertpapierdienstleistungsunternehmens zum Gesamthandelsvolumen in einem bestimmten Finanzinstrument in der Europäischen Union; nähere Bestimmungen enthalten die Artikel 12 bis 17 der Delegierten Verordnung (EU) 2017/565. 5Die Voraussetzungen der systematischen Internalisierung sind erst dann erfüllt, wenn sowohl die Obergrenze für den häufigen systematischen Handel als auch die Obergrenze für den Handel in erheblichem Umfang überschritten werden oder wenn ein Unternehmen sich freiwillig den für die systematische Internalisierung geltenden Regelungen unterworfen und eine Erlaubnis zum Betreiben der systematischen Internalisierung bei der Bundesanstalt beantragt hat. 6Als Wertpapierdienstleistung gilt auch die Anschaffung und Veräußerung von Finanzinstrumenten für eigene Rechnung, die keine Dienstleistung für andere im Sinne des Satzes 1 Nr. 2 darstellt (Eigengeschäft). 7Der Finanzportfolioverwaltung gleichgestellt ist hinsichtlich der §§ 63 bis 83 und 85 bis 92 dieses Gesetzes sowie des Artikels 20 Absatz 1 der Verordnung (EU) Nr. 596/2014, des Artikels 26 der Verordnung (EU) Nr. 600/2014 und der Artikel 72 bis 76 der Delegierten Verordnung (EU) 2017/565 die erlaubnispflichtige Anlageverwaltung nach § 1 Absatz 1a Satz 2 Nummer 11 des Kreditwesengesetzes.

(9) Wertpapiernebendienstleistungen im Sinne dieses Gesetzes sind

1.die Verwahrung und die Verwaltung von Finanzinstrumenten für andere, einschließlich Depotverwahrung und verbundener Dienstleistungen wie Cash-Management oder die Verwaltung von Sicherheiten mit Ausnahme der Bereitstellung und Führung von Wertpapierkonten auf oberster Ebene (zentrale Kontenführung) gemäß Abschnitt A Nummer 2 des Anhangs zur Verordnung (EU) Nr. 909/2014 (Depotgeschäft),

2.die Gewährung von Krediten oder Darlehen an andere für die Durchführung von Wertpapierdienstleistungen, sofern das Unternehmen, das den Kredit oder das Darlehen gewährt, an diesen Geschäften beteiligt ist,

3.die Beratung von Unternehmen über die Kapitalstruktur, die industrielle Strategie sowie die Beratung und

das Angebot von Dienstleistungen bei Unternehmenskäufen und Unternehmenszusammenschlüssen,

4.Devisengeschäfte, die in Zusammenhang mit Wertpapierdienstleistungen stehen,

5.das Erstellen oder Verbreiten von Empfehlungen oder Vorschlägen von Anlagestrategien im Sinne des Artikels 3 Absatz 1 Nummer 34 der Verordnung (EU) Nr. 596/2014 (Anlagestrategieempfehlung) oder von Anlageempfehlungen im Sinne des Artikels 3 Absatz 1 Nummer 35 der Verordnung (EU) Nr. 596/2014 (Anlageempfehlung),

6.Dienstleistungen, die im Zusammenhang mit dem Emissionsgeschäft stehen,

7.Dienstleistungen, die sich auf einen Basiswert im Sinne des Absatzes 2 Nr. 2 oder Nr. 5 beziehen und im Zusammenhang mit Wertpapierdienstleistungen oder Wertpapiernebendienstleistungen stehen.

(10) Wertpapierdienstleistungsunternehmen im Sinne dieses Gesetzes sind Kreditinstitute, Finanzdienstleistungsinstitute und nach § 53 Abs. 1 Satz 1 des Kreditwesengesetzes tätige Unternehmen, die Wertpapierdienstleistungen allein oder zusammen mit Wertpapiernebendienstleistungen gewerbsmäßig oder in einem Umfang erbringen, der einen in kaufmännischer Weise eingerichteten Geschäftsbetrieb erfordert.

§ 3 Ausnahmen; Verordnungsermächtigung

(1) 1Als Wertpapierdienstleistungsunternehmen gelten nicht

1～6号 (略)

7.Unternehmen, die als Wertpapierdienstleistung für andere ausschließlich die Anlageberatung und die Anlagevermittlung zwischen Kunden und

a)Instituten im Sinne des Kreditwesengesetzes,

b)Instituten oder Finanzunternehmen mit Sitz in einem anderen Staat des Europäischen Wirtschaftsraums, die die Voraussetzungen nach § 53b Abs. 1 Satz 1 oder Abs. 7 des Kreditwesengesetzes erfüllen,

c)Unternehmen, die aufgrund einer Rechtsverordnung nach § 53c des Kreditwesengesetzes gleichgestellt oder freigestellt sind,

d)Kapitalverwaltungsgesellschaften, extern verwalteten Investmentgesellschaften, EU-Verwaltungsgesellschaften oder ausländischen AIF-Verwaltungsgesellschaften oder

e)Anbietern oder Emittenten von Vermögensanlagen im Sinne des § 1 Absatz 2 des Vermögensanlagengesetzes

betreiben, sofern sich diese Wertpapierdienstleistungen auf Anteile oder Aktien von inländischen Investmentvermögen, die von einer Kapitalverwaltungsgesellschaft ausgegeben werden, die eine Erlaubnis nach § 7 oder § 97 Absatz 1 des Investmentgesetzes in der bis zum 21. Juli 2013 geltenden Fassung hat, die für den in § 345 Absatz 2 Satz 1, Absatz 3 Satz 2, in Verbindung mit Absatz 2 Satz 1, oder Absatz 4 Satz 1 des Kapitalanlagegesetzbuchs vorgesehenen Zeitraum noch fortbesteht, oder die eine Erlaubnis nach den §§ 20, 21 oder den §§ 20, 22 des Kapitalanlagegesetzbuchs hat, oder die von einer EU-Verwaltungsgesellschaft ausgegeben werden, die eine Erlaubnis nach Artikel 6 der Richtlinie 2009/65/EG des Europäischen Parlaments und des Rates vom 13. Juli 2009 zur Koordinierung der Rechts- und Verwaltungsvorschriften betreffend bestimmte Organismen für gemeinsame Anlagen in Wertpapieren (OGAW) (ABl. L 302 vom 17.11.2009, S. 32, L 269 vom 13.10.2010, S. 27), die zuletzt durch die Richtlinie 2014/91/EU (ABl. L 257 vom 28.8.2014, S. 186) geändert worden ist, oder nach Artikel 6 der Richtlinie 2011/61/EU des Europäischen Parlaments und des Rates vom 8. Juni 2011 über die Verwalter alternativer Investmentfonds und zur Änderung der Richtlinien 2003/41/EG und 2009/65/EG und der Verordnungen (EG) Nr. 1060/2009 und (EU) Nr. 1095/2010 (ABl. L 174 vom 1.7.2011, S. 1, L 115 vom 27.4.2012, S. 35), die zuletzt durch die Richtlinie 2014/65/EU (ABl. L 173 vom 12.6.2014, S. 349, L 74 vom 18.3.2015, S. 38) geändert worden ist, hat, oder auf Anteile oder Aktien an EU-Investmentvermögen oder ausländischen AIF, die nach dem Kapitalanlagegesetzbuch vertrieben werden dürfen, mit Ausnahme solcher AIF, die nach § 330a des Kapitalanlagegesetzbuchs vertrieben werden dürfen, oder auf Vermögensanlagen im Sinne des § 1 Absatz 2 des Vermögensanlagengesetzes, die erstmals öffentlich angeboten werden, beschränken und die Unternehmen nicht befugt sind, sich bei der Erbringung dieser Finanzdienstleistungen Eigentum oder Besitz an Geldern oder Anteilen von Kunden zu verschaffen, es sei denn, das Unternehmen beantragt und erhält eine entsprechende Erlaubnis nach § 32 Abs. 1 des Kreditwesengesetzes; Anteile oder Aktien an Hedgefonds im Sinne des § 283 des Kapitalanlagegesetzbuchs gelten nicht als Anteile an Investmentvermögen im Sinne dieser Vorschrift,

8～11号　(略)

12.Unternehmen, die als Wertpapierdienstleistung ausschließlich die Anlageberatung im Rahmen einer anderen beruflichen Tätigkeit erbringen, ohne sich die Anlageberatung gesondert vergüten zu lassen,

(以下、略)

§ 63　Allgemeine Verhaltensregeln; Verordnungsermächtigung

(1) Ein Wertpapierdienstleistungsunternehmen ist verpflichtet, Wertpapierdienstleistungen und Wertpapiernebendienstleistungen ehrlich, redlich und professionell im bestmöglichen Interesse seiner Kunden zu erbringen.

(2) 1Ein Wertpapierdienstleistungsunternehmen hat einem Kunden, bevor es Geschäfte für ihn durchführt, die allgemeine Art und Herkunft von Interessenkonflikten und die zur Begrenzung der Risiken der Beeinträchtigung der Kundeninteressen unternommenen Schritte eindeutig darzulegen, soweit die organisatorischen Vorkehrungen nach § 80 Absatz 1 Satz 2 Nummer 2 nicht ausreichen, um nach vernünftigem Ermessen zu gewährleisten, dass das Risiko der Beeinträchtigung von Kundeninteressen vermieden wird. 2Die Darlegung nach Satz 1 muss

1.mittels eines dauerhaften Datenträgers erfolgen und

2.unter Berücksichtigung der Einstufung des Kunden im Sinne des § 67 so detailliert sein, dass der Kunde in die Lage versetzt wird, seine Entscheidung über die Wertpapierdienstleistung oder Wertpapiernebendienstleistung, in deren Zusammenhang der Interessenkonflikt auftritt, in Kenntnis der Sachlage zu treffen.

(3) 1Ein Wertpapierdienstleistungsunternehmen muss sicherstellen, dass es die Leistung seiner Mitarbeiter

nicht in einer Weise vergütet oder bewertet, die mit seiner Pflicht, im bestmöglichen Interesse der Kunden zu handeln, kollidiert. 2Insbesondere darf es bei seinen Mitarbeitern weder durch Vergütungsvereinbarungen noch durch Verkaufsziele oder in sonstiger Weise Anreize dafür setzen, einem Privatkunden ein bestimmtes Finanzinstrument zu empfehlen, obwohl das Wertpapierdienstleistungsunternehmen dem Privatkunden ein anderes Finanzinstrument anbieten könnte, das den Bedürfnissen des Privatkunden besser entspricht.

(4) 1Ein Wertpapierdienstleistungsunternehmen, das Finanzinstrumente zum Verkauf an Kunden konzipiert, muss sicherstellen, dass diese Finanzinstrumente so ausgestaltet sind, dass

1.sie den Bedürfnissen eines bestimmten Zielmarktes im Sinne des § 80 Absatz 9 entsprechen und

2.die Strategie für den Vertrieb der Finanzinstrumente mit diesem Zielmarkt vereinbar ist.

2Das Wertpapierdienstleistungsunternehmen muss zumutbare Schritte unternehmen, um zu gewährleisten, dass das Finanzinstrument an den bestimmten Zielmarkt vertrieben wird.

(5) 1Ein Wertpapierdienstleistungsunternehmen muss die von ihm angebotenen oder empfohlenen Finanzinstrumente verstehen. 2Es muss deren Vereinbarkeit mit den Bedürfnissen der Kunden, denen gegenüber es Wertpapierdienstleistungen erbringt, beurteilen, auch unter Berücksichtigung des in § 80 Absatz 9 genannten Zielmarktes, und sicherstellen, dass es Finanzinstrumente nur anbietet oder empfiehlt, wenn dies im Interesse der Kunden liegt.

(6) 1Alle Informationen, die Wertpapierdienstleistungsunternehmen Kunden zugänglich machen, einschließlich Marketingmitteilungen, müssen redlich und eindeutig sein und dürfen nicht irreführend sein. 2Marketingmitteilungen müssen eindeutig als solche erkennbar sein. 3 § 302 des Kapitalanlagegesetzbuchs, Artikel 22 der Verordnung (EU) 2017/1129 und § 7 des Wertpapierprospektgesetzes bleiben unberührt.

(7) 1Wertpapierdienstleistungsunternehmen sind verpflichtet, ihren Kunden rechtzeitig und in verständlicher Form angemessene Informationen über das Wertpapierdienstleistungsunternehmen und seine Dienstleistungen, über die Finanzinstrumente und die vorgeschlagenen Anlagestrategien, über Ausführungsplätze und alle Kosten und Nebenkosten zur Verfügung zu stellen, die erforderlich sind, damit die Kunden nach vernünftigem Ermessen die Art und die Risiken der ihnen angebotenen oder von ihnen nachgefragten Arten von Finanzinstrumenten oder Wertpapierdienstleistungen verstehen und auf dieser Grundlage ihre Anlageentscheidung treffen können. 2Die Informationen können auch in standardisierter Form zur Verfügung gestellt werden. 3Die Informationen nach Satz 1 müssen folgende Angaben enthalten:

1.hinsichtlich der Arten von Finanzinstrumenten und der vorgeschlagenen Anlagestrategie unter Berücksichtigung des Zielmarktes im Sinne des Absatzes 3 oder 4:

a)geeignete Leitlinien zur Anlage in solche Arten von Finanzinstrumenten oder zu den einzelnen Anlagestrategien,

b)geeignete Warnhinweise zu den Risiken, die mit dieser Art von Finanzinstrumenten oder den einzelnen Anlagestrategien verbunden sind, und

c)ob die Art des Finanzinstruments für Privatkunden oder professionelle Kunden bestimmt ist;

2.hinsichtlich aller Kosten und Nebenkosten:

a)Informationen in Bezug auf Kosten und Nebenkosten sowohl der Wertpapierdienstleistungen als auch der Wertpapiernebendienstleistungen, einschließlich eventueller Beratungskosten,

b)Kosten der Finanzinstrumente, die dem Kunden empfohlen oder an ihn vermarktet werden sowie

c)Zahlungsmöglichkeiten des Kunden einschließlich etwaiger Zahlungen durch Dritte.

4Informationen zu Kosten und Nebenkosten, einschließlich solchen Kosten und Nebenkosten im Zusammenhang mit der Wertpapierdienstleistung und dem Finanzinstrument, die nicht durch ein zugrunde liegendes Marktrisiko verursacht werden, muss das Wertpapierdienstleistungsunternehmen in zusammengefasster Weise darstellen, damit der Kunde sowohl die Gesamtkosten als auch die kumulative Wirkung der Kosten auf die Rendite der Anlage verstehen kann. 5Auf Verlangen des Kunden muss das Wertpapierdienstleistungsunternehmen eine Aufstellung, die nach den einzelnen Posten aufgegliedert ist, zur Verfügung stellen. 6Solche Informationen sollen dem Kunden unter den in Artikel 50 Absatz 9 der Delegierten Verordnung (EU) 2017/565 genannten Voraussetzungen regelmäßig, mindestens jedoch jährlich während der Laufzeit der Anlage zur Verfügung gestellt werden. 7Die §§ 293 bis 297, 303 bis 307 des Kapitalanlagegesetzbuchs bleiben unberührt. 8Bei zertifizierten Altersvorsorge- und Basisrentenverträgen im Sinne des Altersvorsorgeverträge-Zertifizierungsgesetzes gilt die Informationspflicht nach diesem Absatz durch Bereitstellung des individuellen Produktinformationsblattes nach § 7 des Altersvorsorgeverträge-Zertifizierungsgesetzes als erfüllt. 9Dem Kunden sind auf Nachfrage die nach diesem Absatz erforderlichen Informationen über Kosten und Nebenkosten zur Verfügung zu stellen. 10Der Kunde ist bei Bereitstellung des individuellen Produktinformationsblattes nach § 7 des Altersvorsorgeverträge-Zertifizierungsgesetzes ausdrücklich auf dieses Recht hinzuweisen. 11Wird einem Kunden ein standardisiertes Informationsblatt nach § 64 Absatz 2 Satz 3 zur Verfügung gestellt, sind dem Kunden die Informationen hinsichtlich aller Kosten und Nebenkosten nach den Sätzen 4 und 5 unverlangt unter Verwendung einer formalisierten Kostenaufstellung zur Verfügung zu stellen.

(8) Die Absätze 6 und 7 gelten nicht für Wertpapierdienstleistungen, die als Teil eines Finanzprodukts angeboten werden, das in Bezug auf die Informationspflichten bereits anderen Bestimmungen des Europäischen Gemeinschaftsrechts, die Kreditinstitute und Verbraucherkredite betreffen, unterliegt.

(9) 1Bietet ein Wertpapierdienstleistungsunternehmen Wertpapierdienstleistungen verbunden mit anderen Dienstleistungen oder anderen Produkten als Gesamtpaket oder in der Form an, dass die Erbringung der Wertpapierdienstleistungen, der anderen Dienstleistungen oder der Geschäfte über die anderen Produkte Bedingung für die Durchführung der jeweils anderen Bestandteile oder des Abschlusses der anderen Vereinbarungen ist, muss es den Kunden darüber informieren, ob die einzelnen Bestandteile auch getrennt voneinander bezogen werden können und dem Kunden für jeden Bestandteil getrennt Kosten und Gebühren nachweisen. 2Besteht die Wahrscheinlichkeit, dass die mit dem Gesamtpaket oder der Gesamtvereinbarung verknüpften Risiken von den mit den einzelnen Bestandteilen verknüpften Risiken abweichen, hat es Privatkunden in angemessener Weise über die einzelnen Bestandteile, die mit ihnen verknüpften Risiken und die Art und Weise, wie ihre Wechselwirkung das Risiko beeinflusst, zu informieren.

(10) 1Vor der Erbringung anderer Wertpapierdienstleistungen als der Anlageberatung oder der Finanzportfolioverwaltung hat ein Wertpapierdienstleistungsunternehmen von den Kunden Informationen einzuholen über Kenntnisse und Erfahrungen der Kunden in Bezug auf Geschäfte mit bestimmten Arten von Finanzinstrumenten oder Wertpapierdienstleistungen, soweit diese Informationen erforderlich sind, um die Angemessenheit der Finanzinstrumente oder Wertpapierdienstleistungen für die Kunden beurteilen zu können. 2Sind verbundene Dienstleistungen oder Produkte im Sinne des Absatzes 9 Gegenstand des Kundenauftrages, muss das Wertpapierdienstleistungsunternehmen beurteilen, ob das gesamte verbundene Geschäft für den Kunden angemessen ist. 3Gelangt ein Wertpapierdienstleistungsunternehmen auf Grund der nach Satz 1 erhaltenen Informationen zu der Auffassung, dass das vom Kunden gewünschte Finanzinstrument oder die Wertpapierdienstleistung für den Kunden nicht angemessen ist, hat es den Kunden darauf hinzuweisen. 4Erlangt das Wertpapierdienstleistungsunternehmen nicht die erforderlichen Informationen, hat es den Kunden darüber zu informieren, dass eine Beurteilung der Angemessenheit im Sinne des Satzes 1 nicht möglich ist. 5Näheres zur Angemessenheit und zu den Pflichten, die im Zusammenhang mit der Beurteilung der Angemessenheit geltenden Pflichten regeln die Artikel 55 und 56 der Delegierten Verordnung (EU) 2017/565. 6Der Hinweis nach Satz 3 und die Information nach Satz 4 können in standardisierter Form erfolgen.

(11) Die Pflichten nach Absatz 10 gelten nicht, soweit das Wertpapierdienstleistungsunternehmen

1.auf Veranlassung des Kunden Finanzkommissionsgeschäft, Eigenhandel, Abschlussvermittlung oder Anlagevermittlung erbringt in Bezug auf

a)Aktien, die zum Handel an einem organisierten Markt, an einem diesem gleichwertigen Markt eines Drittlandes oder an einem multilateralen Handelssystem zugelassen sind, mit Ausnahme von Aktien an AIF im Sinne von § 1 Absatz 3 des Kapitalanlagegesetzbuchs, und von Aktien, in die ein Derivat eingebettet ist,

b)Schuldverschreibungen und andere verbriefte Schuldtitel, die zum Handel an einem organisierten Markt, einem diesem gleichwertigen Markt eines Drittlandes oder einem multilateralen Handelssystem zugelassen sind, mit Ausnahme solcher, in die ein Derivat eingebettet ist und solcher, die eine Struktur aufweisen, die es dem Kunden erschwert, die mit ihnen einhergehenden Risiken zu verstehen,

c)Geldmarktinstrumente, mit Ausnahme solcher, in die ein Derivat eingebettet ist, und solcher, die eine Struktur aufweisen, die es dem Kunden erschwert, die mit ihnen einhergehenden Risiken zu verstehen,

d)Anteile oder Aktien an OGAW im Sinne von § 1 Absatz 2 des Kapitalanlagegesetzbuchs, mit Ausnahme der in Artikel 36 Absatz 1 Unterabsatz 2 der Verordnung (EU) Nr. 583/2010 genannten strukturierten OGAW,

e)strukturierte Einlagen, mit Ausnahme solcher, die eine Struktur aufweisen, die es dem Kunden erschwert, das Ertragsrisiko oder die Kosten des Verkaufs des Produkts vor Fälligkeit zu verstehen oder

f)andere nicht komplexe Finanzinstrumente für Zwecke dieses Absatzes, die die in Artikel 57 der Delegierten Verordnung (EU) 2017/565 genannten Kriterien erfüllen,

2.diese Wertpapierdienstleistung nicht gemeinsam mit der Gewährung eines Darlehens als Wertpapiernebendienstleistung im Sinne des § 2 Absatz 7 Nummer 2 erbringt, außer sie besteht in der Ausnutzung einer Kreditobergrenze eines bereits bestehenden Darlehens oder eines bereits bestehenden

Darlehens, das in der Weise gewährt wurde, dass der Darlehensgeber in einem Vertragsverhältnis über ein laufendes Konto dem Darlehensnehmer das Recht einräumt, sein Konto in bestimmter Höhe zu überziehen (Überziehungsmöglichkeit) oder darin, dass der Darlehensgeber im Rahmen eines Vertrages über ein laufendes Konto, ohne eingeräumte Überziehungsmöglichkeit die Überziehung des Kontos durch den Darlehensnehmer duldet und hierfür vereinbarungsgemäß ein Entgelt verlangt, und

3.den Kunden ausdrücklich darüber informiert, dass keine Angemessenheitsprüfung im Sinne des Absatzes 10 vorgenommen wird, wobei diese Information in standardisierter Form erfolgen kann.

(12) 1Wertpapierdienstleistungsunternehmen müssen ihren Kunden in geeigneter Weise auf einem dauerhaften Datenträger über die erbrachten Wertpapierdienstleistungen berichten; insbesondere müssen sie nach Ausführung eines Geschäftes mitteilen, wo sie den Auftrag ausgeführt haben. 2Die Pflicht nach Satz 1 beinhaltet einerseits nach den in den Artikeln 59 bis 63 der Delegierten Verordnung (EU) 2017/565 näher bestimmten Fällen regelmäßige Berichte an den Kunden, wobei die Art und Komplexität der jeweiligen Finanzinstrumente sowie die Art der erbrachten Wertpapierdienstleistungen zu berücksichtigen ist, und andererseits, sofern relevant, Informationen zu den angefallenen Kosten. 3Bei zertifizierten Altersvorsorge- und Basisrentenverträgen im Sinne des Altersvorsorgeverträge-Zertifizierungsgesetzes gilt die Informationspflicht gemäß Satz 1 bei Beachtung der jährlichen Informationspflicht nach § 7a des Altersvorsorgeverträge-Zertifizierungsgesetzes als erfüllt. 4Dem Kunden sind auf Nachfrage die nach diesem Absatz erforderlichen Informationen über Kosten und Nebenkosten zur Verfügung zu stellen. 5Der Kunde ist bei Bereitstellung der jährlichen Information nach § 7a des Altersvorsorgeverträge-Zertifizierungsgesetzes ausdrücklich auf dieses Recht hinzuweisen.

(13) Nähere Bestimmungen zu den Absätzen 1 bis 3, 6, 7, 10 und 12 ergeben sich aus der Delegierten Verordnung (EU) 2017/565, insbesondere zu

1.der Verpflichtung nach Absatz 1 aus den Artikeln 58, 64, 65 und 67 bis 69,

2.Art, Umfang und Form der Offenlegung nach Absatz 2 aus den Artikeln 34 und 41 bis 43,

3.der Vergütung oder Bewertung nach Absatz 3 aus Artikel 27,

4.den Voraussetzungen, unter denen Informationen im Sinne von Absatz 6 Satz 1 als redlich, eindeutig und nicht irreführend angesehen werden aus den Artikeln 36 und 44,

5.Art, Inhalt, Gestaltung und Zeitpunkt der nach Absatz 7 notwendigen Informationen für die Kunden aus den Artikeln 38, 39, 41, 45 bis 53, 61 und 65,

6.Art, Umfang und Kriterien der nach Absatz 10 von den Kunden einzuholenden Informationen aus den Artikeln 54 bis 56,

7.Art, Inhalt und Zeitpunkt der Berichtspflichten nach Absatz 12 aus den Artikeln 59 bis 63.

(14) 1Das Bundesministerium der Finanzen kann im Einvernehmen mit dem Bundesministerium der Justiz und für Verbraucherschutz durch Rechtsverordnung, die nicht der Zustimmung des Bundesrates bedarf, nähere Bestimmungen zu Inhalt und Aufbau der formalisierten Kostenaufstellung nach Absatz 7 Satz 11 erlassen. 2Das Bundesministerium der Finanzen kann die Ermächtigung durch Rechtsverordnung auf die Bundesanstalt

übertragen.

§ 64 Besondere Verhaltensregeln bei der Erbringung von Anlageberatung und Finanzportfolioverwaltung; Verordnungsermächtigung

(1) 1Erbringt ein Wertpapierdienstleistungsunternehmen Anlageberatung, muss es den Kunden zusätzlich zu den Informationen nach § 63 Absatz 7 rechtzeitig vor der Beratung und in verständlicher Form darüber informieren

1.ob die Anlageberatung unabhängig erbracht wird (Unabhängige Honorar-Anlageberatung) oder nicht;

2.ob sich die Anlageberatung auf eine umfangreiche oder eine eher beschränkte Analyse verschiedener Arten von Finanzinstrumenten stützt, insbesondere, ob die Palette an Finanzinstrumenten auf Finanzinstrumente beschränkt ist, die von Anbietern oder Emittenten stammen, die in einer engen Verbindung zum Wertpapierdienstleistungsunternehmen stehen oder zu denen in sonstiger Weise rechtliche oder wirtschaftliche Verbindungen bestehen, die so eng sind, dass das Risiko besteht, dass die Unabhängigkeit der Anlageberatung beeinträchtigt wird, und

3.ob das Wertpapierdienstleistungsunternehmen dem Kunden regelmäßig eine Beurteilung der Geeignetheit der empfohlenen Finanzinstrumente zur Verfügung stellt.

2 § 63 Absatz 7 Satz 2 und bei Vorliegen der dort genannten Voraussetzungen die Ausnahme nach § 63 Absatz 8 gelten entsprechend.

(2) 1Im Falle einer Anlageberatung hat das Wertpapierdienstleistungsunternehmen einem Privatkunden rechtzeitig vor dem Abschluss eines Geschäfts über Finanzinstrumente, für die kein Basisinformationsblatt nach der Verordnung (EU) Nr. 1286/2014 erstellt werden muss,

1.über jedes Finanzinstrument, auf das sich eine Kaufempfehlung bezieht, ein kurzes und leicht verständliches Informationsblatt,

2.in den Fällen des Satzes 3 ein in Nummer 1 genanntes Informationsblatt oder wahlweise ein standardisiertes Informationsblatt oder

3.in den Fällen des Satzes 4 ein dort genanntes Dokument anstelle des in Nummer 1 genannten Informationsblatts

zur Verfügung zu stellen. 2Die Angaben in den Informationsblättern nach Satz 1 dürfen weder unrichtig noch irreführend sein und müssen mit den Angaben des Prospekts vereinbar sein. 3Für Aktien, die zum Zeitpunkt der Anlageberatung an einem organisierten Markt gehandelt werden, kann anstelle des Informationsblattes nach Satz 1 Nummer 1 ein standardisiertes Informationsblatt verwendet werden. 4An die Stelle des Informationsblattes treten

1.bei Anteilen oder Aktien an OGAW oder an offenen Publikums-AIF die wesentlichen Anlegerinformationen nach den § § 164 und 166 des Kapitalanlagegesetzbuchs,

2.bei Anteilen oder Aktien an geschlossenen Publikums-AIF die wesentlichen Anlegerinformationen nach den

§ § 268 und 270 des Kapitalanlagegesetzbuchs,

3.bei Anteilen oder Aktien an Spezial-AIF die wesentlichen Anlegerinformationen nach § 166 oder § 270 des Kapitalanlagegesetzbuchs, sofern die AIF-Kapitalverwaltungsgesellschaft solche gemäß § 307 Absatz 5 des Kapitalanlagegesetzbuchs erstellt hat,

4.bei EU-AIF und ausländischen AIF die wesentlichen Anlegerinformationen nach § 318 Absatz 5 des Kapitalanlagegesetzbuchs,

5.bei EU-OGAW die wesentlichen Anlegerinformationen, die nach § 298 Absatz 1 Satz 2 des Kapitalanlagegesetzbuchs in deutscher Sprache veröffentlicht worden sind,

6.bei inländischen Investmentvermögen im Sinne des Investmentgesetzes in der bis zum 21. Juli 2013 geltenden Fassung, die für den in § 345 Absatz 6 Satz 1 des Kapitalanlagegesetzbuchs genannten Zeitraum noch weiter vertrieben werden dürfen, die wesentlichen Anlegerinformationen, die nach § 42 Absatz 2 des Investmentgesetzes in der bis zum 21. Juli 2013 geltenden Fassung erstellt worden sind,

7.bei ausländischen Investmentvermögen im Sinne des Investmentgesetzes in der bis zum 21. Juli 2013 geltenden Fassung, die für den in § 345 Absatz 8 Satz 2 oder § 355 Absatz 2 Satz 10 des Kapitalanlagegesetzbuchs genannten Zeitraum noch weiter vertrieben werden dürfen, die wesentlichen Anlegerinformationen, die nach § 137 Absatz 2 des Investmentgesetzes in der bis zum 21. Juli 2013 geltenden Fassung erstellt worden sind,

8.bei Vermögensanlagen im Sinne des § 1 Absatz 2 des Vermögensanlagengesetzes das Vermögensanlagen-Informationsblatt nach § 13 des Vermögensanlagengesetzes, soweit der Anbieter der Vermögensanlagen zur Erstellung eines solchen Vermögensanlagen-Informationsblatts verpflichtet ist,

9.bei zertifizierten Altersvorsorge- und Basisrentenverträgen im Sinne des Altersvorsorgeverträge-Zertifizierungsgesetzes das individuelle Produktinformationsblatt nach § 7 Absatz 1 des Altersvorsorgeverträge-Zertifizierungsgesetzes sowie zusätzlich die wesentlichen Anlegerinformationen nach Nummer 1, 3 oder Nummer 4, sofern es sich um Anteile an den in Nummer 1, 3 oder Nummer 4 genannten Organismen für gemeinsame Anlagen handelt und

10.bei Wertpapieren im Sinne des § 2 Nummer 1 des Wertpapierprospektgesetzes das Wertpapier-Informationsblatt nach § 4 des Wertpapierprospektgesetzes, soweit der Anbieter der Wertpapiere zur Erstellung eines solchen Wertpapier-Informationsblatts verpflichtet ist.

(3) 1Das Wertpapierdienstleistungsunternehmen muss von einem Kunden alle Informationen

1.über Kenntnisse und Erfahrungen des Kunden in Bezug auf Geschäfte mit bestimmten Arten von Finanzinstrumenten oder Wertpapierdienstleistungen,

2.über die finanziellen Verhältnisse des Kunden, einschließlich seiner Fähigkeit, Verluste zu tragen, und

3.über seine Anlageziele, einschließlich seiner Risikotoleranz,

einholen, die erforderlich sind, um dem Kunden ein Finanzinstrument oder eine Wertpapierdienstleistung empfehlen zu können, das oder die für ihn geeignet ist und insbesondere seiner Risikotoleranz und seiner Fähigkeit, Verluste zu tragen, entspricht. 2Ein Wertpapierdienstleistungsunternehmen darf seinen Kunden nur

Finanzinstrumente und Wertpapierdienstleistungen empfehlen oder Geschäfte im Rahmen der Finanzportfolioverwaltung tätigen, die nach den eingeholten Informationen für den Kunden geeignet sind. 3Näheres zur Geeignetheit und den im Zusammenhang mit der Beurteilung der Geeignetheit geltenden Pflichten regeln die Artikel 54 und 55 der Delegierten Verordnung (EU) 2017/565. 4Näheres zur Geeignetheit von Verbriefungen und den im Zusammenhang mit der Beurteilung der Geeignetheit geltenden Pflichten regelt Artikel 3 der Verordnung (EU) 2017/2402 des Europäischen Parlaments und des Rates vom 12. Dezember 2017 zur Festlegung eines allgemeinen Rahmens für Verbriefungen und zur Schaffung eines spezifischen Rahmens für einfache, transparente und standardisierte Verbriefung und zur Änderung der Richtlinien 2009/65/EG, 2009/138/EG, 2011/61/EU und der Verordnungen (EG) Nr. 1060/2009 und (EU) Nr. 648/2012 (ABl. L 347 vom 28.12.2017, S. 35). 5Erbringt ein Wertpapierdienstleistungsunternehmen eine Anlageberatung, bei der verbundene Produkte oder Dienstleistungen im Sinne des § 63 Absatz 9 empfohlen werden, gilt Satz 2 für das gesamte verbundene Geschäft entsprechend.

(4) 1Ein Wertpapierdienstleistungsunternehmen, das Anlageberatung erbringt, muss dem Privatkunden auf einem dauerhaften Datenträger vor Vertragsschluss eine Erklärung über die Geeignetheit der Empfehlung (Geeignetheitserklärung) zur Verfügung stellen. 2Die Geeignetheitserklärung muss die erbrachte Beratung nennen sowie erläutern, wie sie auf die Präferenzen, Anlageziele und die sonstigen Merkmale des Kunden abgestimmt wurde. 3Näheres regelt Artikel 54 Absatz 12 der Delegierten Verordnung (EU) 2017/565. 4Wird die Vereinbarung über den Kauf oder Verkauf eines Finanzinstruments mittels eines Fernkommunikationsmittels geschlossen, das die vorherige Übermittlung der Geeignetheitserklärung nicht erlaubt, darf das Wertpapierdienstleistungsunternehmen die Geeignetheitserklärung ausnahmsweise unmittelbar nach dem Vertragsschluss zur Verfügung stellen, wenn der Kunde zugestimmt hat, dass ihm die Geeignetheitserklärung unverzüglich nach Vertragsschluss zur Verfügung gestellt wird und das Wertpapierdienstleistungsunternehmen dem Kunden angeboten hat, die Ausführung des Geschäfts zu verschieben, damit der Kunde die Möglichkeit hat, die Geeignetheitserklärung zuvor zu erhalten.

(5) 1Ein Wertpapierdienstleistungsunternehmen, das Unabhängige Honorar-Anlageberatung erbringt,

1.muss bei der Beratung eine ausreichende Palette von auf dem Markt angebotenen Finanzinstrumenten berücksichtigen, die

a)hinsichtlich ihrer Art und des Emittenten oder Anbieters hinreichend gestreut sind und

b)nicht beschränkt sind auf Finanzinstrumente, die das Wertpapierdienstleistungsunternehmen selbst emittiert oder anbietet oder deren Anbieter oder Emittenten in einer engen Verbindung zum Wertpapierdienstleistungsunternehmen stehen oder in sonstiger Weise so enge rechtliche oder wirtschaftliche Verbindung zu diesem unterhalten, dass die Unabhängigkeit der Beratung dadurch gefährdet werden könnte;

2.darf sich die Unabhängige Honorar-Anlageberatung allein durch den Kunden vergüten lassen.

2Es dürfen nach Satz 1 Nummer 2 im Zusammenhang mit der Unabhängigen Honorar-Anlageberatung keinerlei nichtmonetäre Zuwendungen von einem Dritten, der nicht Kunde dieser Dienstleistung ist oder von dem Kunden dazu beauftragt worden ist, angenommen werden. 3Monetäre Zuwendungen dürfen nur dann angenommen werden, wenn das empfohlene Finanzinstrument oder ein in gleicher Weise geeignetes Finanzinstrument ohne Zuwendung nicht erhältlich ist. 4In diesem Fall sind die monetären Zuwendungen so schnell wie nach vernünftigem Ermessen möglich, nach Erhalt und in vollem Umfang an den Kunden auszukehren. 5Vorschriften über die Entrichtung von Steuern und Abgaben bleiben davon unberührt. 6Das Wertpapierdienstleistungsunternehmen muss Kunden über die ausgekehrten monetären Zuwendungen unterrichten. 7Im Übrigen gelten die allgemeinen Anforderungen für die Anlageberatung.

(6) 1Bei der Empfehlung von Geschäftsabschlüssen in Finanzinstrumenten, die auf einer Unabhängigen Honorar-Anlageberatung beruhen, deren Anbieter oder Emittent das Wertpapierdienstleistungsunternehmen selbst ist oder zu deren Anbieter oder Emittenten eine enge Verbindung oder sonstige wirtschaftliche Verflechtung besteht, muss das Wertpapierdienstleistungsunternehmen den Kunden rechtzeitig vor der Empfehlung und in verständlicher Form informieren über

1.die Tatsache, dass es selbst Anbieter oder Emittent der Finanzinstrumente ist,

2.das Bestehen einer engen Verbindung oder einer sonstigen wirtschaftlichen Verflechtung zum Anbieter oder Emittenten sowie

3.das Bestehen eines eigenen Gewinninteresses oder des Interesses eines mit ihm verbundenen oder wirtschaftlich verflochtenen Emittenten oder Anbieters an dem Geschäftsabschluss.

2Ein Wertpapierdienstleistungsunternehmen darf einen auf seiner Unabhängigen Honorar-Anlageberatung beruhenden Geschäftsabschluss nicht als Geschäft mit dem Kunden zu einem festen oder bestimmbaren Preis für eigene Rechnung (Festpreisgeschäft) ausführen. 3Ausgenommen sind Festpreisgeschäfte in Finanzinstrumenten, deren Anbieter oder Emittent das Wertpapierdienstleistungsunternehmen selbst ist.

(7) 1Ein Wertpapierdienstleistungsunternehmen, das Finanzportfolioverwaltung erbringt, darf im Zusammenhang mit der Finanzportfolioverwaltung keine Zuwendungen von Dritten oder für Dritte handelnder Personen annehmen und behalten. 2Abweichend von Satz 1 dürfen nichtmonetäre Vorteile nur angenommen werden, wenn es sich um geringfügige nichtmonetäre Vorteile handelt,

1.die geeignet sind, die Qualität der für den Kunden erbrachten Wertpapierdienstleistung und Wertpapiernebendienstleistungen zu verbessern und

2.die hinsichtlich ihres Umfangs, wobei die Gesamthöhe der von einem einzelnen Unternehmen oder einer einzelnen Unternehmensgruppe gewährten Vorteile zu berücksichtigen ist, und ihrer Art vertretbar und verhältnismäßig sind und daher nicht vermuten lassen, dass sie die Pflicht des Wertpapierdienstleistungsunternehmens, im bestmöglichen Interesse ihrer Kunden zu handeln, beeinträchtigen,

wenn diese Zuwendungen dem Kunden unmissverständlich offengelegt werden, bevor die betreffende Wertpapierdienstleistung oder Wertpapiernebendienstleistung für die Kunden erbracht wird. 3Die Offenlegung kann in Form einer generischen Beschreibung erfolgen. 4Monetäre Zuwendungen, die im Zusammenhang mit der Finanzportfolioverwaltung angenommen werden, sind so schnell wie nach vernünftigem Ermessen möglich nach Erhalt und in vollem Umfang an den Kunden auszukehren. 5Vorschriften

über die Entrichtung von Steuern und Abgaben bleiben davon unberührt. 6Das Wertpapierdienstleistungsunternehmen muss den Kunden über die ausgekehrten monetären Zuwendungen unterrichten.

(8) Erbringt ein Wertpapierdienstleistungsunternehmen Finanzportfolioverwaltung oder hat es den Kunden nach Absatz 1 Satz 1 Nummer 3 darüber informiert, dass es die Geeignetheit der empfohlenen Finanzinstrumente regelmäßig beurteilt, so müssen die regelmäßigen Berichte gegenüber Privatkunden nach § 63 Absatz 12 insbesondere eine Erklärung darüber enthalten, wie die Anlage den Präferenzen, den Anlagezielen und den sonstigen Merkmalen des Kunden entspricht.

(9) Nähere Bestimmungen zu den Absätzen 1, 3, 5 und 8 ergeben sich aus der Delegierten Verordnung (EU) 2017/565, insbesondere zu

1.Art, Inhalt, Gestaltung und Zeitpunkt der nach den Absätzen 1 und 5, auch in Verbindung mit § 63 Absatz 7, notwendigen Informationen für die Kunden aus den Artikeln 52 und 53,

2.der Geeignetheit nach Absatz 3, den im Zusammenhang mit der Beurteilung der Geeignetheit geltenden Pflichten sowie zu Art, Umfang und Kriterien der nach Absatz 3 von den Kunden einzuholenden Informationen aus den Artikeln 54 und 55,

3.der Erklärung nach Absatz 4 aus Artikel 54 Absatz 12,

4.der Anlageberatung nach Absatz 5 aus Artikel 53,

5.Art, Inhalt und Zeitpunkt der Berichtspflichten nach Absatz 8, auch in Verbindung mit § 63 Absatz 12, aus den Artikeln 60 und 62.

(10) 1Das Bundesministerium der Finanzen kann durch Rechtsverordnung, die nicht der Zustimmung des Bundesrates bedarf, nähere Bestimmungen erlassen

1.im Einvernehmen mit dem Bundesministerium der Justiz und für Verbraucherschutz zu Inhalt und Aufbau sowie zu Art und Weise der Zurverfügungstellung der Informationsblätter im Sinne des Absatzes 2 Satz 1 und zu Inhalt und Aufbau sowie Art und Weise der Zurverfügungstellung des standardisierten Informationsblattes im Sinne des Absatzes 2 Satz 3,

2.zu Art, inhaltlicher Gestaltung, Zeitpunkt und Datenträger der nach Absatz 6 notwendigen Informationen für die Kunden,

3.zu Kriterien dazu, wann geringfügige nichtmonetäre Vorteile im Sinne des Absatzes 7 vorliegen.

2Das Bundesministerium der Finanzen kann die Ermächtigung durch Rechtsverordnung auf die Bundesanstalt übertragen.

§ 65 Selbstauskunft bei der Vermittlung des Vertragsschlusses über eine Vermögensanlage im Sinne des § 2a des Vermögensanlagengesetzes

(1) 1Ein Wertpapierdienstleistungsunternehmen hat vor der Vermittlung des Vertragsschlusses über eine Vermögensanlage im Sinne des § 2a des Vermögensanlagengesetzes von dem Kunden insoweit eine Selbstauskunft über dessen Vermögen oder dessen Einkommen einzuholen, wie dies erforderlich ist, um prüfen

zu können, ob der Gesamtbetrag der Vermögensanlagen desselben Emittenten, die von dem Kunden erworben werden, folgende Beträge nicht übersteigt:

1.10 000 Euro, sofern der jeweilige Anleger nach seiner Selbstauskunft über ein frei verfügbares Vermögen in Form von Bankguthaben und Finanzinstrumenten von mindestens 100 000 Euro verfügt, oder

2.den zweifachen Betrag des durchschnittlichen monatlichen Nettoeinkommens des jeweiligen Anlegers, höchstens jedoch 25 000 Euro.

2Satz 1 gilt nicht, wenn der Gesamtbetrag der Vermögensanlagen desselben Emittenten, die von dem Kunden erworben werden, 1 000 Euro nicht überschreitet. 3Ein Wertpapierdienstleistungsunternehmen darf einen Vertragsschluss über eine Vermögensanlage im Sinne des § 2a des Vermögensanlagengesetzes nur vermitteln, wenn es geprüft hat, dass der Gesamtbetrag der Vermögensanlagen desselben Emittenten, die von dem Kunden erworben werden, 1 000 Euro oder die in Satz 1 Nummer 1 und 2 genannten Beträge nicht übersteigt. 4Die Sätze 1 und 3 gelten nicht, wenn der Anleger eine Kapitalgesellschaft ist oder eine GmbH & Co. KG, deren Kommanditisten gleichzeitig Gesellschafter der GmbH oder an der Entscheidungsfindung der GmbH beteiligt sind, sofern die GmbH & Co. KG kein Investmentvermögen und keine Verwaltungsgesellschaft nach dem Kapitalanlagegesetzbuch ist.

(2) Soweit die in Absatz 1 genannten Informationen auf Angaben des Kunden beruhen, hat das Wertpapierdienstleistungsunternehmen die Fehlerhaftigkeit oder Unvollständigkeit der Angaben seines Kunden nicht zu vertreten, es sei denn, die Unvollständigkeit oder Unrichtigkeit der Kundenangaben ist ihm bekannt oder infolge grober Fahrlässigkeit unbekannt.

§ 68 Geschäfte mit geeigneten Gegenparteien; Verordnungsermächtigung

(1) 1Wertpapierdienstleistungsunternehmen, die das Finanzkommissionsgeschäft, die Anlage- und Abschlussvermittlung und den Eigenhandel sowie damit in direktem Zusammenhang stehende Wertpapiernebendienstleistungen gegenüber geeigneten Gegenparteien erbringen, sind nicht an die Vorgaben von § 63 Absatz 1, 3 bis 7, 9, 10, § 64 Absatz 3, 5 und 7, § 69 Absatz 1, der § § 70, 82, 83 Absatz 2 und § 87 Absatz 1 und 2 gebunden. 2Satz 1 ist nicht anwendbar, sofern die geeignete Gegenpartei mit dem Wertpapierdienstleistungsunternehmen für alle oder für einzelne Geschäfte vereinbart hat, als professioneller Kunde oder als Privatkunde behandelt zu werden. 3Wertpapierdienstleistungsunternehmen müssen in ihrer Beziehung mit geeigneten Gegenparteien auf eine Art und Weise kommunizieren, die redlich, eindeutig und nicht irreführend ist und müssen dabei der Form der geeigneten Gegenpartei und deren Geschäftstätigkeit Rechnung tragen.

(2) Nähere Bestimmungen zu Absatz 1, insbesondere zu der Form und dem Inhalt einer Vereinbarung nach Absatz 1 Satz 2 und zur Art und Weise der Zustimmung nach § 67 Absatz 4 Satz 2 ergeben sich aus Artikel 71 der Delegierten Verordnung (EU) 2017/565.

§ 80 Organisationspflichten; Verordnungsermächtigung

(1) Ein Wertpapierdienstleistungsunternehmen muss die organisatorischen Pflichten nach § 25a Absatz 1 und § 25e des Kreditwesengesetzes einhalten. Darüber hinaus muss es

1. angemessene Vorkehrungen treffen, um die Kontinuität und Regelmäßigkeit der Wertpapierdienstleistungen und Wertpapiernebendienstleistungen zu gewährleisten;

2. auf Dauer wirksame Vorkehrungen für angemessene Maßnahmen treffen, um Interessenkonflikte bei der Erbringung von Wertpapierdienstleistungen und Wertpapiernebendienstleistungen oder einer Kombination davon zwischen einerseits ihm selbst einschließlich seiner Geschäftsleitung, seiner Mitarbeiter, seiner vertraglich gebundenen Vermittler und der mit ihm direkt oder indirekt durch Kontrolle im Sinne des Artikels 4 Absatz 1 Nummer 37 der Verordnung (EU) Nr. 575/2013 verbundenen Personen und Unternehmen und andererseits seinen Kunden oder zwischen seinen Kunden untereinander zu erkennen und zu vermeiden oder zu regeln; dies umfasst auch solche Interessenkonflikte, die durch die Annahme von Zuwendungen Dritter sowie durch die eigene Vergütungsstruktur oder sonstige Anreizstrukturen des Wertpapierdienstleistungsunternehmens verursacht werden;

3. im Rahmen der Vorkehrungen nach Nummer 2 Grundsätze oder Ziele, die den Umsatz, das Volumen oder den Ertrag der im Rahmen der Anlageberatung empfohlenen Geschäfte unmittelbar oder mittelbar betreffen (Vertriebsvorgaben), derart ausgestalten, umsetzen und überwachen, dass Kundeninteressen nicht beeinträchtigt werden;

4. über solide Sicherheitsmechanismen verfügen, die die Sicherheit und Authentifizierung der Informationsübermittlungswege gewährleisten, das Risiko der Datenverfälschung und des unberechtigten Zugriffs minimieren und verhindern, dass Informationen bekannt werden, so dass die Vertraulichkeit der Daten jederzeit gewährleistet ist.

Nähere Bestimmungen zur Organisation der Wertpapierdienstleistungsunternehmen enthalten die Artikel 21 bis 26 der Delegierten Verordnung (EU) 2017/565.

(2) Ein Wertpapierdienstleistungsunternehmen muss zusätzlich die in diesem Absatz genannten Bestimmungen einhalten, wenn es in der Weise Handel mit Finanzinstrumenten betreibt, dass ein Computeralgorithmus die einzelnen Auftragsparameter automatisch bestimmt, ohne dass es sich um ein System handelt, das nur zur Weiterleitung von Aufträgen zu einem oder mehreren Handelsplätzen, zur Bearbeitung von Aufträgen ohne die Bestimmung von Auftragsparametern, zur Bestätigung von Aufträgen oder zur Nachhandelsbearbeitung ausgeführter Aufträge verwendet wird (algorithmischer Handel). Auftragsparameter im Sinne des Satzes 1 sind insbesondere Entscheidungen, ob der Auftrag eingeleitet werden soll, über Zeitpunkt, Preis oder Quantität des Auftrags oder wie der Auftrag nach seiner Einreichung mit eingeschränkter oder überhaupt keiner menschlichen Beteiligung bearbeitet wird. Ein Wertpapierdienstleistungsunternehmen, das algorithmischen Handel betreibt, muss über Systeme und Risikokontrollen verfügen, die sicherstellen, dass

1. seine Handelssysteme belastbar sind, über ausreichende Kapazitäten verfügen und angemessenen

Handelsschwellen und Handelsobergrenzen unterliegen;

2. die Übermittlung von fehlerhaften Aufträgen oder eine Funktionsweise des Systems vermieden wird, durch die Störungen auf dem Markt verursacht oder ein Beitrag zu diesen geleistet werden könnten;

3. seine Handelssysteme nicht für einen Zweck verwendet werden können, der gegen die europäischen und nationalen Vorschriften gegen Marktmissbrauch oder die Vorschriften des Handelsplatzes verstößt, mit dem es verbunden ist. Ein Wertpapierdienstleistungsunternehmen, das algorithmischen Handel betreibt, muss ferner über wirksame Notfallvorkehrungen verfügen, um mit unvorgesehenen Störungen in seinen Handelssystemen umzugehen, und sicherstellen, dass seine Systeme vollständig geprüft sind und ordnungsgemäß überwacht werden. Das Wertpapierdienstleistungsunternehmen zeigt der Bundesanstalt und den zuständigen Behörden des Handelsplatzes, dessen Mitglied oder Teilnehmer es ist, an, dass es algorithmischen Handel betreibt.

(3) Ein Wertpapierdienstleistungsunternehmen, das algorithmischen Handel im Sinne des Artikels 18 der Delegierten Verordnung (EU) 2017/565 betreibt, hat ausreichende Aufzeichnungen zu den in Absatz 2 genannten Angelegenheiten für mindestens fünf Jahre aufzubewahren. Nutzt das Wertpapierdienstleistungsunternehmen eine hochfrequente algorithmische Handelstechnik, müssen diese Aufzeichnungen insbesondere alle von ihm platzierten Aufträge einschließlich Auftragsstornierungen, ausgeführten Aufträge und Kursnotierungen an Handelsplätzen umfassen und chronologisch geordnet aufbewahrt werden. Auf Verlangen der Bundesanstalt sind diese Aufzeichnungen herauszugeben.

(4) Betreibt ein Wertpapierdienstleistungsunternehmen algorithmischen Handel im Sinne des Absatzes 2 unter Verfolgung einer Market-Making-Strategie, hat es unter Berücksichtigung der Liquidität, des Umfangs und der Art des konkreten Marktes und der konkreten Merkmale des gehandelten Instruments

1. dieses Market-Making während eines festgelegten Teils der Handelszeiten des Handelsplatzes kontinuierlich zu betreiben, abgesehen von außergewöhnlichen Umständen, so dass der Handelsplatz regelmäßig und verlässlich mit Liquidität versorgt wird,

2. einen schriftlichen Vertrag mit dem Handelsplatz zu schließen, in dem zumindest die Verpflichtungen nach Nummer 1 festgelegt werden, sofern es nicht den Vorschriften des § 26c des Börsengesetzes unterliegt, und

3. über wirksame Systeme und Kontrollen zu verfügen, durch die gewährleistet wird, dass es jederzeit diesen Verpflichtungen nachkommt.

(5) Ein Wertpapierdienstleistungsunternehmen, das algorithmischen Handel betreibt, verfolgt eine Market-Making-Strategie im Sinne des Absatzes 4, wenn es Mitglied oder Teilnehmer eines oder mehrerer Handelsplätze ist und seine Strategie beim Handel auf eigene Rechnung beinhaltet, dass es in Bezug auf ein oder mehrere Finanzinstrumente an einem einzelnen Handelsplatz oder an verschiedenen Handelsplätzen feste, zeitgleiche Geld- und Briefkurse vergleichbarer Höhe zu wettbewerbsfähigen Preisen stellt.

(6) Ein Wertpapierdienstleistungsunternehmen muss bei einer Auslagerung von Aktivitäten und Prozessen sowie von Finanzdienstleistungen die Anforderungen nach § 25b des Kreditwesengesetzes einhalten. Die Auslagerung darf nicht die Rechtsverhältnisse des Unternehmens zu seinen Kunden und seine Pflichten, die

nach diesem Abschnitt gegenüber den Kunden bestehen, verändern. Die Auslagerung darf die Voraussetzungen, unter denen dem Wertpapierdienstleistungsunternehmen eine Erlaubnis nach § 32 des Kreditwesengesetzes erteilt worden ist, nicht verändern. Nähere Bestimmungen zu den Anforderungen an die Auslagerung ergeben sich aus den

Artikeln 30 bis 32 der Delegierten Verordnung (EU) 2017/565.

(7) Ein Wertpapierdienstleistungsunternehmen darf die Anlageberatung nur dann als Unabhängige Honorar-Anlageberatung erbringen, wenn es ausschließlich Unabhängige Honorar-Anlageberatung erbringt oder wenn es die Unabhängige Honorar-Anlageberatung organisatorisch, funktional und personell von der übrigen Anlageberatung trennt. Wertpapierdienstleistungsunternehmen müssen Vertriebsvorgaben im Sinne des Absatzes 1 Nummer 3 für die Unabhängige Honorar-Anlageberatung so ausgestalten, dass in keinem Falle Interessenkonflikte mit Kundeninteressen entstehen können. Ein Wertpapierdienstleistungsunternehmen, das Unabhängige Honorar-Anlageberatung erbringt, muss auf seiner Internetseite angeben, ob die Unabhängige Honorar-Anlageberatung in der Hauptniederlassung und in welchen inländischen Zweigniederlassungen angeboten wird.

(8) Ein Wertpapierdienstleistungsunternehmen, das Finanzportfolioverwaltung oder Unabhängige Honorar-Anlageberatung erbringt, muss durch entsprechende Grundsätze sicherstellen, dass alle monetären Zuwendungen, die im Zusammenhang mit der Finanzportfolioverwaltung oder Unabhängigen Honorar-Anlageberatung von Dritten oder von für Dritte handelnden Personen angenommen werden, dem jeweiligen Kunden zugewiesen und an diesen weitergegeben werden.

(9) Ein Wertpapierdienstleistungsunternehmen, das Finanzinstrumente zum Verkauf konzipiert, hat ein Verfahren für die Freigabe jedes einzelnen Finanzinstruments und jeder wesentlichen Anpassung bestehender Finanzinstrumente zu unterhalten, zu betreiben und zu überprüfen, bevor das Finanzinstrument an Kunden vermarktet oder vertrieben wird (Produktfreigabeverfahren). Das Verfahren muss sicherstellen, dass für jedes Finanzinstrument für Endkunden innerhalb der jeweiligen Kundengattung ein bestimmter Zielmarkt festgelegt wird. Dabei sind alle einschlägigen Risiken für den Zielmarkt zu bewerten. Darüber hinaus ist sicherzustellen, dass die beabsichtigte Vertriebsstrategie dem nach Satz 2 bestimmten Zielmarkt entspricht.

(10) Ein Wertpapierdienstleistungsunternehmen hat von ihm angebotene oder vermarktete Finanzinstrumente regelmäßig zu überprüfen und dabei alle Ereignisse zu berücksichtigen, die wesentlichen Einfluss auf das potentielle Risiko für den bestimmten Zielmarkt haben könnten. Zumindest ist regelmäßig zu beurteilen, ob das Finanzinstrument den Bedürfnissen des nach Absatz 9 Satz 2 bestimmten Zielmarkts weiterhin entspricht und ob die beabsichtigte Vertriebsstrategie zur Erreichung dieses Zielmarkts weiterhin geeignet ist.

(11) Ein Wertpapierdienstleistungsunternehmen, das Finanzinstrumente konzipiert, hat allen Vertriebsunternehmen sämtliche erforderlichen und sachdienlichen Informationen zu dem Finanzinstrument und dem Produktfreigabeverfahren nach Absatz 9 Satz 1, einschließlich des nach Absatz 9 Satz 2 bestimmten Zielmarkts, zur Verfügung zu stellen. Vertreibt ein Wertpapierdienstleistungsunternehmen Finanzinstrumente

oder empfiehlt es diese, ohne sie zu konzipieren, muss es über angemessene Vorkehrungen verfügen, um sich die in Satz 1 genannten Informationen vom konzipierenden Wertpapierdienstleistungsunternehmen oder vom Emittenten zu verschaffen und die Merkmale sowie den Zielmarkt des Finanzinstruments zu verstehen.

(12) Ein Wertpapierdienstleistungsunternehmen, das Finanzinstrumente anzubieten oder zu empfehlen beabsichtigt und das von einem anderen Wertpapierdienstleistungsunternehmen konzipierte Finanzinstrumente vertreibt, hat geeignete Verfahren aufrechtzuerhalten und Maßnahmen zu treffen, um sicherzustellen, dass die Anforderungen nach diesem Gesetz eingehalten werden. Dies umfasst auch solche Anforderungen, die für die Offenlegung, für die Bewertung der Eignung und der Angemessenheit, für Anreize und für den ordnungsgemäßen Umgang mit Interessenkonflikten gelten. Das Wertpapierdienstleistungsunternehmen ist zu besonderer Sorgfalt verpflichtet, wenn es als Vertriebsunternehmen ein neues Finanzprodukt anzubieten oder zu empfehlen beabsichtigt oder wenn sich die Dienstleistungen ändern, die es als Vertriebsunternehmen anzubieten oder zu empfehlen beabsichtigt.

(13) Das Wertpapierdienstleistungsunternehmen hat seine Produktfreigabevorkehrungen regelmäßig zu überprüfen, um sicherzustellen, dass diese belastbar und zweckmäßig sind und zur Umsetzung erforderlicher Änderungen geeignete Maßnahmen zu treffen. Es hat sicherzustellen, dass seine gemäß Artikel 22 Absatz 2 der Delegierten Verordnung (EU) 2017/565 eingerichtete Compliance-Funktion die Entwicklung und regelmäßige Überprüfung der Produktfreigabevorkehrungen überwacht und etwaige Risiken, dass Anforderungen an den Produktüberwachungsprozess nicht erfüllt werden, frühzeitig erkennt.

(14) Das Bundesministerium der Finanzen kann durch Rechtsverordnung, die nicht der Zustimmung des Bundesrates bedarf, nähere Bestimmungen zur Anwendung der Delegierten Verordnung (EU) 2017/565 sowie zur Umsetzung der Delegierten Richtlinie (EU) 2017/593 der Kommission vom 7. April 2016 zur Ergänzung der Richtlinie 2014/65/EU des Europäischen Parlaments und des Rates im Hinblick auf den Schutz der Finanzinstrumente und Gelder von Kunden, Produktüberwachungspflichten und Vorschriften für die Entrichtung beziehungsweise Gewährung oder Entgegennahme von Gebühren, Provisionen oder anderen monetären oder nicht-monetären Vorteilen (ABl. L 87 vom 31.3.2017, S. 500), in der jeweils geltenden Fassung, und den organisatorischen Anforderungen nach Absatz 1 Satz 2 und Absatz 7, den Anforderungen an das Produktfreigabeverfahren und den Produktvertrieb nach Absatz 9 und das Überprüfungsverfahren nach Absatz 10 sowie den nach Absatz 11 zur Verfügung zu stellenden Informationen und damit zusammenhängenden Pflichten der Wertpapierdienstleistungsunternehmen erlassen. Das Bundesministerium der Finanzen kann die Ermächtigung durch Rechtsverordnung auf die Bundesanstalt übertragen.

§ 87 Einsatz von Mitarbeitern in der Anlageberatung, als Vertriebsbeauftragte, in der Finanzportfolioverwaltung oder als Compliance-Beauftragte; Verordnungsermächtigung

(1) Ein Wertpapierdienstleistungsunternehmen darf einen Mitarbeiter nur dann mit der Anlageberatung betrauen, wenn dieser sachkundig ist und über die für die Tätigkeit erforderliche Zuverlässigkeit verfügt. Das Wertpapierdienstleistungsunternehmen muss der Bundesanstalt

1. den Mitarbeiter und,

2. sofern das Wertpapierdienstleistungsunternehmen über Vertriebsbeauftragte im Sinne des Absatzes 4 verfügt, den auf Grund der Organisation des Wertpapierdienstleistungsunternehmens für den Mitarbeiter unmittelbar zuständigen Vertriebsbeauftragten anzeigen, bevor der Mitarbeiter die Tätigkeit nach Satz 1 aufnimmt. Ändern sich die von dem Wertpapierdienstleistungsunternehmen nach Satz 2 angezeigten Verhältnisse, sind die neuen Verhältnisse unverzüglich der Bundesanstalt anzuzeigen. Ferner sind der Bundesanstalt, wenn auf Grund der Tätigkeit des Mitarbeiters eine oder mehrere Beschwerden im Sinne des Artikels 26 der Delegierten Verordnung (EU) 2017/565 durch Privatkunden gegenüber dem Wertpapierdienstleistungsunternehmen erhoben werden,

1. jede Beschwerde,

2. der Name des Mitarbeiters, auf Grund dessen Tätigkeit die Beschwerde erhoben wird, sowie,

3. sofern das Wertpapierdienstleistungsunternehmen mehrere Zweigstellen, Zweigniederlassungen oder sonstige Organisationseinheiten hat, die Zweigstelle, Zweigniederlassung oder Organisationseinheit, welcher der Mitarbeiter zugeordnet ist oder für welche er überwiegend oder in der Regel die nach Satz 1 anzuzeigende Tätigkeit ausübt, anzuzeigen.

(2) Ein Wertpapierdienstleistungsunternehmen darf einen Mitarbeiter nur dann damit betrauen, Kunden über Finanzinstrumente, strukturierte Einlagen, Wertpapierdienstleistungen oder Wertpapiernebendienstleistungen zu informieren (Vertriebsmitarbeiter), wenn dieser sachkundig ist und über die für die Tätigkeit erforderliche Zuverlässigkeit verfügt.

(3) Ein Wertpapierdienstleistungsunternehmen darf einen Mitarbeiter nur dann mit der Finanzportfolioverwaltung betrauen, wenn dieser sachkundig ist und über die für die Tätigkeit erforderliche Zuverlässigkeit verfügt.

(4) Ein Wertpapierdienstleistungsunternehmen darf einen Mitarbeiter mit der Ausgestaltung, Umsetzung oder Überwachung von Vertriebsvorgaben im Sinne des § 80 Absatz 1 Satz 2 Nummer 3 nur dann betrauen (Vertriebsbeauftragter), wenn dieser sachkundig ist und über die für die Tätigkeit erforderliche Zuverlässigkeit verfügt. Das Wertpapierdienstleistungsunternehmen muss der Bundesanstalt den Mitarbeiter anzeigen, bevor dieser die Tätigkeit nach Satz 1 aufnimmt. Ändern sich die von dem Wertpapierdienstleistungsunternehmen nach Satz 2 angezeigten Verhältnisse, sind die neuen Verhältnisse unverzüglich der Bundesanstalt anzuzeigen.

(5) Ein Wertpapierdienstleistungsunternehmen darf einen Mitarbeiter nur dann mit der Verantwortlichkeit für die Compliance-Funktion im Sinne des Artikels 22 Absatz 2 der Delegierten Verordnung (EU) 2017/565 und für die Berichte an die Geschäftsleitung nach Artikel 25 Absatz 2 der Delegierten Verordnung (EU) 2017/565 betrauen (Compliance-Beauftragter), wenn dieser sachkundig ist und über die für die Tätigkeit erforderliche Zuverlässigkeit verfügt. Das Wertpapierdienstleistungsunternehmen muss der Bundesanstalt den Mitarbeiter anzeigen, bevor der Mitarbeiter die Tätigkeit nach Satz 1 aufnimmt. Ändern sich die von dem Wertpapierdienstleistungsunternehmen nach Satz 2 angezeigten Verhältnisse, sind die neuen Verhältnisse unverzüglich der Bundesanstalt anzuzeigen.

(6) Liegen Tatsachen vor, aus denen sich ergibt, dass ein Mitarbeiter 1. nicht oder nicht mehr die Anforderungen nach Absatz 1 Satz 1, Absatz 2, 3, 4 Satz 1, jeweils auch in Verbindung mit § 96, oder Absatz 5 Satz 1 erfüllt, kann die Bundesanstalt unbeschadet ihrer Befugnisse nach § 6 dem Wertpapierdienstleistungsunternehmen untersagen, den Mitarbeiter in der angezeigten Tätigkeit einzusetzen, solange dieser die gesetzlichen Anforderungen nicht erfüllt, oder

2. gegen Bestimmungen dieses Abschnittes verstoßen hat, deren Einhaltung bei der Durchführung seiner Tätigkeit zu beachten sind, kann die Bundesanstalt unbeschadet ihrer Befugnisse nach § 6 a) das Wertpapierdienstleistungsunternehmen und den Mitarbeiter verwarnen oder b) dem Wertpapierdienstleistungsunternehmen für eine Dauer von bis zu zwei Jahren untersagen, den Mitarbeiter in der angezeigten Tätigkeit einzusetzen. Die Bundesanstalt kann unanfechtbar gewordene Anordnungen im Sinne des Satzes 1 auf ihrer Internetseite öffentlich bekannt machen, es sei denn, diese Veröffentlichung wäre geeignet, den berechtigten Interessen des Unternehmens zu schaden. Die öffentliche Bekanntmachung nach Satz 2 hat ohne Nennung des Namens des betroffenen Mitarbeiters zu erfolgen. Widerspruch und Anfechtungsklage gegen Maßnahmen nach Satz 1 haben keine aufschiebende Wirkung.

(7) Die Bundesanstalt führt über die nach den Absätzen 1, 4 und 5 anzuzeigenden Mitarbeiter sowie die ihnen zugeordneten Beschwerdeanzeigen nach Absatz 1 und die ihre Tätigkeit betreffenden Anordnungen nach Absatz 6 eine interne Datenbank.

(8) Die Absätze 1 bis 7 sind nicht anzuwenden auf diejenigen Mitarbeiter eines Wertpapierdienstleistungsunternehmens, die ausschließlich in einer Zweigniederlassung im Sinne des § 24a des Kreditwesengesetzes oder in mehreren solcher Zweigniederlassungen tätig sind.

(9) Das Bundesministerium der Finanzen kann durch Rechtsverordnung, die nicht der Zustimmung des Bundesrates bedarf, die näheren Anforderungen an

1. den Inhalt, die Art, die Sprache, den Umfang und die Form der Anzeigen nach den Absätzen 1, 4 oder 5,

2. die Sachkunde und die Zuverlässigkeit nach Absatz 1 Satz 1, den Absätzen 2, 3, 4 Satz 1, jeweils auch in Verbindung mit § 96, sowie Absatz 5 Satz 1 sowie

3. den Inhalt der Datenbank nach Absatz 7 und die Dauer der Speicherung der Einträge

einschließlich des jeweiligen Verfahrens regeln. In der Rechtsverordnung nach Satz 1 kann insbesondere bestimmt werden, dass dem jeweiligen Wertpapierdienstleistungsunternehmen ein schreibender Zugriff auf die für das Unternehmen einzurichtenden Einträge in die Datenbank nach Absatz 7 eingeräumt und ihm die Verantwortlichkeit für die Richtigkeit und Aktualität dieser Einträge übertragen wird. Das Bundesministerium der Finanzen kann die Ermächtigung durch Rechtsverordnung ohne Zustimmung des Bundesrates auf die Bundesanstalt übertragen.

(10) Die Absätze 1 bis 3 gelten nicht für Immobiliar-Verbraucherdarlehensverträge, die an die Vorbedingung geknüpft sind, dass dem Verbraucher eine Wertpapierdienstleistung in Bezug auf gedeckte Schuldverschreibungen, die zur Besicherung der Finanzierung des Kredits begeben worden sind und denen dieselben Konditionen wie dem Immobiliar-Verbraucherdarlehensvertrag zugrunde liegen, erbracht wird, und

wenn damit das Darlehen ausgezahlt, refinanziert oder abgelöst werden kann.

§ 94 Bezeichnungen zur Unabhängigen Honorar-Anlageberatung

(1) Die Bezeichnungen „Unabhängiger Honorar-Anlageberater“, „Unabhängige Honorar-Anlageberaterin“,„Unabhängige Honorar-Anlageberatung“ oder „Unabhängiger Honoraranlageberater“, „Unabhängige Honoraranlageberaterin“, „Unabhängige Honoraranlageberatung“ auch in abweichender Schreibweise oder eine Bezeichnung, in der diese Wörter enthalten sind, dürfen, soweit durch Gesetz nichts anderes bestimmt ist, in der Firma, als Zusatz zur Firma, zur Bezeichnung des Geschäftszwecks oder zu Werbezwecken nur Wertpapierdienstleistungsunternehmen führen, die im Register Unabhängiger Anlageberater nach § 93 eingetragen sind.

(2) Absatz 1 gilt nicht für Unternehmen, die die dort genannten Bezeichnungen in einem Zusammenhang führen, der den Anschein ausschließt, dass sie Wertpapierdienstleistungen erbringen. Wertpapierdienstleistungsunternehmen mit Sitz im Ausland dürfen bei ihrer Tätigkeit im Inland die in Absatz 1 genannten Bezeichnungen in der Firma, als Zusatz zur Firma, zur Bezeichnung des Geschäftszwecks oder zu Werbezwecken führen, wenn sie zur Führung dieser Bezeichnung in ihrem Sitzstaat berechtigt sind und sie die Bezeichnung um einen auf ihren Sitzstaat hinweisenden Zusatz ergänzen.

(3) Die Bundesanstalt entscheidet in Zweifelsfällen, ob ein Wertpapierdienstleistungsunternehmen zur Führung der in Absatz 1 genannten Bezeichnungen befugt ist. Sie hat ihre Entscheidungen dem Registergericht mitzuteilen.

(4) Die Vorschrift des § 43 des Kreditwesengesetzes ist entsprechend anzuwenden mit der Maßgabe, dass an die Stelle der Erlaubnis nach § 32 des Kreditwesengesetzes die Eintragung in das Register Unabhängiger Honorar-Anlageberater nach § 93 tritt.

以上

資料7

COMMITTEE OF EUROPEAN SECURITIES REGULATORS

Date: 19 April 2010
Ref.: CESR/10-293

Question & Answers

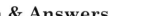

Understanding the definition of advice under MiFID

CESR, 11-13 avenue de Friedland, 75008 Paris, France - Tel +33 (0)1 58 36 43 21, web site: www.cesr.eu

Table of contents

Executive Summary

On 14 October 2009, CESR published a consultation paper (CP) entitled "Understanding the definition of advice under MiFID" (Ref. CESR/09-665). In that CP, CESR consulted on Questions and Answers designed to clarify and illustrate situations where firms will, or will not, be considered as providing investment advice. Investment advice is an investment service under MiFID, which is why the distinction is important.

This set of Questions and Answers reflects CESR's statement of its policy following its consultation paper. In parallel to this Q&A, CESR also publishes its Feedback Statement (Ref. CESR/10-294) responding to comments it received in response to the CP and would recommend that these documents be read in conjunction.

The main questions for consideration, when determining whether a particular service amounts to investment advice, are laid out in 'Diagram: the five key tests for investment advice' in the Introduction (see page 6). This diagram illustrates the five key tests that are set out in MiFID, with issues to consider in relation to each test. CESR wishes to stress that all five of these tests have to be met for a service to be considered as investment advice.

Key subjects covered in this Q&A include:

- The provision of personal recommendations and whether other forms of presenting information such as 'investment research', filtering, general recommendations, generic advice, presenting multiple products or access to model investment portfolios could constitute investment advice.
- The presentation of a recommendation as suitable for a client or based on the client's circumstances, including making recommendations to become a client of a particular firm, making recommendations which are clearly unsuitable in light of knowledge about the client, definitions of a 'person's circumstances' and when recommendations will be viewed as based on a view of a person's circumstances.
- Perimeter issues around the definition of personal recommendation, including disclaimers to the client and failing to use known customer information.
- Issues around the form of communication, including whether the Internet is always a 'distribution channel', messages to multiple clients, distinguishing corporate finance and investment advice and whether these are mutually exclusive.

II. Introduction

1. The Markets in Financial Instruments Directive (2004/39/EC), or 'MiFID', identifies investment advice as an investment service, the provision of which, on a professional basis, generally requires authorisation as an investment firm[1]. Together, MiFID and the MiFID Implementing Directive (2006/73/EC) place various requirements on firms when they provide investment advice that do not apply when providing many other investment services, notably including requirements to ensure that any personal recommendations made to clients and potential clients are suitable for them.

2. In the light of this distinction, it is important to provide as much clarity as possible about the definition of investment advice, to help firms to ascertain whether or not the services that they provide are subject to the requirements on investment advice.

3. This document does not form part of the MiFID review. It is a Level 3 paper designed to further harmonisation in the interpretation of the EU rules on the definition of investment advice as it currently stands under MiFID

Examining the definition of investment advice

4. According to MiFID, investment advice means the provision of personal recommendations to a client, either upon his request or at the initiative of the investment firm, in respect of one or more transactions relating to financial instruments (Article 4(4)). For the purposes of the definition of investment advice, that recommendation must be presented as suitable for that person or must be based on a consideration of the circumstances of that person (Article 52 of the MiFID Implementing Directive). The Directive also sets out a number of other tests for firms to consider in determining whether they are providing such personal recommendations, which we examine and discuss in this paper.

5. The diagram on page 6 illustrates how the five key tests work together and hence the thought process that a firm will need to go through to determine whether its services constitute investment advice. All five tests shown in the diagram have to be met in order for a service to be considered investment advice under MiFID. The following pages of this paper then use Questions and Answers to clarify and illustrate situations where firms will, or will not, be considered as meeting each of the tests and hence providing investment advice. Where the Questions and Answers describe a situation where a particular test is met, the reader should bear in mind that all four of the other tests would also have to be met for the service described to be considered as advice.

Considering an investor's view of whether advice is being given (Test 3)

6. MiFID identifies the importance of presentation in determining whether investment advice is being given: one of the tests that the Directive sets out is whether a recommendation is *presented* as suitable, rather than whether it is *actually* suitable for the client. CESR believes that it is, therefore, important to take account of whether it would be reasonable to think that a personal recommendation is being made in determining whether investment advice is being given. So, if a recommendation is put forward in such a way that a reasonable observer would view it as being based on a consideration of a client's circumstances or presented as suitable then – subject to the other four tests being met – this will amount to investment advice.

[1] Some exemptions are provided in MiFID, including exemptions for the 'incidental' provision of the service (Article 2(1)(c)) and the provision of the service in such a way that it is not 'specifically remunerated' (Article 2(1)(j)). These exemptions are not examined in detail in this paper.

7. Despite the fact that MiFID requires that all information addressed by the investment firm to clients or potential clients shall be fair, clear and not misleading, CESR recognises that a particular client's understanding of the nature of the service he is receiving will not always be accurate. For this reason, whether or not a particular client feels that he is receiving a personal recommendation will not determine, on its own, whether or not investment advice is actually being given.

Advice given to professional clients

8. Many of the examples used in this paper will be of most relevance to firms dealing with retail clients. This reflects the fact that, in many cases, services to professional clients are likely to include the provision of investment research, as well as other general recommendations that do not amount to investment advice. In practice, firms can often place greater reliance on the ability of professional clients to understand whether or not they are receiving investment advice. However, the overall concepts and analyses in this paper will still be of relevance in relation to services given to professional clients and, in particular, regarding the distinction between investment advice and corporate finance advice.

Information for firms that do not wish to provide investment advice

9. If a firm wishes to verify that the service it is providing is not investment advice, it can do so by considering whether or not its service meets the five tests illustrated on the next page. A firm that does not intend to give advice can seek to avoid doing so inadvertently by making sure that its internal systems and controls, its staff training and its information to clients appropriately and consistently reflect the nature of the service it is providing. (Firms should bear in mind that describing a service as non-advised in their documentation will not be sufficient, on its own to ensure that the services given do not amount to advice – this is reflected in the Questions and Answers in this paper.)

10. In reviewing its training, a key point for a firm to consider will be whether its customer-facing staff understand that when they provide information to clients, they should not give their own views or recommendations about the suitability for the client of any particular financial instrument. By reflecting the firm's intention not to give advice in training and oversight of staff, firms can seek to manage the risk of individuals making personal recommendations. It is particularly difficult for a firm to manage the risk that a client will be given advice in a face-to-face situation, but the possibility of giving advice inadvertently also arises in relation to other distribution mechanisms. Firms that interact with clients on-line, for example, will need to make sure that staff involved in designing and operating web systems understand the nature of the service that they should, and should not, be providing.

Assumptions made in preparing this paper

11. It is taken as given throughout the following Questions and Answers that when a firm is providing investment advice under MiFID, it will be subject to all of the Directive requirements that apply in relation to investment advice (e.g. the suitability requirements in Article 19(4) of MiFID and Article 35 of the MiFID Implementing Directive), so this point is not reiterated for examples individually. References to 'clients' or 'investors' made throughout the rest of this paper can also be read as applying to potential clients or potential investors.

Diagram: the five key tests for investment advice

Is it investment advice?	Examples of issues to consider:	Page
1. Does the service being offered constitute a recommendation?	• the difference between information and a recommendation • whether assisting a client to filter information amounts to a recommendation	7
YES		
2. Is the recommendation in relation to one or more transactions in financial instruments?	• how to distinguish generic advice and general recommendations from investment advice • whether recommending a firm or a service can amount to investment advice	9
YES		
3. Is the recommendation at least one of the following… …a) presented as suitable? …b) based on a consideration of the person's circumstances?	• how a financial instrument might implicitly be presented as suitable • the impact of disclaimers • what it means to consider a person's circumstances	11
YES		
4. Is the recommendation issued otherwise than exclusively through distribution channels or to the public?	• assessing recommendations delivered via the Internet • assessing recommendations given to multiple clients at once • distributing investment research	13
YES		
5. Is the recommendation made to a person in his capacity as one of the following… …a) an investor or potential investor? …b) an agent for an investor or potential investor?	• identifying investors and their agents • the distinction between corporate finance advice and investment advice	15
YES		
INVESTMENT ADVICE		

III. Part 1: Does the service being offered constitute a recommendation?

What constitutes a recommendation?

12. Under MiFID, a personal recommendation is a recommendation that is made to a person in his capacity as an investor or potential investor, or in his capacity as an agent for an investor or personal investor.

13. In specifying that a service will only amount to investment advice if it constitutes a recommendation, the Directive draws a distinction between providing advice and simply providing information. It should be noted that a recommendation may be made on the initiative of the investment firm or of the investor. The fact that a recommendation is being given does not have to be made explicit to the investor – and the investor does not have to act upon the recommendation – for it to be regarded as a recommendation

What is the difference between providing information and providing a recommendation?

14. A recommendation requires an element of opinion on the part of the adviser. In effect, advice involves a recommendation as to a course of action, which may be presented to be in the interest of the investor.

15. Information, on the other hand, involves statements of fact or figures. In general terms, simply giving objective information without making any comment or value judgement on its relevance to decisions which an investor may make, is not a recommendation.

When could the provision of information to a client constitute a recommendation?

16. Giving information may amount to giving a recommendation if the circumstances in which the information is provided give it the force of a recommendation. While a firm may not intend to provide a recommendation to a client, it may find that it does so if it allows the information it provides to become subjective, such that it actually leads the customer to one particular product over others.

17. For example, if a person places special emphasis on the advantages of one product over others for a client, in a way that would tend to influence the decision of the recipient to select that particular product over others presented, this could amount to a personal recommendation rather than the mere provision of information.

18. We can also think of situations where the wider context in which information is provided will determine whether or not advice is given. The following are some examples of objective information that might be given to a client, without amounting to a personal recommendation:

- listings of share and unit prices;
- company news or announcements;
- an explanation of the terms and conditions of an investment;
- a comparison of the benefits and risks of one investment as compared to another;
- league tables showing the performance of investments of a particular kind against set published criteria;
- alerts about the happening of certain events (for example, certain shares reaching a certain price);
- details of directors' dealings in the shares of their own companies.

19. Taking the information in the last two bullet points above as examples we can, however, imagine the following situations where providing a client with the information could involve giving a personal recommendation:

- a person may offer to tell a client when certain shares reach a certain value on the basis of a prior recommendation to purchase or to sell at that price; or
- a person may offer to provide information on directors' dealings on the basis that, in his opinion, were directors to buy or sell investors would do well to follow suit.

20. The communication about the instrument reaching the target price, or the one about the directors' dealings, could be viewed as mere information if it were considered in isolation. But, as this communication should be considered as part of a multiple step recommendation process, providing the information should be regarded as giving a personal recommendation to the client.

21. The question of whether a communication to a client constitutes a recommendation may be closely related to the question of whether a recommendation is presented as suitable (see Section 3a for related Questions and Answers on presenting a recommendation implicitly).

Can a firm guide a client through a set of filtering questions about the investment products it offers without this constituting a recommendation?

22. The fact that a firm enables a client to filter the information that he receives about different financial instruments – for example, by choosing from a set of options on a website, or even following a decision-tree process with a member of staff – does not automatically mean that a recommendation is being given by the firm that provides the information. But where a firm uses a mechanism to filter the information that it provides investors, the circumstances of such a case should be taken into account in determining whether a recommendation is being made.

23. Factors that may be relevant in deciding whether the process involves a recommendation may include:

- any representations made by the questioner at the start of the questioning relating to the service he is to provide;
- the context in which the questioning takes place;
- the stage in the questioning at which the opinion is offered and its significance;
- the role played by the questioner who guides a person through the questions;
- the type of questions and whether they infer the use of opinion or judgment by the firm;
- the outcome of the questioning (whether particular products are highlighted, how many of them, who provides them, their relationship to the questioner and so on); and
- whether the questions and answers have been provided by, and are clearly the responsibility of, an unconnected third party, and all that the questioner has done is help the person understand what the questions or options are and how to determine which option applies to his particular circumstances.

24. A critical factor would be whether the process is limited to assisting the person to make his own choice of product which has particular features which the person regards as important: if this is the case then it is unlikely that the process will involve a personal recommendation.

25. As an example, price comparison websites commonly collect information from clients and about their circumstances and allow them to filter the information that they view as a result, without necessarily giving investment advice. The website may enable a client to enter information to generate a list of investment products for which they are eligible, or that meet criteria they have chosen, without providing a recommendation. In such cases, the ability of the client to make their own choices about the features they are looking for, and the absence of apparent judgement about which features or products they should choose, would make it unlikely that the service offered would be viewed as investment advice.

If a firm gives investors access to model investment portfolios, which are composed of different financial instruments that it can sell them, is this investment advice?

26. Whether or not providing a client with access to a model investment portfolio amounts to investment advice will depend on the particular circumstances, just as was described in the question about other forms of filtering of information (above). Different factors would need to be assessed, on a case-by-case basis, to determine whether or not investment advice is being given.

27. If we consider a situation where a firm provides, on its website or through another medium, the possibility for investors to determine their investment profile (e.g. dynamic, conservative etc.) and for each profile discloses a related model portfolio, composed of different financial instruments, we can certainly envisage situations in which providing such a service is likely to amount to investment advice. If buying, or subscribing for, the financial instruments identified in the model portfolio is positioned as the appropriate action for the investor to take, the overall service might be viewed as a recommendation rather than merely the provision of information.

28. The following sections of this paper will clearly also be relevant in determining whether investment advice is being given when a firm gives clients access to model investment portfolios. For example, if a website provider collects information about a specific investor's circumstances; uses an element of opinion in translating this into a risk profile and then to identify a particular set of products; and presents the portfolio using phrases such as "this might be appropriate for you", it is possible that all the tests described in this paper might be met and the service provided would amount to investment advice.

IV. Part 2: Is the recommendation in relation to one or more transactions in financial instruments?

What does it mean to make recommendations in relation to transactions in financial instruments?

29. MIFID sets out the 'transactions' that a recommendation could be in relation to:

- buying, selling, subscribing for, exchanging, redeeming, holding or underwriting a particular financial instrument; or

- exercising or not exercising any right conferred by such an instrument to buy, sell, subscribe for, exchange or redeem a financial instrument.

30. This test means that, in general, any advice that relates to particular financial instruments – whether or not transactions ultimately go ahead – could be considered as investment advice under MiFID.

31. Subject to also fulfilling the other four tests described in this paper, a recommendation not to buy a financial instrument can also constitute the provision of a personal recommendation for the purposes of MiFID.

32. According to MIFID, the definition of recommendations does not necessarily involve the adviser reviewing a wide range of financial instruments. Advice can also be based, for example, on a review of just a firm's own products or a restricted list of financial instruments.[2]

[2] In this context, the client can select the intermediary having regard to the features of the advice service that is going to be provided. To this extent, MiFID requires that investment firms provide clients before they are bound by any agreement for the provision of investment services with information about the terms of such agreement (Article 29(1)(a) of the Implementing Directive).

33. In contrast, generic advice about a type of financial instrument and general recommendations are not investment advice under the Directive.

What is generic advice?

34. Advice that does not relate a particular investment or investments should be regarded as generic advice. Examples of generic advice may include:

- advice on the merits of investing in one geographical zone rather than another (for example, Japan rather than Europe); or

- advice on the merits of investing in certain asset classes rather than in others (for example, bonds rather than shares).

35. See Recital 81 of the MiFID Implementing Directive for further information of the definition of generic advice and the rules applying when generic advice is being provided.

What is a general recommendation?

36. A general recommendation is a recommendation about a transaction in a financial instrument or a type of financial instrument which is intended for distribution channels or the public (see Recital 83 of the MiFID Implementing Directive). General recommendations include investment research and financial analysis, and are an ancillary service under Section B(5) of Annex I of MiFID.

37. Being addressed to the public in general, a general recommendation is not, by definition, based on an evaluation of the personal circumstances of a particular person, nor does it appear to be presented as suitable for that person. Further information about when an instrument is issued exclusively through distribution channels or to the public can be found in Section 4.

38. For more details regarding the definition of investment research, financial analysis or other forms of general recommendation relating to transactions in financial instruments, reference should be made to Article 24 of the MiFID Implementing Directive.

Can investment advice involve presenting several alternative financial instruments, rather than recommending just one?

39. Yes, a recommendation can involve the presentation of several specific financial instruments that are, together, recommended over other possible choices. The fact that more than one financial instrument is being recommended does not stop the service being offered from being advice.

40. For instance, where a firm giving advice recommends that an investor takes a particular action in relation to any one of a group of specific financial instruments, which are presented as equally suitable (e.g. the firm might state that "share A, share B or share C are equally suitable for your needs") this will constitute investment advice.

Does a firm give advice when it discusses the merits of different product types for the customer?

41. It is possible for a client to ask for and receive information about different types of financial instruments without advice being given on one or more specific financial instruments. For example, advice about whether it would be best for a client to invest directly in shares or through a collective investment scheme (CIS) could be given without investment advice being given.

42. Advice looking only at which asset class would be better for an investor would normally qualify as generic advice rather than as investment advice. If, further to advice regarding an asset class

being given, the firm also indicates a particular instrument within that asset class this would be regarded as investment advice.

Is a recommendation to become a client of a particular investment firm investment advice?

43. Advice to become the client of a particular investment firm (e.g. a particular portfolio manager), or to use its services in a certain way, would need to relate to one or more specific financial instruments in order to be considered as investment advice under MiFID.

44. Recital 60 of the MiFID Implementing Directive notes that advice given by a portfolio manager to a client to the effect that the client should give or alter a mandate to the portfolio manager that defines the limits of the portfolio manager's discretion should be considered a recommendation within the meaning of Article 19(4) of MiFID. This Recital makes clear that advice in relation to a portfolio management mandate is subject to the requirements on assessing suitability (although it is not necessarily a personal recommendation).

V. Part 3a: Is the recommendation presented as suitable?

Can a financial instrument be implicitly presented as suitable?

45. Yes. A financial instrument might be presented as suitable for the investor in an explicit or implicit form. In both cases the firm will be providing investment advice, if the other tests are also met. For instance, a financial instrument might be explicitly presented as suitable using words such as "this product would be the best option for you". Alternatively, the recommendation could be implicit, but clearly influence the client to take action in relation to a specific financial instrument over others presented (for example, several products might be presented, with one of them highlighted for the client by a phrase such as "people like you tend to buy this product").

46. As noted earlier, if a person places special emphasis on the advantages of one product over others for a client, in a way that would tend to influence the decision of the recipient to select that particular product over others presented, this could amount to a personal recommendation. It is not necessary for a firm to tell a client that a recommendation it is making is suitable for him in order for its recommendation to be viewed as being presented as suitable.

47. For example, an investment firm might contact clients that hold units in a particular fund and present to them as suitable the idea of selling those assets and purchasing units in another particular fund. In such a context, we could imagine an implicit recommendation being given through a form of words like "Our research indicates that Fund X is no longer performing as our clients would wish. We have identified Fund Y as a replacement investment, which can be used to achieve the same investment outcomes".

Could the presentation of a financial instrument as suitable for an investor constitute advice even if the firm is aware that it is not suitable for that investor?

48. Yes, a financial instrument can be presented as suitable for an investor without this actually being the case. In such a case, before making the recommendation the firm should have obtained the necessary information regarding the client's knowledge and experience, his financial situation and his investment objectives so as to recommend a financial instrument that is suitable for him. While a recommendation of a product that is not suitable for the investor would constitute a breach of the rules on suitability (in Article 19(4) of MiFID and Article 35 of the MiFID Implementing Directive) it would not stop the recommendation from being presented as suitable or constituting investment advice.

Can a firm avoid providing investment advice using a disclaimer in its communications?

49. It is important that firms provide clients with appropriate information in a comprehensible form about their services (see Article 19(3) of the MiFID Implementing Directive) and CESR recognises that disclaimers can be of some use. For example, if a firm has been asked to provide an existing client with information, but is aware that the client has received recommendations from the firm in the past, it might make use of a disclaimer to confirm the nature of the service being provided when it presents the information.

50. It is important to remember, though, that even if a clear, prominent and understandable disclaimer is provided stating that no advice or recommendation is being given, a firm could still be viewed as having presented a recommendation as suitable for the client. For example, if a firm stated that its product would suit a particular client's needs, the inclusion of a disclaimer saying that this was not advice would be unlikely to change the nature of the communication. If the other tests are also met, the firm would be viewed as providing investment advice.

51. While disclaimers may be of some use to firms seeking to ensure that they do not inadvertently present financial instruments as suitable for particular clients, they will also need to take other steps to achieve this. As noted earlier (see paragraphs 9 and 10), a firm that does not intend to give advice will need to ensure that, for example, its internal systems and controls and staff training appropriately reflect this.

VI. Part 3b: Is the recommendation based on a consideration of the person's circumstances?

What do we mean when we talk about a person's circumstances?

52. Information about a person's circumstances could include both factual information (e.g. their address, income or marital status) and more subjective information about their wants and needs (e.g. their overall risk appetite, short- and long-term investment objectives or their desire for protection from particular risks). Any such information could be considered as part of a person's circumstances.

When will a firm be viewed as basing a recommendation on a consideration of a person's circumstances?

53. Whether or not a firm will be viewed as providing a recommendation based on a consideration of person's circumstances is likely to depend on factors such as:

    - the nature of the information it collects; and
    - the way that it presents its questions.

54. For example, if a firm has collected information from a client on his investment objectives or financial situation, if he returns to the firm through the same channel for a follow-on service, it could reasonably be expected that this information is being used to create a picture of his needs and wants to form the basis of a recommendation. Other elements, such as the following, could lead to consider that it is reasonable to expect that the information previously given is being used: the contact point with the firm is the same and the nature of the service is similar to that given in the past.

55. In other cases, it would not be reasonable to expect that a firm will access and use all of the information that it may happen to hold about a client's circumstances. For example, if a client gave the firm information when purchasing a mortgage, he could not reasonably assume that the information was being accessed and made use of when he makes use of the execution only service provided by the firm through its online channel.

56. On certain occasions a firm will be forbidden from using information it holds about clients as a consequence of the operation of information barriers to manage conflicts of interest. For example,

certain information held by a corporate finance team providing investment services related to securities offering by the firm's client will not be able to be used by the sales and trading part of the firm. Despite the lack of such confidential information, the sales and trading staff of the firm will be considered to provide investment advice to the client if all the relevant conditions are satisfied.

Can a firm avoid being viewed as making a personal recommendation by failing to use information about a person's circumstances?

57. No, not if a firm has accumulated relevant information on a person's circumstances – either during a single interview or during the course of an ongoing relationship – and it can reasonably be expected that this information is being taken into account (as discussed in the question above). In this case, any recommendation made will be treated as being based on a consideration of the person's circumstances.

58. This situation is perhaps most likely to arise if a firm collects potentially relevant information from a client through one contact point, as part of an established relationship. In this situation, the firm could be held responsible for giving the impression that it is basing its later recommendations on information about the person's circumstances collected earlier.

59. In the same way as was described earlier (see paragraphs 49 to 51) disclaimers may be of some use in providing clients with information about their services. However, adding a disclaimer to a client agreement or order noting that information collected will not be used to make a recommendation will not be sufficient to prevent the firm from being treated as having given a personal recommendation, if it is clear that the client could reasonably have expected that the recommendation was based on a consideration of his or her circumstances. If the other tests are also met, in such a situation, the service will amount to investment advice.

VII. Part 4: Is the recommendation issued otherwise than exclusively through distribution channels or to the public?

What does it mean to make a recommendation exclusively through distribution channels or to the public?

60. A recommendation concerning financial instruments made exclusively through newspapers, magazines or in any other publication addressed to the public (including a public webpage on the Internet), or during a television or a radio programme should be regarded as a recommendation made through a distribution channel or to the public. The same would apply to marketing campaigns, such as those made through posters or folders that can be seen in places accessible to the public (e.g. on public transport or at a firm's agencies).

61. Newspapers, magazines or any other publication addressed to the public, as well as television or radio are examples of distribution channels. A distribution channel is a channel through which information is, or is likely to become, publicly available – i.e. a large number of persons have access to it (see Article 1(7) of Commission Directive 2003/125/EC, to which the MiFID Implementing Directive refers).

62. According to Article 52 of the MiFID Implementing Directive, a recommendation is not a personal recommendation if it is issued exclusively through distribution channels or to the public.

Does publishing a list of "best products" or "funds of the month" on a public page of a website or in a newspaper count as investment advice?

63. Publishing a list of "best products" or "funds of the month" would not, in itself, normally be regarded as investment advice. Assuming that such a communication is not addressed to a

person as such but rather to the public in general, it would normally not be presented as suitable for a particular person; be based on a consideration of the circumstances of that person; or, indeed, involve a recommendation. Furthermore, if the information is provided on a public page of a website or in a newspaper, for example, this can also be considered as a distribution channel (within the meaning of Article 2(1) of the MiFID Implementing Directive).

64. Of course, if a list of best products was provided to one or more individual clients, rather than distributed through a distribution channel or to the public, it is possible that such a communication could meet the different tests described in this paper and amount to investment advice.

Would a medium such as the Internet always be seen as a distribution channel?

65. According to Article 52 of the MiFID Implementing Directive, "a recommendation is not a personal recommendation if it is issued exclusively through distribution channels or to the public". CESR is of the opinion that this exemption only applies when the recommendation issued through distribution channels or to the public *is addressed to the public in general.*

66. When a recommendation is addressed to a particular person and is presented as suitable for that person or based on a consideration of the circumstances of that person, CESR believes that it does not fulfil the conditions to benefit from the exemption under Article 52 of the MiFID Implementing Directive. This includes situations where a webpage, or indeed e-mail correspondence, is used to provide personalised information, rather than to address information to the public in general.

67. By way of example, Section 1 of this paper also describes how providing a model portfolio to client, such as through the Internet, could amount to investment advice.

Can a message sent to several clients, for example through emails or letters, be considered as investment advice?

68. While many messages that are sent to batches of clients are unlikely to amount to investment advice, the fact that a recommendation is made to multiple clients would not automatically mean that it could not be a personal recommendation. Advice can be provided in many ways, including: face to face; orally to a group; by telephone; by correspondence (including email); using a website; or through the provision of an interactive software system.

69. In order to assess whether a message sent to several clients amounts to investment advice, different elements should be taken into account: the target audience, the content of the message and the language used:

    - Target audience: the way the firm selects the clients to whom the message will be sent can have an incidence on the qualification of that message as investment advice. For example, when the internal procedures of a firm specify that a financial instrument may only be sold to a sample of clients selected on the basis of certain factors, such as clients under a certain age or who hold no similar products, the selection of the target audience will not automatically mean that the firm is providing investment advice. However, highlighting the particular personal circumstances that led the individual to be contacted, for example, is very likely to mean that the product is being presented as suitable for the particular investor.

    - Content of the message: if the message contains a solicitation, a recommendation, an opinion or a judgment, for example, regarding the advisability of a transaction, this could mean that it is regarded as investment advice.

    - Language: if the language is such that it strongly suggests an instrument, this will have an impact. Thus, the tone of the message and the way would it could be understood by the client are important elements when determining if a message amounts to investment advice.

70. In the sorts of situations described above, messages addressed to clients would be unlikely to be considered as issued exclusively through distribution channels or to the public (within the meaning of Article 52 of the MiFID Implementing Directive).

Does distributing investment research amount to investment advice?

71. Investment research under MiFID is research or other information recommending or suggesting an investment strategy concerning one or several financial instruments or the issuers of financial instruments, including any opinion as to the present or future value or price of such instruments, intended for distribution channels or for the public. From this definition it results that investment research is separate from investment advice and that firms can use distribution channels to provide their clients with investment research without this amounting to a personal recommendation.

72. Sending research to a client may not commonly amount to giving investment advice but, as we illustrated in Section 1 with other examples, information can be provided in such a way that this amounts to a personal recommendation. For example, if the sales force of a firm emails investment research to a number of clients and subsequently engages in telephone calls to discuss the merits of a particular financial instrument that the research identifies for the client in question, then this will amount to a personal recommendation.

VIII. Part 5a: Is the recommendation made to a person in his capacity as an investor or potential investor?

What does it mean to make a recommendation to a person in his capacity as an investor?

73. Article 52 of the implementing directive indicates that a personal recommendation may be provided either to a person acting in his capacity as an investor or potential investor, or to a person acting in his capacity as an agent for an investor or potential investor. It follows that where a recommendation is provided to a person acting in another capacity (neither investor nor agent for an investor), it is not a personal recommendation and consequently does not constitute investment advice.

74. The concept of a person acting in his capacity as an investor (or potential investor) will almost always be perfectly clear, both to the investment firm and to the client. Where an investment firm makes a recommendation to a person to buy or sell a financial instrument, it should be assumed that the person is an investor or potential investor unless particular circumstances clearly demonstrate otherwise. Where the primary motivation behind a recommendation is, for example, to hedge a risk such as the loss in value of the client's portfolio or the client's interest rate exposure (rather than more common investment aims of achieving income growth or capital accumulation) the client will still be acting in his capacity as an investor.

75. Under MIFID, it is not relevant for the purposes of advice definition whether a client is specifically paying for the advice or if advice is provided as part of a wider package of investment services (for which the investment firm might even be remunerated via a third party).

Compared to investment advice, what is the ancillary service of corporate finance advice?

76. Whilst investment advice is an investment service the provision of which on a professional basis generally requires authorisation as an investment firm, "corporate finance advice" is an ancillary service for which MiFID does not require authorisation. Unlike investment advice, "corporate finance advice" provided by an investment firm (as for any other ancillary service) is only subject, as appropriate to certain conduct of business obligations under Article 19 of MiFID. This includes the general requirement to act honestly, fairly and professionally in accordance with the best interests of the client.

77. The service often called "corporate finance advice" is described in Section B(3) of Annex I of MiFID as the provision of "advice to undertakings on capital structure, industrial strategy and related matters and advice and services relating to mergers and the purchase of undertakings".

In practice, how should corporate finance advice be distinguished from investment advice?

78. The only provisions of MiFID capable of assisting investment firms and their clients in drawing a line between these two categories of advice are the definition of investment advice and the above description of the ancillary service (in Section B(3) of Annex I of MiFID).

79. It is important to consider that investment advice will be provided only where a recommendation is made to a person in his capacity as an investor or potential investor (or in his capacity as an agent for an investor or potential investor). It follows from this that advice to an undertaking to issue securities is not investment advice. It is also clear from the MiFID provisions that corporate finance advice will be provided when advice is given with regard to "capital structure, industrial strategy and related matters".

80. CESR acknowledges that beyond these two conclusions that result clearly from the provisions of MiFID, firms may face some uncertainty trying to determine whether or not they are providing investment advice when providing corporate finance services. To assist in determining the type of advice to provide, CESR recommends that firms consider the objective pursued by the client when seeking advice from a firm.

81. Where the client's primary purpose for seeking advice is in order to generate a financial return on an investment or to hedge a risk, the client's objective is patrimonial in nature and the advice provided would be investment advice. Conversely, where the client's primary purpose for requesting the advice is for an industrial, strategic or entrepreneurial purpose rather than to receive a financial return or hedge a risk, the advice provided would be corporate finance advice. The context relative to the request for advice may be used to determine the primary purpose for the request.

82. In situations where it is impossible to identify the primary purpose because both a patrimonial and a strategic/industrial/entrepreneurial purpose are present and neither purpose outweighs the other in importance, CESR understands that the client would receive investment advice, perhaps simultaneously with corporate finance advice. This is notwithstanding the situations where a firm (such as a law firm or accounting firm) is providing investment advice in an incidental manner in the course of another professional activity not covered by MiFID provided that this activity is regulated and/or the provision of the advice is not remunerated, in accordance with Articles 2 1(c) and (j) of Level 1 MiFID.

83. When an undertaking approaches a firm for advice, through an individual authorised to act on behalf of the undertaking, for instance the Chief Executive Officer or the Chief Finance Officer, for the purpose of capital raising, a merger or acquisition, the disposal of a subsidiary or a management buyout, the advice provided to the client will fall under the corporate finance advice category, because the primary purpose of soliciting the advice relates to the present or future strategy of the undertaking.

84. In the context of private equity and venture capital, the industrial purpose of the firms providing these services is purely financial. Where individuals authorised to act on behalf of these firms seek advice, their primary objective is likely to be mainly entrepreneurial, and also aligned to the industrial purpose of the private equity or venture capital firms i.e. to generate a return. That is, why, where such clients seek advice in this context CESR considers it to be corporate finance advice.

85. Where an undertaking is family-owned, advice on whether to sell shares in the undertaking may involve the provision of both corporate finance advice and investment advice, perhaps for different members of the family. In this situation, the firm will have to look at the reasons for

the client's request for advice. For instance, one member of the family may be the controlling shareholder and heavily involved in the running of the business and his request for advice on whether and/or under what conditions to sell his shares is likely to primarily involve a future decision to continue or not to continue to pursue his strategic or entrepreneurial objective. Therefore the advice given is likely to be corporate finance advice, provided however that the consideration for the sale of his shares is cash only and does not include securities. On the other hand another family member who may or may not be involved in the running of the undertaking but whose primary concern is the investment in the undertaking may need to decide whether or not to sell his shares and in this case the purpose of the decision is primarily to generate a financial return, and therefore the client would be the recipient of investment advice.

86. CESR understands that the 'primary purpose test' as described above is not definitive, rather it is a tool that firms can use to help them determine whether they are likely to be providing investment advice. It is every firm's responsibility to establish and analyse all relevant factors that enable them to assess whether they are providing investment advice.

Are investment advice and corporate finance advice mutually exclusive?

87. As illustrated above, the provision of "corporate finance advice" and the provision of investment advice, can, in certain situations, overlap and this may occur with respect to the same client in circumstances where both the strategic and patrimonial purposes are equally important for the client. However, CESR understands that it is possible for a firm to structure itself as a specialist corporate finance firm and fall outside of the remit of MiFID. When a firm wishes to do so, it has to ensure that its documentation, internal structure, organisation, training and personnel are very clear as to what services the firm can and cannot perform.

IX. Part 5b: Is the recommendation made to a person in his capacity as an agent for an investor or potential investor?

What does it mean to make a recommendation to a person in his capacity as agent for an investor?

88. In most cases the concept of a person acting in his capacity as agent for an investor or potential investor will be perfectly clear, for example where a person holds a power of attorney to act in the name of his or her spouse or child.

89. There are circumstances, however, where it will not always be clear that an agency relationship within the meaning of Article 52 of the MiFID Implementing Directive exists. For example, where an investment firm provides a recommendation to a portfolio manager, it will usually be the case that the investment firm is not giving investment advice to the portfolio manager's client but is simply providing a general recommendation, such as an investment tip. However, there may be cases where a firm such as a portfolio manager *does* commission advice for a client from a third party – such as from a specialist adviser on a particular subject area – and in doing so acts as an agent. In such cases, it will be important for the firms involved to be clear about the fact that the portfolio manager is acting for a particular client (or a particular group of clients) and to ensure that the investment firm commissioned possesses the necessary information about the clients involved.

90. In CESR's view, the reference in Article 52 to the recommendation being presented as suitable "for that person" or based on a consideration of the circumstances "of that person" should, by inference, be read as meaning for that person (or where the person in question is an agent, for the person for whom he is the agent)

資料8

esma European Securities and Markets Authority

Guidelines

Guidelines for the assessment of knowledge and competence

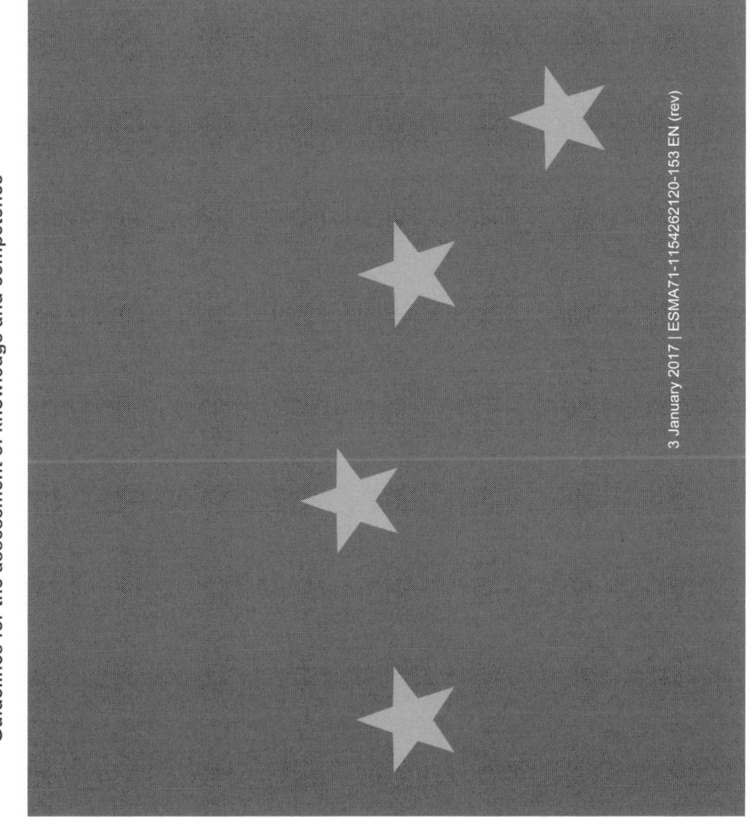

Table of Contents

I. Scope

Who?

1. These guidelines apply to:

a. Competent Authorities and

b. Firms.

What?

2. These guidelines apply in relation to the provision of the investment services and activities listed in Section A, and the ancillary services listed in Section B of Annex I of MiFID II.

When?

3. These guidelines apply from 3 January 2018.

II. References, abbreviations and definitions

Legislative references

AIFMD	Directive 2011/16/EU of the European Parliament and of the Council of 8 June 2011 on Alternative Investment Fund Manager and amending Directive 2003/41/EC and 2009/65/EC and Regulations (EC) No 1060/2009 and (EU) No 1095/2010.
ESMA Regulation	Regulation (EU) No 1095/2010 of the European Parliament and of the Council of 24 November 2010 establishing an European Supervisory Authority (European Securities and Markets Authority), amending Decision No 716/2009/EC and repealing Commission Decision 2009/77/EC.
MiFID	Directive 2004/39/EC of the European Parliament and of the Council of 21 April 2004 on markets in financial instruments amending Council Directives 85/611/EEC and 93/6/EEC and Directive 2000/12/EC of the European Parliament and of the Council and repealing Council Directive 93/22/EEC.
MiFID II	Directive 2014/65/EU of the European Parliament and of the Council of 15 May 2014 on markets in financial instruments and amending Directive 2002/92/EC and Directive 2011/61/EU (recast).

Abbreviations

AIFMD	Alternative Investment Fund Manager Directive
CA	Competent Authority
CP	Consultation Paper
EC	European Commission
EU	European Union
ESMA	European Securities and Markets Authority
MiFID	Markets in Financial Instruments Directive

Definitions

4. Unless otherwise specified, terms used in MiFID II have the same meaning in these guidelines. In addition, the following definitions apply:

a. Competent authority (or CA) means an authority designated under Article 67 of MiFID II.

b. 'Firms' means investment firms, as defined in Article 4(1)(1) of MiFID II, credit institutions (as defined in Article 4(1)(27) of MiFID II) when providing investment services as well as investment firms and credit institutions when selling or advising clients in relation to structured deposits, UCITS management companies and external Alternative Investment Fund Managers (AIFMs) insofar as they are providing the investment services of individual portfolio management or non-core services and only in connection to the provision of these services (respectively within the meaning of Article 6(3)(a) and (b) of the UCITS Directive and Article 6(4)(a) and (b) of the AIFMD).

c. 'Staff' means natural persons (including tied agents) providing relevant services to clients on behalf of the firm.

d. 'Relevant services' means providing investment advice or giving information about financial instruments, structured deposits, investment services or ancillary services to clients.

e. 'Giving information' means directly providing information to clients about financial instruments, structured deposits, investment services or ancillary services, either upon the request of the client or at the initiative of the firm, in the context of the provision by the staff member to the client of any of the services and activities listed in the section A and B of Annex I of MiFID II.

f. 'Knowledge and competence' means having acquired an appropriate qualification and appropriate experience to fulfil obligations in Article 24 and 25 MiFID II in order to provide the relevant services.

g. 'Appropriate qualification' means a qualification or other test or training course that meets the criteria set out by the guidelines.

h. 'Appropriate experience' means that a member of staff has successfully demonstrated the ability to perform the relevant services through previous work. This work must have been performed, on a full time equivalent basis, for a minimum period of 6 months. Beyond this minimum period, the CA can differentiate the period of experience required, depending on the appropriate qualification attained by staff and also depending on the relevant services being provided.

i. 'Investment products' means financial instruments and structured deposits as defined in MiFID II.

j. 'Under supervision' means providing the relevant services to clients under the responsibility of a staff member who has both an appropriate qualification and appropriate experience. The staff member can work under supervision for a maximum period of 4 years except where a shorter period is determined by the CA.

III. Purpose

5. The purpose of these guidelines is to specify the criteria for the assessment of knowledge and competence required under Article 25(1) of MiFID II, in accordance with Article 25(9) of the same Directive.

6. ESMA expects these guidelines to promote greater convergence in the knowledge and competence of staff providing investment advice or information about financial instruments, structured deposits, investment services or ancillary services to clients, and competent authorities to assess the adequacy of the compliance with such requirements. These guidelines set important standards to assist firms in meeting their obligations to act in the best interest of their clients and to assist CAs to adequately assess how firms meet these obligations.

7. These guidelines establish minimum standards for the assessment of knowledge and competence for staff providing relevant services. Consequently, CAs can require greater levels of knowledge and competence for staff giving advice and/or for staff giving information.

8. In complying with these guidelines, ESMA anticipates a corresponding strengthening of investor protection. Annex I includes a number of illustrative examples of how a firm might apply the guidelines. These examples do not form part of the guidelines but instead aim to assist firms in identifying practical examples of how the requirements in the guidelines can be met.

IV. Compliance and reporting obligations

Status of the guidelines

9. This document contains guidelines issued under Article 16 of the ESMA Regulation and required under Article 25(9) of MiFID II. In accordance with Article 16(3) of the ESMA Regulation, competent authorities and financial market participants must make every effort to comply with the guidelines.

10. Competent authorities to whom the guidelines apply should comply by incorporating them into their supervisory practices, including where particular guidelines are directed primarily at financial market participants.

Reporting requirements

11. Competent authorities to which these guidelines apply must notify ESMA whether they comply or intend to comply with the guidelines, stating their reasons for non-compliance, within two months of the date of publication by ESMA to KCguidelines1886@esma.europa.eu. In the absence of a response by this deadline, competent authorities will be considered as non-compliant. A template for notifications is available from the ESMA website.

12. Firms to which these guidelines apply are not required to report to ESMA whether they comply with these guidelines.

V. Guidelines

V.I General

13. The level and intensity of knowledge and competence expected for those providing investment advice should be of a higher standard than those that only give information on investment products and services.

14. Firms should ensure that staff providing relevant services possess the necessary knowledge and competence to meet relevant regulatory and legal requirements and business ethics standards.

15. Firms should ensure that staff know, understand and apply firm's internal policies and procedures designed to ensure compliance with MiFID II. In order to ensure a proportionate application of knowledge and competence requirements, firms should ensure that staff have the necessary levels of knowledge and competence to fulfil their obligations, reflecting the scope and degree of the relevant services provided.

16. The compliance function should assess and review compliance with these guidelines. This review should be included in the report to the management body on the implementation and effectiveness of the overall control environment for investment services and activities.

V.II Criteria for knowledge and competence for staff giving information about investment products, investment services or ancillary services

17. Firms should ensure that staff giving information about investment products, investment services or ancillary services that are available through the firm have the necessary knowledge and competence to:

a. understand the key characteristics, risk and features of those investment products available through the firm, including any general tax implications and costs to be incurred by the client in the context of transactions. Particular care should be taken when giving information with respect to products characterised by higher levels of complexity;

b. understand the total amount of costs and charges to be incurred by the client in the context of transactions in an investment product, or investment services or ancillary services;

c. understand the characteristics and scope of investment services or ancillary services;

d. understand how financial markets function and how they affect the value and pricing of investment products on which they provide information to clients;

e. understand the impact of economic figures, national/regional/global events on markets and on the value of investment products on which they provide information;

f. understand the difference between past performance and future performance scenarios as well as the limits of predictive forecasting;

g. understand issues relating to market abuse and anti-money laundering;

h. assess data relevant to the investment products on which they provide information to clients such as Key Investor Information Documents, prospectuses, financial statements, or financial data;

i. understand specific market structures for the investment products on which they provide information to clients and, where relevant, their trading venues or the existence of any secondary markets;

j. have a basic knowledge of valuation principles for the type of investment products in relation to which the information is provided.

V.III Criteria for knowledge and competence for staff giving investment advice

18. Firms should ensure that staff giving investment advice have the necessary knowledge and competence to:

a. understand the key characteristics, risk and features of the investment products being offered or recommended, including any general tax implications to be incurred by the client in the context of transactions. Particular care should be taken when providing advice with respect to products characterised by higher levels of complexity;

b. understand the total costs and charges to be ncurred by the client in the context of the type of investment product being offered or recommended and the costs related to the provision of the advice and any other related services being provided;

c. fulfil the obligations required by firms in relation the suitability requirements including the obligations as set out in the Guidelines on certain aspects of the MiFID suitability requirements[1];

d. understand how the type of investment product provided by the firm may not be suitable for the client, having assessed the relevant information provided by the client against potential changes that may have occurred since the relevant information was gathered;

[1] http://www.esma.europa.eu/system/files/2012-387.pdf

e. understand how financial markets function and how they affect the value and pricing investment products offered or recommended to clients;

f. understand the impact of economic figures, national/regional/global events on markets and on the value of investment products being offered or recommended to clients;

g. understand the difference between past performance and future performance scenarios as well as the limits of predictive forecasting;

h. understand issues relating to market abuse and anti-money laundering;

i. assess data relevant to the type investment products offered or recommended to clients such as Key Investor Information Documents, prospectuses, financial statements, or financial data;

j. understand specific market structures for the type investment products offered or recommended to clients and where relevant their trading venues or the existence of any secondary markets;

k. have a basic knowledge of valuation principles for the type of investment products offered or recommended to clients;

l. understand the fundamentals of managing a portfolio, including being able to understand the implications of diversification regarding individual investment alternatives.

V.IV Organisational requirements for assessment, maintenance and updating of knowledge and competence

19. Firms should set out the responsibilities of staff and ensure that, where relevant, in accordance with the services provided by the firm and its internal organisation, there is a clear distinction in the description of responsibilities between the roles of giving advice and giving information.

20. Firms should:

a. ensure that staff providing relevant services to clients are assessed through the successful completion of an appropriate qualification and having gained appropriate experience in the provision of relevant services to clients;

b. carry out an internal or external review, on at least an annual basis, of staff members' development and experience needs, assess regulatory developments and take action necessary to comply with these requirements. This review should also ensure that staff possess an appropriate qualification and maintain and update their knowledge and competence by undertaking continuous professional development or training for the appropriate qualification as well as specific training required in advance of any new investment products being offered by the firm;

c. ensure that they submit to their CA, on request, records concerning knowledge and competence of staff providing relevant services to clients. These records shall contain information that enables the CA to assess and verify compliance with these guidelines;

d. ensure that when a member of staff has not acquired the necessary knowledge and competence in the provision of the relevant services, this staff member cannot provide the relevant services. However, where this member of staff has not acquired the appropriate qualification or the appropriate experience to provide the relevant services or both, this staff member can only provide the relevant services under supervision. The level and intensity of supervision should reflect the relevant qualification and experience of the staff member being supervised and this could include, where appropriate, supervision during clients meeting and other forms of communication such as telephone calls and e-mails;

e. ensure that, in situations under letter d., the staff member supervising other staff has the necessary knowledge and competence required by these guidelines and the necessary skills and resources to act as a competent supervisor;

f. ensure that the supervision provided is tailored to the services to be provided by that staff member and cover the requirements of these guidelines relevant to those services;

g. ensure that the supervisor takes responsibility for the provision of the relevant services when the staff member under supervision is providing relevant services to a client, as if the supervisor is providing the relevant services to the client, including signing-off the suitability report where advice is being provided;

h. ensure that the staff member, who has not acquired the necessary knowledge or competence in the provision of the relevant services, cannot provide those relevant services under supervision for a period exceeding 4 years (or shorter if required by the CA).

V.V Publication of information by Competent Authorities

21. When a list of the specific appropriate qualifications that meet the criteria of the guidelines is not published by the CA or other national bodies identified in the Member State, the CA must publish the criteria of these guidelines as well as the characteristics that an appropriate qualification needs to meet in order to comply with those criteria.

22. CAs should also publish: (i) information on the period of time required to gain appropriate experience; (ii) the maximum period of time under which a staff member

lacking appropriate qualification or appropriate experience is allowed to work under supervision; and (iii) whether the review of staff member's appropriate qualification should be carried out by the firm or an external body.

23. Information in paragraph 21 and 22 shall be published on the website of the CA.

VI. Annex I

Illustrative examples of the application of certain aspects of the guidelines

Examples relating to the scope of the guidelines

The following examples set out instances where a staff member would not fall within the scope of the guidelines:

- employees only pointing out where clients can find information;
- employees distributing brochures and leaflets to clients without giving additional information with regards to its content or providing any follow up investment services to those clients;
- employees who only hand over information such as KIID at the client's request without giving any additional information with regards to its content or providing any follow up investment services to those clients; and
- employees who perform back-office functions and do not have direct contact with the clients.

Examples relating to the scope of the guidelines

Firm should consider that regarding the distinction between staff providing information and staff providing investment advice, that the Q&A issued by CESR[2] be taken into consideration.

General example relating to part V.I:

A firm provides regular mandatory training to staff in the area of MiFID conduct of business, and organisational requirements.

General example relating to part V.I:

The firm adopts a code of ethics to set forth the standards of business conduct and behaviour necessary for the proper provision of relevant services and obtain written acknowledgements from staff that they have read, understood and complied with it.

Examples relating to part V.I, V.II and V.III:

A firm provides regular mandatory training to staff in the features and characteristics, including potential risks, of the products offered by the firm. This comprises training about products newly offered by the firm.

[2] http://www.esma.europa.eu/system/files/10_293.pdf

esma

A firm ensures staff are familiar with the situations in which conflicts of interest arise and how to apply the rules regarding the management of conflicts of interest.

A firm ensures staff are familiar with the situations as to when a firm may pay or receive an inducement and the relevant legal requirements regulating inducements.

Examples relating to part V.III and V.IV

A firm regularly monitors the suitability assessments provided by staff to assess whether the staff member has considered all aspects of the suitability requirements, against the specific details of the investment product.

A firm regularly monitors that relevant staff giving advice demonstrate:

- ability to ask appropriate questions to the client to understand her/his investment objectives, financial situation and knowledge and experience;
- ability to explain the risks and rewards of a particular product or strategy to the client;
- ability to compare selected products with regards to terms and risks, to be able to select the product best suited to the client profile.

Examples relating to part V.IV

The firm documents staff roles and responsibilities and evaluates their performance against key set criteria contained in the description of responsibilities.

Firms communicate publicly, in a way that is consistent and meaningful to clients, their criteria for demonstrating how staff comply with these guidelines.

Continuous or on-going professional development is required in order for staff to hold the "appropriate qualification". This ongoing assessment will contain updated material and will test staff on their knowledge of, for example, regulatory changes, new products and services available on the market. This ongoing assessment:

- may involve training in the form of courses, seminars, independent studies or learning; and
- includes verification questions demonstrating that staff has necessary knowledge and competence.

Firms verify the relevance of continuous on-ongoing development being provided to staff providing relevant services.

II

(Non-legislative acts)

REGULATIONS

COMMISSION DELEGATED REGULATION (EU) 2017/565

of 25 April 2016

supplementing Directive 2014/65/EU of the European Parliament and of the Council as regards organisational requirements and operating conditions for investment firms and defined terms for the purposes of that Directive

(Text with EEA relevance)

THE EUROPEAN COMMISSION,

Having regard to the Treaty on the Functioning of the European Union,

Having regard to Directive 2014/65/EU of the European Parliament and of the Council of 15 May 2014 on markets in financial instruments and amending Directive 2002/92/EC and Directive 2011/61/EU [1], and in particular Article 2(3), the second subparagraph of Article 4(1)(2), and Articles 4(2), 16(12), 23(4), 24(13), 25(8), 27(9), 28(3), 30(5), 31(4), 32(4), 33(8), 52(4), 54(4), 58(6), 64(7), 65(7) and 79(8) thereof,

Whereas:

(1) Directive 2014/65/EU establishes the framework for a regulatory regime for financial markets in the Union, governing operating conditions relating to the performance by investment firms of investment services and, where appropriate, ancillary services and investment activities; organisational requirements for investment firms performing such services and activities, for regulated markets and data reporting services providers; reporting requirements in respect of transactions in financial instruments; position limits and position management controls in commodity derivatives; transparency requirements in respect of transactions in financial instruments.

(2) Directive 2014/65/EU empowers the Commission to adopt a number of delegated acts. It is important that all the detailed supplementing rules regarding the authorisation, ongoing operation, market transparency and integrity, which are inextricably-linked aspects inherent to the taking up and pursuit of the services and activities covered by Directive 2014/65/EU, begin to apply at the same time as Directive 2014/65/EU so that the new requirements can operate effectively. To ensure coherence and to facilitate a comprehensive view and compact access to the provisions by persons subject to those obligations as well as by investors, it is desirable to include the delegated acts related to the above-mentioned rules in this Regulation.

(3) It is necessary to further specify the criteria to determine under what circumstances contracts in relation to wholesale energy products must be physically settled for the purposes of the limitation of scope set out in Section C(6) of Annex I to Directive 2014/65/EU. In order to ensure that the scope of this exemption is limited to avoid loopholes it is necessary that such contracts require that both buyer and seller should have proportionate arrangements in place to make or receive delivery of the underlying commodity upon the expiry of the contract. In order to avoid loopholes in case of balancing agreements with the Transmission System Operator in the areas

[1] OJ L 173, 12.6.2014, p. 349.

of electricity and gas, such balancing arrangements should only be considered as a proportionate arrangement if the parties to the arrangement have the obligation to physically deliver electricity or gas. Contracts should also establish clear obligations for physical delivery which cannot be offset whilst recognising that forms of operational netting as defined in Regulation (EU) No 1227/2011 of the European Parliament and of the Council [1] or national law should not considered as offsetting. Contracts which must be physically settled should be permitted to deliver in a variety of methods however all methods should involve a form of transfer of right of an ownership nature of the relevant underlying commodity or a relevant quantity thereof.

(4) In order to clarify when a contract in relation to wholesale energy product must be physically settled, it is necessary to further specify when certain circumstances such as force majeure or bona fide inability to settle provisions are present, and which should not alter the characterisation of those contracts as 'must be physically settled'. It is important to also clarify how oil and coal energy derivatives should be understood for the purposes of Section C(6) of Annex I to Directive 2014/65/EU. In this context, contracts related to oil shale should not be understood to be coal energy derivatives.

(5) A derivative contract should only be considered to be a financial instrument under Section C(7) of Annex I to Directive 2014/65/EU if it relates to a commodity and meets a set of criteria for determining whether a contract should be considered as having the characteristics of other derivative financial instruments and as not being for commercial purposes. This should include contracts which are standardised and traded on venues, or contracts equivalent thereof where all the terms of such contracts are equivalent to contracts traded on venues. In this case, terms of these contracts should also be understood to include provisions such as quality of the commodity or place of delivery.

(6) In order to provide clarity on the definitions of contracts relating to underlying variables set out in Section C(10) of Directive 2014/65/EU, criteria should be provided relating to their terms and underlying variables in those contracts. The inclusion of actuarial statistics in the list of underlyings should not be understood as extending the scope of those contracts to insurance and reinsurance.

(7) Directive 2014/65/EU establishes the general framework for a regulatory regime for financial markets in the Union, setting out in Section C of Annex I the list of financial instruments covered. Section C(4) of Annex I to Directive 2014/65/EU includes financial instruments relating to a currency which are therefore under the scope of this Directive.

(8) In order to ensure the uniform application of Directive 2014/65/EU, it is necessary to clarify the definitions laid down in Section C(4) of Annex I to Directive 2014/65/EU for other derivative contracts relating to currencies and to clarify that spot contracts relating to currencies are not other derivative instruments for the purposes of Section C(4) of Annex I to Directive 2014/65/EU.

(9) The settlement period for a spot contract is generally accepted in most main currencies as taking place within 2 days or less, but where this is not market practice it is necessary to make provision to allow settlement to take place in accordance with normal market practice. In such cases, physical settlement does not require the use of paper money and can include electronic settlement.

(10) Foreign exchange contracts may also be used for the purpose of effecting payment and those contracts should not be considered financial instruments provided they are not traded on a trading venue. Therefore it is appropriate to consider as spot contracts those foreign exchange contracts that are used to effect payment for financial instruments where the settlement period for those contracts is more than 2 trading days and less than 5 trading days. It is also appropriate to consider as means of payments those foreign exchange contracts that are entered into for the purpose of achieving certainty about the level of payments for goods, services and real investment. This will result in excluding from the definition of financial instruments foreign exchange contracts entered into by non-financial firms receiving payments in foreign currency for exports of identifiable goods and services and non-financial firms making payments in foreign currency to import specific goods and services.

[1] Regulation (EU) No 1227/2011 of the European Parliament and of the Council of 25 October 2011 on wholesale energy market integrity and transparency (OJ L 326, 8.12.2011, p. 1).

(11) Payment netting is essential to the effective and efficient operation of currency settlement systems and therefore the classification of a foreign currency contract as a spot transaction should not require that each foreign currency spot contract is settled independently.

(12) Non deliverable forwards are contracts for the difference between an exchange rate agreed before and the actual spot rate at maturity and therefore should not be considered to be spot contracts, regardless of their settlement period.

(13) A contract for the exchange of one currency against another currency should be understood as relating to a direct and unconditional exchange of those currencies. In the case of a contract with multiple exchanges, each exchange should be considered separately. However an option or a swap on a currency should not be considered a contract for the sale or exchange of a currency and therefore could not constitute either a spot contract or means of payment regardless of the duration of the swap or option and regardless of whether it is traded on a trading venue or not.

(14) Advice about financial instruments addressed to the general public should not be considered as a personal recommendation for the purposes of the definition of 'investment advice' in Directive 2014/65/EU. In view of the growing number of intermediaries providing personal recommendations through the use of distribution channels, it should be clarified that a recommendation issued, even exclusively, through distribution channels, such as internet, could qualify as a personal recommendation. Therefore, situations in which, for instance, email correspondence is used to provide personal recommendations to a specific person, rather than to address information to the public in general, may amount to investment advice.

(15) Generic advice about a type of financial instrument is not considered investment advice for the purposes of Directive 2014/65/EU. However, if an investment firm provides generic advice to a client about a type of financial instrument which it presents as suitable for, or based on a consideration of the circumstances of, that client, and that advice is not in fact suitable for the client, or is not based on a consideration of his circumstances, the firm is likely to be acting in contravention of Article 24(1) or (3) of Directive 2014/65/EU In particular, a firm which gives a client such advice would be likely to contravene the requirement of Article 24(1) to act honestly, fairly and professionally in accordance with the best interests of its clients. Similarly or alternatively, such advice would be likely to contravene the requirement of Article 24(3) that information addressed by a firm to a client should be fair, clear and not misleading.

(16) Acts carried out by an investment firm that are preparatory to the provision of an investment service or carrying out an investment activity should be considered as an integral part of that service or activity. This would include, for example, the provision of generic advice by an investment firm to clients or potential clients prior to or in the course of the provision of investment advice or any other investment service or activity.

(17) The provision of a general recommendation about a transaction in a financial instrument or a type of financial instrument constitutes the provision of an ancillary service within Section B(5) of Annex I to Directive 2014/65/EU, and consequently Directive 2014/65/EU and its protections apply to the provision of that recommendation.

(18) In order to ensure the objective and effective application of the definition of systematic internalisers in the Union in accordance with Article 4(1)(20) of Directive 2014/65/EU, further specifications should be provided on the applicable pre-set limits for the purposes of what constitutes frequent systematic and substantial over the counter (OTC) trading. Pre-set limits should be set at an appropriate level to ensure that OTC trading of such a size that it had a material effect on price formation is within scope while at the same time excluding OTC trading of such a small size that it would be disproportionate to require the obligation to comply with the requirements applicable to systematic internalisers.

(19) Pursuant to Directive 2014/65/EU, a systematic internaliser should not be allowed to bring together third party buying and selling interests in functionally the same way as a trading venue. A systematic internaliser should not consist of an internal matching system which executes client orders on a multilateral basis, an activity which

requires authorisation as a multilateral trading facility (MTF). An internal matching system in this context is a system for matching client orders which results in the investment firm undertaking matched principal transactions on a regular and not occasional basis.

(20) For reasons of clarity and legal certainty and to ensure a uniform application, it is appropriate to provide supplementary provisions in relation to the definitions in relation to algorithmic trading, high frequency algorithmic trading techniques and direct electronic access. In automated trading, various technical arrangements are deployed. It is essential to clarify how those arrangements are to be categorised in relation to the definitions of algorithmic trading and direct electronic access. The trading processes based on direct electronic access are not mutually exclusive to those involving algorithmic trading or its sub-segment high frequency algorithmic trading technique. The trading of a person having direct electronic access may therefore also fall under the algorithmic trading including the high frequency algorithmic trading technique definition.

(21) Algorithmic trading in accordance with Article 4(1)(39) of Directive 2014/65/EU should include arrangements where the system makes decisions, other than only determining the trading venue or venues on which the order should be submitted, at any stage of the trading processes including at the stage of initiating, generating, routing or executing orders. Therefore, it should be clarified that algorithmic trading, which encompasses trading with no or limited human intervention, should refer not only to the automatic generation of orders but also to the optimisation of order-execution processes by automated means.

(22) Algorithmic trading should encompass smart order routers (SORs) where such devices use algorithms for optimisation of order execution processes that determine parameters of the order other than the venue or venues where the order should be submitted. Algorithmic trading should not encompass automated order routers (AOR) where, although using algorithms, such devices only determine the trading venue or venues where the order should be submitted without changing any other parameter of the order.

(23) High frequency algorithmic trading technique in accordance with Article 4(1)(40) of Directive 2014/65/EU, which is a subset of algorithmic trading, should be further specified through the establishment of criteria to define high message intraday rates which constitutes orders quotes or modifications or cancellations thereof. Using absolute quantitative thresholds on the basis of messaging rates provides legal certainty by allowing firms and competent authorities to assess the individual trading activity of firms. The level and scope of these thresholds should be sufficiently broad to cover trading which constitute high frequency trading technique, including those in relation to single instruments and multiple instruments.

(24) Since the use of high frequency algorithmic trading technique is predominantly common in liquid instruments, only instruments for which there is a liquid market should be included in the calculation of high intraday message rate. Also, given that high frequency algorithmic trading technique is a subset of algorithmic trading, messages introduced for the purpose of trading that fulfil the criteria in Article 17(4) of Directive 2014/65/EU should be included in the calculation of intraday message rates. In order not to capture trading activity other than high frequency algorithmic trading techniques, having regard to the characteristics of such trading as set out in recital 61 of Directive 2014/65/EU, in particular that such trading is typically done by traders using their own capital to implement more traditional trading strategies such as market making or arbitrage through the use of sophisticated technology, only messages introduced for the purposes of dealing on own account, and not those introduced for the purposes of receiving and transmitting orders or executing orders of behalf of clients, should be included in the calculation of high intraday message rates. However, messages introduced through other techniques than those relying on trading on own account should be included in the calculation of high intraday message rate where, viewed as a whole and taking into account all circumstances, the execution of the technique is structured in such a way as to avoid the execution taking place on own account, such as through the transmission of orders between entities within the same group. In order to take into account, when determining what constitutes high message intra-day rates, the identity of the client ultimately behind the activity, messages which were originated by clients of DEA providers should be excluded from the calculation of high intraday message rate in relation to such providers.

(25) The definition of direct electronic access should be further specified. The definition of direct electronic access should not encompass any other activity beyond the provision of direct market access and sponsored access. Therefore, arrangements where client orders are intermediated through electronic means by members or participants of a trading venue such as online brokerage and arrangements where clients have direct electronic access to a trading venue should be distinguished.

(26) In case of order intermediation, submitters of orders do not have sufficient control over the parameters of the arrangement for market access and should therefore not fall within scope of direct electronic access. Therefore, arrangements that allow clients to transmit orders to an investment firm in an electronic format, such as online brokerage, should be not be considered direct electronic access provided that clients do not have the ability to determine the fraction of a second of order entry and the life time of orders within that time frame.

(27) Arrangements where the client of a member or participant of a trading venue, including the client of a direct clients of organised trading facilities (OTFs), submit their orders through arrangements for optimisation of order execution processes that determine parameters of the order other than the venue or venues where the order should be submitted through SORs embedded into the provider's infrastructure and not on the client's infrastructure should be excluded from the scope of direct electronic access since the client of the provider does not have control over the time of submission of the order and its lifetime. The characterisation of direct electronic access when deploying smart order routers should therefore be dependent on whether the smart order router is embedded in the clients' systems and not in that of the provider.

(28) The rules for the implementation of the regime governing organisational requirements for investment firms performing investment services and, where appropriate, ancillary services and investment activities on a professional basis, for regulated markets, and data reporting services providers should be consistent with the aim of Directive 2014/65/EU. They should be designed to ensure a high level of integrity, competence and soundness among investment firms and entities that operate regulated markets, MTFs or OTFs, and to be applied in a uniform manner.

(29) It is necessary to specify concrete organisational requirements and procedures for investment firms performing such services or activities. In particular, rigorous procedures should be provided for with regard to matters such as compliance, risk management, complaints handling, personal transactions, outsourcing and the identification, management and disclosure of conflicts of interest.

(30) The organisational requirements and conditions for authorisation for investment firms should be set out in the form of a set of rules that ensures the uniform application of the relevant provisions of Directive 2014/65/EU. This is necessary in order to ensure that investment firms have equal access on equivalent terms to all markets in the Union and to eliminate obstacles, linked to authorisation procedures, to cross-border activities in the field of investment services.

(31) The rules for the implementation of the regime governing operating conditions for the performance of investment and ancillary services and investment activities should reflect the aim underlying that regime. They should be designed to ensure a high level of investor protection to be applied in a uniform manner through the introduction of clear standards and requirements governing the relationship between an investment firm and its client. On the other hand, as regards investor protection, and in particular the provision of investors with information or the seeking of information from investors, the retail or professional nature of the client or potential client concerned should be taken into account.

(32) In order to ensure the uniform application of the various relevant provisions of Directive 2014/65/EU, it is necessary to establish a harmonised set of organisational requirements and operating conditions for investment firms.

(33) Investment firms vary widely in their size, their structure and the nature of their business. A regulatory regime should be adapted to that diversity while imposing certain fundamental regulatory requirements which are appropriate for all firms. Regulated entities should comply with their high level obligations and design and adopt measures that are best suited to their particular nature and circumstances.

(34) It is appropriate to set out common criteria for assessing whether an investment service is provided by a person in an incidental manner in the course of a professional activity, in order to ensure a harmonised and strict implementation of the exemption granted by Directive 2014/65/EU. The exemption should only apply if the investment service has an intrinsic connection to the main area of the professional activity and is subordinated thereto.

(35) The organisational requirements established under Directive 2014/65/EU should be without prejudice to systems established by national law for the registration or monitoring by competent authorities or firms of individuals working within investment firms.

(36) For the purposes of requiring an investment firm to establish, implement and maintain an adequate risk management policy, the risks relating to the firm's activities, processes and systems should include the risks associated with the outsourcing of critical or important functions. Those risks should include those associated with the firm's relationship with the service provider, and the potential risks posed where the outsourced functions of multiple investment firms or other regulated entities are concentrated within a limited number of service providers.

(37) The fact that risk management and compliance functions are performed by the same person does not necessarily jeopardise the independent functioning of each function. The conditions that persons involved in the compliance function should not also be involved in the performance of the functions that they monitor, and that the method of determining the remuneration of such persons should not be likely to compromise their objectivity, may not be proportionate in the case of small investment firms. However, they would only be disproportionate for larger firms in exceptional circumstances.

(38) Clients or potential clients should be enabled to express their dissatisfaction with investment services provided by investment firms in the interests of investor protection as well as strengthening investment firms' compliance with their obligations. Clients' or potential clients' complaints should be handled effectively and in an independent manner by a complaints management function. In line with the principle of proportionality, that function could be carried out by the compliance function.

(39) Investment firms are required to collect and maintain information relating to clients and services provided to clients. Where those requirements involve the collection and processing of personal data, the respect of the right to the protection of personal data in accordance with Directive 95/46/EC of the European Parliament and of the Council ([1]) and Directive 2002/58/EC of the European Parliament and of the Council ([2]) which govern the processing of personal data carried out in application of this Directive should be ensured. Processing of personal data by the European Securities and Markets Authority (ESMA) in the application of this Regulation is subject to Regulation (EC) No 45/2001 of the European Parliament and of the Council ([3]).

(40) A definition of remuneration should be introduced in order to ensure the efficient and consistent application of the conflicts of interest and conduct of business requirements in the area of remuneration and should include all forms of financial or non-financial benefits or payments provided directly or indirectly by firms to relevant persons in the provision of investment or ancillary services to clients, such as cash, shares, options, cancellations of loans to relevant persons at dismissal, pension contributions, remuneration by third parties for instance through carried interest models, wage increases or promotions, health insurance, discounts or special allowances, generous expense accounts or seminars in exotic destinations.

(41) In order to ensure that clients' interests are not impaired, investment firms should design and implement remuneration policies to all persons who could have an impact on the service provided or corporate behaviour of the firm, including persons who are front-office staff, sales force staff or other staff indirectly involved in the provision of investment or ancillary services. Persons overseeing the sales forces, such as line managers, who may be incentivised to pressure sales staff, or financial analysts whose literature may be used by sales staff to entice clients to make investment decisions or persons involved in complaints-handling or in product design and development should also be included in the scope of relevant persons concerned by remuneration rules. Relevant persons should also include tied agents. When determining the remuneration for tied agents, firms should take the tied agents' special status and the respective national specificities into consideration. However, in such cases, firms' remuneration policies and practices should still define appropriate criteria to be used to assess the performance of relevant persons, including qualitative criteria encouraging the relevant persons to act in the best interests of the client.

(42) Where successive personal transactions are carried out on behalf of a person in accordance with prior instructions given by that person, obligations relating to personal transactions should not apply separately to

([1]) Directive 95/46/EC of the European Parliament and of the Council of 24 October 1995 on the protection of individuals with regard to the processing of personal data and on the free movement of such data (OJ L 281, 23.11.1995, p. 31).
([2]) Directive 2002/58/EC of the European Parliament and of the Council of 12 July 2002 concerning the processing of personal data and the protection of privacy in the electronic communications sector (OJ L 201, 31.7.2002, p. 37).
([3]) Regulation (EC) No 45/2001 of the European Parliament and of the Council of 18 December 2000 on the protection of individuals with regard to the processing of personal data by the Community institutions and bodies and on the free movement of such data (OJ L 8, 12.1.2001, p. 1).

each such successive transaction if those instructions remain in force and unchanged. Similarly, those obligations should not apply to the termination or withdrawal of such instructions, provided that any financial instruments which had previously been acquired pursuant to the instructions are not disposed of at the same time as the instructions terminate or are withdrawn. However, those obligations should apply in relation to a personal transaction, or the commencement of successive personal transactions, carried out on behalf of the same person if those instructions are changed or if new instructions are issued.

(43) Competent authorities should not make the authorisation to provide investment services or activities subject to a general prohibition on the outsourcing of one or more critical or important functions. Investment firms should be allowed to outsource such functions if the outsourcing arrangements established by the firm comply with certain conditions.

(44) The outsourcing of investment services or activities or critical and important functions is capable of constituting a material change of the conditions for the authorisation of the investment firm, as referred to in Article 21(2) of Directive 2014/65/EU. If such outsourcing arrangements are to be put in place after the investment firm has obtained an authorisation according to Chapter I of Title II of Directive 2014/65/EU, those arrangements should be notified to the competent authority where required by Article 21(2) of that Directive.

(45) The circumstances which should be treated as giving rise to a conflict of interest should cover cases where there is a conflict between the interests of the firm or certain persons connected to the firm or the firm's group and the duty the firm owes to a client; or between the differing interests of two or more of its clients, to each of whom the firm owes a duty. It is not enough that the firm may gain a benefit if there is not also a possible disadvantage to a client, or that one client to whom the firm owes a duty may make a gain or avoid a loss without there being a concomitant possible loss to another such client.

(46) Conflicts of interest should be regulated only where an investment service or ancillary service is provided by an investment firm. The status of the client to whom the service is provided — as either retail, professional or eligible counterparty — should be irrelevant for that purpose.

(47) In complying with its obligation to draw up a conflict of interest policy under Directive 2014/65/EU which identifies circumstances which constitute or may give rise to a conflict of interest, the investment firm should pay special attention to the activities of investment research and advice, proprietary trading, portfolio management and corporate finance business, including underwriting or selling in an offering of securities and advising on mergers and acquisitions. In particular, such special attention is appropriate where the firm or a person directly or indirectly linked by control to the firm performs a combination of two or more of those activities.

(48) Investment firms should aim to identify and prevent or manage the conflicts of interest arising in relation to their various business lines and their group's activities under a comprehensive conflicts of interest policy. While disclosure of specific conflicts of interest is required by Article 23(2) of Directive 2014/65/EU, it should be a measure of last resort to be used only where the organisational and administrative arrangements established by the investment firm to prevent or manage its conflicts of interest in accordance with Article 23(1) of Directive 2014/65/EU are not sufficient to ensure, with reasonable confidence, that the risks of damage to the interests of the client are prevented. Over-reliance on disclosure without adequate consideration as to how conflicts may appropriately be prevented or managed should not be permitted. The disclosure of conflicts of interest by an investment firm should not exempt it from the obligation to maintain and operate the effective organisational and administrative arrangements required under Article 16(3) of Directive 2014/65/EU.

(49) Firms should always comply with the inducements rules under Article 24 of Directive 2014/65/EU, including when providing placing services. In particular, fees received by investment firms placing the financial instruments issued to its investment clients should comply with these provisions and laddering and spinning should be considered as abusive practices.

(50) Investment research should be a sub-category of the type of information defined as a recommendation in Regulation (EU) No 596/2014 of the European Parliament and of the Council (¹) (market abuse).

(¹) Regulation (EU) No 596/2014 of the European Parliament and of the Council of 16 April 2014 on market abuse (market abuse Regulation) and repealing Directive 2003/6/EC of the European Parliament and of the Council and Commission Directives 2003/124/EC, 2003/125/EC and 2004/72/EC (OJ L 173, 12.6.2014, p. 1).

(51) The measures and arrangements adopted by an investment firm to manage the conflicts of interests that might arise from the production and dissemination of material that is presented as investment research should be appropriate to protect the objectivity and independence of financial analysts and of the investment research they produce. Those measures and arrangements should ensure that financial analysts enjoy an adequate degree of independence from the interests of persons whose responsibilities or business interests may reasonably be considered to conflict with the interests of the persons to whom the investment research is disseminated.

(52) Persons whose responsibilities or business interests may reasonably be considered to conflict with the interests of the persons to whom investment research is disseminated should include corporate finance personnel and persons involved in sales and trading on behalf of clients or the firm.

(53) Exceptional circumstances in which financial analysts and other persons connected with the investment firm who are involved in the production of investment research may, with prior written approval, undertake personal transactions in instruments to which the research relates should include those circumstances where, for personal reasons relating to financial hardship, the financial analyst or other person is required to liquidate a position.

(54) Fees, commissions, monetary or non-monetary benefits received by the firm providing investment research from any third party should only be acceptable when they are provided in accordance with requirements specified in Article 24(9) of Directive 2014/65/EU and Article 13 of Commission Delegated Directive (EU) 2017/593 (¹).

(55) The concept of dissemination of investment research to clients or the public should not include dissemination exclusively to persons within the group of the investment firm. Current recommendations should be considered to be those recommendations contained in investment research which have not been withdrawn and which have not lapsed. The substantial alteration of investment research produced by a third party should be governed by the same requirements as the production of research.

(56) Financial analysts should not engage in activities other than the preparation of investment research where engaging in such activities are inconsistent with the maintenance of that person's objectivity. These include participating in investment banking activities such as corporate finance business and underwriting, participating in 'pitches' for new business or 'road shows' for new issues of financial instruments; or being otherwise involved in the preparation of issuer marketing.

(57) Given the specificities of underwriting and placing services and the potential for conflicts of interest to arise in relation to such services, more detailed and tailored requirements should be specified in this Regulation. In particular, such requirements should ensure that the underwriting and placing process is managed in a way which respects the interests of different actors. Investment firms should ensure that their own interests or interests of their other clients do not improperly influence the quality of services provided to the issuer client. Such arrangements should be explained to that client, along with other relevant information about the offering process, before the firm accepts to undertake the offering.

(58) Investment firms engaged in underwriting or placing activities should have appropriate arrangements in place to ensure that the pricing process, including book-building, is not detrimental to the issuer's interests.

(59) The placing process involves the exercise of judgement by an investment firm as to the allocation of an issue, and is based on the particular facts and circumstances of the arrangements, which raises conflicts of interest concerns. The firm should have in place effective organisational requirements to ensure that allocations made as part of the placing process do not result in the firm's interest being placed ahead of the interests of the issuer client, or the interests of one investment client over those of another investment client. In particular, firms should clearly set out the process for developing allocation recommendations in an allocation policy.

(60) Requirements imposed by this Regulation, including those relating to personal transactions, to dealing with knowledge of investment research and to the production or dissemination of investment research, should apply without prejudice to requirements of Directive 2014/65/EU and Regulation (EU) No 596/2014 and their respective implementing measures.

(¹) Commission Delegated Directive (EU) 2017/593 of 7 April 2016 supplementing Directive 2014/65/EU of the European Parliament and of the Council with regard to safeguarding of financial instruments and funds belonging to clients, product governance obligations and the rules applicable to the provision or reception of fees, commissions or any monetary or non-monetary benefits (see page 500 of this Official Journal).

(61) This Regulation sets out requirements regarding information addressed to clients or potential clients, including marketing communications, in order to ensure that such information be fair, clear and not misleading in accordance with Article 24(3) of Directive 2014/65/EU.

(62) Nothing in this Regulation requires competent authorities to approve the content and form of marketing communications. However, neither does it prevent them from doing so, insofar as any such pre-approval is based only on compliance with the obligation in Directive 2014/65/EU that information to clients or potential clients, including marketing communications, should be fair, clear and not misleading.

(63) Information requirements should be established which take account of the status of a client as either retail, professional or eligible counterparty. An objective of Directive 2014/65/EU is to ensure a proportionate balance between investor protection and the disclosure obligations which apply to investment firms. To this end, it is appropriate to establish less stringent specific information requirements with respect to professional clients than to retail clients.

(64) Investment firms should provide clients or potential clients with the necessary information on the nature of financial instruments and the risks associated with investing in them so that their clients are properly informed The level of detail of the information to be provided may vary according to whether the client is a retail client or a professional client and the nature and risk profile of the financial instruments that are being offered, but should always include any essential elements. Member States may specify the precise terms, or the contents, of the description of risks required under this Regulation, taking into account the information requirements set out in Regulation (EU) No 1286/2014 of the European Parliament and of the Council [1].

(65) The conditions with which information addressed by investment firms to clients and potential clients must comply in order to be fair, clear and not misleading should apply to communications intended for retail or professional clients in a way that is appropriate and proportionate, taking into account, for example, the means of communication, and the information that the communication is intended to convey to the clients or potential clients. In particular, it would not be appropriate to apply such conditions to marketing communications which consist only of one or more of the following: the name of the firm, a logo or other image associated with the firm, a contact point, a reference to the types of investment services provided by the firm.

(66) In order to improve the consistency of information received by investors, investment firms should ensure that the information provided to each client is consistently presented in the same language throughout all forms of information and marketing material provided to that client. However, this should not imply a requirement for firms to translate prospectuses, prepared in accordance with Directive 2003/71/EC of the European Parliament and of the Council [2] or Directive 2009/65/EC of the European Parliament and of the Council [3], provided to clients.

(67) In order to provide a fair and balanced presentation of benefits and risks, investment firms should always give a clear and prominent indication of any relevant risks, including drawbacks and weaknesses, when referencing any potential benefits of a service or financial instrument.

(68) Information should be considered to be misleading if it has a tendency to mislead the person or persons to whom it is addressed or by whom it is likely to be received, regardless of whether the person who provides the information considers or intends it to be misleading.

(69) In cases where an investment firm is required to provide information to a client before the provision of a service, each transaction in respect of the same type of financial instrument should not be considered as the provision of a new or different service.

(70) Detailed information on whether investment advice is provided on an independent basis, on the broad or restricted analysis of different types of instruments and on the selection process used should help clients assess the scope of the advice provided. Sufficient details on the number of financial instruments analysed by the firms

(1) Regulation (EU) No 1286/2014 of the European Parliament and of the Council of 26 November 2014 on key information documents for packaged retail and insurance-based investment products (PRIIPs) (OJ L 352, 9.12.2014, p. 1).
(2) Directive 2003/71/EC of the European Parliament and of the Council of 4 November 2003 on the prospectus to be published when securities are offered to the public or admitted to trading and amending Directive 2001/34/EC (OJ L 345, 31.12.2003, p. 64).
(3) Directive 2009/65/EC of the European Parliament and of the Council of 13 July 2009 on the coordination of laws, regulations and administrative provisions relating to undertakings for collective investment in transferable securities (UCITS) (OJ L 302, 17.11.2009, p. 32).

should be provided to clients. The number and variety of financial instruments to be considered, other than the ones provided by the investment firm or entities close to the firm, should be proportionate to the scope of the advice to be given, client preferences and needs. However, irrespective of the scope of services offered, all assessments should be based on an adequate number of financial instruments available on the market to allow an appropriate consideration of what the market offers as alternatives.

(71) The scope of the advice given by investment firms on an independent basis could range from broad and general to specialist and specific. In order to ensure that the scope of the advice allows for a fair and appropriate comparison between different financial instruments, investment advisers specialising in certain categories of financial instruments and focusing on criteria that are not based on the technical structure of the instrument per se, such as 'green' or 'ethical' investments, should comply with certain conditions if they present themselves as independent advisers.

(72) Enabling the same adviser to provide both independent and non-independent advice could create confusion for the client. In order to ensure clients' understanding of the nature and basis of investment advice provided, certain organisational requirements should also be established.

(73) The provision by an investment firm to a client of a copy of a prospectus that has been drawn up and published in accordance with Directive 2003/71/EC should not be treated as the provision by the firm of information to a client for the purposes of the operating conditions under Directive 2014/65/EU which relate to the quality and contents of such information, if the firm is not responsible under that Directive for the information given in the prospectus.

(74) Directive 2014/65/EU strengthens investment firms' obligations to disclose information on all costs and charges and extends these obligations to relationships with professional clients and eligible counterparties. In order to ensure that all categories of clients benefit from such increased transparency on costs and charges, investment firms should be allowed, in certain situations, when providing investment services to professional clients or eligible counterparties, to agree with these clients to limit the detailed requirements set out in this Regulation. This however should never lead to disapplying the obligations imposed on investment firms pursuant to Article 24(4) of Directive 2014/65/EU. In this respect, investment firms should inform professional clients about all costs and charges as set out in this Regulation, when the services of investment advice or portfolio management are provided or when, irrespective of the investment service provided, the financial instruments concerned embed a derivative. Investment firms should also inform eligible counterparties about all costs and charges as set out in this Regulation when, irrespective of the investment service provided, the financial instrument concerned embeds a derivative and intends to be distributed to their clients. However, in other cases, when providing investment services to professional clients or eligible counterparties, investment firms may agree, for instance, at the request of the client concerned, not to provide the illustration showing the cumulative effect of costs on return or an indication of the currency involved and the applicable conversion rates and costs where any part of the total costs and charges is expressed in foreign currency.

(75) Taking into account the overarching obligation to act in accordance with the best interest of clients and the importance of informing clients, on an *ex-ante* basis, of all costs and charges to be incurred, the reference to financial instruments recommended or marketed should include in particular investment firms providing investment advice or portfolio management services, firms providing general recommendation concerning financial instruments or promoting certain financial instruments in the provision of investment and ancillary services to clients. This would for instance be the case for investment firms that have entered into distribution or placement agreements with a product manufacturer or issuer.

(76) In accordance with the overarching obligation to act in accordance with the best interest of clients and taking into account the obligations resulting from specific Union legislation regulating certain financial instruments (in particular, units in collective investment undertakings and packaged retail and insurance-based investment products (PRIIPs) investment firms should disclose and aggregate all costs and charges, including the costs of the financial instrument, in all cases where investment firms are obliged to provide the client with information about the costs of a financial instrument in accordance with Union legislation.

(77) Where investment firms have not marketed or recommended a financial instrument or are not required under Union law to provide clients with information about costs of a financial instrument, they may not be in the position to take into account all the costs associated with that financial instrument. Even in these residual instances, investment firms should inform clients, on an ex-ante basis, about all costs and charges associated to

the investment service and the price of acquiring the relevant financial instrument. Furthermore, investment firms should comply with any other obligations to provide appropriate information about the risks of the relevant financial instrument in accordance with Article 24(4)(b) of Directive 2014/65/EU or to provide clients, on an ex-post basis, with adequate reports on the services provided in accordance with Article 25(6) of Directive 2014/65/EU, including cost elements.

(78) In order to ensure clients' awareness of all costs and charges to be incurred as well as evaluation of such information and comparison with different financial instruments and investment services, investment firms should provide clients with clear and comprehensible information on all costs and charges in good time before the provision of services. *Ex-ante* information about the costs related to the financial instrument or ancillary service can be provided based on an assumed investment amount. However, the costs and charges disclosed should represent the costs the client would actually incur based on that assumed investment amount. For example, if an investment firm offers a range of ongoing services with different charges associated with each service, the firm should disclose the costs associated with the service the client subscribed to. For ex-post disclosures, information related to costs and charges should reflect the client's actual investment amount at the time the disclosure is produced.

(79) In order to ensure investors receive information about all costs and charges pursuant to Article 24(4) of Directive 2014/65/EU, the underlying market risk should be understood as relating only to movements in the value of capital invested caused directly by movements in the value of underlying assets. Transactions costs and ongoing charges on financial instruments should therefore also be included in the required aggregation of costs and charges and should be estimated using reasonable assumptions, accompanied by an explanation that such estimations are based on assumptions and may deviate from costs and charges that will actually be incurred. Following the same objective of full disclosure, practices where there is 'netting' of costs should not be excluded from the obligation to provide information on costs and charges. The costs and charges disclosure is underpinned by the principle that every difference between the price of a position for the firm and the respective price for the client should be disclosed, including mark-ups and mark-downs.

(80) While investment firms should aggregate all costs and charges in accordance with Article 24(4) of Directive 2014/65/EU and provide clients with the overall costs expressed both as a monetary amount and as a percentage, investment firms should, in addition, be allowed to provide clients or prospective clients with separate figures comprising aggregated initial costs and charges, aggregated on-going costs and charges and aggregated exit costs.

(81) Investment firms distributing financial instruments, in relation to which information on costs and charges is insufficient, should additionally inform their clients about those costs as well as all the other costs and associated charges relating to the provision of investment services in relation to those financial instruments in order to safeguard clients' rights to full disclosure of costs and charges. This would be the case for investment firms distributing units in collective investment undertakings for which transaction costs have not been provided by for example units in UCITS management company. In such cases, the investment firms should liaise with UCITS management companies to obtain the relevant information.

(82) In order to improve transparency for clients on the associated costs of their investments and the performance of their investments against the relevant costs and charges over time, periodic *ex-post* disclosure should also be provided where the investment firms have or have had an ongoing relationship with the client during the year. *Ex-post* disclosure on all the relevant costs and charges should be provided on a personalised basis. The *ex-post* periodic disclosure may be made by building on existing reporting obligations, such as obligations for firms providing execution of orders other than portfolio management, portfolio management or holding client financial instruments or funds.

(83) The information which an investment firm is required to give to clients concerning costs and associated charges includes information about the arrangements for payment or performance of the agreement for the provision of investment services and any other agreement relating to a financial instrument that is being offered. For this purpose, arrangements for payment will generally be relevant where a financial instrument contract is terminated by cash settlement. Arrangements for performance will generally be relevant where, upon termination, a financial instrument requires the delivery of shares, bonds, a warrant, bullion or another instrument or commodity.

(84) It is necessary to introduce different requirements for the application of the suitability assessment set out in Article 25(2) of Directive 2014/65/EU and the appropriateness assessment set out in Article 25(3) of that Directive. These tests are different in scope with regards to the investment services to which they relate, and have different functions and characteristics.

(85) Investment firms should include in the suitability report and draw clients' attention to information on whether the recommended services or instruments are likely to require the retail client to seek a periodic review of their arrangements. This includes situations where a client is likely to need to seek advice to bring a portfolio of investments back in line with the original recommended allocation where there is a probability that the portfolio could deviate from the target asset allocation.

(86) In order to take market developments into account and ensure the same level of investor protection, it should be clarified that investment firms should remain responsible for undertaking suitability assessments where investment advice or portfolio management services are provided in whole or in part through an automated or semi-automated system.

(87) In accordance with the suitability assessment requirement under Article 25(2) of Directive 2014/65/EU, it should also be clarified that investment firms should undertake a suitability assessment not only in relation to recommendations to buy a financial instrument are made but for all decisions whether to trade including whether or not to buy, hold or sell an investment.

(88) For the purposes of Article 25(2) of Directive 2014/65/EU, a transaction may be unsuitable for the client or potential client due to the risks of the associated financial instruments, the type of transaction, the characteristics of the order or the frequency of the trading. A series of transactions, each of which are suitable when viewed in isolation may be unsuitable if the recommendation or the decisions to trade are made with a frequency that is not in the best interests of the client. In the case of portfolio management, a transaction might also be unsuitable if it would result in an unsuitable portfolio.

(89) A recommendation or request made, or advice given, by a portfolio manager to a client to the effect that the client should give or alter a mandate to the portfolio manager that defines the limits of the portfolio manager's discretion should be considered a recommendation as referred to in of Article 25(2) of Directive 2014/65/EU.

(90) In order to provide legal certainty and enable clients to better understand the nature of the services provided, investment firms that provide investment or ancillary services to clients should enter into a written basic agreement with the client, setting out the essential rights and obligations of the firm and the client.

(91) This Regulation should not require competent authorities to approve the content of the basic agreement between an investment firm and its clients. Nor should it prevent them from doing so, insofar as any such approval is based only on the firm's compliance with its obligations under Directive 2014/65/EU to act honestly, fairly and professionally in accordance with the best interests of its clients, and to establish a record that sets out the rights and obligations of investment firms and their clients, and the other terms on which firms will provide services to their clients.

(92) The records an investment firm is required to keep should be adapted to the type of business and the range of investment services and activities performed, provided that the record-keeping obligations set out in Directive 2014/65/EU, Regulation (EU) No 600/2014 of the European Parliament and of the Council (1), Regulation (EU) No 596/2014, Directive 2014/57/EU of the European Parliament and of the Council (2) and this Regulation are fulfilled and that competent authorities are able to fulfil their supervisory tasks and perform enforcement actions in view of ensuring both investor protection and market integrity.

(93) In light of the importance of reports and periodic communications for all clients, and the extension of Article 25(6) of Directive 2014/65/EU to the relationship to eligible counterparties, the reporting requirements set in this Regulation should apply to all categories of clients. Taking into account the nature of the interactions with eligible counterparties, investment firms should be allowed to enter into agreements determining the specific content and timing of reporting different from the ones applicable for retail and professional clients.

(1) Regulation (EU) No 600/2014 of the European Parliament and of the Council of 15 May 2014 on markets in financial instruments and amending Regulation (EU) No 648/2012 (OJ L 173, 12.6.2014, p. 84).
(2) Directive 2014/57/EU of the European Parliament and of the Council of 16 April 2014 on criminal sanctions for market abuse (market abuse directive) (OJ L 173, 12.6.2014, p. 179).

(94) In cases where an investment firm providing portfolio management services is required to provide clients or potential clients with information on the types of financial instruments that may be included in the client portfolio and the types of transactions that may be carried out in such instruments, such information should state separately whether the investment firm will be mandated to invest in financial instruments not admitted to trading on a regulated market, in derivatives, or in illiquid or highly volatile instruments; or to undertake short sales, purchases with borrowed funds, securities financing transactions, or any transactions involving margin payments, deposit of collateral or foreign exchange risk.

(95) Clients should be informed of the performance of their portfolio and depreciations of their initial investments. In the case of portfolio management, this trigger should be set at the depreciation of 10 %, and thereafter at multiples of 10 %, of the overall value of the overall portfolio and should not apply to individual holdings.

(96) For the purposes of the reporting obligations in respect of portfolio management, a contingent liability transaction should involve any actual or potential liability for the client that exceeds the cost of acquiring the instrument.

(97) For the purposes of the provisions on reporting to clients, a reference to the type of the order should be understood as referring to its status as a limit order, market order, or other specific type of order.

(98) For the purposes of the provisions on reporting to clients, a reference to the nature of the order should be understood as referring to orders to subscribe for securities, or to exercise an option, or similar client order.

(99) When establishing its execution policy in accordance with Article 27(4) of Directive 2014/65/EU, an investment firm should determine the relative importance of the factors mentioned in Article 27(1) of that Directive, or at least establish the process by which it determines the relative importance of these factors, so that it can deliver the best possible result to its clients. In order to give effect to that policy, an investment firm should select the execution venues that enable it to obtain on a consistent basis the best possible result for the execution of client orders. In order to comply with the legal obligation of best execution, investment firms, when applying the criteria for best execution for professional clients, will typically not use the same execution venues for securities financing transactions (SFTs) and other transactions. This is because the SFTs are used as a source of funding subject to a commitment that the borrower will return equivalent securities on a future date and the terms of SFTs are typically defined bilaterally between the counterparties ahead of the execution. Therefore, the choice of execution venues for SFTs is more limited than in the case of other transactions, given that it depends on the particular terms defined in advance between the counterparties and on whether there is a specific demand on those execution venues for the financial instruments involved. As a result, the order execution policy established by investment firms should take into account the particular characteristics of SFTs and it should list separately execution venues used for SFTs. An investment firm should apply its execution policy to each client order that it executes with a view to obtaining the best possible result for the client in accordance with that policy.

(100) In order to ensure that investment firms who transmit or place clients' orders with other entities for execution act in the best interest of their clients in accordance with Article 24(1) of Directive 2014/65/EU and with Article 24(4) of Directive 2014/65/EU to provide appropriate information to clients on the firm and its services, investment firms should provide clients with appropriate information on the top five entities for each class of financial instruments to which they transmit or place clients' orders and provide clients with information on the execution quality, in accordance with Article 27(6) of Directive 2014/65/EU and respective implementing measures. Investment firms transmitting or placing orders with other entities for execution may select a single entity for execution only where they are able to show that this allows them to obtain the best possible result for their clients on a consistent basis and where they can reasonably expect that the selected entity will enable them to obtain results for clients that are at least as good as the results that they reasonably could expect from using alternative entities for execution. This reasonable expectation should be supported by relevant data published in accordance with Article 27 of Directive 2014/65/EU or by internal analysis conducted by these investment firms.

(101) For the purposes of ensuring that an investment firm obtains the best possible result for the client when executing a retail client order in the absence of specific client instructions, the firm should take into consideration all factors that will allow it to deliver the best possible result in terms of the total consideration, representing the price of the financial instrument and the costs related to execution. Speed, likelihood of execution and settlement,

the size and nature of the order, market impact and any other implicit transaction costs may be given precedence over the immediate price and cost consideration only insofar as they are instrumental in delivering the best possible result in terms of the total consideration to the retail client.

(102) When an investment firm executes an order following specific instructions from the client, it should be treated as having satisfied its best execution obligations only in respect of the part or aspect of the order to which the client instructions relate. The fact that the client has given specific instructions which cover one part or aspect of the order should not be treated as releasing the investment firm from its best execution obligations in respect of any other parts or aspects of the client order that are not covered by such instructions. An investment firm should not induce a client to instruct it to execute an order in a particular way, by expressly indicating or implicitly suggesting the content of the instruction to the client, when the firm ought reasonably to know that an instruction to that effect is likely to prevent it from obtaining the best possible result for that client. However, this should not prevent a firm inviting a client to choose between two or more specified trading venues, provided that those venues are consistent with the execution policy of the firm.

(103) Dealing on own account with clients by an investment firm should be considered as the execution of client orders, and therefore subject to the requirements under Directive 2014/65/EU and this Regulation and, in particular, those obligations in relation to best execution. However, if an investment firm provides a quote to a client and that quote would meet the investment firm's obligations under Article 27(1) of Directive 2014/65/EU if the firm executed that quote at the time the quote was provided, then the firm should meet those same obligations if it executes its quote after the client accepts it, provided that, taking into account the changing market conditions and the time elapsed between the offer and acceptance of the quote, the quote is not manifestly out of date.

(104) The obligation to deliver the best possible result when executing client orders applies in relation to all types of financial instruments. However, given the differences in market structures or the structure of financial instruments, it may be difficult to identify and apply a uniform standard of and procedure for best execution that would be valid and effective for all classes of instrument. Best execution obligations should therefore be applied in a manner that takes into account the different circumstances associated with the execution of orders related to particular types of financial instruments. For example, transactions involving a customised OTC financial instrument that involve a unique contractual relationship tailored to the circumstances of the client and the investment firm may not be comparable for best execution purposes with transactions involving shares traded on centralised execution venues. As best execution obligations apply to all financial instruments, irrespective of whether they are traded on trading venues or OTC, investment firms should gather relevant market data in order to check whether the OTC price offered for a client is fair and delivers on best execution obligation.

(105) The provisions of this Regulation as to execution policy should be without prejudice to the general obligation of an investment firm under Article 27(7) of Directive 2014/65/EU to monitor the effectiveness of its order execution arrangements and policy and assess the venues in its execution policy on a regular basis.

(106) This Regulation should not require a duplication of effort as to best execution between an investment firm which provides the service of reception and transmission of order or portfolio management and any investment firm to which that investment firm transmits its orders for execution.

(107) The best execution obligation under Directive 2014/65/EU requires investment firms to take all sufficient steps to obtain the best possible result for their clients. The quality of execution, which includes aspects such as the speed and likelihood of execution such as fill rate) and the availability and incidence of price improvement, is an important factor in the delivery of best execution. Availability, comparability and consolidation of data related to execution quality provided by the various execution venues is crucial in enabling investment firms and investors to identify those execution venues that deliver the highest quality of execution for their clients. In order to obtain best execution result for a client, investment firms should compare and analyse relevant data including that made public in accordance with Article 27(3) of Directive 2014/65/EU and respective implementing measures.

(108) Investment firms executing orders should be able to include a single execution venue in their policy only where they are able to show that this allows them to obtain best execution for their clients on a consistent basis. Investment firms should select a single execution venue only where they can reasonably expect that the selected execution venue will enable them to obtain results for clients that are at least as good as the results that they

reasonably could expect from using alternative execution venues. This reasonable expectation must be supported by relevant data published in accordance with Article 27 of Directive 2014/65/EU or by other internal analyses conducts by the firms.

(109) The reallocation of transactions should be considered as detrimental to a client if, as an effect of that reallocation, unfair precedence is given to the investment firm or to any particular client.

(110) Without prejudice to Regulation (EU) No 596/2014, for the purposes of the provisions of this Regulation concerning client order handling, client orders should not be treated as otherwise comparable if they are received by different media and it would not be practicable for them to be treated sequentially. Any use by an investment firm of information relating to a pending client order in order to deal on own account in the financial instruments to which the client order relates, or in related financial instruments, should be considered a misuse of that information. However, the mere fact that market makers or bodies authorised to act as counterparties confine themselves to pursuing their legitimate business of buying and selling financial instruments, or that persons authorised to execute orders on behalf of third parties confine themselves to carrying out an order dutifully, should not in itself be deemed to constitute a misuse of information.

(111) When assessing whether a market fulfils the requirement laid down in point (a) of Article 33(3) of Directive 2014/65/EU that at least 50 % of the issuers admitted to trading on that market are small and medium-size enterprises (SMEs), a flexible approach should be taken by competent authorities with regard to markets with no previous operating history, newly created SMEs whose financial instruments have been admitted to trading for less than three years and issuers exclusively of non-equity financial instruments.

(112) Given the diversity in operating models of existing MTFs with a focus on SMEs in the Union, and to ensure the success of the new category of SME growth market, it is appropriate to grant SME growth markets an appropriate degree of flexibility in evaluating the appropriateness of issuers for admission on their venue. In any case, an SME growth market should not have rules that impose greater burdens on issuers than those applicable to issuers on regulated markets.

(113) With regard to the content of the admission document which an issuer is required to produce upon initial admission to trading of its securities on an SME growth market, where the requirement to publish a prospectus pursuant to Directive 2003/71/EC does not apply, it is appropriate that competent authorities retain discretion to assess whether the rules set out by the operator of the SME growth market achieve the proper information of investors. While full responsibility for the information featured in the admission document should lie with the issuer, it should be for the operator of an SME growth market to define how the admission document should be appropriately reviewed. This should not necessarily involve a formal approval by the competent authority or the operator.

(114) The publication by issuers of annual and half-yearly financial reports represents an appropriate minimum standard of transparency which is coherent with the prevailing best practice in existing markets focusing on SMEs. As to the content of financial reports, the operator of an SME growth market should be free to prescribe the use of International Financial Reporting Standards or financial reporting standards permitted by local laws and regulations, or both, by issuers whose financial instruments are traded on its venue. Deadlines for publishing financial reports should be less onerous than those prescribed by Directive 2004/109/EC of the European Parliament and of the Council ([1]) as less stringent timeframes appear better suited to the needs and circumstances of SMEs.

(115) Since the rules on dissemination of information about issuers on regulated markets under Directive 2004/109/EC would be too burdensome for issuers on SME growth markets, it is appropriate that the website of the operator of the SME growth market becomes the point of convergence for investors seeking information on the issuers traded on that venue. A publication on the website of the operator of the SME growth market can also be effected by providing a direct link to the website of the issuer in case the information is published there, if the link goes directly to the relevant part of the website of the issuer where the regulatory information can be easily found by investors.

([1]) Directive 2004/109/EC of the European Parliament and of the Council of 15 December 2004 on the harmonisation of transparency requirements in relation to information about issuers whose securities are admitted to trading on a regulated market and amending Directive 2001/34/EC (OJ L 390, 31.12.2004, p. 38).

(116) It is necessary to further specify when a suspension or a removal from trading of a financial instrument is likely to cause significant damages to the investor's interest or to the orderly functioning of the market. Convergence in that field is necessary to ensure that market participants in a Member State where trading in financial instruments has been suspended or financial instruments have been removed are not disadvantaged in comparison to market participants in another Member State, where trading is still ongoing.

(117) To ensure the necessary level of convergence, it is appropriate to specify a list of circumstances constituting significant damage to investors' interests and the orderly functioning of the market which could be the basis of a decision by a national competent authority, a market operator operating a regulated market or an investment firm or a market operator operating an MTF or an OTF not to demand the suspension or removal of a financial instrument from trading, or not to follow a notification thereto. It is appropriate for such a list to be non-exhaustive as it will thus provide national competent authorities with a framework for the exercise of their judgement and will leave them a necessary degree of flexibility in the assessment of individual cases.

(118) Articles 31(2) and 54(2) of Directive 2014/65/EU respectively require investment firms and market operators operating an MTF or an OTF, and market operators of regulated markets to immediately inform their national competent authorities under certain circumstances. This requirement is intended to ensure that national competent authorities can fulfil their regulatory tasks and are informed in a timely manner about relevant incidents which may have a negative impact on the functioning and integrity of the markets. The information received from operators of trading venues should enable national competent authorities to identify and assess the risks for the markets and their participants as well as to react efficiently and to take action if necessary.

(119) It is appropriate to set up a non-exhaustive list of high-level circumstances where significant infringements of the rules of a trading venue, disorderly trading conditions or system disruptions in relation to a financial instrument may be assumed, thus triggering the obligation for the operators of trading venues to immediately inform their competent authorities as set out in Articles 31(2) and 54(2) of Directive 2014/65/EU. For that purpose, reference to the 'rules of a trading venue' should be understood in a broad sense and should comprise all rules, rulings, orders as well as general terms and conditions of contractual agreements between the trading venue and its participants which contain the conditions for trading and admission to the trading venue.

(120) With regard to conduct that may indicate abusive behaviour within the scope of Regulation (EU) No 596/2014, it is also appropriate to set up a non-exhaustive list of signals of insider dealing and market manipulation which should be taken into account by the operator of a trading venue when examining transactions or orders to trade in order to determine whether the obligation to inform the relevant national competent authority applies, as set out in Articles 31(2) and 54(2) of Directive 2014/65/EU. For that purpose, reference to 'order to trade' should encompass all types of orders, including initial orders, modifications, updates and cancellations of orders, irrespective of whether or not they have been executed and irrespective of the means used to access the trading venue.

(121) The list of signals of insider dealing and market manipulation should be neither exhaustive nor determinative of market abuse or attempts of market abuse, as each of the signals may not necessarily constitute market abuse or attempts of market abuse *per se*. Transactions or orders to trade meeting one or more signals may be conducted for legitimate reasons or in compliance with the rules of the trading venue.

(122) In order to provide transparency to market stakeholders whilst preventing market abuse and preserving confidentiality of the identities of position holders, the publication of aggregate weekly position reports on positions referred to in Article 58(1)(a) of Directive 2014/65/EU should only apply to contracts that are traded by a certain number of persons, above certain sizes as specified in this Regulation.

(123) In order to ensure that market data is provided on a reasonable commercial basis in a uniform manner in the Union, this Regulation specifies the conditions that APAs and CTPs must fulfil. These conditions are based on the objective to ensure that the obligation to provide market data on a reasonable commercial basis is sufficiently clear to allow for an effective and uniform application whilst taking into account different operating models and costs structures of data providers.

(124) To ensure that fees for market data are set at a reasonable level, the fulfilment of the obligation to provide market data on a reasonable commercial basis requires that prices be based on a reasonable relationship to the cost of producing and disseminating that data. Therefore, without prejudice to the application of competition rules, data providers should determine their fees on the basis of their costs whilst being allowed to obtain a reasonable margin, based on factors such as the operating profit margin, the return on costs, the return on operating assets and the return on capital. Where data providers incur joint costs for data provision and the provision of other services, costs of data provision may include an appropriate share of costs arising from any other relevant service provided. Since specifying the exact cost is very complex, cost allocation and cost apportionment methodologies should be specified instead, leaving the specification of those costs to the discretion of market data providers.

(125) Market data should be provided on a non-discriminatory basis, which requires that the same price and other terms and conditions should be offered to all customers who are in the same category according to published objective criteria.

(126) To allow data users to obtain market data without having to buy other services, market data should be offered unbundled from other services. To avoid that data users are charged more than once for the same market data when buying data from different market data distributors, market data should be offered on a per user basis unless doing so would be disproportionate to the cost of such way of offering that data in respect of the scale and the scope of the market data provided by the APA and the CTP.

(127) In order to allow for data users and competent authorities to effectively assess whether market data is provided on a reasonable commercial basis, it is necessary that all the essential conditions for its provision are disclosed to the public. Data providers should therefore disclose information about their fees and the content of the market data As well as the cost accounting methodologies used to determine their costs without having to disclose their actual costs.

(128) It is appropriate to set the criteria for determining when the operations of a regulated market, an MTF or an OTF are of substantial importance in a host Member State so as to avoid creating an obligation on a trading venue to deal with or be made subject to the supervision of more than one competent authority where this would not be necessary according to Directive 2014/65/EU. For MTFs and OTFs, it is appropriate that only MTFs and OTFs with a significant market share be considered as being of substantial importance, so that not any relocation or acquisition of an economically insignificant MTF or OTF automatically triggers the establishment of the cooperation arrangements set out in Article 79(2) of Directive 2014/65/EU.

(129) This Regulation respects the fundamental rights and observes the principles recognised in the Charter of Fundamental Rights of the European Union (Charter). Accordingly, this Regulation should be interpreted and applied in accordance with those rights and principles in particular the right to protection of personal data, the freedom to conduct business, the right to consumer protection, the right to effective remedy and to a fair trial. Any processing of personal data under this Regulation should respect fundamental rights, including the right to respect for private and family life and the right to protection of personal data under Articles 7 and 8 of the Charter of Fundamental Rights of the European Union and must be in compliance with the Directive 95/46/EC and Regulation (EC) No 45/2001.

(130) ESMA, established by Regulation (EU) No 1095/2010 of the European Parliament and of the Council [1] has been consulted for technical advice.

(131) In order to allow competent authorities and investment firms to adapt to the new requirements contained in this Regulation so that they can be applied in an efficient and effective manner, the starting date of application of this Regulation should be aligned with the entry into application date of Directive 2014/65/EU,

[1] Regulation (EU) No 1095/2010 of the European Parliament and of the Council of 24 November 2010 establishing a European Supervisory Authority (European Securities and Markets Authority), amending Decision No 716/2009/EC and repealing Commission Decision 2009/77/EC (OJ L 331, 15.12.2010, p. 84).

HAS ADOPTED THIS REGULATION:

CHAPTER I

SCOPE AND DEFINITIONS

Article 1

Subject-matter and scope

1. Chapter II, and Sections 1 to 4, Articles 59(4) and 60 and Sections 6 and 8 of Chapter III and, to the extent they relate to those provisions, Chapter I and Section 9 of Chapter III and Chapter IV of this Regulation shall apply to management companies in accordance with Article 6(4) of Directive 2009/65/EC and Article 6(6) of Directive 2011/61/EU of the European Parliament and of the Council [1].

2. References to investment firms shall encompass credit institutions and references to financial instruments shall encompass structured deposits in relation to all the requirements referred to in Article 1(3) and 1(4) of Directive 2014/65/EU and their implementing provisions as set out under this Regulation.

Article 2

Definitions

For the purposes of this Regulation, the following definitions shall apply:

(1) 'relevant person' in relation to an investment firm, means any of the following:

(a) a director, partner or equivalent, manager or tied agent of the firm;

(b) a director, partner or equivalent, or manager of any tied agent of the firm;

(c) an employee of the firm or of a tied agent of the firm, as well as any other natural person whose services are placed at the disposal and under the control of the firm or a tied agent of the firm and who is involved in the provision by the firm of investment services and activities;

(d) a natural person who is directly involved in the provision of services to the investment firm or to its tied agent under an outsourcing arrangement for the purpose of the provision by the firm of investment services and activities;

(2) 'financial analyst' means a relevant person who produces the substance of investment research;

(3) 'outsourcing' means an arrangement of any form between an investment firm and a service provider by which that service provider performs a process, a service or an activity which would otherwise be undertaken by the investment firm itself;

(3a) 'person with whom a relevant person has a family relationship' means any of the following:

(a) the spouse of the relevant person or any partner of that person considered by national law as equivalent to a spouse;

(b) a dependent child or stepchild of the relevant person;

(c) any other relative of the relevant person who has shared the same household as that person for at least one year on the date of the personal transaction concerned;

(4) 'securities financing transaction' means security financing transaction as defined in Article 3(11) of Regulation (EU) 2015/2365 of the European Parliament and of the Council [2].

(5) 'remuneration' means all forms of payments or financial or non-financial benefits provided directly or indirectly by firms to relevant persons in the provision of investment or ancillary services to clients;

(6) 'commodity' means any goods of a fungible nature that are capable of being delivered, including metals and their ores and alloys, agricultural products, and energy such as electricity.

[1] Directive 2011/61/EU of the European Parliament and of the Council of 8 June 2011 on Alternative Investment Fund Managers and amending Directives 2003/41/EC and 2009/65/EC and Regulations (EC) No 1060/2009 and (EU) No 1095/2010 (OJ L 174, 1.7.2011, p. 1).

[2] Regulation (EU) 2015/2365 of the European Parliament and of the Council of 25 November 2015 on transparency of securities financing transactions and of reuse and amending Regulation (EU) No 648/2012 (OJ L 337, 23.12.2015, p. 1).

Article 3

Conditions applying to the provision of information

1. Where, for the purposes of this Regulation, information is required to be provided in a durable medium as defined in Article 4(1) point 62 of Directive 2014/65/EU investment firms shall have the right to provide that information in a durable medium other than on paper only if:

(a) the provision of that information in that medium is appropriate to the context in which the business between the firm and the client is, or is to be, carried on; and

(b) the person to whom the information is to be provided, when offered the choice between information on paper or in that other durable medium, specifically chooses the provision of the information in that other medium.

2. Where, pursuant to Article 46, 47, 48, 49, 50 or 66(3) of this Regulation, an investment firm provides information to a client by means of a website and that information is not addressed personally to the client, investment firms shall ensure that the following conditions are satisfied:

(a) the provision of that information in that medium is appropriate to the context in which the business between the firm and the client is, or is to be, carried on;

(b) the client must specifically consent to the provision of that information in that form;

(c) the client must be notified electronically of the address of the website, and the place on the website where the information may be accessed;

(d) the information must be up to date;

(e) the information must be accessible continuously by means of that website for such period of time as the client may reasonably need to inspect it.

3. For the purposes of this Article, the provision of information by means of electronic communications shall be treated as appropriate to the context in which the business between the firm and the client is, or is to be, carried on where there is evidence that the client has regular access to the internet. The provision by the client of an e-mail address for the purposes of the carrying on of that business shall be treated as such evidence.

Article 4

Provision of investment service in an incidental manner

(Article 2(1) of Directive 2014/65/EU)

For the purpose of the exemption in point (c) of Article 2(1) of Directive 2014/65/EU, an investment service shall be deemed to be provided in an incidental manner in the course of a professional activity where the following conditions are satisfied:

(a) a close and factual connection exists between the professional activity and the provision of the investment service to the same client, such that the investment service can be regarded as accessory to the main professional activity;

(b) the provision of investment services to the clients of the main professional activity does not aim to provide a systematic source of income to the person providing the professional activity; and

(c) the person providing the professional activity does not market or otherwise promote his ability to provide investment services, except where these are disclosed to clients as being accessory to the main professional activity.

Article 5

Wholesale energy products that must be physically settled

(Article 4(1)(2) of Directive 2014/65/EU)

1. For the purposes of Section C(6) of Annex I to Directive 2014/65/EU, a wholesale energy product must be physically settled where all the following conditions are satisfied:

(a) it contains provisions which ensure that parties to the contract have proportionate arrangements in place to be able to make or take delivery of the underlying commodity; a balancing agreement with the Transmission System Operator in the area of electricity and gas shall be considered a proportionate arrangement where the parties to the agreement have to ensure physical delivery of electricity or gas.

(b) it establishes unconditional, unrestricted and enforceable obligations of the parties to the contract to deliver and take delivery of the underlying commodity;

(c) it does not allow either party to replace physical delivery with cash settlement;

(d) the obligations under the contract cannot be offset against obligations from other contracts between the parties concerned, without prejudice to the rights of the parties to the contract, to net their cash payment obligations.

For the purposes of point (d), operational netting in power and gas markets shall not be considered as offsetting of obligations under a contract against obligations from other contracts.

2. Operational netting shall be understood as any nomination of quantities of power and gas to be fed into a gridwork upon being so required by the rules or requests of a Transmission System Operator as defined in Article 2(4) of Directive 2009/72/EC of the European Parliament and of the Council [1] for an entity performing an equivalent function to a Transmission System Operator at the national level. Any nomination of quantities based on operational netting shall not be at the discretion of the parties to the contract.

3. For the purposes of Section C(6) of Annex I to Directive 2014/65/EU, force majeure shall include any exceptional event or a set of circumstances which are outside the control of the parties to the contract, which the parties to the contract could not have reasonably foreseen or avoided by the exercise of appropriate and reasonable due diligence and which prevent one or both parties to the contract from fulfilling their contractual obligations.

4. For the purposes of Section C(6) of Annex I to Directive 2014/65/EU bona fide inability to settle shall include any event or set of circumstances, not qualifying as force majeure as referred to in paragraph 3, which are objectively and expressly defined in the contract terms, for one or both parties to the contract, acting in good faith, not to fulfil their contractual obligations.

5. The existence of force majeure or bona fide inability to settle provisions shall not prevent a contract from being considered as 'physically settled' for the purposes of Section C(6) of Annex I to Directive 2014/65/EU.

6. The existence of default clauses providing that a party is entitled to financial compensation in the case of non- or defective performance of the contract shall not prevent the contract from being considered as 'physically settled' within the meaning of Section C(6) of Annex I to Directive 2014/65/EU.

7. The delivery methods for the contracts being considered as 'physically settled' within the meaning of Section C(6) of Annex I to Directive 2014/65/EU shall include at least:

(a) physical delivery of the relevant commodities themselves;

(b) delivery of a document giving rights of an ownership nature to the relevant commodities or the relevant quantity of the commodities concerned;

(c) other methods of bringing about the transfer of rights of an ownership nature in relation to the relevant quantity of goods without physically delivering them, including notification, scheduling or nomination to the operator of an energy supply network, that entitles the recipient to the relevant quantity of the goods.

Article 6

Energy derivative contracts relating to oil and coal and wholesale energy products

(Article 4(1)(2) of Directive 2014/65/EU)

1. For the purposes of Section C(6) of Annex I to Directive 2014/65/EU, energy derivative contracts relating to oil shall be contracts with mineral oil, of any description and petroleum gases, whether in liquid or vapour form, including products, components and derivatives of oil and oil transport fuels, including those with biofuel additives, as an underlying.

[1] Directive 2009/72/EC of the European Parliament and of the Council of 13 July 2009 concerning common rules for the internal market in electricity and repealing Directive 2003/54/EC (OJ L 211, 14.8.2009, p. 55).

2. For the purposes of Section C(6) of Annex I to Directive 2014/65/EU, energy derivative contracts relating to coal shall be contracts with coal, defined as a black or dark-brown combustible mineral substance consisting of carbonised vegetable matter, used as a fuel, as an underlying.

3. For the purposes of Section C(6) of Annex I to Directive 2014/65/EU derivative contracts that have the characteristics of wholesale energy products as defined in Article 2(4) of Regulation (EU) No 1227/2011 shall be derivatives with electricity or natural gas as an underlying, in accordance with points (b) and (d) of Article 2(4) of that Regulation.

Article 7

Other derivative financial instruments

(Article 4(1)(2) of Directive 2014/65/EU)

1. For the purposes of Section C(7) of Annex I to Directive 2014/65/EU, a contract which is not a spot contract in accordance with paragraph 2 and which is not for commercial purposes as laid down in paragraph 4 shall be considered as having the characteristics of other derivative financial instruments where it satisfies the following conditions:

(a) it meets one of the following criteria:

(i) it is traded on a third country trading venue that performs a similar function to a regulated market, an MTF or an OTF;

(ii) it is expressly stated to be traded on, or is subject to the rules of, a regulated market, an MTF, an OTF or such a third country trading venue;

(iii) it is equivalent to a contract traded on a regulated market, MTF, an OTF or such a third country trading venue, with regards to the price, the lot, the delivery date and other contractual terms;

(b) it is standardised so that the price, the lot, the delivery date and other terms are determined principally by reference to regularly published prices, standard lots or standard delivery dates.

2. A spot contract for the purposes of paragraph 1 shall be a contract for the sale of a commodity, asset or right, under the terms of which delivery is scheduled to be made within the longer of the following periods:

(a) 2 trading days;

(b) the period generally accepted in the market for that commodity, asset or right as the standard delivery period.

A contract shall not be considered a spot contract where, irrespective of its explicit terms, there is an understanding between the parties to the contract that delivery of the underlying is to be postponed and not to be performed within the period referred to in paragraph 2.

3. For the purposes of Section C(10) of Annex I to Directive 2004/39/EC of the European Parliament and of the Council [1], a derivative contract relating to an underlying referred to in that Section or in Article 8 of this Regulation shall be considered to have the characteristics of other derivative financial instruments where one of the following conditions is satisfied:

(a) it is settled in cash or may be settled in cash at the option of one or more of the parties, otherwise than by reason of a default or other termination event;

(b) it is traded on a regulated market, an MTF, an OTF, or a third country trading venue that performs a similar function to a regulated market, MTF or an OTF;

(c) the conditions laid down in paragraph 1 are satisfied in relation to that contract.

[1] Directive 2004/39/EC of the European Parliament and of the Council of 21 April 2004 on markets in financial instruments amending Council Directives 85/611/EEC and 93/6/EEC and Directive 2000/12/EC of the European Parliament and of the Council and repealing Council Directive 93/22/EEC (OJ L 145, 30.4.2004, p. 1).

4. A contract shall be considered to be for commercial purposes for the purposes of Section C(7) of Annex I to Directive 2014/65/EU, and as not having the characteristics of other derivative financial instruments for the purposes of Sections C(7) and (10) of that Annex, where the following conditions are both met:

(a) it is entered into with or by an operator or administrator of an energy transmission grid, energy balancing mechanism or pipeline network,

(b) it is necessary to keep in balance the supplies and uses of energy at a given time, including the case when the reserve capacity contracted by an electricity transmission system operator as defined in Article 2(4) of Directive 2009/72/EC is being transferred from one prequalified balancing service provider to another prequalified balancing service provider with the consent of the relevant transmission system operator.

Article 8

Derivatives under Section C(10) of Annex I to Directive 2014/65/EU

(Article 4(1)(2) of Directive 2014/65/EU)

In addition to derivative contracts expressly referred to in Section C(10) of Annex I to Directive 2014/65/EU, a derivative contract shall be subject to the provisions in that Section where it meets the criteria set out in that Section and in Article 7(3) of this Regulation and it relates to any of the following:

(a) telecommunications bandwidth;

(b) commodity storage capacity;

(c) transmission or transportation capacity relating to commodities, whether cable, pipeline or other means with the exception of transmission rights related to electricity transmission cross zonal capacities when they are, on the primary market, entered into with or by a transmission system operator or any persons acting as service providers on their behalf and in order to allocate the transmission capacity;

(d) an allowance, credit, permit, right or similar asset which is directly linked to the supply, distribution or consumption of energy derived from renewable resources, except where the contract is already within the scope of Section C of Annex I to Directive 2014/65/EU;

(e) a geological, environmental or other physical variable, except if the contract is relating to any units recognised for compliance with the requirements of Directive 2003/87/EC of the European Parliament and of the Council [1];

(f) any other asset or right of a fungible nature, other than a right to receive a service, that is capable of being transferred;

(g) an index or measure related to the price or value of, or volume of transactions in any asset, right, service or obligation;

(h) an index or measure based on actuarial statistics.

Article 9

Investment advice

(Article 4(1)(4) of Directive 2014/65/EU)

For the purposes of the definition of 'investment advice' in Article 4(1)(4) of Directive 2014/65/EU, a personal recommendation shall be considered a recommendation that is made to a person in his capacity as an investor or potential investor, or in his capacity as an agent for an investor or potential investor.

That recommendation shall be presented as suitable for that person, or shall be based on a consideration of the circumstances of that person, and shall constitute a recommendation to take one of the following sets of steps:

(a) to buy, sell, subscribe for, exchange, redeem, hold or underwrite a particular financial instrument;

[1] Directive 2003/87/EC of the European Parliament and of the Council of 13 October 2003 establishing a scheme for greenhouse gas emission allowance trading within the Community and amending Council Directive 96/61/EC (OJ L 275, 25.10.2003, p. 32).

(b) to exercise or not to exercise any right conferred by a particular financial instrument to buy, sell, subscribe for, exchange, or redeem a financial instrument.

A recommendation shall not be considered a personal recommendation if it is issued exclusively to the public.

Article 10

Characteristics of other derivative contracts relating to currencies

1. For the purposes of Section C(4) of Annex I to Directive 2014/65/EU, other derivative contracts relating to a currency shall not be a financial instrument where the contract is one of the following:

(a) a spot contract within the meaning of paragraph 2 of this Article,

(b) a means of payment that:

(i) must be settled physically otherwise than by reason of a default or other termination event;

(ii) is entered into by at least a person which is not a financial counterparty within the meaning of Article 2(8) of Regulation (EU) No 648/2012 of the European Parliament and of the Council ([1]);

(iii) is entered into in order to facilitate payment for identifiable goods, services or direct investment; and

(iv) is not traded on a trading venue.

2. A spot contract for the purposes of paragraph 1 shall be a contract for the exchange of one currency against another currency, under the terms of which delivery is scheduled to be made within the longer of the following periods:

(a) 2 trading days in respect of any pair of the major currencies set out in paragraph 3;

(b) for any pair of currencies where at least one currency is not a major currency, the longer of 2 trading days or the period generally accepted in the market for that currency pair as the standard delivery period;

(c) where the contract for the exchange of those currencies is used for the main purpose of the sale or purchase of a transferable security or a unit in a collective investment undertaking, the period generally accepted in the market for the settlement of that transferable security or a unit in a collective investment undertaking as the standard delivery period or 5 trading days, whichever is shorter.

A contract shall not be considered a spot contract where, irrespective of its explicit terms, there is an understanding between the parties to the contract that delivery of the currency is to be postponed and not to be performed within the period set out in the first subparagraph.

3. The major currencies for the purposes of paragraph 2 shall only include the US dollar, Euro, Japanese yen, Pound sterling, Australian dollar, Swiss franc, Canadian dollar, Hong Kong dollar, Swedish krona, New Zealand dollar, Singapore dollar, Norwegian krone, Mexican peso, Croatian kuna, Bulgarian lev, Czech koruna, Danish krone, Hungarian forint, Polish złoty and Romanian leu.

4. For the purposes of paragraph 2, a trading day shall mean any day of normal trading in the jurisdiction of both the currencies that are exchanged pursuant to the contract for the exchange of those currencies and in the jurisdiction of a third currency where any of the following conditions are met:

(a) the exchange of those currencies involves converting them through that third currency for the purposes of liquidity;

(b) the standard delivery period for the exchange of those currencies references the jurisdiction of that third currency.

([1]) Regulation (EU) No 648/2012 of the European Parliament and of the Council of 4 July 2012 on OTC derivatives, central counterparties and trade repositories (OJ L 201, 27.7.2012, p. 1).

Article 11

Money-market instruments

(Article 4(1)(17) of Directive 2014/65/EU)

Money-market instruments in accordance with Article 4(1)(17) of Directive 2014/65/EU, shall include treasury bills, certificates of deposits, commercial papers and other instruments with substantively equivalent features where they have the following characteristics:

(a) they have a value that can be determined at any time;

(b) they are not derivatives;

(c) they have a maturity at issuance of 397 days or less.

Article 12

Systematic internalisers for shares, depositary receipts, ETFs, certificates and other similar financial instruments

(Article 4(1)(20) of Directive 2014/65/EU)

An investment firm shall be considered to be a systematic internaliser in accordance with Article 4(1)(20) of Directive 2014/65/EU in respect of each share, depositary receipt, exchange traded fund (ETF), certificate and other similar financial instrument where it internalises according to the following criteria:

(a) on a frequent and systematic basis in the financial instrument for which there is a liquid market as defined in Article 2(1)(17)(b) of Regulation (EU) No 600/2014 where during the past 6 months:

(i) the number of OTC transactions carried out by it on own account when executing client orders is equal to or larger than 0,4 % of the total number of transactions in the relevant financial instrument executed in the Union on any trading venue or OTC during the same period;

(ii) the OTC transactions carried out by it on own account when executing client orders in the relevant financial instrument take place on average on a daily basis;

(b) on a frequent and systematic basis in the financial instrument for which there is not a liquid market as defined in Article 2(1)(17)(b) of Regulation (EU) No 600/2014 where during the past 6 months the OTC transactions carried out by it on own account when executing client orders takes place on average on a daily basis;

(c) on a substantial basis in the financial instrument where the size of OTC trading carried out by it on own account when executing client orders is, during the past 6 months, equal to or larger than either:

(i) 15 % of the total turnover in that financial instrument executed by the investment firm on own account or on behalf of clients and executed on a trading venue or OTC;

(ii) 0,4 % of the total turnover in that financial instrument executed in the Union on a trading venue or OTC.

Article 13

Systematic internalisers for bonds

(Article 4(1)(20) of Directive 2014/65/EU)

An investment firm shall be considered to be a systematic internaliser in accordance with Article 4(1)(20) of Directive 2014/65/EU in respect of all bonds belonging to a class of bonds issued by the same entity or by any entity within the same group where, in relation to any such bond, it internalises according to the following criteria:

(a) on a frequent and systematic basis in a bond for which there is a liquid market as defined in Article 2(1)(17)(a) of Regulation (EU) No 600/2014 where during the past 6 months:

(i) the number of OTC transactions carried out by it on own account when executing client orders is equal to or larger than 2,5 % of the total number of transactions in the relevant bond executed in the Union on any trading venue or OTC during the same period;

(ii) the OTC transactions carried out by it on own account when executing client orders in the relevant financial instrument take place on average once a week;

(b) on a frequent and systematic basis in a bond for which there is not a liquid market as defined in Article 2(1)(17)(a) of Regulation (EU) No 600/2014 where during the past 6 months the OTC transactions carried out by it on own account when executing client orders take place on average once a week;

(c) on a substantial basis in a bond where the size of OTC trading carried out by it on own account when executing client orders is, during the past 6 months, equal to or larger than any of the following:

(i) 25 % of the total turnover in that bond executed by the investment firm on own account or on behalf of clients and executed on a trading venue or OTC;

(ii) 1 % of the total turnover in that bond executed in the Union on a trading venue or OTC.

Article 14

Systematic internalisers for structured finance products

(Article 4(1)(20) of Directive 2014/65/EU)

An investment firm shall be considered to be a systematic internaliser in accordance with Article 4(1)(20) of Directive 2014/65/EU in respect of all structured finance products belonging to a class of structured finance products issued by the same entity or by any entity within the same group where, in relation to any such structured finance product, it internalises according to the following criteria:

(a) on a frequent and systematic basis in a structured finance product for which there is a liquid market as defined in Article 2(1)(17)(a) of Regulation (EU) No 600/2014 where during the past 6 months:

(i) the number of OTC transactions carried out by it on own account when executing client orders is equal to or larger than 4 % of the total number of transactions in the relevant structured finance product executed in the Union on any trading venue or OTC during the same period;

(ii) the OTC transactions carried out by it on own account when executing client orders in the relevant financial instrument take place on average once a week;

(b) on a frequent and systematic basis in a structured finance product for which there is not a liquid market as defined in Article 2(1)(17)(a) of Regulation (EU) No 600/2014 where during the past 6 months the OTC transactions carried out by it on own account when executing client orders take place on average once a week;

(c) on a substantial basis in a structured finance product where the size of OTC trading carried out by it on own account when executing client orders is, during the past 6 months, equal to or larger than any of the following:

(i) 30 % of the total turnover in that structured finance product executed by the investment firm on own account or on behalf of clients and executed on a trading venue or OTC;

(ii) 2,25 % of the total turnover in that structured finance product executed in the Union on a trading venue or OTC.

Article 15

Systematic internalisers for derivatives

(Article 4(1)(20) of Directive 2014/65/EU)

An investment firm shall be considered to be a systematic internaliser in accordance with Article 4(1)(20) of Directive 2014/65/EU in respect of all derivatives belonging to a class of derivatives where, in relation to any such derivative, it internalises according to the following criteria:

(a) on a frequent and systematic basis in a derivative for which there is a liquid market as defined in Article 2(1)(17)(a) of Regulation (EU) No 600/2014 where during the past 6 months:

(i) the number of OTC transactions carried out by it on own account when executing client orders is equal to or larger than 2,5 % of the total number of transactions in the relevant class of derivatives executed in the Union on any trading venue or OTC during the same period;

(ii) the OTC transactions carried out by it on own account when executing client orders in this class of derivatives take place on average once a week;

(b) on a frequent and systematic basis in a derivative for which there is not a liquid market as defined in Article 2(1)(17)(a) of Regulation (EU) No 600/2014 where during the past 6 months the OTC transactions carried out by it on own account in the relevant class of derivative when executing client orders takes place on average once a week;

(c) on a substantial basis in a derivative where the size of OTC trading carried out by it on own account when executing client orders is, during the past 6 months, equal to or larger than any of the following:

(i) 25 % of the total turnover in that class of derivatives executed by the investment firm on own account or on behalf of clients and executed on a trading venue or OTC; or

(ii) 1 % of the total turnover in that class of derivatives executed in the Union on a trading venue or OTC.

Article 16

Systematic internalisers for emission allowances

(Article 4(1)(20) of Directive 2014/65/EU)

An investment firm shall be considered to be a systematic internaliser in accordance with Article 4(1)(20) of Directive 2014/65/EU in respect of emission allowances where, in relation to any such instrument, it internalises according to the following criteria:

(a) on a frequent and systematic basis in an emission allowance for which there is a liquid market as defined in Article 2(1)(17)(a) of Regulation (EU) No 600/2014 where during the past 6 months:

(i) the number of OTC transactions carried out by it on own account when executing client orders is equal to or larger than 4 % of the total number of transactions in the relevant type of emission allowances executed in the Union on any trading venue or OTC during the same period;

(ii) the OTC transactions carried out by it on own account when executing client orders in this type of emission allowances take place on average once a week;

(b) on a frequent and systematic basis in an emission allowance for which there is not a liquid market as defined in Article 2(1)(17)(a) of Regulation (EU) No 600/2014 where during the past 6 months the OTC transactions carried out by it on own account in the relevant type of emission allowances when executing client orders takes place on average once a week;

(c) on a substantial basis in an emission allowance where the size of OTC trading carried out by it on own account when executing client orders is, during the past 6 months, equal to or larger than any of the following:

(i) 30 % of the total turnover in that type of emission allowances executed by the investment firm on own account or on behalf of clients and executed on a trading venue or OTC;

(ii) 2,25 % of the total turnover in that type of emission allowance executed in the Union on a trading venue or OTC.

Article 17

Relevant assessment periods

(Article 4(1)(20) of Directive 2014/65/EU)

The conditions set out in Articles 12 to 16 shall be assessed on a quarterly basis on the basis of data from the past 6 months. The assessment period shall start on the first working day of the months of January, April, July and October.

Newly issued instruments shall only be considered in the assessment when historical data covers a period of at least three months in the case of shares, depositary receipts, ETFs, certificates and other similar financial instruments, and six weeks in the case of bonds, structured finance products and derivatives.

Article 18

Algorithmic trading

(Article 4(1)(39) of Directive 2014/65/EU)

For the purposes of further specifying the definition of algorithmic trading in accordance with Article 4(1)(39) of Directive 2014/65/EU, a system shall be considered as having no or limited human intervention where, for any order or quote generation process or any process to optimise order-execution, an automated system makes decisions at any of the stages of initiating, generating, routing or executing orders or quotes according to pre-determined parameters.

Article 19

High frequency algorithmic trading technique

(Article 4(1)(40) of Directive 2014/65/EU)

1. A high message intraday rate in accordance with Article 4(1)(40) of Directive 2014/65/EU shall consist of the submission on average of any of the following:

(a) at least 2 messages per second with respect to any single financial instrument traded on a trading venue;

(b) at least 4 messages per second with respect to all financial instruments traded on a trading venue.

2. For the purposes of paragraph 1, messages concerning financial instruments for which there is a liquid market in accordance with Article 2(1)(17) of Regulation (EU) No 600/2014 shall be included in the calculation. Messages introduced for the purpose of trading that fulfil the criteria in Article 17(4) of Directive 2014/65/EU shall be included in the calculation.

3. For the purposes of paragraph 1, messages introduced for the purpose of dealing on own account shall be included in the calculation. Messages introduced through other trading techniques than those relying on dealing on own account shall be included in the calculation where the firm's execution technique is structured in such a way as to avoid that the execution takes place on own account.

4. For the purposes of paragraph 1, for the calculation of high message intraday rate in relation to DEA providers, messages submitted by their DEA clients shall be excluded from the calculations.

5. For the purposes of paragraph 1, trading venues shall make available to the firms concerned, on request, estimates of the average number of messages per second on a monthly basis two weeks after the end of each calendar month, thereby taking into account all messages submitted during the preceding 12 months.

Article 20

Direct electronic access

(Article 4(1)(41) of Directive 2014/65/EU)

1. A person shall be considered not capable of electronically transmitting orders relating to a financial instrument directly to a trading venue in accordance with Article 4(1)(41) of Directive 2014/65/EU where that person cannot exercise discretion regarding the exact fraction of a second of order entry and the lifetime of the order within that timeframe.

2. A person shall be considered not capable of such direct electronic order transmission where it takes place through arrangements for optimisation of order execution processes that determine the parameters of the order other than the venue or venues where the order should be submitted, unless these arrangements are embedded into the clients' systems and not into those of the member or participant of a regulated market or of an MTF or a client of an OTF.

CHAPTER II

ORGANISATIONAL REQUIREMENTS

SECTION 1

Organisation

Article 21

General organisational requirements

(Article 16(2) to (10) of Directive 2014/65/EU)

1. Investment firms shall comply with the following organisational requirements:

(a) establish, implement and maintain decision-making procedures and an organisational structure which clearly and in documented manner specifies reporting lines and allocates functions and responsibilities;

(b) ensure that their relevant persons are aware of the procedures which must be followed for the proper discharge of their responsibilities;

(c) establish, implement and maintain adequate internal control mechanisms designed to secure compliance with decisions and procedures at all levels of the investment firm;

(d) employ personnel with the skills, knowledge and expertise necessary for the discharge of the responsibilities allocated to them;

(e) establish, implement and maintain effective internal reporting and communication of information at all relevant levels of the investment firm;

(f) maintain adequate and orderly records of their business and internal organisation;

(g) ensure that the performance of multiple functions by their relevant persons does not and is not likely to prevent those persons from discharging any particular function soundly, honestly, and professionally.

When complying with the requirements set out in the this paragraph, investment firms shall take into account the nature, scale and complexity of the business of the firm, and the nature and range of investment services and activities undertaken in the course of that business.

2. Investment firms shall establish, implement and maintain systems and procedures that are adequate to safeguard the security, integrity and confidentiality of information, taking into account the nature of the information in question.

3. Investment firms shall establish, implement and maintain an adequate business continuity policy aimed at ensuring, in the case of an interruption to their systems and procedures, the preservation of essential data and functions, and the maintenance of investment services and activities, or, where that is not possible, the timely recovery of such data and functions and the timely resumption of their investment services and activities.

4. Investment firms shall establish, implement and maintain accounting policies and procedures that enable them, at the request of the competent authority, to deliver in a timely manner to the competent authority financial reports which reflect a true and fair view of their financial position and which comply with all applicable accounting standards and rules.

5. Investment firms shall monitor and, on a regular basis, evaluate the adequacy and effectiveness of their systems, internal control mechanisms and arrangements established in accordance with paragraphs 1 to 4, and take appropriate measures to address any deficiencies.

Article 22

Compliance

(Article 16(2) of Directive 2014/65/EU)

1. Investment firms shall establish, implement and maintain adequate policies and procedures designed to detect any risk of failure by the firm to comply with its obligations under Directive 2014/65/EU, as well as the associated risks, and put in place adequate measures and procedures designed to minimise such risk and to enable the competent authorities to exercise their powers effectively under that Directive.

Investment firms shall take into account the nature, scale and complexity of the business of the firm, and the nature and range of investment services and activities undertaken in the course of that business.

2. Investment firms shall establish and maintain a permanent and effective compliance function which operates independently and which has the following responsibilities:

(a) to monitor on a permanent basis and to assess, on a regular basis, the adequacy and effectiveness of the measures, policies and procedures put in place in accordance with the first subparagraph of paragraph 1, and the actions taken to address any deficiencies in the firm's compliance with its obligations;

(b) to advise and assist the relevant persons responsible for carrying out investment services and activities to comply with the firm's obligations under Directive 2014/65/EU;

(c) to report to the management body, on at least an annual basis, on the implementation and effectiveness of the overall control environment for investment services and activities, on the risks that have been identified and on the complaints-handling reporting as well as remedies undertaken or to be undertaken;

(d) to monitor the operations of the complaints-handling process and consider complaints as a source of relevant information in the context of its general monitoring responsibilities.

In order to comply with points (a) and (b) of this paragraph, the compliance function shall conduct an assessment on the basis of which it shall establish a risk-based monitoring programme that takes into consideration all areas of the investment firm's investment services, activities and any relevant ancillary services, including relevant information gathered in relation to the monitoring of complaints handling. The monitoring programme shall establish priorities determined by the compliance risk assessment ensuring that compliance risk is comprehensively monitored.

3. In order to enable the compliance function referred to in paragraph 2 to discharge its responsibilities properly and independently, investment firms shall ensure that the following conditions are satisfied:

(a) the compliance function has the necessary authority, resources, expertise and access to all relevant information;

(b) a compliance officer is appointed and replaced by the management body and is responsible for the compliance function and for any reporting as to compliance required by Directive 2014/65/EU and Article 25(2) of this Regulation;

(c) the compliance function reports on an ad-hoc basis directly to the management body where it detects a significant risk of failure by the firm to comply with its obligations under Directive 2014/65/EU;

(d) the relevant persons involved in the compliance function are not involved in the performance of services or activities they monitor;

(e) the method of determining the remuneration of the relevant persons involved in the compliance function does not compromise their objectivity and is not likely to do so.

4. An investment firm shall not be required to comply with point (d) or point (e) of paragraph 3 where it is able to demonstrate that in view of the nature, scale and complexity of its business, and the nature and range of investment services and activities, the requirements under point (d) or (e) are not proportionate and that its compliance function continues to be effective. In that case, the investment firm shall assess whether the effectiveness of the compliance function is compromised. The assessment shall be reviewed on a regular basis.

Article 23

Risk management

(Article 16(5) of Directive 2014/65/EU)

1. Investment firms shall take the following actions relating to risk management:

(a) establish, implement and maintain adequate risk management policies and procedures which identify the risks relating to the firm's activities, processes and systems, and where appropriate, set the level of risk tolerated by the firm;

(b) adopt effective arrangements, processes and mechanisms to manage the risks relating to the firm's activities, processes and systems, in light of that level of risk tolerance;

(c) monitor the following:

(i) the adequacy and effectiveness of the investment firm's risk management policies and procedures;

(ii) the level of compliance by the investment firm and its relevant persons with the arrangements, processes and mechanisms adopted in accordance with point (b);

(iii) the adequacy and effectiveness of measures taken to address any deficiencies in those policies, procedures, arrangements, processes and mechanisms, including failures by the relevant persons to comply with such arrangements, processes and mechanisms or follow such policies and procedures.

2. Investment firms shall, where appropriate and proportionate in view of the nature, scale and complexity of their business and the nature and range of the investment services and activities undertaken in the course of that business, establish and maintain a risk management function that operates independently and carries out the following tasks:

(a) implementation of the policy and procedures referred to in paragraph 1;

(b) provision of reports and advice to senior management in accordance with Article 25(2).

Where an investment firm does not establish and maintain a risk management function under the first sub-paragraph, it shall be able to demonstrate upon request that the policies and procedures which it is has adopted in accordance with paragraph 1 satisfy the requirements therein.

Article 24

Internal audit

(Article 16(5) of Directive 2014/65/EU)

Investment firms shall, where appropriate and proportionate in view of the nature, scale and complexity of their business and the nature and range of investment services and activities undertaken in the course of that business, establish and maintain an internal audit function which is separate and independent from the other functions and activities of the investment firm and which has the following responsibilities:

(a) establish, implement and maintain an audit plan to examine and evaluate the adequacy and effectiveness of the investment firm's systems, internal control mechanisms and arrangements;

(b) issue recommendations based on the result of work carried out in accordance with point (a) and verify compliance with those recommendations;

(c) report in relation to internal audit matters in accordance with Article 25(2).

Article 25

Responsibility of senior management

(Article 16(2) of Directive 2014/65/EU)

1. Investment firms shall, when allocating functions internally, ensure that senior management, and, where applicable, the supervisory function, are responsible for ensuring that the firm complies with its obligations under Directive 2014/65/EU. In particular, senior management and, where applicable, the supervisory function shall be required to assess and periodically review the effectiveness of the policies, arrangements and procedures put in place to comply with the obligations under Directive 2014/65/EU and to take appropriate measures to address any deficiencies.

The allocation of significant functions among senior managers shall clearly establish who is responsible for overseeing and maintaining the firm's organisational requirements. Records of the allocation of significant functions shall be kept up-to-date.

2. Investment firms shall ensure that their senior management receive on a frequent basis, and at least annually, written reports on the matters covered by Articles 22, 23 and 24 indicating in particular whether the appropriate remedial measures have been taken in the event of any deficiencies.

3. Investment firms shall ensure that where there is a supervisory function, it receives written reports on the matters covered by Articles 22, 23 and 24 on a regular basis.

4. For the purposes of this Article, the supervisory function shall be the function within an investment firm responsible for the supervision of its senior management.

Article 26

Complaints handling

(Article 16(2) of Directive 2014/65/EU)

1. Investment firms shall establish, implement and maintain effective and transparent complaints management policies and procedures for the prompt handling of clients' or potential clients' complaints. Investment firms shall keep a record of the complaints received and the measures taken for their resolution.

The complaints management policy shall provide clear, accurate and up-to-date information about the complaints-handling process. This policy shall be endorsed by the firm's management body.

2. Investment firms shall publish the details of the process to be followed when handling a complaint. Such details shall include information about the complaints management policy and the contact details of the complaints management function. The information shall be provided to clients or potential clients, on request, or when acknowledging a complaint. Investment firms shall enable clients and potential clients to submit complaints free of charge.

3. Investment firms shall establish a complaints management function responsible for the investigation of complaints. This function may be carried out by the compliance function.

4. When handling a complaint, investment firms shall communicate with clients or potential clients clearly, in plain language that is easy to understand and shall reply to the complaint without undue delay.

5. Investment firms shall communicate the firm's position on the complaint to clients or potential clients and inform the clients or potential clients about their options, including that they may be able to refer the complaint to an alternative dispute resolution entity, as defined in Article 4(h) of Directive 2013/11/EU of the European Parliament and the Council [1] on consumer ADR or that the client may be able to take civil action.

6. Investment firms shall provide information on complaints and complaints-handling to the relevant competent authorities and, where applicable under national law, to an alternative dispute resolution (ADR) entity.

7. Investment firms' compliance function shall analyse complaints and complaints-handling data to ensure that they identify and address any risks or issues.

Article 27

Remuneration policies and practices

(Articles 16, 23 and 24 of Directive 2014/65/EU)

1. Investment firms shall define and implement remuneration policies and practices under appropriate internal procedures taking into account the interests of all the clients of the firm, with a view to ensuring that clients are treated fairly and their interests are not impaired by the remuneration practices adopted by the firm in the short, medium or long term.

Remuneration policies and practices shall be designed in such a way so as not to create a conflict of interest or incentive that may lead relevant persons to favour their own interests or the firm's interests to the potential detriment of any client.

(1) Directive 2013/11/EU of the European Parliament and the Council of 21 May 2013 on alternative dispute resolution for consumer disputes and amending Regulation (EC) No 2006/2004 and Directive 2009/22/EC (Directive on consumer ADR) (OJ L 165, 18.6.2013, p. 63).

2. Investment firms shall ensure that their remuneration policies and practices apply to all relevant persons with an impact, directly or indirectly, on investment and ancillary services provided by the investment firm or on its corporate behaviour, regardless of the type of clients, to the extent that the remuneration of such persons and similar incentives may create a conflict of interest that encourages them to act against the interests of any of the firm's clients.

3. The management body of the investment firm shall approve, after taking advice from the compliance function, the firm's remuneration policy. The senior management of the investment firm shall be responsible for the day-to-day implementation of the remuneration policy and the monitoring of compliance risks related to the policy.

4. Remuneration and similar incentives shall not be solely or predominantly based on quantitative commercial criteria, and shall take fully into account appropriate qualitative criteria reflecting compliance with the applicable regulations, the fair treatment of clients and the quality of services provided to clients.

A balance between fixed and variable components of remuneration shall be maintained at all times, so that the remuneration structure does not favour the interests of the investment firm or its relevant persons against the interests of any client.

Article 28

Scope of personal transactions

(Article 16(2) of Directive 2014/65/EU)

For the purposes of Article 29 and Article 37, a personal transaction shall be a trade in a financial instrument effected by or on behalf of a relevant person, where at least one of the following criteria are met:

(a) the relevant person is acting outside the scope of the activities he carries out in his professional capacity;

(b) the trade is carried out for the account of any of the following persons:

  (i) the relevant person;

  (ii) any person with whom he has a family relationship, or with whom he has close links;

  (iii) a person in respect of whom the relevant person has a direct or indirect material interest in the outcome of the trade, other than obtaining a fee or commission for the execution of the trade.

Article 29

Personal transactions

(Article 16(2) of Directive 2014/65/EU)

1. Investment firms shall establish, implement and maintain adequate arrangements aimed at preventing the activities set out in paragraphs 2, 3 and 4 in the case of any relevant person who is involved in activities that may give rise to a conflict of interest, or who has access to inside information within the meaning of Article 7(1) of Regulation (EU) No 596/2014 or to other confidential information relating to clients or transactions with or for clients by virtue of an activity carried out by him on behalf of the firm.

2. Investment firms shall ensure that relevant persons do not enter into a personal transaction which meets at least one of the following criteria:

(a) that person is prohibited from entering into it under Regulation (EU) No 596/2014;

(b) it involves the misuse or improper disclosure of that confidential information;

(c) it conflicts or is likely to conflict with an obligation of the investment firm under Directive 2014/65/EU.

3. Investment firms shall ensure that relevant persons do not advise or recommend, other than in the proper course of employment or contract for services, any other person to enter into a transaction in financial instruments which, if it were a personal transaction of the relevant person, would be covered by paragraph 2 or Article 37(2)(a) or (b) or Article 67(3).

4. Without prejudice to Article 10(1) of Regulation (EU) No 596/2014, investment firms shall ensure that relevant persons do not disclose, other than in the normal course of his employment or contract for services, any information or opinion to any other person where the relevant person knows, or reasonably ought to know, that as a result of that disclosure that other person will or would be likely to take either of the following steps:

(a) to enter into a transaction in financial instruments which, if it were a personal transaction of the relevant person, would be covered by paragraphs 2 or 3 or Article 37(2)(a) or (b) or Article 67(3);

(b) to advise or procure another person to enter into such a transaction.

5. The arrangements required under paragraph 1 shall be designed to ensure that:

(a) each relevant person covered by paragraphs 1, 2, 3 and 4 is aware of the restrictions on personal transactions, and of the measures established by the investment firm in connection with personal transactions and disclosure, in accordance with paragraphs 1, 2,3 and 4.

(b) the firm is informed promptly of any personal transaction entered into by a relevant person, either by notification of that transaction or by other procedures enabling the firm to identify such transactions;

(c) a record is kept of the personal transaction notified to the firm or identified by it, including any authorisation or prohibition in connection with such a transaction.

In the case of outsourcing arrangements, the investment firm shall ensure that the firm to which the activity is outsourced maintains a record of personal transactions entered into by any relevant person and provides that information to the investment firm promptly on request.

6. Paragraphs 1 to 5 shall not apply to the following personal transactions:

(a) personal transactions effected under a discretionary portfolio management service where there is no prior communication in connection with the transaction between the portfolio manager and the relevant person or other person for whose account the transaction is executed;

(b) personal transactions in undertakings for collective investments in transferable securities (UCITS) or AIFs that are subject to supervision under the law of a Member State which requires an equivalent level of risk spreading in their assets, where the relevant person and any other person for whose account the transactions are effected are not involved in the management of that undertaking.

SECTION 2

Outsourcing

Article 30

Scope of critical and important operational functions

(Article 16(2) and first subparagraph of Article 16(5) of Directive 2014/65/EU)

1. For the purposes of the first subparagraph of Article 16(5) of Directive 2014/65/EU, an operational function shall be regarded as critical or important where a defect or failure in its performance would materially impair the continuing compliance of an investment firm with the conditions and obligations of its authorisation or its other obligations under Directive 2014/65/EU, or its financial performance, or the soundness or the continuity of its investment services and activities.

2. Without prejudice to the status of any other function, the following functions shall not be considered as critical or important for the purposes of paragraph 1:

(a) the provision to the firm of advisory services, and other services which do not form part of the investment business of the firm, including the provision of legal advice to the firm, the training of personnel of the firm, billing services and the security of the firm's premises and personnel;

(b) the purchase of standardised services, including market information services and the provision of price feeds.

Article 31

Outsourcing critical or important operational functions

(Article 16(2) and of Article 16(5) first subparagraph of Directive 2014/65/EU)

1. Investment firms outsourcing critical or important operational functions shall remain fully responsible for discharging all of their obligations under Directive 2014/65/EU and shall comply with the following conditions:

(a) the outsourcing does not result in the delegation by senior management of its responsibility;

(b) the relationship and obligations of the investment firm towards its clients under the terms of Directive 2014/65/EU is not altered;

(c) the conditions with which the investment firm must comply in order to be authorised in accordance with Article 5 of Directive 2014/65/EU, and to remain so, are not undermined;

(d) none of the other conditions subject to which the firm's authorisation was granted is removed or modified.

2. Investment firms shall exercise due skill, care and diligence when entering into, managing or terminating any arrangement for the outsourcing to a service provider of critical or important operational functions and shall take the necessary steps to ensure that the following conditions are satisfied:

(a) the service provider has the ability, capacity, sufficient resources, appropriate organisational structure supporting the performance of the outsourced functions, and any authorisation required by law to perform the outsourced functions, reliably and professionally;

(b) the service provider carries out the outsourced services effectively and in compliance with applicable law and regulatory requirements, and to this end the firm has established methods and procedures for assessing the standard of performance of the service provider and for reviewing on an ongoing basis the services provided by the service provider;

(c) the service provider properly supervises the carrying out of the outsourced functions, and adequately manage the risks associated with the outsourcing;

(d) appropriate action is taken where it appears that the service provider may not be carrying out the functions effectively or in compliance with applicable laws and regulatory requirements;

(e) the investment firm effectively supervises the outsourced functions or services and manage the risks associated with the outsourcing and to this end the firm retains the necessary expertise and resources to supervise the outsourced functions effectively and manage those risks;

(f) the service provider has disclosed to the investment firm any development that may have a material impact on its ability to carry out the outsourced functions effectively and in compliance with applicable laws and regulatory requirements;

(g) the investment firm is able to terminate the arrangement for outsourcing where necessary, with immediate effect when this is in the interests of its clients, without detriment to the continuity and quality of its provision of services to clients;

(h) the service provider cooperates with the competent authorities of the investment firm in connection with the outsourced functions;

(i) the investment firm, its auditors and the relevant competent authorities have effective access to data related to the outsourced functions, as well as to the relevant business premises of the service provider, where necessary for the purpose of effective oversight in accordance with this article, and the competent authorities are able to exercise those rights of access;

(j) the service provider protects any confidential information relating to the investment firm and its clients;

(k) the investment firm and the service provider have established, implemented and maintained a contingency plan for disaster recovery and periodic testing of backup facilities, where that is necessary having regard to the function, service or activity that has been outsourced;

(l) the investment firm has ensured that the continuity and quality of the outsourced functions or services are maintained also in the event of termination of the outsourcing either by transferring the outsourced functions or services to another third party or by performing them itself.

3. The respective rights and obligations of the investment firms and of the service provider shall be clearly allocated and set out in a written agreement. In particular, the investment firm shall keep its instruction and termination rights, its rights of information, and its right to inspections and access to books and premises. The agreement shall ensure that outsourcing by the service provider only takes place with the consent, in writing, of the investment firm.

4. Where the investment firm and the service provider are members of the same group, the investment firm may, for the purposes of complying with this Article and Article 32, take into account the extent to which the firm controls the service provider or has the ability to influence its actions.

5. Investment firms shall make available on request to the competent authority all information necessary to enable the authority to supervise the compliance of the performance of the outsourced functions with the requirements of Directive 2014/65/EU and its implementing measures.

Article 32

Service providers located in third countries

(Article 16(2) and first subparagraph of Article 16(5) of Directive 2014/65/EU)

1. In addition to the requirements set out in Article 31, where an investment firm outsources functions related to the investment service of portfolio management provided to clients to a service provider located in a third country, that investment firm ensures that the following conditions are satisfied:

(a) the service provider is authorised or registered in its home country to provide that service and is effectively supervised by a competent authority in that third country;

(b) there is an appropriate cooperation agreement between the competent authority of the investment firm and the supervisory authority of the service provider.

2. The cooperation agreement referred to in point (b) of paragraph 1 shall ensure that the competent authorities of the investment firm are able, at least, to:

(a) obtain on request the information necessary to carry out their supervisory tasks pursuant to Directive 2014/65/EU and Regulation (EU) No 600/2014;

(b) obtain access to the documents relevant for the performance of their supervisory duties maintained in the third country;

(c) receive information from the supervisory authority in the third country as soon as possible for the purpose of investigating apparent breaches of the requirements of Directive 2014/65/EU and its implementing measures and Regulation (EU) No 600/2014;

(d) cooperate with regard to enforcement, in accordance with the national and international law applicable to the supervisory authority of the third country and the competent authorities in the Union in cases of breach of the requirements of Directive 2014/65/EU and its implementing measures and relevant national law.

3. Competent authorities shall publish on their website a list of the supervisory authorities in third countries with which they have a cooperation agreement referred to in point (b) of paragraph 1.

Competent authorities shall update cooperation agreements concluded before the date of entry into application of this Regulation within six months from that date.

SECTION 3

Conflicts of interest

Article 33

Conflicts of interest potentially detrimental to a client

(Articles 16(3) and 23 of Directive 2014/65/EU)

For the purposes of identifying the types of conflict of interest that arise in the course of providing investment and ancillary services or a combination thereof and whose existence may damage the interests of a client, investment firms shall take into account, by way of minimum criteria, whether the investment firm or a relevant person, or a person directly or indirectly linked by control to the firm, is in any of the following situations, whether as a result of providing investment or ancillary services or investment activities or otherwise:

(a) the firm or that person is likely to make a financial gain, or avoid a financial loss, at the expense of the client;

(b) the firm or that person has an interest in the outcome of a service provided to the client or of a transaction carried out on behalf of the client, which is distinct from the client's interest in that outcome;

(c) the firm or that person has a financial or other incentive to favour the interest of another client or group of clients over the interests of the client;

(d) the firm or that person carries on the same business as the client;

(e) the firm or that person receives or will receive from a person other than the client an inducement in relation to a service provided to the client, in the form of monetary or non-monetary benefits or services.

Article 34

Conflicts of interest policy

(Articles 16(3) and 23 of Directive 2014/65/EU)

1. Investment firms shall establish, implement and maintain an effective conflicts of interest policy set out in writing and appropriate to the size and organisation of the firm and the nature, scale and complexity of its business.

Where the firm is a member of a group, the policy shall also take into account any circumstances, of which the firm is or should be aware, which may give rise to a conflict of interest arising as a result of the structure and business activities of other members of the group.

2. The conflicts of interest policy established in accordance with paragraph 1 shall include the following content:

(a) it must identify, with reference to the specific investment services and activities and ancillary services carried out by or on behalf of the investment firm, the circumstances which constitute or may give rise to a conflict of interest entailing a risk of damage to the interests of one or more clients;

(b) it must specify procedures to be followed and measures to be adopted in order to prevent or manage such conflicts.

3. The procedures and measures referred to in paragraph 2(b) shall be designed to ensure that relevant persons engaged in different business activities involving a conflict of interest of the kind specified in paragraph 2(a) carry on those activities at a level of independence appropriate to the size and activities of the investment firm and of the group to which it belongs, and to the risk of damage to the interests of clients.

For the purposes of paragraph 2(b), the procedures to be followed and measures to be adopted shall include at least those items in the following list that are necessary for the firm to ensure the requisite degree of independence:

(a) effective procedures to prevent or control the exchange of information between relevant persons engaged in activities involving a risk of a conflict of interest where the exchange of that information may harm the interests of one or more clients;

(b) the separate supervision of relevant persons whose principal functions involve carrying out activities on behalf of, or providing services to, clients whose interests may conflict, or who otherwise represent different interests that may conflict, including those of the firm;

(c) the removal of any direct link between the remuneration of relevant persons principally engaged in one activity and the remuneration of, or revenues generated by, different relevant persons principally engaged in another activity, where a conflict of interest may arise in relation to those activities;

(d) measures to prevent or limit any person from exercising inappropriate influence over the way in which a relevant person carries out investment or ancillary services or activities;

(e) measures to prevent or control the simultaneous or sequential involvement of a relevant person in separate investment or ancillary services or activities where such involvement may impair the proper management of conflicts of interest.

4. Investment firms shall ensure that disclosure to clients, pursuant to Article 23(2) of Directive 2014/65/EU, is a measure of last resort that shall be used only where the effective organisational and administrative arrangements established by the investment firm to prevent or manage its conflicts of interest in accordance with Article 23 of Directive 2014/65/EU are not sufficient to ensure, with reasonable confidence, that risks of damage to the interests of the client will be prevented.

The disclosure shall clearly state that the organisational and administrative arrangements established by the investment firm to prevent or manage that conflict are not sufficient to ensure, with reasonable confidence, that the risks of damage to the interests of the client will be prevented. The disclosure shall include specific description of the conflicts of interest that arise in the provision of investment and/or ancillary services, taking into account the nature of the client to whom the disclosure is being made. The description shall explain the general nature and sources of conflicts of interest, as well as the risks to the client that arise as a result of the conflicts of interest and the steps undertaken to mitigate these risks, in sufficient detail to enable that client to take an informed decision with respect to the investment or ancillary service in the context of which the conflicts of interest arise.

5. Investment firms shall assess and periodically review, on an at least annual basis, the conflicts of interest policy established in accordance with paragraphs 1 to 4 and shall take all appropriate measures to address any deficiencies. Over-reliance on disclosure of conflicts of interest shall be considered a deficiency in the investment firm's conflicts of interest policy.

Article 35

Record of services or activities giving rise to detrimental conflict of interest

(Article 16(6) of Directive 2014/65/EU)

Investment firms shall keep and regularly update a record of the kinds of investment or ancillary service or investment activity carried out by or on behalf of the firm in which a conflict of interest entailing a risk of damage to the interests of one or more clients has arisen or, in the case of an ongoing service or activity, may arise.

Senior management shall receive on a frequent basis, and at least annually, written reports on situations referred to in this Article.

Article 36

Investment research and marketing communications

(Article 24(3) of Directive 2014/65/EU)

1. For the purposes of Article 37 investment research shall be research or other information recommending or suggesting an investment strategy, explicitly or implicitly, concerning one or several financial instruments or the issuers of financial instruments, including any opinion as to the present or future value or price of such instruments, intended for distribution channels or for the public, and in relation to which the following conditions are met:

(a) the research or information is labelled or described as investment research or in similar terms, or is otherwise presented as an objective or independent explanation of the matters contained in the recommendation;

(b) if the recommendation in question were made by an investment firm to a client, it would not constitute the provision of investment advice for the purposes of Directive 2014/65/EU.

2. A recommendation of the type covered by point (35) of Article 3(1) of Regulation (EU) No 596/2014 that does not meet the conditions set out in paragraph 1 shall be treated as a marketing communication for the purposes of Directive 2014/65/EU and investment firms that produce or disseminate that recommendation shall ensure that it is clearly identified as such.

Additionally, firms shall ensure that any such recommendation contains a clear and prominent statement that (or, in the case of an oral recommendation, to the effect that) it has not been prepared in accordance with legal requirements designed to promote the independence of investment research, and that it is not subject to any prohibition on dealing ahead of the dissemination of investment research.

Article 37

Additional organisational requirements in relation to investment research or marketing communications

(Article 16(3) of Directive 2014/65/EU)

1. Investment firms which produce, or arrange for the production of, investment research that is intended or likely to be subsequently disseminated to clients of the firm or to the public, under their own responsibility or that of a member of their group, shall ensure the implementation of all the measures set out in Article 34(3) in relation to the financial analysts involved in the production of the investment research and other relevant persons whose responsibilities or business interests may conflict with the interests of the persons to whom the investment research is disseminated.

The obligations in the first subparagraph shall also apply in relation to recommendations referred to in Article 36(2).

2. Investment firms referred to in the first subparagraph of paragraph 1 shall have in place arrangements designed to ensure that the following conditions are satisfied:

(a) financial analysts and other relevant persons do not undertake personal transactions or trade, other than as market makers acting in good faith and in the ordinary course of market making or in the execution of an unsolicited client order, on behalf of any other person, including the investment firm, in financial instruments to which investment research relates, or in any related financial instruments, with knowledge of the likely timing or content of that investment research which is not publicly available or available to clients and cannot readily be inferred from information that is so available, until the recipients of the investment research have had a reasonable opportunity to act on it;

(b) in circumstances not covered by point (a), financial analysts and any other relevant persons involved in the production of investment research do not undertake personal transactions in financial instruments to which the investment research relates, or in any related financial instruments, contrary to current recommendations, except in exceptional circumstances and with the prior approval of a member of the firm's legal or compliance function;

(c) a physical separation exists between the financial analysts involved in the production of investment research and other relevant persons whose responsibilities or business interests may conflict with the interests of the persons to whom the investment research is disseminated or, when considered not appropriate to the size and organisation of the firm as well as the nature, scale and complexity of its business, the establishment and implementation of appropriate alternative information barriers;

(d) the investment firms themselves, financial analysts, and other relevant persons involved in the production of the investment research do not accept inducements from those with a material interest in the subject-matter of the investment research;

(e) the investment firms themselves, financial analysts, and other relevant persons involved in the production of the investment research do not promise issuers favourable research coverage;

(f) before the dissemination of investment research issuers, relevant persons other than financial analysts, and any other persons are not permitted to review a draft of the investment research for the purpose of verifying the accuracy of factual statements made in that research, or for any purpose other than verifying compliance with the firm's legal obligations, where the draft includes a recommendation or a target price.

For the purposes of this paragraph, 'related financial instrument' shall be any financial instrument the price of which is closely affected by price movements in another financial instrument which is the subject of investment research, and includes a derivative on that other financial instrument.

3. Investment firms which disseminate investment research produced by another person to the public or to clients shall be exempt from complying with paragraph 1 if the following criteria are met:

(a) the person that produces the investment research is not a member of the group to which the investment firm belongs;

(b) the investment firm does not substantially alter the recommendations within the investment research;

(c) the investment firm does not present the investment research as having been produced by it;

(d) the investment firm verifies that the producer of the research is subject to requirements equivalent to the requirements under this Regulation in relation to the production of that research, or has established a policy setting such requirements.

Article 38

Additional general requirements in relation to underwriting or placing

(Articles 16(3), 23 and 24 of Directive 2014/65/EU)

1. Investment firms which provide advice on corporate finance strategy, as set out in Section B(3) of Annex I, and provide the service of underwriting or placing of financial instruments, shall, before accepting a mandate to manage the offering, have arrangements in place to inform the issuer client of the following:

(a) the various financing alternatives available with the firm, and an indication of the amount of transaction fees associated with each alternative;

(b) the timing and the process with regard to the corporate finance advice on pricing of the offer;

(c) the timing and the process with regard to the corporate finance advice on placing of the offering;

(d) details of the targeted investors, to whom the firm intends to offer the financial instruments;

(e) the job titles and departments of the relevant individuals involved in the provision of corporate finance advice on the price and allotment of financial instruments; and

(f) firm's arrangements to prevent or manage conflicts of interest that may arise where the firm places the relevant financial instruments with its investment clients or with its own proprietary book.

2. Investment firms shall have in place a centralised process to identify all underwriting and placing operations of the firm and record such information, including the date on which the firm was informed of potential underwriting and placing operations. Firms shall identify all potential conflicts of interest arising from other activities of the investment firm, or group, and implement appropriate management procedures. In cases where an investment firm cannot manage a conflict of interest by way of implementing appropriate procedures, the investment firm shall not engage in the operation.

3. Investment firms providing execution and research services as well as carrying out underwriting and placing activities shall ensure adequate controls are in place to manage any potential conflicts of interest between these activities and between their different clients receiving those services.

Article 39

Additional requirements in relation to pricing of offerings in relation to issuance of financial instruments

(Articles 16(3), 23 and 24 of Directive 2014/65/EU)

1. Investment firms shall have in place systems, controls and procedures to identify and prevent or manage conflicts of interest that arise in relation to possible under-pricing or over-pricing of an issue or involvement of relevant parties in the process. In particular, investment firms shall as a minimum requirement establish, implement and maintain internal arrangements to ensure both of the following:

(a) that the pricing of the offer does not promote the interests of other clients or firm's own interests, in a way that may conflict with the issuer client's interests; and

(b) the prevention or management of a situation where persons responsible for providing services to the firm's investment clients are directly involved in decisions about corporate finance advice on pricing to the issuer client.

2. Investment firms shall provide clients with information about how the recommendation as to the price of the offering and the timings involved is determined. In particular, the firm shall inform and engage with the issuer client about any hedging or stabilisation strategies it intends to undertake with respect to the offering, including how these strategies may impact the issuer clients' interests. During the offering process, firms shall also take all reasonable steps to keep the issuer client informed about developments with respect to the pricing of the issue.

Article 40

Additional requirements in relation to placing

(Articles 16(3), 23 and 24 of Directive 2014/65/EU)

1. Investment firms placing financial instruments shall establish, implement and maintain effective arrangements to prevent recommendations on placing from being inappropriately influenced by any existing or future relationships.

2. Investment firms shall establish, implement and maintain effective internal arrangements to prevent or manage conflicts of interests that arise where persons responsible for providing services to the firm's investment clients are directly involved in decisions about recommendations to the issuer client on allocation.

3. Investment firms shall not accept any third-party payments or benefits unless such payments or benefits comply with the inducements requirements laid down in Article 24 of Directive 2014/65/EU. In particular, the following practices shall be considered not compliant with those requirements and shall therefore be considered not acceptable:

(a) an allocation made to incentivise the payment of disproportionately high fees for unrelated services provided by the investment firm ('laddering'), such as disproportionately high fees or commissions paid by an investment client, or disproportionately high volumes of business at normal levels of commission provided by the investment client as a compensation for receiving an allocation of the issue;

(b) an allocation made to a senior executive or a corporate officer of an existing or potential issuer client, in consideration for the future or past award of corporate finance business ('spinning');

(c) an allocation that is expressly or implicitly conditional on the receipt of future orders or the purchase of any other service from the investment firm by an investment client, or any entity of which the investor is a corporate officer.

4. Investment firms shall establish, implement and maintain an allocation policy that sets out the process for developing allocation recommendations. The allocation policy shall be provided to the issuer client before agreeing to undertake any placing services. The policy shall set out relevant information that is available at that stage, about the proposed allocation methodology for the issue.

5. Investment firms shall involve the issuer client in discussions about the placing process in order for the firm to be able to understand and take into account the client's interests and objectives. The investment firm shall obtain the issuer client's agreement to its proposed allocation per type of client for the transaction in accordance with the allocation policy.

Article 41

Additional requirements in relation to advice, distribution and self-placement

(Articles 16(3), 23 and 24 of Directive 2014/65/EU)

1. Investment firms shall have in place systems, controls and procedures to identify and manage the conflicts of interest that arise when providing investment service to an investment client to participate in a new issue, where the investment firm receives commissions, fees or any monetary or non-monetary benefits in relation to arranging the issuance. Any commissions, fees or monetary or non-monetary benefits shall comply with the requirements in Article 24(7), 24(8) and 24(9) of Directive 2014/65/EU and be documented in the investment firm's conflicts of interest policies and reflected in the firm's inducements arrangements.

2. Investment firms engaging in the placement of financial instruments issued by themselves or by entities within the same group, to their own clients, including their existing depositor clients in the case of credit institutions, or investment funds managed by entities of their group, shall establish, implement and maintain clear and effective arrangements for the identification, prevention or management of the potential conflicts of interest that arise in relation to this type of activity. Such arrangements shall include consideration of refraining from engaging in the activity, where conflicts of interest cannot be appropriately managed so as to prevent any adverse effects on clients.

3. When disclosure of conflicts of interest is required, investment firms shall comply with the requirements in Article 34(4), including an explanation of the nature and source of the conflicts of interest inherent to this type of activity, providing details about the specific risks related to such practices in order to enable clients to make an informed investment decision.

4. Investment firms which offer financial instruments issued that are by themselves or other group entities to their clients and that are included in the calculation of prudential requirements specified in Regulation (EU) No 575/2013 of the European Parliament and of the Council (1), Directive 2013/36/EU of the European Parliament and of the Council (2) or Directive 2014/59/EU of the European Parliament and of the Council (3), shall provide those clients with additional information explaining the differences between the financial instrument and bank deposits in terms of yield, risk, liquidity and any protection provided in accordance with Directive 2014/49/EU of the European Parliament and of the Council (4).

Article 42

Additional requirements in relation to lending or provision of credit in the context of underwriting or placement

(Articles 16(3), 23 and 24 of Directive 2014/65/EU)

1. Where any previous lending or credit to the issuer client by an investment firm, or an entity within the same group, may be repaid with the proceeds of an issue, the investment firm shall have arrangements in place to identify and prevent or manage any conflicts of interest that may arise as a result.

2. Where the arrangements taken to manage conflicts of interest prove insufficient to ensure that the risk of damage to the issuer client would be prevented, investment firms shall disclose to the issuer client the specific conflicts of interest that have arisen in relation to their, or group entities', activities in a capacity of credit provider, and their activities related to the securities offering.

(1) Regulation (EU) No 575/2013 of the European Parliament and of the Council of 26 June 2013 on prudential requirements for credit institutions and investment firms and amending Regulation (EU) No 648/2012 (OJ L 176, 27.6.2013, p. 1).
(2) Directive 2013/36/EU of the European Parliament and of the Council of 26 June 2013 on access to the activity of credit institutions and the prudential supervision of credit institutions and investment firms, amending Directive 2002/87/EC and repealing Directives 2006/48/EC and 2006/49/EC (OJ L 176, 27.6.2013, p. 338).
(3) Directive 2014/59/EU of the European Parliament and of the Council of 15 May 2014 establishing a framework for the recovery and resolution of credit institutions and investment firms and amending Council Directive 82/891/EEC, and Directives 2001/24/EC, 2002/47/EC, 2004/25/EC, 2005/56/EC, 2007/36/EC, 2011/35/EU, 2012/30/EU and 2013/36/EU, and Regulations (EU) No 1093/2010 and (EU) No 648/2012, of the European Parliament and of the Council (OJ L 173, 12.6.2014, p. 190).
(4) Directive 2014/49/EU of the European Parliament and of the Council of 16 April 2014 on deposit guarantee schemes (OJ L 173, 12.6.2014, p. 149).

3. Investment firms' conflict of interest policy shall require the sharing of information about the issuer's financial situation with group entities acting as credit providers, provided this would not breach information barriers set up by the firm to protect the interests of a client.

Article 43

Record keeping in relation to underwriting or placing

(Articles 16(3), 23 and 24 of Directive 2014/65/EU)

Investment firms shall keep records of the content and timing of instructions received from clients. A record of the allocation decisions taken for each operation shall be kept to provide for a complete audit trail between the movements registered in clients' accounts and the instructions received by the investment firm. In particular, the final allocation made to each investment client shall be clearly justified and recorded. The complete audit trail of the material steps in the underwriting and placing process shall be made available to competent authorities upon request.

CHAPTER III

OPERATING CONDITIONS FOR INVESTMENT FIRMS

SECTION 1

Information to clients and potential clients

Article 44

Fair, clear and not misleading information requirements

(Article 24(3) of Directive 2014/65/EU)

1. Investment firms shall ensure that all information they address to, or disseminate in such a way that it is likely to be received by, retail or professional clients or potential retail or professional clients, including marketing communications, satisfies the conditions laid down in paragraphs 2 to 8.

2. Investment firm shall ensure that the information referred to in paragraph 1 complies with the following conditions:

(a) the information includes the name of the investment firm,

(b) the information is accurate and always gives a fair and prominent indication of any relevant risks when referencing any potential benefits of an investment service or financial instrument,

(c) the information uses a font size in the indication of relevant risks that is at least equal to the predominant font size used throughout the information provided, as well as a layout ensuring such indication is prominent,

(d) the information is sufficient for, and presented in a way that is likely to be understood by, the average member of the group to whom it is directed, or by whom it is likely to be received,

(e) the information does not disguise, diminish or obscure important items, statements or warnings,

(f) the information is consistently presented in the same language throughout all forms of information and marketing materials that are provided to each client, unless the client has accepted to receive information in more than one language,

(g) the information is up-to-date and relevant to the means of communication used.

3. Where the information compares investment or ancillary services, financial instruments, or persons providing investment or ancillary services, investment firms shall ensure that the following conditions are satisfied:

(a) the comparison is meaningful and presented in a fair and balanced way;

(b) the sources of the information used for the comparison are specified;

(c) the key facts and assumptions used to make the comparison are included.

4. Where the information contains an indication of past performance of a financial instrument, a financial index or an investment service, investment firms shall ensure that the following conditions are satisfied:

(a) that indication is not the most prominent feature of the communication;

(b) the information must include appropriate performance information which covers the preceding 5 years, or the whole period for which the financial instrument has been offered, the financial index has been established, or the investment service has been provided where less than five years, or such longer period as the firm may decide, and in every case that performance information is based on complete 12-month periods;

(c) the reference period and the source of information is clearly stated;

(d) the information contains a prominent warning that the figures refer to the past and that past performance is not a reliable indicator of future results;

(e) where the indication relies on figures denominated in a currency other than that of the Member State in which the retail client or potential retail client is resident, the currency is clearly stated, together with a warning that the return may increase or decrease as a result of currency fluctuations;

(f) where the indication is based on gross performance, the effect of commissions, fees or other charges are disclosed.

5. Where the information includes or refers to simulated past performance, investment firms shall ensure that the information relates to a financial instrument or a financial index, and the following conditions are satisfied:

(a) the simulated past performance is based on the actual past performance of one or more financial instruments or financial indices which are the same as, or substantially the same as, or underlie, the financial instrument concerned;

(b) in respect of the actual past performance referred to in point (a), the conditions set out in points (a) to (c), (e) and (f) of paragraph 4 are satisfied;

(c) the information contains a prominent warning that the figures refer to simulated past performance and that past performance is not a reliable indicator of future performance.

6. Where the information contains information on future performance, investment firms shall ensure that the following conditions are satisfied:

(a) the information is not based on or refer to simulated past performance;

(b) the information is based on reasonable assumptions supported by objective data;

(c) where the information is based on gross performance, the effect of commissions, fees or other charges is disclosed;

(d) the information is based on performance scenarios in different market conditions (both negative and positive scenarios), and reflects the nature and risks of the specific types of instruments included in the analysis;

(e) the information contains a prominent warning that such forecasts are not a reliable indicator of future performance.

7. Where the information refers to a particular tax treatment, it shall prominently state that the tax treatment depends on the individual circumstances of each client and may be subject to change in the future.

8. The information shall not use the name of any competent authority in such a way that would indicate or suggest endorsement or approval by that authority of the products or services of the investment firm.

Article 45

Information concerning client categorisation

(Article 24(4) of Directive 2014/65/EU)

1. Investment firms shall notify new clients, and existing clients that the investment firm has newly categorised as required by Directive 2014/65/EU, of their categorisation as a retail client, a professional client or an eligible counterparty in accordance with that Directive.

2. Investment firms shall inform clients in a durable medium about any right that client has to request a different categorisation and about any limitations to the level of client protection that a different categorisation would entail.

3. Investment firms may, either on their own initiative or at the request of the client concerned treat a client in the following manner:

(a) as a professional or retail client where that client might otherwise be classified as an eligible counterparty pursuant to Article 30(2) of Directive 2014/65/EU;

(b) a retail client where that client that is considered a professional client pursuant to Section I of Annex II to Directive 2014/65/EU.

Article 46

General requirements for information to clients

(Article 24(4) of Directive 2014/65/EU)

1. Investment firms shall, in good time before a client or potential client is bound by any agreement for the provision of investment services or ancillary services or before the provision of those services, whichever is the earlier to provide that client or potential client with the following information:

(a) the terms of any such agreement;

(b) the information required by Article 47 relating to that agreement or to those investment or ancillary services.

2. Investment firms shall, in good time before the provision of investment services or ancillary services to clients or potential clients, to provide the information required under Articles 47 to 50.

3. The information referred to in paragraphs 1 and 2 shall be provided in a durable medium or by means of a website (where it does not constitute a durable medium) provided that the conditions specified in Article 3(2) are satisfied.

4. Investment firms shall notify a client in good time about any material change to the information provided under Articles 47 to 50 which is relevant to a service that the firm is providing to that client. That notification shall be given in a durable medium if the information to which it relates is given in a durable medium.

5. Investment firms shall ensure that information contained in a marketing communication is consistent with any information the firm provides to clients in the course of carrying on investment and ancillary services.

6. Marketing communications containing an offer or invitation of the following nature and specifying the manner of response or including a form by which any response may be made, shall include such of the information referred to in Articles 47 to 50 as is relevant to that offer or invitation:

(a) an offer to enter into an agreement in relation to a financial instrument or investment service or ancillary service with any person who responds to the communication;

(b) an invitation to any person who responds to the communication to make an offer to enter into an agreement in relation to a financial instrument or investment service or ancillary service.

However, the first subparagraph shall not apply if, in order to respond to an offer or invitation contained in the marketing communication, the potential client must refer to another document or documents, which, alone or in combination, contain that information.

Article 47

Information about the investment firm and its services for clients and potential clients

(Article 24(4) of Directive 2014/65/EU)

1. Investment firms shall provide clients or potential clients with the following general information, where relevant:

(a) the name and address of the investment firm, and the contact details necessary to enable clients to communicate effectively with the firm;

(b) the languages in which the client may communicate with the investment firm, and receive documents and other information from the firm;

(c) the methods of communication to be used between the investment firm and the client including, where relevant, those for the sending and reception of orders;

(d) a statement of the fact that the investment firm is authorised and the name and contact address of the competent authority that has authorised it;

(e) where the investment firm is acting through a tied agent, a statement of this fact specifying the Member State in which that agent is registered;

(f) the nature, frequency and timing of the reports on the performance of the service to be provided by the investment firm to the client in accordance with Article 25(6) of Directive 2014/65/EU;

(g) where the investment firm holds client financial instruments or client funds, a summary description of the steps which it takes to ensure their protection, including summary details of any relevant investor compensation or deposit guarantee scheme which applies to the firm by virtue of its activities in a Member State;

(h) a description, which may be provided in summary form, of the conflicts of interest policy maintained by the firm in accordance with Article 34;

(i) at the request of the client, further details of that conflicts of interest policy in a durable medium or by means of a website (where that does not constitute a durable medium) provided that the conditions set out Article 3(2) are satisfied.

The information listed in points (a) to (i) shall be provided in good time before the provision of investment services or ancillary services to clients or potential clients.

2. When providing the service of portfolio management, investment firms shall establish an appropriate method of evaluation and comparison such as a meaningful benchmark, based on the investment objectives of the client and the types of financial instruments included in the client portfolio, so as to enable the client for whom the service is provided to assess the firm's performance.

3. Where investment firms propose to provide portfolio management services to a client or potential client, they shall provide the client, in addition to the information required under paragraph 1, with such of the following information as is applicable:

(a) information on the method and frequency of valuation of the financial instruments in the client portfolio;

(b) details of any delegation of the discretionary management of all or part of the financial instruments or funds in the client portfolio;

(c) a specification of any benchmark against which the performance of the client portfolio will be compared;

(d) the types of financial instrument that may be included in the client portfolio and types of transaction that may be carried out in such instruments, including any limits;

(e) the management objectives, the level of risk to be reflected in the manager's exercise of discretion, and any specific constraints on that discretion.

The information listed in points (a) to (e) shall be provided in good time before the provision of investment services or ancillary services to clients or potential clients.

Article 48

Information about financial instruments

(Article 24(4) of Directive 2014/65/EU)

1. Investment firms shall provide clients or potential clients in good time before the provision of investment services or ancillary services to clients or potential clients with a general description of the nature and risks of financial instruments, taking into account, in particular, the client's categorisation as either a retail client, professional client or eligible counterparty. That description shall explain the nature of the specific type of instrument concerned, the functioning and performance of the financial instrument in different market conditions, including both positive and negative conditions, as well as the risks particular to that specific type of instrument in sufficient detail to enable the client to take investment decisions on an informed basis.

2. The description of risks referred to in paragraph 1 shall include, where relevant to the specific type of instrument concerned and the status and level of knowledge of the client, the following elements:

(a) the risks associated with that type of financial instrument including an explanation of leverage and its effects and the risk of losing the entire investment including the risks associated with insolvency of the issuer or related events, such as bail in;

(b) the volatility of the price of such instruments and any limitations on the available market for such instruments;

(c) information on impediments or restrictions for disinvestment, for example as may be the case for illiquid financial instruments or financial instruments with a fixed investment term, including an illustration of the possible exit methods and consequences of any exit, possible constraints and the estimated time frame for the sale of the financial instrument before recovering the initial costs of the transaction in that type of financial instruments;

(d) the fact that an investor might assume, as a result of transactions in such instruments, financial commitments and other additional obligations, including contingent liabilities, additional to the cost of acquiring the instruments;

(e) any margin requirements or similar obligations, applicable to instruments of that type.

3. Where an investment firm provides a retail client or potential retail client with information about a financial instrument that is the subject of a current offer to the public and a prospectus has been published in connection with that offer in accordance with Directive 2003/71/EC, that firm shall in good time before the provision of investment services or ancillary services to clients or potential clients inform the client or potential client where that prospectus is made available to the public.

4. Where a financial instrument is composed of two or more different financial instruments or services, the investment firm shall provide an adequate description of the legal nature of the financial instrument, the components of that instrument and the way in which the interaction between the components affects the risks of the investment.

5. In the case of financial instruments that incorporate a guarantee or capital protection, the investment firm shall provide a client or a potential client with information about the scope and nature of such guarantee or capital protection. When the guarantee is provided by a third party, information about the guarantee shall include sufficient detail about the guarantor and the guarantee to enable the client or potential client to make a fair assessment of the guarantee.

Article 49

Information concerning safeguarding of client financial instruments or client funds

(Article 24(4) of Directive 2014/65/EU)

1. Investment firms holding financial instruments or funds belonging to clients shall provide those clients or potential clients with the information specified in paragraphs 2 to 7 where relevant.

2. The investment firm shall inform the client or potential client where the financial instruments or funds of that client may be held by a third party on behalf of the investment firm and of the responsibility of the investment firm under the applicable national law for any acts or omissions of the third party and the consequences for the client of the insolvency of the third party.

3. Where financial instruments of the client or potential client may, if permitted by national law, be held in an omnibus account by a third party, the investment firm shall inform the client of this fact and shall provide a prominent warning of the resulting risks.

4. The investment firm shall inform the client or potential client where it is not possible under national law for client financial instruments held with a third party to be separately identifiable from the proprietary financial instruments of that third party or of the investment firm and shall provide a prominent warning of the resulting risks.

5. The investment firm shall inform the client or potential client where accounts that contain financial instruments or funds belonging to that client or potential client are or will be subject to the law of a jurisdiction other than that of a Member State and shall indicate that the rights of the client or potential client relating to those financial instruments or funds may differ accordingly.

6. An investment firm shall inform the client about the existence and the terms of any security interest or lien which the firm has or may have over the client's financial instruments or funds, or any right of set-off it holds in relation to those instruments or funds. Where applicable, it shall also inform the client of the fact that a depository may have a security interest or lien over, or right of set-off in relation to those instruments or funds.

7. An investment firm, before entering into securities financing transactions in relation to financial instruments held by it on behalf of a client, or before otherwise using such financial instruments for its own account or the account of another client shall in good time before the use of those instruments provide the client, in a durable medium, with clear, full and accurate information on the obligations and responsibilities of the investment firm with respect to the use of those financial instruments, including the terms for their restitution, and on the risks involved.

Article 50

Information on costs and associated charges

(Article 24(4) of Directive 2014/65/EU)

1. For the purposes of providing information to clients on all costs and charges pursuant to Article 24(4) of Directive 2014/65/EU, investment firms shall comply with the detailed requirements in paragraphs 2 to 10.

Without prejudice to the obligations set out in Article 24(4) of Directive 2014/65/EU, investment firms providing investment services to professional clients shall have the right to agree to a limited application of the detailed requirements set out in this Article with these clients. Investment firms shall not be allowed to agree such limitations when the services of investment advice or portfolio management are provided or when, irrespective of the investment service provided, the financial instruments concerned embed a derivative.

Without prejudice to the obligations set out in Article 24(4) of Directive 2014/65/EU, investment firms providing investment services to eligible counterparties shall have the right to agree to a limited application of the detailed requirements set out in this Article, except when, irrespective of the investment service provided, the financial instruments concerned embed a derivative and the eligible counterparty intends to offer them to its clients.

2. For ex-ante and ex-post disclosure of information on costs and charges to clients, investment firms shall aggregate the following:

(a) all costs and associated charges charged by the investment firm or other parties where the client has been directed to such other parties, for the investment services(s) and/or ancillary services provided to the client; and

(b) all costs and associated charges associated with the manufacturing and managing of the financial instruments.

Costs referred to in points (a) and (b) are listed in Annex II to this Regulation. For the purposes of point (a), third party payments received by investment firms in connection with the investment service provided to a client shall be itemised separately and the aggregated costs and charges shall be totalled and expressed both as a cash amount and as a percentage.

3. Where any part of the total costs and charges is to be paid in or represents an amount of foreign currency, investment firms shall provide an indication of the currency involved and the applicable currency conversion rates and costs. Investments firms shall also inform about the arrangements for payment or other performance.

4. In relation to the disclosure of product costs and charges that are not included in the UCITS KIID, the investment firms shall calculate and disclose these costs, for example, by liaising with UCITS management companies to obtain the relevant information.

5. The obligation to provide in good time a full ex-ante disclosure of information about the aggregated costs and charges related to the financial instrument and to the investment or ancillary service provided shall apply to investment firms in the following situations:

(a) where the investment firm recommends or markets financial instruments to clients; or

(b) where the investment firm providing any investment services is required to provide clients with a UCITS KIID or PRIIPs KID in relation to the relevant financial instruments, in accordance with relevant Union legislation.

6. Investment firms that do not recommend or market a financial instrument to the client or are not obliged to provide the client with a KID/KIID in accordance with relevant Union legislation shall inform their clients about all costs and charges relating to the investment and/or ancillary service provided.

7. Where more than one investment firm provides investment or ancillary services to the client, each investment firm shall provide information about the costs of the investment or ancillary services it provides. An investment firm that recommends or markets to its clients the services provided by another firm, shall aggregate the cost and charges of its services together with the cost and charges of the services provided by the other firm. An investment firm shall take into account the costs and charges associated to the provision of other investment or ancillary services by other firms where it has directed the client to these other firms.

8. Where calculating costs and charges on an ex-ante basis, investment firms shall use actually incurred costs as a proxy for the expected costs and charges. Where actual costs are not available, the investment firm shall make reasonable estimations of these costs. Investment firms shall review ex-ante assumptions based on the ex-post experience and shall make adjustment to these assumptions, where necessary.

9. Investment firms shall provide annual ex-post information about all costs and charges related to both the financial instrument(s) and investment and ancillary service(s) where they have recommended or marketed the financial instrument(s) or where they have provided the client with the KID/KIID in relation to the financial instrument(s) and they have or have had an ongoing relationship with the client during the year. Such information shall be based on costs incurred and shall be provided on a personalised basis.

Investment firms may choose to provide such aggregated information on costs and charges of the investment services and the financial instruments together with any existing periodic reporting to clients.

10. Investment firms shall provide their clients with an illustration showing the cumulative effect of costs on return when providing investment services. Such an illustration shall be provided both on an ex-ante and ex-post basis. Investment firms shall ensure that the illustration meets the following requirements:

(a) the illustration shows the effect of the overall costs and charges on the return of the investment;

(b) the illustration shows any anticipated spikes or fluctuations in the costs; and

(c) the illustration is accompanied by a description of the illustration.

Article 51

Information provided in accordance with Directive 2009/65/EU and Regulation (EU) No 1286/2014

(Article 24(4) of Directive 2014/65/EU)

Investment firms distributing units in collective investment undertakings or PRIIPs shall additionally inform their clients about any other costs and associated charges related to the product which may have not been included in the UCITS KID or PRIIPs KID and about the costs and charges relating to their provision of investment services in relation to that financial instrument.

SECTION 2

Investment advice

Article 52

Information about investment advice

(Article 24(4) of Directive 2014/65/EU)

1. Investment firms shall explain in a clear and concise way whether and why investment advice qualifies as independent or non-independent and the type and nature of the restrictions that apply, including, when providing investment advice on an independent basis, the prohibition to receive and retain inducements.

Where advice is offered or provided to the same client on both an independent and non-independent basis, investment firms shall explain the scope of both services to allow investors to understand the differences between them and not present itself f as an independent investment adviser for the overall activity. Firms shall not give undue prominence to their independent investment advice services over non-independent investment services in their communications with clients.

2. Investment firms providing investment advice, on an independent or non-independent basis, shall explain to the client the range of financial instruments that may be recommended, including the firm's relationship with the issuers or providers of the instruments.

3. Investment firms shall provide a description of the types of financial instruments considered, the range of financial instruments and providers analysed per each type of instrument according to the scope of the service, and, when providing independent advice, how the service provided satisfies the conditions for the provision of investment advice on an independent basis and the factors taken into consideration in the selection process used by the investment firm to recommend financial instruments, such as risks, costs and complexity of the financial instruments.

4. When the range of financial instruments assessed by the investment firm providing investment advice on an independent basis includes the investment firm's own financial instruments or those issued or provided by entities having close links or any other close legal or economic relationship with the investment firm as well as other issuers or providers which are not linked or related, the investment firm shall distinguish, for each type of financial instrument, the range of the financial instruments issued or provided by entities not having any links with the investment firm.

5. Investments firms providing a periodic assessment of the suitability of the recommendations provided pursuant to Article 54(12) shall disclose all of the following:

(a) the frequency and extent of the periodic suitability assessment and where relevant, the conditions that trigger that assessment;

(b) the extent to which the information previously collected will be subject to reassessment; and

(c) the way in which an updated recommendation will be communicated to the client.

Article 53

Investment advice on an independent basis

(Article 24(4) and 24(7) of Directive 2014/65/EU)

1. Investment firms providing investment advice on an independent basis shall define and implement a selection process to assess and compare a sufficient range of financial instruments available on the market in accordance with Article 24(7)(a) of Directive 2014/65/EU. The selection process shall include the following elements:

(a) the number and variety of financial instruments considered is proportionate to the scope of investment advice services offered by the independent investment adviser;

(b) the number and variety of financial instruments considered is adequately representative of financial instruments available on the market;

(c) the quantity of financial instruments issued by the investment firm itself or by entities closely linked to the investment firm itself is proportionate to the total amount of financial instruments considered; and

(d) the criteria for selecting the various financial instruments shall include all relevant aspects such as risks, costs and complexity as well as the characteristics of the investment firm's clients, and shall ensure that the selection of the instruments that may be recommended is not biased.

Where such a comparison is not possible due to the business model or the specific scope of the service provided, the investment firm providing investment advice shall not present itself as independent.

2. An investment firm that provides investment advice on an independent basis and that focuses on certain categories or a specified range of financial instruments shall comply with the following requirements:

(a) the firm shall market itself in a way that is intended only to attract clients with a preference for those categories or range of financial instruments;

(b) the firm shall require clients to indicate that they are only interested in investing in the specified category or range of financial instruments; and

(c) prior to the provision of the service, the firm shall ensure that its service is appropriate for each new client on the basis that its business model matches the client's needs and objectives, and the range of financial instruments that are suitable for the client. Where this is not the case the firm shall not provide such a service to the client.

3. An investment firm offering investment advice on both an independent basis and on a non-independent basis shall comply with the following obligations:

(a) in good time before the provision of its services, the investment firm has informed its clients, in a durable medium, whether the advice will be independent or non-independent in accordance with Article 24(4)(a) of Directive 2014/65/EU and the relevant implementing measures;

(b) the investment firm has presented itself as independent for the services for which it provides investment advice on an independent basis;

(c) the investment firms has adequate organisational requirements and controls in place to ensure that both types of advice services and advisers are clearly separated from each other and that clients are not likely to be confused about the type of advice that they are receiving and are given the type of advice that is appropriate for them. The investment firm shall not allow a natural person to provide both independent and non-independent advice.

SECTION 3

Assessment of suitability and appropriateness

Article 54

Assessment of suitability and suitability reports

(Article 25(2) of Directive 2014/65/EU)

1. Investment firms shall not create any ambiguity or confusion about their responsibilities in the process when assessing the suitability of investment services or financial instruments in accordance with Article 25(2) of Directive 2014/65/EU. When undertaking the suitability assessment, the firm shall inform clients or potential clients, clearly and simply, that the reason for assessing suitability is to enable the firm to act in the client's best interest.

Where investment advice or portfolio management services are provided in whole or in part through an automated or semi-automated system, the responsibility to undertake the suitability assessment shall lie with the investment firm providing the service and shall not be reduced by the use of an electronic system in making the personal recommendation or decision to trade.

2. Investment firms shall determine the extent of the information to be collected from clients in light of all the features of the investment advice or portfolio management services to be provided to those clients. Investment firms shall obtain from clients or potential clients such information as is necessary for the firm to understand the essential facts about the client and to have a reasonable basis for determining, giving due consideration to the nature and extent of the service provided, that the specific transaction to be recommended, or entered into in the course of providing a portfolio management service, satisfies the following criteria:

(a) it meets the investment objectives of the client in question, including client's risk tolerance;

(b) it is such that the client is able financially to bear any related investment risks consistent with his investment objectives;

(c) it is such that the client has the necessary experience and knowledge in order to understand the risks involved in the transaction or in the management of his portfolio.

3. Where an investment firm provides an investment service to a professional client it shall be entitled to assume that in relation to the products, transactions and services for which it is so classified, the client has the necessary level of experience and knowledge for the purposes of point (c) of paragraph 2.

Where that investment service consists in the provision of investment advice to a professional client covered by Section 1 of Annex II to Directive 2014/65/EU, the investment firm shall be entitled to assume for the purposes of point (b) of paragraph 2 that the client is able financially to bear any related investment risks consistent with the investment objectives of that client.

4. The information regarding the financial situation of the client or potential client shall include, where relevant, information on the source and extent of his regular income, his assets, including liquid assets, investments and real property, and his regular financial commitments.

5. The information regarding the investment objectives of the client or potential client shall include, where relevant, information on the length of time for which the client wishes to hold the investment, his preferences regarding risk taking, his risk profile, and the purposes of the investment.

6. Where a client is a legal person or a group of two or more natural persons or where one or more natural persons are represented by another natural person, the investment firm shall establish and implement policy as to who should be subject to the suitability assessment and how this assessment will be done in practice, including from whom information about knowledge and experience, financial situation and investment objectives should be collected. The investment firm shall record this policy.

Where a natural person is represented by another natural person or where a legal person having requested treatment as professional client in accordance with Section 2 of Annex II to Directive 2014/65/EU is to be considered for the suitability assessment, the financial situation and investment objectives shall be those of the legal person or, in relation to the natural person, the underlying client rather than of the representative. The knowledge and experience shall be that of the representative of the natural person or the person authorised to carry out transactions on behalf of the underlying client.

7. Investment firms shall take reasonable steps to ensure that the information collected about their clients or potential clients is reliable. This shall include, but shall not be limited to the following:

(a) ensuring clients are aware of the importance of providing accurate and up-to-date information;

(b) ensuring all tools, such as risk assessment profiling tools or tools to assess a client's knowledge and experience, employed in the suitability assessment process are fit-for-purpose and are appropriately designed for use with their clients, with any limitations identified and actively mitigated through the suitability assessment process;

(c) ensuring questions used in the process are likely to be understood by clients, capture an accurate reflection of the client's objectives and needs, and the information necessary to undertake the suitability assessment; and

(d) taking steps, as appropriate, to ensure the consistency of client information, such as by considering whether there are obvious inaccuracies in the information provided by clients.

Investment firms having an on-going relationship with the client, such as by providing an ongoing advice or portfolio management service, shall have, and be able to demonstrate, appropriate policies and procedures to maintain adequate and up-to-date information about clients to the extent necessary to fulfil the requirements under paragraph 2.

8. Where, when providing the investment service of investment advice or portfolio management, an investment firm does not obtain the information required under Article 25(2) of Directive 2014/65/EU, the firm shall not recommend investment services or financial instruments to the client or potential client.

9. Investment firms shall have, and be able to demonstrate, adequate policies and procedures in place to ensure that they understand the nature, features, including costs and risks of investment services and financial instruments selected for their clients and that they assess, while taking into account cost and complexity, whether equivalent investment services or financial instruments can meet their client's profile.

10. When providing the investment service of investment advice or portfolio management, an investment firm shall not recommend or decide to trade where none of the services or instruments are suitable for the client.

11. When providing investment advice or portfolio management services that involve switching investments, either by selling an instrument and buying another or by exercising a right to make a change in regard to an existing instrument, investment firms shall collect the necessary information on the client's existing investments and the recommended new investments and shall undertake an analysis of the costs and benefits of the switch, such that they are reasonably able to demonstrate that the benefits of switching are greater than the costs.

12. When providing investment advice, investment firms shall provide a report to the retail client that includes an outline of the advice given and how the recommendation provided is suitable for the retail client, including how it meets the client's objectives and personal circumstances with reference to the investment term required, client's knowledge and experience and client's attitude to risk and capacity for loss.

Investment firms shall draw clients' attention to and shall include in the suitability report information on whether the recommended services or instruments are likely to require the retail client to seek a periodic review of their arrangements.

Where an investment firm provides a service that involves periodic suitability assessments and reports, the subsequent reports after the initial service is established may only cover changes in the services or instruments involved and/or the circumstances of the client and may not need to repeat all the details of the first report.

13. Investment firms providing a periodic suitability assessment shall review, in order to enhance the service, the suitability of the recommendations given at least annually. The frequency of this assessment shall be increased depending on the risk profile of the client and the type of financial instruments recommended.

Article 55

Provisions common to the assessment of suitability or appropriateness

(Article 25(2) and 25(3) of Directive 2014/65/EU)

1. Investment firms shall ensure that the information regarding a client's or potential client's knowledge and experience in the investment field includes the following, to the extent appropriate to the nature of the client, the nature and extent of the service to be provided and the type of product or transaction envisaged, including their complexity and the risks involved:

(a) the types of service, transaction and financial instrument with which the client is familiar;

(b) the nature, volume, and frequency of the client's transactions in financial instruments and the period over which they have been carried out;

(c) the level of education, and profession or relevant former profession of the client or potential client.

2. An investment firm shall not discourage a client or potential client from providing information required for the purposes of Article 25(2) and (3) of Directive 2014/65/EU.

3. An investment firm shall be entitled to rely on the information provided by its clients or potential clients unless it is aware or ought to be aware that the information is manifestly out of date, inaccurate or incomplete.

Article 56

Assessment of appropriateness and related record-keeping obligations

(Article 25(3) and 25(5) of Directive 2014/65/EU)

1. Investment firms, shall determine whether that client has the necessary experience and knowledge in order to understand the risks involved in relation to the product or investment service offered or demanded when assessing whether an investment service as referred to in Article 25(3) of Directive 2014/65/EU is appropriate for a client.

An investment firm shall be entitled to assume that a professional client has the necessary experience and knowledge in order to understand the risks involved in relation to those particular investment services or transactions, or types of transaction or product, for which the client is classified as a professional client.

2. Investment firms shall maintain records of the appropriateness assessments undertaken which shall include the following:

(a) the result of the appropriateness assessment;

(b) any warning given to the client where the investment service or product purchase was assessed as potentially inappropriate for the client, whether the client asked to proceed with the transaction despite the warning and, where applicable, whether the firm accepted the client's request to proceed with the transaction;

(c) any warning given to the client where the client did not provide sufficient information to enable the firm to undertake an appropriateness assessment, whether the client asked to proceed with the transaction despite this warning and, where applicable, whether the firm accepted the client's request to proceed with the transaction.

Article 57

Provision of services in non-complex instruments

(Article 25(4) of Directive 2014/65/EU)

A financial instrument which is not explicitly specified in Article 25(4)(a) of Directive 2014/65/EU shall be considered as non-complex for the purposes of Article 25(4)(a)(vi) of Directive 2014/65/EU if it satisfies the following criteria:

(a) it does not fall within Article 4(1)(44)(c) of, or points (4) to (11) of Section C of Annex I to Directive 2014/65/EU;

(b) there are frequent opportunities to dispose of, redeem, or otherwise realise that instrument at prices that are publicly available to market participants and that are either market prices or prices made available, or validated, by valuation systems independent of the issuer;

(c) it does not involve any actual or potential liability for the client that exceeds the cost of acquiring the instrument;

(d) it does not incorporate a clause, condition or trigger that could fundamentally alter the nature or risk of the investment or pay out profile, such as investments that incorporate a right to convert the instrument into a different investment;

(e) it does not include any explicit or implicit exit charges that have the effect of making the investment illiquid even though there are technically frequent opportunities to dispose of, redeem or otherwise realise it;

(f) adequately comprehensive information on its characteristics is publicly available and is likely to be readily understood so as to enable the average retail client to make an informed judgment as to whether to enter into a transaction in that instrument.

Article 58

Retail and Professional Client agreements

(Article 24(1) and 25(5) of Directive 2014/65/EU)

Investment firms providing any investment service or the ancillary service referred to in Section B(1) of Annex I to Directive 2014/65/EU to a client after the date of application of this Regulation shall enter into a written basic agreement with the client, in paper or another durable medium, with the client setting out the essential rights and obligations of the firm and the client. Investment firms providing investment advice shall comply with this obligation only where a periodic assessment of the suitability of the financial instruments or services recommended is performed.

The written agreement shall set out the essential rights and obligations of the parties, and shall include the following:

(a) a description of the services, and where relevant the nature and extent of the investment advice, to be provided;

(b) in case of portfolio management services, the types of financial instruments that may be purchased and sold and the types of transactions that may be undertaken on behalf of the client, as well as any instruments or transactions prohibited; and

(c) a description of the main features of any services referred to in Section B(1) of Annex I to Directive 2014/65/EU to be provided, including where applicable the role of the firm with respect to corporate actions relating to client instruments and the terms on which securities financing transactions involving client securities will generate a return for the client.

SECTION 4

Reporting to clients

Article 59

Reporting obligations in respect of execution of orders other than for portfolio management

(Article 25(6) of Directive 2014/65/EU)

1. Investment firms having carried out an order on behalf of a client, other than for portfolio management, shall, in respect of that order:

(a) promptly provide the client, in a durable medium, with the essential information concerning the execution of that order;

(b) send a notice to the client in a durable medium confirming execution of the order as soon as possible and no later than the first business day following execution or, where the confirmation is received by the investment firm from a third party, no later than the first business day following receipt of the confirmation from the third party.

Point (b) shall not apply where the confirmation would contain the same information as a confirmation that is to be promptly dispatched to the client by another person.

Points (a) and (b) shall not apply where orders executed on behalf of clients relate to bonds funding mortgage loan agreements with the said clients, in which case the report on the transaction shall be made at the same time as the terms of the mortgage loan are communicated, but no later than one month after the execution of the order.

2. In addition to the requirements under paragraph 1, investment firms shall supply the client, on request, with information about the status of his order.

3. In the case of client orders relating to units or shares in a collective investment undertaking which are executed periodically, investment firms shall either take the action specified in point (b) of paragraph 1 or provide the client, at least once every six months, with the information listed in paragraph 4 in respect of those transactions.

4. The notice referred to in point (b) of paragraph 1 shall include such of the following information as is applicable and, where relevant, in accordance with the regulatory technical standards on reporting obligations adopted in accordance with Article 26 of Regulation (EU) No 600/2014:

(a) the reporting firm identification;

(b) the name or other designation of the client;

(c) the trading day;

(d) the trading time;

(e) the type of the order;

(f) the venue identification;

(g) the instrument identification;

(h) the buy/sell indicator;

(i) the nature of the order if other than buy/sell;

(j) the quantity;

(k) the unit price;

(l) the total consideration;

(m) a total sum of the commissions and expenses charged and, where the client so requests, an itemised breakdown including, where relevant, the amount of any mark-up or mark-down imposed where the transaction was executed by an investment firm when dealing on own account, and the investment firm owes a duty of best execution to the client;

(n) the rate of exchange obtained where the transaction involves a conversion of currency;

(o) the client's responsibilities in relation to the settlement of the transaction, including the time limit for payment or delivery as well as the appropriate account details where these details and responsibilities have not previously been notified to the client;

(p) where the client's counterparty was the investment firm itself or any person in the investment firm's group or another client of the investment firm, the fact that this was the case unless the order was executed through a trading system that facilitates anonymous trading.

For the purposes of point (k), where the order is executed in tranches, the investment firm may supply the client with information about the price of each tranche or the average price. Where the average price is provided, the investment firm shall supply the client with information about the price of each tranche upon request.

5. The investment firm may provide the client with the information referred to in paragraph 4 using standard codes if it also provides an explanation of the codes used.

Article 60

Reporting obligations in respect of portfolio management

(Article 25(6) of Directive 2014/65/EU)

1. Investments firms which provide the service of portfolio management to clients shall provide each such client with a periodic statement in a durable medium of the portfolio management activities carried out on behalf of that client unless such a statement is provided by another person.

2. The periodic statement required under paragraph 1 shall provide a fair and balanced review of the activities undertaken and of the performance of the portfolio during the reporting period and shall include, where relevant, the following information:

(a) the name of the investment firm;

(b) the name or other designation of the client's account;

(c) a statement of the contents and the valuation of the portfolio, including details of each financial instrument held, its market value, or fair value if market value is unavailable and the cash balance at the beginning and at the end of the reporting period, and the performance of the portfolio during the reporting period;

(d) the total amount of fees and charges incurred during the reporting period, itemising at least total management fees and total costs associated with execution, and including, where relevant, a statement that a more detailed breakdown will be provided on request;

(e) a comparison of performance during the period covered by the statement with the investment performance benchmark (if any) agreed between the investment firm and the client;

(f) the total amount of dividends, interest and other payments received during the reporting period in relation to the client's portfolio;

(g) information about other corporate actions giving rights in relation to financial instruments held in the portfolio;

(h) for each transaction executed during the period, the information referred to in Article 59(4)(c) to (l) where relevant, unless the client elects to receive information about executed transactions on a transaction-by-transaction basis, in which case paragraph 4 of this Article shall apply.

3. The periodic statement referred to in paragraph 1 shall be provided once every three months, except in the following cases:

(a) where the investment firm provides its clients with access to an online system, which qualifies as a durable medium, where up-to-date valuations of the client's portfolio can be accessed and where the client can easily access the information required by Article 63(2) and the firm has evidence that the client has accessed a valuation of their portfolio at least once during the relevant quarter;

(b) in cases where paragraph 4 applies, the periodic statement must be provided at least once every 12 months;

(c) where the agreement between an investment firm and a client for a portfolio management service authorises a leveraged portfolio, the periodic statement must be provided at least once a month.

The exception provided for in point (b) shall not apply in the case of transactions in financial instruments covered by Article 4(1)(44)(c) of, or any of points 4 to 11 of Section C in Annex I to Directive 2014/65/EU.

4. Investment firms, in cases where the client elects to receive information about executed transactions on a transaction-by-transaction basis, shall provide promptly to the client, on the execution of a transaction by the portfolio manager, the essential information concerning that transaction in a durable medium.

The investment firm shall send the client a notice confirming the transaction and containing the information referred to in Article 59(4) no later than the first business day following that execution or, where the confirmation is received by the investment firm from a third party, no later than the first business day following receipt of the confirmation from the third party.

The second subparagraph shall not apply where the confirmation would contain the same information as a confirmation that is to be promptly dispatched to the client by another person.

Article 61

Reporting obligations in respect of eligible counterparties

(Article 24(4) and Article 25(6) of Directive 2014/65/EU)

The requirements applicable to reports for retail and professional clients under Articles 49 and 59 shall apply unless investment firms enter into agreements with eligible counterparties to determine content and timing of reporting.

Article 62

Additional reporting obligations for portfolio management or contingent liability transactions

(Article 25(6) of Directive 2014/65/EU)

1. Investment firms providing the service of portfolio management shall inform the client where the overall value of the portfolio, as evaluated at the beginning of each reporting period, depreciates by 10 % and thereafter at multiples of 10 %, no later than the end of the business day in which the threshold is exceeded or, in a case where the threshold is exceeded on a non-business day, the close of the next business day.

2. Investment firms that hold a retail client account that includes positions in leveraged financial instruments or contingent liability transactions shall inform the client, where the initial value of each instrument depreciates by 10 % and thereafter at multiples of 10 %. Reporting under this paragraph should be on an instrument-by-instrument basis, unless otherwise agreed with the client, and shall take place no later than the end of the business day in which the threshold is exceeded or, in a case where the threshold is exceeded on a non-business day, the close of the next business day.

Article 63

Statements of client financial instruments or client funds

(Article 25(6) of Directive 2014/65/EU)

1. Investment firms that hold client financial instruments or client funds shall send at least on a quarterly basis, to each client for whom they hold financial instruments or funds, a statement in a durable medium of those financial instruments or funds unless such a statement has been provided in any other periodic statement. Upon client request, firms shall provide such statement more frequently at a commercial cost.

The first subparagraph shall not apply to a credit institution authorised under Directive 2000/12/EC of the European Parliament and of the Council [1] in respect of deposits within the meaning of that Directive held by that institution.

[1] Directive 2000/12/EC of the European Parliament and of the Council of 20 March 2000 relating to the taking up and pursuit of the business of credit institutions (OJ L 126, 26.5.2000, p. 1).

2. The statement of client assets referred to in paragraph 1 shall include the following information:

(a) details of all the financial instruments or funds held by the investment firm for the client at the end of the period covered by the statement;

(b) the extent to which any client financial instruments or client funds have been the subject of securities financing transactions;

(c) the extent of any benefit that has accrued to the client by virtue of participation in any securities financing transactions, and the basis on which that benefit has accrued;

(d) a clear indication of the assets or funds which are subject to the rules of Directive 2014/65/EU and its implementing measures and those that are not, such as those that are subject to Title Transfer Collateral Agreement;

(e) a clear indication of which assets are affected by some peculiarities in their ownership status, for instance due to a security interest;

(f) the market or estimated value, when the market value is not available, of the financial instruments included in the statement with a clear indication of the fact that the absence of a market price is likely to be indicative of a lack of liquidity. The evaluation of the estimated value shall be performed by the firm on a best effort basis.

In cases where the portfolio of a client includes the proceeds of one or more unsettled transactions, the information referred to in point (a) may be based either on the trade date or the settlement date, provided that the same basis is applied consistently to all such information in the statement.

The periodic statement of client assets referred to in paragraph 1 shall not be provided where the investment firm provides its clients with access to an online system, which qualifies as a durable medium, where up-to-date statements of client's financial instruments or funds can be easily accessed by the client and the firm has evidence that the client has accessed this statement at least once during the relevant quarter.

3. Investment firms which hold financial instruments or funds and which carry out the service of portfolio management for a client may include the statement of client assets referred to in paragraph 1 in the periodic statement it provides to that client pursuant to Article 60(1).

SECTION 5

Best execution

Article 64

Best execution criteria

(Articles 27(1) and 24(1) of Directive 2014/65/EU)

1. When executing client orders, investment firms shall take into account the following criteria for determining the relative importance of the factors referred to in Article 27(1) of Directive 2014/65/EU:

(a) the characteristics of the client including the categorisation of the client as retail or professional;

(b) the characteristics of the client order, including where the order involves a securities financing transaction (SFT);

(c) the characteristics of financial instruments that are the subject of that order;

(d) the characteristics of the execution venues to which that order can be directed.

For the purposes of this Article and Articles 65 and 66, 'execution venue' includes a regulated market, an MTF, an OTF, a systematic internaliser, or a market maker or other liquidity provider or an entity that performs a similar function in a third country to the functions performed by any of the foregoing.

2. An investment firm satisfies its obligation under Article 27(1) of Directive 2014/65/EU to take all sufficient steps to obtain the best possible result for a client to the extent that it executes an order or a specific aspect of an order following specific instructions from the client relating to the order or the specific aspect of the order.

3. Investment firms shall not structure or charge their commissions in such a way as to discriminate unfairly between execution venues.

4. When executing orders or taking decision to deal in OTC products including bespoke products, the investment firm shall check the fairness of the price proposed to the client, by gathering market data used in the estimation of the price of such product and, where possible, by comparing with similar or comparable products.

Article 65

Duty of investment firms carrying out portfolio management and reception and transmission of orders to act in the best interests of the client

(Article 24(1) and 24(4) of Directive 2014/65/EU)

1. Investment firms, when providing portfolio management, shall comply with the obligation under Article 24(1) of Directive 2014/65/EU to act in accordance with the best interests of their clients when placing orders with other entities for execution that result from decisions by the investment firm to deal in financial instruments on behalf of its client.

2. Investment firms, when providing the service of reception and transmission of orders, shall comply with the obligation under Article 24(1) of Directive 2014/65/EU to act in accordance with the best interests of their clients when transmitting client orders to other entities for execution.

3. In order to comply with paragraphs 1 or 2, investment firms shall comply with paragraphs 4 to 7 of this Article and Article 64(4).

4. Investment firms shall take all sufficient steps to obtain the best possible result for their clients taking into account the factors referred to in Article 27(1) of Directive 2014/65/EU. The relative importance of these factors shall be determined by reference to the criteria set out in Article 64(1) and, for retail clients, to the requirement under Article 27(1) of Directive 2014/65/EU.

An investment firm satisfies its obligations under paragraph 1 or 2, and is not required to take the steps mentioned in this paragraph, to the extent that it follows specific instructions from its client when placing an order with, or transmitting an order to, another entity for execution.

5. Investment firms shall establish and implement a policy that enables them to comply with the obligation in paragraph 4. The policy shall identify, in respect of each class of instruments, the entities with which the orders are placed or to which the investment firm transmits orders for execution. The entities identified shall have execution arrangements that enable the investment firm to comply with its obligations under this Article when it places or transmits orders to that entity for execution.

6. Investment firms shall provide information to their clients on the policy established in accordance with paragraph 5 and paragraphs 2 to 9 of Article 66. Investment firms shall provide clients with appropriate information about the firm and its services and the entities chosen for execution. In particular, when the investment firm select other firms to provide order execution services, it shall summarise and make public, on an annual basis, for each class of financial instruments, the top five investment firms in terms of trading volumes where it transmitted or placed client orders for execution in the preceding year and information on the quality of execution obtained. The information shall be consistent with the information published in accordance with the technical standards developed under Article 27(10)(b) of Directive 2014/65/EU.

Upon reasonable request from a client, investment firms shall provide its clients or potential clients with information about entities where the orders are transmitted or placed for execution.

7. Investment firms shall monitor on a regular basis the effectiveness of the policy established in accordance with paragraph 5 and, in particular, shall monitor the execution quality of the entities identified in that policy and, where appropriate, correct any deficiencies.

Investment firms shall review the policy and arrangements at least annually. Such a review shall also be carried out whenever a material change occurs that affects the firm's ability to continue to obtain the best possible result for their clients.

Investment firms shall assess whether a material change has occurred and shall consider making changes to the execution venues or entities on which they place significant reliance in meeting the overarching best execution requirement.

A material change shall be a significant event that could impact parameters of best execution such as cost, price, speed, likelihood of execution and settlement, size, nature or any other consideration relevant to the execution of the order.

8. This Article shall not apply where the investment firm that provides the service of portfolio management or reception and transmission of orders also executes the orders received or the decisions to deal on behalf of its client's portfolio. In those cases Article 27 of Directive 2014/65/EU shall apply.

Article 66

Execution policy

(Article 27(5) and (7) of Directive 2014/65/EU)

1. Investment firms shall review, at least on an annual basis execution policy established pursuant to Article 27(4) of Directive 2014/65/EU, as well as their order execution arrangements.

Such a review shall also be carried out whenever a material change as defined in Article 65(7) occurs that affects the firm's ability to continue to obtain the best possible result for the execution of its client orders on a consistent basis using the venues included in its execution policy. An investment firm shall assess whether a material change has occurred and shall consider making changes to the relative importance of the best execution factors in meeting the overarching best execution requirement.

2. The information on the execution policy shall be customised depending on the class of financial instrument and type of the service provided and shall include information set out in paragraphs 3 to 9.

3. Investment firms shall provide clients with the following details on their execution policy in good time prior to the provision of the service:

(a) an account of the relative importance the investment firm assigns, in accordance with the criteria specified in Article 59(1), to the factors referred to in Article 27(1) of Directive 2014/65/EU, or the process by which the firm determines the relative importance of those factors.

(b) a list of the execution venues on which the firm places significant reliance in meeting its obligation to take all reasonable steps to obtain on a consistent basis the best possible result for the execution of client orders and specifying which execution venues are used for each class of financial instruments, for retail client orders, professional client orders and SFTs;

(c) a list of factors used to select an execution venue, including qualitative factors such as clearing schemes, circuit breakers, scheduled actions, or any other relevant consideration, and the relative importance of each factor; The information about the factors used to select an execution venue for execution shall be consistent with the controls used by the firm to demonstrate to clients that best execution has been achieved in a consistent basis when reviewing the adequacy of its policy and arrangements;

(d) how the execution factors of price costs, speed, likelihood of execution and any other relevant factors are considered as part of all sufficient steps to obtain the best possible result for the client;

(e) where applicable, information that the firm executes orders outside a trading venue, the consequences, for example counterparty risk arising from execution outside a trading venue, and upon client request, additional information about the consequences of this means of execution;

(f) a clear and prominent warning that any specific instructions from a client may prevent the firm from taking the steps that it has designed and implemented in its execution policy to obtain the best possible result for the execution of those orders in respect of the elements covered by those instructions;

(g) a summary of the selection process for execution venues, execution strategies employed, the procedures and process used to analyse the quality of execution obtained and how the firms monitor and verify that the best possible results were obtained for clients.

That information shall be provided in a durable medium, or by means of a website (where that does not constitute a durable medium) provided that the conditions specified in Article 3(2) are satisfied.

4. Where investment firms apply different fees depending on the execution venue, the firm shall explain these differences in sufficient detail in order to allow the client to understand the advantages and the disadvantages of the choice of a single execution venue.

5. Where investment firms invite clients to choose an execution venue, fair, clear and not misleading information shall be provided to prevent the client from choosing one execution venue rather than another on the sole basis of the price policy applied by the firm.

6. Investment firms shall only receive third-party payments that comply with Article 24(9) of Directive 2014/65/EU and shall inform clients about the inducements that the firm may receive from the execution venues. The information shall specify the fees charged by the investment firm to all counterparties involved in the transaction, and where the fees vary depending on the client, the information shall indicate the maximum fees or range of the fees that may be payable.

7. Where an investment firm charges more than one participant in a transaction, in compliance with Article 24(9) of Directive 2014/65/EU and its implementing measures, the firm shall inform its clients of the value of any monetary or non-monetary benefits received by the firm.

8. Where a client makes reasonable and proportionate requests for information about its policies or arrangements and how they are reviewed to an investment firm, that investment firm shall answer clearly and within a reasonable time.

9. Where an investment firm executes orders for retail clients, it shall provide those clients with a summary of the relevant policy, focused on the total costs they incur. The summary shall also provide a link to the most recent execution quality data published in accordance with Article 27(3) of Directive 2014/65/EU for each execution venue listed by the investment firm in its execution policy.

SECTION 6

Client order handling

Article 67

General principles

(Articles 28(1) and 24(1) of Directive 2014/65/EU)

1. Investment firms shall satisfy the following conditions when carrying out client orders:

(a) ensure that orders executed on behalf of clients are promptly and accurately recorded and allocated;

(b) carry out otherwise comparable client orders sequentially and promptly unless the characteristics of the order or prevailing market conditions make this impracticable, or the interests of the client require otherwise;

(c) inform a retail client about any material difficulty relevant to the proper carrying out of orders promptly upon becoming aware of the difficulty.

2. Where an investment firm is responsible for overseeing or arranging the settlement of an executed order, it shall take all reasonable steps to ensure that any client financial instruments or client funds received in settlement of that executed order are promptly and correctly delivered to the account of the appropriate client.

3. An investment firm shall not misuse information relating to pending client orders, and shall take all reasonable steps to prevent the misuse of such information by any of its relevant persons.

Article 68

Aggregation and allocation of orders

(Articles 28(1) and 24(1) of Directive 2014/65/EU)

1. Investment firms shall not carry out a client order or a transaction for own account in aggregation with another client order unless the following conditions are met:

(a) it is unlikely that the aggregation of orders and transactions will work overall to the disadvantage of any client whose order is to be aggregated;

(b) it is disclosed to each client whose order is to be aggregated that the effect of aggregation may work to its disadvantage in relation to a particular order;

(c) an order allocation policy is established and effectively implemented, providing for the fair allocation of aggregated orders and transactions, including how the volume and price of orders determines allocations and the treatment of partial executions.

2. Where an investment firm aggregates an order with one or more other client orders and the aggregated order is partially executed, it shall allocate the related trades in accordance with its order allocation policy.

Article 69

Aggregation and allocation of transactions for own account

(Articles 28(1) and 24(1) of Directive 2014/65/EU)

1. Investment firms which have aggregated transactions for own account with one or more client orders shall not allocate the related trades in a way that is detrimental to a client.

2. Where an investment firm aggregates a client order with a transaction for own account and the aggregated order is partially executed, it shall allocate the related trades to the client in priority to the firm.

Where an investment firm is able to demonstrate on reasonable grounds that without the combination it would not have been able to carry out the order on such advantageous terms, or at all, it may allocate the transaction for own account proportionally, in accordance with its order allocation policy referred to in Article 68(1)(c).

3. As part of the order allocation policy referred to in Article 68(1)(c), investment firms shall put in place procedures designed to prevent the reallocation, in a way that is detrimental to the client, of transactions for own account which are executed in combination with client orders.

Article 70

Prompt fair and expeditious execution of client orders and publication of unexecuted client limit orders for shares traded on a trading venue

(Article 28 of Directive 2014/65/EU)

1. A client limit order in respect of shares admitted to trading on a regulated market or traded on a trading venue which have not been immediately executed under prevailing market conditions as referred to in Article 28(2) of Directive 2014/65/EU shall be considered available to the public when the investment firm has submitted the order for execution to a regulated market or a MTF or the order has been published by a data reporting services provider located in one Member State and can be easily executed as soon as market conditions allow.

2. Regulated markets and MTFs shall be prioritised according to the firm's execution policy to ensure execution as soon as market conditions allow.

SECTION 7

Eligible counterparties

Article 71

Eligible counterparties

(Article 30 of Directive 2014/65/EU)

1. In addition to the categories which are explicitly set out in Article 30(2) of Directive 2014/65/EU, Member States may recognise as eligible counterparty, in accordance with Article 30(3) of that Directive, an undertaking falling within a category of clients who are to be considered professional clients in accordance with paragraphs 1, 2 and 3 of Section I of Annex II to that Directive.

2. Where, pursuant to the second subparagraph of Article 30(2) of Directive 2014/65/EU, an eligible counterparty requests treatment as a client whose business with an investment firm is subject to Articles 24, 25, 27 and 28 of that Directive, the request should be made in writing, and shall indicate whether the treatment as retail client or professional client refers to one or more investment services or transactions, or one or more types of transaction or product.

3. Where an eligible counterparty requests treatment as a client whose business with an investment firm is subject to Articles 24, 25, 27 and 28 of Directive 2014/65/EU, but does not expressly request treatment as a retail client, the firm shall treat that eligible counterparty as a professional client.

4. Where the eligible counterparty expressly requests treatment as a retail client, the investment firm shall treat the eligible counterparty as a retail client, applying the provisions in respect of requests of non-professional treatment specified in the second, third and fourth sub-paragraphs of Section I of Annex II to Directive 2014/65/EU.

5. Where a client requests to be treated as an eligible counterparty, in accordance with Article 30(3) of Directive 2014/65/EU, the following procedure shall be followed:

(a) the investment firm shall provide the client with a clear written warning of the consequences for the client of such a request, including the protections they may lose;

(b) the client shall confirm in writing the request to be treated as an eligible counterparty either generally or in respect of one or more investment services or a transaction or type of transaction or product and that they are aware of the consequences of the protection they may lose as a result of the request.

SECTION 8

Record-keeping

Article 72

Retention of records

(Article 16(6) of Directive 2014/65/EU)

1. The records shall be retained in a medium that allows the storage of information in a way accessible for future reference by the competent authority, and in such a form and manner that the following conditions are met:

(a) the competent authority is able to access them readily and to reconstitute each key stage of the processing of each transaction;

(b) it is possible for any corrections or other amendments, and the contents of the records prior to such corrections or amendments, to be easily ascertained;

(c) it is not possible for the records otherwise to be manipulated or altered;

(d) it allows IT or any other efficient exploitation when the analysis of the data cannot be easily carried out due to the volume and the nature of the data; and

(e) the firm's arrangements comply with the record keeping requirements irrespective of the technology used.

2. Investment firms shall keep at least the records identified in Annex I to this Regulation depending upon the nature of their activities.

The list of records identified in Annex I to this Regulation is without prejudice to any other record-keeping obligations arising from other legislation.

3. Investment firms shall also keep records of any policies and procedures they are required to maintain pursuant to Directive 2014/65/EU, Regulation (EU) No 600/2014, Directive 2014/57/EU and Regulation (EU) No 596/2014 and their respective implementing measures in writing.

Competent authorities may require investment firms to keep additional records to the list identified in Annex I to this Regulation.

Article 73

Record keeping of rights and obligations of the investment firm and the client

(Article 25(5) of Directive 2014/65/EU)

Records which set out the respective rights and obligations of the investment firm and the client under an agreement to provide services, or the terms on which the firm provides services to the client, shall be retained for at least the duration of the relationship with the client.

Article 74

Record keeping of client orders and decision to deal

(Article 16(6) of Directive 2014/65/EU)

An investment firm shall, in relation to every initial order received from a client and in relation to every initial decision to deal taken, immediately record and keep at the disposal of the competent authority at least the details set out in Section 1 of Annex IV to this Regulation to the extent they are applicable to the order or decision to deal in question.

Where the details set out in Section 1 of Annex IV to this Regulation are also prescribed under Articles 25 and 26 of Regulation (EU) No 600/2014, these details should be maintained in a consistent way and according to the same standards prescribed under Articles 25 and 26 of Regulation (EU) No 600/2014.

Article 75

Record keeping of transactions and order processing

(Article 16(6) of Directive 2014/65/EU)

Investment firms shall, immediately after receiving a client order or making a decision to deal to the extent they are applicable to the order or decision to deal in question, record and keep at the disposal of the competent authority at least the details set out in Section 2 of Annex IV.

Where the details set out in Section 2 of Annex IV are also prescribed under Articles 25 and 26 of Regulation (EU) No 600/2014, they shall be maintained in a consistent way and according to the same standards prescribed under Articles 25 and 26 of Regulation (EU) No 600/2014.

Article 76

Recording of telephone conversations or electronic communications

(Article 16(7) of Directive 2014/65/EU)

1. Investment firms shall establish, implement and maintain an effective recording of telephone conversations and electronic communications policy, set out in writing, and appropriate to the size and organisation of the firm, and the nature, scale and complexity of its business. The policy shall include the following content:

(a) the identification of the telephone conversations and electronic communications, including relevant internal telephone conversations and electronic communications, that are subject to the recording requirements in accordance with Article 16(7) of Directive 2014/65/EU; and

(b) the specification of the procedures to be followed and measures to be adopted to ensure the firm's compliance with the third and eighth subparagraphs of Article 16(7) of Directive 2014/65/EU where exceptional circumstances arise and the firm is unable to record the conversation/communication on devices issued, accepted or permitted by the firm. Evidence of such circumstances shall be retained and shall be accessible to competent authorities.

2. Investment firms shall ensure that the management body has effective oversight and control over the policies and procedures relating to the firm's recording of telephone conversations and electronic communications.

3. Investment firms shall ensure that the arrangements to comply with recording requirements are technology-neutral. Firms shall periodically evaluate the effectiveness of the firm's policies and procedures and adopt any such alternative or additional measures and procedures as are necessary and appropriate. At a minimum, such adoption of alternative or additional measures shall occur when a new medium of communication is accepted or permitted for use by the firm.

4. Investment firms shall keep and regularly update a record of those individuals who have firm devices or privately owned devices that have been approved for use by the firm.

5. Investment firms shall educate and train employees in procedures governing the requirements in Article 16(7) of Directive 2014/65/EU.

6. To monitor compliance with the recording and record-keeping requirements in accordance with Article 16(7) of Directive 2014/65/EU, investment firms shall periodically monitor the records of transactions and orders subject to these requirements, including relevant conversations. Such monitoring shall be risk based and proportionate.

7. Investment firms shall demonstrate the policies, procedures and management oversight of the recording rules to the relevant competent authorities upon request.

8. Before investment firms provide investment services and activities relating to the reception, transmission and execution of orders to new and existing clients, firms shall inform the client of the following:

(a) that the conversations and communications are being recorded; and

(b) that a copy of the recording of such conversations with the client and communications with the client will be available on request for a period of five years and, where requested by the competent authority, for a period of up to seven years.

The information referred to in the first sub-paragraph shall be presented in the same language(s) as that used to provide investment services to clients.

9. Investment firms shall record in a durable medium all relevant information related to relevant face-to-face conversations with clients. The information recorded shall include at least the following:

(a) date and time of meetings;

(b) location of meetings;

(c) identity of the attendees;

(d) initiator of the meetings; and

(e) relevant information about the client order including the price, volume, type of order and when it shall be transmitted or executed.

10. Records shall be stored in a durable medium, which allows them to be replayed or copied and must be retained in a format that does not allow the original record to be altered or deleted.

Records shall be stored in a medium so that they are readily accessible and available to clients on request.

Firms shall ensure the quality, accuracy and completeness of the records of all telephone recordings and electronic communications.

11. The period of time for the retention of a record shall begin on the date when the record is created.

SECTION 9

SME growth markets

Article 77

Qualification as an SME

(Article 4(1)(13) of Directive 2014/65/EU)

1. An issuer whose shares have been admitted to trading for less than three years shall be deemed an SME for the purpose of point (a) of Article 33(3) of Directive 2014/65/EU where its market capitalisation is below EUR 200 million based on any of the following:

(a) the closing share price of the first day of trading, if its shares have been admitted to trading for less than one year;

(b) the last closing share price of the first year of trading, if its shares have been admitted to trading for more than one year but less than two years;

(c) the average of the last closing share prices of each of the first two years of trading, if its shares have been admitted to trading for more than two years but less than three years.

2. An issuer which has no equity instrument traded on any trading venue shall be deemed an SME for the purpose of Article 4(1)(13) of Directive 2014/65/EU if, according to its last annual or consolidated accounts, it meets at least two of the following three criteria: an average number of employees during the financial year of less than 250, a total balance sheet not exceeding EUR 43 000 000 and an annual net turnover not exceeding EUR 50 000 000.

Article 78

Registration as an SME growth market

(Article 33(3) of Directive 2014/65/EU)

1. When determining whether at least 50 % of the issuers admitted to trading on an MTF are SMEs for the purposes of registration as an SME growth market in accordance with point (a) of Article 33(3) of Directive 2014/65/EU, the competent authority of the home Member State of the operator of an MTF shall calculate the average ratio of SMEs over the total number of issuers whose financial instruments are admitted to trading on that market. The average ratio shall be calculated on 31 December of the previous calendar year as the average of the twelve end-of-month ratios of that calendar year.

Without prejudice to the other conditions for registration specified in points (b) to (g) of Article 33(3) of Directive 2014/65/EU, the competent authority shall register as an SME growth market an applicant with no previous operating history and, after three calendar years have elapsed, shall verify that it complies with the minimum proportion of SMEs, as determined in accordance with the first subparagraph.

2. With regard to the criteria laid out in points (b), (c), (d) and (f) of Article 33(3) of Directive 2014/65/EU, the competent authority of the home Member State of the operator of an MTF shall not register the MTF as an SME growth market unless it is satisfied that the MTF:

(a) has established and applies rules providing for objective and transparent criteria for the initial and ongoing admission to trading of issuers on its venue;

(b) has an operating model which is appropriate for the performance of its functions and ensures the maintenance of fair and orderly trading in the financial instruments admitted to trading on its venue;

(c) has established and applies rules that require an issuer seeking admission of its financial instruments to trading on the MTF, to publish, in cases where Directive 2003/71/EC does not apply, an appropriate admission document, drawn up under the responsibility of the issuer and clearly stating whether or not it has been approved or reviewed and by whom;

(d) has established and applies rules that define the minimum content of the admission document referred to under point (c), in such a way that sufficient information is provided to investors to enable them to make an informed assessment of the financial position and prospects of the issuer, and the rights attaching to its securities;

(e) requires the issuer to state, in the admission document referred to under point (c), whether or not, in its opinion, its working capital is sufficient for its present requirements or, if not, how it proposes to provide the additional working capital needed;

(f) has made arrangements for the admission document referred to under point (c) to be subject to an appropriate review of its completeness, consistency and comprehensibility;

(g) requires the issuers whose securities are traded on its venue to publish annual financial reports within 6 months after the end of each financial year, and half yearly financial reports within 4 months after the end of the first 6 months of each financial year;

(h) ensures dissemination to the public of prospectuses drawn up in accordance with Directive 2003/71/EC, admission documents referred to under point (c), financial reports referred to under point (g) and information defined in Article 7(1) of Regulation (EU) No 596/2014 publicly disclosed by the issuers whose securities are traded on its venue, by publishing them on its website, or providing thereon a direct link to the page of the website of the issuers where such documents, reports and information are published;

(i) ensures that the regulatory information referred to under point (h) and direct links remain available on its website for a period of at least five years.

Article 79

Deregistration as an SME growth market

(Article 33(3) of Directive 2014/65/EU)

1. With regard to the proportion of SMEs, and without prejudice to the other conditions specified in points (b) to (g) of Article 33(3) of Directive 2014/65/EU and in Article 78(2) of this Regulation, an SME growth market shall only be deregistered by the competent authority of its home Member State where the proportion of SMEs, as determined in accordance with the first subparagraph of Article 78(1) of this Regulation, falls below 50 % for three consecutive calendar years.

2. With regard to the conditions specified in points (b) to (g) of Article 33(3) of Directive 2014/65/EU and in Article 78(2) of this Regulation, the operator of an SME growth market shall be deregistered by the competent authority of its home Member State where such conditions are no longer satisfied.

CHAPTER IV

OPERATING OBLIGATIONS FOR TRADING VENUES

Article 80

Circumstances constituting significant damage to investors' interests and the orderly functioning of the market

(Articles 32(1), 32(2), 52(1) and 52(2) of Directive 2014/65/EU)

1. For the purpose of Articles 32(1), 32(2), 52(1) and 52(2) of Directive 2014/65/EU, a suspension or a removal from trading of a financial instrument shall be deemed likely to cause significant damage to investors' interests or the orderly functioning of the market at least in the following circumstances:

(a) where it would create a systemic risk undermining financial stability, such as where the need exists to unwind a dominant market position, or where settlement obligations would not be met in a significant volume;

(b) where the continuation of trading on the market is necessary to perform critical post-trade risk management functions when there is a need for the liquidation of financial instruments due to the default of a clearing member under the default procedures of a CCP and a CCP would be exposed to unacceptable risks as a result of an inability to calculate margin requirements;

(c) where the financial viability of the issuer would be threatened, such as where it is involved in a corporate transaction or capital raising.

2. For the purpose of determining whether a suspension or a removal is likely to cause significant damage to the investors' interest or the orderly functioning of the markets in any particular case, the national competent authority, a market operator operating a regulated market or an investment firm or a market operator operating an MTF or an OTF shall consider all relevant factors, including:

(a) the relevance of the market in terms of liquidity where the consequences of the actions are likely to be more significant where those markets are more relevant in terms of liquidity than in other markets;

(b) the nature of the envisaged action where actions with a sustained or lasting impact on the ability of investors to trade a financial instrument on trading venues, such as removals, are likely to have a greater impact on investors than other actions;

(c) the knock-on effects of a suspension or removal of sufficiently related derivatives, indices or benchmarks for which the removed or suspended instrument serves as an underlying or constituent;

(d) the effects of a suspension on the interests of market end users who are not financial counterparties, such as entities trading in financial instruments to hedge commercial risks.

3. The factors set out in paragraph 2 shall also be taken into consideration where a national competent authority, a market operator operating a regulated market or an investment firm or a market operator operating an MTF or an OTF decides not to suspend or remove a financial instrument on the basis of circumstances not covered by the list of paragraph 1.

Article 81

Circumstances where significant infringements of the rules of a trading venue or disorderly trading conditions or system disruptions in relation to a financial instrument may be assumed

(Articles 31(2) and 54(2) of Directive 2014/65/EU)

1. When assessing whether the requirement to immediately inform their competent authorities of significant infringements of the rules of their trading venue or disorderly trading conditions or system disruptions in relation to a financial instrument applies, operators of trading venues shall consider the signals listed in Section A of Annex III to this Regulation.

2. Information shall only be required in cases of significant events which have the potential to jeopardise the role and function of trading venues as part of the financial market infrastructure.

Article 82

Circumstances where a conduct indicating behaviour that is prohibited under Regulation (EU) No 596/2014 may be assumed

(Articles 31(2) and 54(2) of Directive 2014/65/EU)

1. When assessing whether the requirement to immediately inform their competent authorities of conduct that may indicate behaviour that is prohibited under Regulation (EU) No 596/2014 applies, operators of trading venues shall consider the signals listed in Section B of Annex III to this Regulation.

2. The operator of one or several trading venues where a financial instrument and/or related financial instrument are traded shall apply a proportionate approach and shall exercise judgment on the signals triggered, including any relevant signals not specifically included in Section B of Annex III to this Regulation, before informing the relevant national competent authority, taking into account the following:

(a) the deviations from the usual trading pattern of the financial instruments admitted to trading or traded on its trading venue; and

(b) the information available or accessible to the operator, whether that be internally as part of the operations of the trading venue or publicly available.

3. The operator of one or several trading venues shall take into account front running behaviours, which consist in a market member or participant trading, for its own account, ahead of its client, and shall use for that purpose the order book data required to be recorded by the trading venue pursuant to Article 25 of Regulation (EU) No 600/2014, in particular those relating to the way the member or participant conducts its trading activity.

CHAPTER V

POSITION REPORTING IN COMMODITY DERIVATIVES

Article 83

Position reporting

(Article 58(1) of Directive 2014/65/EU)

1. For the purpose of the weekly reports referred to in Art 58(1)(a) of Directive 2014/65/EU, the obligation for a trading venue to make public such a report shall apply when both of the following two thresholds are met:

(a) 20 open position holders exist in a given contract on a given trading venue; and

(b) the absolute amount of the gross long or short volume of total open interest, expressed in the number of lots of the relevant commodity derivative, exceeds a level of four times the deliverable supply in the same commodity derivative, expressed in number of lots.

Where the commodity derivative does not have a physically deliverable underlying asset and for emission allowances and derivatives thereof, point (b) shall not apply.

2. The threshold set out in point (a) of paragraph 1 shall apply in aggregate on the basis of all of the categories of persons regardless of the numbers of position holders in any single category of persons.

3. For contracts where there are less than five position holders active in a given category of persons, the number of position holders in that category shall not be published.

4. For contracts that meet the conditions set out in points (a) and (b) of paragraph 1 for the first time, trading venues shall publish the contracts first weekly report as soon as it is feasibly practical, and in any event no later than 3 weeks from the date on which the thresholds are first triggered.

5. Where the conditions set out in points (a) and (b) of paragraph 1 are no longer met, trading venues shall continue to publish the weekly reports for a period of three months. The obligation to publish the weekly report no longer applies where the conditions set out in points (a) and (b) of paragraph 1 have not been met continuously upon expiry of that period.

CHAPTER VI

DATA PROVISION OBLIGATIONS FOR DATA REPORTING SERVICE PROVIDERS

Article 84

Obligation to provide market data on a reasonable commercial basis

(Article 64(1) and 65(1) of Directive 2014/65/EU)

1. For the purposes of making market data containing the information set out in Articles 6, 20 and 21 of Regulation (EU) No 600/2014 available to the public on a reasonable commercial basis in accordance with Articles 64(1) and 65(1) of Directive 2014/65/EU, approved publication arrangements (APAs) and consolidated tape providers (CTPs) shall comply with the obligations set out in Articles 85 to 89.

2. Articles 85, 86(2), 87, 88(2) and 89 shall not apply to APAs or CTPs that make market data available to the public free of charge.

Article 85

Provision of market data on the basis of cost

(Article 64(1) and 65(1) of Directive 2014/65/EU)

1. The price of market data shall be based on the cost of producing and disseminating such data and may include a reasonable margin.

2. The costs of producing and disseminating market data may include an appropriate share of joint costs for other service provided by APAs and CTPs.

Article 86

Obligation to provide market data on a non-discriminatory basis

(Article 64(1) and 65(1) of Directive 2014/65/EU)

1. APAs and CTPs shall make market data available at the same price and on the same terms and conditions to all customers falling within the same category in accordance with published objective criteria.

2. Any differentials in prices charged to different categories of customers shall be proportionate to the value which the market data represent to those customers, taking into account:

(a) the scope and scale of the market data including the number of financial instruments covered and trading volume;

(b) the use made by the customer of the market data, including whether it is used for the customer's own trading activities, for resale or for data aggregation.

3. For the purposes of paragraph 1, APAs and CTPs shall have scalable capacities in place to ensure that customers can obtain timely access to market data at all times on a non-discriminatory basis.

Article 87

Per user fees

(Article 64(1) and 65(1) of Directive 2014/65/EU)

1. APAs and CTPs shall charge for the use of market data on the basis of the use made by individual end-users of the market data ('per user basis'). APAs and CTPs shall have arrangements in place to ensure that each individual use of market data is charged only once.

2. By way of derogation from paragraph 1, APAs and CTPs may decide not to make market data available on a per user basis where to charge on a per user basis is disproportionate to the cost of making market data available, having regard to the scale and scope of the market data.

3. APAs or CTPs shall provide grounds for the refusal to make market data available on a per user basis and shall publish those grounds on their webpage.

Article 88

Unbundling and disaggregating market data

(Article 64(1) and 65(1) of Directive 2014/65/EU)

1. APAs and CTPs shall make market data available without being bundled with other services.

2. Prices for market data shall be charged on the basis of the level of market data disaggregation provided for in Article 12(1) of Regulation (EU) No 600/2014 as further specified in Articles of Commission Delegated Regulation (EU) 2017/572 [1].

Article 89

Transparency obligation

(Article 64(1) and 65(1) of Directive 2014/65/EU)

1. APAs and CTPs shall disclose and make easily available to the public the price and other terms and conditions for the provision of the market data in a manner which is easily accessible.

2. The disclosure shall include the following:

(a) current price lists, including the following information:

(i) fees per display user;

(ii) non-display fees;

(iii) discount policies;

(iv) fees associated with licence conditions;

(v) fees for pre-trade and for post-trade market data;

(vi) fees for other subsets of information, including those required in accordance with the regulatory technical standards pursuant to Article 12(2) of Regulation (EU) No 600/2014;

(vii) other contractual terms and conditions;

(b) advance disclosure with a minimum of 90 days' notice of future price changes;

(c) information on the content of the market data including the following information:

(i) the number of instruments covered;

(ii) the total turnover of instruments covered;

(iii) pre-trade and post-trade market data ratio;

(iv) information on any data provided in addition to market data;

(v) the date of the last licence fee adaption for market data provided;

(d) revenue obtained from making market data available and the proportion of that revenue compared to total revenue of the APA or CTP;

(e) information on how the price was set, including the cost accounting methodologies used and information about the specific principles according to which direct and variable joint costs are allocated and fixed joint costs are apportioned, between the production and dissemination of market data and other services provided by APAs and CTPs.

CHAPTER VII

COMPETENT AUTHORITIES AND FINAL PROVISIONS

Article 90

Determination of the substantial importance of the operations of a trading venue in a host Member State

(Article 79(2) of Directive 2014/65/EU)

1. The operations of a regulated market in a host Member State shall be considered to be of substantial importance for the functioning of the securities markets and the protection of investors in that host Member State where at least one of the following criteria is met:

(a) the host Member State has formerly been the home Member State of the regulated market in question;

[1] Commission Delegated Regulation (EU) 2017/572 of 2 June 2016 supplementing Regulation (EU) No 600/2014 of the European Parliament and of the Council with regard to regulatory technical standards on the specification of the offering of pre-and post-trade data and the level of disaggregation of data (see page 142 of this Official Journal).

(b) the regulated market in question has acquired through merger, takeover, or any other form of transfer of the whole or part of the business of a regulated market which was previously operated by a market operator which had its registered office or head office in the host Member State.

2. The operations of an MTF or OTF in a host Member State shall be considered to be of substantial importance for the functioning of the securities markets and the protection of investors in that host Member State where at least one of the criteria laid down in paragraph 1 is met in regard to that MTF or OTF and at least one of the following additional criteria is met:

(a) before one of the situations set out in paragraph 1 occurred in regard to the MTF or OTF, the trading venue had a market share of at least 10 % of trading in terms of total turnover in monetary terms in on-venue trading and systematic internaliser trading in the host Member State in at least one asset class subject to the transparency obligations of Regulation (EU) No 600/2014;

(b) the MTF or OTF is registered as an SME growth market.

CHAPTER VIII

FINAL PROVISIONS

Article 91

Entry into force and application

This Regulation shall enter into force on the twentieth day following that of its publication in the *Official Journal of the European Union*.

It shall apply from the date that appears first in the second subparagraph of Article 93(1) of Directive 2014/65/EU.

This Regulation shall be binding in its entirety and directly applicable in all Member States.

Done at Brussels, 25 April 2016.

For the Commission

The President

Jean-Claude JUNCKER

ANNEX I

Record-keeping

Minimum list of records to be kept by investment firms depending upon the nature of their activities

Nature of obligation	Type of record	Summary of content	Legislative reference
Client assessment			
	Information to clients	Content as provided for under Article 24(4) of Directive 2014/65/EU and Articles 39 to 45 of this Regulation	Article 24(4) MIFID II Articles 39 to 45 of this Regulation
	Client agreements	Records as provided for under Article 25(5) of Directive 2014/65/EU	Article 25(5) MIFID II Article 53 of this Regulation
	Assessment of suitability and appropriateness	Content as provided for under Article 25(2) and (3) of Directive 2014/65/EU and Article 50 of this Regulation	Article 25(2) and (3) of Directive 2014/65/EU Articles 35, 36 and 37 of this Regulation
Order handling			
	Client order-handling — Aggregated transactions	Records as provided for under Articles 63 to 66 of this Regulation	Articles 24(1) and 28(1) of Directive 2014/65/EU Articles 63 to 66 of this Regulation
	Aggregation and allocation of trans-actions for own account	Records as provided for under Article 65 of this Regulation	Articles 28(1) and 24(1) of Directive 2014/65/EU Article 65 of this Regulation
Client Orders and transactions			
	Record keeping of client orders or decision to deal	Records as provided for under Article 69 of this Regulation	Article 16(6) of Directive 2014/65/EU Article 69 of this Regulation
	Record keeping of transactions and order processing	Records as provided for under Article 70 of this Regulation	Article 16(6) of Directive 2014/65/EU Article 70 of this Regulation
Reporting to clients			
	Obligation in respect of services provided to clients	Contents as provided for under Articles 53 to 58 of this Regulation	Article 24(1) and (6) and Article 25(1) and (6) of Directive 2014/65/EU Articles 53 to 58 of this Regulation
Safeguarding of client assets			
	Client financial instruments held by an investment firm	Records as provided for under Article 16(8) of Directive 2014/65/EU and under Article 2 of Commission Delegated Directive (EU) 2017/593	Article 16(8) of Directive 2014/65/EU Article 2 of Delegated Directive (EU) 2017/593

Nature of obligation	Type of record	Summary of content	Legislative reference
	Client funds held by an investment firm	Records as provided for under Article 16(9) of Directive 2014/65/EU and under Article 2 of Delegated Directive (EU) 2017/593	Article 16(9) of Directive 2014/65/EU Article 2 of Delegated Directive (EU) 2017/593
	Use of client financial instruments	Records provided for under Article 5 of Delegated Directive (EU) 2017/593	Article 16(8) to (10) of Directive 2014/65/EU Article 5 of Delegated Directive (EU) 2017/593

Communication with clients

Nature of obligation	Type of record	Summary of content	Legislative reference
	Information about Costs and associated charges	Contents as provided for under Article 45 of this Regulation	Article 24(4)(c) of Directive 2014/65/EU Article 45 of this Regulation
	Information about the investment firm and its services, financial instruments and safe-guarding of client assets	Content as provided for under Articles 45 and 46 of this Regulation	Article 24(4) of Directive 2014/65/EU Articles 45 and 46 of this Regulation
	Information to clients	Records of communication	Article 24(3) of Directive 2014/65/EU Article 39 of this Regulation
	Marketing communications (except in oral form)	Each marketing communication issued by the investment firm (except in oral form) as provided under Articles 36 and 37 of this Regulation	Article 24(3) of Directive 2014/65/EU Articles 36 and 37 of this Regulation
	Investment advice to retail clients	(i) The fact, time and date that investment advice was rendered and (ii) the financial instrument that was recommended (iii) the suitability report provided to the client	Article 25(6) of Directive 2014/65/EU Article 54 of this Regulation
	Investment research	Each item of investment research issued by the investment firm in a durable medium	Article 24(3) of Directive 2014/65/EU Articles 36 and 37 of this Regulation

Organisational requirements

Nature of obligation	Type of record	Summary of content	Legislative reference
	The firm's business and internal organisation	Records as provided for under Article 21(1)(h) of this Regulation	Article 16(2) to (10) of Directive 2014/65/EU Article 21(1)(h) of this Regulation
	Compliance reports	Each compliance report to management body	Article 16(2) of Directive 2014/65/EU Article 22(2)(b) and Article 25(2) of this Regulation
	Conflict of Interest record	Records as provided for under Article 35 of this Regulation	Article 16(3) of Directive 2014/65/EU Article 35 of this Regulation

Nature of obligation	Type of record	Summary of content	Legislative reference
	Inducements	The information dis-closed to clients under Article 24(9) of Directive 2014/65/EU	Article 24(9) of Directive 2014/65/EU Article 11 of Delegated Directive (EU) 2017/593
	Risk management reports	Each risk management report to senior management	Article 16(5) of Directive 2014/65/EU Article 23(1)(b) and Article 25(2) of this Regulation
	Internal audit reports	Each internal audit report to senior management	Article 16(5) of Directive 2014/65/EU Article 24 and Article 25(2) of this Regulation
	Complaints-handling records	Each complaint and the complaint handling measures taken to address the complaint	Article 16(2) of Directive 2014/65/EU Article 26 of this Regulation
	Records of personal transactions	Records as provided for under Article 29(2)(c) of this Regulation	Article 16(2) of Directive 2014/65/EU Article 29(2)(c) of this Regulation

ANNEX II

Costs and charges

Identified costs that should form part of the costs to be disclosed to the clients [1]

Table 1 — All costs and associated charges charged for the investment service(s) and/or ancillary services provided to the client that should form part of the amount to be disclosed

Cost items to be disclosed		Examples:
One-off charges related to the provision of an investment service	All costs and charges paid to the investment firm at the beginning or at the end of the provided investment service(s).	Deposit fees, termination fees and switching costs [1].
Ongoing charges related to the provision of an investment service	All ongoing costs and charges paid to investment firms for their services provided to the client.	Management fees, advisory fees, custodian fees.
All costs related to transactions initiated in the course of the provision of an investment service	All costs and charges that are related to transactions performed by the investment firm or other parties.	Broker commissions [2], entry- and exit-charges paid to the fund manager, platform fees, mark ups (embedded in the transaction price), stamp duty, transactions tax and foreign exchange costs.
Any charges that are related to ancillary services	Any costs and charges that are related to ancillary services that are not included in the costs mentioned above.	Research costs. Custody costs.
Incidental costs		Performance fees

(1) Switching costs should be understood as costs (if any) that are incurred by investors by switching from one investment firm to another investment firm.
(2) Broker commissions should be understood as costs that are charged by investment firms for the execution of orders.

Table 2 — All costs and associated charges related to the financial instrument that should form part of the amount to be disclosed

Cost items to be disclosed		Examples:
One-off charges	All costs and charges (included in the price or in addition to the price of the financial instrument) paid to product suppliers at the beginning or at the end of the investment in the financial instrument.	Front-loaded management fee, structuring fee [1], distribution fee.
Ongoing charges	All ongoing costs and charges related to the management of the financial product that are deducted from the value of the financial instrument during the investment in the financial instrument.	Management fees, service costs, swap fees, securities lending costs and taxes, financing costs.
All costs related to the transactions	All costs and charges that incurred as a result of the acquisition and disposal of investments.	Broker commissions, entry- and exit-charges paid by the fund, mark ups embedded in the transaction price, stamp duty, transactions tax and foreign exchange costs.
Incidental costs		Performance fees

(1) Structuring fees should be understood as fees charged by manufacturers of structured investment products for structuring the products. They may cover a broader range of services provided by the manufacturer.

(1) It should be noted that certain cost items appear in both tables but are not duplicative since they respectively refer to costs of the product and costs of the service. Examples are the management fees (in table 1, this refers to management fees charged by an investment firm providing the service of portfolio management to its clients while in Table 2 it refers to management fees charged by an investment fund manager to its investor) and broker commissions (in Table 1, they refer to commissions incurred by the investment firm when trading on behalf of its clients while in Table 2 they refer to commissions paid by investment funds when trading on behalf of the fund).

ANNEX III

Requirement for operators of trading venues to immediately inform their national competent authority

SECTION A

Signals that may indicate significant infringements of the rules of a trading venue or disorderly trading conditions or system disruptions in relation to a financial instrument

Significant infringements of the rules of a trading venue

1. Market participants infringe rules of the trading venue which aim to protect the market integrity, the orderly functioning of the market or the significant interests of the other market participants; and

2. A trading venue considers that an infringement is of sufficient severity or impact to justify consideration of disciplinary action.

Disorderly trading conditions

3. The price discovery process is interfered with over a significant period of time;

4. The capacities of the trading systems are reached or exceeded;

5. Market makers/liquidity providers repeatedly claim mis-trades; or

6. Breakdown or failure of critical mechanisms under Article 48 of Directive 2014/65/EU and its implementing measures which are designed to protect the trading venue against the risks of algorithmic trading.

System disruptions

7. Any major malfunction or breakdown of the system for market access that results in participants losing their ability to enter, adjust or cancel their orders;

8. Any major malfunction or breakdown of the system for the matching of transactions, that results in participants losing certainty over the status of completed transactions or live orders as well as unavailability of information indispensable for trading (e.g., index value dissemination for trading certain derivatives on that index);

9. Any major malfunction or breakdown of the systems for the dissemination of pre- and post-trade transparency and other relevant data published by trading venues in accordance with their obligations under Directive 2014/65/EU and Regulation (EU) No 600/2014;

10. Any major malfunction or breakdown of the systems of the trading venue to monitor and control the trading activities of the market participants; and any major malfunction or breakdown in the sphere of other interrelated services providers, in particular CCPs and CSDs, that has repercussions on the trading system.

SECTION B

Signals that may indicate abusive behaviour under Regulation (EU) No 596/2014

Signals of possible insider dealing or market manipulation

1. Unusual concentration of transactions and/or orders to trade in a particular financial instrument with one member/participant or between certain members/participants.

2. Unusual repetition of a transaction among a small number of members/participants over a certain period of time.

Signals of possible insider dealing

3. Unusual and significant trading or submission of orders to trade in the financial instruments of a company by certain members/participants before the announcement of important corporate events or of price sensitive information relating to the company; orders to trade/transactions resulting in sudden and unusual changes in the volume of orders/transactions and/or prices before public announcements regarding the financial instrument in question.

4. Whether orders to trade are given or transactions are undertaken by a market member/participant before or immediately after that member/participant or persons publicly known as linked to that member/participant produce or disseminate research or investment recommendations that are made publicly available.

Signals of possible market manipulation

The signals described below in points 18 to 23 are particularly relevant in an automated trading environment.

5. Orders to trade given or transactions undertaken which represent a significant proportion of the daily volume of transactions in the relevant financial instrument on the trading venue concerned, in particular when these activities lead to a significant change in the price of the financial instruments.

6. Orders to trade given or transactions undertaken by a member/participant with a significant buying or selling interest in a financial instrument which lead to significant changes in the price of the financial instrument on a trading venue.

7. Orders to trade given or transactions undertaken which are concentrated within a short time span in the trading session and lead to a price change which is subsequently reversed.

8. Orders to trade given which change the representation of the best bid or offer prices in a financial instrument admitted to trading or traded on a trading venue, or more generally the representation of the order book available to market participants, and are removed before they are executed.

9. Transactions or orders to trade by a market/participant with no other apparent justification than to increase/decrease the price or value of, or to have a significant impact on the supply of or demand for a financial instrument, namely near the reference point during the trading day, e.g. at the opening or near the close.

10. Buying or selling of a financial instrument at the reference time of the trading session (e.g. opening, closing, settlement) in an effort to increase, to decrease or to maintain the reference price (e.g. opening price, closing price, settlement price) at a specific level (usually known as marking the close).

11. Transactions or orders to trade which have the effect of, or are likely to have the effect of increasing/decreasing the weighted average price of the day or of a period during the session.

12. Transactions or orders to trade which have the effect of, or are likely to have the effect of, setting a market price when the liquidity of the financial instrument or the depth of the order book is not sufficient to fix a price within the session.

13. Execution of a transaction, changing the bid-offer prices when this spread is a factor in the determination of the price of another transaction whether or not on the same trading venue.

14. Entering orders representing significant volumes in the central order book of the trading system a few minutes before the price determination phase of the auction and cancelling these orders a few seconds before the order book is frozen for computing the auction price so that the theoretical opening price might look higher or lower than it otherwise would do.

15. Engaging in a transaction or series of transactions which are shown on a public display facility to give the impression of activity or price movement in a financial instrument (usually known as painting the tape).

16. Transactions carried out as a result of the entering of buy and sell orders to trade at or nearly at the same time, with the very similar quantity and similar price by the same or different but colluding market members/participants (usually known as improper matched orders).

17. Transactions or orders to trade which have the effect of, or are likely to have the effect of bypassing the trading safeguards of the market (e.g. as regards volume limits; price limits; bid/offer spread parameters; etc.).

18. Entering of orders to trade or a series of orders to trade, executing transactions or series of transactions likely to start or exacerbate a trend and to encourage other participants to accelerate or extend the trend in order to create an opportunity to close out/open a position at a favourable price (usually know as momentum ignition).

19. Submitting multiple or large orders to trade often away from the touch on one side of the order book in order to execute a trade on the other side of the order book. Once that trade has taken place, the manipulative orders will be removed (usually known as layering and spoofing).

20. Entry of small orders to trade in order to ascertain the level of hidden orders and particularly used to assess what is resting on a dark platform (usually know as ping order).

21. Entry of large numbers of orders to trade and/or cancellations and/or updates to orders to trade so as to create uncertainty for other participants, slowing down their process and to camouflage their own strategy (usually known as quote stuffing).

22. Posting of orders to trade, to attract other market members/participants employing traditional trading techniques ('slow traders'), that are then rapidly revised onto less generous terms, hoping to execute profitably against the incoming flow of 'slow traders' orders to trade (usually known as smoking).

23. Executing orders to trade or a series of orders to trade, in order to uncover orders of other participants, and then entering an order to trade to take advantage of the information obtained (usually known as phishing).

24. The extent to which, to the best knowledge of the operator of a trading venue, orders to trade given or transactions undertaken show evidence of position reversals in a short period and represent a significant proportion of the daily volume of transactions in the relevant financial instrument on the trading venue concerned, and might be associated with significant changes in the price of a financial instrument admitted to trading or traded on the trading venue.

Signals for cross-product market manipulation, including across different trading venues

The signals described below should be particularly considered by the operator of a trading venue where both a financial instrument and related financial instruments are admitted to trading or traded or where the above mentioned instruments are traded on several trading venues operated by the same operator.

25. Transactions or orders to trade which have the effect of, or are likely to have the effect of increasing/decreasing/maintaining the price of a financial instrument during the days preceding the issue, optional redemption or expiry of a related derivative or convertible;

26. Transactions or orders to trade which have the effect of, or are likely to have the effect of maintaining the price of the underlying financial instrument below or above the strike price, or other element used to determine the pay-out (e.g. barrier), of a related derivative at expiration date;

27. Transactions which have the effect of, or are likely to have the effect of modifying the price of the underlying financial instrument so that it surpasses/not reaches the strike price, or other element used to determine the pay-out (e.g. barrier), of a related derivative at expiration date;

28. Transactions which have the effect of, or are likely to have the effect of modifying the settlement price of a financial instrument when this price is used as a reference/determinant, namely, in the calculation of margins requirements;

29. Orders to trade given or transactions undertaken by a member/participant with a significant buying or selling interest in a financial instrument which lead to significant changes in the price of the related derivative or underlying asset admitted to trading on a trading venue;

30. Undertaking trading or entering orders to trade in one trading venue or outside a trading venue (including entering indications of interest) with a view to improperly influencing the price of a related financial instrument in another or in the same trading venue or outside a trading venue (usually known as cross-product manipulation (trading on financial instrument to improperly position the price of a related financial instrument in another or in the same trading venue or outside a trading venue)).

31. Creating or enhancing arbitrage possibilities between a financial instrument and another related financial instrument by influencing reference prices of one of the financial instruments can be carried out with different financial instruments (like rights/shares, cash markets/derivatives markets, warrants/shares, …). In the context of rights issues, it could be achieved by influencing the (theoretical) opening or (theoretical) closing price of the rights.

ANNEX IV

SECTION 1

Record keeping of client orders and decision to deal

1. Name and designation of the client
2. Name and designation of any relevant person acting on behalf of the client
3. A designation to identify the trader (Trader ID) responsible within the investment firm for the investment decision
4. A designation to identify the algorithm (Algo ID) responsible within the investment firm for the investment decision;
5. B/S indicator;
6. Instrument identification
7. Unit price and price notation;
8. Price
9. Price multiplier
10. Currency 1
11. Currency 2
12. Initial quantity and quantity notation;
13. Validity period
14. Type of the order;
15. Any other details, conditions and particular instructions from the client;
16. The date and exact time of the receipt of the order or the date and exact time of when the decision to deal was made. The exact time must be measured according to the methodology prescribed under the standards on clock synchronisation under Article 50(2) of Directive 2014/65/EU.

SECTION 2

Record keeping of transactions and order processing

1. name and designation of the client;
2. name and designation of any relevant person acting on behalf of the client;
3. a designation to identify the trader (Trader ID) responsible within the investment firm for the investment decision;
4. a designation to identify the Algo (Ago ID) responsible within the investment firm for the investment decision
5. Transaction reference number
6. a designation to identify the order (Order ID)
7. the identification code of the order assigned by the trading venue upon receipt of the order;
8. a unique identification for each group of aggregated clients' orders (which will be subsequently placed as one block order on a given trading venue). This identification should indicated 'aggregated_X' with X representing the number of clients whose orders have been aggregated.
9. the segment MIC code of the trading venue to which the order has been submitted.

10. the name and other designation of the person to whom the order was transmitted
11. designation to identify the Seller & the Buyer
12. the trading capacity
13. a designation to identify the Trader (Trader ID) responsible for the execution
14. a designation to identify the Algo (Algo ID) responsible for the execution
15. B/S indicator;
16. instrument identification
17. ultimate underlying
18. Put/Call identifier
19. Strike price
20. Up-front payment
21. Delivery type
22. Option style
23. Maturity date
24. unit price and price notation;
25. price
26. price multiplier
27. Currency 1
28. Currency 2
29. remaining quantity
30. modified quantity
31. executed quantity
32. the date and exact time of submission of the order or decision to deal. The exact time must be measured according to the methodology prescribed under the standards on clock synchronisation under Article 50(2) of Directive 2014/65/EU
33. the date and exact time of any message that is transmitted to and received from the trading venue in relation to any events affecting an order. The exact time must be measured according to the methodology prescribed under Commission Delegated Regulation (EU) 2017/574 [1]
34. the date and exact time any message that is transmitted to and received from another investment firm in relation to any events affecting an order. The exact time must be measured according to the methodology prescribed under the standards on clock synchronisation under Article 50(2) of Directive 2014/65/EU
35. Any message that is transmitted to and received from the trading venue in relation to orders placed by the investment firm;
36. Any other details and conditions that was submitted to and received from another investment firm in relation with the order;

[1] Commission Delegated Regulation (EU) 2017/574 of 7 June 2016 supplementing Directive 2014/65/EU of the European Parliament and of the Council with regard to regulatory technical standards for the level of accuracy of business clocks (see page 148 of this Official Journal).

37. Each placed order's sequences in order to reflect the chronology of every event affecting it, including but not limited to modifications, cancellations and execution;

38. Short selling flag

39. SSR exemption flag;

40. Waiver flag

金融商品取引法研究会名簿

（令和３年３月16日現在）

会　　長	神作裕之	東京大学大学院法学政治学研究科教授
会長代理	弥永真生	筑波大学ビジネスサイエンス系 ビジネス科学研究科教授
委　　員	飯田秀総	東京大学大学院法学政治学研究科准教授
〃	大崎貞和	野村総合研究所未来創発センターフェロー
〃	尾崎悠一	東京都立大学大学院法学政治学研究科教授
〃	加藤貴仁	東京大学大学院法学政治学研究科教授
〃	河村賢治	立教大学大学院法務研究科教授
〃	小出　篤	学習院大学法学部教授
〃	後藤　元	東京大学大学院法学政治学研究科教授
〃	武井一浩	西村あさひ法律事務所パートナー弁護士
〃	中東正文	名古屋大学大学院法学研究科教授
〃	藤田友敬	東京大学大学院法学政治学研究科教授
〃	松井智予	東京大学大学院法学政治学研究科教授
〃	松井秀征	立教大学法学部教授
〃	松尾健一	大阪大学大学院高等司法研究科教授
〃	松尾直彦	松尾国際法律事務所弁護士
〃	宮下　央	ＴＭＩ総合法律事務所弁護士
オブザーバー	三井秀範	預金保険機構理事長
〃	太田原和房	金融庁企画市場局市場課長
〃	岸田吉史	野村ホールディングス執行役員
〃	森　忠之	大和証券グループ本社経営企画部担当部長兼法務課長
〃	森　正孝	ＳＭＢＣ日興証券法務部長
〃	田中秀樹	みずほ証券法務部長
〃	窪　久子	三菱ＵＦＪモルガン・スタンレー証券法務部長
〃	島村昌征	日本証券業協会常務執行役政策本部共同本部長
〃	松本昌男	日本証券業協会自主規制本部長
〃	横田　裕	日本証券業協会自主規制本部自主規制企画部長
〃	塚﨑由寛	日本取引所グループ総務部法務グループ課長
研究所	増井喜一郎	日本証券経済研究所理事長
〃	髙木　隆	日本証券経済研究所常務理事
〃（幹事）	石川真衣	日本証券経済研究所研究員

（敬称略）

［参考］ 既に公表した「金融商品取引法研究会（証券取引法研究会）研究記録」

第１号「裁判外紛争処理制度の構築と問題点」 2003年11月
報告者　森田章同志社大学教授

第２号「システム障害と損失補償問題」 2004年１月
報告者　山下友信東京大学教授

第３号「会社法の大改正と証券規制への影響」 2004年３月
報告者　前田雅弘京都大学教授

第４号「証券化の進展に伴う諸問題(倒産隔離の明確化等)」 2004年６月
報告者　浜田道代名古屋大学教授

第５号「EUにおける資本市場法の統合の動向
—投資商品、証券業務の範囲を中心として—」 2005年７月
報告者　神作裕之東京大学教授

第６号「近時の企業情報開示を巡る課題
—実効性確保の観点を中心に—」 2005年７月
報告者　山田剛志新潟大学助教授

第７号「プロ・アマ投資者の区分—金融商品・
販売方法等の変化に伴うリテール規制の再編—」 2005年９月
報告者　青木浩子千葉大学助教授

第８号「目論見書制度の改革」 2005年11月
報告者　黒沼悦郎早稲田大学教授

第９号「投資サービス法(仮称)について」 2005年11月
報告者　三井秀範金融庁総務企画局市場課長
松尾直彦金融庁総務企画局
投資サービス法(仮称)法令準備室長

第10号「委任状勧誘に関する実務上の諸問題
—委任状争奪戦（proxy fight）の文脈を中心に—」 2005年11月
報告者　太田洋 西村ときわ法律事務所パートナー・弁護士

第11号「集団投資スキームに関する規制について
—組合型ファンドを中心に—」 2005年12月
報告者　中村聡 森・濱田松本法律事務所パートナー・弁護士

第12号「証券仲介業」 2006年３月
報告者　川口恭弘同志社大学教授

第 13 号「敵対的買収に関する法規制」　2006 年 5 月
報告者　中東正文名古屋大学教授

第 14 号「証券アナリスト規制と強制情報開示・不公正取引規制」　2006 年 7 月
報告者　戸田暁京都大学助教授

第 15 号「新会社法のもとでの株式買取請求権制度」　2006 年 9 月
報告者　藤田友敬東京大学教授

第 16 号「証券取引法改正に係る政令等について」　2006 年 12 月
（ＴＯＢ、大量保有報告関係、内部統制報告関係）
報告者　池田唯一　金融庁総務企画局企業開示課長

第 17 号「間接保有証券に関するユニドロア条約策定作業の状況」　2007 年 5 月
報告者　神田秀樹　東京大学大学院法学政治学研究科教授

第 18 号「金融商品取引法の政令・内閣府令について」　2007 年 6 月
報告者　三井秀範　金融庁総務企画局市場課長

第 19 号「特定投資家・一般投資家について―自主規制業務を中心に―」　2007 年 9 月
報告者　青木浩子　千葉大学大学院専門法務研究科教授

第 20 号「金融商品取引所について」　2007 年 10 月
報告者　前田雅弘　京都大学大学院法学研究科教授

第 21 号「不公正取引について－村上ファンド事件を中心に－」　2008 年 1 月
報告者　太田 洋 西村あさひ法律事務所パートナー・弁護士

第 22 号「大量保有報告制度」　2008 年 3 月
報告者　神作裕之　東京大学大学院法学政治学研究科教授

第 23 号「開示制度（Ⅰ）―企業再編成に係る開示制度および集団投資スキーム持分等の開示制度―」　2008 年 4 月
報告者　川口恭弘 同志社大学大学院法学研究科教授

第 24 号「開示制度（Ⅱ）―確認書、内部統制報告書、四半期報告書―」　2008 年 7 月
報告者　戸田　暁　京都大学大学院法学研究科准教授

第 25 号「有価証券の範囲」　2008 年 7 月
報告者　藤田友敬　東京大学大学院法学政治学研究科教授

第 26 号「民事責任規定・エンフォースメント」　2008 年 10 月
報告者　近藤光男　神戸大学大学院法学研究科教授

第 27 号「金融機関による説明義務・適合性の原則と金融商品販売法」2009 年 1 月
報告者　山田剛志　新潟大学大学院実務法学研究科准教授

第 28 号「集団投資スキーム（ファンド）規制」　2009 年 3 月
報告者　中村聡 森・濱田松本法律事務所パートナー・弁護士

第29号「金融商品取引業の業規制」　2009年4月
報告者　黒沼悦郎　早稲田大学大学院法務研究科教授

第30号「公開買付け制度」　2009年7月
報告者　中東正文　名古屋大学大学院法学研究科教授

第31号「最近の金融商品取引法の改正について」　2011年3月
報告者　藤本拓資　金融庁総務企画局市場課長

第32号「金融商品取引業における利益相反　2011年6月
—利益相反管理体制の整備業務を中心として—」
報告者　神作裕之　東京大学大学院法学政治学研究科教授

第33号「顧客との個別の取引条件における特別の利益提供に関する問題」2011年9月
報告者　青木浩子　千葉大学大学院専門法務研究科教授
松本譲治　ＳＭＢＣ日興証券　法務部長

第34号「ライツ・オファリングの円滑な利用に向けた制度整備と課題」2011年11月
報告者　前田雅弘　京都大学大学院法学研究科教授

第35号「公開買付規制を巡る近時の諸問題」　2012年2月
報告者　太田 洋 西村あさひ法律事務所弁護士・NY州弁護士

第36号「格付会社への規制」　2012年6月
報告者　山田剛志　成城大学法学部教授

第37号「金商法第6章の不公正取引規制の体系」　2012年7月
報告者　松尾直彦　東京大学大学院法学政治学研究科客員
教授・西村あさひ法律事務所弁護士

第38号「キャッシュ・アウト法制」　2012年10月
報告者　中東正文　名古屋大学大学院法学研究科教授

第39号「デリバティブに関する規制」　2012年11月
報告者　神田秀樹　東京大学大学院法学政治学研究科教授

第40号「米国JOBS法による証券規制の変革」　2013年1月
報告者　中村聡 森・濱田松本法律事務所パートナー・弁護士

第41号「金融商品取引法の役員の責任と会社法の役員の責任　2013年3月
—虚偽記載をめぐる役員の責任を中心に—」
報告者　近藤光男　神戸大学大学院法学研究科教授

第42号「ドッド=フランク法における信用リスクの保持ルールについて」　2013年4月
報告者　黒沼悦郎　早稲田大学大学院法務研究科教授

第43号「相場操縦の規制」　2013年8月
報告者　藤田友敬　東京大学大学院法学政治学研究科教授

第 44 号「法人関係情報」 2013年10月
報告者　川口恭弘　同志社大学大学院法学研究科教授
平田公一　日本証券業協会常務執行役

第 45 号「最近の金融商品取引法の改正について」 2014 年 6 月
報告者　藤本拓資　金融庁総務企画局企画課長

第 46 号「リテール顧客向けデリバティブ関連商品販売における民事責任 2014 年 9 月
—「新規な説明義務」を中心として—」
報告者　青木浩子　千葉大学大学院専門法務研究科教授

第 47 号「投資者保護基金制度」 2014年10月
報告者　神田秀樹　東京大学大学院法学政治学研究科教授

第 48 号「市場に対する詐欺に関する米国判例の動向について」 2015 年 1 月
報告者　黒沼悦郎　早稲田大学大学院法務研究科教授

第 49 号「継続開示義務者の範囲—アメリカ法を中心に—」 2015 年 3 月
報告者　飯田秀総　神戸大学大学院法学研究科准教授

第 50 号「証券会社の破綻と投資者保護基金 2015 年 5 月
—金融商品取引法と預金保険法の交錯—」
報告者　山田剛志　成城大学大学院法学研究科教授

第 51 号「インサイダー取引規制と自己株式」 2015 年 7 月
報告者　前田雅弘　京都大学大学院法学研究科教授

第 52 号「金商法において利用されない制度と利用される制度の制限」 2015 年 8 月
報告者　松尾直彦　東京大学大学院法学政治学研究科
客員教授・弁護士

第 53 号「証券訴訟を巡る近時の諸問題 2015年10月
—流通市場において不実開示を行った提出会社の責任を中心に—」
報告者　太田 洋 西村あさひ法律事務所パートナー・弁護士

第 54 号「適合性の原則」 2016 年 3 月
報告者　川口恭弘　同志社大学大学院法学研究科教授

第 55 号「金商法の観点から見たコーポレートガバナンス・コード」 2016 年 5 月
報告者　神作裕之　東京大学大学院法学政治学研究科教授

第 56 号「ＥＵにおける投資型クラウドファンディング規制」 2016 年 7 月
報告者　松尾健一　大阪大学大学院法学研究科准教授

第 57 号「上場会社による種類株式の利用」 2016 年 9 月
報告者　加藤貴仁　東京大学大学院法学政治学研究科准教授

第 58 号「公開買付前置型キャッシュアウトにおける　2016年11月
価格決定請求と公正な対価」
報告者　藤田友敬　東京大学大学院法学政治学研究科教授

第 59 号「平成26年会社法改正後のキャッシュ・アウト法制」2017 年 1 月
報告者　中東正文　名古屋大学大学院法学研究科教授

第 60 号「流通市場の投資家による発行会社に対する証券訴訟の実態」2017 年 3 月
報告者　後藤　元　東京大学大学院法学政治学研究科准教授

第 61 号「米国における投資助言業者（investment adviser）　2017 年 5 月
の負う信認義務」
報告者　萬澤陽子　専修大学法学部准教授･当研究所客員研究員

第 62 号「最近の金融商品取引法の改正について」　2018 年 2 月
報告者　小森卓郎　金融庁総務企画局市場課長

第 63 号「監査報告書の見直し」　2018 年 3 月
報告者　弥永真生　筑波大学ビジネスサイエンス系
ビジネス科学研究科教授

第 64 号「フェア・ディスクロージャー・ルールについて」　2018 年 6 月
報告者　大崎貞和　野村総合研究所未来創発センターフェロー

第 65 号「外国為替証拠金取引のレバレッジ規制」　2018 年 8 月
報告者　飯田秀総　東京大学大学院法学政治学研究科准教授

第 66 号「一般的不公正取引規制に関する一考察」　2018 年12月
報告者　松井秀征　立教大学法学部教授

第 67 号「仮想通貨・ＩＣＯに関する法規制・自主規制」　2019 年 3 月
報告者　河村賢治　立教大学大学院法務研究科教授

第 68 号「投資信託･投資法人関連法制に関する問題意識について」2019 年 5 月
報告者　松尾直彦　東京大学大学院法学政治学研究科
客員教授・弁護士

第 69 号「「政策保有株式」に関する開示規制の再構築について」2019 年 7 月
報告者　加藤貴仁　東京大学大学院法学政治学研究科教授

第 70 号「複数議決権株式を用いた株主構造のコントロール」2019 年11月
報告者　松井智予　上智大学大学院法学研究科教授

第 71 号「会社法・証券法における分散台帳の利用　2020 年 2 月
―デラウェア州会社法改正などを参考として」
報告者　小出　篤　学習院大学法学部教授

第 72 号「スチュワードシップコードの目的とその多様性」　2020 年 5 月
報告者　後藤　元　東京大学大学院法学政治学研究科教授

第73号「インデックスファンドとコーポレートガバナンス」2020年7月
報告者　松尾健一　大阪大学大学院高等司法研究科教授

第74号「株対価M&A/株式交付制度について」　2020年8月
報告者　武井一浩　西村あさひ法律事務所パートナー弁護士

第75号「取締役の報酬に関する会社法の見直し」　2021年2月
報告者　尾崎悠一　東京都立大学大学院法学政治学研究科教授

購入を希望される方は、一般書店または当研究所までお申し込み下さい。
当研究所の出版物案内は研究所のホームページ https://www.jsri.or.jp/ にてご覧いただけます。

金融商品取引法研究会研究記録　第76号
投資助言業に係る規制
—ドイツ法との比較を中心として—
令和3年6月9日
定価550円（本体500円+税10%）

編　者　金融商品取引法研究会
発行者　公益財団法人　日本証券経済研究所
東京都中央区日本橋2-11-2
〒103-0027
電話　03（6225）2326代表
URL: https://www.jsri.or.jp

ISBN978-4-89032-692-1 C3032